Secondary Education

Secondary Education:
An Introduction

David G. Armstrong
Texas A&M University

Tom V. Savage
Texas A&M University

MACMILLAN PUBLISHING CO., INC.
New York

COLLIER MACMILLAN PUBLISHERS
London

Macmillan Publishing Co., Inc.
866 Third Avenue, New York, New York 10022

Collier Macmillan Canada, Inc.

Library of Congress Cataloging in Publication Data

Armstrong, David G.
   Secondary education.

   Includes bibliographies and index.
   1. Education, Secondary.   I. Savage, Tom V.
II. Title.
LB1607.A75   373   82-15333
ISBN 0-02-304070-X   AACR2

Printing: 1 2 3 4 5 6 7 8   Year: 3 4 5 6 7 8 9 0

ISBN   0-02-304070-X

Preface

The complexion of secondary education is changing. True, secondary schools continue to serve youngsters who have completed their elementary school years. True, many of the courses offered today have been in the secondary schools for years. But, despite the presence of many traditional features, secondary education today must address itself to responsibilities little dreamed of by secondary school educators of a generation ago.

Together, these changes have made secondary school teaching a complex and challenging calling. For example, partisans of the accountability movement increasingly demand evidence of clear relationships between monies spent on schooling and student learning. At the same time, other interests seek to extend the rights of students to determine the contents of school programs. Given the conflicting agendas of these interests, many teachers feel themselves caught between one force demanding that they assume more responsibility for the individual student's learning and one force demanding that the individual student be given more responsibility for his or her program. These forces and other interests demanding special attention for the needs of the gifted and talented, the handicapped, nonnative speakers of English, and other special groups in the school have made it difficult for secondary school teachers to know with confidence that the directions they pursue are appropriate.

Secondary Education: An Introduction seeks to provide those who are considering a career in secondary school teaching with a realistic grasp of the field's complexity. We hope that, as a consequence of information presented here, readers will learn to perform their diverse roles confidently and competently.

We realize that, as a result of some material introduced in the book, certain readers may decide that secondary school teaching is not for them. In our view, not everyone *ought* to be a secondary school teacher. Those who do decide upon a career in this difficult field should make their choices on the basis of a clear understanding of the kinds of responsibilities they will assume as secondary school teachers. Consequently, we have made no attempt to gloss over some of the more difficult aspects of teaching in middle schools, junior high schools, and senior high schools.

The book is divided into four major sections. The first focuses on the relationship between society and the secondary school. Chapters in this section provide background material related to the growth and development of the senior high school and the intermediate school. Additional emphases are placed on a number of issues and innovations related to secondary education today.

The second section focuses on the extremely critical topic of instructional planning. Individual chapters prepare teachers to use a systems approach to instructional planning. Special attention is devoted to diagnosing students, selecting content and preparing objectives, identifying instructional techniques, motivating students and implementing programs, and measuring, evaluating, and reporting student progress.

The third section focuses on secondary school students themselves. The first chapter in this part of the book provides a profile of today's secondary school population. Other chapters deal with student rights, programs for gifted and talented youngsters and handicapped students, and reading difficulties of secondary school students.

The final section includes chapters focusing on secondary school teachers. The first chapter features a description of the general population of secondary school teachers. The next two deal, respectively, with the challenging topics of classroom management and discipline and the many roles that must be assumed by today's secondary teachers. The final chapter is directed toward the individual seeking his or her initial teaching position. It introduces systematic procedures to follow in searching for and obtaining that all-important first job.

As with any endeavor of this magnitude, preparation of this book involved the assistance of a large number of people. We want to extend a special thank you to several who are very special to us. Ford Button, a long-time high school art teacher in Rochester, New York and a well-known professional cartoonist, contributed a number of original cartoons for the book. As important, he provided us with considerable encouragement as the writing process went forward. We appreciate his thoughtfulness and, of course, his keen sense of humor.

In addition, we want to thank professors Ronald D. Anderson of the University of Colorado, Robert H. Pinney of Western Washington University, and Jon Wiles of the University of South Florida for their comments on early drafts of the manuscript. We believe that the final version of the book benefited enormously from their wise counsel.

Lloyd Chilton of Macmillan has been of inestimable help to us in conceptualizing this project and in supporting us during the long period when ideas moved from the speculative stage into completed chapter form. He has been ever willing to have his work interrupted by a phone call and to offer constructive assistance.

We also wish to extend our appreciation to Beth Van Cleave, who helped us with typing and proofreading of the manuscript. Additionally, as a person who works with us every day, she has had the grace to put up with our sometimes bizarre senses of humor. For her help and her tolerance, a big "thank you, Beth" is more than due. Valerie Birdwell provided fine assistance to us in typing the index. We thank her for her good help.

Certainly other colleagues, friends, and our respective families provided an environment that allowed us to complete this project. To all of you, we wish to extend our sincerest appreciation.

David G. Armstrong
Tom V. Savage

Contents

PART II: Instruction in the Secondary School

PART III: Students in the Secondary School

PART IV: Teachers in the Secondary School

17 Profiles of Secondary School Teachers   389

18 Teachers' Roles and Responsibilities   406

19 Teachers and Discipline   424

20   Finding a Teaching Position   447

Author Index   467

Subject Index   471

Secondary Education

I

SOCIETY AND THE SECONDARY SCHOOL

The Senior High School

FUNKY WINKERBEAN by Tom Batiuk © 1973. Field Enterprises, Inc. Courtesy of Field Newspaper Syndicate.

Objectives

This chapter provides information to help the reader to

1. Recognize historical antecedents of the senior high school.
2. Describe the general purposes of the comprehensive high school.
3. Point out several criticisms that have been made of the comprehensive high school in recent years.
4. Realize that senior high schools constitute a kind of minisociety with very strict, if unwritten, rules about what sorts of behaviors are acceptable and how status is won and distributed.
5. Suggest some emerging changes in the public's attitudes toward education in general and senior high schools in particular.

Pretest

Directions: Using your own paper, answer each of the following true/false questions. For each correct statement write the word ''true.'' For each incorrect statement, write the word ''false.''

_____ 1. Early high schools had a curriculum that differed dramatically from that offered in the secondary academies.

　　　　　　　　2. Public secondary school education in this country has a history going back just as far as public elementary school education.

　　　　　　　　3. Evidence is overwhelming that the senior high school has been a public agency that has been able to solve many deeply rooted social problems.

　　　　　　　　4. In school year 1919–1920, only slightly over 10 percent of all students in school were enrolled in grades 9 through 12.

　　　　　　　　5. The length of the school term has generally decreased in this country since the 1800s.

　　　　　　　　6. Supporters of the "comprehensive" high school traditionally have seen high school as an institution designed only to meet the needs of college- and university-bound youngsters.

　　　　　　　　7. In the 1920s, people were little concerned about any supposed drop in the quality of students enrolled in high schools.

　　　　　　　　8. There is evidence that large numbers of high school students are very concerned about their status within their own age group.

　　　　　　　　9. The first high school was the English Classical School, established in Boston in 1821.

　　　　　　　10. In the second half of the eighteenth century, the dominant type of American secondary school was the public high school.

INTRODUCTION

Suppose that a group of sociologists had received a grant to study how strangers behave in groups. Part of the money was used to select at random a group of 50 people from the entire adult population of the United States. Once selected, these people were transported to a site in a city in the middle of the country. This site was a large pavilionlike structure. Individuals in the group were shepherded into the center of a huge high-ceilinged room. They were given these simple instructions: "Get to know one another."

From watching posts in nearby rooms fitted with one-way glass, sociologists observed the scene. First, there was a good deal of awkward shuffling, staring at the floor, craning of necks, and uncomfortable scratching behavior. A few glad-hander types made tentative efforts to introduce themselves around, but, in general, the group remained rather chilly and reserved. This was, after all, a mixed group of people, none of whom had ever before seen anyone else in the room. As the sociologists noted on their pads, the group seemed to be getting off to a painfully slow start. Then, quite by accident, someone in the group backed into a folding metal chair. The chair careened for an instant on one leg and then fell crashing to the floor. The clatter resulted in some visible wincing in this crowd of increasingly anxious strangers.

Then, someone in the group shouted out, "Sounds like a banging high school locker." At once heads perked up, smiles began to appear, and nods of agreement began sweeping across the crowd. There were murmurs of "Sure did," "By Gawd, yes!" "Uh huh," and "Yes, indeed" from people in scattered parts of the room.

From the center of the room, a middle-aged man commented, "Maybe that's how *you* remember lockers, but not me. In my school they were really loud. One of the highlights of my school day was watching old Mr. Feldon leap from his seat and charge for the hall when I let fly hard with my locker door. Of course I was always around the corner before he got there." These remarks prompted recollections from others in the room. Soon the 50 strangers in the room were involved in animated conversations focusing on the general theme of "How I survived high school."

In their observation rooms the sociologists' pens moved relentlessly forward prompted by visions of professional articles, speeches, and who knows, maybe even a book.

Although the story about the sociologists and the 50 randomly selected Americans who found a sense of community in the realization that all had had somewhat similar experiences during their high school years is imaginary, it does depict one aspect of the high school experience in the United States. High school programs in all parts of the country are remarkably similar. Perhaps even more significantly, the football teams, cheerleaders, pep clubs and other adolescent societies reflect a pattern that varies little among different geographical regions of the nation. In short, the senior high school provides American young people with a common experience that, in a sense, serves as a social glue that can provide an important communications bond even among people who grow up in widely separated parts of the country. Indeed, it may not be too much to say that part of becoming an American is wrapped up in the cluster of experiences that young people encounter as students in senior high schools.

The senior high school is a genuinely American phenomenon (see Figure 1-1). With some modifications, it exists in Canada in a parallel form. Beyond Canada, however, similarities to U.S. patterns fade quickly. Indeed, to many Europeans, the American senior high school is a phenomenon that almost defies understanding. Even in the English-speaking British Isles, a prominent American entertainer who had written songs including lyrics referencing certain aspects of high school life found it necessary to provide his audience with a glossary of terms that would be recognized immediately by any American high school graduate (Keyes 1976).

Figure 1-1

WE ARE WHAT WE WERE AT DEAR OLD FILL-IN-THE-BLANK HIGH

High schools are ghettos. They cram together hordes of 14- to 17-year-olds who are shut off from contact with the real world. They are minisocieties with their own rules, regulations, and codes of conduct. They identify heroes and goats on criteria that are quite unknown to the "great outside."

Exposure to the high school experience creates an indelible imprint from which Americans, even as adults, do not escape. The pecking order in high school tends to condition adults to see themselves in certain ways. The student who was an "also ran" in high school begins adult life with some heavy negative emotional baggage. He or she may well have to overcome a great deal of self-doubt before whatever talents are truly there will bloom. Others, who for reasons difficult to fathom by outsiders have flowered brilliantly in the hothouse atmosphere of high school society, may well make adjustments more easily to the social environment of the post-high school world.

That people are conditioned by their high school experiences is beyond dispute. But the permanence of this conditioning has prompted a good deal of debate. Some say that high school is simply a burden that cannot be shed. Others suggest that a psychic "rebirth" after high school is possible. Regardless of whether ultimate victory is possible or not, many young adults seem to spend a good deal of time thinking about how to change the status accorded to them by the adolescent subculture that the calendar says they have outgrown but that clings yet to their self-images.

YOUR OPINION, PLEASE

Read the comments above. Then, respond to these questions.

1. Are high schools ghettos? Why, or why not?
2. Do high school students have their own rules for according status? If so, what are some of these rules? What chances does an individual have to achieve high status?
3. Do people carry an adult image of themselves that is somewhat similar to their self-image as a student in high school? How do you know?
4. To what extent do you think people can change after high school? Why do you think so?
5. What positive and negative influences do you think your high school experience had on how you view yourself today?

In the sections that follow, we will look at the historical evolution of the senior high school. Then, we will examine some key contemporary issues relating to the comprehensive high school. Finally, we will take a look at the American high school as a social phenomenon.

DEVELOPMENT OF THE AMERICAN HIGH SCHOOL

Secondary education has a long history in this country. However, *public* secondary education has been with us only since the nineteenth century. The early settlers of Puritan New England established the first recorded secondary school on the North American continent, the Boston Public Latin Grammar School, in 1635.

The Boston Public Latin Grammar School, which served an elite group of male students, was designed to prepare young men for positions of political and religious leadership in the Massachusetts Bay Colony. More specifically, the program was designed to prepare young men for more advanced study at Harvard. For nearly 50 years, the Boston Public Latin Grammar School was the only secondary school in Boston. Two more were added in 1682 (Barry 1961).

The use of the word "public" in the name Boston Public Latin Grammar School needs some elaboration. In this context, "public" meant that the school was technically open to any who could enroll and pay the fees, a condition that contrasted to practices that limited school enrollments to students falling within a given category (members of a certain religious denomination, for example). However, the term "public" in this context did not imply free or tax supported; it was simply meant to suggest that those who could afford to attend would be welcome to attend.

Although enrollments in individual schools were not large, opportunities for students of means to pursue education at the secondary level continued to expand throughout the late seventeenth century and on into the eighteenth. By 1700, there were about 35 Latin schools in New England, and their popularity continued for a good many years. It was the dominant form of secondary education in North America until the middle of the eighteenth century (Barry 1961).

These schools featured a heavy emphasis on classical subjects. Materials were read in the original Latin or Greek, the purpose being to prepare young men for college. Vocational or other "practical" subjects were missing from the curricula of these schools. In general, students were the sons of the well-to-do who were being groomed for positions of leadership.

Not everyone was satisfied with the curriculum of the Latin schools. One of the foremost critics was Benjamin Franklin, whose concern focused on the growing new country's need for individuals who were educated in technical and practical arts. Clearly the classical studies offered by the Latin schools were not responsive to this need. In 1751, Franklin and others of like mind were instrumental in establishing the Philadelphia Public Academy.*

Franklin's academy had a much broader curriculum than did the Latin schools. Subjects taught included reading, writing, arithmetic, geometry, history, geography, chronology, public speaking, morality, and agriculture. The school originally included three "departments": English, Latin, and mathematics. Not long after the school was founded, a fourth department, philosophical studies, was added (Barry 1961). There is evidence that the present practice by senior high schools of organizing related subject fields into units called departments stemmed from the initial experience at the academy founded by Franklin.

---

*Again, in this case the term "public" meant only that the school was open to those who could come and pay the tuition. The school was a private operation and derived none of its support from tax revenues.

The academy idea caught on with the American public after the Revolutionary War. The following figures illustrate the rapid growth of this model of secondary education in the years through 1850 in the state of Massachusetts.

Year	Number of Academies
1797	15
1830	55
1850	403

Source: Thomas Newman Barry, "Origin and Development of the American Public High School in the Nineteenth Century," unpublished doctoral dissertation. Stanford University, 1961, p. 45.

The success of the academy seems related in part at least to an American bias toward preparing people to work with real-world problems as opposed to preparing people for a life of scholarship; individuals trained in the academies were capable of moving relatively smoothly into the mainstream of American commerce. In general, the curricular orientation of the academy was much admired.

For some, however, the academy suffered a major deficiency: namely, that secondary education was not being provided to all the youngsters who could benefit from such instruction. The academies, it must be remembered, were private institutions.* Therefore, students tended to come primarily from the families of the middle and upper classes. Youngsters from less affluent families simply were not able to attend. In the end, a recognition that too narrow a population of youngsters was being served prompted support for secondary education that was tax supported and, hence, available to many more young people.

The academy movement, Barry tells us, reached its peak in 1850 when there were 6,085 such schools in the country (1961, p. 46). Although there were never again so many academies, the approach to secondary education by no means faded away overnight. Academies continued to be very popular alternatives to tax-supported secondary schools for many years after 1850.

Recognition that there ought to be nonprivate secondary schools came long before the peak year of the academies in 1850. The first public high school in the United States, established in 1821, was the Boston English Classical School. The inclusion of the word "classical" in the name deserves some special mention. In fact, the curriculum of the school was not classical at all. That is, students did not simply read the same works in English translation that youngsters had read in the original Latin and Greek in the Latin grammar schools. Rather, the curriculum was very practical. The use of the term "classical" may have been little more than a public relations ploy to give the school a certain respectability among those in the population who were skeptical of the practical arts and convinced that the only real education was a classical education.

The courses studied at the Boston English Classical School were almost a carbon copy of those presented at the academies of the day. That is, they emphasized the useful and practical subjects and attended less to subjects that were seen to have less obvious connections to the demands of daily living. The similarity of the curricula of the early high schools and those of the academies suggests that proponents of the tax-supported high school were not interested in revolutionary change in the secondary school curriculum. The practical academy curriculum was seen as good. (Consider this discussion

---

*Some academies received modest state support. But in no cases did such support establish an institution like the high school open to all comers on a no-tuition basis.

Figure 1-2

A NATION WITHOUT HIGH SCHOOLS

Suppose that the tax-supported high school never had come into existence. Suppose, too, that the predominant model of secondary education today was the academy. Were this the case, we might well expect there to be tremendous numbers of academies in the country. Doubtless large numbers of students would be served. But in every likelihood American secondary education would be different from today's prevailing patterns.

YOUR OPINION, PLEASE

Read the paragraph above. Then, respond to these questions.

1. If we had only academies, would there be any difference in the size of the secondary school population from what we have today in our high schools? Why, or why not?
2. To what extent would characteristics of students in these academies be similar to the characteristics of students enrolled in our high schools?
3. To what extent would characteristics of students in these academies be different from the characteristics of students enrolled in our high schools?
4. What advantages do you see for a system where the academy represented the only option for a student interested in secondary education?
5. What disadvantages do you see for a system where the academy represented the only option for a student interested in secondary education?
6. Do you think that the role academies would play as a rallying point for the local community would be different from that of the tax-supported high school? Why, or why not?
7. How would you react to a proposal to convert our tax-supported high school pattern of secondary education to a system where academies represented the only available path for students completing the elementary school program? Why do you feel this way?

---

as you think about questions raised in Figure 1-2.) Barry (1961, p. 179) speaks to this point as follows:

> *The American public high school grew up in the nineteenth century not because of the desire for a type of education different from that being provided by the contemporary academies, but because the people wished to extend the opportunities for that kind of education more widely.*

Establishment of the first high school in Boston did not result in an immediate storm of interest in this new approach to secondary education. As has been noted, academies continued to grow in numbers through the year 1850. Expansion of the high school idea proceeded very slowly. Some of the very earliest high schools established were these:

Place	Name	Year Established
New York, N.Y.	New York High School	1825
Bridgeport, Conn.	Bridgeport High School	1827
Portsmouth, N.H.	Portsmouth High School	1827
Portland, Maine	English High School	1829
Cincinnati, Ohio	Woodward High School	1831

Source: Thomas Newman Barry, "Origin and Development of the American Public High School in the Nineteenth Century," unpublished doctoral dissertation, Stanford University, 1961, p. 7.

A number of reasons contributed to the rather slow initial growth of high schools. First, there was by no means universal agreement that there was a need for a dramatic expansion of educational opportunity for youngsters beyond the elementary school years. Further, where such a need was felt, growth of academies, in the minds of many, was sufficient to accommodate the demand for students educated through the secondary school level.

Second, the community of individuals interested in education was much more diffuse than it is today. In the 1820s, there really was no tightly organized national community of individuals vitally interested in education. National organizations interested in education did not evolve until much later in the century. The few individuals such as Horace Mann who spoke out on educational issues tended to be much more interested in promoting the spread of elementary education than with secondary education. In the United States in the 1820s, there simply was no way to disseminate information about the Boston English Classical School, the nation's first high school, quickly. The list of early high schools points to a very slow migration of the innovation from its birthplace in eastern Massachusetts, to other New England states, and only then to more distant areas of the country.

Perhaps the most important barrier to the rapid spread of the high school centered on the idea that the institution should be supported largely by tax money. The principle of public support for elementary education went back to colonial times. But, for many years, there was doubt about the legality of using tax money to support secondary schools. A key decision in this area was the famous *Kalamazoo* case of 1874 [*Stuart* v. *School District No. 1 of the Village of Kalamazoo,* 30 Mich. 69 (1874)], which supported the right of state legislatures to pass laws permitting local communities to levy taxes to support secondary as well as elementary schools. The assurance of a legally sound financial base had to come before any broad expansion of secondary schools was possible.

The importance of the principle of tax support can be seen in the very modest growth in the numbers of secondary schools in the country until after the 1870s. Note the following figures:

Year	No. of High Schools in the United States
1860	40
1870	160
1880	800
1890	2,526
1900	6,005

Source: Thomas Newman Barry, "Origin and Development of the American Public High School in the Nineteenth Century," unpublished doctoral dissertation, Stanford University, 1961, p. 70.

Growth of public high schools after the *Kalamazoo* case was dramatic. For example, in 1880 there were only 110,000 students in secondary schools; by 1900 the figure had jumped to 519,000, by 1920 there were 2,200,000 youngsters enrolled, and 20 years later, in 1940, enrollments totaled 6,601,000 students. Today, between 12 and 13 million youngsters are enrolled in secondary schools*

*Figures are from the U.S. Department of Commerce, Bureau of the Census, *Historical Statistics of the United States: Colonial Times to 1970,* Part 1, Bicentennial edition (Washington, D.C.: U.S. Government Printing Office, 1975), p. 375, and U.S. Department of Education, *The Condition of Education, 1980* (Washington, D.C.: National Center for Education Statistics, 1980), p. 56.

PROBLEMS OF HIGH SCHOOLS IN THE LATE NINETEENTH AND EARLY TWENTIETH CENTURIES

As the number of high schools began to increase, more attention was focused on the nature of high school programs and what high schools ought to do. To understand some of the basic issues at stake, we need to review briefly the character of the academy, the secondary institution that predominated before the rise of the high school.

Although academies had sprung up initially to provide instruction oriented toward the more practical arts and away from classical studies, they had always strived to meet another objective as well. Proponents of the academy realized that some students who finished the programs would go on to pursue advanced work at colleges and universities. Therefore, the academy attempted to equip students with the essentials necessary to gain admittance to institutions of higher learning. Throughout its history as an institution, there was concern about whether instruction at individual academies was weighted too heavily toward practical arts or toward college preparation instruction. This general debate continued as the high school emerged as the most common secondary education institution.

Since they were tax-supported schools, it seemed likely that high schools would respond quite readily to expressions of political will. Presumably this will would be reflective of the community at large. In general, evidence suggests that, in the years following the Civil War, high school curricula, to some extent at least, did respond to changing social, political and economic conditions in the country.

For example, between the end of the Civil War and the 1890s, manual training programs were introduced in a number of high schools. This was a clear response to a national need for skilled workers to move into responsible work positions in a time of general economic expansion. Further, there was a great increase in the number of commercial or business courses offered in high schools during this time. In general, the number of courses offered expanded significantly.

In part, this expansion seems to have resulted from a conviction "that the greater the variety and number of programs the more chance the pupil would have of finding the areas in which his capabilities might lie" (Tanner and Tanner 1975, p. 182). Additionally, the high school, as an institution with a relatively short history, was not overburdened with tradition. Proposals to change the curriculum did not prompt howls of protest from older generations who were concerned that "it wasn't done this way when we were in school." During this time innovations in the secondary curriculum could be installed with much less resistance than is true today, when years of familiarity with certain practices has prompted a view that existing approaches have "stood the test of time" and should not be changed.

Speaking to the efforts of high schools to expand the range of high school course offerings during this period, Tanner and Tanner (1975, p. 182) have commented that:

> It was an attempt to provide equality of educational opportunity; to make it possible for every boy and girl to discover and develop his or her talents. An intense faith in popular education and a, perhaps fortuitous, lack of agreement on the functions and purposes of the high school led to the development of programs in classical, industrial, commercial, cultural, scientific, and literary fields. ... The expanding curriculum reflected the aim of the high school to meet changing social needs.

The thrust toward expanding the range of course offerings in the high schools was not supported universally. In particular, university people were concerned that proliferation of new courses in high schools might result in programs that would ill suit the student who, upon graduation, would embark upon further study in a college or university. There was even a fear that, by refusing to teach certain courses, high schools would force colleges to alter their admission requirements (Tanner and Tanner 1975).

From their perspective, high school administrators were concerned that colleges and universities themselves were by no means in agreement with regard to which courses students ought to take in high school to qualify for admission to institutions of higher learning. There was a good deal of grumbling about the necessity to work up different kinds of documentation on students seeking admission to different institutions. As Tanner and Tanner have noted, this activity resulted in high school officials' spending a good deal of their time managing paperwork related to college-bound students, which took away time that could have been directed toward the needs of noncollege-bound youngsters.

Concerns about the lack of coordination between high school programs and college and university entrance requirements prompted the formation in the 1890s of the National Education Association's famous Committee of Ten. The Committee of Ten was dominated by individuals who viewed the high school predominantly as a school to prepare youngsters for college and university work. The committed recommended that high schools focus on nine major subjects that were thought to provide adequate foundational experiences for students intending to go on to colleges and universities. These nine were (1) Latin; (2) Greek; (3) English; (4) other modern languages; (5) mathematics; (6) physics, astronomy, and chemistry; (7) natural history; (8) history, civil government, and political economy; and (9) geography (Tanner and Tanner 1975; National Education Association 1983).

Although in its report the Committee of Ten made pointed reference to the idea that secondary schools have responsibilities beyond preparing youngsters for colleges and universities, there was no suggestion that subjects other than those designed for college- and university-bound youngsters be included in the high school curriculum. Thus, despite the lip service paid to the ideal of a high school serving the interests of the college-bound as well as the noncollege-bound student, the suggested program of study included no mention of practical or enrichment courses for those students whose formal education would stop upon high school graduation (see Figure 1-3). The report of the Committee of Ten represented a high tide for the point of view that the high school properly was a college preparatory institution.

Today, the Committee of Ten's view seems narrow to anyone familiar with contemporary high schools. How could such a position have been espoused by so august a body? There are many reasons. But perhaps paramount among them was the prevalent view that for the vast majority of the population formal education ended with the completion of elementary school. To bring this situation into focus, let us consider some information from school year 1889–1890.

In this year, of *all* students enrolled in public schools in the United States, a mere 1.6 percent were enrolled in grades 9 through 12. In the spring of 1890, there were only 22,000 graduating high school seniors in the entire country. Total high school enrollment was only 203,000 as compared with a total elementary school enrollment of 12,520,000 (U.S. Department of Health, Education, and Welfare 1979). Clearly, high school students represented only a tiny fraction of all students enrolled in school. Many of these youngsters tended to be academically talented. Given their small numbers and a perception that they were well-endowed intellectually, perhaps it was not surprising that large numbers of Americans in fact did see high school primarily as a preparation ground for college. Such a small percentage of the total population of young people was enrolled in high school that it was difficult for a good many people to see the high school as an institution that needed to provide learning experiences broader than those needed by the college bound.

Although the Committee of Ten's view of the high school as a college preparatory institution had a good deal of support, by no means was this support universal. Critics of this view noted that each year high school enrollments were increasing. Higher and

Figure 1-3

THE SOPHOMORE YEAR IN HIGH SCHOOL AS ENVISIONED BY THE 1893 COMMITTEE OF TEN

In 1893, the Committee of Ten proposed that the following subjects be taken by students in the second year of high school.*

    Latin
    Greek
    English Literature
    English Composition
    German (continued from the freshman year)
    Beginning French
    †Algebra
    Geometry
    Botany or Zoology
    English History to 1688

†Students could substitute bookkeeping or commercial arithmetic.

YOUR OPINION, PLEASE

1. How do you think most people today would react to a proposal to install the program listed above as requirements for all high school sophomores? Why do you think so?
2. If such a program were required of all students, how do you think most students would fare?
3. Would homework expectations likely be different if such a program were required of all students? If so, in what ways?
4. How would you personally have reacted had your own high school required all of these subjects to be taken by sophomores?

*Committee of Ten, *Report of the Committee of Ten on Secondary School Studies* (Washington, D.C.: National Education Association, 1893), p. 4.

---

higher percentages of the total 14- to 17-year-old age group were enrolling in high schools with each passing year. This trend suggested that more and more youngsters who were in high schools would not be going on for further study to colleges and universities. Moreover, the old arguments that a technically developing society needed people trained beyond the elementary school level with practical world-of-work skills was used to attack the position taken by the Committee of Ten.

In the early years of the twentieth century, the view that high schools ought to do more than prepare youngsters for college grew in influence. Reflecting this change, the National Education Association's Committee of Nine, formed in 1910, developed a final report in 1911 that suggested a much broader purpose for the high school. The report was among the first to suggest that high schools had a responsibility for producing individuals who were "socially efficient." By "socially efficient" was meant a person who was committed to fundamental American values and capable of making a real contribution to the technical and social development of the country. Clearly this concept of the function of high school education differed significantly from the view that had been promoted by the Committee of Ten in 1893. The Committee of Nine's position was stated in this way in the group's final report (National Education Association 1911, p. 560):

> *Not only is it the duty of the high school to lay the foundations of good citizenship and to help in the wise choice of a vocation, but it is equally important that the high school should make specific contribution to the efficiency of the individual*

along various broad lines. In our industrial democracy the development of individual aptitude and unique gifts is quite as important as the development of the common elements of the culture.

There was concern, too, that the high school should serve as a mechanism for promoting understanding among people who, as adults, would pursue different vocational and career interests. Some feared that a high school dedicated to a scholarly precollege curriculum would produce a class of students who would constitute a standoffish elite who would be unable to communicate with people of a more practical bent. Addressing this issue, the Committee of Nine noted: "By means of excessively bookish curricula false ideals of culture are developed. A chasm is created between the producers of material wealth and the distributors and consumers thereof (p. 560).

The work of the Committee of Nine reflected a growing sense of need to define the purposes of the high school more broadly. Note that nothing in the statements of the Committee of Nine suggested that college preparation should be abandoned as one of the purposes of the high school program. Rather, the committee suggested that college preparation should not be the *only* purpose of the high school. This concern continued to stimulate a great deal of thought during the World War I years. Finally, the famous National Education Association's Commission on the Reorganization of Secondary Education in its 1918 report laid down the principles underlying the broad-based high school. This broadly based or "comprehensive" high school is the dominant model in the United States today.

THE HIGH SCHOOL BECOMES COMPREHENSIVE

The report of the National Education Association's Commission on the Reorganization of Secondary Education of 1918 is a seminal document in the evolution of American secondary education. It is the intellectual source for nearly every argument that has been made in support of the view that properly public high school ought to be "comprehensive" high schools. In its report, the commission attempted to build a bridge between those who saw the high school as a college preparatory institution and those who saw the high school as an institution devoted to training youngsters in the more practical arts. In its inspired use of the term "comprehensive," the commission suggested that the high school could meet both objectives. The commission envisioned a high school curriculum broad enough to accommodate the needs and interests of a student body as wide and as varied as the general population of the country. Given this conception, the high school program was to be devoted to preparing young people of all kinds for appropriate and responsible adult roles.

This broad view of the high school's purpose was perhaps best expressed in the commission's (1918) description of the "cardinal principles" of secondary education. These cardinal principles, promoted as goals to be promoted by a high school education, were

1. Health
2. Command of fundamental processes
3. Worthy home membership
4. Vocational preparation
5. Citizenship
6. Worthy use of leisure time
7. Ethical character

The cardinal principles provided a rationale for the expansion of curricular offerings in secondary schools to meet the increasingly varied interests and needs of the rapidly expanding high school population. The commission's work resulted in a tremendous increase in the numbers of high schools that described themselves as comprehensive.

A number of motives were behind the effort to establish the comprehensive high school as the national norm. Although numbers of secondary students in the years before 1920 and into the 1920s remained small when compared with elementary school enrollments, these enrollments were expanding. Even children of immigrant parents were beginning to enter secondary school classrooms. Especially during the 1920s, when there was great concern the unacceptable foreign values might corrupt what many saw as a fragile American democracy, there was an interest in using the high school to teach all youngsters the "American way." One manifestation of this interest was the development of a new course, called civics, that became a standard feature of many high school curricula.

A second influence was the work of John Dewey and his followers, who suggested that learning ought to center on the individual and that learning included all life experiences, not just those traditionally defined by academic subjects in the school. Further, Dewey's contention that learning required practical application if transfer to new settings was to occur supported the idea of broadening the kind of experiences to which students were exposed in school.

Third, there was a growing belief that secondary schools were a logical extension of the elementary school program. Reacting to this conviction, state legislatures by the 1920s had enacted laws requiring students to stay in school at least through the first few years of the high school program. These laws assured that a good proportion of the students in high schools would profit from a curriculum broader than one directed only at the college-bound student.

Broadening of the high school curriculum in the 1920s and 1930s was by no means accomplished without criticism. Many of the adults of the 1920s who had graduated from high school in the 1880s, 1890s, or early 1900s lamented the trend as something that would "debase" the integrity of the high school diploma. These concerns were raised even though by present-day standards only a very small percentage of youngsters of high school age were actually in high school. Let us look at some figures from the early 1920s. In school year 1919–1920, high school students represented only slightly over 10 percent of all students in school. In other words, nearly 90 percent of youngsters in schools were enrolled in grades 1 through 8 (U.S. Department of Health, Education, and Welfare 1979). These figures mean that, as late as 1920, tremendous numbers of youngsters were completing their education at the end (or even before the end) of the eighth grade.

Further, of those who did enter high school, dropout rates were very high. Of students who entered high school as freshmen in 1920, only 46 percent remained to be seniors in 1923 (Krug 1972). In short, high schools in the early 1920s continued to enroll a very narrow cross section of American youth. But, to adults of the time, the high schools seemed enormously crowded as compared with the schools of their own day. Further, they sensed that such an enrollment increase must necessarily have been accompanied by a decline in quality. It is instructive to reflect that those few older citizens who today are outspoken in their attacks on the "watered-down" experience that, they allege, today's high schoolers receive, were themselves considered to be getting highly inferior high school education by many critics of high school education in the 1920s and 1930s. Krug (1972, pp. 107–108) has commented on this point as follows:

> *Today's older people would not be flattered by what was said about them then. According to the pedagogical rhetoric of the 1920s, the academic quality of the students then in high school represented a calamitous decline from the heights of excellence that had been occupied by their predecessors before the war.*
>
> *Even though the students of the twenties were only a fraction of all youth, there*

were large numbers of them, many more than before. It was assumed that when large numbers were involved many of them had to be stupid.

Despite the concerns of some that the comprehensive high school was providing an intellectually "soft" experience compared with earlier high schools that had served a narrower audience of college-bound students, the comprehensive high school came to be the standard American model. At various times there were efforts to place more emphases on programmatic areas within the total high school curriculum and less on others. For example, given the limited job opportunities through much of the 1930s, many high schools placed much less emphasis on vocational preparation programs than they had during the late 1920s. These changes in degree of emphasis almost never resulted in broad-based demands that the comprehensive high school as an idea be scrapped. It seemed to be a model that met the general American need very well.

Today, the comprehensive high school continues to be the American norm. But whether this will continue to be the case in the future is open to dispute. We are beginning to hear today people raising serious questions about whether the comprehensive high school is truly doing what it is supposed to be doing (see Figure 1-4, for example). In the next section, we will examine a brief history of some of the present criticisms being made of the comprehensive high school.

Figure 1-4

THEY AIN'T WHAT THEY USED TO BE

On a late-night talk show, a caller phones in and makes these comments:

When I was in school we had to work. It was five, I mean *five,* solid subjects. When I was a sophomore I took Latin, geometry, English, biology, and world history. I had p.e. three times a week and a study hall twice a week. Teachers in those days really cared. They knew what an educated person had to know, and by golly they saw to it we found out what that was too.

Now my son's in high school. He's taking basic pottery, some nebulous thing called "language arts," business math, career appreciation, and some other ill-defined course called "problems in democracy." He never seems to have any homework. He is just going through school like it's one big frivolous party.

Now, I am paying taxes for my son's education. So are a lot of other folks. I really wonder what we're getting. There is simply no way he is going to know what I knew when I got out of high school. I am really concerned, too, that he'll lack the skills to get in and dig when he matures a bit and finds out that there are some things he's got to really study to understand. I think our high schools have become just a sham. They are a national disgrace. We need to do something.

YOUR OPINION, PLEASE

Read the comments above. Then, respond to these questions.

1. Are high schools "too easy" on students? Why, or why not? How would you define "too easy"?
2. Do high schools give students a false set of expectations of what "life is really all about"? Why, or why not?
3. What do you suppose the basic purpose was of the curriculum the caller experienced in high school? Should that have been (or should it be) the curriculum for all students? Why, or why not?
4. What do you suppose is the basic purpose of the curriculum that seems to be presented to the caller's son? Should it be the curriculum for all students? Why, or why not?
5. Are high schools a national disgrace? Why, or why not?
6. If you could change one thing in the high school curriculum you experienced, what would that be? Why would you change it? Would every student in the school benefit from this change? Why, or why not?

STATUS OF THE COMPREHENSIVE HIGH SCHOOL TODAY

The comprehensive high school emerged to become the most common American secondary school, but at no time has it received the unanimous support of the American public. For example, individuals believing strongly that separate institutions ought to exist for training vocationally and academically oriented youngsters have criticized the idea that the needs of both groups can be served properly in a comprehensive high school. Despite these and other concerns raised by critics, the preponderance of comprehensive high schools suggests that a majority of Americans interested in education have preferred comprehensive high schools to other kinds of more specialized high schools. It is fair to say, however, that the debate over the adequacy of the comprehensive school has heated up in recent years. To understand why this has happened, let us review a few trends that have developed over the last 30 to 40 years.

Shortly after World War II, some observers noted that the comprehensive high schools were doing a reasonably good job of preparing the 20 percent or so of high school students who were going on to college and the 20 percent or so who had keen vocational interests and who were enrolled in specific vocational training courses. However, it was alleged, the 60 percent of the students who did not fit into either the college preparation category or the vocational category were not being well served. These people included many female students who were expected to grow up to be homemakers (remember, this was the 1940s before women's liberation and the view that women's career aspirations could and should be as broad as men's), students who would work in blue-collar trades, and others who would find a niche in the world of business, in the government bureaucracy, or in some other line of work. Because the specific employment futures of these people could not be predicted with accuracy, the school vocational program was not a good choice for them. Since they would not be going on to college, the college preparation program was determined to be inadequate. What was needed, so the critics suggested, was a curriculum designed to prepare them for the general kinds of decisions they would have to make as adults, regardless of the particular kinds of adult roles in which they came to find themselves.

Concern for this so-called "forgotten 60 percent" led to a movement for the high school to include courses designed to help students meet the demands of daily living they would face as adults. This came to be known as the "life adjustment" curriculum. As the name suggested, courses were to be offered in schools that would smooth the adjustment of students to the world they would confront after graduation.

For a time in the late 1940s and into the 1950s, there was a good deal of support for life adjustment efforts on the part of many leaders in secondary education. A difficulty with the approach was the failure of many leaders of the movement to suggest just what sorts of specific courses ought to be included. Simply stated, there was a tendency for national leaders to articulate a general need for a life adjustment program and to leave it to state and local authorities to decide just what kinds of courses should be included in the high schools to promote this general end. Many states and local communities set up special commissions to determine exactly what should be taught. Often the result was a hodgepodge of suggestions for courses that, while attempting to teach some so-called "adult need," appeared potentially very weak in terms of substance. For example, in some places such courses as "Finding a Reliable Dentist" and "Good Cosmetic Selection" were recommended. (Think about this discussion as you review questions raised in Figure 1-5.)

It is doubtful whether such courses were what the national leaders of the life adjustment idea had in mind, but their failure to provide specific course suggestions led to a proliferation of courses at the state and local level that varied enormously in quality. Some of these courses provided a field day for people who were critical of the comprehensive high school as an institution. Critics supporting the view that high schools should be directed primarily to preparing students for college were outraged by

Figure 1-5

PLANNING A LIFE ADJUSTMENT CURRICULUM
  Suppose that you were a high school administrator in a large school district. A survey conducted revealed that large numbers of your students were not profiting from the school program. In thinking about this problem, you decided that the time might be ripe to introduce a program consistent with the life adjustment point of view.

YOUR OPINION, PLEASE
In thinking about the program of courses you would establish, how would you respond to these questions?

1. How, exactly, would you go about determining what an adult who was "adjusted" to life has to be able to do?
2. How could you be sure that your program would prepare students who might move away from the local area after graduation?
3. Would you be able to respond effectively to individuals critical of a life adjustment approach? Why, or why not?
4. How would your teacher recruitment practices have to be changed to get teachers capable of teaching your new program?
5. How receptive do you think students might be to the new program? On what do you base your judgment?
6. Would there be a need to organize new departments? If so, what might those departments be? What courses would be taught by teachers in each?

---

the life adjustment perspective. Stories about courses in basket weaving circulated among the cocktail party set. Comedians were presented with a gold mine of new material in the form of some of the more bizarre courses suggested by some state and local partisans of life adjustment.

  As a result, the very term "life adjustment" came to suggest to large numbers of people that schools were taking on some of the characteristics of a comic opera. This perception tended to change the character of criticism of the high school. Prior to life adjustment, various factions had debated whether high schools should have this emphasis or that emphasis. But, usually, all factions agreed that the high school was a serious institution and that, by extension, educational leaders charged with administering and managing high schools were intelligent and responsible people. With the advent of the life adjustment movement and the resultant jokes about some suggested new courses, the high school came to be seen as a less serious institution. As a less serious institution, fewer people than ever stood in awe of what educational leaders were suggesting. It became psychologically easier for people to criticize openly high schools and high school programs.

  By the middle 1950s, the perception that high schools had gone soft had spread to the point that the term "life adjustment" was purged from the vocabularies of careful school administrators. The final blow to the life adjustment concept was dealt in 1957, when the Soviets launched the world's first earth satellite, Sputnik I. This watershed event set off a barrage of criticism of American schools, particularly American high schools. Critics such as Admiral Rickover spoke out against high school curricula that they saw as pathetically weak as compared with the more academically rigorous requirements of European secondary schools. These critics were especially concerned that the level of training in mathematics and the sciences in our high schools fell far short of what Europeans in general and the Soviets in particular were providing for their young people.

These criticisms began to have an impact on high school curricula. While the idea that high schools should be comprehensive was not attacked directly in most cases, there was great pressure on the schools to emphasize the college preparatory portion of the high school program more heavily. During this period, a very important book appeared that was widely read by a broad cross section of the American public and that influenced a good deal of thinking about the nature of the high school. The book was James B. Conant's *The American High School Today.*

Conant (1959) commented that mathematics, foreign languages, technical course training, and other areas of the high school curriculum should be strengthened. But his final conclusion suggested that there was no need to establish new kinds of secondary schools. The comprehensive high school, he noted, was still a good idea. Basically what was required was a little internal tinkering with the array of course offerings.

Implicit in the remarks of Conant, of Rickover, and of nearly every other individual of this period who articulated a position on an issue related to high school education was an important fundamental assumption. This assumption was that the high school was an institution that, when organized properly, could provide programs that would solve important national problems. A testament to this basic faith in high schools' ability to respond effectively to a national need was the passage of the National Defense Education Act in 1958.

The National Defense Education Act (NDEA) resulted in the expenditure of vast amounts of federal money to improve education. Some of this money went to underwrite costs of national curriculum development projects. Initially, the emphases were on mathematics, sciences, and foreign languages. Later, programs in the social sciences were included, and special workshops for teachers designed to upgrade teachers skills were established. In short, the National Defense Education Act represented a massive effort to use the schools to solve what many considered to be a problem of "academic weakness" in American schools.

Results of efforts launched by National Defense Education Act were not as promising as many supporters of more rigor in high school education had hoped. For one thing, although many teachers were reached by these efforts, the vast majority was not. Many teachers continued to operate much as they always had. Second, the programs, in the eyes of many, seemed directed almost exclusively toward an academic elite of high school students. There were many complaints that the new materials were simply too difficult for large numbers of high school youngsters. Finally, a good number of the new NDEA-sponsored programs did not respond well to the issue of motivation. Some students simply were not interested in them.

Although there was not substantial lasting impact on school programs as a result of the National Defense Education Act, the idea the schools could solve important social problems was little attacked as a consequence of the failure to transform the nature of American high schools. One implication drawn from this failure was the finding that the NDEA programs and materials were not adequate to serve all students needs. Few questioned that the school as an institution might not be able to solve important social problems. This view was reinforced during the youth revolts of the 1960s and early 1970s.

In the early and middle 1960s, the tide of feeling that schools were capable of resolving deep-seated problems reached its high. Passage of the Elementary and Secondary Education Act of 1965 (ESEA) dramatically increased the level of federal involvement in education by establishing federal monetary support for a number of specialized programs. The clear presumption of those favoring passage of this bill was that a better society could logically be expected as an end result of better school programs.

The act also set another important precedent. In its attempt to target specific aspects of the school program for special attention, it started a trend for special school efforts to be directed toward promoting the specific interests of particular parts of the school and school program rather than toward promoting the more generalized interest of the school as a whole. Subsequent to passage of ESEA, the federal government (and states and local authorities, too) increasingly imposed requirements on schools designed to serve needs of specific groups of youngsters. For example, mandated programs came to be required for students whose native language was not English and for students suffering from a number of handicapping conditions. A result of this trend has been a great proliferation of the kinds of needs schools seek to accommodate. Some critics suggest that today the schools are being asked to do too much. Certainly the issue is one that is being widely debated.

While the comprehensive school, as an institution designed to meet the needs of all youngsters, should have no philosophical problem in adding new programs to meet specialized needs, there is increasing concern that these needs are not being met well in practice. The National Panel on High School and Adolescent Education in its final report (1976) noted that "in attempting to meet the needs of all American youth, the high school today is often failing to respond adequately to the needs of individual students" (p. 1).

Even where high schools have been observed to offer courses that seem to provide important services needed by a specific portion of the student population, results have not always been impressive. After many years of emphasis on vocational programs, "investigators report that graduates of vocational programs tend *not* to be employed in the field of their training, that their earnings do not exceed those of nonvocational students, that materials and equipment used and skills taught in vocational courses tend to be out of date, and that little effort is made to relate training to job needs or to provide help in placement" (1976, p. 6). Similar concerns have been raised about the effectiveness of other school programs directed toward special groups. One general criticism that has been made in this connection is that such programs tend to become isolated from reality because students are taught away from members of the adult population in a cocoonlike environment called a high school. Some critics have suggested a need to provide educational opportunities for high-school-aged youngsters in situations where they would come into more frequent and more direct contact with adults (National Panel 1976).

Criticisms, too, have been made about the substance of efforts supposedly designed to broaden curricular offerings to serve well the interests of all of the students in high school. Although evidence suggests that there has been a great expansion of the numbers of courses being offered in today's high schools as compared with those of 20 years ago, there is additional evidence that these courses may not be meeting the needs of a broader cross section of students. One report revealed that the tendency to expand numbers of course offerings resulted more frequently than not in an increase in the numbers of specialized electives available for college-bound students rather than in an increase in the numbers of courses designed to meet the specialized requirements of other students.

Perhaps the most serious criticism being made today against the comprehensive high school has to do with the challenge to the assumption that programs in such a school can be realistically expected to solve serious social problems. In its final report, the National Panel on High School and Adolescent Education made this comment (1976, p. 26):

> *The comprehensive school seems to emphasize the class and racial differences in society. Merely bringing all these elements under one roof on the assumption that this action will counteract successfully the effects of stratification in society is naive at best. The evidence indicates that the comprehensive high school serves to* reinforce *the class and race stratification of society.*

Increasingly there is a perception that high schools are part of whatever social problems embroil the entire society. Whatever difficulties society wrestles with are also problems for the school. Some argue, then, that it is illogical for the high school, alone, or education, alone, to be expected to solve social problems. Robert D. Barr (1979, p. 86) speaks to this issue as follows:

> *Our entire culture seems eaten away and ripped apart with one dramatic prob-*
> *lem after another. We live in an age where there is almost never any good news.*
> *If education is in trouble, then we look at the religious institutions, the political*
> *institutions, the economic institutions . . . and even the nuclear family. Something*
> *seems to have slipped in this great nation of ours and suddenly all our cultural*
> *institutions seem out of sync and off beat. The slow death of the Puritan ethic in*
> *the market place has crept into the classroom to gnaw away at motivation, the*
> *drive for personal excellence and educational ideals. The misuse of alcohol and*
> *drugs, the rampant vandalism and violence, the commonplace suicide and prom-*
> *iscuity in schools is only a reflection of the frustration, fear, and anger that typifies*
> *so much of contemporary life.*

Today, high schools find themselves awash in a sea of criticism. On the one hand, some people who say they are interested in "quality" education fear that college preparatory programs are being weakened as a result of the introduction of so many courses directed toward the needs of special groups in the high school student population. They point to such so-called "measures of decline" as decreases in student scores on the Scholastic Aptitude Test.

From the students themselves comes pressure to mount programs that are responsive to their own interests and needs. Though perhaps less strident in formulating these demands than they were in the late 1960s and the early 1970s, students in high schools still continue to push for courses that interest them.

State legislators, citing their constituents' horror stories about high school graduates who cannot read, write, or compute, charge that schools are not giving sufficient emphasis to basic skills. Increasingly they are requiring schools to show evidence that high school students are profiting from their school experience as measured by a performance on a test of minimum competency.

Squeezed by inflation, taxpayer groups have joined the chorus of criticism of school programs by alleging that many of them are simply too expensive. Cost control has become a paramount concern of those interested in avoiding dramatic escalations in property tax rates. (Schools receive a very high percentage of their operating revenues from property taxes.)

In summary, the comprehensive high school is being monitored today by many different groups in the society. It has proved to be an exceptionally resilient institution. And it seems likely that the institution is in no immediate danger of being replaced by another kind of high school. But pressures from one organized group or another may result in some changes in emphases in comprehensive school programs in the years ahead. Figure 1-6 addresses this concern in more detail.

THE SENIOR HIGH SCHOOL AS A SOCIAL PHENOMENON

Ask adults to recall something about their high school years and most will make only a few guarded references to what they learned in classes and how teachers taught courses. But you are likely to hear a great deal about football games, clubs, interpersonal relationships, and extracurricular activities of all kinds. The essentially social aspects of this peculiarly American institution tend to have a profound and lasting impact on many people.

In his delightful book, *Is There Life After High School?*, Ralph Keyes (1976) points out that the senior high school embraces a very special population of American youngsters. It includes students at an age when society expects them to begin breaking off lines of dependency on parental authority (and even on more generalized adult authority of all kinds). Yet these youngsters retain a need for status and personal rec-

Figure 1-6

SHOULD WE HAVE A SYSTEM OF SMALLER, MORE SPECIALIZED HIGH SCHOOLS?
The Panel would shift the emphasis away from the *comprehensive school* toward *comprehensive education*, arguing that the confines of one building are no longer enough to contain all the valuable and necessary experiences for today's young person. What is needed is greater diversity in formal
· education which reflects the actual diversity of the learning situations and the variety of experience that living in today's world demands.*

YOUR OPINION, PLEASE
Read the materal above. Then, respond to these questions.

1. Would you favor splitting up today's large comprehensive high schools into a number of smaller, more specialized schools? Why, or why not?
2. What changes in student life in high schools would you foresee if today's comprehensive high schools were broken up into a number of smaller units?
3. Can a single school building of any kind do an adequate job of preparing a high school student for the "real world"? Why, or why not?
4. If you decided that students in high school need more real-world experience, how would you provide for it?
5. If you were to predict what high schools 30 years from now would look like, would you expect there to be more or less emphasis on the comprehensive high school than we have today? On what do you base your opinion?

*National Panel on High School and Adolescent Education, *The Education of Adolescents,* Final Report and Recommendations (Washington, D.C.: U.S. Department of Health, Education, and Welfare, 1976), p. 8.

---

ognition. Since this recognition among adolescents cannot (for many youngsters, at least) come from adults, it must come from other young people. What we have, then, is a high school filled with young people who desperately seek recognition and status in a situation that has only a limited amount of status to award. Clearly not everyone can be a cheerleader. Clearly not everyone can be a star athlete. Clearly not everyone can be a leader in the most prestigious clubs. The result of all this, notes Keyes, is a social pressure cooker where a small group of students whom he describes as the "ins" ride high and where a much larger number who Keyes styles "the outs" muddle, often resentfully, through their high school years.

Keyes points out that the "sense of place" that many students get in high schools may stick with them long after they have left school. Although there is little evidence to suggest that someone who was low on the social pecking order in high school is condemned to that kind of a status after leaving school, some people continue to define themselves as they were in high school when interacting with old classmates. Potential embarrassment about what one was or was not in high school has led to this unwritten rule of social conduct among newly introduced adults (Keyes 1976, p. 8):

> *If you don't ask me what I was like in high school, I won't ask you.*

Keyes suggests that high school is a time when a student senses himself or herself to be constantly undergoing systematic evaluation on the part of all with whom he or she comes into contact (see Figure 1-7). Speaking to this issue, he comments as follows (p. 21):

> *As the most tribal experience many of us will ever have, high school must be memorable. Never again are we ranked so precisely by those around us, and on so many scales. Through the popularity polls of our classmates, and their inexperi-*

Figure 1-7

___

WHO ARE THE HIGH-STATUS AND LOW-STATUS STUDENTS?

Ralph Keyes (1976) has suggested that high schools are very closed societies where certain kinds of student behaviors are rewarded and others are punished. Only a few students emerge as "winners" in this setting. Most go though school feeling that if they are not outright "losers" then they at best are "not winners."

YOUR OPINION, PLEASE

Think about this point of view. Then, respond to these questions.

1. Was there a rigid social system in your high school? What evidence supports your view?
2. What sorts of students were treated as winners or high-status people by other students in school?
3. How were high-status students treated? What special privileges were they accorded?
4. How did one get to be a high-status student? Was the selection process fair? Why, or why not?
5. What kind of behaviors were considered high status and low status? (For example, was riding a bike to school a high-status or a low-status behavior?)
6. How would you feel personally if you received news that the most pushy cheerleader from your high school senior class had ballooned to 250 pounds and was selling candy in a dime store?
7. In general, do you think that people in high school who were high status will be greater achievers in midlife than will those who were of either intermediate status or low status? Why do you think so?
8. Did you see yourself as high status, intermediate status, or low status in high school? How did you "know your place"? How did you feel about your place? Did you ever do anything specific in high school to change your relative social standing? If so, what? Were you successful?

___

ence at tact, daily feedback was conveyed about how we were coming across. Such merciless judgment is not easily forgotten, the last time of life we know just where we stand in the scrutinizing eyes around us.

The perception that there is this kind of constant review and evaluation process going on contributes to adolescents' sense personal anxiety. This anxiety tends to be promoted also by the reality that the high school years are a very dangerous time of life in a physical sense. Because adult control mechanisms are not yet developed fully, youngsters in this age group take chances, and they do get hurt with a much higher frequency than do either younger children or adults. Dangers come not only from too great a willingness to "take a chance" but also from badgering by other youngsters. Who among us (at least those of us who made up the great majority of small and averaged-sized "outs") cannot remember our tightening stomach muscles as a few muscle-bound giants edged their way in our direction at a high school dance? High school students, at least a great many of them, do have a real basis for their anxieties. In many ways their world is much more dangerous than the one they will face as adults when they move out into a world governed by a different set of rules.

We do not wish to belabor the nature of the social world of the high school students. Youngsters, after all, have been graduating from high school for years with no debilitating emotional scars. But those planning to work as teachers in high schools, we believe, do need to be sensitive to the special social world that exists in the high school. Events in this adolescent social world may well have a great impact on how certain students behave in class and on the kinds of academic difficulties some may be having. Our intent here is to suggest that a high school teacher may well increase his or her effectiveness by sharpening his or her sensitivities to the social environment within which students exist in the outside-of-class world of the high school.

Posttest

Directions: Using your own paper, answer each of the following true/false questions. For each correct statement write the word "true." For each incorrect statement, write the word "false."

_____ 1. Early high schools had a curriculum that differed dramatically from that offered in the secondary academies.

_____ 2. Public secondary school education in this country has a history going back just as far as public elementary school education.

_____ 3. Evidence is overwhelming that the senior high school has been an agency that has been able to solve many deeply rooted social problems.

_____ 4. In school year 1919–1920, only slightly over 10 percent of all students in school were enrolled in grades 9 through 12.

_____ 5. The length of the school term has generally decreased in this country since the 1800s.

_____ 6. Supporters of the "comprehensive" high school traditionally have seen high school as an institution designed only to meet the needs of college- and university-bound youngsters.

_____ 7. In the 1920s, people were little concerned about any supposed drop in the quality of students enrolled in high schools.

_____ 8. There is evidence that large numbers of high school students are very concerned about their status within their own age group.

_____ 9. The first high school was the English Classical School, established in Boston in 1821.

_____ 10. In the second half of the eighteenth century, the dominant type of American secondary school was the public high school.

Key Ideas in Review

1. Today's high schools are unique American institutions. Despite some slight differences from place to place, high school academic and extracurricular programs tend to follow a very similar pattern throughout the country. In a sense, the common high school experience provides a strong social bond to which Americans in widely separated parts of the country can relate.

2. Public concern for secondary education, as opposed to elementary education, developed rather slowly in this country. Early secondary schools, frequently termed Latin grammar schools, were funded privately. They were targeted toward an elite group of students who were expected to go on to colleges and universities upon completion of the secondary school program.

3. The academy was a secondary school that evolved from a conviction that secondary education of a more practical nature than that afforded by Latin grammar schools was needed. Typically funded by private sources, the academies became very popular in this country in the years following the Revolutionary War. The academy reached its height of popularity in 1850 (Barry 1961, p. 46).

4. The first high school supported by public funds was the Boston English Classical School, established in 1821. The high school curricula of this and other early high schools paralleled closely curricula offered by the private academies. At first, high schools expanded rather slowly. One reason for this was the concern about whether tax money could be used legally to support secondary schools as well as elementary schools. The famous *Kalamazoo* case of 1874 established a legal precedent in this regard. After the legal environment was established, high schools grew in number at a rapid rate.

5. In the earlier years of this century, small numbers of students enrolled in high schools. Only in relatively recent times has the vast majority of students in the 14- to 17-year-old age group been enrolled in high schools. Today between 12 and 13 million students attend high schools in this country.

6. In the early years of this century (and even before) there was a great debate over whether high schools should serve only college-bound students or whether they should serve other students as well. Partisans of serving a cross section of youngsters broader than the college bound generally emerged victorious. The comprehensive high school, in theory at least dedicated to serving *all* youngsters of secondary school age, has become the American norm.

7. In recent years, debate over whether the comprehensive high school can indeed serve all youngsters well has heated up. Some suggest that, by attempting to serve all groups, no groups get served very well. Others complain that the comprehensive high school has been charged not only with teaching youngsters specific subjects but with reforming society as well. Some critics suggest that this latter aim is unrealistic. Some talk is being heard about the desirability of abandoning the comprehensive high school and replacing it with a number of smaller schools, each of which would have a narrower responsibility. However, given the long-standing tradition of comprehensive high schools, it seems more likely that emphases within the programs offered by comprehensive high schools will be forced to change from time to time in response to the political envirionment. The institution, itself, seems in little immediate danger of being eliminated.

8. High schools consist of a tight social world for students that coexists with the world of classes and schedules that teachers know. High school awards and denies status to certain individuals according to "rules" known to the adolescent community that comprise the social world of the school. Because only a limited number of students can savor the rewards in this system, many find themselves to be social outsiders. This can influence how they view themselves and how they act in class. It is sound practice for a secondary school teacher to learn as much about the social structure of the student community in the school as he or she can. Such information can shed light on how given youngsters behave in formal classroom settings.

SUMMARY

The high school is an American institution. Today, high schools enroll an overwhelming percentage of youngsters in the 14- to 17-year-old age group. Despite certain differences, basic patterns of academic and nonacademic life persist across vast reaches of territory. People from far-flung areas of the country are likely to have had very similar kinds of experiences during their high school years.

The presumption that all students will stay in school through their secondary school years is relatively new to the American scene. In the early years of our country, public education was provided only for a relatively few and generally only for a few elementary school years. Some early attention to secondary education came with the establishment of Latin grammar schools, which sought to train young men to study at colleges and universities. Later, privately sponsored academies were established. These privately funded institutions offered more practical courses with a view to preparing young people for the technical demands of a rapidly expanding industrial society.

The first public high school did not emerge until 1821. The high school was not especially popular until the second half of the nineteenth century. There was some concern about the legality of using public funds to support secondary schools. After the courts decided that tax money could be so used, the number of high schools began to expand at a rapid rate. But, even as late as 1900, only a small fraction of all students in public schools were enrolled in high schools. By the early 1920s about 30 to 40 percent of the age-eligible youngsters were in high school. Surprisingly, it has been only within the last 30 years that the high school has enrolled more than 50 percent of the nation's adolescents. Today, well over 90 percent of youngsters in the 14- to 17-year-old age group attend high schools.

High schools comprise not only a place where students take courses but also a unique adolescent social system. The culture of the high school awards status for certain behavior and denies it for certain behavior. Some authorities suggest that the anxiety many high school students experience results, in part at least, from their existence in a social system that seems constantly to be holding them up for purposes of ascertaining their appropriate place in the adolescent pecking order. Certainly, how an individual student stands in the eyes of his or her classroom may have implications for how he or she acts in class. Teachers then need to be students not only of their subjects and of generalized learning psychology, but also of the adolescent social system of the American high school.

References

Barr, Robert D. "Secondary Schools: New Optimism in a Time of Trouble," in Robert D. Barr and Christine I. Bennett, eds., "Secondary Education: A Time of Crisis and Creativity," *Viewpoints in Teaching and Learning*. Bloomington: University of Indiana, School of Education, Spring 1977, pp. 85–93.

Barry, Thomas Newman. "Origin and Development of the American Public High School in the Nineteenth Century." Unpublished doctoral dissertation. Stanford University, 1961.

Commission on the Reorganization of Secondary Education. *Cardinal Principles of Secondary Education*. Washington, D.C.: U.S. Government Printing Office, 1918.

Conant, James B. *The American High School Today*. New York: McGraw-Hill Book Company, 1959.

Keyes, Ralph. *Is There Life After High School?* Boston: Little, Brown Company, 1976.

Krug, Edward A. *The Shaping of the American High School*. Vol. 2, 1920–1941. Madison; University of Wisconsin Press, 1972.

National Education Association. *Report of the Committee of Ten on Secondary School Studies*. Washington, D.C.: NEA, 1893.

National Education Association. *Addresses and Proceedings*. Washington, D.C.: NEA, July 11, 1911.

National Panel on High School and Adolescent Education. *The Education of Adolescents*. Final Report and Recommendations. Washington, D.C.: U.S. Department of Health, Education, and Welfare, 1976.

O'Bryan, Sharon. "Reports on the Reform of Secondary Education: An In-Depth Analysis," in Robert D. Barr and Christine I. Bennett, eds., "Secondary Education: A Time of Crisis and Creativity," *Viewpoints in Teaching and Learning*. Bloomington: University of Indiana, School of Education, Spring 1979, pp. 53–66.

Raubinger, Frederick M.; Rowe, Harold G.; Piper, Donald L.; and West, Charles K. *The Development of Secondary Education*. New York: Macmillan Publishing Co., Inc., 1969.

Tanner, Daniel, and Tanner, Laurel N. *Curriculum Development: Theory into Practice*. New York: Macmillan Publishing Co., Inc., 1975.

U.S. Department of Commerce, Bureau of the Census. *Historical Statistics of the United States: Colonial Times to 1870*. Part I, Bicentennial edition. Washington, D.C.: U.S. Government Printing Office, 1975.

U.S. Department of Education. *The Condition of Education, 1980*. Washington, D.C.: National Center for Education Statistics, 1980.

U.S. Department of Health, Education, and Welfare. *Digest of Education Statistics, 1979*. Washington, D.C.: U.S. Government Printing Office, 1979.

2

The Intermediate School

"Talk about a waste of money . . . this building takes the cake! I say we should send them off to live in caves until they come back semi-civilized at 15 or 16!"

Objectives

This chapter provides information to help the reader to

1. Identify reasons behind the initial establishment of intermediate schools.
2. Suggest a number of criticisms of junior high schools that have been made over the years.
3. Differentiate between junior high schools and middle schools.

4. Suggest a number of characteristics of learners of intermediate school age.
5. Point out some implications for teachers of characteristics of the intermediate school setting.

Pretest

Directions: Using your own paper, answer each of the following true/false questions. For each correct statement, write the word "true." For each incorrect statement, write the word "false."

_____ 1. Intermediate schools have had as long a history in this country as have elementary schools and senior high schools.

_____ 2. Scientists have discovered that the human brain grows not continuously but rather in a predictable series of growth stages and nongrowth plateaus from birth to maturity.

_____ 3. The junior high school has been criticized for attempting to provide a program too similar to that of the senior high school.

_____ 4. The middle school has a shorter history as an intermediate school than does the junior high school.

_____ 5. Many youngsters during their intermediate school years are engaged in a search for personal identity and personal independence.

_____ 6. Because youngsters have few distinctive characteristics at this stage of their lives, there is little need for special preparation programs for future teachers of intermediate school youngsters.

_____ 7. At the intermediate school level, there should be little emphasis on application of newly learned information.

_____ 8. When new buildings are being constructed in a given district, it is much more common for new middle schools or junior high school buildings to be constructed than for new high school buildings to be constructed.

_____ 9. Some teachers have felt that it is less prestigious to teach in a middle school or junior high school than in a senior high school.

_____ 10. In general, students at the intermediate school level need individualized attention and personal counseling.

INTRODUCTION

Intermediate schools are relative newcomers to the American educational scene. The first public intermediate schools were not established until the early years of the twentieth century. Despite their relatively short history, however, intermediate schools almost from the start have drawn a good deal of public attention. Indeed, it may not be too much to say that no school type has been surrounded by so much controversy as has the intermediate school. Much of this controversy has been prompted because of varying conceptions about what responsibilities ought to be discharged by intermediate schools.

Historically, the movement to establish intermediate schools began late in the nineteenth century, when large numbers of public high schools were being built. Although, by present standards, only a very small percentage of the school-aged population was enrolling in high schools, still these numbers were dramatically higher than what they had been in earlier years. Generally high schools of this time were seen as much more academically demanding institutions than elementary schools. As a result, many felt a need for a school that would bridge the gap between the elementary school and the high school. The intermediate school was proposed as an appropriate remedy.

In addition to a growing belief in a need for a school that would provide a smooth intellectual transition from elementary to high school, a number of influential psychologists were drawing attention to new-found principles of child growth and development. And their work led many well-read adults to begin to develop new views regarding the condition of childhood. Increasingly, people were coming to understand that youngsters' development followed a sequential pattern. Further, the kinds of tasks that a youngster logically could be expected to perform were coming to be viewed as related to the approximate age of the youngster. This view tended to support the establishment of an intermediate school in which youngsters in the preadolescent and early-adolescent age groups could be presented with learning experiences consistent with their levels of intellectual development.

In summary, then, two basic forces were at work to establish a new school unit, an intermediate school to serve the years between elementary and high school. One of these forces saw the new school primarily as a training ground for the academic challenges of high school. The other saw the new school as serving the unique needs of the youngsters enrolled and was much less concerned with the role of the intermediate school as a preparatory experience for high-school-level academics. Clearly these two views of the intermediate school were in conflict. In general, the debate between those seeing the intermediate school as primarily a training ground for high school and those who see it as an institution designed to fulfill the unique needs of the age groups it serves has continued unabated since the very first discussions related to establishment of intermediate schools. We will consider some contemporary issues associated with this debate in a subsequent section of this chapter.

THE ESTABLISHMENT OF THE JUNIOR HIGH SCHOOL

The first intermediate school to be established in response to the forces mentioned was founded in Berkeley, California in 1909. In this city, the superintendent of schools proposed to the board of education the establishment of a 6-3-3 organizational pattern. The first six grades would comprise the elementary school unit, the next three grades the intermediate school unit, and the final three grades the high school unit (Popper 1967). This pattern soon was copied by large numbers of school districts throughout the country.

Initially, there was a good deal of debate regarding what name should be applied to the intermediate school. In the early years, such names as "subhigh school," "upper grammar school," "higher primary school," "departmental school," and "intermediate school" were used. In time, however, most of these alternatives gave way to the term "junior high school." The choice of this name may have influenced the development of programs at the intermediate school level. It is interesting to speculate about differences that might have emerged had a name such as upper grammar school been adopted.

The Emerging Character of the Junior High School

By the end of World War I, most junior high schools had become clearly identified as academic preparatory institutions for the senior high school. Although some lip service continued to be paid to "serving the special needs of preadolescents and early adolescents," mastery of subject matter had become the order of the day.

Teachers in junior high schools came to these schools from university and college preparation programs that were oriented heavily toward the senior high school. With few exceptions, teachers in junior high schools were required to have secondary as opposed to elementary teaching certificates. Large numbers of junior high school teachers saw teachers in high school as ideal professional role models. Many of them hoped some day to teach at the senior high school level. Ever sensitive to negative comments that might come their way from teachers in the senior high school, many junior high school teachers worked hard to demonstrate to potential skeptics that there was nothing "academically soft" about junior high school programs.

One consequence of all this was to divert attention away from specialized needs of youngsters who were students in junior high schools. This situation always prompted criticism from parents and educators who were concerned about human growth and development issues and the special needs of preadolescent and early-adolescent youngsters. Numbers of these critics swelled appreciably in the years following World War II when the partisans of the "life adjustment" movement promoted the idea that schools should seek to produce adults who would become productive contributing members of society. Individuals who subscribed to this view condemned the idea that the junior high school curriculum should be all academics. In time, critics who saw junior high schools as too narrowly aping the perspectives of the senior high school began to consider the possibility of establishing an entirely new institution to serve preadolescent and early-adolescent youngsters. Drawing on work of developmental psychologists and physiologists for an intellectual rationale for change, supporters of reform by the early 1960s proposed borrowing a term from European education, "middle school," to serve as a new intermediate school to replace the junior high school.

THE ADVENT OF THE MIDDLE SCHOOL

The middle school concept began to catch on during the decade of the 1960s. In general, middle schools are organized in such a way as to have at least three but not more than five grades that must include grades 6 and 7 (Lounsbury and Vars 1978). However, the focus in middle schools is not on grade levels so much as on individual students. Leaders of the middle school movement are strong proponents of program flexibility to meet individual youngster's needs (something they see lacking in many junior high schools). Consequently, then, there is fairly wide support for the view that "the middle school is not a grouping by grades but a grouping of ages, normally ages 11 through 14" (Egnatuck et al. 1975, p. 7).

In school year 1967–1968, a total of 1,101 middle schools were in operation. By 1976, the popularity of the middle school had increased their number to 4,060. Even larger numbers exist today. Clearly middle schools are displacing junior high schools as the dominant American intermediate school type. Today the National Middle School Association claims over 5,000 members, and the group is growing.* (Further questions on this topic are raised in Figure 2-1.)

In addition to some general opposition to programs in junior high school that many middle school supporters view as "too high school oriented," there are some specific positives they see associated with the middle school response to intermediate education. Let us examine several of the more common themes that run through the professional middle school literature.

Administrative Arrangements to Meet Special Needs of Middle School Youngsters

The junior high school was organized, in part at least, for the purpose of achieving a convenient division of the secondary grades (7 through 12) into two equal parts. Thus, grades 7, 8, and 9 became junior high school grades, and grades 10, 11, 12 became

---

*To keep these numbers in perspective, we note that the National Association of Secondary School Principals has a membership of about 35,000 and the National Association of Elementary School Principals has a membership of about 20,000. Although the membership in the middle school group still is relatively small compared with these other organizations, it is experiencing dramatic growth. Professionals who are active in the National Middle School Association believe there is potential, at least, for this group to become as large and powerful as the elementary and secondary organizations.

Figure 2-1

HOW SHOULD A SCHOOL SYSTEM BE ORGANIZED?
  Throughout the twentieth century, there have been numerous proposals for organizing American schools. Generally, there is agreement that there should be three distinct kinds of schools: elementary schools, intermediate schools, senior high schools. But there has been a good deal of debate about which grades should be assigned to which level.

YOUR OPINION, PLEASE
Read the paragraph above. Then, respond to these questions.

1. Should the present three-school structure be kept? Why do you think so? If you do not favor keeping this three-school structure, what alternative do you propose? Why do you think it would be better?
2. Some taxpayers argue that we should go back to a school system where we had a grades K through 8 elementary school and a grades 9 through 12 senior high school. Two buildings, they contend, would cost less to operate than three. What is your reaction to this proposal? What evidence supports your stand?
3. What kind of an intermediate school structure did you experience? (What grades were included in your junior high school or your middle school?) What strengths and weaknesses to this scheme can you comment on?
4. If you were called upon to identify an ideal structure for an intermediate school (that is, identify the grades to be included), what would that structure be? Why would you view such a scheme as ideal?
5. If you were to make a prediction about which grades typically would be included in most American intermediate schools in the year 2000, what would that prediction be? On what is it based? What might happen to make your prediction come true? Be off target?

senior high school grades. "Conceptually, then, the junior high school was not an educational response to learner needs as much as it was an attempt to improve educational management of learning in the secondary grades" (Toepfer 1980b, p. 32).

Middle school educators argue that certain psychological and physiological characteristics of youngsters in the 11- to 14-year-old group require a unique set of educational conditions in the school. The idea here is that there is something special about the task of educating youngsters of this age. This task can be accomplished most efficiently when the school is organized in such a way that special needs of these youngsters are supported by the administrative structure of the school.

More specifically, middle school administrators are charged with supporting instructional practices that respond to some specific needs of the 11- to 14-year-old. Among recommendations for work with youngsters of this age are the following:

1. Teachers must be prepared to listen to and talk informally with youngsters outside of regular class meetings. Youngsters of this age need ample opportunity to interact positively with adults (Toepfer 1980b).
2. Great options in subject matter and in modes of presentation must be provided to accommodate differences in youngsters' abilities and levels of development (Hurd 1978).
3. Specific learner characteristics must be diagnosed.
4. Correctives for deficiencies in the basic skill areas of reading, mathematics, and communication must be provided (Hurd 1978).
5. Linkages among subjects and between the school setting and the real world must be encouraged (Hurd 1978).

For middle school administrators, the charge is not to simply recognize these needs but to take specific steps to ensure that the program has real potential for accommodating them.

Physiological and Psychological Development of Middle School Youngsters

Individuals who have argued for an intermediate school that is clearly distinct both from the elementary school and the high school have based their view on the belief that youngsters in the preadolescent and early-adolescent age groups have certain unique characteristics. Some early discussion favoring the establishment of a middle school cited evidence that children were experiencing changes leading to sexual maturity at younger ages than had been the case with earlier generations (Toepfer 1980b). This information provided some rationale for grouping youngsters as young as fifth-graders in middle schools.

This early development was thought by some educators to harbor potential dangers for youngsters enrolled in traditional junior high schools (see Figure 2-2). Some felt that many junior high schools had developed activity programs including dances and other social events that too closely paralleled those in the senior high school. While physiologically many youngsters in the 11- to 14-year-old age group might appear

---

Figure 2-2

SHOULD MIDDLE SCHOOLS PROTECT YOUNGSTERS FROM THE "WORLD" OR HELP THEM REACH OUT TO THE "WORLD"?

SPEAKER A: We know that 10- and 11-year-olds are bigger and more mature today than ever before. Many of them are already going through processes leading them to social maturity. They are much more "savvy" about what's going on in the world than we were as kids. The kinds of films, books, and other information sources available to them today use language and portray events that tend to make them "streetwise" at a much younger age than was true for us. What we need is a middle school program that recognizes this reality. We need to get these kids involved in social situations and other kinds of issues that used to be reserved for high school students. We are kidding ourselves if we think we can shelter them from "reality." Many of them know a shocking amount of reality already. We need to tackle this thing head on and help them deal with it in a responsible way. So, let's have dances, let's have open discussions of social diseases, let's deal with real issues with these youngsters. In the end, they'll be stronger for it.

SPEAKER B: We have witnessed a regrettable trend in this country of trying to make our kids adults too soon. I have seen the information about how youngsters are going through sexual maturity earlier than they used to. But I am unconvinced that that fact has anything whatever to do with their emotional maturity to deal with their own emerging sexuality. It is one thing to have the biological capability to function in an adult manner. It is quite another to have the maturity to handle this capability in a responsible manner. I am very disturbed about middle school and junior high school dating. I don't think organized social dances are appropriate for these kids. We are rushing them too fast. We need to hold them back a little. We need to give them time to grow. There is going to be plenty of time for all of this in high school. If they get jaded on dancing and social affairs in their intermediate school years, I shudder to think what it will take to excite them when they get to high school.

YOUR OPINION, PLEASE
Read the comments above. Then, respond to these questions.

1. What are the primary concerns of Speaker A? How valid are they? Why do you think so?
2. What are the primary concerns of Speaker B? How valid are they? Why do you think so?
3. With which speaker do you identify most closely with personally? Why?
4. How do you remember your own intermediate school years? Were you pushed too fast? Not fast enough? Why do you think so?

ready for such social outlets, some authorities feared that emotionally they were not yet mature enough to engage in such activities. This view was reflected in a report of the Michigan Association of Middle School Educators as follows (Egantuck et al. 1975, p. 5):

> *While the junior high school was originally intended as protection for the young adolescent through a paced introduction into the complexities of senior high school, the present emphasis appears to be one of earlier and earlier participation in adult activities for which youth at this age are ill-prepared.*

In recent years, some fascinating research has supported the view that there is something special about youngsters in the 11- to 14-year-old age group. Epstein (1978) has reported conclusive evidence that the human brain does not grow in a regular, continuous, incremental fashion from birth to adulthood. Rather, the brain tends to grow in spurts. The primary periods or stages of brain growth occur during these chronological age intervals: (1) 3 to 10 months, (2) 2 to 4 years, (3) 6 to 8 years, (4) 10 to 12 or 13 years, and (5) 14 to 16 or 17 years (p. 344).

Toepfer (1980b), commenting on Epstein's work, points out that 85 to 90 percent of youngsters experience a brain growth stage between the ages of 10 and 12. However, a similar percentage experience a temporary cessation of brain growth during years 12 and 14, a time when most youngsters will be in grades 7 and 8 in school (p. 30). As Toepfer (1980b) points out, this information has important implications for middle school educators. There is evidence that youngsters cannot profit from instruction requiring them to develop new kinds of thinking abilities when they are going through a temporary cessation of brain growth. Rather, during these times, "the middle school curricula should seek after the maturation of skills already initiated and use these existing skills to learn new facts" (p. 30).

In general then, researchers have established patterns of development that suggest that youngsters in the 11- to 14-year-old age group have characteristics that make them different both from younger and from older students. Middle school educators seek to respond to these differences with programs designed to fit the particular requirements of individuals in this age group (see Figure 2-3).

The Middle School as a Response to Civil Rights Concerns

Aside from a feeling that the middle school may be able to respond to individual youngster's needs better than the traditional junior high school, public policy has tended to bolster the middle school movement. During the 1960s and 1970s, civil rights groups interested in racial desegregation stepped up their activities. As a consequence, federal courts increasingly were asked to scrutinize public school districts to determine whether school attendance guidelines were in violation of civil rights statutes. Traditionally, six-grade elementary schools were located in neighborhoods that tended to be relatively homogeneous in terms of racial makeup. Consequently, many such schools enrolled youngsters who were all white, all black, all Chicano, or all something else, depending on the particular neighborhood in which the school was located.

Some school administrators, as they recognized that the courts were looking with disfavor on schools enrolling a preponderance of youngsters of one race, may have been attracted to the middle school as a mechanism for solving this problem. Recall that nearly all middle schools enroll youngsters at grade 6 and that many enroll fifth-graders as well. Middle schools tend to draw students from several elementary schools. Thus, with some careful attention to drawing of attendance boundaries, middle schools can be organized in such a way that they include youngsters from a variety of racial groups in their student bodies. The middle school, then, was seen by some school leaders as an institution that could accomplish racial integration two years earlier than

Figure 2-3

SHOULD WE ESTABLISH NEW MIDDLE SCHOOL PROGRAMS NOW OR SHOULD WE WAIT UNTIL WE HAVE MORE INFORMATION?

There is compelling information arriving daily on the desks of intermediate school educators from researchers who have established conclusively that the human brain grows in a series of stages or steps. Basically, these researchers have found that individuals who are between growth phases cannot profit from instruction requiring them to use complex new mental processes. Rather, it is better for them to spend this time building upon what they already know. The best time for complex learning is when a brain growth stage is occurring.

Impressive as this information is, we can see the stirrings . . . the undesirable stirrings in our view . . . of the educational bureaucracy. We envision grandiose proposals for projects designed to purchase special kinds of instructional materials for both youngsters who are between brain growth phases and those who are undergoing a brain growth phase. Not yet, we would caution, not yet.

Interesting as the new research information is, much remains to be established before any attempt to revise school practices ought to be undertaken. First of all, no one yet has come up with a way of identifying whether an *individual* youngster is in a between brain growth phase or in a brain growth phase. Further, there is a lamentable lack of specificity about what kinds of instructional materials and instruction ought to be provided when an individual is "building upon what he or she knows" or, alternatively, "being exposed to complex learning." When we have this information, *then* we will look seriously at proposals to reform present school practices. In the meantime, let's not be too hasty to change a system that in general has served us well.

An editorial appearing in a daily newspaper

YOUR OPINION, PLEASE
Read the editorial above. Then, respond to these questions.

1. In general, what is your reaction to the case made by the writer of this editorial? What is the basis for your reaction?
2. Some proponents of middle school suggest that what we already know about brain growth is sufficient for us to presume that there are special instructional needs characterizing youngsters of middle school age. Do you agree? Why, or why not?
3. How do you react to the phrase, "let's not be too hasty to change a system that in general has served us well." Why do you react as you do?
4. Suppose that you were to write a letter to the editor regarding this editorial. What would you say?

---

would have been the case if youngsters had not left their neighborhood elementary school until after having completed the sixth grade.

THE JUNIOR HIGH SCHOOL AND THE MIDDLE SCHOOL: SOME CAUTIONS

In viewing individual junior high schools and middle schools, we believe it is necessary to look at what is going on in the school rather than to rely on some generalized conceptions of what a junior high school is or what a middle school is. For example, although middle school leaders promote a model of middle school education that calls for school programs that are student centered and very responsive to individual differences, certainly not all middle school programs reflect these objectives in practice. Similarly, some schools called junior high schools have programs that are eminently sensitive to youngsters' special needs and are clearly concerned with issues other than academics. It is by the nature of their programs, then, that individual intermediate schools should be evaluated. Whether they are called junior high schools or middle schools is a much less important issue.

HOW ARE INTERMEDIATE SCHOOLS VIEWED?

Intermediate schools, by whatever name known, generally have not enjoyed the same prestige or status as have senior high schools. No one reason, by itself, provides an adequate explanation for this phenomenon. Let us examine some ideas that have been put forward by those who have pondered this issue.

Some observers have noted that a large number of people harbor a mistaken assumption that "not much can be done with intermediate school youngsters." While this conviction is not often made explicit, it underlies such frequently heard comments as "Let's build a new lab at the high school. I'm sure folks at the junior high can get along with what they have now." This position assumes that intermediate school programs do not need to be first rate because youngsters at this age are not ready to profit from a truly high-quality program (see Figure 2-4).

The absence of logic in this view may well be traced to hasty readings of developmental psychologists and physiologists who have noted that there are significant maturational changes experienced by young people during their intermediate school years. A hasty reading of an authority such as Epstein (1980) and his citation of evidence that there are times when the brain pauses before continuing its growth may have led to an erroneous impression that intermediate school youngsters cease intellectual functioning during this time of their lives. If a person accepts this untenable premise, it is a short jump to making a case for assigning a low priority to middle school or junior high school programs.

Some school district administrative practices have contributed to a spread of the view that intermediate school education is not terribly important. One school district personnel officer, known to the authors, frequently commented in public that he liked to place new secondary school teachers in a middle school or a junior high school for "seasoning." Presumably, after a few years of working in the intermediate school, these

Figure 2-4

SHOULD WE BOTHER ABOUT INTERMEDIATE SCHOOLS?

Recently, a caller to a late-night radio talk show made these comments:

> Our beloved School Board has gone and done it again. Now we all know that a basic qualification for election to the School Board is an absence of common sense. But with this latest thing they all should be issued *bona fide* "certificates of ignorance."
>
> I mean they want to spend ten million dollars for a new junior high school. You heard it right . . . *junior high school!* Now that's what I call a real waste. Remember how you were in junior high school? I sure do. I mean, you know, junior high kids are just borderline civilized . . . just *borderline*. I can't remember *one thing* I learned in junior high school. I can't believe these kids today are much different. My father had an answer for this age group. Take them when they're 12 and ship them off to some caves until they come back with some sense around 15 or 16. Well, I know we can't do that. But we sure don't need an expensive new school for these kids. If it was a senior high school, maybe OK. But a junior high school, *no way!*

YOUR OPINION, PLEASE

Read the comments above. Then, respond to these questions.

1. What does this speaker, in general, think about junior high school students?
2. Would you consider this speaker's views to be typical or atypical?
3. Suppose that you were the next caller on this program and you had heard what this speaker had to say. How would you respond to what this speaker said?
4. How was the junior high school or the middle school viewed in your own community? What accounted for these views?

---

individuals would be sent up to the senior high school where quality teaching could make a difference. This practice was founded on the assumption that junior high school and middle school teachers would learn from their mistakes. Further, these mistakes were thought to come at no real cost in that even a totally inept teacher could not do much real harm to intermediate school youngsters who were presumed to be in some sort of an intellectual holding pattern.

In many districts, decisions about new buildings to be constructed have reflected a bias against intermediate schools. While we do not wish to suggest that no new middle schools and junior high schools have been built, still there has been a pattern of favoring construction of senior high schools over intermediate schools when a choice had to be made.

Traditionally teachers working at the intermediate school level have not sensed their work to be as worthy or important as that performed by their colleagues at the senior high school level. (This situation, however, may be changing, given the active work of the fast-growing National Middle School Association.) A number of long-standing school district practices have contributed to potential status difficulties of intermediate school teachers. For example, the terminology used to describe teachers reassigned from a middle school or junior high school to a senior high school suggests something about how teaching at each level is perceived. Often a teacher going from a junior high or middle school to a senior high school is said to be "moving up" to the high school. On the other hand, a teacher going from a senior high school to a junior high or middle school is said to be "moving down" to the new level.

In addition to problems associated with this kind of language, intermediate school teachers usually have not received as high a level of remuneration for their involvement in extracurricular activities and athletics as have high school teachers. Given these differences, it has been natural that talented teachers in certain specializations (coaching and music, for example) have tended to see their involvement in intermediate school education simply as a way station en route to better things at the senior high school level.

We would like to conclude this short section with the observation that large numbers of teachers do find great happiness and personal satisfaction at the intermediate school level. Almost every school district is blessed with some middle school or junior high school teachers who would resign rather than accept a transfer to a senior high school. Many intermediate school youngsters have been influenced profoundly and positively by these dedicated people. Perhaps, given the growth in interest in school programs uniquely tailored to the needs of preadolescents and early adolescents, we may begin to see more people committed to career-long work with youngsters in the intermediate schools.

WHAT DO INTERMEDIATE SCHOOL TEACHERS NEED TO KNOW?

Despite the increase in college and university programs designed to provide special training for intermediate school teachers, it is still fair to say that the majority of teachers working in these schools have not been prepared specifically to work with youngsters in this age group. Traditionally, colleges of education have divided their teacher preparation programs into the two broad categories of elementary education and secondary education. Most intermediate school teachers have come out of general secondary education programs. These, by and large, have been oriented heavily toward the preparation of senior high school teachers.

A concern for providing intermediate school teachers with some specific kinds of understandings related to the nature of the intermediate school child and the intermediate school setting has been an issue of long standing in educational circles. Although recommendations have varied over time, certain proposals have been mentioned repeatedly by educators interested in improving the quality of instruction in intermediate schools. Gradually, these proposals are beginning to influence changes in college and university teacher preparation programs.

In a survey of some 30 years of recommendations for improved training for intermediate school teachers, Armstrong (March 1977) found recurring emphasis on four basic themes. Armstrong's review reported that intermediate school teachers should come to their initial teaching positions with some background in these areas (pp. 249–50):

1. *Psychology of adolescence and guidance*
2. *Reading*
3. *Application of knowledge*
4. *Experience with early adolescents*

Regarding the area of psychology of adolescence and guidance, students preparing for careers in intermediate school teaching may well wish to supplement required course work with additional elective study. Youngsters in intermediate schools are at a stage of life when they are attempting to come to terms with themselves and with the social world in which they live. Teachers with some sensitivity and understanding of the peculiar psychological and emotional needs of these youngsters are likely to work more productively with this age group than are teachers lacking such specialized training.

Textual materials with which youngsters are expected to work as they move into their intermediate school years tend to be much more demanding than those they encountered during their elementary school years. Part of this difficulty may stem from a tendency of most writers of school texts to be oriented toward either an elementary school population or a senior high school population. Particularly in years gone by, many junior high school texts started life as high school books. In the absence of materials written for the intermediate school age group, some publishers simply enlarged the typeface slightly, added some illustrations, and did a little rewriting to convert a high school text to a reborn junior high or middle school text. Consequently, much of the print material available for use at the intermediate school level was simply too sophisticated for many youngsters at this age.

Today, there has been a good deal of improvement in the quality of texts and other print material designed for use in middle schools and junior high schools. Publishers, for example, are now checking the readability level of their publications to ensure that intermediate school youngsters are not being asked to learn from materials requiring a high-school-level reading competence. Still, many intermediate school teachers report that their youngsters experience difficulty in the area of reading. Teachers at this level find it useful to have some professional background in the area of developmental reading as they attempt to identify and design reading materials with which their students can succeed. Thus it makes sense for prospective intermediate school teachers to enroll in some professional reading courses as part of their undergraduate training program.

Many youngsters in intermediate schools are not yet sufficiently developed intellectually to deal well with learning tasks that require abstract thinking. In very general terms, leading developmental psychologists have told us that youngsters progress gradually through various stages of thinking as they mature. Only during their later intermediate school years (and, in some cases, into the early high school years) do youngsters begin to develop some real facility with abstract reasoning. (More specific information regarding stages of intellectual development is introduced in Chapter 12, "Profiles of Secondary Students.")

Difficulties that many intermediate school youngsters experience with abstract thinking suggest a need for teachers at this level to provide opportunities for students to deal with concrete examples whenever possible. Physical manipulation of tangible material is considered to be a great asset to learning, particularly at this age. Consider, for example, a junior high school teacher interested in teaching youngsters how to read and interpret contour maps. With only verbal instruction, many youngsters have difficulty in visualizing the terrain when it is represented by different contour patterns. However, if clay or some other medium can be used to construct a representation, more students will come to grasp the connection between the abstract lines on the map and the real-world terrain patterns that those contour lines depict.

Although few undergraduate courses focus specifically on development of models and other kinds of application activities, prospective intermediate school teachers should give some thought as to how instruction on topics they expect to teach can be made more concrete. Journal articles written by practicing intermediate school teachers and conversations with intermediate school teachers are sources that might be tapped for information of this sort.

Finally, most administrators and teachers in middle schools and junior high schools believe that intermediate school youngsters are a special breed. Principals, in particular, often are reluctant to hire new teachers who have done their student teaching at the senior high school level. "Mr. Jones," they may say, "may have done a super job at the high school. But that doesn't mean a thing here. This is a whole new ball game. I want somebody who has a good student teaching record with these younger kids." It should be acknowledged that many prospective teachers who have engaged in student teaching at the high school level *do* accept initial employment in middle schools and junior high schools. Many make a successful transition. But large numbers of intermediate school administrators do prefer to hire first-year teachers who have done student teaching in middle schools and junior high schools, when they can get them (see Figure 2-5).

In addition to student teaching at the intermediate school level, individuals who have had other kinds of direct leadership experience with early adolescents tend to be given some employment preference. Consequently, undergraduates looking toward intermediate school teaching might seek out opportunities to work with youngsters of this age during their undergraduate years. Frequently opportunities are available to work with scouting units, campfire groups, and other young people's organizations.

SPECIALIZED TRAINING FOR INTERMEDIATE SCHOOL TEACHERS

Considering the interest of educators through the years in identifying some of the kinds of expertise needed by successful intermediate school teachers, one might suppose that specialized training programs for individuals wishing to teach youngsters of this age would be numerous. As we noted earlier, such programs, though growing in number, are still not available on every campus. Let us examine some reasons for this.

Recall that nearly all colleges and universities offering undergraduate teacher preparation programs tend to be organized into departments or programs of (1) elementary education and (2) secondary education. Intermediate school education, though typically assigned to the secondary program area, has not fitted well either with the central interests of the secondary education specialists (who tend to focus on the senior high school) or with the central interests of the elementary education specialists (who tend to focus on the primary and intermediate grades of elementary schools). Traditionally, then, the intermediate school has not had a specific university department or program constituency that has been charged with looking after its exclusive interests.

The basic pattern in colleges and universities of dividing programs into either elementary education units or secondary education units paralleled an historic division among national professional interests of educators. For years, many national professional groups served educators who thought of themselves as part of "elementary education" or of "secondary education." For example, at the administrative level, elementary school principals belong to the National Association of Elementary School

Figure 2-5

___

HOW DIFFERENT *ARE* INTERMEDIATE SCHOOL YOUNGSTERS?

SPEAKER A: So now all the principals at the intermediate school buildings are saying they won't hire anybody who hasn't done student teaching in a middle school or a junior high school. Seems like a bunch of self-serving baloney to me. I mean, think about it. They'll have to process just a fraction of the applications that are on file in the personnel office. All those people who did student teaching in high schools are out, *o u t,* out.

And I don't buy for a minute this idea that intermediate school kids are so different that somebody who has done student teaching with high school youngsters can't work with them. Nonsense! Good teachers are by nature flexible. A competent person will make the necessary adjustments to get the job done with these younger students. To my mind, this whole policy smacks of lazy administrators jealously guarding a territory that is seen as unique by no one except themselves.

SPEAKER B: These teachers at the junior high are turning over *too fast.* We just aren't getting any continuity of program. Most of them make no bones about wanting to jump up to the high school level at the first opportunity. They just don't like working with these younger kids.

Seems to me that the only way to break this cycle is to hire people who have been trained to work with the junior high school group. We should absolutely *insist* that any new junior high school teacher who is hired has done student teaching at the intermediate school level. They need to know what they are getting into. Indeed, they should *want* to get into what they are getting into. As far as I'm concerned, a person needs to "know the territory" before he or she can make an honest commitment. Let's have no more of these high-school-trained teachers who make themselves miserable while waiting two or three years for a high-school-level vacancy.

YOUR OPINION, PLEASE
Read the remarks above. Then, respond to these questions.

1. What strengths and weaknesses do you note in the comments of Speaker A?
2. What strengths and weaknesses do you note in the comments of Speaker B?
3. How do you feel personally about a requirement that all teachers hired at a junior high school must have done student teaching at the intermediate school level?

___

Principals and secondary school principals belong to the National Association of Secondary School Principals. These are large, established organizations. Only in relatively recent times has a strong intermediate school group, the National Middle School Association, begun to emerge. The growth of this group and the availability of new publications such as *Transescence: The Journal of Emerging Adolescent Development* are indicators of an enlarged professional support structure for intermediate education. The expansion of interest in intermediate school education in terms of organizations and publications with a unique focus on preadolescents and early adolescents represents an important force supporting expansion of specialized college and university training for intermediate school teachers.

Traditional patterns of teacher education have inhibited the development of programs to prepare middle school and junior high school professionals. Historically, teachers have followed programs terminating in the award of either elementary certificates valid for grades K through 6 or secondary certificates valid in grades 7 through 12. (There have been some exceptions to these grade ranges.) The existence of a certification system that allowed teachers to emerge from their training with only two certificate options, elementary or secondary, inhibited the development of specialized training programs for intermediate school teachers.

Today, there is a trend for states to establish specialized certificates for intermediate school teachers (see Figure 2-6). About half the states either have such certificates or are contemplating establishing them. Professional educators with interests in intermediate school education believe that the existence of special intermediate school teaching certificates will provide an additional inducement to colleges of education to develop specialized training programs for future middle and junior high school teachers.

In summary, then, there is a trend toward expanding the numbers of programs in colleges and universities that are directed toward the preparation of intermediate school teachers. These efforts are being supported by the development of active national professional organizations, specialized publications, and college and university preparation programs focusing on the unique needs of preadolescent and early-adolescent youngsters.

DECIDING TO TEACH AT THE INTERMEDIATE SCHOOL LEVEL

Even successful practitioners in middle schools and junior high schools acknowledge that intermediate school youngsters at times are difficult. Part of the challenge in working with these students involves dealing with the unpredictability of boys and girls at this time of their lives. At times, they reflect great insights and exhibit a behavioral maturity similar to that more typical of senior high school students. At other times, their actions are consistent with what we might expect from an aroused group of third- or fourth-graders.

Physiological and psychological changes sometimes combine to make it difficult for these youngsters to attend to school tasks. As increasingly they sense themselves to

Figure 2-6

ARE SPECIAL INTERMEDIATE SCHOOL CERTIFICATES THE ANSWER?

Several years ago, interested educators in one state mounted an effort to establish a special middle school certificate. After fighting many battles in the legislature, such a certificate was adopted. But the final legislation differed greatly from what the interested legislatures would have liked to have had.

The new middle school certificate enabled a teacher to instruct in grades 5 through 8 *only* in a school with the words "middle school" in its name. On the other hand, the old elementary certificate that enabled a holder to teach grades K to 8 in *any* school remained on the books. Similarly, the old secondary certificate that enabled the holder to teach grades 7 through 12 in *any* school also remained an available option.

YOUR OPINION, PLEASE
Read the paragraphs above. Then, respond to these questions.

1. How popular do you think that the middle school certificate was with undergraduate teacher education candidates in this state? On what do you base your opinion?
2. What certificate would you suppose the majority of individuals interested in teaching intermediate school youngsters in this state would prefer to hold? Why?
3. How do you account for the rather limited authority granted by the middle school certificate? What forces might have been at work contributing to the imposition of these conditions?
4. If you would look down the road ten years in this state, would you expect to see a dramatic increase in the number of teachers holding middle school certificates? (Assume that present certification laws remain unchanged.)
5. If you were to start a campaign in this state to remove the requirement that a holder of a middle school certificate could teach in a school only with the words "middle school" in its name, what kind of resistance would you be likely to meet? How would you counter this resistance?

---

be grown up, intermediate school students test the limits of their authority. Sometimes this behavior results in confrontations with their teachers. ("This is a really *dumb* assignment. And I'm not going to do it," etc.) Usually nothing personal is directed at the teacher in these outbursts. The teacher is simply a handy adult target for the emerging adolescent who is beginning to probe the extent to which the adult world will take him or her seriously. Teachers who recognize what is going on develop ways of defusing confrontations without, at the same time, diminishing the self-esteem of the youngsters involved. There is no magic formula for doing this. But, in general, it includes the development of a set of responses that communicate to youngsters "Yes, I hear you, but there are still some things you must do that, for now, may seem frustrating and unimportant to you."

Certainly we do not wish to suggest that there are no rewards in working with intermediate school youngsters. Indeed there are. Unlike some of their older high-school-aged brethren who like to affect a studied boredom with "anything related to something as pedestrian as *school*," youngsters in the intermediate school still possess some of the enthusiasm of elementary school youngsters. They are capable of becoming very excited about a topic or issue. Some teachers take great pleasure in encouraging these enthusiasms as they watch their students grow and mature. Many teachers, too, derive much satisfaction from their understanding that they have been an important help to students at a critical stage of their personal development. Large numbers of adults can look back appreciatively and recall some sensitive support they received from a caring teacher during their middle school or junior high school years.

Posttest

Directions: Using your own paper, answer each of the following true/false questions. For each correct statement, write the word "true." For each incorrect statement, write the word "false."

_____   1. Intermediate schools have had as long a history in this country as have elementary schools and senior high schools.

_____   2. Scientists have discovered that the human brain does not grow continuously but rather in a predictable series of growth stages and nongrowth plateaus from birth to maturity.

_____   3. The junior high school has been criticized for attempting to provide a program too similar to that of the senior high school.

_____   4. The middle school has a shorter history as an intermediate school than does the junior high school.

_____   5. Many youngsters during their intermediate school years are engaged in a search for personal identity and personal independence.

_____   6. Because youngsters have few distinctive characteristics at this stage of their lives, there is little need for special preparation programs for future teachers of intermediate school youngsters.

_____   7. At the intermediate school level, there should be little emphasis on application of newly learned information.

_____   8. When new buildings are being constructed in a given district, it is much more common for new middle school or junior high school buildings to be constructed than for new high school buildings to be constructed.

_____   9. Some teachers have felt that it is less prestigious to teach in a middle school or junior high school than in a senior high school.

_____ 10. In general, students at the intermediate school level need individualized attention and personal counseling.

Key Ideas in Review

1. Intermediate schools are much newer additions to the public school systems of this country than are elementary schools and senior high schools. They came into existence beginning only in the years preceding World War I. They were designed to bridge the gap between elementary education and what was perceived to be a much more difficult high school program.

2. Junior high schools were the predominant variety of intermediate school during the first 50 years of intermediate education. In more recent years middle schools have become more popular. Professional educators favoring the middle school contend that middle schools are well suited to develop programs to accommodate what developmental physiologists and psychologists tell us about learners in this age group.

3. In the past, teachers who have worked in middle schools in many cases have not enjoyed the status associated with teaching at the senior high school level. For a variety of reasons, some people felt that teaching at this level was simply not as important as teaching at the high school level. There is evidence that this perception is diminishing as more and more information becomes available regarding specialized needs of youngsters who are preadolescents or early adolescents.

4. A growing professional support structure is beginning to work in behalf of intermediate school educators, particularly those working in middle schools. Consequently, colleges and universities are expanding the numbers of preparation programs for individuals seeking to specialize in intermediate school education. Further, there are moves to establish special certificates for individuals desiring to work at the intermediate school level.

5. Teachers in intermediate schools are thought to require specialized skills. Particularly widespread have been recommendations for demonstrated skills in these four areas: (a) psychology of adolescence and guidance, (b) reading, (c) application of knowledge, and (d) experience with early adolescents.

SUMMARY

Traditionally, intermediate education has been something of a stepchild in American education. From the beginning of the intermediate education movement, there have been debates regarding what intermediate schools should do. Although these debates continue, today there is increasing evidence that preadolescent and early-adolescent youngsters have characteristics that distinguish them clearly from pupils in the elementary school and students in the senior high school. The remarkable spread of the middle school, an institution designed to meet the specialized needs of the 11- to 14-year-old youngster, testifies to the broadening commitment to serve the intermediate school population well.

In recent years there has been a dramatic broadening of the research base supporting the view that intermediate school youngsters have special needs. The work of such figures as Epstein (1980), for example, has demonstrated conclusively the existence of brain stage cycles having important instructional implications for youngsters in the 11- to 14-year-old age group. A number of individual professionals as well as intermediate school organizations are building on this growing research and theory base to produce more sophisticated guidelines for intermediate school instructional practices.

Colleges and universities are expanding the numbers of specialized training programs for individuals seeking careers in intermediate schools. Similarly, there is a trend for states to develop special intermediate school teaching certificates. Specialized publications are beginning to appear in larger numbers that have a focus on the problems of intermediate school youngsters and intermediate school teaching.

To conclude, then, interest in intermediate schools is increasing. And, at this point in time, it seems reasonable to suggest that increasingly educators will come to think of education as divided among three branches of elementary, intermediate, and secondary education rather than between the two branches (elementary and secondary) that traditionally have framed much thinking about public education in this country.

References

Armstrong, David G. "Specialized Training for Middle School and Junior High School Teachers: Prescriptions, Problems, and Prospects," *The High School Journal* (March 1977): 247–254.

——. "The Intermediate School: Whither Education's Ugly Duckling?" *Peabody Journal of Education* (April 1977): 207–210.

Egnatuck, Tony; Georgiady, Nicolas P.; Muth, C. Robert; and Romano, Louis G. *The Middle School*. East Lansing: Michigan Association of Middle School Educators, 1975.

Eichhorn, Donald H. *The Middle School*. New York: The Center for Applied Research in Education, 1966.

Epstein, Herman T. "Growth Spurts During Brain Development: Implications for Educational Policy and Practice," in Jeanne S. Chall and Allan F. Mirsky, (eds)., *Education and the Brain*. The seventy-seventh yearbook of the National Society for the Study of Education. Chicago: NSSE, 1978, pp. 343–370.

Howell, Bruce. "The School in the Middle . . . What's So Special About It?" Unpublished paper presented at the Annual Meeting of the National Association of Secondary School Principals. Miami Beach, Florida, January 1980.

Hurd, Paul DeHart (panel leader). *Final Report of the National Science Foundation Early Adolescence Panel Meeting*. Washington, D.C.: National Science Foundation, July 1978.

James, Michael. "Early Adolescent Ego Development," *The High School Journal* (March 1980): 244–249.

Johnston, J. Howard. "Middle School Research: What We Know and What We Need to Find Out," in Christina K. McCann, ed., *Perspectives on Middle School Research*. Cincinnati, Ohio: University of Cincinnati, College of Education, 1980.

Lounsbury, John H., and Vars, Gorden E. *Curriculum for the Middle Years*. New York: Harper & Row, Publishers, Inc., 1978.

Lynch, James J. "A Primer on a Current Trend: The Middle School." Educational Resources Information Clearinghouse document, ED 168 183, 1978.

McGlasson, Maurice. *The Middle School: Where? What? Whither?* Bloomington, Ind.: Phi Delta Kappa Educational Foundation, 1973.

Popper, Samuel H. *The American Middle School: An Organizational Analysis*. Waltham, Mass.: Blaisdell Publishing Company, 1967.

Thornburg, Hershel D. "Early Adolescents: Their Developmental Characteristics," *The High School Journal* (March 1980): 212–221.

Toepfer, Conrad F., Jr. "Brain Growth Periodization Data: Some Implications for Re-Thinking Middle Grades Education," *The High School Journal* (March 1980a): 222–227.

——. "What We Know: Reactions," in Christina K. McCann, ed., *Perspectives on Middle School Research*. Cincinnati, Ohio: University of Cincinnati, College of Education, 1980b, pp. 27–36.

3

Current Issues in Secondary Education

"After an exhaustive study of your new curriculum which evaluated all available data, using multivariable longitudinal analysis with particular attention to IQ, SES, and academic-cognitive and affective-social factors as they relate to stated goal-orientation, I find that you were doing it better before."

Objectives

This chapter provides information to help the reader to

1. Identify certain forces that may have contributed to a decline in public confidence in public education.
2. Differentiate among several types of alternative schools.
3. Describe arguments favoring and opposing the accountability and competency testing movements.

4. Suggest possible consequences of a massive adoption of educational voucher plans.

5. Point out some changes in the schools that have come about as a result of attempts to equalize educational opportunities for all youngsters.

6. Identify key arguments made both by proponents and opponents of mandated bilingual education programs.

Pretest

Directions: Using your own paper, answer each of the following true/false questions. For each correct statement, write the word ''true.'' For each incorrect statement, write the word ''false.''

_____ 1. In general, it is fair to say that in recent years there has developed an increasing tendency for teachers to be held responsible for the achievement of the students under their charge.

_____ 2. The concept of alternative school is broad enough to include some schools that place a very heavy emphasis on certain basic subjects.

_____ 3. Certain proponents of competency testing argue that its introduction into a school has potential for increasing students' motivation to learn.

_____ 4. In part, the voucher system seeks to improve education by introducing an element of competition among various schools in a district.

_____ 5. A watershed decision in the area of school desegregation was *Brown* v. *Board of Education.*

_____ 6. Magnet schools represent one response to the need to integrate schools.

_____ 7. Some critics of bilingual education allege that bilingual programs may result in a slowdown in the rate of acquisition of proficiency in English on the part of students who come to school as nonspeakers of English.

_____ 8. The role of the federal government has changed but little throughout the entire history of American education.

_____ 9. Some professional educators have pointed out that, today, schools are being asked to do more things at the same time that school budgets are growing tighter.

_____ 10. In recent years, many court decisions have had impacts on secondary school programs.

INTRODUCTION

Pick up a newspaper. Scan a news magazine. Flip on a television or a radio. Do one or all of these things and you will find considerable coverage of secondary schools. For a variety of reasons, public education has become a hot topic; as such, it is receiving more media attention today than at any other time in our history.

In general, this attention centers on two basic public concerns: quality and equity. To citizens who ask "How good are our schools," many critics who have examined the schools have concluded that "they aren't as good as they should be." There is a perception that quality (however defined) of secondary school programs has declined.

To those concerned with the issue of fairness, the basic question might be stated as: "Do all youngsters receive fair and equal treatment in our secondary schools?" Critics of present practices have often answered this question with a resounding "No!"

Concerns for quality and for equity have engendered considerable debate on how secondary schools might be made better. This debate has been conducted in the halls of Congress, in the courts, in parent-teacher meetings, in faculty lounges, in bars, in church assemblies, and in every other imaginable setting where two or more people have come together to discuss the issues of the day. These discussions seem certain to be with us for years to come. In the sections that follow, we will highlight some positions that have been taken with regard to a selection of issues related to school quality and school equity.

PUBLIC CONFIDENCE IN SECONDARY SCHOOLS

One of the most pressing issues facing secondary school educators today is the decline in public confidence in the quality of secondary school programs. While there have always been skeptics of secondary schools programs, in general, the large American middle class tended to see secondary education in general and high school education in particular as essentially good. In part, this view resulted from a conviction that access to public secondary education provided youngsters coming from a variety of backgrounds with an opportunity to enjoy an ultimate social and economic status that was limited only by their own talents and ambitions.

Historically, then, secondary education was viewed as providing opportunities for students to attain the American dream. Graduation from high school was seen as essential for those seeking upward social and economic mobility. Given a conviction that secondary education had the potential, at least, to change the nature of students' lives for the better, secondary schools, as institutions, enjoyed very high esteem. Although they were not well rewarded in a financial sense, public educators generally were regarded as eminently respectable individuals. Few serious challenges to their authority were mounted.

Over the past 20 or so years, this favorable view of secondary education and secondary school administrators and teachers has been changing. No single factor explains this shift in public perceptions. A number of events have contributed to the change. Let us look now at some of the factors that might be contributing to the trend for people to look with an increasingly skeptical eye at secondary education.

During the decade of the 1960s, teachers, acting through their professional organizations, became increasingly militant in their demands for better salaries and improved working conditions. For the first time, teacher strikes became common. (There had been strikes before. But they tended to be few in number and concentrated in small numbers of districts.) To many members of the middle class, it became difficult to reconcile their former image of a teacher as a selfless professional dedicated to the interests of the young with the picture of a teacher as a militant on a picket line seeming to pursue only his or her self-interests. Certainly not everyone developed negative images of teachers because of teacher involvement in labor disputes. But many did.

Although perhaps more subtle in its potential impact on public attitudes toward secondary education than the issue of teacher militancy, the tendency for secondary schools to become ever larger entities may well have contributed to a certain loss of confidence in secondary education. Decisions to build larger schools often made good sense on economic and programmatic grounds. Consolidated schools could be managed by one rather than by several administrations. Further, the arrays of courses offered to students in such buildings greatly exceeded in numbers those that could be provided in smaller buildings. On the other side of the ledger, however, larger schools meant increasing physical distances between homes of many of the parents and individual school buildings. Teachers in large buildings were much less likely to be close neighbors than was the case when buildings were smaller and designed to serve smaller populations. One result of this development was a decline in parent-teacher interaction in the community, which had enabled them to become well acquainted in nonschool settings. The trend toward larger buildings tended to make the teacher something of an anonymous figure about whom parents knew little. It became much easier to find fault with this kind of an individual than with a teacher who parents knew as a friend and neighbor.

Another change that has evolved over the past several decades has been the development of certain youth subcultures that parents have found to be very disturbing. While most parents probably knew students who drank a little (and sometimes more than a little) beer or hard liquor occasionally, the idea of students using drugs was foreign to the experience of these adults who were in high school before the mid-1960s. (At least, it is foreign to the experience of most.) Many parents read reports that students were taking drugs, protesting certain traditional school practices, and in other ways behaving in ways that were different from student behaviors when parents were in school. Some parents concluded that these behaviors resulted because principals and teachers were unwilling to exercise appropriate control over students in the school. Concerns centering on the issue of discipline contributed to a decline in confidence in the competence of public school educators.

Beginning in the 1970s and continuing to the present, suspicions that educators were not getting the job done were further advanced by revelations that students' scores and standardized tests of achievement were declining. Whether declines in scores are due to a deterioration in school programs or to other factors is very much open to debate *within* the educational community. But, to the public at large, the evidence seems clear. "Schools," many people allege, "simply are not doing as good a job as they used to do."

Certainly there are factors in addition to those mentioned here that have contributed to a public perception that all is not well with public education. The cumulative impact of all the factors that have played a part in the development of this declining confidence trend is revealed in the annual Gallup poll on education. In 1974, 48 percent of the individuals sampled gave the schools a grade of "A" or "B." In 1980, only 35 percent of those polled awarded grades of "A" or "B" to the schools. At the other end of the scale, in 1974, only 11 percent gave the schools grades of "D" or "F." In 1980, 18 percent of the respondents gave schools "D" or "F" grades (Gallup 1980).

The public has not remained passive as suspicions about the quality of secondary school education have grown (see Figure 3-1). Numerous proposals to "remedy" the situation have been put forward. A number of these are introduced in the subsections that follow.

Alternative Schools

During the late 1960s and early 1970s, there was a great deal of interest in "alternative schools." Alternative schools, in public education, were established for many different reasons and to serve many different purposes. But a common thread running through all these schools was a conviction that traditional secondary schools were not serving the needs of students.

Growth in numbers of alternative schools as component parts of public school systems has been dramatic. In 1970, for example, there were at most a few dozen formal alternative schools within public school systems. But, by 1980, there were thousands of them (Smith 1981). Alternative schools have become particularly popular in larger school systems. Smith notes that "at least 90% of our larger school systems provide alternative schools" (p. 546). Smaller districts too, increasingly, have seen the wisdom of establishing alternative schools. One recent estimate suggests that more than a third of smaller systems have them (Smith 1981).

In the early years of the alternative school movement, that is, in the late 1960s and early 1970s, such schools tended to be established to meet the emotional needs of youngsters who were "turned off" by what they regarded as insensitive treatment in traditional school programs. Many such schools placed heavy emphases on participatory democracy and organizational schemes that involved students in the decision-making process. In general, there was an effort to make the alternative school a more humane place than many critics of the traditional school perceived that institution to be.

Figure 3-1

HOW BAD ARE THE SECONDARY SCHOOLS?

I visited a high school last week. I had a short meeting on a business matter with the principal. When it was over, I decided just as a matter of curiosity to walk around the halls.

I was absolutely *appalled* at what I saw. In the first place, these kids looked like they had been airlifted in from some sort of refugee camp. I mean, they had on the scraggliest collection of unkempt clothing I've ever seen. Some of the boys had long greasy hair. A few had untrimmed beards. They were a mess!

And you simply wouldn't *believe* the foul language. I simply couldn't repeat it over the air. And, to make the situation worse, all of this garbage talk was going on within clear hearing range of some of the teachers who were acting as hall monitors. The teachers didn't do a thing. What's the matter with them? Don't they care?

Well, I came away very very depressed. Things have certainly changed since I was in school. It seems to me that these school people are letting us down. They just are not doing their jobs. The kids are running the schools now. And the whole thing has degenerated to the point that the individuals with the lowest personal standards are setting the low level that all the youngsters are aspiring to. It just makes me sick.

Statement by a caller to a radio talk show

YOUR OPINION, PLEASE
Read the comments above. Then, respond to these questions.

1. Do you agree with the general comments made by this caller? If so, why?
2. Do you disagree with the general comments made by this caller? If so, why?
3. Do you think that the situation reported by this caller is typical of what one might encounter in many secondary schools today? Why, or why not?
4. Could the principal or the teachers change any of the situations mentioned? Which ones?
5. Do you think that teachers and administrators have more or less freedom of action today than they had formerly? Why do you think so?

Today, alternative schools represent a much broader range of perspectives than they did in the early days. Individual alternative schools, for example, have been established to serve missions as diverse as providing for violence-free instructional atmospheres, teaching basic skills competently by tailoring programs to students' individual needs, accommodating varying parental preferences regarding classroom control, and responding programmatically to concerns that youngsters not be denied access to quality education merely because of their place of residence. Alternative schools have sought after a good many other missions as well.

In a sense, alternative schools have represented a challenge to the traditional secondary school. Some have welcomed the challenge. Others have viewed the growth of the alternative school with dismay.

Arguments Favoring Alternative Schools.   The American population is diverse. It is simply impossible for a single kind of school to meet all the needs of all the children. Our traditional high schools may call themselves "comprehensive schools," but in reality they are anything but comprehensive. Administrative necessity ensures that most programs will be targeted toward the so-called "average" learner. Youngsters with special needs must conform to this program if they are to be served at all.

As a result, it makes good sense for us to establish a large number of tax-supported alternative schools. Each of these can be designed to serve a specific subgroup within the total school population. Parents of youngsters who differ markedly from the "average" served by the traditional school will have an institution available that will be sensitive to their youngsters' special needs.

When students attend alternative schools that are responsive to their own needs and consistent with desires of their parents, discipline problems diminish. Further, youngsters are likely to be much more motivated to learn. The decline in discipline problems and the accompanying increase in student motivation provide an environment in which youngsters can learn. Consequently, achievement levels are likely to go up. Given improved student performance and a feeling among parents that public education is being truly responsive to youngsters' real needs, an improvement in public confidence in education may well ensue.

Teachers as well as students can profit when alternative schools are available. Teacher personalities range across a broad spectrum. Some prefer to work in a highly structured, controlled environment. Others welcome ambiguity. Given the availability of a variety of alternative schools, it would be possible for teachers to find teaching positions in schools where environments meshed well with their own personalities. Teachers' performances seem likely to improve when they find a teaching environment with which they are philosophically attuned.

Finally, a system that supports larger number of alternative schools would suggest a secondary school system characterized by much smaller buildings than those that house today's traditional middle schools, junior high schools, and senior high schools. This situation would make teacher-parent contact easier and certainly more comfortable. Further, if individual alternative schools were given a great deal of autonomy in organizing their school programs, parental influence on the programs of individual alternative schools might well be substantial. An increase in this influence might correlate with more positive parental attitudes toward public education.

Arguments Opposing Alternative Schools.   While there is a certain intellectual appeal to the ideal of building alternative schools focusing on special needs of certain groups of students, there are practical limitations to the idea. For example, the number of individual differences among students is almost beyond calculation. Yet even the most affluent school district cannot afford to construct more than a few alternative schools with special emphases. Large number of youngsters having special needs will be served no better than they are at present.

Further, even supposing the arrival of an economic millennium that would allow districts to build as many schools as they wished, the idea of building dozens of small secondary schools to replace today's larger buildings is not a good one. A final result of such an effort would be a system of secondary education characterized by a loose conglomeration of ideologically narrow alternative schools. Each would have relatively homogeneous populations. Student contacts with youngsters from a variety of backgrounds would be minimized. This kind of a scheme represents an unhealthy challenge to a fundamental premise of American education: namely, that schools, in part, ought to provide opportunities for youngsters from all strata of society to come together in the school for the purpose of developing tolerance and understanding for perspectives other than those they bring with them from home. An ultimate result of a secondary school system where we might have, for example, schools for liberals, schools for those of different religious persuasions, schools for conservatives, and so forth would be a fragmentation of American society. Nobody wants that.

Further, if we had a system of scattered alternative schools, it would be extremely difficult to monitor quality. Since each school would be pursuing its own ends, what common threads could be measured? This situation would promote the development of unsound educational practices as educators in individual schools came to understand that their practices were beyond the review of any external authorities.

What would happen to graduates of alternative schools? Certainly many students would face difficulties in terms of seeking admission to institutions of higher learning or in terms of convincing employers to hire them. The present structure of secondary education assures that all students will have at least some exposure to certain required course work. Levels of performance in these courses as reflected on school transcripts provides a method whereby relative achievement of different students can be compared. In the absence of this kind of a baseline, it would be extremely difficult for employers and admissions officials in colleges and universities to make judgments relative to qualifications of individual graduates.

There is a very substantial financial argument to make in opposition to alternative schools. Any system calling for large numbers of smaller buildings to replace smaller numbers of larger buildings will add significantly to already strained school budgets. Beyond costs incurred to construct new buildings, operating costs would be much higher. For example, it is much more efficient to heat one large building than to heat a number of smaller buildings. Costs seem certain to rise.

Finally, the assumption that individual students would learn more in a secondary school system characterized by fragmented alternative schools than in a system characterized by larger comprehensive schools has not been clearly demonstrated. Where is the evidence for improvement? There simply isn't any. At the present time no solid research base points to the need for abandoning today's comprehensive secondary schools.

Alternative Schools: Present Status.   The great expansion in the number of public alternative schools over the past ten years suggests that the alternative school is an innovation that is here to stay. It seems fair to suggest that alternative schools are a mechanism whereby the special needs of individual youngsters can be met in fact. Although projections of present trends are hazardous, it appears likely that alternative schools will grow in numbers in the years ahead.

Today, there is an accelerating public concern about what youngsters are learning in schools. Newspaper and television reports have provided a great deal of coverage to the issue of declining student scores on tests of academic achievement. In general, when public schools are faulted today, it is because they are expecting too little, in an academic sense, from students rather than pushing students too hard and, in the process, denying youngsters certain freedoms of choice. It is not surprising then that many of the most popular alternative schools today place a heavy emphasis on academics.

One special type alternative school has grown up in a number of large school districts over the past few years and deserves special mention. This is the so-called "magnet school." Magnet schools were developed initially as a response to pressures to desegregate schools. School district officials desperately sought ways of achieving a better racial mix of students without going to forced busing, an historically unpopular solution for many parents. The magnet school represented one such attempt.

A magnet school is a school in a district that organizes the curriculum around a given theme. While such a school may offer a broad range of courses, typically each magnet school is set up to be especially strong in a particular area. For example, a magnet school might specialize in music and theater arts, another in programs for the gifted and talented, still another in mathematics and the sciences, and so forth. On a voluntary basis, students from the *entire* school district may request to attend a particular magnet school. Students from every part of the district will be bused to the magnet school. This has potential to achieve a racial balance in the magnet school since attendance lines are district wide rather than based on traditional neighborhood lines. (Where attendance boundaries follow neighborhood lines, schools tend to be racially unbalanced because of de facto separation of races in many residential areas.)

Despite the limited numbers of magnet schools, those that have been established have been reasonably successful. It would also be fair to say that the most successful have been those with a clearly defined theme that has appealed to a relatively small number of very committed students. While the schools themselves have been successful, ordinarily the establishment of magnet schools alone has not proved sufficient to meet requirements for achieving racial balance in public schools of large districts. But they do provide an attractive alternative to certain youngsters that would not have been available to them a few years ago (see Figure 3-2).

Accountability

In recent years, we have heard much about "accountability." While the term is somewhat difficult to define, in general, accountability refers to the idea that educators bear some direct responsibility for what students learn in school. People concerned about accountability therefore have been very much interested in different kinds of measures that can be used to determine how much a given youngster has learned from his or her experiences in the classroom.

Interest in accountability, in large measure, has come about because of wide publicity given to two simultaneous phenomena: the rising costs of education and the declining test scores of students. On the one hand, school tax rates have climbed dramatically in many parts of the country to meet rising costs. On the other hand, scores of students on certain well-known standardized tests of achievement have been coming down. (See Figure 3-3 for one point of view.) To many, the combination of higher school taxes and lower average test scores has suggested that schools are costing more, but are doing less. This perception has prompted an interest in holding educators to account for youngsters' academic performances in schools.

Figure 3-2

SHOULD SECONDARY SCHOOLS BE BROKEN INTO SMALLER UNITS?

Do this. Do that. Then do this again. That's all you get from these teachers. I mean this high school is a crock. I feel like I'm in some kind of a Gestapo camp. Where do these people get off telling me how to lead *my* life? I've got my head together. I know what I want to do.

Way I see it is this. See, there're just too many of us for them to really teach or even get to know. So they respond by acting like sheep herders. A little prod here. A little prod there. Move the bodies. Sit them down. Ring the bell. Stand them up. Move them out and through the chutes to the next class.

I wish we had a small quiet building. I wish I could just get together with a couple of my friends and one or two of these teachers that maybe are on my wavelength. Then, maybe school would be O.K. It's sure nothing to get excited about now.

Statement made to an interviewer by a high school student

YOUR OPINION, PLEASE
Read the comments above. Then, respond to these questions.

1. Were there students with attitudes like the one presented here in your school? Were they numerous or few in number?
2. Do you think that the student is justified or not justified in the opinions cited in the interview? Why do you think so?
3. What about the student's suggestion to develop a small school building for similar students? Is this a good idea or a bad idea? Why do you think so?
4. How do you feel personally about the attitudes expressed by this student about his/her treatment in school? Did you have some experiences in high school that led to your feelings?
5. Do you think that the attitudes expressed by this student are typical of those held by high school students today? Why, or why not?

Figure 3-3

SHOULD TEACHERS BE EVALUATED ON THE BASIS OF THEIR STUDENTS' TEST SCORES?

I'm just getting sick and tired of this business. I mean, *really* sick and tired. This is the *third* time since school started that Ms. Smith, my son's English teacher, has sent a dittoed note home to me that is full of misspelled words. I just can't believe we have to put up with this kind of incompetence.

When my husband visited Ms. Smith's room during the open house, he said that there were misspellings all over the material for student notes on the blackboard. He came home shaking his head and wondering what had happened to standards for teachers since the two of us were in school.

I talked to Mrs. Wright, the school principal. I told her that surely something could be done. She listened politely, but then went on to point out that she really didn't have any specific evidence to show that the spelling problem was interfering with what students were learning. I told her that they ought to give these kids a really tough test at the end of the year that would include some spelling words. I told Mrs. Wright that I would bet Ms. Smith's students would not do as well as those taught by some of the other teachers. I think if we did this kind of testing, we could build a case for getting rid of some of these illiterates who are teaching our kids.

Statement made by a parent at a neighborhood party

YOUR OPINION, PLEASE

Read the comments above. Then, respond to these questions.

1. What kind of impact do you think the teacher who has been described will have on students? Why do you think so?
2. The parent suggests using a standardized test to see how well youngsters in this class do. Further, it is suggested that low scores will be taken as evidence that this teacher is not doing a good job. Do you agree with this suggestion? Why, or why not?
3. If you do not wish to use standardized tests to weed out (or at least identify) weak and incompetent teachers, how would you identify such people?
4. Did you ever have a teacher who was incompetent? If so, what is the basis for your judgment? How did such a teacher manage to survive as an employee of the school system? If you were in a position of responsibility in the schools, how would you deal with the issue of teacher incompetence?

Interest in accountability has prompted legislative action in many states. In general, such legislation has called upon schools to provide clear evidence that learners are making satisfactory progress toward established educational goals. Passage of this kind of legislation has led to increasing use of standardized tests to ascertain levels of student progress. Some people who have studied the issue contend that this kind of legislation has great potential to improve public education. Others contend that public education will be hurt by these laws. A few of the arguments on both sides of the issue are introduced in the sections that follow.

Arguments for Accountability.   Accountability legislation is an idea that is long overdue. For too long we have allowed educators to evade criticisms of weak instructional programs by contending that truly worthwhile educational goals cannot be measured by standardized tests. These educators have asked the public to take it on faith that teachers in the school were acting in a responsible manner and that students were learning all that they logically could be expected to learn. While many dedicated teachers have worked hard to do their best for students, some have not put forth a responsible effort. Indeed, irresponsible teacher behavior has been encouraged in an environment where teachers have not been called upon to provide specific evidence that youngsters under their charge are learning.

A net result of a past failure to use standardized tests to determine which teachers are getting the job done has been that incompetent teachers have been allowed to keep working side-by-side with competent teachers. The transparent incompetence of many of these people has tended to undermine public confidence in *all* teachers. Good teachers as well as bad have been tarred with a general suspicion that "teachers simply are not acting professionally."

Good teachers have nothing to fear from accountability legislation. First, their students are likely to perform at very satisfactory levels on standardized tests of achievement. Second, they will receive valuable feedback from standardized tests highlighting areas in which students did well and areas in which they did rather poorly. Good teachers will welcome this information as baseline data they can use to strengthen instruction in identified areas of weakness.

Another great advantage of accountability legislation is perhaps more psychological than educational. These laws have great potential for improving levels of public confidence in the schools. When the public is provided with information revealing that substantiated learning has occurred (as evidenced by respectable test scores), criticisms of teachers and of school programs should diminish.

Students, recognizing that they will have to take rigorous standardized tests, may well be more motivated to learn. If student motivation increases, teachers may find teaching to be easier than has frequently been true in the past. If teachers have to worry less about motivation and discipline problems, their efficiency in transmitting content may well improve.

Another benefit of accountability legislation for teachers is that such laws may reduce the range of teacher responsibilities. Most standardized tests have focused on academic content. It may be that public expectations regarding what schools should do will constrict to include chiefly, if not exclusively, the teaching of academic subject matter. The broader roles of the school in such areas as social training and personal development may be diminished. Should this indeed be the case, teachers may find themselves responsible for a smaller, but more manageable, array of tasks.

Arguments Against Accountability.   Certainly teachers should be held responsible for their behavior. But accountability legislation represents a narrow and simplistic approach to this issue. It is probably not stretching the truth to say that accountability laws have much more potential to harm than to save public education in this country.

Accountability legislation almost invariably mandates the use of some kind of standardized tests to measure the effectiveness of schools and of teachers. Typically, achievement scores of students are used as the criterion on which judgments of acceptability are made. Anyone who is at all conversant with professional test design and construction will testify that it is folly to make broad judgments based only on a single measure (such as a standardized test score.)

Further, even supposing that a single score might be an adequate measure of achievement, is such an indicator alone a realistic measure of the worth of a given teacher or school? Clearly it is not. Certainly most fair-minded observers support the idea that formal and informal instruction directed toward such diverse ends as promoting positive student attitudes toward school and encouraging development of sophisticated decision-making skills is equally as important as teaching specifics of academic subjects. Yet standardized test scores rarely focus on nonsubject-matter-specific outcomes of instruction. Because of their failure to do so, there is a likelihood that accountability legislation will force teachers and schools to teach only what is tested. If this happens, youngsters and, ultimately, all in our society will be the worse for it.

The claim that youngsters will work harder and be more motivated when they know that they will face taking standardized tests is not supported by solid research evidence. Indeed, a contrary case might well be made. Some theorists postulate that individuals, and young people in particular, do less well when they are placed under conditions of tension and stress. The implicit threat to do well on a standardized test for many youngsters may result in diminished enthusiasm for the school program. If this occurs, teachers might well find themselves faced with increased discipline problems in the classroom.

A fundamental fallacy of the accountability legislation argument is that teachers alone should be held responsible for achievement of students under their charge. Clearly many things influence youngsters' achievement levels other than teachers. For example, are parents at home supportive of the aims and programs of the school? Do they encourage the youngster to do his or her school assignments? What health factors are involved? Does the youngster take medications that interfere with his or her concentration levels at school. What about nutritional levels. Does the youngster eat enough of the right kinds of foods? Answers to questions such as these have a great bearing on how a given individual might do on a standardized achievement test. Certainly it is irresponsible to suggest that teachers alone should be held to account for learning of youngsters in their classes.

Finally, the accountability movement as it is being applied in education is inconsistent with the way in which accountability is determined in other human service professions. For example, a physician is not held responsible for curing all his or her patients. Neither is a lawyer expected to win all his or her cases. Rather, they are held to account in terms of whether they exercised reasonable care in the discharge of their duties. This is the kind of standard that is appropriate for teachers. We should look to see whether they have acted in a professional and a responsible manner in delivering programs to students. But we should not hold them personally responsible for the *results* of these programs as reflected in students' performances. To do so places the teacher in an untenable position. He or she is asked to bear the responsibility for a condition that comes about as a result of interactions among many variables over which he or she may have no control. Certainly this cannot be justice.

Accountability: Present Status. The accountability movement continues to gain strength. Many states now have some accountability legislation. States that do not have such laws are giving serious consideration to enacting them. In general, teachers in public schools increasingly will be teaching in areas covered by some sort of accountability legislation.

At this time, it appears that standardized tests will remain the dominant tool used to assess the adequacy of performance of schools and of teachers. A number of new standardized tests may well be developed. But most seem likely to maintain the focus on school subjects that characterizes most existing standardized tests. At this juncture, there appears to be little legislative interest in making quality judgments about schools based on measures taking into account learning outcomes that cannot be associated readily with the academic curriculum. Whether, in the end, this will be a positive or negative influence on public education remains to be seen. What is certain is that accountability legislation will be a topic of heated debate over the next several years, both within and without professional education.

The Voucher System

The "voucher system" like accountability legislation, has been proposed because of certain criticisms that have been made of public school education. Under the voucher system, a parent would be given a voucher, something like a check, that could be turned in for educational services for his or her children to any school of the parent's choice. Money represented by the voucher would be used by the school to defray the cost of educating the student (or students).

The amount of the voucher would be determined as follows. Total tax monies for educating youngsters in a given district would be computed. Then this total would be divided by the total number of students. Thus, if it were determined that $2,000 in tax revenues were required to educate each child, the $2,000 would be the value of a voucher for each child in a family. If a family had three students in school, then vouchers totaling $6,000 would be presented to the parents. These would be spent at schools of their choice. (Vouchers would have to be turned in to schools. They could not be cashed by the parents.)

According to the voucher plan, parents should be able to place youngsters in schools in which they have confidence. Presumably, the best schools would attract the largest number of vouchers. Other schools in the district, seeing what was happening, would work to improve their programs to attract more students. In the end, better programs and programs more consistent with the wishes of parents and students would ensue—or at least so argue supporters of the voucher plan. As might be imagined, the voucher plan has prompted a good deal of discussion in educational circles. The arguments of proponents and opponents are outlined in the sections that follow.

Arguments for the Voucher Plan. Parents are the best judge of what is good for their own youngsters. Given freedom of choice, parents will learn a great deal about school programs and select a school that will provide learning experiences for their youngsters that are consistent with their own views regarding what constitutes good education. For example, if a given parent believes that his or her child would learn best in a school characterized by very strict discipline and heavy reliance on lecture method instruction and homework, then he or she could "spend" the educational voucher at such a school and enroll his or her child at that institution.

The present practice of assigning students to schools on bases not associated with the nature of programs assures that many youngsters will not profit from offered instruction. Because of this lack of fit between student and school program, a fertile environment develops for the development of apathy, hostility, and alienation. But, when students have freedom of choice with regard to which school they attend, motivation for the school program is likely to be enhanced. Consequently student achievement levels are likely to improve.

The voucher system has potential to introduce healthy competition among schools in a district. As schools begin to compete for vouchers, they will have to develop programs that will attract students. They will do a better job of communicating with parents. Further, administrators will pay much more attention to rewarding effective teachers. The reputations of these teachers will be critically important incentives for parents to select specific schools in which to enroll their youngsters. This may well result in improved salaries for teachers who are truly outstanding in the classroom. On the other hand, this system would prompt a quick identification of ineffective teachers. Salary levels could be set in such a way as to discourage their continuance in the profession.

Finally, public education traditionally has done a very poor job of providing equal educational opportunities. Wealthy sections of school districts have provided outstanding educational services for students in those districts. But the poor generally have not been able to take advantage of these schools, because they have been trapped by traditional attendance boundaries within parts of districts having inadequate facilities. The voucher system would enable parents, regardless of place of residence within a district, to send youngsters to any school in the district. This would provide a major step forward in the effort to provide fair treatment to all constituents in a district.

Arguments Against the Voucher Plan.   The voucher plan has the potential to destroy public education. It will promote fragmentation of the student population into separate schools where narrow interests are served. The function of the school as a meetingplace for all elements within the society will be lost. This has serious implications for the society at large. Because students during their formative years in school will not rub shoulders with a cross section of the population, as adults they may well be much less tolerant of individuals with perspectives different from their own. In time, this could lead to dangerous factionalism within the adult population. Potentially even political stability could be threatened.

The voucher plan would lead to dangerous competitive practices among schools. These surely would result in reduced levels of innovation and of creative teaching in the schools. Teachers would be ever fearful of alienating parents and, hence, losing their sons and daughters as students (and the revenues represented by the vouchers attached to these sons and daughters). Consequently, teachers would be disinclined to engage in daring, provocative, and stimulating teaching. Instruction would settle at some kind of blah, noncontroversial norm.

The voucher plan assumes that individual parents to be the best judge of what constitutes good education. While many parents have the training and understanding necessary to make sound choices regarding the education of their youngsters, others do not. Certainly in this vast population, there are many parents who have little idea about how to recognize schools providing good educational services. Educational hucksters would have a field day selling low-quality school programs to parents lacking the skills to discriminate between sound and unsound educational practices. Indeed, the voucher plan has potential to inhibit sons and daughters of the uneducated and the poor by encouraging parents to enroll such youngsters in low-quality programs. Social mobility seems certain to be served less well by the voucher plan that it is by present practices.

The Voucher Plan: Present Status.   There has been much more discussion about the voucher plan than there has been implementation. Concerns of certain spokespersons for minority students relating to possible resegregation of schools should voucher plans be adopted have weighed heavily on school administrators who have considered such a plan. Other worries relate to the possibility that a vast new bureaucratic structure might have to be created to administer such a plan. Further, there has been consternation with regard to how schools would conduct long-range planning in an environment where the numbers of youngsters to be served might vary dramatically from year to year. Teachers' professional groups have not been enthusiastic about, in effect, pitting one professional against another in a competitive effort to attract students. Other concerns have been voiced as well. In general, given the complexity of the issues associated with implementing a voucher plan system, it probably is reasonable to conclude that widespread adoption of the scheme is not imminent.

EQUALIZATION OF EDUCATIONAL OPPORTUNITIES

From the earliest days of public education, to a great extent schools have been viewed as social equalizers. An abiding premise has been that schools ought to enable students from different social and economic backgrounds to come together to learn not only school subjects but about one another as well. This experience, it has been argued, would produce adult citizens who would respect individual differences.

Further, schools have been seen as promoters of social mobility. Although a youngster might come from the humblest of backgrounds, the traditional myth of American public education suggested that he or she, by dint of hard study, could lift himself or herself to the particular economic or social plateau to which he or she might aspire. That the schools could accomplish such transformations was questioned little throughout much of the history of American public education.

In recent years, certain critics have begun to look beyond what public education has promised to do in the area of promoting social equity to examine what, in fact, public education has done. From such examinations, large numbers of individuals have concluded that the schools have not served well many of the subgroups within the total school population. In particular, many have felt that public schools have not been doing a good job of serving certain youngsters from minority ethnic backgrounds, those from homes where English is not the first language, and youngsters who are females. A number of proposals to provide educational equity for individuals in these (and other) groups have been put forward. Some of these now have the force of law. A few have been implemented for quite some time. A number of others are still in the talking stage. In almost every case, these proposals have prompted a good deal of discussion. In the subsections that follow, a selection of these proposals and associated arguments is introduced.

Racial Segregation and Busing

In 1954, the Supreme Court in the famous *Brown* v. *Board of Education* case [*Brown* v. *Board of Education,* 347 U.S. 483 (1954)] overturned the then-prevailing "separate but equal doctrine" that had provided the legal basis for racially segregated school systems. Although the *Brown* decision represented a giant step forward in the effort to desegregate public schools, this decision alone by no means led to all schools having racially mixed populations. As critics pointed out, neighborhood attendance lines in many instances assured that many schools would remain predominantly white or pre-dominantly black (white in white neighborhoods and black in black neighborhoods). Segregation in the schools was not being maintained because of laws requiring it (the *Brown* decision, in effect, ruled such laws null and void) but rather by de facto seg-regation in neighborhoods and a tradition of neighborhood attendance boundaries for schools.

During the 1960s (and, to some extent, continuing to the present time), spokes-persons for racial minorities began to demand that school segregation based on racial makeups of neighborhoods be ended. A number of the lawsuits filed claimed that school segregation caused by neighborhood attendance boundaries created a situation that was inherently unequal for minority youngsters. In general, the courts supported this view and directed school districts to take action to ensure some semblance of racial balance within all schools within their boundaries.

In a few cases, school districts were able to comply with these rulings by slightly shifting attendance boundaries in such a way that a better racial balance in each school resulted. This approach, however, did not prove feasible, particularly in large cities where large numbers of minorities resided. The solution (adopted in many cases as a result of specific court orders) was to require students living in one part of a district to be bused to schools in other parts of the district. In this way, some black students could be bused to schools in predominantly white neighborhoods and some white students could be bused to schools in predominantly black neighborhoods. The result would be sufficient mixing of the races to ensure that schools would be in compliance with deseg-regation guidelines. The busing solution has proved to be extremely controversial (see Figure 3-4). Some arguments related to the issue are introduced in the sections that follow.

Arguments for Busing.   Busing represents the only practical way in which to achieve racial integration in the schools. Obviously we cannot rely on the old way of allowing students to attend schools in their own neighborhoods. Neighborhoods, in general, have always been and remain today racially segregated. There is no

Figure 3-4

IS CONCERN FOR WEAR AND TEAR ON THEIR CHILDREN THE REAL ISSUE WHEN WHITES COMPLAIN ABOUT BUSING?

These arguments that the white parents are putting out against busing are just so much bunk. "Busing is too hard on the kids" or "Busing deprives them of extracurricular activities time," they say. Baloney! Simple baloney!

I mean those things may be true, but concern for the kids is not the *real* issue. Look, kids have been bused for years. Rural kids have ridden buses for generations. Did we hear loud complaints? We did *not!* But, now that white kids are to be bused to predominantly black schools, we get this great outcry. Why aren't these parents honest with themselves? What they are really opposed to is not the bus ride but what waits for their kids at the end of the line. It's simply more respectable for them to oppose the bus ride than to come right out and and say they don't want their young-sters going to school with black kids. Opposition to busing is simply a front for antiblack racism. That's what it is, pure and simple.

Statement by a black parent at a school board meeting

YOUR OPINION, PLEASE

Read the comments above. Then, respond to these questions.

1. If you were to respond to this parent's statements, what would you say?
2. Is opposition to busing simply racism in disguise? Why, or why not?
3. How do you react to the argument that nobody got excited about busing students until it was done for the purpose of promoting racial integration?
4. What is your personal reaction to busing? Why do you feel as you do?
5. Suppose that you were a chief administrator of a large school district. You were under court order to achieve racial balance (or at least a close approximation of racial balance) in your district's schools. What, besides busing, might you recommend to the school board?

---

evidence that this pattern is changing. Theoretically, it might be possible for the government to force people, on the basis of race, to change residences with a view to producing more racially integrated neighborhoods. (In that case, of course, neighborhood schools would be integrated.) Such a policy would require massive relocations and clearly would be much more disruptive than any busing proposal.

In the past, minority groups have borne more than their share of what might be called social inconveniences. For example, until relatively recent times blacks in many places were required to sit in poor locations in theaters, ride in the back of buses, and use specially designated water fountains. Even in areas of the country with less for-malized restrictions, blacks (and certain other minorities) knew that their presence in certain places was unwelcome, understood that their choices of residential housing were limited, and perceived that their access to better paying jobs was limited. Given this sad history, it is certainly not too much to ask some white youngsters to be slightly inconvenienced by requiring them to ride buses to schools located outside their home neighborhoods.

The fear that busing will result in diminished parental involvement in school affairs is nonsense. The vase majority of parents have automobiles. They think nothing of driving these cars across town to shop, to go to the theater, or to dine at a restaurant. When something as important as the education of their youngsters is at stake, certainly they will find a way to get to the school.

Arguments Against Busing.   The neighborhood school is the social center of the local community. Without it, neighborhoods lose their individual identities. When neighborhoods seek to have a distinct sense of place, they begin to die. Busing represents a direct assault on one of the institutions that has bound people together: the neighborhood school. This represents nothing less than an assault on the basic values of neighborliness and caring that have contributed so much to the nation's greatness.

Students who are bused to schools have much less pride in their schools than do those who attend schools in their home neighborhoods. A tradition of support for the local school on the part of parents, relatives, and neighbors in an important factor in building loyalties of today's students. When students are bused, they are cut off from this tradition of support. There is evidence that youngsters who have little pride in their school are more likely to engage in vandalism and other socially unacceptable practices. In the classroom, they are more likely to be discipline problems.

Students who must travel on buses long distances to school are often denied the opportunity to participate in extracurricular activities, which constitute an important part of the secondary education experience. When they are not available, the schooling of youngsters is not complete. Further, in the absence of an opportunity to get involved in these activities, academic work becomes the sole focus of school attendance. For many youngsters, a school in which "nothing happens but classes" is a dreary place at best. Clearly it is not an institution likely to be viewed with much warmth and affection.

Busing students is expensive. When neighborhood schools were the norm, large numbers of youngsters could walk to school. But busing requirements have meant that many must now ride buses to schools at considerable distances from their homes. In an era of escalating fuel cost, such a policy diverts scarce school tax dollars from the important tasks of instructing students to the doubtfully worthy objective of providing them long rides on buses.*

Busing is detrimental to the cause of integration. What happens when busing is adopted as official school policy is a "white flight" from the school district. This tends to result in even greater concentrations of minority students in the district than was true before establishment of the busing policy. The ultimate result of white flight can be a district that is populated so heavily with minority students that it will be impossible to integrate the schools. For example, if a district has 90 percent black students and 10 percent white students, it will be extremely difficult to achieve any kind of meaningful integration in the district's schools.

Racial Segregation and Busing: Present Status.   Busing has been extremely unpopular with a broad cross section of the public. Indeed, many political figures have found it to their advantage to go public with their opposition to busing as a way to achieve integration in the schools. A number of legislative proposals that have been mounted would prevent federal funds from being used to support busing programs.

What seems to be at stake here is a conflict between court decisions that have required school districts to achieve racial integration and a very unpopular method of acting to conform to these court decisions, namely, busing. Although the entire issue continues to be debated hotly, it seems clear that many school districts are searching desperately for ways in which to achieve racial integration that do not require mandatory busing of students to accomplish this objective. Some large districts are banking on the success of magnet school programs to desegregate their schools. Others are trying still other approaches. At this time, districts are by no means agreed on how they will respond to the need to integrate schools without relying on the very unpopular response of forced busing. The issue seems certain to be a thorny one for educators for years to come.

---

*During the 1978–1979 school year, the Los Angeles school district spent $12 million on busing. (Summers 1979).

Language Discrimination

Historically, schools were seen as social forges capable of melting youngsters from a variety of ethnic backgrounds into the pure American alloy. To accomplish this goal, it was presumed that students should be expected to become functional in English as quickly as possible. Thus, youngsters who did not come to school speaking acceptable English (or, perhaps, not speaking any English at all) were required to take all instruction in the English language. In some cases, youngsters were forbidden by strict school rules from speaking any language except English during the school day.

In recent years, some individuals have pointed out that the tradition of "English only" at school has placed youngsters who come to school as nonnative speakers of English at a severe disadvantage. In the landmark court case of *Lau* v. *Nichols* [414 U.S. 563 (1974)], it was determined that requiring students who did not understand English to use the same materials and facilities as English-speaking students constituted unequal treatment. This decision led to the establishment of bilingual programs in the school.

The term "bilingual" may be misleading to those not familiar with its use in the schools. Bilingual does not mean that all students are to become fluent in two languages; rather, bilingual programs seek to provide youngsters who are nonnative speakers of English with school instruction in their native languages until such time as their proficiency in English is roughly equal to that of native speakers of English. In this way, it is felt, youngsters who do not speak fluent English when they come to school initially will be able to make acceptable progress in learning of academic subjects.

In meeting bilingual education guidelines, school districts generally begin by identifying students who come from homes where English is not the dominant language. These students are tested. If their English proficiency is below a specified level, the district attempts to provide school instruction in their primary language. Efforts to deal with nonnative speakers of English in the schools by providing school instruction in primary languages have been surrounded by controversy. (Figure 3-5 presents one point of view.) Some of the arguments that have been put forward relating to this issue are described in the sections that follow.

Arguments for Bilingual Education.　Bilingual education is the only acceptable way in which to put the nonnative speaker of English and the native speaker of English on an equal footing. Obviously a youngster who comes to school with a deficient understanding of the language of instruction cannot be expected to profit as much from the instructional program as the student who has a sound understanding of the language of instruction. This kind of inequity is removed when schools provide all youngsters initial instruction in their primary languages.

There is an important psychological argument to be made in support of bilingual education as well. Traditionally, when non–English-speaking or marginally English-speaking youngsters came to school, they did not perform so well as their native English speaking counterparts. Further, there was a tendency for at least some native speakers of English to poke fun at youngsters who spoke English poorly. All these factors contributed to give children coming from families where English was not the primary language low self-images. Bilingual education promotes self-esteem of nonnative speakers of English.

The traditional way of dealing with nonnative speakers of English, by placing them in specialized courses designed to teach them English quickly ("English as a Second Language" courses, for example), has not proved effective. First, dropout rates from such courses have been high. Second, to attend such courses, students frequently have had to miss some of their regular academic content courses. As a result, academic achievement of these youngsters has been impaired. It is far better to provide a bilin-

Figure 3-5

IS BILINGUAL EDUCATION DANGEROUS?

To the north my friends, look to the north! "Vive Quebec Libre," and all of that. We see a society bent on tearing itself apart. We see a sad Canada at war with itself. And it can happen here. Indeed, given some strange goings on regarding this bilingual education business, it may well happen here.

Look, it's like this. A language is more than a way of just saying hello. A language is the bearer of an entire cultural tradition. Speakers of English see the world in ways that are different from speakers of other languages. Individual languages promote unity among their speakers. Countries where multiple languages are spoken hang together with difficulty. The potential for discord is always there. Look at your Belgiums, your Hollands, your Yugoslavias, if you want a non-Canadian example.

Now, what bothers me is this bilingual business. It seems to me we're encouraging people to avoid a complete conversion to reliance on English. It seems to me we're saying to them that it's "OK" to go through life more fluent in Spanish, for example, than English. This is a *terrible mistake*. We are going to end up in a few years with a significant percentage of our adult population not thinking of English as the "real" language of this country. When that day comes, we are in for trouble. I can foresee a time when Texas and adjacent areas may seek to go the same way as Quebec. There is a real possibility that divisive regionalism built on language lines is building in this country. It is a prospect to ponder with some concern.

Statement made to a school board by a district patron

YOUR OPINION, PLEASE

Read the comments above. Then, respond to these questions.

1. Does the speaker, in your view, have an accurate impression of the purposes of bilingual education? Why, or why not?
2. Do you see evidence that "language regionalism" is building in this country? If so, where? How has it come about?
3. Will bilingual programs result in a sizable percentage of the population developing or retaining perspectives that are incompatible with those of native speakers of English?
4. Will bilingual education lead to divisiveness along the lines experienced in Canada? Why, or why not?
5. If you were asked to make a general response to this speaker's comments, what would you say?

---

gual program in which students are taught mathematics in the Spanish language, for example, just as native speakers of English are taught mathematics in the English language.

Certainly bilingual programs are expensive. But the social costs of students who drop out of school programs because of language-associated problems are even higher. Bilingual programs enable youngsters who are nonnative speakers of English to take full advantage of what public education has to offer. By so doing, their chances of completing their educations and joining the adult population as competent, trained adults are enhanced. When this happens, the entire society benefits.

Arguments Against Bilingual Education. Immigrants came to the United States and learned to speak fluent English successfully for centuries before anyone suggested the need for bilingual education. People in Minnesota speak excellent English today even though many early settlers arrived speaking only Scandinavian languages or German. Learning English just is not as complex, confusing, or time consuming as advocates of bilingual education would have us believe.

Although proponents of bilingual education claim that their interest is to teach youngsters in their primary languages only until they become fluent in English, such programs have potential to delay acquisition of functional fluency in English. Formerly, when all instruction was in English, students (and their parents) had an interest in mastering English as quickly as possible. Today, when a youngster who does not speak English fluently comes to school, he or she knows that it is not necessary to work hard to learn English. Instruction will be provided in the primary language. Why hurry to learn English?

There is a real possibility that bilingual programs will result in some students failing *ever* to become fluent speakers of English. Such an eventuality is a real tragedy. The youngster who fails to acquire fluency in English loses much of his or her potential mobility within American society. True, he or she may find a home in a minority language enclave in a large city where it is perfectly possible to function with no knowledge of English, but his or her geographic range will be severely limited as opposed to that enjoyed by people who are fluent speakers of English.

Another difficulty with bilingual education relates to cost. Framers of some of the initial legislation in this area had no idea of the number of primary languages that are spoken by families sending youngsters to public school. For example, the Houston Independent School District found 89 distinct languages being spoken in students' homes in a 1978 language survey. Problems associated with finding teachers who are fluent in languages such as Tagalog, Bulgarian, and Punjabi and, at the same time, qualified to teach required school subjects are considerable. Obviously there are not many certified teachers with these kinds of language competencies. Training native speakers of these languages so that they qualify for teacher certification would be expensive. Further, even if such training could be accomplished, some teachers would find themselves working only with one or two youngsters. This would hardly be a cost-effective way to spend scarce instructional dollars.

Bilingual Education: Present Status.   Bilingual education finds itself in something of a confused state today. In the later days of the Carter administration, much pressure was put on local school districts to offer bilingual education programs. Many districts did install such programs.

But in early 1981 the Reagan administration indicated that less federal pressure would be placed on local school districts as to the kinds of bilingual instruction that would be considered appropriate. In essence, federal authorities seemed to be saying that local school officials were in a better position than were federal officials to determine how special needs of language minority youngsters would be best served. If this general federal direction persists, a wider variety of bilingual programs might be expected to emerge as districts begin to assess their own needs and develop their own programmatic responses.

What is clear at this point is that the position outlined by the Supreme Court in the *Lau* v. *Nichols* case still stands. That is, schools are expected to do *something* to ensure that language minority children are not placed at a disadvantage vis-à-vis native speakers of English. But the decisions are not yet in in terms of how this general objective will be accomplished.

Sex Discrimination

Title IX of Public Law 92-318, the Education Amendments of 1972, prohibited discrimination based on sex. The opening sentence of Title IX reads as follows (*United States Statutes at Large* 1973, p. 373):

> *No person in the United States, shall, on the basis of sex, be excluded from participation in, be denied the benefits of, or be subjected to discrimination under any education program or activity receiving Federal financial assistance . . .*

Title IX and follow-up legislation have impacted all parts of the school program. In general, sex equity laws have attempted to open up all aspects of public education to students of either sex. Clearly this has constituted a break with many traditional practices. The effort has gone forward in an atmosphere of considerable controversy. Some positions of individuals who have favored and opposed sex equity legislation are introduced in the subsections that follow.

Arguments for Sex Equity Legislation.   For years, girls received inferior services than boys from public schools. Differences were particularly striking in vocational programs and athletics. In the area of vocational offerings, traditionally, girls were tracked into home economics classes. There was little, if any, expectation that any girl would seriously be interested in pursuing an adult role other than that of wife and homemaker. Boys, on the other hand, could participate in a variety of shop and other vocationally oriented classes that could lead to a variety of interesting and monetarily rewarding careers.

A very serious side effect of the traditional practice of "boys-only" vocational programs was an erosion of girls' self-confidence in the kinds of things they could do and accomplish as adults. Too many female students were conditioned to believe that they were somehow "genetically inferior" to male students and could not, therefore, hope to hold demanding skill positions as adults. In essence these programs conditioned half the student population (the female half) to set artificially low career objectives. As a consequence, the whole society suffered because females tended not to develop their talents to their full potential. Sex equity legislation that has encouraged girls to enter a variety of vocational fields represents a step to ensure that talented females make maximum use of their gifts.

In the area of athletics, budgets for girls' programs traditionally represented a small fraction of budgets for boys' programs. At the varsity level, boys' teams were provided with the finest equipment and were taken, at district expense, to play teams in cities far distant from their home communities. Few girls' teams received this kind of support. Indeed, it was not uncommon at all for girls' teams, if they existed at all, to be dependent on parent car pools to get to games. In general, there was an unstated assumption that females were "delicate" and that athletics were "not appropriate for someone who is *really* feminine." Although not often stated openly, there were whispers that females with serious athletic interests had homosexual tendencies.

Today, we know that there are very few genetic limitations on what women can do. Today, we recognize that, given opportunities, women can make as many contributions as men. It has taken sex equity legislation to force school officials to recognize what leading medical authorities have known for some time (that there are few limits on what women can do). This very important legislation has opened many doors to female students (see Figure 3-6). In the end, these students and the society at large will both be the better for it.

Arguments Against Sex Equity Legislation.   Nobody is against providing female students with sound educational programs. The argument here is not one in favor of the principle of sex discrimination. The argument is about the pernicious side effects of sex equity legislation. Let us consider, first, the issue of athletics.

Nobody argues anymore that girls' athletics are unfeminine. Everybody agrees that girls interested in athletic programs should be encouraged to participate. But sex equity legislation tends to go much beyond this kind of encouragement. Some legislation seems to imply that, if a school has an approximately equal number of male and female students, the athletic budget should be split down the middle. That is, half should go to support boys' athletics and half to support girls' athletics. While the framers of the legislation may have had good intents, they failed to recognize that a good deal of money for the total athletic budget comes in the form of revenues from ticket

Figure 3-6

"MY NAME IS SALLY, AND I WANT TO PLAY QUARTERBACK"

My name is Sally. And I have some news for you. *I don't want to play volleyball. I don't want to play volleyball.* I want a contact sport. I'm smart. I've got fast hands. I can throw a ball 50 yards. I want to play football. I want to play quarterback.

Statement made by a female student to her school principal

YOUR OPINION, PLEASE

Read the statement above. Then, respond to these questions.

1. In the name of sex equity, should females be allowed to try out for traditional male sports and males be allowed to try out for traditional female sports?
2. Suppose that the principal pointed out that dressing facilities had been set up under the assumption that only students of one sex would be playing football. How would you counter this objection to females playing alongside males on the football team?
3. If the principal went along with Sally's desire, what special changes might have to be made in traditional ways of working with students trying out for football?
4. What is your general reaction to the suggestion that any student of any sex should be allowed to try out for any school athletic team? On what do you base your decision?

---

sales at athletic events. With few exceptions (girls' basketball in Iowa, for example), revenues from athletic contests between girls' teams bring in only a fraction of the money that results from ticket sales to athletic contests between boys' teams. It hardly seems fair then that boys' athletics, which bring in the lion's share of revenue to the total athletic budget, should not be supported by more money than girls' athletics, which bring in fewer dollars.

Sex equity legislation has the potential to put girls at a great disadvantage as compared with boys in certain parts of the school curriculum. For example, should the assumptions of these laws be carried to their logical conclusions, all references to sex-based performance standards would disappear. Think about what this might mean in a program such as weight lifting. If a common criterion for grading failed to make distinctions between male and female students, on average, females would likely receive lower grades than males. (Certainly there would be a few exceptions. But, because of general size and weight differences, most boys can lift more than girls.)

Although many more careers are open to females today than was once the case, still more men than women are supporting one or more dependents. Sex equity legislation, by opening all secondary school vocational classes to both boys and girls, has the potential for excluding large numbers of boys from such programs. This legislation makes no provisions for extra money to support expansions of vocational programs. Hence, what we tend to get is a larger number of students competing for a given number of spaces in these classes. Because of school authorities fear of being accused of noncompliance with sex equity laws, there is a tendency to admit most girls who apply. A regrettable consequence is that many boys, who have a higher likelihood in later life than girls of being called upon to support dependents, may be denied the opportunity to obtain skills that can lead to well-paying work.

Finally, framers of sex equity laws, though well intentioned, simply have not considered how this legislation may be interfering with some long-standing school traditions. For example, lawsuits in recent years in some school districts have sought to prevent schools from holding such traditional affairs as mother-daughter or father-son banquets. Certainly this kind of nonsense represents an inexcusable intrusion of legislators into school affairs.

Figure 3-7

CAN WE HAVE BOTH QUALITY AND EQUITY IN THE SCHOOLS?

Schools have been placed in a ''no-win'' situation. On the one hand, representatives of the great interest lobbies have placed new requirements on school officials to assure fair treatment of such groups as ethnic and racial minorities, women, and handicapped youngsters. On the other hand, members of the upwardly mobile middle class point with disgust at declining student scores on tests of academic achievement.

In considering present trends, we must ask ourselves, ''Have the schools been asked to do too much?'' ''Is there a fundamental inconsistency between the goal of equity and the goal of quality?'' We believe there is. The effort to achieve equity has required massive disruptions in traditional school programs. These have served the principle of equity well. But they may well have interfered with efforts to serve the other objective of educational quality. As a nation, it appears to us, a choice must be made. Either we continue to push ahead with programs to get equity and trade off quality in the bargain, or we take a position that a great deal of equity has been achieved and desist in efforts to extend the principle. By so doing, we can provide an educational environment where ''quality'' can be nurtured. We believe such a commitment to quality, even at the expense of equity, to be in the national interest at this time.

Part of a newspaper editorial

YOUR OPINION, PLEASE

Read the paragraphs above. Then, respond to these questions.

1. Can you think of examples where efforts to promote ''equity'' have interfered with efforts to promote quality?
2. Is it possible for schools to provide both equity and quality? Why, or why not?
3. Do you agree with the general position taken in this editorial? Express your position in the form of a short letter to the editor you might write.
4. In the years ahead, would you expect schools to be placed under more pressure to improve educational equity or more pressure to improve educational quality? Why do you think so?

Sex Equity Legislation: Present Status.   This area continues to be debated hotly. In general, nearly all areas of school curricula are now open to members of either sex. Enrollments of boys in such traditional female areas as home economics are up. Enrollments of girls in such traditionally male courses as automechanics are up. In general, schools are making an effort to avoid suggesting to a given student that any activity or career option may be inappropriate for him or her based on the criterion of gender.

A great deal of discussion continues in the area of what schools must do to comply with sex equity legislation in the area of athletics. In general, schools have not simply cut athletic budgets down the middle and reserved one half for boys' athletic programs and one half for girls' athletic programs. A number of complicated formulas have been devised that take into account such things as numbers of students involved in different athletic activities, equipment costs, and so forth. (For a discussion on quality and equity, see Figure 3-7.)

Posttest

Directions: Using your own paper, answer each of the following true/false questions. For each correct statement, write the word ''true.'' For each incorrect statement, write the word ''false.''

_____ 1. In general, it is fair to say that in recent years there has developed an increasing tendency for teachers to be held responsible for the achievement of the students under their charge.

_____ 2. The concept of alternative school is broad enough to include some schools that place a very heavy emphasis on certain basic subjects.

_____ 3. Certain proponents of competency testing argue that its introduction into a school has potential for increasing students' motivation to learn.

_____ 4. In part, the voucher system seeks to improve education by introducing an element of competition among various schools in a district.

_____ 5. A watershed decision in the area of school desegregation was *Brown* v. *Board of Education.*

_____ 6. Magnet schools represent one response to the need to integrate schools.

_____ 7. Some critics of bilingual education allege that bilingual programs may result in a slowdown in the rate of acquisition of proficiency in English on the part of students who come to school as nonspeakers of English.

_____ 8. The role of the federal government has changed but little throughout the entire history of American education.

_____ 9. Some professional educators have pointed out that, today, schools are being asked to do more things at the same time that school budgets are growing tighter.

_____ 10. In recent years, many court decisions have had impacts on secondary school programs.

Key Ideas in Review

1. Today, citizens are asking two general questions about schools. First, they are asking, "Are the schools doing a good job?" Second, they are asking, "Are the schools treating all youngsters fairly?" The issues of educational quality and educational equity have spawned numerous proposals for school reform. A number of these have been introduced. All have been accompanied by a good deal of controversy. That controversy continues today.

2. Alternative schools represent a response to a lack of confidence of some segments of the public in traditional school curricula and organizational schemes. Many different kinds of alternative schools have been tried. There has been a tremendous growth in the number of public alternative schools in the last ten years. One especially important alternative school is the magnet school. Magnet schools, located in large districts, attempt to attract students from throughout an entire district by offering exemplary programs in specialized areas.

3. The idea that educators should be accountable has received a good deal of currency in recent years. In general, accountability refers to the idea that the teacher bears some direct responsibility for the learning of youngsters under their charge. This view has been challenged by some teachers who argue that learning is influenced by many variables other than the quality of classroom instruction. Certainly this issue is one of the most hotly debated in education today.

4. The voucher system proposes to give parents a choice in terms of where their youngsters go to school. Each parent is given a voucher that can be spent on the education of his or her child in any school in the district. In this system, revenues of a given school would be tied directly to the number of vouchers "spent" at this school by parents. According to proponents of the plan, the voucher system would result in competition among schools to mount quality programs that would attract the interest of large numbers of parents. The scheme has been much debated. But, for various reasons, it has been little implemented.

5. Mandatory busing of students has been one response to meeting federal demands that schools be desegregated. Busing has been seen as necessary because residential patterns of

neighborhoods typically do not reflect an adequate racial mix. Busing proposals have been extremely controversial. School officials find themselves (at least in many districts) caught between a legal order to integrate and violent parental opposition to busing, the only way many authorities see as viable for achieving this required integration.

6. In recent years, court decisions and related policy decisions of the executive branch have promoted the view that youngsters who come to schools as nonnative speakers of English should receive instruction in their home languages until such time as they are fluent in English. Proponents of these bilingual programs point out that nonnative speakers of English can hardly be expected to profit from instruction if they do not know the language the teacher is using. Opponents point to such things as potential costs of such programs and possibilities of delaying acquisition of English competencies by allowing youngsters to function in school in their primary languages (not English).

7. Beginning with the passage of Title IX of Public Law 92-318 in 1972, schools have been under pressure to avoid sex discrimination in their programs. In general, this has resulted in the opening up of the entire school curriculum to all students. Special courses for boys and girls have disappeared. The effort to promote sexual equity has generated a great deal of debate. The discussion has been very heated in the area of athletics, particularly when issues such as distributions of funds for girls' teams and boys' teams have come up.

"Back to basics, I guess."

SUMMARY

There is evidence that public esteem for the schools has declined in recent years. In general, this decline appears related to two specific issues. On the one hand, there is a feeling that the quality of educational services has declined. On the other hand, there is a perception that certain students have not been treated fairly. A number of proposals have been put forward and implemented with a view to remedying what critics have seen to be weaknesses in more traditional school practices.

A number of the proposed remedies to "the problems of the schools" have themselves prompted at least as much debate as that surrounding the original problems. For example, while the issue of integrating schools received a great deal of attention, one might argue that the proposed solution — mandatory busing — has generated at least as much discussion. A basic problem in the whole debate about how to improve the schools is that there may be some mutual incompatibility between seeking quality and equity simultaneously. Some individuals suggest that programs that serve one of these objectives may conflict with the principle represented by the other. Whether this is true or not, we can assert with some confidence that proposals to reform school programs will continue to stimulate great public interest in the years ahead.

References

Butts, R. Freeman. "Educational Vouchers: The Private Pursuit of the Public Purse," *Phi Delta Kappan* (September 1979): 7–9.

Conant, James B. *The American High School Today.* New York: McGraw-Hill Book Company, 1959.

Coombs, Jerrold R. "Can Minimum Competency Testing Be Justified?" *The High School Journal* (January 1979): 175–180.

Gallup, George H. "The 12th Annual Gallup Poll of the Public's Attitudes Toward the Public Schools," *Phi Delta Kappan* (September 1980): 33–48.

Gilman, David Alan. "The Logic of Minimal Competency Testing," *National Association of Secondary School Principals Bulletin* (September 1978): 56–63.

Goodlad, John I. "Can Our Schools Get Better?" *Phi Delta Kappan* (January 1979): 342–347.

Hodgkinson, Harold. "What's Right with Education?" *Phi Delta Kappan* (November 1979): 159–162.

Seely, David S. "Reducing the Confrontation over Teacher Accountability," *Phi Delta Kappan* (December 1979): 248–151.

Smith, Vernon H. "Alternative Education is Here to Stay," *Phi Delta Kappan* (April 1981): 546–547.

Summers, Alex. "Angels in Purgatory: Los Angeles Awaits Two Decisions on Mandatory Busing for Desegregation," *Phi Delta Kappan* (June 1979): 718–723.

United States Statutes at Large. Vol. 86 (1972). Washington, D.C.: U.S. Government Printing Office, 1973.

Valverde, Leonard A., ed. *Bilingual Education for Latinos.* Washington, D.C.: Association for Supervision and Curriculum Development, 1978.

Yaffe, Elaine. "Public Education: Society's Band Aid," *Phi Delta Kappan* (March 1980): 452–454.

4

Selected Innovations

"I think I've lost the will to innovate!"

Objectives

This chapter provides information to help the reader to

1. Note the relationship between the American cultural milieu and the receptivity of educators to innovations.
2. Identify several innovations associated with teaching, program organization, and time management.
3. Point out "advantages" of selected innovations as those advantages are seen by supporters of these innovations.
4. Suggest some pitfalls associated with implementation of selected innovations.

Pretest

Directions: Using your own paper, answer each of the following true/false questions. For each correct statement, write the word "true." For each incorrect statement, write the word "false."

_____ 1. School leaders have been pleased to find that, when year-round school plans have been implemented, youngsters have been very eager to attend school during the summer months.

_____ 2. In this country, innovations are tested thoroughly before they are tried in schools.

_____ 3. There is almost universal agreement that innovation is "good for education."

_____ 4. Computer-assisted instruction can be installed in the school program without requiring teachers to change their traditional roles.

_____ 5. Time for team planning is a characteristic of successful team-teaching schemes.

_____ 6. At present, minicourses seem to be increasing in popularity in an overwhelming majority of secondary school programs.

_____ 7. In continuous progress programs, grade-level designations are removed and students progress through the curriculum at their own individual rates.

_____ 8. Modular scheduling can provide for great flexibility in planning schedules for individual students.

_____ 9. Revolving schedules allow more courses to be offered without requiring additional physical space.

_____ 10. The most popular plan for extending the length of the traditional nine-month school year is the mandatory four-quarter plan.

INTRODUCTION

Americans are receptive to change. As a people, we are fascinated by innovations of all kinds. We are quick to adapt whatever is new and make it a part of our daily lives. The impact of innovation on our lives over the past several decades reflects some astonishing changes. Who, for example, when he or she was slogging away in school trying to learn how to calculate square roots would have imagined the development of small inexpensive devices that would blink out a correct answer at the press of a button? Who, too, would have imagined the possibility of live televised coverage of events anywhere in the world via instantaneous transmissions from orbiting earth satellites? Certainly many other examples might be cited.

Those of us who live in a culture that is receptive to change sometimes think little about what existence in such a social climate means. A willingness to accept new things and, indeed, to look forward to what might come along next is a feature of life in America. It is not so everywhere. For example, Milton Friedman (1979) points out that in parts of India the local culture has been so resistant to change that weaving continues to be done using long-outdated hand methods. While this has assured a continuity of tradition, it has come at a great social cost. Productivity of the community has been kept low, and poverty has been perpetuated. In this country, on the other hand, the willingness of people to embrace change has produced great prosperity. Some argue that this may come at a great cost to tradition. (And the issue *is* debated. For example, consider the fights between developers and environmental groups.) But, in general, our society continues to look on change as a positive thing.

This perspective affects education. Few meetings of educators go by without some proposals to modify present practices to improve education. Indeed, some critics of education suggest that educators have not moved fast enough to install needed changes. Some claim that technological advances of recent years have not been adapted to school use as quickly as they might have been. For example, the school calendar, teaching methods, and administrative organization have not changed drastically since the beginning of the twentieth century—or, at least, so allege the critics.

On the other hand, some believe that change and innovation in the schools have progressed at too rapid a rate. They note that some teachers and administrators have developed an allegiance to change for the sake of change. These critics point to dust-catching teaching machines from the early 1960s sitting on schools' supply-room shelves as evidence that schools are too willing to jump on a bandwagon when innovations become available. They charge that school people have been too eager to embrace untested innovations. As a consequence, some critics allege, we now are faced with a population of youngsters who do not do as well on standardized tests of learning as did their counterparts of some years ago who studied in schools "unencumbered" by many of today's "educational novelties" (see Figure 4-1, for example).

In summary, the issue of innovation and the schools has generated a good deal of debate. And we expect this debate to continue into the future. In the sections that follow, we will describe a number of innovative practices that have been installed in some secondary schools in recent years. Comments related to some advantages and disadvantages of each will be provided. Specifically, we will be examining innovations related to (1) teaching, (2) program organization, (3) the school day, and (4) the school year.

Figure 4-1

___

ARE INNOVATIONS HARMFUL?

Picked up the paper last night. Had an article there about SAT scores. Noticed they are down again. They had scores for last year and for a bunch of previous years. I saw that last year's scores were down 20 points from what they were when I was in high school. This got me to thinking.

Now my kid's a junior in high school. In his history class, he's in one of these team-teaching set-ups. You know, they put about 150 kids in a big lecture hall a time or two a week. Then one of the teachers holds forth and the kids take notes. Then, the other days, they work in smaller groups with their individual teachers.

Well, when I was in school, we had one teacher. We had a fairly small group. Maybe 25 to 30. We met that teacher every day. We got to know the teacher, and the teacher got to know us. And I think we learned more. I think if we'd get rid of some of these so-called ''wonder'' methods like team teaching our kids would learn a lot more. The old way certainly didn't hurt me or any of my friends when we were in school.

Statement by a parent calling a radio talk show

YOUR OPINION, PLEASE

Read the paragraphs above. Then, respond to these questions.

1. What is your general reaction to this parent's comments? Why do you react in this way?
2. Suppose that all teaching methods in use in the schools today were abandoned excepting those that were also in use 30 years ago. What would be the likely result in terms of student scores on standardized tests of learning? Why do you think so?
3. Do you think that there might be other reasons for the differences in the SAT scores of this parent's class and those of today than simply the differences in teaching methods? If so, what?
4. Were any innovative teaching methods used when you were in school? What made them innovative? Were they successful or unsuccessful? On what do you base your judgment?

___

INNOVATIONS RELATED TO TEACHING

The traditional system of delivering content to youngsters in American schools has included two components: teacher and textbook. In this system, the teacher has played a dominant role. Ordinarily the teacher has planned the lessons, acted as an authority figure as lessons have unfolded, controlled interactions between teacher and student (and among students), and disseminated and collected materials. Some critics of this pattern have spoken out against this time-honored arrangement.

There has been a concern that the system presumes that all teachers are competent individuals. While undergraduate preparation programs have made respectable enough intellectual demands on individuals headed for a career in teaching, the breadth of the content teachers have to teach often has stretched severely the limits of their subject matter competence. This has been especially true in cases when teachers, out of administrative necessity, have had to be assigned to teach courses well out of their areas of undergraduate preparation. Consider, for example, the social studies teacher asked to deal with a senior-level course in economics. Many social studies teachers have sufficient experience in history, political science, and geography. But it is the rare social studies teacher who, as an undergraduate, will have completed more than a course or two in economics (and many will have had no work at all in this area).

Even assuming that teachers have had adequate undergraduate training, the demands of teaching tend to make it very difficult for them to keep current in their major subject areas. Although many try to read widely and take occasional courses, they simply do not have time for concentrated study while they are teaching.

Problems associated with teacher subject matter competence have been recognized for years. Traditionally, the feeling was that any gaps in the teacher's understanding could be compensated for by providing students with textbooks. Whatever the teacher did not know, so the logic went, the textbook could fill in. Critics have pointed out a number of flaws in this argument. A frequent one these days is that many youngsters do not have reading skills sufficient to deal with the textbooks provided to them in their classes. (Publishers are making valiant attempts to deal with this problem, but many youngsters continue to experience difficulties with texts.)

Beyond the readability issue, textbooks cannot deliver current content. This is so because it takes several years for a book to go through the cycle of writing, responding to critiques of the manuscript, rewriting, and publication. For example, a book published in 1983 likely existed as a completed manuscript no later than 1981. Consequently, a textbook cannot be regarded as a completely up-to-date source of information.

A second criticism in this area is that schools do not purchase textbooks every year. Because of budget limitations, a textbook must last several years. Even in the best of economic times, textbooks rarely are purchased more frequently than once every five years. Clearly, then, a teacher may be using a book with information that is very much out of date. Given problems inherent with school textbooks, it seems clear to many who have studied the matter that educators cannot rely on the textbook to supplement any content deficiencies a teacher might have.

Aside from textbooks and their own difficulties in keeping current, other factors in the teaching situation create problems for teachers as they seek to work effectively with youngsters. For example, large classes make it difficult for teachers to diagnose problems of individual students and to arrange for specially designed programs of instruction to meet the needs of each youngster. These conditions, too, make it difficult for teachers to manage the needed paperwork and, at the same time, provide adequate attention to the need to provide youngsters with direct instruction.

A number of proposals have been made with a view to helping teachers to overcome their problems of keeping current in their subject areas and in delivering content to youngsters expeditiously. In the sections that follow, we will take a look at some of these innovations.

Computer-Assisted Instruction

Computer-assisted instruction, often referred to by educators as CAI, enjoys a large number of advocates within the community of professional educators. Proponents of CAI point out that many traditional problems of teachers can be overcome through judicious use of computer-based instructional procedures. For example, computers have tremendous capacities for information storage and information can be retrieved quickly. New information can be placed into the system much more quickly and efficiently than teachers and textbooks can be updated. Further, it is argued, computers can be programmed to diagnose students' entry-level abilities with a view to making recommendations about where a given youngster should start and what kind of learning experiences should be provided to him or her. The computer can store this, as well as learner progress, information with no strain whatever and can retrieve it upon request of the teacher or the student.

Early attempts to apply computer technology to education of 20 or so years ago were not notably successful. For one thing, costs were prohibitive. Few schools could afford to install the necessary equipment, pay for programmers, and purchase the necessary software. Further, computer programs that were available in those early days often were not instructionally sound. Few teachers who were familiar with the content that needed to be taught were well versed in computer technology. Consequently, many early computer programs included content developed by noneducators. A good deal of this material was of an inferior quality.

Another problem that contributed to a lack of acceptance of the early computer-assisted instructional programs had to do with resistance from many teachers. This came about because some overzealous promoters of computers in the classroom went so far as to suggest that computers could replace teachers. Naturally, teachers who wondered how they would make a living when this "happy day" arrived felt threatened by such talk.

Today, the conditions associated with computer-assisted instruction are much different from those in the early days. No one (or at least no one who is a serious student of the matter) suggests that computers can or should replace teachers. There is an almost universal agreement that computers, when they are used in the schools, will supplement and complement the work of teachers, not eliminate a need for teacher services. Further, many more of today's teachers have developed some familiarity with computer use and computer programming than was formerly the case. Given this kind of understanding, today's teachers see computers as far less intimidating than did their predecessors. Given these changes, perhaps it is not surprising that nearly 2 million students today are involved in some kind of computer-assisted instruction.

It is clear that we are far short of tapping the potential use of computers in the classroom. Prices of computer technology are coming down. More teachers than ever before are familiar with computers. Yet massive applications of computers to public education would require teachers to reconceptualize their roles. Teachers making heavy use of computers tend to function as instructional managers. They need to be skilled in such areas as preparing computer-based diagnostic programs, organizing programs for computer instruction consistent with their readings of resultant diagnostic information, and to be capable of determining when specialists need to be called in to change computer programs. Although sizable numbers of teachers are doing these things today, given the total population of secondary schools they remain a distinct minority.

A shift to massive use of computer-assisted instruction would also entail changes in attitudes of students. Relatively few students today are used to working with computers. They are much more familiar with learning in a classroom setting where other youngsters are present and where a teacher oversees activities that, in large measure, tend to be common to the whole group. A curriculum oriented heavily toward computer-based instruction requires youngsters in schools to develop a different conception of what a student is and does.

Additionally, a move to wide use of computers would have implications for scheduling of students' time. The usual practice of assigning a given number of students to a teacher for a specific increment of time (perhaps for 50 or 55 minutes) and dividing the day into numbered periods would not be needed. New patterns of scheduling would be devised to assign students to computer terminals according to their own instructional needs and the availability of equipment and teachers.

Tradition remains a potent force in American education. (Consider these points as you respond to questions raised in Figure 4-2.) Because a massive shift to computer-based instruction would require so many changes, it is unlikely that such a shift is imminent. It does seem likely, however, that there will be a gradual expansion of the use of computers in secondary schools as equipment is improved and as more educators and students become familiar with its use. Evidence suggests that these developments

Figure 4-2

SHOULD STUDENTS BE TAUGHT BY COMPUTERS?

Now look. The *only* purpose of the school is to teach some*thing* to some*body*. Right? Of course, it's right! And are the schools charging ahead to do this as efficiently as possible? I'll tell you *they are not.*

We're teaching these kids just like they were taught in 1900. A teacher lays on a lecture. An assignment is made in a textbook. And after some discussion over the material, a test is given. Education is barely into the twentieth century!

As I see it, we need to get on the ball and install banks of computers with individual terminals for student use in the schools. We can fire about half of the teachers, keep the good ones, and use up-to-the-minute computer technology to get the job done. I mean if computer-based instruction is good enough for the airlines to use in training pilots, it is *more* than good enough to teach the more modest kinds of learning we provide public school kids.

I know the teachers will howl and scream and talk about "dehumanization of education." But we know that's just a cheap shot to save their own hides. Most of those who scream the loudest are going to be much more interested in saving their jobs than in "quality education," despite what they may say. For myself, I believe we have to put the kids first. Let's get some computers in the schools. Let's take advantage of what we know how to do today. Let's make education join the twentieth century!

Statement by a parent at a school board meeting

YOUR OPINION, PLEASE

Read the comments above. Then, respond to these questions.

1. Are schools still operating with nineteenth-century or early-twentieth-century technology? Why do you think so?
2. Is there a conspiracy to keep modern technology out of the schools? On what do you base your opinion?
3. Is the "only purpose of the school to teach some*thing* to some*body*"? Why do you think so?
4. The speaker suggests that teachers are being less than honest when they suggest that heavy use of computers might be "dehumanizing." How do you react to this charge? What is the basis for your reaction?
5. Twenty or 25 years from now, would you expect to find use of computers in school to be dramatically greater than the level of computer use today? Why, or why not?

will not diminish the need for classroom teachers. But teachers who work with computers may well find themselves doing different kinds of things as they work with their students.

Team Teaching

Team teaching is an innovation that has been around since the late 1950s. The approach, in part, was developed as a means of redressing some areas of alleged teacher weakness. According to one argument of early proponents of team teaching, teachers in the classroom must deal with more content than they, individually, know well. Therefore, it would make sense to organize groups of teachers into teams in such a fashion that some teachers in each team would have some real depth in each major topic treated in a course. In this way, individuals in a team would be free to teach those things they really knew well. Conversely, they would be released from instructional responsibilities when topics being treated ranged beyond the limits of their expertise. As early-day proponents of team teaching saw it, this approach would provide students with better instruction while, at the same time, it would make life easier for individual teachers.

Another early argument supporting team teaching was that the innovation would increase teachers' professionalism because each team member would have an opportunity to profit from insights of individuals expert in different areas of academic strength. Further, given the likelihood that other team members as well as students would be in the class when presentations were made, proponents of team teaching suggested that teachers would spend more time preparing to ensure that they did a credible job in front of their professional colleagues.

Although team teaching continues to be extremely popular in many schools, it has not been the panacea that some of the more ardent proponents of the approach have suggested. For example, some teachers have been forced to join teams against their will. When this has happened, a great deal of dissatisfaction has developed. Teachers' personalities vary tremendously. Some simply prefer to work in their own classroom with a group of students for which they alone are responsible. When such individuals have been pushed to join teams, a good deal of personal frustration has resulted.

Another difficulty that has faced team teaching concerns the issue of scheduling. When several teachers work together, they must coordinate their respective schedules and activities carefully. For example, if three teachers working with a large group agree to work with one third of the students in a class for 15 minutes and then rotate them to another teacher, each teacher must be sure that he or she starts and stops at the same time. Failure to do so can result in chaos. Some teachers who have worked in teaming situations for a time have left because they were unable to adjust the instructional time to take advantage of unanticipated events or to respond to numerous student questions. Critics of team teaching have complained that the approach can lead to the schedule's controlling the teacher's behavior in an irresponsible manner. Some have suggested that they enjoy much more flexibility in working with students in single-teacher classrooms.

Critics of team teaching claim that the approach has the potential to degenerate into "turn teaching," with one teacher taking a group of 60 students on one day while the other teacher sits in the faculty lounge and does nothing and then switching roles on the next day. When this happens, youngsters enjoy much less teacher-student contact than is the case in single-teacher classrooms. In effect, a teacher-student ratio of 1 to 30 in a self-contained classroom can be turned into a teacher-student ratio of 1 to 60 in a team teaching situation with two teachers (that has turned into an irresponsible "turn teaching" program).

Space has been a problem in some schools that have attempted to utilize team-teaching approaches. Older high school buildings in particular generally have classrooms of a fairly uniform size. These classrooms were constructed under the assumption that one teacher would be working with, on average, about 30 students. Teaming arrangements ordinarily require much larger groups of students to come together at least some of the time. Some older schools have tried to use cafeterias, gymnasiums, and other spaces for such purposes. Frequently acoustical problems, classroom equipment problems, and other difficulties have restricted the capability of teams to function effectively in such environments. Many newer buildings have been designed to include some classrooms capable of accommodating large groups of youngsters. In general, it has been an easier task to manage team teaching in these buildings than in older secondary school buildings.

In summary, team teaching is an innovation of some years' standing. The approach, in terms of its impacts on students, can best be judged as neutral (Armstrong 1977). Certainly there are important implementation problems. But there is evidence that some teachers enjoy working jointly with other professionals.

In some districts, team teaching has been in use for years. In other districts, the approach has been used sparingly, if at all. Some districts that have not had team teaching doubtless will try it. Others that have may use the approach less extensively. Although practices may vary from place to place, the innovation seems destined to be used in many school districts in the years ahead (refer to Figure 4-3).

INNOVATIONS RELATED TO PROGRAM ORGANIZATION

Throughout history, curricula in secondary schools have undergone changes. Frequently, changes in emphases have been associated with changes in society's view

---

Figure 4-3

BY WHAT CRITERIA SHOULD WE JUDGE INNOVATIONS?

TEACHER A: I just *love* working on a teaching team. There are three of us, and we get along fabulously. I go home every night pumped up about what has gone on at school that day. When I'm responsible for the instruction, I give it my best. I want to do well for my colleagues as well as for the students. I just *know* I'm doing a better job than I would if I worked alone. I can see it on the faces of the kids too. We really turn them on! That's all the evidence I need. Team teaching works!

TEACHER B: The only *real* test of team teaching is student learning. If the youngsters who are team taught learn more, then the innovation is a good one. If they don't, then there is nothing special to commend it. There is nothing that *I* have seen that convinces me that team teaching results in superior learning for youngsters. I know there is a lot of "creepy-feely" stuff about how teachers and youngsters feel good about team teaching. But I haven't seen the hard evidence about learning that I'm looking for. As far as I'm concerned, team teaching hasn't made its case.

YOUR OPINION, PLEASE

Read the comments above. Then, respond to these questions.

1. Should Teacher A be satisfied with team teaching based on the evidence noted in the comments above? Why, or why not?
2. Should Teacher B be dissatisfied with team teaching because of the evidence or lack of evidence cited in the comments above? Why, or why not?
3. Do *you* think that a teacher's feeling good about an innovation is sufficient cause for the teacher to support its continued use? Why, or why not?
4. How do *you* feel about judging the adequacy of an innovation only on the basis of how the innovation affects students' learning? Why do you feel this way?
5. How do you think that Teacher A and Teacher B would get along if a decision were made requiring them to work on the same teaching team?

---

regarding what the schools should do. For example, in the early years of the American nation, secondary schools were regarded largely as institutions designed to serve the learning needs of children of the upper classes. Study of Latin, Greek, and other classical subjects that were thought to be essential learnings for an educated member of the upper class was emphasized. In time, a broader cross section of the population began to see a need for making secondary education available to a larger percentage of the nation's children. With this concern came pressure to shape the secondary curriculum to provide more practical and more career-oriented subjects.

Throughout the latter half of the nineteenth century, pressures exerted resulted in a dramatic expansion in the number of publicly supported high schools. Because of concerns of colleges and universities that high school graduates begin study in institutions of higher learning with some common knowledge base, efforts were undertaken to establish common curricular patterns in high schools. This effort was supported as well by secondary school administrators' need for a convenient means of fitting transfer students into their school programs. Clearly, this process was much easier when school programs from school to school tended to have a good number of common elements. A consequence of these efforts was the development of a rather stable secondary school curriculum by the second decade of the twentieth century. (For a fuller treatment of these developments see Chapter 1, "The Senior High School.")

This stability of content came under great pressure as the percentage of youngsters of secondary school age in the total population who actually attended secondary schools increased. By the late 1920s and early 1930s it was evident that large numbers of high school graduates were not headed for colleges and universities. From this period forward, high school curricula, in particular, tended to expand to include many noncollege preparatory courses. For many years, the need to expand the services provided by high schools was accommodated by simply increasing the number of electives.

By the late 1960s and early 1970s, this response to pressures for change began to come under severe strains. For one thing, many saw knowledge expanding faster than the schools' abilities to introduce and staff new courses. For example, areas such as the behavioral sciences were expanding rapidly during this period. Specialists in these areas were demanding inclusion of such subjects as anthropology, psychology, and sociology (and many others) in secondary school curricula. Given school curricula that were already choked with courses, such pressures caused severe problems for school administrators.

These problems surfaced at a time in our national history when young people (and a good many adults, too) were questioning traditional American institutions. It was a time when many practices of long standing were subjected to a not always friendly public scrutiny. In short, it was an era when proposals for change were likely to receive a friendly hearing from a good many people. Not surprisingly, school administrators found this to be a time when some innovative responses to the difficulties associated with delivering content to students could be installed without too much political risk.

Several responses to the need to do something about the need to reorganize the means of organizing and disseminating content were introduced. Some of these innovations were tried in only a few places. Others, at least for a time, enjoyed fairly wide popularity. In the sections that follow, we will look at two of these innovative approaches.

Minicourses

Minicourses were developed to introduce a wider variety of content into the secondary school program. A minicourse is a course of relatively short duration, perhaps three to six weeks in length. This length contrasts sharply with the more traditional semester-long or year-long courses generally offered by secondary schools. The idea of the minicourse is to enable students to take a much broader array of courses than he or she could have taken under the traditional semester-long and year-long course arrangement. For example, rather than taking a one-semester course in geography, a student in a minicourse program might take three minicourses in (1) "The History of Revolutions," (2) "Alternative Life-styles," and (3) "Women in American History," respectively.

Although specific patterns vary from program to program, most provide students with a great many options. While they may be required to take certain minicourses, they also have opportunities to choose freely from among an array of alternatives (see Figure 4-4). The breadth of choice is thought to allow youngsters to enroll in courses that they will enjoy taking. Under these conditions, allege supporters of minicourses, students are likely to do well because they will be motivated to learn.

Minicourse programs have presented administrators with some thorny problems. One difficulty has to do with scheduling. It requires much more planning to arrange schedules in a minicourse program where youngsters may be changing their schedules every three or five weeks rather than once a semester. A second difficulty relates to budgets for student learning materials. Clearly budgets will not support separate texts for dozens of separate minicourses. Often this situation has required teachers to produce themselves or buy out of their own pockets materials for their courses. Administrators have had to face numerous teacher complaints arising from this situation.

Some critics of minicourse programs point out that they permit students to escape much basic and essential content by providing them with too many free options. These critics suggest that content of many minicourses is frivolous and reflects an attempt to please and entertain students rather than to educate them. This, so say the critics, leads to circumstances in which high school graduates cannot be counted on to have had certain kinds of basic learning experiences acquired during their school years. Because minicourses allow students to take so many different kinds of courses, students cannot

Figure 4-4

SHOULD STUDENTS TAKE ONLY WHAT THEY WANT TO TAKE?

I resent all of these high school graduation requirements. Take U.S. history, for example. Who needs it? Yuck! Just a bunch of garbage about dead guys and happenings nobody cares about. I'll tell you this, my dad could buy or sell my history teacher ten times over. And he doesn't know a thing about history, not a *thing!*

Seems to me we ought to be able to take what we want. I mean it's my life isn't it? If I want to take it, I should take it. If I don't, well then I shouldn't. I tell you if they only taught courses we wanted, we'd run off some of these jerk teachers in a hurry. They wouldn't last a minute if there weren't some law saying we had to take their worthless courses.

Statement of a high school junior

YOUR OPINION, PLEASE

Read the comments above. Then, respond to these questions.

1. Are certain high school requirements needed? If so, which ones? Why are they needed?
2. Suppose that schools agreed that students could take any courses they wanted to take. Nothing would be required. Would this be a good thing or a bad thing? Why?
3. This student implies that state requirements prescribing that all students take certain courses are there just to provide certain teachers with job security. Do you agree or disagree? Why?
4. How did students feel about required courses when you were in school? Do you think today's students feel the same way?
5. If you were to predict how things would be 30 years from now, would you expect students would have fewer choices or more choices of courses during their secondary school years? On what evidence do you base your prediction?

be held accountable for a specific body of learning. According to some critics, this creates an intolerable situation whereby schools and school programs cannot be called to account when graduates lack certain basic skills.

It is difficult to generalize about the popularity of minicourses today. In some districts, critics of declining standardized test scores have attacked minicourses as mechanisms that fragment the school programs and, hence, result in poorer test performance on the part of students. In other districts, minicourses have been hailed as a mechanism for assuring that specialized needs of individual youngsters are being met. In some districts, then, we are likely to see more minicourses; and in others, fewer.

Continuous Progress Programs

Some critics of organizing secondary school programs into courses that are offered for a given number of hours per week for a given period of calendar time have argued that such arrangements ignore individual student differences. Youngsters, they argue, do not learn at similar rates. For some students, a 16-week semester may be too short a time for them to master content in a course such as introductory economics. For others, the content could be mastered in a much shorter period of time.

Present arrangements, some feel, place especially heavy burdens on students who do not learn rapidly. Suppose, for example, that a given student could master introductory economics if he or she had 20 weeks to spend on the course. In an arrangement where only 16 weeks were provided, the student likely would be rewarded with a very low grade. This grade, it is argued, may be a poor measure of the student's real ability in economics. It may show only that economics is not a subject the individual can learn as rapidly as some other students. In response to situations of this kind, some secondary schools have developed continuous progress programs.

As the name implies, students in a continuous progress program work through the school program at their own individual rates. There are no grade-level or course time limits that establish an end point for study of any subject. To gain an appreciation for how this system might work, let us consider a hypothetical mathematics program. In a traditional arrangement, a student would take a series of mathematics courses. Each would be offered for a definite period of calendar time, typically for a single school semester or for one school year. In a continuous progress mathematics program, curriculum professionals would identify learning objectives for the entire secondary mathematics program. These would be organized in a sequence from most simple through most complex. Instructional experiences would be designed for each objective. Students, then, would begin with the simplest objectives and, working at their own individual rates, progress through increasingly complex objectives. For example, in a given period of time, some students might complete work associated with 10 such objectives whereas others may have completed as few as 2 or 3 or as many as 15 or 16.

Continuous progress programs place significant demands on teachers. Because youngsters are not all at the same place, examinations are rarely given to an entire class at the same time. Teachers must be prepared to test an individual student whenever he or she has completed work associated with a given learning objective. This requirement necessitates very careful record keeping. It is essential that the teacher know exactly what objective is being pursued by each youngster.

Because of these very considerable management difficulties, relatively few continuous progress programs have been implemented in secondary schools. Some authorities, however, suggest that with the spread of computer technology some of these management difficulties can be overcome. If this is so, there may well be an expansion of interest in continuous progress programs. Further, some pressures are being placed on the schools to demonstrate that real efforts are being made to meet individual learner needs. (See, for example, the discussion in Chapter 15, "Teaching Handicapped Students," regarding the impact of Public Law 94-142.) These pressures, too, may bring renewed attention to continuous progress programs.

INNOVATIONS RELATED TO ORGANIZATION OF THE SCHOOL DAY

A number of efforts have been made to make school programs more responsive to students' needs by changing methods of allocating students' time during the school day. Changes in time arrangements have been relatively common in secondary schools. However, large numbers of such schools continue to organize time by cutting it into traditional "periods" of fixed lengths of time that occur in a fixed sequence every day. In the sections that follow, we will examine a number of approaches that have been taken to modify this traditional practice.

Modular Schedules

Modular schedules have been developed to deal with the traditional common length of the school period. Traditionally, periods in schools have each been alloted a fixed amount of time. Ordinarily time periods of between 40 and 55 minutes in length have been selected. For example, in a senior high school, each period might run 55 minutes, with 5-minute time schedules for passing from one class to the next. Modular schedules provide much more flexibility in planning students' time than do these more traditional period schedules.

In preparing a modular scheduling plan, the entire school day is thought of as being divided into a number of small units of time called "modules." For example, there might be 22 modules of time, each 20 minutes in length, from 8:00 A.M. to 3:20 P.M. Each module is numbered sequentially beginning with the first one in the morning. For example, the module of time from 8:00 to 8:20 would be module 1, the module from 8:20 to 8:40 would be module 2, and so forth until the day would conclude with module 22 running from 3:00 to 3:20 P.M. See Figure 4-5 for an example of a modular schedule.

In scheduling students in schools that use modules, individual students' needs are considered. Further, teachers' preferences for amounts of time necessary to provide instruction over a given topic are considered. When all relevant information is in hand, administrators prepare (utilizing computer programs) schedules for each student. Ordinarily a new schedule is prepared about once a week. Some schools prepare them more frequently; some less frequently. To appreciate how this might work, let us suppose that a teacher wishes to present some basic information related to a new area by giving a series of short lectures. Under a modular schedule, this need could be reflected in schedules of this teacher's students. They might be scheduled with this teacher for two back-to-back modules each day of the week for a total of 40 minutes each day (assuming modules of 20 minutes).

Modular scheduling, then, allows for a good deal of flexibility. When a chemistry teacher needs to provide laboratory experiences for youngsters, he or she can request that students be assigned for four or five continuous modules (80 or 100 minutes). This arrangement allows the teacher to maximize actual hands-on experience in the laboratory. Many science teachers, forced to work within the framework of traditional 45- or 50-minute periods, despair over the time that is lost setting up laboratories at the beginning of the period and putting equipment away and cleaning up at the end of the period. Clearly a modular schedule, with the flexibility to provide students with an opportunity to work longer in laboratory settings, can minimize this time-lost problem.

Modular schedules require teachers and administrators to work closely. Because such schemes depend heavily on computers, teachers must get time requests submitted on time so that data needed to produce new student schedules can be fed into the computers along with requests of all other teachers. To implement modular schedules, school districts must invest heavily in computer technology. It is not possible to operate a large-scale modular scheduling program without computers. While the dependency on computers provides a capability to generate new student schedules at frequent intervals, it can also create problems. Teachers who work in buildings where modular schedules are used tell horror stories about problems encountered on the day "the com-

Figure 4-5

SAMPLE MODULAR SCHEDULE

NUMBERS AND TIMES OF MODULES

1.	8:00– 8:20	12.	11:40–12:00
2.	8:20– 8:40	13.	12:00–12:20
3.	8:40– 9:00	14.	12:20–12:40
4.	9:00– 9:20	15.	12:40– 1:00
5.	9:20– 9:40	16.	1:00– 1:20
6.	9:40–10:00	17.	1:20– 1:40
7.	10:00–10:20	18.	1:40– 2:00
8.	10:20–10:40	19.	2:00– 2:20
9.	10:40–11:00	20.	2:20– 2:40
10.	11:00–11:20	21.	2:40– 3:00
11.	11:20–11:40	22.	3:00– 3:20

SCHEDULE OF JOHN JONES FOR WEEK OF NOVEMBER 10.

MONDAY
Spanish (1–5) language lab
Break (6)
Algebra (7–8) lecture
Geography (9–11) work session
Lunch (12–14)
English (15–17) class presentation
Chemistry (18–21) lab experiments

TUESDAY
Geography (1–4) film
Algebra (5–6) work session
Break (7)
English (8–11) class presentation
Lunch (12–14)
Chemistry (15–19) class presentation and lab
Spanish (20–22) work with teacher

WEDNESDAY
Spanish (1–3) language lab
Study Hall (4–7)
English (8–10) test
Lunch (11–13)
Geography (14–16) class presentation
Algebra (17–18) review session with teacher
Chemistry (19–21) extra credit lab

THURSDAY
Chemistry (1–9) field trip
Spanish (10–12) class presentation
Lunch (13–15)
Algebra (16–18)
English (19–21) work session

FRIDAY
Study Hall (1–3)
Spanish (4–7) test
Algebra (8–10) class presentation
Geography (11–12) work session
Lunch (13–15)
English (16–20) film

---

puter went on the blink." Despite these potential pitfalls, however, the desire of educators to provide students with greater time flexibility and the increasing sophistication of computer systems suggest that more secondary schools may be adopting modular schedules in the future.

Revolving Schedules

The revolving schedule permits schools to add additional courses to the school program without adding to available space or offering courses before or after normal school hours. This trick is accomplished by setting up a system whereby students do not attend every class every day. For example, a revolving schedule might be set up in such a way that a total of eight courses could be made available even though only six instructional hours would be available each day. To accommodate this situation, only six of the eight courses would meet each day. The revolving schedule establishes a sequence of courses to be taught on a given day and of courses not to be taught on a given day. An example of a revolving schedule is provided in Figure 4-6.

In many traditional high school schedules, teachers are expected to teach classes for five of the six periods in the day. The sixth period is a planning or preparation period. Let us see how a teacher might fare who worked in a building using a rotating schedule where seven instructional periods were fitted into a six-period day. (Refer to Figure 4-6 to see how this can be accomplished.) Ordinarily, in such a setting a teacher would still be expected to teach five classes a day. A schedule for a teacher in this building might look something like this:

Period 1: English I

Period 2: English II

Period 3: preparation period

Period 4: English I

Period 5: preparation period

Period 6: English II

Period 7: Speech I

Figure 4-6

SAMPLE REVOLVING SCHEDULE

CLASS TIMES	MON.	TUES.	WED.	THURS.	FRI.	MON.	TUES.	WED.
8:00– 8:56	1	2	3	4	5	6	7	1
9:00– 9:56	2	3	4	5	6	7	1	2
10:00–10:56	3	4	5	6	7	1	2	3
11:00–11:56	4	5	6	7	1	2	3	4
1:00– 1:56	5	6	7	1	2	3	4	5
2:00– 2:56	6	7	1	2	3	4	5	6

YOUR OPINION, PLEASE
Assume the following schedule of courses for Zelda Zilch.

Period 1: English II
Period 2: Physical Education
Period 3: Study Hall
Period 4: Spanish I
Period 5: Algebra II
Period 6: World History
Period 7: Study Hall

1. How often does Zelda meet each of these courses in one week?
2. What are the advantages? What disadvantages?
3. What problems do you think a teacher might have in working in a rotating schedule plan?

This teacher's schedule for each day of the revolving schedule sequence would look like this:

Monday
8:00–8:56 English I
9:00–9:56 English II
10:00–10:56 preparation
11:00–11:56 English I
1:00–1:56 preparation
2:00–2:56 English II
(no period 7)

Tuesday
8:00–8:56 English II
9:00–9:56 preparation
10:00–10:56 English I
11:00–11:56 preparation
1:00–1:56 English II
2:00–2:56 Speech I
(no period 1)

Wednesday
8:00–8:56 preparation
9:00–9:56 English I
10:00–10:56 preparation
11:00–11:56 English II
1:00–1:56 Speech I
2:00–2:56 English II
(no period 2)

Thursday
8:00–8:56 English I
9:00–9:56 preparation
10:00–10:56 English II
11:00–11:56 Speech I
1:00–1:56 English I
2:00–2:56 English II
(no period 3)

Friday
8:00–8:56 preparation
9:00–9:56 English II
10:00–10:56 Speech I
11:00–11:56 English I
1:00–1:56 English II
2:00–2:56 preparation
(no period 4)

Monday
8:00–8:56 English II
9:00–9:56 Speech I
10:00–10:56 English I
11:00–11:56 English II
1:00–1:56 preparation
2:00–2:56 English I
(no period 5)

Tuesday
8:00–8:56 Speech I
9:00–9:56 English I
10:00–10:56 English II
11:00–11:56 preparation
1:00–1:56 English I
2:00–2:56 preparation
(no period 6)

Note that, in this arrangement, on most days in the cycle the teacher has two preparation periods. In fact, only on two days out of the total of seven required for a complete turnover of the cycle will the teacher have a single preparation period. The capability of revolving schedules to provide teachers with more preparation time makes the system very attractive to those who have experienced this kind of a scheduling system.

In traditional scheduling systems, teachers often complain that they never get to see youngsters in their afternoon classes when they are still "fresh." By late afternoon, some youngsters begin to display evidence of fatigue. It is common for teachers to report difficulties in motivating youngsters as the end of the instructional day approaches. The revolving schedule can help in this regard. Refer again to Figure 4-6. Note that during a given cycle of this revolving schedule the student meets every class once at a different time of the day. For the teacher, this means that each group of students will be met at some time early in the morning when, presumably, their interests and energy levels may be higher than they may be later in the day.

Revolving schedules are not without their problems. Obviously, they require clear communications to both teachers and students regarding the times individual periods are to meet each day. Further, some teachers prefer the security of knowing that a given class will be in session at a specific time each day. Finally, there is some loss of class time by students. In a traditional arrangement, a student over a seven-day time period would meet each class for a total of 392 minutes (56 minutes $\times$ 7 days). In the revolving schedule depicted in Figure 4-6, a student during a seven-day cycle would meet each class for a total of 336 minutes (56 minutes $\times$ 6 days). In essence, this means that in this revolving schedule program a student, on average, would meet his or her classes 48 minutes every day (336 $\div$ 7). Some do not see this 48-minute average a significant reduction from the 56 minutes a day spent in classes under a more conventional schedule. Others would regard this as an important difference in the total amount of student contact. In some places, school laws require a specified amount of student time in each class per week and it is difficult to implement revolving schedules.

INNOVATIONS RELATED TO THE SCHOOL YEAR

In addition to proposals focusing on how time should be allocated during the school day, other innovations adopted in some schools have attempted to modify the traditional nine-month school year. Historically, the pattern of dismissing students during the three summer months stemmed from a need for young people's services at home during the months that crops were sown, cared for, and harvested. Today, given the fact that more than 90 percent of the people are engaged in nonagricultural pursuits, very few families need youngsters' services around the farm during the summer months. This transformation of the United States from an agrarian and rural society to an industrial and urban society has undercut the logic that resulted in the practice of holding school for nine months from fall to spring and dismissing students for the summer months. Because of these altered societal conditions, a number of proposals have come forward to modify the nature of the school calendar. In the sections that follow, we will take a look at some of these proposals.

Mandatory Four-Quarter Plan

The mandatory four-quarter plan proposes that the 12-month year be divided into four parts of 3 months each. School buildings are used the entire year. But each student attends only three of the four quarters. To see how such a plan might operate, let us consider a school district with 4,800 students. The school year could be divided into four parts and students assigned to attend as follows:

Quarter	Months	No. of Students in School
1	September October November	1,200
2	December January February	1,200
3	March April May	1,200
4	June July August	1,200

The word "mandatory" in the mandatory four-quarter plan refers to a policy of requiring or mandating that students attend school during the three quarters of the year to which they are assigned by school authorities. For example, if a student were assigned to attend during quarters 2, 3, and 4, he or she would be obligated to attend during the months from December through August. The vacation period in such a case would run from September through November.

Claimed advantages of the mandatory four-quarter plan are mostly administrative. Suppose, for example, that the district described had physical facilities that, during a traditional nine-month year, could accommodate only 3,600 students. By adopting the mandatory four-quarter plan, the same physical facilities can accommodate 4,800 students.

Where this plan has been proposed, strenuous objections have emanated from parents. At one level, these objections have resulted because of a break with tradition. Parents had summers off when they were in school. They are familiar and comfortable with that practice. The very break with this tradition, in itself, often prompts resistance.

Perhaps more important than the issue of tradition is the havoc that the four-quarter plan can wreak on family vacation plans. For example, a family with large numbers of youngsters in the schools might well have some children on vacation from school at times different from the others. Even when arrangements can be made for all youngsters in a family to be on the same attendance sequence, families whose children might be required to go to school during the summer quarter have expressed opposition. In many parts of the country, parents' vacations are planned for the summer months. Obviously, parents do not want to be on vacation themselves when their youngsters are in school.

Other critics of the mandatory four-quarter plan point out that school maintenance has a potential to suffer under this scheme. Typically, interiors of schools get a thorough going-over during the months when students are not in school. This kind of maintenance would be difficult under conditions when buildings were not vacated for long enough periods to permit time for maintenance and upgrading. In general, given all the objections to the proposal, the mandatory four-quarter plan has not received a favorable hearing in communities where it has been proposed.

Optional Four-Quarter Plan

As the name suggests, the optional four-quarter plan provides students and their parents with some choices or options. As in the mandatory four-quarter arrangement, the school year is divided into four parts or quarters. Similarly, students are expected to be in school during three of the four school quarters. But, unlike under the mandatory four-quarter plan, students are not assigned arbitrarily by school authorities to attend school at certain times of the year. Rather, they and their families can decide which of the three school quarters the students will attend school.

Originators of the optional four-quarter plan hoped that sufficient numbers of students would elect to attend school during the summer term to achieve enrollment totals during this quarter close to those during the other three quarters of the school year. In practice, this has not happened. The tradition of summer being vacation time is so strongly entrenched that attempts to build enrollments on a voluntary basis during this period of the year have not been notably successful.

Another feature of the optional four-quarter plan is that it enables students who wish to do so to remain in school for all four quarters of the year. Youngsters choosing this option can either accelerate their progress through school or take elective courses that, otherwise, they may not be able to fit in their programs. In practice, the number of youngsters who have chosen to attend school all four quarters has remained small. The long-standing practice of students attending school for nine months and then having about three months off has been a difficult pattern to modify. In general, because of difficulties associated with securing large summer quarter enrollments and in encouraging significant numbers of youngsters to stay in school all four quarters, the optional four-quarter plan has not enjoyed a high degree of popularity.

Concept Six

Concept Six is an approach that seeks to provide for more learning flexibility for youngsters in the school and to use available school facilities during a greater proportion of the year. In Concept Six districts, the school year is divided into six equal parts. Students elect to attend any four of the six sessions. An example of a Concept Six schedule is provided in Figure 4-7.

Figure 4-7

SAMPLE CONCEPT SIX SCHEDULE

Schedule for hypothetical student, Gabby Goforth.

SESSION	GABBY GOFORTH
Jan.–Feb.	In school
Mar.–Apr.	Vacation
May–June	In school
July–Aug.	Vacation
Sept.–Oct.	In school
Nov.–Dec.	In school

Note that, because of differing lengths of months, numbers of weekends, and distribution of holidays, beginning and ending dates do not fall on the first and the end of months as indicated here. This schedule has been provided to illustrate the general impact of such a plan on an individual student and the options it provides.

In Concept Six programs, every course offered is six weeks in length. That is, it begins and ends within one of the six parts into which the school year is divided. This has important advantages for youngsters who fail a course as compared with the situation in a traditional nine-month school year where courses are either one or two semesters long. For example, suppose that a student failed a one-semester course in mathematics under this system. He or she would have failed half of the school year in this course. But, under a Concept Six program, a failure in a given course would constitute only failure of one sixth of the total year's program in a subject. (Remember that each course begins and ends within a period equaling one sixth of the school year.) Students finding themselves in this kind of a situation could retake the course and, possibly, achieve a passing grade in a much shorter period of time in a Concept Six system.

Supporters of Concept Six point out that the system enables more courses to be offered during the school year than can be offered under conventional nine-month-long two-semester programs. This feature allows students the possibility to sample a much broader variety of content than is the case under more traditional organizational schemes.

Concept Six shares certain problems with other schemes for transforming the traditional school year. There are difficulties associated with scheduling youngsters in the same family so that each will be in school and out of school at the same times during the year. Further, the general resistance parents and students have displayed toward attendance during the summer months suggests difficulties in building enrollments during summer month sessions. Finally, most existing instructional materials, including texts, have been developed under the assumptions that courses last either one semester or two semesters. Certain modifications to these materials are necessary to make them "fit" a situation where courses last only one sixth of the year.

Quinmester Plan

The quinmester plan is somewhat similar in orientation to Concept Six. But, under this scheme, the year is divided into five nine-week sessions. Students may choose to attend any four of these sessions. Or they may attend all five sessions if they wish to accelerate their progress through school. An example of a quinmester schedule is provided in Figure 4-8.

One advantage of the quinmester plan is that a limited summer vacation is provided even for students who choose to attend the summer quinmester. Promoters of the plan have hoped that this feature would entice more students to elect the summer quinmester as one of the four periods of the year they would be in school. In practice, however, significantly smaller numbers of youngsters have chosen to attend during this

Figure 4-8

SAMPLE QUINMESTER PLAN

Quinmester 1:	September 5 through November 6 (45 school days)
Quinmester 2:	November 7 through January 19 (45 school days)
Quinmester 3:	January 22 through March 26 (45 school days)
Quinmester 4:	March 27 through June 4 (45 school days)
Quinmester 5:	June 5 through August 7 (45 school days)

Note that a student can complete the typical 180-day attendance requirement by attending classes during any four quinmesters. Some students who wish to accelerate their progress or take enrichment courses may elect to attend all five quinmesters.

Figure 4-9

SHOULD YEAR-ROUND SCHOOLING BE REQUIRED?

It just bugs me. I see these school buildings standing empty from June until August. I mean there they are . . . these big empty vessels sucking up our tax dollars and providing no services for three months of the year. Then, I look at these kids hanging around on corners doing nothing. I mean, from the 4th of July on most of them are just bored silly. The younger ones can't get jobs. I tell you it's a situation tailor made to encourage kids to get in trouble. We need to get these kids off the street and back in school. The kids would learn more, we'd get a better return on our tax dollars, and everybody would be better off. Why don't they do it?

Comments made by a caller to a call-in radio show

YOUR OPINION, PLEASE

Read the comments above. Then, respond to these questions.

1. Do you agree or disagree with the caller's position? Why, or why not?
2. Suppose that a decision were made to implement a year-round schooling plan in your district. What special problems might you, as a teacher, face? How would you respond to these problems?
3. If you wished to suggest to this caller some problems that have been encountered when attempts have been made to change the traditional school calendar, what would you say?
4. Suppose that you were told to devise a plan that would result in schools being used 12 months of the year. What would your plan be? How would you "sell" it to the public (especially to students and parents)?
5. If you had a crystal ball and could look 40 years into the future, would you expect to find more or fewer schools with extended school year plans than we have today? Why would you make this prediction?

---

quinmester than during the other four. Too many students continue to want their entire summers free from school responsibilities. And many of their parents support this point of view as well.

Attempts to Lengthen the School Year—Summary

In general, plans devised to extend the use of school facilities by changing the school calendar have not proved to be popular. Administrators have faced great difficulty in arranging schedules for youngsters from the same family that allow all to be in school and out of school at the same time. Requirements for some students to be in school during the traditional summer months have led to great resistance both from students and from parents who want their youngsters to be out of school during traditional family vacation times. Finally, curricula for years have been built around the assumption that school courses last either a semester or two semesters. Often, new school calendars have been tried without a parallel reworking of instructional materials to fit new course lengths. This has produced frustration both for teachers and for parents. Consequently, despite the ongoing talk of year-round schooling, there does not appear to be a strong trend to implementing extended-year plans at this time. One opinion is presented in Figure 4-9.

Posttest

Directions: Using your own paper, answer each of the following true/false questions. For each correct statement, write the word "true." For each incorrect statement, write the word "false."

_____ 1. School leaders have been pleased to find that, when year-round school plans have been implemented, youngsters have been very eager to attend school during the summer months.

_____ 2. In this country, innovations are tested thoroughly before they are tried in the schools.

_____ 3. There is almost universal agreement that innovation is "good for education."

_____ 4. Computer-assisted instruction can be installed in the school program without requiring teachers to change their traditional roles.

_____ 5. Time for team planning is a characteristic of successful team-teaching schemes.

_____ 6. At present, minicourses seem to be increasing in popularity in an overwhelming majority of secondary school programs.

_____ 7. In continuous progress programs, grade-level designations are removed and students progress through the curriculum at their own individual rates.

_____ 8. Modular scheduling can provide for great flexibility in planning schedules for individual students.

_____ 9. Revolving schedules allow more courses to be offered without requiring additional physical space.

_____ 10. The most popular plan for extending the length of the traditional nine-month school year is the mandatory four-quarter plan.

Key Ideas in Review

1. Innovation is consistent with the American cultural milieu. In the school setting, this has meant a willingness to try new things to "do the job better." Some critics have suggested that schools often adopt innovations before they are well tested. They allege too great an allegiance to what they view as inappropriate "change for change's sake." Others suggest that the willingness to do new things has kept American educators from falling into sterile patterns supported by no greater logic than tradition.

2. Computer-assisted instruction has the capability to store and update tremendous quantities of information. Further, computers can be programmed to diagnose students' needs and prescribe appropriate instructional responses. Today, prices of computer technology are dropping and increasing numbers of educators are conversant with computer programs and their use in the school. This suggests that increasing use of computers will be seen in education in the future. This by no means suggests that teachers will be replaced. Rather, it is likely that computers will supplement teacher activities in ways that will make teachers' efforts more effective.

3. Team teaching is an innovation that has been used in the schools to some extent since the late 1950s. The approach attempts to take advantages of the specialized talents of two or more teachers who work together as a team. The idea is that instructional responsibilities will be split in such a fashion that each teacher will be doing what he or she does best. Further, supporters of team teaching suggest the approach has potential for enhancing teachers' performances in that they teach not only in front of their students but in front of the other teachers on their team as well. In practice, team teaching requires a great deal of cooperative planning. Careful scheduling of activities is a must. The approach has been difficult to implement in older buildings that lack large instructional spaces.

4. Minicourses represent an attempt to introduce more variety into secondary programs. Typically, these are short courses lasting perhaps two to five weeks each. In many instances, students have had opportunities to select particular minicourses from a wide variety of options. Supporters claim an advantage in permitting youngsters to experience many different kinds of content. Critics suggest that too often minicourse programs have allowed youngsters to take a wide variety of frivolous courses that, collectively, tend not to represent anything

worth knowing. Minicourses also tend to present administrators with difficult scheduling problems.

5. Continuous progress programs allow students to progress through academic content at their own individual rates. Ordinarily, grade-level designations are eliminated. Content in continuous progress programs tends to be organized in terms of sequentially more difficult objectives. As students master given objectives, they are allowed to go on to more difficult topics. Continuous progress programs place heavy demands on teachers who must monitor students who may be working on very different kinds of materials. Some people suggest that, with the expansion of computer technology, some of these difficulties may be diminished in the near future.

6. Modular schedules represent an attempt to introduce flexibility into the process of scheduling students for classes. Simply stated, the school day is divided into a number of time periods of a given length. Each time period, or "module," is assigned a number. Then, based on requests by teachers who can ask to have students assigned to them for different lengths of time each day, computers generate student schedules, usually on a weekly basis, that assign students to classes. The system provides for a great deal of flexibility. But the system depends heavily on working computers. When computer systems fail, conditions in schools using modular schedules can be chaotic.

7. Revolving schedules allow schools to offer additional courses in their buildings without expanding physical facilities or lengthening the school day. This is accomplished by establishing a scheme where every course does not meet every day. There is some trade-off in terms of total amounts of instructional time in a given subject that students receive in a given semester. In a revolving schedule, they receive less instructional time in each subject than they do in conventional scheduling schemes. But, some argue, the loss is not significant and the gains to be had in expanding offerings is more than adequate compensation.

8. There have been numerous attempts to increase use of school buildings and offer students opportunities to complete their programs at different rates by extending the length of the school year. Nearly all these plans involve some expectation that sizable numbers of youngsters will agree to attend school during the summer months. This feature has led to a good deal of resistance to such plans in many areas where they have been proposed. Administrators have found that most students simply do not like to go to school during the summer months. Many parents, too, want their children free to accompany them on family vacations during the summer months. Although discussion about extended school years continues, prospects for rapid expansion of the idea do not appear bright at the present time.

SUMMARY

The American cultural milieu is very supportive of change and innovation. Given this fact, schools have been receptive to innovations. Some critics allege that school people often have been too willing to reject old practices without subjecting suggested replacements to rigorous evaluations before they have been installed. Others argue that school problems are so severe that it is only natural that school people would welcome anything promising some relief. To wait months or even years for definitive proof of an innovation's worth would mean an intolerable delay in introducing something that might solve a pressing immediate problem.

Numerous innovations have been tried with regard to improving mechanisms for introducing learners to new content. These have involved changes in staffing patterns, such as team teaching, to recommendations that exotic new hardware and software be used, as in computer-assisted instruction. Other recommendations have come forth for helping students by reorganizing the way in which they spend their time during the school day. Modular schedules and revolving schedules are among the many alternatives that have been proposed in this regard. Others have suggested that students and the entire society would be better served if the school year were extended. The mandatory four-quarter plan, Concept

Six, and the quinmester plan have been suggested as replacements for the traditional nine-month school year.

There have been great differences in the extent of use of the innovations described in this chapter. But all have shared one common characteristic. They have been put forward by people sincerely wishing to improve the quality of public education. Indeed, it can be said fairly that Americans' willingness to embrace innovations in the school is a testament to their belief that education is "something worth worrying about." While we share the view that some innovations may have been adopted in haste, we also believe that the willingness to introduce change in the school can be viewed as a positive sign of our commitment to make the schools as good as they can be.

Finally, we would caution against a natural tendency to evaluate individual innovations as being universally "good" or "bad." The success of a single innovation tends to be related strongly to the specific setting where it is installed. That is, an innovation that might work well in school A might prove to be a disaster in school B. Any discussion of a given innovation's appropriateness, then, ought to be in terms of how the innovation will work *in a particular setting*.

References

Armstrong, David G. "Open Space vs. Self-Contained," *Educational Leadership* (January 1975): 291–295.

————. "Team Teaching and Academic Achievement," *Review of Educational Research* (Winter 1977): 65–86.

Friedman, Milton, and Friedman, Rose. *Free to Choose*. New York: Harcourt Brace Jovanovich, Inc., 1979.

Glatthorn, Allan. *Alternatives in Education: Schools and Programs*. New York: Harper & Row, Publishers, Inc., 1975.

Parkinson, Daniel S. "Minicourse Approach in Ohio," *Phi Delta Kappan* (April 1976): 551–552.

Roberts, Arthur D., ed. *Educational Innovation: Alternatives in Curriculum and Instruction*. Boston: Allyn & Bacon, Inc. 1975.

Unruh, Glenys G., and Alexander, William M. *Innovations in Secondary Education*. 2nd ed. New York: Holt, Rinehart and Winston, Inc., 1974.

II

INSTRUCTION IN THE SECONDARY SCHOOL

5

A Framework for Planning and Implementing Instruction

B.C. by permission of Johnny Hart and Field Enterprises, Inc.

Objectives

This chapter provides information to help the reader to

1. Recognize the need for a system that enables teachers to examine the effectiveness of their instruction in terms of its impact on students.
2. Point out elements of a framework for instructional planning and implementation.
3. Describe relationships among various elements of a framework for instructional planning and implementation.
4. Recognize that a systematic framework for planning and implementing instruction allows teachers to use assessment techniques to evaluate their instructional programs as well as to evaluate students.

Pretest

Directions: Using your own paper, answer each of the following true/false questions. For each correct statement, write the word ''true.'' For each incorrect statement, write the word ''false.''

_____ 1. Teachers should never use preplanned objectives because they restrict their creativity in the classroom.

_____ 2. If instructional planning is done systematically, it is possible to use test results to evaluate the effectiveness of individual parts of the instructional planning process as well as to evaluate students.

_____ 3. Teachers should draw upon their own instructional strengths in planning lessons for students.

_____ 4. In preparing students to become teachers, it is best that these students be taught to model "ideal" classroom behaviors of certain successful teachers. They should be evaluated in terms of their ability to behave as these model teachers behave.

_____ 5. Teachers have no responsibilities other than planning and implementing instruction in the classroom.

_____ 6. Teaching may be thought of as a series of events requiring decisions.

_____ 7. There should be a logical relationship between stated objectives that guide instruction over a given segment of content and the kinds of test questions and tests administered at the conclusion of this period of instruction.

_____ 8. In selecting which instructional techniques to use, teachers should properly consider every element of the framework for instruction except for the one referring to instructional objectives.

_____ 9. It is possible for different teachers to develop instructional plans for helping students to master a common set of performance objectives that differ dramatically one from the other.

_____ 10. Because the primary purpose of schooling is motivation, each teacher should draw upon his or her own "bag of tricks" to develop lessons students like regardless of whether or not such lessons bear any relationship to stated performance objectives.

INTRODUCTION

Teachers are busy people. They serve as chaperones on student bus trips. They go to football and basketball games to cheer on the home team. They supervise cheerleaders, chess club students, literary societies, and an array of other adolescent activities too numerous to detail here. They attend professional meetings, and they buttonhole politicians in an effort to promote quality education. They grouse about administrators (some of the time anyway). They chortle in faculty lounges over some particularly outrageous student malapropism. They do all of these things—and more. But, most of all, teachers instruct students.

In considering teachers' roles, sometimes there is a tendency to count the numbers of different activities that engage teachers' attention and to presume that each is equally demanding on teachers' time. Nothing could be farther from the truth. Despite their many activities, most teachers continue to spend the vast majority of their professional time in the classroom working with students. Clearly, the instructional role of teaching is central to our whole notion of "teaching" as an activity that is distinct and separate from what other people in our society do. Therefore, it is appropriate for us to take a very detailed look at this pre-eminently important teacher responsibility.

ALTERNATIVE CONCEPTIONS OF TEACHERS' INSTRUCTIONAL ROLES

Teachers are by no means agreed as to what good instruction is. In fact, this topic is much debated in middle school, junior high school, and senior high school faculty lounges. Views of Joseph Barry, a junior high school mathematics teacher, and Vera

Noble, a senior high school English teacher, are representative of two commonly held positions.

Joseph Barry

"What's good teaching, you say? And what's a good classroom like? Well, as I see it, my job is to get the content across to these kids. We've got a pretty decent curriculum guide, and all of us working with the eighth grade know what our kids are supposed to do. We've got the content pretty well outlined. There are some specific objectives for us to have the kids work toward. And there are some procedures for teaching some of these things that some experts have worked out. Oh, I forgot to mention that there are some pretty good tests included too. They've been worked over by some talented measurement people, and we're pretty proud of the reliability of these exams.

"Once or twice a semester, Mr. Willis, our district's math coordinator, gets us all together. He helps us with the teaching techniques suggested in the curriculum guide. Every once in a while he'll call in a specialist from the university or somewhere to show us how to get some of the more difficult material across. I know some of our folks holler about some of these sessions. But I've always felt that I can learn something from a person who has made a scientific study of teaching. And, I mean, teaching ought to be more scientific. Seems to me that I can be more efficient in my classroom when I learn techniques from people who have tested them out on more kids than I'll ever see. As I see it, this scientific approach is my best hope for having my students really learn this content. And, believe me, this is important. You can't imagine the kind of remarks I put up with from those folks at the high school when they get a former student of mine who can't work with fractions."

Vera Noble

"What's good teaching? Well, to get myself off the hook, I suppose I could say simply, 'it depends.' But if you want a little more substance I suppose I can do better than that. Fundamentally, teaching is an art. Teachers are individuals. Students are individuals. The artistry of the teacher takes this frothy and exciting mixture of young people and, through processes that basically are intuitive, builds a program that has meaning. The focus of teaching must always be on the individual. This means that my colleagues and I have to resist imposing our own values. We need to draw out the best from the 'raw clay' that presents itself to us at the beginning of each term.

"Perhaps my position will become clearer if I explain it as it stands in contrast to the idea that teaching is more science than art. This view erroneously supposes that common techniques can be identified that will work equally well with one youngster as with another. My experience has taught me that differences among our kids are much more profound than similarities. Frankly, I have found no common principles that can be applied with confidence to all (or even to most) students. Since there really can be no science of teaching, what is left to me and to my colleagues is art. The best teachers are those who are the best artists. Now, just what is a 'good' artist? Well, the criteria are a bit elusive. But just about everyone will agree that some teachers in a building have a certain 'something' that places them head and shoulders above the others. And this 'something' has much to do with their ability to 'read' and respond to individual student differences and almost nothing to do with their mastery of so-called 'scientific' instructional principles."

Although exaggerated somewhat so as to make a clear distinction, the points of view of Joseph Barry and Vera Noble reflect the basic division between those who view instruction either as "science" or as "art." Strong proponents of each fundamental position can be found in nearly every secondary school. Only rarely does a case-hardened supporter of one of these basic positions become a convert to the other fundamental view. Probably it is fair to suggest that those who engage in debates over the issue do so as much out of enjoyment of the heat and the fire of opinionated discussion as out of real hope of snaring a convert.

For teachers who have not thought much about whether teachers function properly as "scientists" or "artists" when they instruct students, arguments on both sides of the issue can be confusing. Particularly for new teachers, it is not unusual to leave a passionate argument for the "teaching-as-science" position utterly convinced of the merits of the logic supporting this view only to have a complete change of opinion a day or two later after being collared and preached to by a proponent of the "teaching-as-art" school of thought.

From our own vantage point, it makes little sense for teachers to be to worry excessively about the justice of either the teaching-as-art or the teaching-as-science point of view. Must one opt for either one or the other of these fundamental positions? We think not. In our view, teachers' instructional practices are characterized by both art and science. The proper blend of these two perspectives has to be achieved by the individual teacher. No particular blend is better than another. Further, a given teacher's excellence may have little to do with the extent to which his or her instructional practices derive from art or science.

In approaching their instructional responsibilities, all teachers, regardless of the degree to which they view themselves as scientists or artists, have certain things they wish to communicate to youngsters. We believe that the measure of good teaching ought to be their success in accomplishing their objective of helping youngsters learn what it is that the teachers intend to teach. For some, this may mean drawing almost exclusively upon instructional principles that have been validated using solid scientific methodologies. For others, this may mean using the more intuitive approach of the sensitive artist. For still others (probably a majority), this may mean striking a balance of some kind between approaches that derive alternatively from science and art.

In thinking about their instructional responsibilities, then, teachers, we believe, ought to begin by identifying what they would like their youngsters to have accomplished at the conclusion of a given section of instruction. For example, if a teacher plans to introduce the War of 1812, what, exactly, should an attentive student be able to show the teacher he or she knows at the conclusion of instruction? If the topic is to be the sixteenth-century classic theater, what sorts of things will the teacher be looking for at the end as indicators that students have mastered the content? When these "end-of-instruction" expectations are identified at the very beginning of the instructional process, teachers have some basis for weighing the utility of a number of instructional approaches that might help students to master the skills and understandings needed to perform as expected at the end.

Different teachers may well select very different kinds of techniques to achieve their instructional intentions. Some of these may tend more toward science, some more toward art. The worth of a given set of procedures is not based on the nature of the individual procedures. Rather, the acid test comes when students' learning is measured at the end of the period of instruction. If students' learning comes up to teachers' expectations, then it is fair to assume that the selected techniques were "good." If not, then logically it can be assumed that there were some problems. Summarizing, then, the assessment of good or not-so-good instruction turns on the question, "Have youngsters learned?" (See Figure 5-1.)

PLANNING FOR PURPOSEFUL INSTRUCTION

Instruction that results in student learning is not haphazard. Learning does not come about because of some mystical quality possessed by "good" teachers that somehow has

Figure 5-1

REMARKS OF DR. PERCIVAL JAMISON AT A STATE TEACHERS' MEETING

I am delighted to point out to this group that members of my research staff have just completed a report on the impact of simulation games on students' learning in eleventh-grade U.S. history classes. You will remember that this study involved some 5,000 youngsters in schools in low, medium, and high socioeconomic districts in rural, suburban, and urban districts throughout the United States.

The results are just astounding. We found that youngsters who played with the simulations scored significantly higher on tests of understanding focusing on the Civil War period and the Great Depression period. For those of you who remember your statistics, these results were significant at the 0.001 level. For those of you who don't recall what that means, let me just say that it means that the reasons for these students' better performance on the tests seem overwhelmingly related to their exposure to the simulations.

An important implication from these results, I think, is that we all should make every effort to use simulation games in our U.S. history classes, particularly when we are covering the Civil War period and the Great Depression period. The results indicate an overwhelming improvement in the learning of students who have an opportunity to work with these simulations. The opportunity seems too good to pass up.

YOUR OPINION, PLEASE

Read the remarks above. Then, respond to these questions.

1. Suppose that your principal came back from hearing this speaker and insisted that you begin using simulation games. How would you respond? Why?
2. In your opinion, would it make a difference whether a teacher had had prior experience using simulations in his or her classroom when studying the Civil War period and the Great Depression period? Why, or why not?
3. What impact might a teacher's personal attitude toward simulations have on whether they worked well in his or her classroom?
4. Suppose that you wished to write to Dr. Jamison to take issue with his recommendation. What would you say? How do you think he might counter your argument?

---

been denied to "not-so-good" teachers. Rather, it occurs because successful teachers are better able to apply sound principles of teaching.

One principle that is being supported increasingly in the research literature of education is that the amount of student-engaged time on a learning task is related positively to achievement. This simply means that students who spend time working actively on learning tasks learn more than do those whose attentions are not engaged actively by learning tasks.

Student-engaged time is *not* the same as the total time allocated for learning. For example, we may gain nothing by increasing the amount of time for students to read supplementary materials in a history class we are teaching if youngsters in the class fail to spend their time engaged in reading these materials. An implication of student-engaged time research is that we, as teachers, must devise ways of getting our youngsters to focus their attentions on the instructional experiences we are providing and to keep their attentions involved actively.

Systematic instructional planning is necessary if student-engaged time is to be maximized. Sometimes people who visit a polished teacher's classroom fail to recognize the planning that has gone on in preparation for his or her performance. For example, it is not unusual for visitors to report, after visiting such a classroom, that the teacher "just seemed to talk calmly to students and engage them in easy discussion. The teacher and students seemed so relaxed."

An experienced classroom teacher often *does* appear to be interacting with youngsters in a totally spontaneous manner. In reality, a great deal of planning, formal and informal, has preceded the act of teaching. A more sophisticated observer who visits this classroom might note that, while the atmosphere appeared relaxed, the teacher was working to maintain students' focus on the lesson topic. He or she was monitoring events carefully to ensure a smooth flow from point to point. Further, the individual was listening carefully to student comments and was responding quickly to provide corrective feedback. It is likely that this teacher spent little time during the lesson seated at his or her desk keeping records or correcting papers. Keeping students engaged in learning also requires that the teacher stay engaged while the youngsters are in the classroom. (This does not mean that the teacher must always be in front of the group. He or she might well be wandering through the classroom to check on individual students.) The point here is that the teacher must take some active role to ensure that students' are maintaining a focus on instructional tasks.

First-year teachers who have concluded erroneously that systematic planning is unnecessary frequently face problems. Often they find themselves confronting students who are confused, unmotivated, and generally difficult to manage. Basically, their problem results from their attempt to play the role of a professional without doing the work of the professional. Professionalism in instruction just as professionalism in anything else results from mastery of certain basic principles. While challenging to newcomers, these mysteries are not infinite. They can be mastered by those seeking to enter the profession, though not without some effort.

We like to think that, in planning for instruction, teachers need to master techniques for dealing with six important areas. In our view, successful instructional sequences always involve teacher decisions regarding each of the following instructional tasks:

1. Diagnosing students' needs
2. Selecting content and establishing objectives
3. Identifying instructional techniques
4. Formalizing unit and lesson plans
5. Motivating students and implementing programs
6. Measuring, evaluating, and reporting on student progress

Instructional planning, then, is a sequential series of steps. It involves decisions respecting each of the six tasks. Each task bears a relationship to the entire instructional planning effort. When all these tasks are accomplished successfully, prospects that students will master the material that has been taught are excellent. In thinking about the issue of instructional planning, we like to think about the interrelationship among these tasks as displayed in a framework for planning and implementing instruction. The framework is introduced here in Figure 5-2.

THE FRAMEWORK FOR PLANNING AND IMPLEMENTING INSTRUCTION

The framework for planning and implementing instruction involves a sequence of steps useful to teachers in preparing for and executing instructional plans. The framework is an attractive planning vehicle for several reasons. First, it limits the number of specific tasks to be accomplished by the teacher to only six. For new teachers, in particular, this relatively small number provides some reassurance as they deal with their feelings about entering a profession "where there seems so much to learn."

Let us look at the framework and see what it tells us about the relationship of the six tasks to one another. Note that the first task is "diagnosing students' needs." This tells us that we need to pay attention to the particular youngsters in our classroom. What are their individual interests, needs, and capabilities? How can we find out?

Figure 5-2

A FRAMEWORK FOR PLANNING AND IMPLEMENTING INSTRUCTION

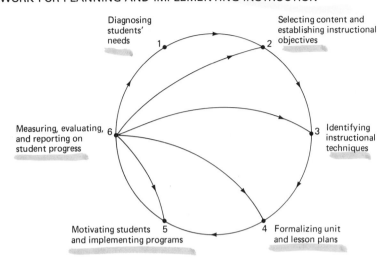

How should our materials be selected and presented to capitalize on these characteristics? Answers to these questions help us as we move on to the second task, "selecting content and establishing objectives."

Our instructional objectives describe what it is that we expect students to be able to do at the conclusion of our instructional sequence that will convince us that they have learned. We will need to consider information we have gathered about individual differences and the nature of the subject we are teaching. Next, we will move on to the task of "identifying instructional techniques." Because we already know our objectives, we will have a basis for making a decision in this area. We are free to select any instructional technique that, in our professional judgment, seems promising as a vehicle for helping students to achieve the objectives we have established.

Next, we move our planning to the task of "formalizing unit and lesson plans." Essentially what we are doing here is organizing information about decisions we have made about individual students, objectives, and instructional techniques into more or less formal documents that we can refer to as instruction goes forward.

The fifth task involves planning for "motivating students and implementing programs." Planning at this stage prepares us for some of the specific motivational techniques we will use and administrative procedures we will follow in putting our instructional plan into action. One important kind of decision we need to make that relates to this task has to do with the kinds of transitions we will make from one part of a day's lesson to another.

The sixth and final task relates to plans focusing on "measuring, evaluating, and grading." This task involves development of plans for testing and for making judgments about performances of individual students. Note the relationship of measuring, evaluating, and grading to other tasks in the framework. This task is related directly to each of the others. For this reason, information we gather about students' learning at the conclusion of an instructional sequence can be used to evaluate the entire instructional program as well as to evaluate individual students.

The Framework's Importance to the Teacher

Perhaps the most important value of this systematic planning framework for the teacher is that it can enhance his or her instructional efficiency. Suppose, for example, that a classroom teacher was making the following comments to a faculty lounge filled with sympathetic colleagues:

"I'm just going to give up on these classroom debates. I've worked myself to a frazzle getting materials ready. This 'ho hum' attitude they have just really gets to me. And, to make matters worse, nobody *listened when the debaters were talking. Finally, the crowning blow came this afternoon. I gave a test over the debate topic. Would you believe, 40 percent failed? On Monday, it's back to lecture and take notes."*

Whether we agree or disagree with this teacher's conclusion and the suggested remedy, the comments reflect a common pattern of complaint among teachers who do not use a systematic planning framework of some kind. The conclusion of the teacher in the faculty lounge is all too frequently to "abandon the whole program as a mistake." (See Figure 5-3 for a related discussion.) This is a terribly disappointing alternative, particularly when a great deal of effort has gone into the development of some novel approach. More regrettably, from our perspective, it is an unnecessary conclusion.

For teachers who do not plan systematically, there is no reliable way in which to examine specific parts of the instructional planning process that might explain why the idea just didn't work. Lacking such a capability, many teachers conclude that little is to be done but to scrap the entire approach. But consider a teacher who *had* planned using a framework similar to that depicted in Figure 5-2. In this event, the comments in the faculty lounge might have been more along these lines:

"My friends, I appear to have blown it again. My best planned efforts down the tube. The heralded 'great' debate did not turn them on. Few listened. Many were bored. And, cruelty of cruelties, the test scores were abysmal. So, I'll have to check my plan again.

Figure 5-3

THE TROUBLE WITH INSTRUCTIONAL PLANNING

You would not believe the in-service session I went to yesterday. Another one of these "pillow heads" from the university. During the part when I was still awake, he was holding forth on planning. A very sexy topic, right?

Well, anyway, he said we should diagnose our kids, lay out objectives, select instructional techniques, and all that *before* we start teaching. Can you *believe* such nonsense? I mean, I don't know my objective until I start teaching and get a "feel" for how the kids are reacting. This man would turn me into some kind of a faceless machine. We might as well stand our youngsters in front of the computer and have them push buttons if that's how we're supposed to teach. I mean, it's just too dehumanizing.

Statement made recently by a teacher in a secondary school teacher's lounge

YOUR OPINION, PLEASE

Please read the statement above. Then, respond to these questions.

1. Will preplanning result in a loss of teachers' creativity? Why, or why not?
2. Is teachers' creativity important? Why, or why not?
3. Is instructional planning dehumanizing? On what do you base your opinion?
4. What kind of flexibility do you suppose teachers might retain even after elaborate instructional plans have been made? Will they still be able to react to the ebb and flow of interaction in the classroom? Why or why not?

"I thought I knew these students, but I'm going to go back and see if there is some diagnostic information I missed. I think, too, the objectives I laid out may have been a little too much for this group. I know I'm going to have to rethink my choice of a classroom debate. And I want to check my lesson plans to see if the sequence could be improved. I may have created a problem for myself by not digging in hard enough when I was trying to 'sell' the new procedure to the class at the beginning. Some of the transitions may have been a bit shaky too. Finally, I simply have to recheck some of those test items. I have a sinking feeling in my stomach that some of those questions didn't relate much to what we were doing in class."

Teachers whose instruction has been preceded by planning that has gone forward in a systematic way, perhaps involving decisions related to tasks such as those included in the "framework for planning and implementing instruction," are in a much better position to identify the source of their instructional problems than are teachers whose planning, if it exists at all, is haphazard. Often, it develops that a very simple change will transform a given sequence of instruction from a loser to a winner. This is particularly heartening to teachers who have spent much time in preparing for instruction and who may be devastated when they see no alternative but to abandon an entire instructional sequence.

Clearly teachers' time is better spent in making minor repairs to an instructional program that is basically sound but that has one or two soft spots than to begin anew with an entirely different program when they are unable to pinpoint weaknesses in what they are doing. Use of the framework for planning and implementing instruction provides a mechanism for teachers to enhance their efficiency by being able to isolate probable causes for instructional programs that, in practice, are not working out so well as they had hoped.

In addition to helping teachers use their scarce time efficiently, many find that use of a systematic planning scheme allows them to take advantage of their own strengths. Once objectives have been established, teachers are free to select instructional techniques with which they are familiar. They need not worry if some outside authority thinks a given technique is good or bad so long as they can make a case for the technique as something that will help students to master the identified objectives. For some teachers, this may mean a heavy reliance on simulations. For others, small-group approaches may be best. Others may be comfortable with independent study schemes. The choice is the teacher's. And he or she is free to choose approaches with which he or she is familiar and in which he or she has personal confidence. This kind of flexibility is encouraged by the use of the framework for planning and implementing instruction. Once they become accustomed to using the framework, many teachers develop a great appreciation for the creativity it permits them in planning for classroom instruction.

THE TASKS OF INSTRUCTIONAL PLANNING

In this chapter, we have made very brief reference to six important instructional tasks. Although the number is not large, we are convinced that teachers need a thoroughly professional understanding of the dimensions of each. Given such an understanding, they have the tools necessary to develop and implement instructional programs that take advantage of individual teacher strengths and that help teachers to make wise and efficient use of their valuable time. So important is each of these tasks that we have devoted an entire chapter to each.

We recognize that individuals vary in terms of their familiarity with these tasks. For this reason, we will provide brief descriptions of each in this section as an introduction and suggest which of the chapters that deal with detailed treatments of individual tasks should be read with particular care.

Task 1: Diagnosing Students' Needs

In very simple terms, diagnosis helps us to find out who the students are and what they logically might be expected to do. In general, there are two purposes of diagnosis. Some teachers have interest in diagnostic information to accomplish only one of these purposes; some have an interest in accomplishing both.

The first purpose of diagnosis is to gather information related to student differences that may bear some relationship to their abilities to accomplish certain kinds of academic tasks. The second purpose of diagnosis is to gather information about students' attitudes and interests. These attitudes and interests may or may not relate to subjects to be taught in a given course (see Figure 5-4).

Generally teachers' relative interest in diagnostic information of one type or the other is associated with the kinds of courses they are teaching. Some courses have content that is prescribed by state or district regulation or by school policy. In such cases, individual teachers have little flexibility over what is to be taught. Teachers of courses of this kind tend to be more interested in diagnostic information that will reveal differences among students in terms of strengths and weaknesses related to the skills and understandings that they will need to deal with this prescribed content.

On the other hand, in many secondary courses decisions about the specific content to be taught are left to the teacher. For example, whereas an eighth-grade mathematics teacher may be required to limit his or her instruction pretty closely to the established curriculum, a twelfth-grade crafts teacher may have a good deal of flexibility in selecting what individual students in his or her class might do. The crafts teacher may well be interested in diagnostic information that will illuminate interests and enthusiasms of individual youngsters in the classroom.

Systematic procedures are available for teachers to use to gather information both about student capabilities as they relate to subject matter content and to differences in student interests. In general, there are more techniques available for teachers interested in student differences related to their individual abilities to cope with specific types of subject matter.

Figure 5-4

THINKING ABOUT DIAGNOSIS

You are a beginning teacher. Several days before school starts, you get a roster for your classes. You will teach six classes a day. Classes average 30 students each. All will be in your major area of academic training.

YOUR OPINION, PLEASE

Think about the kinds of diagnostic information about these youngsters you would like to have. Then, respond to these questions.

1. Exactly what would you like to know about these students?
2. Would you have more interest in knowing about their capabilities as they relate to some specifics of the subject you will be teaching or in their general interests and attitudes?
3. Describe at least four ways in which you might go about gathering diagnostic information about these students.
4. Do you have any ideas about how you might organize the information you gather so that you can refer to it quickly and easily when the occasion arises?
5. What sorts of "weaknesses" do you suppose you might uncover? What would you do to help students overcome these weaknesses?

In general, diagnostic information-gathering techniques are of two basic types: techniques that involve administration of a test or some less formal instrument to an entire class of students and techniques that involve a focus on only a single student or on a small group of students at one time. Clearly these techniques vary enormously in terms of the amount of teacher time required to administer them. For example, a teacher interested in knowing about youngsters' abilities to locate cities using coordinates of longitude and latitude could develop a short test, administer it to a class, and correct it in a relatively short time. On the other hand, a decision to learn about general student attitudes toward the high school physics course by interviewing separately every student in a class could be time consuming.

The potential for certain diagnostic techniques to consume a great amount of teacher time, in practice, forces teachers to accept some trade-offs. For example, a teacher may decide to give a test to the entire class that can be evaluated quickly, even though more information about each student could be gathered by conducting a series of indepth personal interviews. On the other hand, a teacher may decide to forego gathering extensive diagnostic information on an entire group of students in favor of collecting extensive information related to a relatively small group of youngsters in the classroom.

Whatever decisions a teacher makes regarding which diagnostic information is to be obtained and how it will be gathered, the information needs to be organized systematically. This information will be important when instructional objectives are being planned. Therefore, it is necessary that the results of diagnosis be easily accessible. A number of procedures for accomplishing this will be introduced in Chapter 6, "Diagnosing Students' Needs."

Finally, there is a tendency for many beginning teachers to become so intrigued with the potentials of diagnosis and so fascinated by the options available for gathering diagnostic information that they spend entirely too much time on the process. Although diagnosis is important, it must be accomplished expeditiously. To do otherwise robs valuable time from other important parts of the instructional planning process. For a more detailed treatment of diagnosis, refer to Chapter 6.

Task 2: Selecting Content and Establishing Instructional Objectives

The content we select pinpoints the general topic on which we will focus in a given instructional unit. The objectives state specifically what sorts of student behaviors we will look for as evidence that learning has taken place. In recent years, the trend has been for teachers to describe objectives in very precise terms. Rarely, today, for example, is it considered sufficient for a teacher to keep an objective at so general a level as "Each student will learn to appreciate literature." Today's objectives tend to reference more clearly observable student behaviors, such as, for example, "Each student will cite specific examples of the author's use of alliteration by . . .".

In part, this trend toward specificity arose because of a suspicion that the vaguer objectives of former times often functioned as little more than public relations window dressing. Schools and teachers may have derived some benefit from the community at large for proclaiming an interest in helping students to "appreciate" or "know" or "understand" something. But these verbs are so nonspecific that it was all but impossible to determine whether objectives in which they occurred were met. How, for example, do we ever truly determine that a given student "appreciates" poetry? "Appreciation" is an abstract concept. No single behavior can automatically be taken as evidence of appreciation.

To remedy this difficulty, many educational leaders today take the position that objectives that use such imprecise verbs as "understand," "know," and "appreciate" ought to be avoided. As noted, achievement or nonachievement of such objectives is very difficult to assess. Second, they do not provide specific targets for students to pursue as they begin dealing with new content in their classes.

The ability to guide students' learning is one of the central functions of instructional objectives. Many educational leaders are convinced that students suffer not so much from a lack of information as from an inability to determine which information is important and which is unimportant. When teachers develop clear instructional objectives and provide them to students, students have a basis for making decisions about the relative importance of the different pieces of information they encounter during their study of a new topic. For students, then, instructional objectives provide a means of focusing attention on relevant material.

For teachers, instructional objectives provide a foundation for all remaining instructional planning. Developed after a careful consideration of diagnostic information, instructional objectives are referents that teachers can use to include or reject certain instructional techniques, learning materials, and testing procedures. They establish a mechanism for determining the relevancy of options that might be selected for inclusion during a given instructional sequence. In general, once instructional objectives have been determined, the teacher, in considering other elements of the program, asks this question: "Will this alternative help students to achieve the objective?" If the answer is "yes," then there is a logical basis for selecting the option. If the answer is "no," then this option likely would be a poor choice.

In general, teachers use three major categories of instructional objectives. The first includes objectives with a focus on the academic side of learning. The second includes objectives relating to students' skill development. The third relates to the feelings and attitudes of the learners. Regardless of the subject being taught, teachers may find it necessary to develop some instructional objectives in each of the three categories. But, depending on the subject being taught, it is likely that there will be more instructional objectives in one of these major categories than in the others. Much more detailed treatments of these categories and specific procedures for developing instructional objectives are provided in Chapter 7, "Selecting Content and Establishing Instructional Objectives."

Task 3: Identifying Instructional Techniques

Instructional techniques include all those planned activities that teachers select to help learners to achieve stated instructional objectives. They include, but most certainly are not limited to, such techniques as lectures, simulations, classroom discussions, independent study, team learning, questioning, role playing, brainstorming, and telelecture.

Properly, instructional techniques are selected after careful consideration of the instructional objectives that the teacher has established. These objectives state what youngsters ought to be able to do at the conclusion of the instructional sequence. The instructional techniques are methodologies that the teacher selects because he or she believes that they have potential for enabling students to perform as expected at the conclusion of the instructional experience. The worth then of any given technique depends upon its value in helping students to learn what the teacher hopes they will learn.

This point, we believe, deserves some elaboration. Many beginning teachers make the mistake of presuming that some techniques are good whereas others are bad. It must be remembered that there is nothing good or bad about any given technique. The appropriateness of a given technique is contextual. That is, it must be judged in terms of the instructional objective it is supposed to help students to master. For example, it is quite possible that a lecture would be a bad technique to help students master some kinds of objectives while it might be a good technique to help them master other kinds of objectives.

In considering a given instructional objective, different teachers may well identify different instructional techniques as appropriate. This is a perfectly logical expectation. We know that a number of techniques may be appropriate for helping students to achieve a single objective. Further, we know that individual teachers vary in terms of their familiarity with different instructional techniques. It makes good sense for a teacher, then, to select an instructional technique in which he or she has confidence. Part of the artistry of teaching involves the teacher's creativity in adapting instructional techniques of his or her own choosing to stated instructional objectives.

While teachers' efforts to identify imaginative approaches to help students learn new material is laudable, it is essential that these techniques bear a logical relationship to stated instructional objectives. Some beginning teachers have a tendency to become so excited about one technique, say, simulation, that they choose the technique because of the pleasure they derive from its use rather than because of its relationship to an instructional objective. We believe that this represents an unhappy victory of process over substance. In the short run students in such classrooms may appear to be happy and excited as lessons unfold. But, in time, this condition may change as test and examination scores reveal that they have failed to acquire some of the information for which, at this point, they are held accountable.

Successful classroom teachers are familiar with a large number of instructional techniques. When they establish instructional objectives, they are able to select rationally from among a number of alternative techniques that logically might help youngsters in their classrooms to master these objectives. In general, teachers tend to prefer techniques with which they have some familiarity. Clearly their flexibility is enhanced as they learn the procedures for using an increasing variety of procedures. Specific information relating to a selection of techniques is provided in Chapter 8, "Instructional Techniques."

Task 4: Formalizing Unit and Lesson Plans

Unit and lesson plans provide guideposts for teachers to use as instruction unfolds. Typically, they will reference the instructional objectives, the intended instructional techniques, some needed materials, and proposed evaluation procedures. One of the most important functions of unit and lesson plans is to lay out the sequence of what the teacher and students will be doing as instruction unfolds.

Unit plans tend to cover a longer period of instruction than do lesson plans. A unit comprises a given coherent portion of content within a course. For example, a physics course might have a unit on electricity. An English literature course might have a unit on muckrakers. A social studies course might have a unit on settlement of the Great Plains. Complete unit plans provide teachers with a framework for guiding instruction over a given period of time. Units vary greatly in length. Many would fall somewhere in the three to eight weeks' range. But some will be shorter, others longer.

Typically a unit will begin with some breakdown of the major content to be covered. Instructional objectives for students will be listed. A selection of appropriate instructional techniques, tied clearly to these objectives, will be described, and a list of needed materials will be included. Some units also suggest alternative testing procedures.

Although some commercially prepared units are available, most are developed by individual teachers or groups of teachers. They provide a mechanism for teachers to organize course contents systematically. Units enable teachers to draw together in a coherent fashion information from a variety of sources. When teachers have good units, they tend to be much less dependent on the scope and sequence of topics as they are arranged in the textbooks they are using. Units, in effect, put teachers in the driver's seat. This results because, as they develop units, teachers make decisions about which contents are to be emphasized, how they are to be taught, and what kind of a sequence makes sense. Units then can have a liberating influence on classroom teachers.

Lesson plans detail what happens in a classroom over a much shorter span of time than do unit plans. Frequently lessons last only a day. (Indeed, sometimes they are referred to as "daily lesson plans," though some lessons might require more than a single day's instructional time.) Lesson plans typically reference the instructional objective that is guiding the instruction. Frequently a sequence of teacher activities will be mentioned. When this is done, it is also common to find mention of what students will be expected to be doing as instruction unfolds. Materials needed to support the lesson will be mentioned. Finally, evaluation procedures to assess the impact of the lesson on students will be included.

Formal lesson plans help teachers to move smoothly from point to point throughout a lesson. For beginners, in particular, they provide a "vision" of what a logical flow of instruction should look like. When completed lesson plans are available for a quick visual inspection by the teacher as instruction unfolds, the teacher has something to fall back on should he or she get disoriented as the instructional period goes forward. Disorientation is a common feeling, particularly among beginning teachers (see Figure 5-5), when a rapid-fire discussion, an unexpected visitor from the central office, a fire alarm, or something else happens that causes the teacher to lose his or her focus. A quick glance at an available lesson plan helps to get a teacher "back on the track." Specific procedures for preparing lesson plans and units are detailed in Chapter 9, "Formalizing Unit and Lesson Plans."

Figure 5-5

LESSON PLANS AND STUDENT TEACHER ANXIETY

Ms. Knox had taken roll. She was reading some announcements from the office. The ninth-graders were reasonably attentive on this drippy Northwest Coast morning.

At the rear of the room, Harvey Munson yanked on his tie. "Too tight," he thought to himself. "And me, too, I'm too tight." He forced his shoulders to sag a bit in a strained effort to relax. And he listened.

"Class," Ms. Knox said in that big and important message tone of voice she affected when dispensing pattern-shattering information, "Our student teacher, Mr. Munson, is going to begin working with you this morning. I know we'll all appreciate having him here." A nod toward the back of the room. "They're all yours Mr. Munson."

Launch time! Munson, stomach muscles creaking, rose stiffly from his chair. Then, eyeballs straight ahead, he marched through a sea of curious eyes to the front of the room. Thoughts of his lesson on Brazil flashed through his mind. "Damn," he accused himself, "I wish I'd brought some notes." Arriving all too soon at the teacher's desk, he took a deep breath and . . . turned.

"Faces . . . faces . . . faces . . . my God there didn't seem to be so many of them from the back of the room," he thought. Control. Self-control. Oh yes, and smile. That's what Dr. Ennis said, smile. "OK," he thought quickly, "How about a snappy opener."

"Boys and girls," he was off to a good start! "Ah, well . . . I . . . ah. . . ." He was beginning to sink. "It's a nice . . . ah . . . er." Ms. Knox saw the trembling hands, and she began to take notes. "Well, I . . . er . . . ah . . . well . . . I've got . . . a . . . dog at home."

First a puzzled look. Then a giggle in the back. A guffaw somewhere in the front row. Soon the entire classroom rocked with laughter. In despair, Harvey Munson tried to frame yet another sentence.

YOUR OPINION, PLEASE
Respond to these questions.

1. Would a lesson plan of some kind have been helpful to Mr. Munson?
2. Why do you think that Mr. Munson had so much trouble getting started?
3. Do you think that Mr. Munson's situation was typical or unusual? Why do you think so?
4. If you were faced with this kind of situation, what would you do?

Task 5: Motivating Students and Implementing Programs

The fifth task of instruction requires teachers to move beyond identification of what they wish students to learn and how they propose to introduce new material to decisions about exactly how the program will be implemented in the classroom. Successful implementation of instructional plans begins with motivating students.

Motivation consists of specific teacher actions designed to prompt student interest in learning. The question of motivation is a perennial topic of discussion at teachers' conventions. Faculty lounge comments often testify to teachers' frustration as they attempt to capture students' interest. ("These kids just don't care. The students have changed. My fifth-period class isn't interested in *anything*.") While many have felt themselves called on to speak to the need to motivate students, few have ventured to prescribe "fail-safe" motivational techniques. And with good reason.

Students, like the population at large, reflect an enormous diversity. What turns on one student may well put another to sleep. Although we sometimes talk about motivating "classes" of students, what we really mean is motivating individual students within these classes. Successful motivation demands a good understanding of particular interests and aspirations of each student in the classroom. Teachers who possess this kind of knowledge have a basis for planning motivational techniques that have some promise of success (although no teacher motivates 100 percent of the students 100 percent of the time). The more adequate the understanding of individual students in a class, the greater the potential for success of motivational procedures designed in the light of this information.

Beyond the issue of motivation, many other decisions need to be made as instructional plans are implemented in the classroom. For example, physical arrangements of students in the classroom must be considered. We have evidence that suggests that students react in different ways in the classroom according to how they are arranged physically. We need to determine what our purpose is and, using knowledge about the relationship of physical placement of students and likely interaction patterns, to arrange students so that our purpose will be well served.

Decisions about group size represent another important area of consideration. For certain kinds of learning, large-group settings represent the most appropriate choice. For others, students may benefit more when they work in small groups. If a small-group format is selected, we need to make decisions regarding how the work of individual groups will be monitored and how the products of this group work will be shared (if at all) with the class as a whole.

Perhaps one of the most difficult skills for teachers to master in implementing programs has to do with engaging in rapid-fire verbal interactions with students. As teachers, we need to develop an ability to think quickly on our feet, respond to questions, listen for subtle changes in tones of voice used by students that may signal potential control problems, and, in general, make many decisions about transitions from one part of a lesson to another. Many new teachers report feeling pressure as they are forced to make dozens of decisions within every class period. In time, many of these decisions become more routinized. But even experienced teachers sometimes express frustration when class periods do not flow as smoothly as they would like. Detailed information focusing on this dimension of teaching is provided in Chapter 10, "Motivating Students and Implementing Programs."

Task 6: Measuring, Evaluating, and Reporting Student Progress

Today, we are witnessing increasing pressures on schools to demonstrate that students are learning something. These pressures have resulted in the passage of laws in some states requiring schools to provide specific evidence that students are able to perform at a given level of competence before being permitted to graduate from high school.

Rarely throughout the history of American education has there been so heavy an emphasis on evaluation of students' learning. Today, it is critical for teachers to be familiar with defensible procedures for evaluating performance of their students.

The concept of assessment is not limited, however, to a concern for testing students. Assessment encompasses efforts to use both formal and informal procedures to make judgments about the standing both of students and of the instructional program to which they have been exposed. The use of assessment procedures to make judgments about students that are reported to parents in the form of grades is a familiar one. Although some attempts have been made to displace the use of grades with other systems, the force of tradition is so strong that grades will be with us for a long time to come.

Only in relatively recent times have educators begun to take a serious look at the possibility of using the same information they have gathered to assess students' progress to make judgments about the quality of the instructional programs to which students have been exposed. Perhaps one of the most important explanations for the new interest in assessing programs has been the move toward more systematic instructional planning.

Before educators became attracted to adapting the systems approach to instructional planning, much less attention was given to specifying objectives, tying instructional techniques to these objectives, and evaluating in terms of these objectives. Consequently, even if students did not do well on a test or series of tests and teachers felt that something might be amiss in their instructional program, they had no way to pinpoint exactly what might have gone wrong. Today, this situation is much changed.

Consider, for example, a teacher who had planned using the six-part planning framework introduced here. If students did not do well on a test, a teacher might look to specific explanatory causes such as (1) inappropriate diagnostic procedures, (2) poorly selected objectives, (3) unsuitable instructional techniques, (4) poorly prepared lesson plans, (5) failure to motivate students, and/or (6) inappropriate testing techniques. In short, today's systematic instructional planning approaches provide teachers with a capability of being much more specific in their analyses of what might have gone wrong during any given instructional sequence. For details, see Chapter 11, "Measuring, Evaluating, and Reporting Student Progress."

Posttest

Directions: Using your own paper, answer each of the following true/false questions. For each correct statement, write the word "true." For each incorrect statement, write the word "false."

_____ 1. Teachers should never use preplanned objectives because they restrict their creativity in the classroom.

_____ 2. If instructional planning is done systematically, it is possible to use test results to evaluate the effectiveness of individual parts of the instructional planning process as well as to evaluate students.

_____ 3. Teachers should draw upon their own instructional strengths in planning lessons for students.

_____ 4. In preparing students to become teachers, it is best that these students be taught to model "ideal" classroom behaviors of certain successful teachers. They should be evaluated in terms of their ability to behave as these model teachers behave.

_____ 5. Teachers have no responsibilities other than planning and implementing instruction in the classroom.

_____ 6. Teaching may be thought of as a series of events requiring decisions.

_____ 7. There should be a logical relationship between stated objectives that guide instruction over a given segment of content and the kinds of test questions and tests administered at the conclusion of this period of instruction.

_____ 8. In selecting which instructional techniques to use, teachers should properly consider every element of the framework for instruction except for the one referring to instructional objectives.

_____ 9. It is possible for different teachers to develop instructional plans for helping students to master a common set of performance objectives that differ dramatically one from the other.

_____ 10. Because the primary purpose of schooling is motivation, each teacher should draw upon his or her own "bag of tricks" to develop lessons students like regardless of whether or not such lessons bear any relationship to stated performance objectives.

Key Ideas in Review

1. Teachers play many very important roles as they work with young people in the schools. But, even given this diversity, teachers today continue to spend most of their professional lives in their capacity as instructional leaders. It is the instructional role that most clearly differentiates what teachers do from roles played by others in our society.

2. In general, there has been disagreement over whether teaching is an art or a science. Most teachers probably take some sort of middle position on this issue.

3. In thinking about teaching excellence, probably the most important criterion for judgment should be student learning. Outstanding teachers know the content they wish students to acquire, and they succeed in transmitting this content to students.

4. Effective learning is promoted by systematic instructional planning. Systematic planning helps teachers to develop an instructional sequence that is guided by carefully selected objectives. Should students' performance on a final assessment fall below expectations, such a system helps teachers pinpoint possible soft spots in their instructional programs.

5. The framework for planning and implementing instruction provides teachers with a mechanism they can use to plan instructional programs systematically. The framework assumes there to be six primary instructional tasks. These are (a) diagnosing students' needs, (b) selecting content and establishing instructional objectives, (c) identifying instructional techniques, (d) formalizing unit and lesson plans, (e) motivating students and implementing programs, and (f) measuring, evaluating, and reporting student progress.

SUMMARY

Systematic instructional planning promotes learning. Such planning encourages teachers to diagnose students, establish important instructional objectives, develop programs designed to promote mastery of these objectives, and devise evaluation procedures that focus clearly on program objectives. Instructional plans of this kind permit assessment both of individual students and of the instructional program as a whole. This latter capability becomes possible because precise specification of individual program elements enables teachers to look at individual components of their programs to spot potential weak spots as well as program strengths.

A teacher's excellence in large measure relates to how well he or she helps students to learn. There is no specific set of ideal teacher behaviors that will always result in optimum student learning. Individual teachers differ. Individual students and groups of students differ. Given this reality, we believe that teachers should be encouraged to take advantage of their own strengths as they diagnose their students' needs and design programs that they feel have potential to promote learning. The measure of the individual teacher's success, properly, is students' learning. How this learning is best achieved, at bottom, must be determined by the individual teacher as he or she interprets the unique challenges of his or her own instructional setting.

References

Armstrong, David G.; Denton, Jon J.; and Savage, Tom V. *Instructional Skills Handbook.* Englewood Cliffs, N.J.: Educational Technology Publications, 1978.

Briggs, Leslie J., ed. *Instructional Design.* Englewood Cliffs, N.J.: Educational Technology Publications, 1977.

Davies, Ivor K. *Objectives in Curriculum Design.* New York: McGraw-Hill Book Company, 1976.

Hass, Glen. *Curriculum Planning: A New Approach.* 3rd ed. Boston: Allyn & Bacon, Inc., 1980.

Hunkins, Francis P. *Curriculum Development: Program Improvement.* Columbus, Ohio: Charles E. Merrill Publishing Co., 1980.

Joyce, Bruce R., and Harootunian, Berj. *The Structure of Teaching.* Chicago: Science Research Associates, Inc., 1967.

Nicholls, Audrey, and Nicholls, S. Howard. *Developing A Curriculum: A Practical Guide.* London: George Allen & Unwin Ltd., 1976.

Orlosky, Donald E., and Smith, B. Othanel. *Curriculum Development: Issues and Insights.* Chicago: Rand McNally & Company, 1978.

Popham, W. James, and Baker, Eva L. *Systematic Instruction.* Englewood Cliffs, N.J.: Prentice-Hall, Inc., 1970.

6

Diagnosing Students' Needs

"Ms. Stein, trying to find out 'where the learners are' is commendable. But don't you think 13 straight weeks of diagnostic testing is a bit much?"

Objectives

This chapter provides information to help the reader to

1. Recognize purposes of diagnostic information.
2. Implement a selection of diagnostic procedures.

3. Make judgments about the relative merits of certain diagnostic procedures as they relate to varying sets of circumstances.
4. Develop procedures for organizing diagnostic information about individual students.
5. Utilize procedures for organizing diagnostic information related to groups of learners in classrooms.

Pretest

Directions: Using your own paper, answer each of the following true/false questions. For each correct statement, write the word "true." For each incorrect statement, write the word "false."

_____ 1. It is recommended that teachers spend at least as much time gathering diagnostic information about students as they spend instructing students.

_____ 2. A sample of a student's previous work is likely to be a better indicator of his or her present understanding when the work was accomplished relatively recently than when it was accomplished some time ago.

_____ 3. In thinking about which diagnostic procedures to use, teachers are advised to consider the time required to gather the information they want.

_____ 4. The teacher-student conference is recognized widely as the most time-efficient procedure a teacher can use to gather diagnostic information about an entire class of students.

_____ 5. The Cloze procedure is used to assess a student's likelihood of experiencing difficulty with certain mathematical operations.

_____ 6. An interest inventory is used frequently to gather information about students' attitudes.

_____ 7. Information about the frequency of occurrence of a given behavior can be gathered through the use of a checklist.

_____ 8. Diagnostic information sometimes is gathered both about students' mastery of skills and students' levels of subject matter comprehension.

_____ 9. If a teacher wanted to find out whether students understand enough about European geography to comprehend a proposed unit on battlefield movements during World War I, good diagnostic information might be gathered through use of a teacher-prepared test.

_____ 10. While it is desirable for teachers to gather diagnostic information about individual students, it is considered unethical for teachers to develop instructional procedures for students identified as having potential problems that differ from those used with the rest of the class.

INTRODUCTION

Education has been described as a glue that keeps strands of our social fabric in place. While education may indeed cement us together, dramatic differences among the individual pieces remain. Our society is a rich human mosaic. It is in our differences and our appreciation of them that much of our national character is found. So, while our schools are called upon to bind the young to the society, the bond is to a society where a commitment to individual differences is fundamental.

In a culture where individual differences are prized, interests and aptitudes of individual people are diverse almost beyond description. This diversity is reflected in the populations of our public schools. Beginning teachers frequently report being "shocked" at the differences existing among students in their classrooms. Secondary school teachers, in particular, must deal with students whose differences sometimes seem more profound than their similarities.

With each succeeding year in school, differences among students increase. The gaps among youngsters that are visible even in early elementary school become absolutely chasmic by the time they reach senior high school. A high school teacher who works with a group of 17-year-olds may well have in the same class students who read only on the third- or fourth-grade level (indeed, some may be functional nonreaders) and others who enjoy the translated essays of Montaigne as recreational reading. A typical class at this level will include those who cannot handle basic addition, subtraction, multiplication, and division skills as well as those who can program a computer. In short, the diversity of talents and interests in our secondary school classrooms comes close to the breadth of talents and interests in the society as a whole.

This diversity presents great challenges to the secondary school teacher. As a practical matter, most teachers are not able to develop individual instructional programs for each student in their classes. In the case of a typical secondary teacher, such an approach might mean as many as 170 or 180 separate programs. But the great variety of students does suggest the necessity of taking into account individual differences as instructional planning goes forward. Such planning can result in the development of procedures that are sufficiently wide ranging that most students in a class will have some realistic prospects for success. When instructional plans reflect an understanding of student differences, the likelihood for students to succeed is enhanced. And success motivates students. In turn, positive student reactions encourage teachers to do their best. Clearly both teachers and students stand to gain when instruction is responsive to individual differences.

Teachers who are interested in responding to these differences must begin with a clear understanding of the nature of the students with whom they are working. For this reason, it is desirable that they have diagnostic information that can shed light on characteristics of students in their classrooms.

In general, there are two basic types of diagnostic information. The first of these concerns diagnostic information about skills. Frequently teachers are interested in knowing individual students' proficiency in certain skills that will be needed for success as the instructional program unfolds. For example, a teacher, regardless of what he or she is going to be teaching, might like to know the reading skills of individuals in a class. Similarly, a teacher might also desire information related to individual students' computational skills.

Once teachers know what they are going to be teaching, they frequently like to have information on students' attitudes about the topic and students' understanding of relevant prerequisite information. Diagnostic information of this kind helps teachers to plan introductory lessons as new material is introduced. Without such information in hand, instructions may be too sophisticated for many of the students. Similarly, if instruction is keyed too low, and the teacher spends time covering what students already know, boredom and consequent discipline problems may arise. The availability of sound diagnostic information helps teachers to plan instructional experiences that are appropriate for students in their classrooms.

Beginning teachers, we have observed, sometimes become too enamoured with diagnostic procedures. They may presume, erroneously, that if they "just get the diagnostic information tight enough" they will be able to reach *every* learner. The objective of reaching every learner is laudable. But it should be regarded as just that: an objective. Given the incredible diversity of human beings with whom a secondary school teacher works, it is asking too much of a teacher to succeed with 100 percent of his or her students. That sort of thing may happen on television. But it is unlikely in the real world. Diagnosis, however, can help teachers to reach more of their students than would be likely in the absence of attention to students' individual differences.

Once a decision to gather diagnostic information has been taken, teachers are faced with decisions about which diagnostic techniques to use to get the information they need. In making this selection, we need to consider two basic questions: (1) Which technique(s) will provide the specific information required? (2) How much time will this technique (these techniques) require? Diagnostic information must be gathered expeditiously. While diagnosis is clearly important, time spent on gathering this information cannot be at the expense of valuable instructional time. The need to get the information and move ahead may well mean that a teacher will make different choices about how to get his or her information. For example, if a teacher wanted to gather diagnostic information about five students working in a group in his or her classroom, he or she might well decide to schedule a personal conference with each student. But, if diagnostic information were needed about all students in five sections of a course, the teacher likely would not want to schedule an individual conference with all 170 students. The time cost would be too high. An alternative procedure for obtaining necessary information would be in order.

Once decisions about which diagnostic procedures have been made and the diagnostic information has been gathered, it needs to be organized. In general, there are two basic types of organization. The first scheme requires the development of a system for arranging diagnostic information about a given individual in such a way that it can be retrieved quickly. The second requires the development of a procedure for collapsing diagnostic information about all students in a class or course so that it can be viewed collectively and patterns of academic strengths and weaknesses, skill-level proficiencies, and attitudes can be inferred quickly.

Sections that follow will introduce a number of procedures for gathering diagnostic information. Strengths and weaknesses of individual procedures will be discussed. Suggestions for organizing diagnostic information as it relates both to individual students and to classes of individual students will also be introduced (see Figure 6-1).

A SELECTION OF DIAGNOSTIC TECHNIQUES

A variety of procedures may be used to gather diagnostic information about students. In fact, potentially useful procedures are far too numerous for us to introduce all of them here. In this section, we will look at a representative sampling of diagnostic procedures. Each technique has its own strengths and limitations.

In selecting which techniques to use, we need to keep a clear focus on the purpose we have in mind for the diagnostic information we desire. Some techniques provide certain kinds of information quickly and efficiently. For other purposes, they are much less suitable. What we are striving for is a selection of techniques that will provide the most useful information in the shortest period of time. This goal is easier stated than achieved. But, with familiarity with available options and some experience, teachers find that they can become quite proficient in organizing a diagnostic program that supplies them with desired information in an efficient manner.

Work Sample

The work sample is frequently used as a source of diagnostic information about individual students. Simply stated, a work sample is an example of previously completed student work (see Figure 6-2). By examining this student work, it is sometimes possible for a teacher to pinpoint specific strengths and weaknesses of the student who produced it. Suppose, for example, we were teaching high school French and were preparing to introduce students to the use of the past tense known as the *passé composé*. Formation of this past tense requires students to be thoroughly familiar with the present tenses of two key French verbs, *être* and *avoir*. Before beginning the work on the *passé composé*, we might wish to examine examples of former student written work using the present

Figure 6-1

DESIRED KINDS OF DIAGNOSTIC INFORMATION

Suppose that the students listed were enrolled in one of your classes. Suppose, too, that all the information you had about them was information related to their ages and to their overall averages in all school course work. (This information is provided.)

Adams, Sandra L.,	age 17,	C— average in all school subjects
Anderson, Larry P.,	age 16,	C average in all school subjects
Boswell, Robert B.,	age 16,	A— average in all school subjects
Benting, Lois L.,	age 16,	C average in all school subjects
Boudreau, Sondra Y.,	age 17,	B+ average in all school subjects
Conroe, Barbara J.,	age 18,	B— average in all school subjects
Cotton, John B.,	age 16,	C average in all school subjects
Cottuletti, Joseph L.,	age 16,	B— average in all school subjects
Dariola, Manuel F.,	age 17,	B average in all school subjects
Epstein, Nathan Q.,	age 16,	B+ average in all school subjects
Fox, Norton N.,	age 17,	D average in all school subjects
Heppelstein, Arthur C.,	age 16,	C— average in all school subjects
Inks, Stella C.,	age 18,	C average in all school subjects
Jensen, Arne C.,	age 17,	B average in all school subjects
Klein, William F.,	age 17,	A average in all school subjects
Lott, Angela A.,	age 16,	B+ average in all school subjects
Muntcliff, Harold O.,	age 16,	C— average in all school subjects
Noble, Nancy C.,	age 16,	B average in all school subjects
Norton, Jeffrey R.,	age 16,	B— average in all school subjects
Ogleby, Oscar Y.,	age 17,	A— average in all school subjects
Prentiss, Pricilla J.,	age 17,	B+ average in all school subjects
Quintana, Arturo O.,	age 16,	A average in all school subjects
Reston, Loise A.,	age 17,	D average in all school subjects
Thompson, Nola V.,	age 16,	C— average in all school subjects
Umphress, Samuel V.,	age 17,	B average in all school subjects
Vick, Marcella L.,	age 16,	C average in all school subjects
Wiggins, Stewart D.,	age 17,	B+ average in all school subjects
Yonce, Peter G.,	age 17,	B— average in all school subjects

YOUR OPINION, PLEASE

Study this information. Then, respond to these questions.

1. What other information do you think you would like to have about these people?
2. Of what specific benefit to you would this information be?
3. What are some alternative ways you might get this information?
4. Of these ways, which would be most costly in terms of teacher time? Which would be least costly?
5. How might you organize this information once you had it available?

Figure 6-2

CHOOSING AN APPROPRIATE WORK SAMPLE

Suppose that you are a senior high school English teacher. You are interested in teaching a unit of instruction on the play "Our Town." During this unit, you will ask individual students to read different parts aloud. Further, there will be class discussions and finally an essay examination that will require students to discuss plot, characterization, and implications of the play for their own lives.

Suppose that you had access to the following work samples (all of these had been completed by students in your class within the last month):

1. Recordings of students reading poetry aloud.
2. Solutions to factoring problems in algebra.
3. Essays on the topic "Symbolism in *War and Peace*."
4. Posters showing the inflation rate changes each year since 1970.
5. Notebooks including outlines of U.S. history textbook chapters.
6. Term papers on topics relating to ecology.
7. Models of the Old Globe Theater.

YOUR OPINION, PLEASE

Read the information above. Then, respond to these questions.

1. Given the availability of these work samples, which one do you think would provide you with the most relevant information? Why?
2. Which one would provide you with the least amount of relevant information? Why?
3. If you had to arrange these work samples in a list from most relevant to least relevant, what would your list look like?
4. Are there any single items on this list that you think to be of no value whatever considering the nature of your proposed unit? If so, which items are they? Why do you feel this way?

---

tense of *être* and *avoir*. By examining these samples, we would be in a position to identify the relative levels of understanding of individual students in the class regarding these important present tense forms.

Diagnostic information of this kind would help to identify students in need of supplementary help with the present tenses of these two key verbs as the new material relating to formation of the *passé composé* was introduced. In short, gathering diagnostic information of this kind and subsequent analysis can help to pinpoint potential problems before they occur. With this information in hand, instructional procedures can be devised that respond to any identified student needs.

In general, the utility of work samples as a source of diagnostic information depends on two factors. First, the work sample must provide information that bears a clear and direct relationship to what is to be taught. Second, the work sample must be current.

Establishing relevancy of a given work sample involves nothing more than the application of common sense. It would make little sense, for example, to look at students' proficiency in tumbling for some indicators as to how they might be expected to fare on a proposed earth science unit on volcanoes. The information about strengths and weaknesses of individual youngsters in tumbling bears almost no connection to the topic of volcanoes. Consequently, little useful diagnostic information would come from an examination of performance in tumbling as a possible indicator of potential student problems on a section of instruction focusing on volcanoes.

Not only must work samples be relevant, they also must be of fairly recent origin. It is almost never legitimate to look at something a student did during a previous year and take the level of performance on that task as a reliable indicator of his or her present level of understanding. Students are exposed to a great many sources of information each day. As time passes since their initial exposure to a certain topic, they may have learned a great deal more about it, they may have stayed the same, or they may have forgotten much of what they once knew. Because of changes in a given student's store of information with the passage of time, a work sample is a useful source of diagnostic information only when the work has been completed fairly recently.

Work samples tend to work best as sources of diagnostic information in courses where new information builds in a clear and logical fashion on previously learned information. Foreign language classes and mathematics classes often proceed in this fashion. In many other courses, however, new units of work may bear scant relationship to previous units. For example, students in a crafts class may finish a unit on throwing pots on a potter's wheel and then begin a unit on tooling leather. Skills demonstrated by individual students on the potter's wheel bear scant relationship to what will be required of them when they begin work on the unit on tooling leather.

Although work samples are not always an appropriate choice as a source of diagnostic information, there are many instances when they can provide very useful insights about students. For example, they are a very time efficient option because the teacher is not required to do anything special to get the information. The work sample is a natural product of previous instruction. It is something that is simply there to be interpreted. Consequently, when work samples are appropriate sources of diagnostic information, there is much to commend their use.

Conference

The conference is nothing more than a one-to-one conversation between a teacher and a student. The conference represents a particularly apt choice as a source of diagnostic information when there is an interest in working with a student who may not feel comfortable in speaking up or participating actively in a large-group setting. Because it is conversational, a conference that is handled properly can put a student at ease and establish a relationship characterized by free and open exchange of information.

Successful conferences do not just happen. They require careful teacher planning. In any conversational setting, the talk may range over a number of topics; in an unplanned conference, then, the conversation may never deal with the issues that prompted the teacher to arrange for the meeting.

Teachers who use the conference technique successfully develop specific objectives that guide their talks with students. These need not be formal. Sometimes even a few lines jotted on a card and placed where they can be seen by the teacher during the conference will suffice. Such notes might include nothing more elaborate than a reference to some general kinds of questions the teacher would like to address with the student. These objectives or guiding questions are particularly important when conferences with more than one student on a given topic are scheduled. The questions prompt teachers to cover the same ground with each student. Analyses of relative strengths, weaknesses, and attitudes of individual students can be made much more reliably when some attention is given to assuring that each student is asked some of the same kinds of questions.

Once conferences are completed, some kind of a written record must be prepared, though beginning teachers tend to overlook this task out of a mistaken belief that they will be able to remember what has been said. Teachers work with tremendous numbers of students, their professional lives are very full, and memories tend to fade, even with the passage of a relatively short period of time. Consequently, some kind of written record of a conference should be completed as soon as possible following the termination of the conference. For example, a teacher who felt that he or she could go one of several directions in a proposed unit on the World War I period might have scheduled conferences to probe student attitudes. A sample summary of one such conference might look something like this:

STUDENT: Leander McKenna

Teacher-Student Conference (March 4, 1982)

Leander and I chatted for about ten minutes this afternoon. He came to see me right after school. With regard to the choice of studying military history, young people on the home front, or technological innovations of war, he seemed to be leaning toward a military history approach. He mentioned that he and his family had visited Gettysburg last year. They went to the museum and saw the map with the lights that accompanied the recorded story of the movements of the various military detachments. He said this experience prompted an interest in military tactics that he'd not had before and that he'd like to learn more about tactics used by World War I participants. In general, he appears quite interested in World War I as a topic.

Written summaries of conferences need not be elaborate. Some may be shorter than this sample, some longer. Information might be placed on index cards and placed in a file box, or a special notebook with one page devoted to conference summaries for each student might be used. The format is much less important than is the decision to prepare a written summary of the conference for future reference. When this is done and a quick reference organizational scheme is developed, the teacher can make some sound diagnostic judgments about individual students in the classroom.

The conference is not without its drawbacks as a diagnostic technique. Perhaps the most important of these is its high cost in terms of teacher time. To be effective, a conference must go on for more than just one or two minutes, but students take a while to warm to the discussion. Few conferences can be accomplished in less than five minutes' time. Ten minutes is probably a more realistic minimum. This time requirement makes it difficult for a teacher to use the conference as a diagnostic technique with an entire class of students. For example, if a teacher decided to hold a ten-minute conference with a class of 30 students, five hours would be required. As a consequence, the conference is best when the teacher feels a special need to speak privately with a small number of students in the classroom.

The conference may engender some classroom management problems as well (or at least it can be accompanied by such difficulties). It is possible for teachers to schedule conferences with students before school, after school, and, possibly, at noon. But, because of bus arrival schedules and after-school work commitments, some conferences may have to be scheduled during regular class time. When this is done, the teacher must provide activities that will engage the attention of other students in the class. This problem is not insurmountable, but it does require some careful attention to planning.

Difficulties associated with the teacher-student conference should not be taken as evidence that the conference is an unsuitable diagnostic technique. When circumstances are appropriate, the conference can provide teachers with a rich and useful store of information.

Anecdotal Record

An anecdotal record is a brief written description about the behavior of a given student. Usually, an anecdotal record will have a specific focus. For example, a teacher interested in establishing a record about a given student's problem behavior in class might focus only on the student's inappropriate actions in the classroom, the purpose being to provide a running record of a given type of student behavior over time. A review of such a record can shed light on the nature of and the persistency of a student characteristic that might be of interest.

Anecdotal records are often used to focus on problem behaviors of students, but by no means are they limited to this purpose. For example, a teacher might be interested in a student's general reaction to essay tests as opposed to multiple-choice tests. Each time a test of either kind is given, the teacher can note the student's reaction in an anecdotal record.

Successful anecdotal records have several key characteristics. First, they tend to have a clear focus. That is, comments in the record tend to relate to a specific topic or theme such as "behavior problems," "patterns of interactions with other students," "interest in science," and so forth. When all comments focus on a selected theme, the collective anecdotal record has potential for telling us something. Lacking such a focus, we are likely to have only a collection of tidbits that tells us very little about an individual student.

Second, when a decision has been made to start an anecdotal record on a given student, it is essential that information be written down when it is fresh. Optimally, the teacher will take a few moments at the end of the class period where the behavior of interest has occurred to add to the anecdotal record. Passage of time tends to erode accuracy of impressions, and the information in the anecdotal record may be less reliable under circumstances where time elapses between the behavior itself and the written comments related to the behavior.

Individual entries in an anecdotal record need not be long. Sometimes a sentence or two will suffice. The records can be kept on index cards, though some teachers prefer to use a notebook.

Anecdotal records present problems, however, when the teachers attempt to maintain them for all students they teach. It simply is not practical to maintain anecdotal records on 160 to 170 students. The tool is best suited for use when a systematic record of the behaviors of a small number of students is desired.

Used properly, the anecdotal record can provide revealing insights relating to attitudes and behavior patterns of individual students. A particularly important feature is its capacity to serve as a "perception check" for the teacher. Although a teacher may think that a given student is behaving in a certain way "all the time," the actual incidence of this behavior may be much less in reality than the teacher thinks. A systematic anecdotal record should demonstrate whether the frequency and nature of the target behavior is what the teacher supposes it to be.

Suppose that a teacher were interested in a student's feelings about the issue of women's rights. Part of the anecdotal record might look something like this:

STUDENT: <u>Roland Allan</u>

Focus: Women's Rights

Dates

2/1   Roland came up after class to ask me why we were going to be "wasting time on this women's rights stuff." He let it be known that the best he could muster was a "ho hum" about the whole subject.

2/2   During class, Roland failed to volunteer during the entire women's rights discussion. He tapped his feet and looked bored throughout the entire period.

2/4   Roland perked up a bit today. He especially took note when the speaker said something about drafting women. He came up to me after class and told me he thought drafting women "is only just." He said something to the effect that if women want to be rewarded as well as men they must face all of the obligations men face. I sense he has been doing a little thinking about the topic.

2/5   I was surprised to find Roland volunteering when I asked for two people to debate this topic on Monday: "Resolved that the women's rights movement is more directed to hurting men then helping women." Roland will be speaking to the affirmative side of the issue.

2/9   Roland came up after class. He thanked me for choosing him to participate in the debate. He indicated he had spent the weekend reading as much as he could on both sides of the issue so he could respond better to some of the arguments. He said the experience had opened him up a bit on the whole question. He said he still leaned a bit on the negative side of the women's rights issue, but he could see some logic at least to the positions being taken by the other side. Clearly he seemed to have developed a genuine interest in the issue as a result of the experience.

The anecdotal record can provide revealing insights about behaviors of individual students as they develop over time. The disadvantage of the approach is that considerable time is required to keep notations for more than a very few students at a time. Consequently, anecdotal records are maintained only on a relatively small number of students whose behaviors a teacher has an interest in tracking in a systematic way.

Checklist

The checklist is a diagnostic technique used to reveal the frequency of occurrence of a specific student behavior of interest to a teacher. A checklist can be used only to measure behavior that can be seen. Further, the behavior has to be something that can be measured at given intervals of time.

Generally a teacher needs an assistant to complete a checklist. It simply is not practical for a teacher to be teaching and interacting with students and, at the same time, to be making notations on a checklist. On the other hand, an observer with no other obligations can complete a checklist quite accurately.

In preparing to complete a checklist, the specific behavior or behaviors to be observed must be identified precisely. Second, a given time span must be determined for each observation. For example, will the observer note what students are doing at a five-minute, ten-minute, or some other time interval? Finally, a total duration for the observation process should be determined. Will the observer be in the classroom only for a single day, a week, or a month or for some other period of time?

A variety of behaviors can be profiled using a checklist. Often they are used when a teacher is concerned with a certain kind of misbehavior. For example, how often is a given student out of his or her seat (without permission) on average during a class period. But checklists can be used for a much wider variety of purposes. Sometimes they are used to determine students' relative interest in different optional activities. Although the "interest" itself cannot be measured directly, a student who spends a great deal of time on one activity is presumed to have a higher preference for this activity than for an alternative.

For purposes of illustration, let us suppose that a teacher in a high school science program provided several activity alternatives to students in his or her classroom. Students would be free to choose from among these activities. The same options would be available to them all week long. Suppose that an observer determined to make a notation once every 15 minutes of what each student was doing. At the end of the week, the observer might have completed a checklist that would look something like the one presented in Figure 6-3. (It is assumed that the observer knows all these students by name.)

A completed checklist can reveal interesting patterns of behavior of the individual students observed. Look, for example, at the sample checklist. There are striking differences among patterns of selected individuals in this class. Note, for instance, that Brent spend the bulk of his time "working at lab stations" or "listening to tape record-

Figure 6-3

SAMPLE CHECKLIST

STUDENTS	Reading Textbook	Reading Supplementary Material	Working at Lab Stations	Viewing Film Loops	Listening to Tape Recordings	Making Models
ALMA	//	////	///	THL /		
BEN	THL //	//			///	///
BETTY	THL //	THL		///		
BRENT			//// //	//	THL /	
CHARLES	THL //	THL ///				
DAVID	THL		THL			THL
DARLA	///	THL	//	//	//	/
EDNA	THL	THL				THL
FARLEY	/	///	////	THL		/
GEORGIA	THL	THL		//		///
HEATHER	THL		THL		THL	
IDA	/	THL	THL	//		//
JAMES	THL	THL	L			
JOANNA			THL		THL	THL
KELLY	//	THL	THL		//	/
LESLIE	THL		///	//	///	//
LARA	THL	THL			THL	
MONTY	//	///	///	//		THL
NORMA	THL	THL		///		//
OLGA	/	//	THL	///	/	///

Tallies were taken at 15-minute intervals (about three per each 50-minute class period) over a five-day period from January 31 through February 4, inclusive.

ings," whereas Norma spent most of her time "reading the textbook" or "reading supplementary material." This information can prove invaluable for the teacher of this class in planning future learning experiences for these two students. Brent seems to indicate a preference for learning via a nonreading mode. Norma, on the other hand, seems to enjoy getting her information from prose materials. With these insights, the teacher can plan instructional experiences that will take into account these individual student characteristics.

Often, a checklist is not kept on an entire class at a time. Sometimes a teacher may have an interest in the behaviors only of a small number of students. The task of the observer becomes somewhat easier under these conditions in that he or she has a smaller number of individuals to watch.

In summary, the checklist can provide useful information. Perhaps the largest drawback to its use is its dependence on the availability of an observer to sit in the classroom and keep a running tally of the numbers of time targeted behaviors occur. But, when arrangements to do this can be made, the checklist can yield some very worthwhile diagnostic information that can be most helpful in planning future learning experiences.

Interest Inventory

Perhaps one of the most difficult areas for teachers to diagnose is in the area of attitudes. Frequently we are interested in how students feel about what we are teaching or are intending to teach. Yet such information is not easy to acquire. One useful tool that can be used to obtain information of this type is the interest inventory.

An interest inventory asks students to rate their relative degree of like or dislike for each of a number of alternatives with which they are presented. Teachers using interest inventories for diagnostic purposes may provide students with lists of different topic or activity options that they are considering introducing in subsequent sections of their courses. They use results as a basis for identifying the specific activities and topics they will feature. In general, they try to accommodate areas of high student interest. (Of course, it never is possible to please all of the students all of the time.)

To see how an interest inventory might work, suppose that a high school English teacher was considering what kinds of things to emphasize during the last quarter of the year. He or she might have identified a number of areas and organized them on an interest inventory such as the one depicted in Figure 6-4.

Once interest inventories such as the one depicted in Figure 6-4 have been completed, the teacher is in a position to identify both areas of interest of individual students

Figure 6-4

SAMPLE INTEREST INVENTORY

YOUR NAME: _____

Directions: Below are listed a number of alternatives we might pursue during the last quarter of the school year. There is a blank provided in front of each choice. Place a "1" in the blank before your highest preference, a "2" in front of your second highest preference, and so forth. Continue this process until you conclude with a "10" in front of your least preferred choice.

_____ Study American short stories.
_____ Write short stories.
_____ Study American plays.
_____ Study European plays.
_____ Write epic poems.
_____ Study structural elements of poetry.
_____ Read a modern novel.
_____ Study nineteenth-century American poetry.
_____ Study short selections of nineteenth-century "realism."
_____ Write one-act plays.

and patterns of interest within the class. This information can be used as the basis for instructional planning. According to the sample, the teacher might identify a cluster of students who would be assigned to work with a modern novel, another that might be assigned to work with some nineteenth-century American poetry, and still another that might be interested in writing some short stories. In short, information from interest inventories can provide a rational basis for teachers to provide a number of instructional alternatives to a class of students.

Teacher Tests

Teacher tests represent a rich source of diagnostic information. Tests used for diagnosis can be of two basic types. On the one hand, they can be regular tests given over previously taught content. On the other hand, they can be specially prepared diagnostic tests that have little or nothing to do with content to which students have been exposed previously.

In general, it is appropriate to use tests over previously taught content for diagnostic purposes when a course is organized in such a way that successive lessons and units build systematically upon what has been taught already. For example, an algebra teacher about to introduce a unit on factoring builds logically on previously taught information about manipulation of algebraic symbols. Thus, a test given earlier over basic information related to manipulation of these basic algebraic symbols may well give the teacher valuable insights regarding which students might be expected to have difficulties during the new instruction focusing on factoring. (Clearly students with a shaky understanding of the more basic processes might be expected to have difficulties with the new, more sophisticated material.)

In using previously administered tests for diagnostic purposes, we need to look not at the total score so much as the individual items each student missed. Suppose that we had just taught a section on basic structure of poetry. We were intending to go into a unit on interpretation of poetry next. At the conclusion of the lesson on the basic structure of poetry we gave students a 25-question multiple-choice test. Five questions focused on each of these major topics: (1) caesura, (2) rhyme scheme, (3) meter, (4) alliteration, and (5) assonance. Suppose that four students scored as following on this test:

	John	Bob	Laura	Jane
CAESURA	5	5	5	5
RHYME SCHEME	4	5	0	0
METER	5	0	5	0
ALLITERATION	4	5	3	0
ASSONANCE	3	5	4	4
	21	20	17	9	TOTAL TEST SCORES

The scores made by each student on each section of the test are depicted in the matrix. Note the information we can gather by looking at the patterns of correct and incorrect answers on each topic area covered by the examination. For example, Bob, who had a fairly good total test score, missed all items relating to meter; clearly he should have help in this area. For Jane, on the other hand, despite a very low total test score, she does indicate reasonably good control over the concepts caesura and assonance; she needs help on rhyme scheme, meter, and alliteration. Clearly an examination of these answer patterns can tell us a good deal about the specific lack of understanding a given student might have. It points up, too, the importance of preparing tests in such a way that individual questions are tied clearly to identifiable content areas.

It is not always practical to use a test given over previously taught material for diagnostic purposes. Such a procedure obviously cannot be followed at the beginning of the year (or at any other time when instruction begins with a new group of students). Clearly there has been no previous instruction at this time. Even at midyear, previous test grades may provide little diagnostic information if new lessons do not build logically on what has been learned in previous units and lessons. Some areas of the subject curriculum are not sequential. For example, a physical education class may spend a few weeks on ballroom dancing and then move on to tumbling. The relationship between ballroom dancing skills and tumbling is certainly not clear and direct. Consequently, little diagnostic information relevant to the new unit on tumbling logically could be expected to result from a systematic analysis of evaluations of students based on their performance during the ballroom dancing unit.

The quality of diagnostic information that can result from examinations of student performances on teacher-prepared tests depends to a great extent on the quality of the test questions themselves. Some guidelines for the preparation of sound test items are introduced in Chapter 11, "Measuring, Evaluating, and Reporting Student Progress."

Cloze Procedure

The range of reading abilities in a given classroom represents a challenge to the great majority of secondary school teachers. Student teachers and first-year teachers often find themselves shocked at the reading deficiencies of many youngsters in their classrooms. In thinking about a new unit of instruction, teachers can estimate likely difficulties of individual students through use of the Cloze procedure.

Developed by Wilson Taylor (1953), the Cloze procedure provides an indication of a given individual's likely reading difficulty with a specific prose item. In using the Cloze procedure, the teacher takes a sample of material from a text (or from other print material that will be used during the new unit). The selected passage should be at least 250 words in length. Somewhat longer passages are desirable in that resultant student scores will tend to be more reliable. These directions should be followed in using a Cloze procedure:

1. A sample passage at least 250 words in length is identified. The teacher types this passage, using double or triple spacing, in such a way that every fifth word is omitted. This rule is followed except when the fifth word falls at the beginning of a sentence. When this happens, the beginning word in the sentence is retained and the second word is omitted. (Following this omission, the count resumes again and every succeeding fifth word is omitted.) In preparing this passage, sufficient space should be left where words have been omitted to allow students to write in omitted words.
2. Students should be provided with the completed test sheets. They should be told to fill in the blanks with words that give the passage good logical sense.
3. To score the tests, count as correct only words that students have provided that are *exactly the same* as those in the original passage. (Accept misspellings. Do not accept synonyms.) Compute the percentage of correct words. For example, given a 250-word passage with 50 blanks, a student with 38 correct responses would have received a percentage-correct score of 76 (38/50 = .76).

Student scores on the completed Cloze procedure should be interpreted as follows:

1. A student receiving a score of 58 percent or higher should be regarded as operating at the *independent level.* This means that he or she should be able to read and master the material from which the sample was drawn with minimal help from the teacher.
2. A student with a percentage score falling in the 44 to 57 percent range should be regarded as operating at the *instructional level.* This means that he or she should be able to read and learn from this material provided that teacher assistance is forthcoming, particularly with the more difficult sections.
3. A student receiving a score of 43 percent or lower should be regarded as operating at the *frustrational level.* Such an individual might be expected to experience great difficulty in reading the material from which the sample was drawn. For the teacher, a score at the frustrational level suggests a need to locate some alternate, less difficult reading materials (of course, they cannot always be located or prepared, but, when available, they should be provided to frustrational-level readers). (Percentage figures are from Bormuth, 1968.)

To see how a Cloze procedure might appear, suppose we were at the beginning of the school year and had been assigned to teach a world geography course. Our assigned text is to be *The Wide World* by Preston E. James and Nelda Davis. Our Cloze procedure would be prepared from a sample taken from this text. An example of a procedure drawn from this material is provided in Figure 6-5.

An advantage of the Cloze procedure is that it provides information not about the general difficulty of a given prose selection but about the prospects for success of individual students who will be working with this material. Once such information is in hand, the teacher can identify youngsters with potential reading difficulties. Other less difficult materials can be found, or certain sections of the material can be rewritten by the teacher at a less sophisticated reading level. (Clearly this latter option does not always represent a practical alternative. Teachers do not have time to rewrite entire textbooks.) Specific procedures for rewriting materials so that they are comprehensible to less able readers and other information about the vexing area of reading are introduced in Chapter 16, "Reading Problems and Secondary Students."

Error-Pattern Analysis

Teachers of mathematics and other areas in which applied mathematics skills are needed have interests in developing students' computational proficiencies. Although these teachers typically experience little difficulty in spotting a student with a problem, the cause for or source of the lack of proficiency has proved difficult to identify. Today, more sophisticated diagnostic tools are becoming available to teachers with interests in this area. One such tool is error-pattern analysis.

Error-pattern analysis, as described by Mattair (1980), provides teachers with a

Figure 6-5

SAMPLE CLOZE PROCEDURE

When you study history, _____ read about how people _____ changed their ways of
                                    1   2

_____ . Sometimes events and sometimes _____ leaders have brought about _____
   3   4   5

in culture. But if _____ look more closely at _____ story of man on _____ earth, you
              6   7   8

will find _____ there were long periods _____ time during which few, _____ any,
        9   10   11

important changes took _____ . In every generation, to _____ sure, there are some
                  12   13

_____ who suggest new ideas _____ ways of doing things. But _____ are many more
  14   15   16

who _____ change and want to _____ things as they are. In _____ long stream of
      17   18   19

history, _____ have been thousands and _____ of years during which _____ basic
      20   21   22

changes took place _____ man's way of living. Then, _____ were periods of very
         23   24

_____ change called *revolutions.*
  25

   Since _____ appearance of *Homo sapiens* _____ or more years ago, _____ have
        26   27   28

been only three _____ revolutions. The first one _____ place before man had _____
        29   30   31

how to keep written _____ . We can find out _____ it only by digging _____ ancient
           32   33   34

ruins, by studying _____ spears or arrowheads and _____ out the dates when _____
         35   36   37

were used, or by _____ the bones of animals _____ by prehistoric campfires. Students
        38   39

_____ ancient man who collect _____ kind of evidence are _____ *archaelogists.*
  40   41   42

   The first great _____ in the story of _____ *sapiens* took place when _____ found
             43   44   45

out how to _____ plants and to domesticate _____ Before man discovered the
        46   47

_____ of agriculture, he lived _____ gathering the fruits and _____ of wild plants. . . .
  48   49   50

KEY

1. you	11. if	21. thousands	31. learned	41. this
2. have	12. place	22. no	32. records	42. called
3. living	13. be	23. in	33. about	43. revolution
4. great	14. people	24. there	34. up	44. *Homo*
5. changes	15. and	25. great	35. broken	45. man
6. you	16. there	26. the	36. figuring	46. cultivate
7. the	17. oppose	27. 50,000	37. they	47. animals
8. the	18. keep	28. there	38. examining	48. secrets
9. that	19. the	29. such	39. charred	49. by
10. of	20. there	30. took	40. of	50. seeds

Source: Preston E. James and Nelda Davis, *The Wide World* (New York: Macmillan Publishing Co., Inc., 1972), pp. 155–156. Reprinted with permission.

mechanism for studying student computational mistakes with a view to spotting repeated patterns. The basic error pattern provides the teacher with an explanation of the specific kind of mistake the student is making in arriving at an incorrect solution to a computational problem. Mattair suggests four basic types of errors. These errors, and their characteristics, are as follows:

Type A: Procedural Errors

1. Student follows an incorrect order of steps.
2. Student fails to complete the entire computational process.

Type B: Conceptual Errors

1. Student fails to understand the meaning and properties of an operation.
2. Student misapprehends the structure of the numeration system.
3. Student makes renaming and regrouping errors.

Type C: Operational Errors

1. Student uses the correct facts for the operation but follows a procedure for a different operation.
2. Student follows a procedure and basic facts that are appropriate for another operation but not for this operation.

Type D: Factual Errors

1. Student uses facts that are incorrect for this operation.

To use this scheme to identify error patterns, suppose that a teacher had asked students to do some multiplication exercises. On John Smith's paper, the teacher noted the following:

$$
\begin{array}{llll}
\text{A.} \quad {}^{1}47 & \text{B.} \quad {}^{1}64 & \text{C.} \quad {}^{2}74 & \text{D.} \quad {}^{2}93 \\
\underline{\times \ 2} & \underline{\times \ 3} & \underline{\times \ 5} & \underline{\times \ 7} \\
\quad 104 & \quad 212 & \quad 450 & \quad 771
\end{array}
$$

Let us look at what this student has done. Note the first problem. He has multiplied 2 times 7 and arrived correctly at 14. He wrote down the 4 correctly below the line. But now his troubles began. Instead of multiplying 2 times 4 and then adding 1 to the total of 8 to give him a 9 and a correct answer of 94, John reversed the order of the operations. That is, he added 1 to 4 first, then proceeded to multiply the resultant 5 by 2. This 10 then was brought down to yield an incorrect answer of 104. This same mistake of reversing the order of the operations occurs in all of these problems. Referring to Mattair's list of error types (1980), we see that this is a clear example of a type A, or procedural, error.

Another student in the class, Sonja Johnson made these mistakes on four problems on the test:

$$
\begin{array}{llll}
\text{A.} \quad 55 & \text{B.} \quad 73 & \text{C.} \quad 47 & \text{D.} \quad 25 \\
\underline{\times \ 32} & \underline{\times \ 74} & \underline{\times \ 36} & \underline{\times \ 54} \\
\quad 110 & \quad 292 & \quad 282 & \quad 100 \\
\underline{\quad 165} & \underline{\quad 511} & \underline{\quad 141} & \underline{\quad 125} \\
\quad 275 & \quad 803 & \quad 423 & \quad 225
\end{array}
$$

Quick inspection of Sonja's work reveals that she failed to shift the product of the second phase of the multiplication on space to the left. That is, the first problem should have been solved as

$$
\begin{array}{r}
55 \\
\times\ 32 \\
\hline
110 \\
165 \\
\hline
1{,}760
\end{array}
$$

Failure to shift appears in all of Sonja's problems. This is a type B, or conceptual, error. The student simply has not learned the properties of the multiplication operation.

Another student in the class, Norman, missed these four problems:

$$
\begin{array}{llll}
\text{A.}\quad {}^{2}88 & \text{B.}\quad {}^{2}27 & \text{C.}\quad {}^{1}46 & \text{D.}\quad {}^{3}26 \\
\underline{\times\ 23} & \underline{\times\ 34} & \underline{\times\ 42} & \underline{\times\ 56} \\
\quad\ 184 & \quad\ 88 & \quad\ 172 & \quad\ 136
\end{array}
$$

Look at the first problem. Norman correctly multiplied 3 times 8, got 24, and wrote down 4. He went astray during the next step. He placed a carry-forward 2 above the 8 in the left-hand column. Then, he multiplied 2 times 8 and added the carry-forward 2 to 16. This yielded 18. He brought down this 18 to produce his final incorrect answer of 184. This same pattern appeared in the other three problems as well. The student has made a type C, or operational, error by mixing inappropriately steps used in multiplication and addition operations.

Another student, Sarah, missed these problems:

$$
\begin{array}{llll}
\text{A.}\quad 56 & \text{B.}\quad 63 & \text{C.}\quad 29 & \text{D.}\quad 296 \\
\underline{\times\ 19} & \underline{\times\ 29} & \underline{\times\ 62} & \underline{\times\ 69} \\
506 & 587 & 58 & 2666 \\
\underline{\ 56\ } & \underline{126} & \underline{176} & \underline{1796} \\
1{,}066 & 1{,}847 & 1{,}818 & 20{,}626
\end{array}
$$

In the first problem, Sarah has multiplied 6 times 9 and arrived at the incorrect answer of 56. This same mistake is repeated in each of the remaining problems. Sarah, evidently, does not have solid control over her basic multiplication tables. Her mistakes are an example of a type D, or factual, error.

Error-pattern analysis can provide teachers with useful information about the types of computational difficulties being experienced by a given student, with the result that the teacher can provide instruction targeted to remedying identified deficiencies.

Examples of error-pattern analysis provided here are rudimentary. The technique has been developed and applied to problems involving the basic operations of addition, subtraction, multiplication, and division of whole numbers. Work has also been done with fractions and decimals and with algebraic and other symbolic representations. New interest in computational skills suggests that a good deal of attention will be given to refining additional diagnostic techniques in this area in the years ahead.

ORGANIZING DIAGNOSTIC INFORMATION

Once diagnostic information has been gathered, some mechanism is needed to organize it systematically. Without some attention to organization, it is difficult for a teacher to gain the maximum benefit from the time that he or she has spent in obtaining the information. Let us see how an organizational scheme might work.

Suppose that Laura Smith had been assigned to teach a course in world geography. At the beginning of the school year, she decided she would like to have some information about a number of selected geographic understandings and about a number of skills. She identified the specific understandings and skills in which she was interested by thinking through the kind of material to which she hoped to expose students and the kinds of presumptions she had about what they ought to know already. She decided that she had an interest in students' grasp of these understandings and skills:

Understandings

1. Locations of major European nations
2. Locations of major Asian nations
3. Locations of major African nations
4. Locations of major South American nations
5. Locations of major nations of the Central and Southern Pacific region
6. The concept "capital"
7. The concept "country"
8. The concept "continent"

Skills

1. Reading skills
2. Skills in locating places using coordinates of latitude and longitude
3. Skills in acquiring information introduced via graphs and charts

Having identified these areas of concern, Ms. Smith selected a number of diagnostic techniques that would provide her with information about how each student in her class stood with respect to each of the identified understanding and skill areas. Once this information was in hand, she developed a diagnostic profile chart on which she noted students with severe difficulties in each understanding and skill area. She devised a scheme of her own to determine exactly how poor a given youngster's level of understanding or skill proficiency would have to be to be labeled a "severe" problem. (There is no clear and objective standard for accomplishing this task. While a teacher interested in something like reading proficiency might decide that a Cloze score indicating frustration-level reading constituted a severe problem, where diagnostic information is gathered via such procedures as individual conferences clear-cut guidelines are lacking. A good deal of subjective teacher judgment is involved.) An example of Ms. Smith's diagnostic profile chart is given in Figure 6-6.

Information gathered together and displayed on a diagnostic profile chart provides a great deal of useful information to the teacher. Note, for example, in the chart that there are vast differences in the numbers of students in the class experiencing difficulties in the various understanding and skill areas. Three areas seem to be difficult for a fairly large number of students in the class. Fully 11 students (out of 23) have problems in identifying locations of major Asian nations. Eight have similar difficulties with regard to nations in Africa. Six have been identified as having severe reading problems. Although other areas posed difficulties for some class members, the diagnostic profile chart suggests that these difficulties tended not to be widespread.

In reviewing this information, our teacher, Ms. Smith, might conclude that, given the large numbers of youngsters with shaky understandings regarding locations of nations in Asia and Africa, a general class review of this information might be in order. Lacking that, some easy-to-read and high-interest student material might be prepared in handout form to share with the youngsters for whom problems in these areas have been noted.

Figure 6-6

DIAGNOSTIC PROFILE CHART

STUDENT*	UNDERSTANDINGS								SKILLS		
	Locations of Major European Nations	Locations of Major Asian Nations	Locations of Major African Nations	Locations of Major South American Nations	Locations of Major Nations of the Central and Southern Pacific Region	Capital	Country	Continent	Severe Reading Skills Problem	Severe Problem in Locating Places Using Latitude and Longitude	Severe Problem in Understanding Information Presented on Graphs and Charts
ALDERSON	X	X								X	
ANDREWS		X	X	X	X			X	X		
BELTONA											X
CAVERA											
DENISOVICH		X									
EPHRAMSON			X						X		

130

Name										
FARLEY			X			X		X	X	
GREGSON			X	X				X	X	
HIGHTOWER	X								X	X
IBANIK										
JOHNSON										
KELLER		X		X	X					
LAVATRONI										
MUELLER										
NORTH								X	X	
O'BANION			X	X			X	X	X	
O'BILLOVICH										
PAULEY									X	
QUENTONSEN								X	X	
RAVELLA	X	X								
STANTON								X	X	
TORELLI			X						X	
URBAN									X	X
TOTALS	3	3	6	3	1	2	2	8	12	3

*Students thought to have severe problems in an area are indicated by "X's."

The information related to reading skills suggests that many youngsters in this class are going to experience considerable difficulty with the text. (This assumes that a label of "severe reading skills problem" was attached to students whose Cloze test scores on a selection taken from the course text were at the frustration level.) An indication of a high incidence of reading difficulty should spur Ms. Smith on to find or develop less sophisticated supplementary reading materials that convey much of the same material as is presented in the adopted course text.

On the positive side, development of a diagnostic profile chart can provide information about areas in which students seem to be well grounded both in understandings and skills. Note, for example, in Ms. Smith's class (see Figure 6-6) that no student seems to have a severe problem with the concept "capital." Very few have problems locating major European nations or South American nations. The concept "country" does not appear to be a severe problem. Finally, most students in the class have an acceptable grasp of locating places using latitude and longitude coordinates and of obtaining information presented on graphs and charts. Diagnostic information of this kind can reduce the time spent on areas that tend to be fairly well understood by students in the class.

In looking at individual students, it is evident that some have no severe deficiencies in any of these areas. Many more have problems only in a very few areas. Some need help on a number of the understanding and skill areas that have been identified. Once the diagnostic profile chart has been prepared, the teacher needs to answer the question "What can I do for each student with a problem?" Some teachers find it useful to prepare a master "prescription list" of possible ways students can be helped. This prescription list contains specific suggestions for helping students with problems to master individual understandings and skills. A sample prescription list is provided in Figure 6-7.

Figure 6-7

SAMPLE PRESCRIPTION LIST

SUBJECT: WORLD GEOGRAPHY

UNDERSTANDINGS

1. Locations of major European nations

   Possible Prescriptions

   a. Listen to European Place Names cassette from "The Wide World" program.
   b. Complete short programmed-learning packet on this subject.
   c. Use atlas and accompanying study guide to identify locations.
   d. Complete a "take-home" map requiring proper identification of locations.

2. Locations of major Asian nations

   Possible Prescriptions

   a. Listen to Asian Place Names cassette from "The Wide World" program.
   b. Complete short programmed-learning packet on this subject.
   c. Use atlas and accompanying study guide to identify locations.
   d. Complete a "take-home" map requiring proper identification of locations.

3. Locations of major African nations

   Possible Prescriptions

   a. Listen to African Place Names cassette from "The Wide World" program.
   b. Complete short programmed-learning packet on this subject.
   c. Use atlas and accompanying study guide to identify locations.
   d. Complete a "take-home" map requiring proper identification of locations.

4. Locations of major South American nations

   Possible Prescriptions

   a. Listen to South American Place Names cassette from "The Wide World" program.
   b. Complete short programmed-learning packet on this subject.
   c. Use atlas and accompanying study guide to identify locations.
   d. Complete a "take-home" map requiring proper identification of locations.

5. Locations of major nations of the Central and Southern Pacific region

   Possible Prescriptions

   a. Listen to Central and Southern Pacific Region Place Names cassette from "The Wide World" program.
   b. Complete short programmed-learning packet on this subject.
   c. Use atlas and accompanying guide to identify locations.
   d. Complete a "take-home" map requiring proper identification of locations.

6. The concept "capital"

   Possible Prescriptions

   None needed. No students with severe deficiencies in this area.

7. The concept "country."

   Possible Prescriptions

   a. Read a short hand-out, readability level grade 6 or below, in which clear distinctions are drawn between the concepts "county," "country," and "continent."
   b. Listen to cassette tape in which concepts "county," "country," and "continent" are defined and examples are provided of each.

8. The concept "continent"

   Possible Prescriptions

   a. Read a short hand-out, readability level grade 6 or below, in which clear distinctions are drawn between the concepts "county," "country," and "continent."
   b. Listen to cassette tape in which concepts "county," "country," and "continent" are defined and examples are provided of each.

SKILLS

1. Severe reading problems

   Possible Prescriptions

   a. Refer student to school reading clinic for assistance.
   b. Prepare tape recordings of key portions of text for student to listen to.
   c. Prepare rewritten versions of key text sections that are easier to read than the textbook itself.

2. Severe problem in location places using latitude and longitude

   Possible Prescriptions

   a. Listen to the cassette tape from "The Wide World" program that explains latitude and longitude and that points out how places can be found using map coordinates.
   b. Complete a short programmed-learning packet focusing on coordinates of longitude and latitude.
   c. Complete the self-study guide on longitude and latitude that accompanies the student at.as.

3. Severe problem in understanding information presented on graphs and charts

   Possible Prescriptions

   a. Complete teacher-prepared hand-out entitled: "How to Read Graphs and Charts."
   b. Work introductory lessons in Educational Research Associates kit entitled "Graphic Literacy Materials."

Once a list of prescriptions has been identified, specific actions for individual students can be prepared. Suppose, for example, that our Ms. Smith was interested in doing something for the student in her class with the last name of Gregson. From Figure 6-6, we see that this person was found to have severe difficulties in four areas. Namely (1) locations of major Asian nations, (2) locations of major African nations, (3) the concept of continent, and (4) textbook reading. A prescription for this person might be formulated from the master prescription list (see Figure 6-7) that would look like this:

STUDENT: Gregson

Prescription List

Problem: Location of major Asian nations.

   Task: Listen to Asian place names cassette from *The Wide Wide World* program.

Problem: Location of major African nations.

   Task: Complete a take-home map requiring proper identification of major African nations.

Problem: Lack of understanding of the concept "continent."

   Task: Listen to cassette tape in which concepts "county," "country," and "continent" are defined and examples are provided of each.

Problem: Severe reading problems (Cloze procedure reveals text is at "frustration level").

   Tasks: Complete remedial work as directed by school reading laboratory.

   Listen to tape recordings prepared by teacher of important textbook passages to supplement reading of the text itself.

Certainly such a prescription cannot guarantee improvement. But it can provide some reasonable assurance to the teacher that a rational response to a student's difficulty has been developed. Provision has been made for the student to engage in learning experiences holding some real promise for remediating difficulties. Although success cannot be assured, a systematic response to identified difficulties raises the chances for closing whatever learning gaps have been identified.

DIAGNOSIS: SOME CAUTIONARY NOTES

We recognize that some of the procedures described in the previous sections, particularly those related to preparing classroom diagnostic profile charts and prescription lists, seem to involve an inordinate amount of teacher time. Certainly, we are *not* advocating the development of diagnostic procedures that are so elaborate that they rob precious time from other important tasks. We know that this can happen. A few teachers in our experience have become so enamoured with elegant diagnostic procedures that their professional focus shifted improperly from instruction of students to a concern for developing visually elegant profiles of students across many dimensions. Such is not the purpose of diagnosis. Figure 6-8 outlines some proper concerns in this area.

Proper diagnosis provides information to teachers in a time-efficient manner that has real practical utility for their own instruction. It helps them to pinpoint problem areas for individual students and, in general, makes for a more productive learning environment. We are convinced that these objectives are achieved most efficiently when some attention is given to systematizing the diagnostic process. That is why we suggest

Figure 6-8

WHAT KIND OF DIAGNOSTIC INFORMATION?

In thinking about what kinds of diagnostic information are needed, a teacher has to consider what he or she already knows about his or her students, the kinds of assumptions he or she is making about what students already know, and the level of sophistication assumed by the producers of the learning materials that will be used. In short, the kinds of diagnostic information that are worthwhile will vary dramatically from situation to situation.

YOUR OPINION, PLEASE

Read the paragraph above. Consider your own academic preparation. Assume that you are about to begin teaching a course that typically is taught by teachers in your subject area specialty. It is the beginning of the school year. Respond to the following questions.

1. What kinds of diagnostic information would you like to have? Specifically, what understandings and skills would it be critical for you to have diagnostic information about?
2. How would you justify your choice to another professional in your field? In general, do you think most in your field would agree or disagree with your choices? Why?
3. There are many ways in which to organize diagnostic information to reveal a general picture of how students in a given class stand. One procedure is depicted in Figure 6-6. Develop a scheme of your own to provide a quick picture of how students in your class stand in terms of the understandings and skills you have identified.
4. What kinds of things would you do to help students with deficiencies? Try your hand at developing a master table of prescriptions. Then, suggest a prescription for an individual youngster.
5. How do you think your suggestions for helping youngsters with problems would be regarded by others in your field?

---

the use of a diagnostic profile sheet for a class and a table of prescriptions. We do not recommend that these profiles and tables of prescriptions be so elaborate that time is invested at the expense of other important instructional responsibilities; rather, we introduce these procedures as suggestions about what a teacher might do to organize and respond to diagnostic information. Certainly modifications of these procedures might work much better for some teachers than those that have been introduced here.

Posttest

Directions: Using your own paper, answer each of the following true/false questions. For each correct statement, write the word ''true.'' For each incorrect statement, write the word ''false.''

_____ 1. It is recommended that teachers spend at least as much time gathering diagnostic information about students as they spend instructing students.

_____ 2. A sample of a student's previous work is likely to be a better indicator of his or her present understanding when the work was accomplished relatively recently than when it was accomplished some time ago.

_____ 3. In thinking about which diagnostic procedures to use, teachers are advised to consider the time required to gather the information they want.

_____ 4. The teacher-student conference is recognized widely as the most time-efficient procedure a teacher can use to gather diagnostic information about an entire class of students.

_____ 5. The Cloze procedure is used to assess a student's likelihood of experiencing difficulty with certain mathematical operations.

_____ 6. An interest inventory is used frequently to gather information about students' attitudes.

_____ 7. Information about the frequency of occurrence of a given behavior can be gathered through the use of a checklist.

_____ 8. Diagnostic information sometimes is gathered both about students' mastery of skills and students' levels of subject matter comprehension.

_____ 9. If a teacher wanted to find out whether students understand enough about European geography to comprehend a proposed unit on battlefield movements during World War I, good diagnostic information might be gathered through use of a teacher-prepared test.

_____ 10. While it is desirable for teachers to gather diagnostic information about individual students, it is considered unethical for teachers to develop instructional procedures for students identified as having potential problems that differ from those used with the rest of the class.

Key Ideas in Review

1. Public schools enroll all comers. This means that the diversity reflected in public schools parallels to a large degree the diversity found in the population at large. Given these differences, teachers need to learn as much as possible about individual students in their classrooms. This information enables them to prepare instructional experiences that are appropriate for individual students. A number of diagnostic approaches are available for teachers interested in gathering information about specific students.

2. Beginning teachers sometimes make the error of spending too much time gathering and interpreting diagnostic information. It is an unwise use of scarce teacher time to become so involved in diagnostic activities that other important responsibilities are slighted. Optimal diagnostic procedures are those that can provide a great deal of information in a time-efficient manner.

3. Differences among individual students in the classroom tend to increase with each succeeding year in school. There are, for example, much more profound differences in aptitudes and interests of high school seniors than in aptitudes and interests of elementary school youngsters. This situation makes it imperative for secondary school teachers to have good diagnostic skills.

4. A variety of special diagnostic techniques are available for teachers to use. Each has advantages and disadvantages. In general, teachers need to use diagnostic techniques that will provide them with the information they want in an efficient manner. These techniques may be divided into two categories. One category is used to provide information about students' understandings; a second category includes procedures designed to provide information about students' proficiency on certain important skills.

5. Once it has been gathered, diagnostic information must be organized. Organized diagnostic information permits a teacher to review special needs of individual students. Further, through use of a device such as a diagnostic profile chart, a teacher can identify general patterns of strengths and weaknesses in the class as a whole.

6. Once students have been identified who have certain learning deficiencies, the teacher must decide what is to be done. One recommended procedure is the development of a master prescription list. A prescription list includes a host of alternative learning experiences that might be provided for learners having difficulty with certain intellectual understandings and skills. Once learners with problems have been identified, the teacher can put together an appropriate remedial program for the individual by drawing items from the prescription list.

SUMMARY

The diversity reflected in America's classrooms suggests that individual students vary tremendously in terms of their interests and attitudes. This diversity is even more pronounced at the secondary school level than during earlier school grades. Differences among students suggest a special need for secondary school teachers to master effective diagnostic techniques. Information gathered during a systematic diagnostic program can provide a basis for instructional planning that truly is differentiated to meet needs of individual students.

A variety of diagnostic techniques is available. In deciding which to use, teachers need to consider the nature of their student population, the nature of the content they will be teaching, and the time available for gathering diagnostic information. In general, diagnostic techniques that permit gathering a great deal of pertinent information in a short period of time are preferred. Diagnosis must be accomplished expeditiously. To spend too much time on diagnosis is to rob essential teacher time from other critical instructional tasks.

Once diagnostic information is in hand, it must be organized. A diagnostic profile sheet or some other device is needed that allows for a quick inspection both of strengths and weaknesses of individual youngsters and of a class as a whole. After such an identification has been made, the teacher can move on to design individual remedial programs for students found to be deficient in terms of intellectual understandings and in terms of skill proficiencies. Some teachers find it profitable to develop a master list of probable prescriptions from which they can draw in planning remedial activities for individual learners.

Finally, diagnosis focuses teachers' attention on individual students. It helps to bring into clear focus the nature of the diversity represented in the classroom. While no diagnostic and remediation program claims to reach 100 percent of the students, still it is safe to say that teachers who diagnose and prescribe carefully reach more students than teachers who do not.

References

Armstrong, David G.; Denton, Jon J.; and Savage, Tom V. *Instructional Skills Handbook*. Englewood Cliffs, N.J.: Educational Technology Publications, 1978.

Blair, Glenn M. *Diagnostic and Remedial Teaching: A Guide to Practice in Elementary and Secondary Schools*. (Rev. ed.) New York: Macmillan Publishing Co., Inc., 1956.

Bormuth, John R. "The Cloze Readability Procedure," *Elementary English* (April 1968): 429–436.

James, Preston E., and Davis, Nelda. *The Wide World*. New York: Macmillan Publishing Co., Inc., 1972.

Lee, Doris M. *Diagnostic Teaching*. Washington, D.C.: National Education Association, 1966.

Mattair, Judy E. M. "The Use of Error-Pattern Analysis in the Diagnosis and Remediation of Computational Difficulties Involving Whole Number Operations." Unpublished doctoral dissertation. Texas A&M University, 1980.

Taylor, Wilson L. "Cloze Procedure: A New Tool for Measuring Readability," *Journalism Quarterly* (Fall 1953): 415–433.

Wilson, John A. R., ed. *Diagnosis of Learning Difficulties*. New York: McGraw-Hill Book Company, 1971.

7

Selecting Content and Establishing Instructional Objectives

''He used to teach mere facts. Then he moved on to concepts. Lately he's been into generalizations. He's striving for the universal galactic principle that governs all things . . . and that's a *fact!*''

Objectives

This chapter provides information to help the reader to

1. Identify content that is to be taught.
2. Distinguish among goals, generalizations, and concepts.
3. Describe the function of instructional objectives.
4. Write instructional objectives using the ABCD format.
5. Differentiate among general characteristics of cognitive, affective, and psychomotor learning.
6. Prepare instructional objectives at different levels of cognitive sophistication.
7. Recognize the relationship between instructional objectives and selected other elements of the overall instructional planning process.

Pretest

Directions: Using your own paper, answer each of the following true/false questions. For each correct statement, write the word "true." For each incorrect statement, write the word "false."

_____ 1. Instructional objectives are developed for use only by teachers as they plan instruction; they should never be shared openly with students.

_____ 2. Educational goals provide learners with specific information about what they are expected to learn from a given instructional sequence.

_____ 3. Typically, instructional objectives are written in such a way that expected student behavior is described precisely. That is, the behavior described is capable of being observed by the teacher.

_____ 4. Instructional objectives focusing on students' attitudes are affective-domain objectives.

_____ 5. Generally, more instructional time is required for students to master an analysis-level instructional objective than a knowledge-level instructional objective.

_____ 6. There should be a clear connection between instructional objectives and what the teacher does in the classroom.

_____ 7. Instructional objectives focusing on students' abilities to complete tasks calling on them to use fine motor skills generally are classified as objectives in the psychomotor domain.

_____ 8. Instructional objectives help to focus students' attention on elements of content that have been identified as relevant and important.

_____ 9. Verbs such as "appreciate," "know," and "understand" are among those most preferred to describe expected student behavior in an instructional objective.

_____ 10. In deciding what to teach, the most professional approach is simply to start at the beginning of the assigned textbook and work chapter by chapter to the end of the assigned textbook.

INTRODUCTION

In thinking about what to teach, all teachers must respond to two key questions: (1) "To what should my students be exposed in this class?" and (2) "What should I expect students to take away from their learning experience?" Answers to these questions are anything but self-evident. They require a great deal of teacher thought. Many beginning teachers find themselves as perplexed about these matters as first-year teacher,

Norman Dalby, felt as he mused in late September about his new position as a world history teacher at Carpenter High School.

Norman Dalby

"Well, I guess I'm launched. Three weeks of school behind me. A few battle scars to show for the effort, but nothing major. My enthusiasm still runs high. I know now I can get through the day and manage the people in my classes. My August nightmares of horrendous discipline problems are happily fading memories. I am finding I can begin to think a little more about 'what' I am teaching now. It's nice to have moved beyond a more elemental concern for physical survival.

"We're tromping our way through Ancient Greece. I've got six notebooks crammed with university lecture notes on the topic. I had two undergraduate courses plus a special senior seminar in the area. I also have half a dozen good books on the subject at home. The subject is just so deep . . . there is so much there. It's tough to know where to begin.

"The text we're using, one of these gems that attempts to compact 3,000 years of historical 'truths' into 600 pages, purports to do Ancient Greece in 10 pages. It seems so irresponsible. I mean we flit into something and then dash madly on to something else. I just don't feel my students are getting much out of it. I want to bring in a lot more background information on my own, but I just don't know how to organize it. And I do recognize that we have to do more than just Ancient Greece in the world history course.

"Compounding my problem is that the text is just too difficult for many of my students. I did some diagnostic work-ups on my people, and lot of them have some severe reading problems. Beyond that, they simply don't have much of a context for a lot of this stuff. I mean, a good many of them don't even know where Greece is. You'll never believe this, but one of them asked me the other day if Greece was a South American country!

"Well, to sum it up at this point, I am still having a good time working with these people. But I find myself frustrated. I just don't know exactly what I should be teaching. And I don't know what a reasonable expectation of performance is for these students. I'd like to be doing better by my students, but I just don't know where to begin."

Concerns such as those expressed by Mr. Dalby are common. Anxieties about "what to teach" and "what to expect of students" disturb many (perhaps most would be more accurate) beginning teachers. Although we certainly would not wish to say that all such anxieties can be eliminated, we do believe that they can be diminished if prospective teachers familiarize themselves with some general procedures related to (1) content selection and (2) development of instructional objectives. Subsequent sections of this chapter will introduce these topics.

SELECTING CONTENT

How do teachers select content? Given the many different kinds of people we have serving as teachers in the schools today, not surprisingly the answer to the question is "in lots of ways." While technically this response is accurate, some practices are much more common than others. Let us look at some relatively high-frequency responses to this problem.

For some teachers, content selection has been turned over entirely to the author (or authors) of the textbook they are using. They simply begin with the first chapter of the text and proceed systematically through the book following the provided sequence of chapters. If all goes well, the students complete work on the final chapter on the final day of the semester or school year. If all does not go so well, instruction might stop at some earlier point, perhaps three fourths or more through the text. (This latter situation for years has been observed often in high school classes on U.S. history where many instructors have found it difficult to get beyond World War II before running out of time at the end of the school year.)

In general, the option of allowing the textbook author to select the content to be taught and the sequence according to which it is presented has little to commend it. There is nothing magical about the content and sequence contained between the covers of any single textbook. The author (or authors) in no case have included it all. They have had to make subjective decisions about which topics to include and about how deeply to treat them. Any review of half a dozen competitive textbooks in a given subject area will reveal dramatic differences in terms of how the material included was organized. Given these differences, beginning teachers in particular ought to approach an adopted textbook with a good deal less awe than has sometimes characterized their responses. It is particularly desirable for new teachers to reflect on perspectives they personally bring to their classroom setting that were unavailable to the authors of any texts they might be using.

For example, a classroom teacher, presuming that some attention has been devoted to gathering diagnostic information, likely will have a much better understanding of the student population to be served than will the authors of any textbooks that will be used. Obviously textbook authors write for a diffuse school audience. They cannot possibly key their texts to the unique characteristics of every classroom. In terms of an understanding of the specific differences characterizing students in a given classroom, the teacher enjoys a significant advantage over any textbook author.

Further, the teacher, assuming that he or she has a respectable academic grounding in the subject areas he or she will teach, has enjoyed exposure to university texts and professionals that may have treated topics from a perspective quite different from those of secondary school textbook authors. Further, as thinking adults, teachers, based on their own training and interactions with other professionals in their fields, are capable of making clear-headed judgments of their own about which contents and sequences deserve emphases in their subject areas.

The bottom line of this discussion is that the classroom teacher ought to play a key role in making decisions about what is taught and the sequence in which it is taught. The teacher stands as a mediator who, in the light of his or her understanding of the students, of the community, and of the subject matter, is best positioned to make responsible decisions about the instructional content and sequence in the classroom. This does not mean, however, that the teacher must act with no outside assistance.

Many school districts have organized curriculum committees that permit teachers and district-level specialists to work collectively to identify content to be taught and suggested sequences for introducing students to this content. Results of these collective efforts frequently are printed and distributed to affected teachers. These documents, called *curriculum guides,* can be of great help to a new teacher. Typically, curriculum guides reference the textbook or textbooks in use, but the references usually include the texts as examples of information sources that teachers are free to use. Curriculum guides are updated periodically. Many districts provide channels that permit teachers to respond to adopted guides so that they do not become rigid, static documents forcing an unproductive pattern of behavior on teachers in the district.

Not all districts have curriculum guides. Under these circumstances, a teacher who is interested in freeing himself or herself from the course textbook needs some understanding of how subject matter content can be broken down and organized in a school program. Some procedures for accomplishing this task will be introduced in the following subsection; Figure 7-1 describes some of the points to consider.

Figure 7-1

IDENTIFYING CONTENT TO BE TAUGHT

Suppose that you were teaching in a district with no curriculum guides in your subject area. Suppose, further, that a disastrous late-summer fire destroyed all textbooks. No replacements can be expected until you have completed half the school year. The school principal comes to see you. He explains that you will have to design your own course.

YOUR OPINION, PLEASE

How would you respond to these questions if you were faced with this situation? (Assume a course lasting 18 weeks.)

1. What major topics would you cover? How would you justify your topic selection?
2. In what sequence would these topics be taught? Do you have any particular reasons for sequencing topics in this way?
3. How much emphasis should each topic receive? In an 18-week program, about how much time would you allocate to each?
4. For each major topic identified, what major concepts or ideas would you want students to grasp? Are any of these ideas more important than others? Why do you think so?

THE BREAKDOWN OF ACADEMIC CONTENT

Textbook writers, developers of curriculum guides, and all others who attempt to identify contents to be covered in school courses use a system to break academic subject matter down in a systematic way. Procedures for accomplishing this task can be sophisticated. Certainly only rarely would a new teacher be expected to identify the scope and sequence of the content to be taught in his or her courses without help. Although the chances that a new teacher will be asked to accomplish this task on his or her own are remote, still there is some utility in understanding how a systematic breakdown of content might proceed.

In general, in breaking down academic content, there is an effort to start with broad topic areas and follow a set of procedures that results in the identification of specific major ideas or concepts to be taught. The following four-step process is typical of many of the schemes used to accomplish this task.

Step 1. Identify topic area.

Step 2. Identify major goals of instruction related to this topic area.

Step 3. Identify generalizations summarizing knowledge related to major goals.

Step 4. Identify major concepts needed for students to grasp the identified generalizations.

Schematically, this set of steps is depicted in Figure 7-2.

Identifying Topic Areas

Topic areas are broad segments of content within a given subject area. For example, topic areas in U.S. history might include "The Revolutionary War Period," "The War of 1812," "The Age of Jackson," and so forth. There is no absolutely uniform pattern for selection of major topics in any subject area. There is an important force at work, however, that tends to make for rather similar sets of topics appearing time after time in breakdowns of individual subject areas.

Figure 7-2

RELATIONSHIP OF STEPS IN A PLAN FOR BREAKING DOWN AN ACADEMIC SUBJECT THAT IS TO BE TAUGHT IN SCHOOL

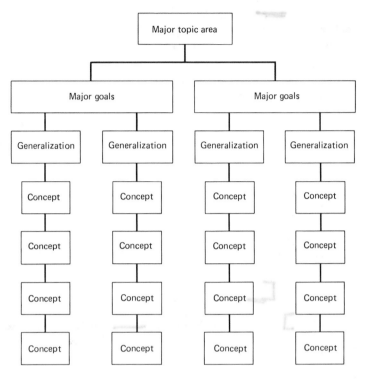

This highly significant force is *tradition*. For example, consider that for years it has been common for history teachers to use important chronological events as major topic areas, introducing first the events most remote in time. Subsequent instruction moves through topics that become progressively more recent. Nothing makes such a pattern of topic selection correct. In fact other patterns exist. For example, sometimes history courses are taught not according to chronological events but according to recurring historical themes such as revolution, war, technological innovations, and so forth. But deviations from the chronological approach are rare. The force of tradition is powerful, and it tends to make for a good deal of uniformity among topics ordinarily treated by large numbers of teachers in a given subject area.

Not surprisingly, specialized school subjects of fairly recent origin tend to be characterized by more topical diversity than are those subjects that have long been in the secondary school curriculum. One would expect to find much more diversity of topical treatment in high school courses in interpersonal communications taught by different teachers than in high school courses in chemistry. The interpersonal communications course, a high school elective encountered only rarely, has too short a history in the curriculum for tradition to have identified those topics that are almost always taught.

In summary, topic selection ordinarily does not prove to be much of a problem for a teacher charged with preparing a breakdown of an academic subject. Because of the influence of tradition, other teachers, district coordinators, and even textbooks are likely sources of information regarding this matter. Certainly the question of what topics are to be taught generates less disagreement than the question of what students should learn from their exposure to these topics.

Identifying Major Goals of Instruction

Some content breakdown schemes suggest identifying major goals even before identifying major topics. Others, such as this one, propose to identify the goals after topics have been identified. Goals are simply broad general statements that make reference to some general feelings about what kinds of benefits should come to students as a consequence of their exposure to a given topic (or, sometimes, given set of topics). Goals represent an attempt to describe what the community at large might generally expect of students exposed to this (or these) topic(s).

Suppose, for example, that one of the topics treated in the seventh-grade mathematics program was "Solving Equations." One related goal for this topic might read

Goal: Students will learn to appreciate the relationship that exists between multiplication and addition as they are exposed to methods for applying this relationship to solving equations.

Consider another example from economics. Suppose that "Inflation" had been selected as a major topic to be treated in the course. One related goal that might be selected for this topic might be

Goal: Students will come to appreciate the forces that are at work to produce the phenomenon we know as inflation.

In summary, then, goals provide very general statements about the level of competence that students are expected to have as a consequence of their exposure to a given topic (or set of topics). They tend to be rather abstract, and they do not reference specific sorts of learnings that students will be expected to master.

Identifying Generalizations

Generalizations are much more specific than goal statements. Sometimes referred to as principles, generalizations are succinct expressions of relationships among important ideas or concepts. Generalizations might be thought of as propositions that have been tested over and over again and that are generally thought to be true. (It is possible in light of some future information, however, that they might have to be revised.) Generalizations represent a kind of idea-dense shorthand for summarizing a large store of knowledge. Generalizations begin to point toward the more specific kinds of learning outcomes toward which students studying a given topic will be directed.

Let us consider again the seventh-grade mathematics course that includes the major topic area "Solving Equations" and see how the breakdown might look through the step of identifying generalizations. (In this example, only one goal and one generalization are included. In reality, there may be more than one of each component related to the major topic.)

Major topic: Solving Equations.

Goal: Students will learn to appreciate the relationship that exists between multiplication and addition as they are exposed to methods for applying this relationship to solving equations.

Generalization: The distributive principle states that the product resulting from the multiplication of a given number and the sum of two others equals the product of this given number multiplied by the first of these two numbers *plus* the product of this given number multiplied by the second of these two numbers. Algebraically, the distributive principle is depicted as

$$a \times (b+c) = (a \times b) + (a \times c)$$

Note the great jump in specificity from the goal statement to the generalization. The generalization begins to provide specific guidance to the teacher in terms of what should be taught. In this example, it is clear that there will be a focus on developing students' ability to apply the distributive principle. But to determine just what students must understand to perform this manipulation, another step is needed.

Identifying Major Concepts

The fourth step in the breakdown of content is identifying major concepts. A concept is a major idea. Concepts sometimes are thought of as definitions. A concept means what it means because it is defined in a given way. Concepts are the building blocks of generalizations. This means that students must understand the concepts included in a generalization before they can be expected to grasp the generalization. Therefore, instruction directed toward helping students to master a generalization begins with a focus on concepts relevant to the generalization. The relevant concepts are those mentioned specifically in the generalization itself and others that the language of the generalization seems to assume students know.

Given the need to focus on concepts, let us look now at a breakdown of the topic "Solving Equations" to the concept level:

Major topic: Solving Equations.

Goal: Students will learn to appreciate the relationship that exists between multiplication and addition as they are exposed to methods for applying this relationship to solving equations.

Generalization: The distributive principle states that the product resulting from the multiplication of a given number and the sum of two others equals the product of this given number multiplied by the second of these two numbers. Algebraically, the distributive principle is depicted as

$$a \times (b+c) = (a \times b) + (a \times c)$$

Concepts:
　　Equation.
　　Addition process.
　　Subtraction process.
　　Multiplication process.
　　Division process.
　　Simplification.

Certainly some of these concepts may be known to students before instruction on this topic begins. A review of diagnostic information would provide some answers regarding entry-level understandings of individual students. Actual instruction would begin with a focus on those concepts with which students were not familiar. It would be with a view to helping students grasp unfamiliar concepts that instruction in this area would go forward.

In summary, then, concepts represent rather specific ideas that result from a systematic breakdown of content that begins with the identification of a major topic. Con-

Figure 7-3

MAKING DISTINCTIONS AMONG GOALS, GENERALIZATIONS, AND CONCEPTS

YOUR OPINION, PLEASE
Look at items in the following list. Which ones are goals? Which ones are generalizations? Which ones are concepts? You may wish to discuss your responses with your instructor.

1. Monsoon wind.
2. Students should come to appreciate the contributions of American poets to the quality of our national life.
3. Onomatopoeia.
4. Students should come to know the properties of real numbers.
5. In technologically advanced societies, innovations tend to be adopted in the largest cities before they are adopted in smaller cities, towns, and rural areas.
6. Successful revolutions result in a shift of political and economic power into the hands of social groups who supported the aims of the revolutionaries.
7. When temperatures go up, objects expand; when temperatures go down, objects contract.
8. Heat of fusion.
9. Moment of illumination.
10. Students should understand how temperature and heat can be measured and how changes in temperature and heat influence the environment.
11. Factoring.

---

cepts provide a basis for teachers to begin planning the kinds of learning experiences that will provide for students within a given topic. Figure 7-3 tests understanding of this discussion.

ESTABLISHING INSTRUCTIONAL OBJECTIVES

Although many new teachers may find the topics, generalizations, and concepts they are to teach identified for them when they assume their first teaching positions, few will be handed pre-established lists of objectives. The vast majority of those teachers who work from objectives have a personal hand in the development of these objectives.

Simply stated, instructional objectives describe what it is that students are supposed to be able to do as a consequence of their exposure to instruction. Today, educators do not think it sufficient to explain to the public only the broad and somewhat vague expectations typically described in goals of instruction. Rather, there is a feeling that some statement is necessary regarding what kind of student performance indicators will be taken as evidence that students are mastering the kinds of content described in these goals. Instructional objectives that describe the kinds of behaviors to be taken as indicators of learning consistent with goals tend to be couched in language that is a good deal more specific than that used in goals' statements.

To see this distinction, consider one of the goals we have seen previously alongside a learning objective that might be one of several identified to suggest kinds of specific student learning that would be consistent with this goal.

Goal: Students will learn to appreciate the relationship that exists between multiplication and addition as they are exposed to methods for applying this relationship to solving equations.

Sample Instructional Objective: Each student will solve correctly at least 11 of 14 problem equations requiring the use of combinations of the addition, subtraction, multiplication, and division processes.

Note that the objective requires students to engage in an *observable behavior* that has been chosen as an indicator of the more general behavior alluded to in the goal. Supplemental objectives might be developed that would be equally valid indicators of student learning consistent with the established goal. No magic number of objectives is right or correct for any given goal statement. A teacher must exercise his or her artistry in developing objectives that provide some indication that students have mastered concepts and generalizations associated with the goal. The number and language of learning objectives identified to accomplish this end will vary greatly from situation to situation.

In general, instructional objectives help teachers in two ways. First, they serve as guideposts for instructional planning. Once a teacher has identified a given set of instructional objectives for a given unit of work, all other instructional planning ties in with these objectives. For example, decisions about which instructional materials to use are made in the light of which materials most clearly seem to have potential to help students master the established instructional objectives. If a film is identified as having potential for providing students with understandings consistent with the established objectives, a good case can be made for including it in the instructional program. If the film has little connection to the kinds of understandings described in the objectives, the teacher can confidently reject the option to use the film. In short, instructional objectives provide teachers with a sound basis on which to identify as appropriate or as inappropriate individual options that might or might not be included in the instructional program.

The second way in which teachers can benefit from the use of instructional objectives has to do with enhanced student learning when objectives are used. Programs planned with objectives in mind tend to be better organized and more purposeful than those in which instruction goes forward without the benefit of a sound planning structure. This kind of careful program planning tends to result in more professional and systematic selection of learning experiences. Consequently, there tends to be less ambiguity in the classroom for students, and some evidence suggests that students' academic performances improve under these conditions. This is particularly likely when teachers provide students with copies of the objectives that they have developed for a given unit of study and discuss these objectives with the class. Given such information, students have a clear idea about the kinds of learning for which they will be held accountable. Under these conditions their study tends to be focused more intensely on relevant information. Some research evidence suggests that students who are provided with instructional objectives perform much better on tests than those who do not have instructional objectives available in advance of instruction (Ferre 1972; Morse and Tillman 1973; Olsen 1973).

Development of instructional objectives represents an important step in the overall planning process. In the planning scheme, preparation of instructional objectives is preceded by identification of topics, goals, generalizations, and concepts. Once they are identified, instructional objectives are followed by decisions in the planning process related to such details as instructional techniques, teacher support materials, student learning materials, and other elements. Taken collectively, these systematically related parts comprise a complete instructional unit. Details regarding unit preparation are introduced in Chapter 9, "Formalizing Unit and Lessons Plans."

An example illustrating the relationship of instructional objectives to major concepts, a generalization, a goal, and a topic is presented in Figure 7-4. Note the effort to ensure that identified major concepts have been referenced in at least one instructional objective.

Figure 7-4

RELATIONSHIP OF LEARNING OBJECTIVES TO MAJOR CONCEPTS, A GENERALIZATION, A GOAL, AND A TOPIC

TOPIC
Solving Equations.

GOAL
Students will learn to appreciate the relationship that exists between multiplication and addition as they are exposed to methods for applying this relationship to solving equations.

GENERALIZATION
The distributive principle states that the product resulting from the multiplication of a given number and the sum of two others equals the product of this given number multiplied by the first of these two numbers *plus* the product of this given number multiplied by the second of these two numbers. Algebraically, the equality suggested by the distributive principle is depicted as follows:

$$a \times (b + c) = (a \times b) + (a \times c)$$

MAJOR CONCEPTS
1. Simplification.
2. Equation.
3. Addition process.
4. Subtraction process.
5. Multiplication process.
6. Division process.
7. Distributive principle.

RELATIONSHIP OF MAJOR CONCEPTS (BY NUMBER) AND INDIVIDUAL

	Concepts						
	1	2	3	4	5	6	7
Objectives	2, 3	2, 3	2, 3	3	2, 3	3	1, 2

INSTRUCTIONAL OBJECTIVES:

1. Each student will respond correctly to 8 of 10 true/false questions related to the nature of the distributive principle.
2. Each student will solve correctly at least 7 of 10 equations requiring them to use a combination of the addition and multiplication processes.
3. Each student will solve correctly at least 11 of 14 problem equations requiring the use of combinations of the addition, subtraction, multiplication, and division processes.
And so forth.

A FORMAT FOR PREPARING INSTRUCTIONAL OBJECTIVES

Of the many formats available for preparing instructional objectives, one we have used for some time is the *ABCD* format. This scheme presumes that a complete instructional objective includes four elements. Reference must be made in the objective to the *audience* (A) to be served, to the *behavior* (B) to be taken as an indicator of appropriate learning, to the *condition* (C) under which this behavior is measured (e.g., kind of assessment procedure to be used), and to the *degree* (D) of competency to be demonstrated before mastery of the objective is assumed. In the next sections we will look at these components of a complete instructional objective one at a time.

A = Audience

The A component of an instructional objective identifies the person or persons to whom the instructional objective is directed. This may be an entire class of students, a group even larger than a class, a small group of students, or even a single student. The purpose of the audience component of an instructional objective is to provide specific information to a given individual regarding whether or not he or she is to be held accountable for mastering the content referenced in a given objective. Typically, the A, or audience, component of an instructional objective will appear as indicated in the following examples:

"Each student will . . ."

"Louisa's group will . . ."

"All students in all sections of U.S. history will . . ."

"All fifth-period physics students will . . ."

"Joanne Smith will . . ."

B = Behavior

The B, or behavior, component of an instructional objective describes the observable performance that will be taken as an indicator that learning has taken place. The behavior in an instructional objective must be described in observable terms. This suggests a need to select verbs that describe performance in precise and specific ways and a need to avoid verbs that describe less readily observable kinds of phenomena. To illustrate this distinction, consider the following choices:

"Each student will appreciate foreign policy differences of the Republican and Democratic presidential candidates by . . ."

"Each student will describe foreign policy differences of the Republican and Democratic presidential candidates by . . ."

In the first example, it is unclear both to the teacher and the student what kind of behavior will be taken as evidence that mastery has occurred. It is not clear what kind of performance signals "appreciation." A student, given an instructional objective with a behavior statement of this kind, might well be confused as to how he or she should study the material. The use of the verb "describe" in the second option is much more precise. "Describe" suggests a behavior that is much more observable and specific than does "appreciate." A student presented with an instructional objective calling upon him or her to describe foreign policy differences can expect to be assessed on his or her ability to provide some clear indication of a familiarity with key policy points of each candidate. The use of the verb "describe" in the instructional objective suggests a need to students to study carefully specific positions of each candidate. It is true that the verb "appreciate" *might* suggest a similar activity to some students. But the meaning of appreciate is much less precise than describe. For example, some students might take the "each student will appreciate" directive to mean that they are to do nothing beyond developing a personal aesthetic satisfaction from the knowledge that, indeed, both candidates have differing foreign policy views. For a student who had this impression, there would be no deeply felt need to become thoroughly familiar with foreign policy positions of each candidate. In summary, then, a good deal of ambiguity is removed when verbs used in the behavior component of an instructional objective reference a relatively specific and an observable kind of student performance (see Figure 7-5).

Figure 7-5

KINDS OF VERBS SUITABLE FOR BEHAVIOR COMPONENT OF AN INSTRUCTIONAL
OBJECTIVE

YOUR OPINION, PLEASE

Below is a list of verbs that might be used in writing instructional objectives. Look at the list. Then
identify those verbs that (1) you think would be suitable for use in an instructional objective and that
(2) you do not think would be suitable for use in an instructional objective. Be prepared to defend your
decisions.

Compute	Note
Apply	Evaluate
Understand	Critique
Comprehend	Select
Describe	Judge
Compare	Identify
Appreciate	Conjecture

The following fragments of complete instructional objectives indicate how the
behavior component might look:

" . . . cite specific examples of . . ."

" . . . describe characteristics of . . ."

" . . . distinguish between . . ."

" . . . name . . ."

" . . . point out . . ."

" . . . compare and contrast . . ."

C = Condition

The C, or condition, component of an instructional objective describes the condition of
assessment. That is, the condition details the kinds of procedures to be followed to
determine whether or not the student can perform in the way described by the behavior
component of the objective. In many instances, the condition is a formal test of some
kind. In other instances, a less formal procedure may be described. The condition component conveys to the student information regarding how his or her learning will be
assessed at the conclusion of the instructional sequence. Typically the C component of
an instructional objective will appear as indicated in the following examples:

" . . . on a multiple-choice test . . ."

" . . . during a five-minute informal conversation with the teacher . . ."

" . . . on an essay examination with use of notes permitted . . ."

" . . . on a formal paper, six to ten pages in length, footnoted properly . . ."

" . . . on a student-prepared, three-color, 3-foot by 4-foot poster . . ."

D = Degree

The D, or degree, component of an instructional objective details the minimum level
of performance that will be acceptable as evidence that the objective has been mastered.

Where such formal assessment procedures as matching tests, true/false tests, and multiple-choice tests are used, the degree frequently is described in terms of either total numbers of items that must be responded to correctly or a percentage of the total number of items that must be responded to correctly. Clearly such a procedure makes no sense for essay items. On essay items, the degree frequently refers to specific categories of content that must be included in responses that will be viewed as indicative of content mastery.

There is a good deal of teacher artistry involved in deciding what degree of competence to describe as minimal evidence a given objective has been achieved. A study by Block (1972) revealed that, when a minimum standard of about 80 percent was assigned to objectives where tests such as true/false, matching, and multiple choice were used, students generally developed a more favorable attitude toward learning than when a minimum standard of 90 percent correct was applied. We would caution, however, that research in this area is in its infancy and that teachers must rely heavily on personal intuition in identifying criterion levels they believe important. The use of criterion levels and instructional objectives' mastery for grading purposes is discussed in some detail in Chapter 11, "Measuring, Evaluating, and Reporting Student Progress."

Typically, the D component of an instructional objective will appear as indicated in the following examples:

" . . . respond correctly to at least 8 of 10 . . ."

" . . . in an essay in which specific references are made to (a) motivations for immigration, (b) domestic resistance to immigration, and (c) psychic rewards of immigration . . ."

" . . . answer correctly 85 percent of the items on a . . ."

" . . . with no mistakes . . ."

Putting It All Together: The ABCD Format

Recall that all complete instructional objectives include references to A, the audience, B, the behavior, C, the condition, and D, the degree. A number of properly prepared objectives are listed below. Individual components of each objective have been underlined and labeled.

     A   B   D   C
1. Each student will solve 8 of 10 problems on a weekly quiz featuring questions about right triangles.

     A   C   B   D
2. Laura's group, on an essay, will cite at least five reasons supporting and five reasons opposing nineteenth-century Swedish migration to the American South.

     A   B
3. The fifth-period class will identify examples of alliteration by responding correctly

       C   D
on a multiple-choice test to at least 8 of 10 items.

Note that the audience, behavior, condition, and degree components may appear in a variety of orders. The order is not critical. What *is* important that all four be included in every instructional objective.

In summary, the ABCD format is an easily learned procedure. Instructional objectives containing all four components (audience, behavior, condition, and degree) are capable of conveying a good deal of information to students about a teacher's expectations. For the teacher, they provide a reminder to keep instruction on track in such a way that learning experiences provided will clearly be consistent with the kinds of expectations reflected in the assessment procedures followed at the conclusion of a given instructional sequence.

KINDS OF INSTRUCTIONAL OBJECTIVES

For some years now, it has been a convention to think of learning as divided into three basic categories or "domains." These are (1) the cognitive domain, (2) the affective domain, and (3) the psychomotor domain. In very general terms, the cognitive domain includes what we might call academic or intellectual kinds of learning (see Figure 7-6). The affective domain includes learning related to values, beliefs, and attitudes. The psychomotor domain includes learning related to the sensorimotor system and fine and large muscle control.

Figure 7-6

DISTINGUISHING AMONG DIFFERENT COGNITIVE LEVELS

YOUR OPINION, PLEASE

On the right-hand side of the page are the six levels in the cognitive Taxonomy (Bloom 1956). On the left-hand side are some tasks students might be asked to do. Look at these tasks. Decide what level of cognitive thinking might be required for students to accomplish each task. Share your responses with the rest of the class and with the instructor.

STUDENT TASKS

A. Describe the likely results of a successful effort to dig a 50-foot wide canal connecting the Mediterranean Sea with the Bay of Biscay in the Atlantic.

B. Identify the individuals who have run for president in this century whom you believe to have been "most qualified" and cite reasons for making your determinations.

C. State from memory the Preamble to the U.S. Constitution.

D. Write a sentence in which you illustrate the use of alliteration.

E. Suggest the relative importance of (1) social forces, (2) political forces, and (3) economic forces as causes of the outbreak of World War I.

F. Describe the characteristics of the halogen family.

G. Suggest procedures that must be followed to obtain a valid driver's license.

H. Name four tragedies by William Shakespeare.

I. Follow directions and build a model airplane.

LEVELS OF THE
COGNITIVE DOMAIN
1. Knowledge
2. Comprehension
3. Application
4. Analysis
5. Synthesis
6. Evaluation

Because the general area of concern of each domain has certain unique features, not surprisingly instructional objectives in each domain tend to be organized in slightly different ways and to be directed toward different purposes. In the sections that follow, some of these differences are introduced.

Instructional Objectives in the Cognitive Domain

The cognitive domain is concerned with rational, systematic, or intellectual thinking. When we think about subject matter content and our expectation that students will learn it, we have in mind the cognitive domain. Much of what we know about thinking in the cognitive domain stems from the work of Benjamin Bloom and others who, in the mid-1950s, set about the task of developing a system for identifying categories of learning in the cognitive domain. Out of their deliberations came a ground-breaking educational document, *Taxonomy of Educational Objectives: Handbook I: Cognitive Domain* (Bloom 1956). Commonly referred to as *Bloom's taxonomy,* this document suggested that there exists a six-step hierarchy of thinking ranging from the most elemental thinking processes to the most sophisticated. Ordered in terms from simplest to most complex, the elements of Bloom's taxonomy are as follows:

Knowledge

Comprehension

Application

Analysis

Synthesis

Evaluation

For teachers, proposed learning experiences can be evaluated in terms of their intellectual complexity by referencing the intellectual demands against Bloom's taxonomy. In general, a task demanding "knowledge-level" performance will challenge students less than a task demanding "synthesis-level" performance. In thinking about instructional planning, teachers find it useful to know something about the kinds of thinking implied by each level of taxonomy. When they have made a decision regarding the kinds of intellectual demands they wish to include in their program, then they need to prepare instructional objectives that clearly are directed toward encouraging student performance at the targeted taxonomical level (knowledge, comprehension, application, analysis, synthesis, and evaluation). Let us look briefly at characteristics of each taxonomical level and at instructional objectives consistent with each.

Knowledge. Knowledge is the simple recall of a piece of previously learned information. At the knowledge level, the student is not required to do anything beyond reproducing something specific to which he or she has been exposed. No manipulation or interpretation of learned material is required. The following are examples of instructional objectives written at the knowledge level:

1. On a multiple-choice test, each student will identify the capitals of countries in NATO by responding correctly to at least 80 percent of the items.
2. Each student, on a matching test, will identify parts of a cell by responding accurately to at least 12 of 15 items.

Comprehension. Comprehension is a slightly more complex mental operation than knowledge. Comprehension requires the student to focus on more than a single piece of previously learned information with a view to understanding certain important relationships. At the comprehension level, a student may be required to change the form of previously learned material or to make a simple interpretation. Note the following examples.

1. Each student will provide literal translations from Russian to English for ten sentences making no errors in at least eight of the sentences translated.
2. Students in Laura's group will select on a matching test the correct connotative meanings of vocabulary words appearing in the first chapter of *The Red Badge of Courage* with a minimal acceptable accuracy of 80 percent correct.

Application. Application involves the use in an unfamiliar context of information that has been learned previously. In short, application requires students to do something with what they have learned. Note the following examples of application-level instructional objectives:

1. Each student in the ninth-grade geography class will compute correct air distances between ten pairs of world cities using a tape measure and a 22-inch globe so that errors of no more than 50 air miles short or long of actual distances are made on any more than two pairs of cities.
2. Each student in the eleventh-grade science class will compute progeny ratios correctly on at least eight of eleven provided problems.

Analysis. Analysis requires students to develop conclusions through a study of the constituent parts of a phenomenon. Through the process of analysis, the students attempt to understand some existing reality by looking carefully at the pieces that go together to make the reality. Some examples of analysis-level instructional objectives follow:

1. Each student will correctly identify the chemical composition of at least 15 of 18 provided unknown compounds.
2. In an essay examination, each student will describe patterns of voting in the recent presidential election on the part of voters of (a) very low incomes, (b) moderately low incomes, (c) average incomes, (d) moderately high incomes, and (e) very high incomes.

Synthesis. Synthesis requires students to take a number of separate pieces of information and combine them to create knowledge that is new (or, more accurately, knowledge that is new to the student). Some examples of synthesis-level instructional objectives follow:

1. Making specific references to possible changes in (a) religious preferences, (b) nature of social hierarchies, (c) typical family structure, and (d) avocational interests, each student, in an essay, will suggest what the culture of Boston might be like today if the preponderance of early settlers had come from (a) Saudi Arabia, (b) Nigeria, (c) Japan, and (d) Spain.
2. In an essay, each student will describe the likely impact on (a) climates, (b) transportation networks, (c) recreational patterns, and (d) dialects of American English were a huge mountain range, with peaks averaging in the 8,000- to 10,000-foot range, to appear along a line running roughly from Omaha to Cincinnati.

Evaluation. At the level of evaluation, students are called upon to make judgments in the light of clearly identified criteria. To be at the evaluation level, it is essential for both the element of judgment and the element of established criteria to be present. Evaluation never calls upon students to engage in simplistic sharings of nonsupported personal opinion. The following instructional objectives are written at the level of evaluation.

1. Each student will compare, contrast, and critique the plays of Racine and Corneille in terms of their adherence to the "rules" of classical drama.
2. Each student will critique a selected painting by Gauguin and a selected painting by Van Gogh and determine which is the superior piece of work by completing an essay in which specific references are made to (a) the degree of coherence observed in each painting, (b) the degree to which each painting is "true" to the medium used, and (c) the degree of emotive pleasure or pain inspired by an observation of each painting.

Cognitive Level of Instructional Objectives and Teaching Time. Not surprisingly there is a relationship between the level of sophistication of thinking a teacher hopes to promote in students and the time required to get them to this level. Generally, there is an increase in instructional time needed as there is an increase in the cognitive level of the instructional objective. For example, it requires less instructional time to teach students to master a knowledge-level objective than it does to prepare them to master an objective at the level of comprehension (or at any higher cognitive level).

Bloom's taxonomy tells us that every higher level contains within it every lower level. This means that a student cannot be expected to think at the level of analysis unless he or she is able to think at the subordinate levels of application, comprehension, and knowledge. This relationship suggests important implications for us in planning for instruction. First, it suggests that, because of time limitations, students will not be expected to operate at higher thinking levels with respect to *all* the content of a course. This simply is unrealistic given time limitations. Consequently, there is a need to select with care those critically important areas where we feel students need to proceed toward mastery at the levels of analysis, synthesis, or even evaluation. When these areas are identified, it is necessary to build systematically the important lower-cognitive-level understandings that are prerequisite to higher-level thinking. This effort requires careful attention to sequencing and to the whole area of lesson and unit planning. Some examples of how a decision to lead students to a higher-level understanding of a given topic area might be reflected in a systematic plan for instruction are provided in Chapter 9, "Formalizing Unit and Lesson Plans."

Instructional Objectives in the Affective Domain

The affective domain, as noted previously, concerns people's values, feelings, and attitudes. Clearly in schools we are concerned about the total development of our students, not just with their mastery of academic content. We need, therefore, to consider the issue of students' values, feelings, and attitudes as the instructional planning process goes forward.

Success in the affective area often associates with success in the cognitive area; in other words, students who like and feel good about what they are doing in school tend to do better in their academic courses than do those who are unhappy in school. This does not mean that instructional planning should be directed exclusively toward the goal of "amusing the students" or "keeping them all happy all the time." What concern for students' values, feelings, and attitudes means is that every effort should be directed toward ensuring that no youngster's sense of self-worth is consciously diminished by something we do as classroom teachers.

The goal of supporting each student's growth toward self-confident and mature adulthood is not inconsistent with an instructional program that makes heavy cognitive demands on students. The critical variable is not the difficulty of the work but, rather, whether the instructional system has been designed in such a way that each youngster has a realistic chance for success. So long as students feel that they are succeeding, attitudes toward school and the teacher generally will remain positive. Success in academic work can itself be an important contributor to students' developing sense of self-worth.

The affective domain involves all areas in which the general emphasis is on values, attitudes, and feelings. But, with regard to planning instructional objectives, our focus will be limited to a small range of concerns within this broader and more general domain. The necessity for limiting our focus here results from the nature of instructional objectives.

Recall that instructional objectives suggest expected, or at least hoped for, outcomes. This purpose becomes something of a problem when we are dealing with the affective area. There is a heavy-handed, possibly authoritarian, ring to the suggestion that a given instructional program is dedicated to shaping students' values in a given way. Certainly in a society that values open discussion and democratic decision making, we have no business establishing instructional objectives that seem to say to students that certain values, attitudes, and feelings are right whereas others are wrong. A teacher who tries to do this is asking for trouble.

In thinking about the possibility of developing instructional objectives in the affective domain, we must ask ourselves this question: "In what area(s) do teachers have a legitimate need to know about students' values, attitudes, and feelings?" Perhaps there are several answers to this question. But the one that has always made the most sense to us is that teachers have a need to know how students are feeling about the instruction to which they are being exposed. For example, do they like the topics selected? How do they feel about the various school subjects? And so forth. If we accept the premise that students who feel disposed toward what is going on in their classes will do better in those classes and, hence, may grow in terms of their own feelings of competence and self-worth, then we have every reason to make some deliberate efforts to gather information that will tell us something about these kinds of student feelings.

A cautionary note is needed here. It is imperative that measures of students' values, feelings, and attitudes never be used as a basis for awarding grades. Information derived from instructional objectives in the affective area is to help the teacher to take a look at how his or her program is being viewed in an attitudinal sense by his or her students. Such information may suggest a need to make changes. It may suggest a need to do nothing at all. But in every case it will provide some indication to the teacher about attitudes of youngsters toward what has been going on in the classroom. It is obvious that any attempt to use such information for grading purposes would soon undermine the reliability of the information. In addition to the ethical problem of grading students' attitudes, any such grading scheme would soon break down as clever students began to report attitudes (whether they truly held them or not) that they believed the teacher wished to hear.

In preparing instructional objectives that relate to the affective domain, it is a common practice to measure a change of attitudes that may have occurred over a period of time. Sometimes a measure of an attitude is taken at the beginning of an instructional unit and then again at the end of the same unit. Let us suppose that we were teaching a high school biology class, that we were about to begin an instructional unit on infectious diseases, and that we expected to spend a good deal of time on the subject of venereal diseases. An affective instructional objective we might prepare could look like this:

> *At the conclusion of the unit on infectious diseases, each student in the biology class will demonstrate greater interest in learning about venereal diseases than at the beginning of the unit as measured by a positive shift in scores from a preunit attitude inventory and a postunit attitude inventory.*

Note that the same ABCD format is used for affective as for cognitive instructional objectives. The reference to an attitude inventory as the condition or means of assessing student attitudes both before the unit and after the unit refers to a procedure according to which students are asked to rank their feelings about a number of provided alternatives. An example of an attitude inventory that we might have used in connection with our sample objective follows:

Attitude Inventory

Topic: Infectious Diseases.

Directions: Listed below are a number of areas studied during a unit on infectious diseases. Look at each area. Then, place a number "1" in the blank before the area in which you have the greatest interest, a "2" in the blank before the area in which you have the second greatest interest, and so forth. Continue this pattern until you conclude with the largest number in the blank before the area in which you have the least personal interest.

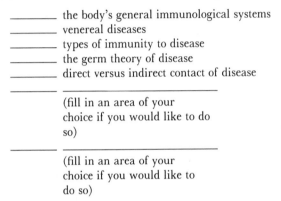

_____ the body's general immunological systems

_____ venereal diseases

_____ types of immunity to disease

_____ the germ theory of disease

_____ direct versus indirect contact of disease

_____ _____

(fill in an area of your
choice if you would like to do
so)

_____ _____

(fill in an area of your
choice if you would like to
do so)

In this attitude inventory, the positive shift would be from a relatively high number on the attitude inventory when it was given before the unit (recall that the higher the number, the lower the interest in the area) to a relatively low number on the attitude inventory given at the conclusion of the unit (recall that the lower the number, the higher the interest in the area).

Clearly we would not hope for a shift on the part of all students. For example, some might already have a high interest in the study of venereal diseases even before we begin studying the unit. Obviously if a student ranked his or her interest in this area "1" on the attitude inventory given before the unit was taught, there could be no positive shift (indicating a change toward a lower number) on the attitude inventory given at the conclusion of the unit. If we had decided that we had a personal interest in prompting students' interest in the study of venereal diseases, our real concern would be to have in hand some evidence that, by the conclusion of the unit, a good many youngsters had developed a greater relative interest in the area than they had had before.

But clearly we would not expect all youngsters to express a high preference for learning about venereal diseases. Nothing would be wrong with students who prized more highly some of the other areas mentioned. Students do, after all, have varied interests. Regardless of how individual students responded, the general profile of students' attitudes regarding the area or areas (in this case, venereal diseases) that we consider important is useful to us as we think through what we did during those sections of the unit that we personally considered to be priority material. If we are displeased with the general way in which students seem to be feeling about this priority material, we may well wish to consider some revisions in our methodologies for introducing this material when teaching the unit again.

In summary, instructional objectives in the affective domain focus properly on students' reactions to the instructional program. Information about students' values, feelings, and attitudes that is derived through the use of affective instructional objectives should never be used for grading. The information is for the use of the teacher as he or she considers the impact of his or her program (or of selected parts of this program) on students' attitudes. This information can provide a basis for productive revision of instructional practices. (For further discussion, see Figure 7-7).

Instructional Objectives in the Psychomotor Domain

The psychomotor domain includes behaviors that require coordination of the body's muscular system. Specific behaviors in this area can range from activities such as run-

Figure 7-7

TEACHING VALUES, ATTITUDES, AND FEELINGS IN SCHOOLS

Recently, a school board heard testimony from citizens regarding whether or not the school program should include instruction directed at teaching certain values, attitudes, and feelings to students. Among the speakers were Ms. Johnson and Mr. Kirby. An abbreviated version of their remarks appears below.

MS. JOHNSON: The schools have *no* business getting into the area of values, attitudes, and feelings. This whole area smacks of indoctrination. Even though we may be told that the objective is to help students understand their own feelings, what is certain to happen is that certain values, attitudes, and feelings will be identified as "right" or "correct." While I have no quarrel with the motives of teachers and administrators, I don't feel they should ever be allowed to "play God" and make clearly judgmental comments regarding very personal values, feelings, and attitudes of individual students. This whole area is something the schools should simply stay out of. It simply is not the business of the schools to poke away at students' individual differences by prying into their personal values and, by implication, weighing those values on some scale of relative merit devised by a teacher, a principal, or some other bureaucrat employed by the school system.

MR. KIRBY: Of course we should be concerned about teaching students certain values, attitudes, and feelings. The idea that we are all so individualistic, so different from one another is simple poppycock. There *are* certain key values that keep us from acting like barbarians. For example, is there anyone in this room who does not believe that murder is a bad thing? Shouldn't we pass this value on to our young people? Can we depend on parents to do the whole job for us without some reinforcement from the schools? I think not. We need to put a stop to this nonsense that the principle of individualism knows no boundaries. Carried to its logical extreme, this position can be used to justify the most outrageous kinds of behaviors. Do we really want a generation who, in reading about the Holocaust, can shrug their shoulders and say, "Oh, well, Hitler was just doing his thing." In my view, we can't allow such unsupportable logic to go unchallenged. We *must* teach values, attitudes, and feelings in the schools.

YOUR OPINION, PLEASE

Read the comments above. Then, respond to these questions.

1. What strengths do you find in Ms. Johnson's comments? What weaknesses?
2. What strengths do you find in Mr. Kirby's comments? What weaknesses?
3. Suppose that you had been asked to state your position before the school board. What would you have said?

---

ning that require intensive use of large muscles to precision-drawing activities that require good control of the body's fine muscle systems. The degree to which an individual teacher may have a need for instructional objectives in the psychomotor domain depends on the extent to which intended learning outcomes require students to demonstrate motor control (control of the body's muscular systems).

In preparing instructional objectives in the psychomotor domain, we can use the same ABCD format introduced earlier. Objectives in this area can be sequenced in terms of increasing difficulty by reference to four stages or levels of psychomotor activity. The simplest of these stages is level 1, the level of awareness. Somewhat akin to the cognitive level of knowledge, awareness demands only that a student be able to describe correctly the movements that need to be made to properly complete a muscular activity.

At level 2, the individual components level, the student is able to correctly demonstrate individual parts of a complex muscular activity. At level 3, the level of integration, the student can perform the entire muscular activity, including all necessary components, with some teacher guidance. Finally, at level 4, the free practice level, the student can perform the muscular activity correctly, in numerous settings, and without any prompting from the teacher. In general, students who achieve level 4 psychomotor objectives can be thought of as having complete mastery of the targeted muscular behavior. Some examples of performance objectives for each of these psychomotor levels follow.

Level 1: Awareness Each student will describe to the teacher, with no errors, the specific hand motions necessary to tie knots needed in preparing a completed Royal Coachman dry fly.

Each student will describe to the teacher, with no errors, the specific foot position changes that occur from beginning to end in a sequence of discus throwing.

Level 2: Individual components Each student, on request, will tie whatever knot called for, with no errors, that represents one knot needed in the preparation of a Royal Coachman dry fly.

Each student will demonstrate, upon the teacher's request and without error, the feet positioning that is correct for a given point in the discus-throwing sequence.

Level 3: Integration Each student will prepare, with some teacher guidance permitted, a complete Royal Coachman dry fly that includes all defining criteria for a dry fly of this type.

Each student will complete a discus throw that includes appropriate feet positioning at each phase of the activity with some teacher guidance permitted.

Level 4: Free practice Each student will prepare, with no supervision from or guidance by the teacher and on several occasions, at least five Royal Coachman dry flies that include all defining criteria for a dry fly of this type.

Each student will complete, with no teacher supervision and guidance and on several occasions, at least six discus throws characterized by appropriate feet positioning at each phase of the activity.

Teachers interested in developing psychomotor objectives need good diagnostic information about individual student capabilities. Lacking such information, it is difficult to plan appropriate objectives in this area. For example, if a student's coordination is less fully developed than we might suppose, the student might have no chance whatever of achieving a psychomotor objective we devised that requires a great deal of muscular coordination.

When students are confronted with a requirement to perform at a level far in excess of their present capacities, some will simply give up and refuse to do anything out of a conviction that "they are beaten before they start." Students' attitudes in the psychomotor area are connected closely to their perception that they have a reasonable chance to succeed. Thus we need to ensure that our requirements in this area are realistic for students' present levels of competence.

Posttest

Directions: Using your own paper, answer each of the following true/false questions. For each correct statement, write the word "true." For each incorrect statement, write the word "false."

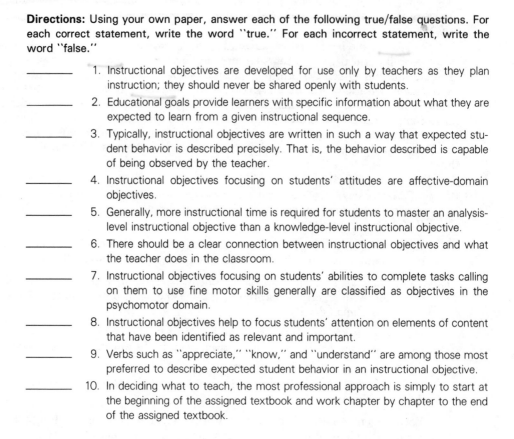

_____ 1. Instructional objectives are developed for use only by teachers as they plan instruction; they should never be shared openly with students.

_____ 2. Educational goals provide learners with specific information about what they are expected to learn from a given instructional sequence.

_____ 3. Typically, instructional objectives are written in such a way that expected student behavior is described precisely. That is, the behavior described is capable of being observed by the teacher.

_____ 4. Instructional objectives focusing on students' attitudes are affective-domain objectives.

_____ 5. Generally, more instructional time is required for students to master an analysis-level instructional objective than a knowledge-level instructional objective.

_____ 6. There should be a clear connection between instructional objectives and what the teacher does in the classroom.

_____ 7. Instructional objectives focusing on students' abilities to complete tasks calling on them to use fine motor skills generally are classified as objectives in the psychomotor domain.

_____ 8. Instructional objectives help to focus students' attention on elements of content that have been identified as relevant and important.

_____ 9. Verbs such as "appreciate," "know," and "understand" are among those most preferred to describe expected student behavior in an instructional objective.

_____ 10. In deciding what to teach, the most professional approach is simply to start at the beginning of the assigned textbook and work chapter by chapter to the end of the assigned textbook.

Key Ideas in Review

1. Selection of content is a problem facing many teachers. It is irresponsible simply to follow the sequence of topics in the adopted course textbook. Such an approach fails to take advantage of the particular content strengths of the teacher and, significantly, of the teacher's ability to diagnose special characteristics of students in his or her classes. Many districts help teachers with content selection by providing curriculum guides. If such documents are lacking, the teacher may find it necessary to accomplish this task by breaking down content using a systematic structure of knowledge approach.

2. One procedure for breaking down academic content in a systematic way involves identification of four major levels of content. First, major topic areas must be identified. Second, goals of instruction related to these topics need to be identified. Third, generalizations must be determined that summarize knowledge related to these major goals. Fourth, major concepts needed for students to grasp the generalizations must be identified.

3. Instructional objectives are statements about what students should be able to do as a consequence of their exposure to a given instructional program. These objectives provide a basis for teacher planning of the instructional program. That is, once objectives have been identified, the teacher then works to develop a plan for instruction that will enable students to master these objectives. There are three general categories of learning for which instructional objectives ordinarily are developed. These are cognitive-domain learning, affective-domain learning, and psychomotor-domain learning.

4. Learning in the cognitive domain refers to academic or subject matter content learning. In this important learning area, a framework for leveling the difficulty of learning in a hierarchy from easiest to most difficult has been identified. Known as *Bloom's taxonomy* (Bloom 1956), this framework provides teachers with a mechanism for scaling the difficulty of their instructional objectives in the cognitive domain. In general, lower-level cognitive-domain objectives require less instructional time than do higher-level cognitive-domain objectives. Some studies have revealed that students who have been provided with lists of cognitive-domain instructional objectives in advance of instruction benefit more from instruction focusing on these objectives than do students who have not seen such objectives in advance of instruction. Therefore, it is recommended that students be provided with the instructional objectives at the beginning of any instructional sequence.

5. Learning in the affective domain refers to values, attitudes, and feelings. Some care must be exercised in this area to assure that students are not subjected to indoctrination into a specific set of values. Our pluralistic society abhors any such attempts to suppress individual differences through systematic imposition of a set of values that some higher authority says is "right." On the other hand, teachers do have a legitimate interest in knowing about students' attitudes toward their course work. Instructional objectives in the affective domain designed to provide this information are worthwhile. Information gained about students as a consequence of their performance on these objectives should be maintained as confidential information for use of the teacher alone. Under no circumstances should performance on an affective-domain objective play any role in determination of students' grades.

6. Learning in the psychomotor domain concerns abilities related to control of the body's muscular systems. Instructional objectives in this area are designed to provide teachers with information about students' relative degrees of control over their large and small muscle systems. Clearly demand for this kind of information will depend greatly on the nature of the subject being taught.

SUMMARY

Even new teachers who are especially well grounded in their content areas frequently find themselves frustrated as they attempt to identify exactly what they should teach to their students. In essence the problem boils down to the question of how to make an acceptable trade-off between responsible treatment of topics and issues and limitations of student interests and capacities and of clock time in secondary school classrooms. Some teachers solve the problem by simply following the scope and sequence of individual textbook chapters. Such a response, however, fails to take advantage of the talents of the individual teacher and of his or her understanding of the special characteristics of students. Some districts (a growing number) provide new teachers with curriculum guides prepared in the district by teachers and central office curriculum specialists that identify patterns of content better tailored to the needs of students in the district than one would expect to find in a textbook. When guides are not available, teachers themselves (with, it is hoped, assistance from specialists) may have to make their own determinations about scope and sequence of content that is taught. Several frameworks are available for breaking down complex academic content systematically.

Once teachers have decided what to teach, they must respond to the issue of what students should learn. Many teachers have found it profitable to formulate instructional objectives that state rather precisely what it is that students should be able to do as a consequence of their exposure to a certain unit of instruction. Once these instructional objectives have been identified, instructional planning that is keyed to these objectives can go forward. That is, teachers can plan for instructional experiences that will enable students to master established objectives.

It is a common practice to think about learning as being divided into three major categories: (1) cognitive learning, (2) affective learning, and (3) psychomotor learning. Cognitive learning refers to what we might call subject matter or academic content learning. Affective learning refers to values, attitudes, and feelings. Psychomotor learning refers to behaviors associated with students' abilities to control the various large and small muscle systems of the body. Appropriate instructional objectives can be designed for each of these three major learning categories.

In summary, instructional objectives might be thought of as a keystone of instructional planning. Once they are in place, teachers have a set of referents they can use to determine the appropriateness or inappropriateness of other alternative elements they are considering placing within a proposed plan for instruction. If those elements are consistent with the objectives, then a case can be made for including them. If there is an inconsistency, then there may well be a need to include something else. A more detailed look at the specific roles played by instructional objectives in the instructional planning process is provided in Chapter 9, ''Formalizing Unit and Lesson Plans.''

References

Armstrong, David G., Denton, Jon J., and Savage, Tom V. *Instructional Skills Handbook.* Englewood Cliffs, N.J.: Educational Technology Publications, 1978.

Block, James H. "Student Learning and the Setting of Mastery Performance Standards," *Educational Horizons* (Summer 1972): 183–191.

Bloom, Benjamin S., ed. *Taxonomy of Educational Objectives: Handbook I: The Cognitive Domain.* New York: David McKay Co., Inc., 1956.

Ferre, Alvin Victor. "Effects of Repeated Performance Objectives upon Student Achievement and Attitude." Ed.D. dissertation. New Mexico State University, 1972.

Gronlund, Norman E. *Stating Objectives for Classroom Instruction.* 2nd ed. New York: Macmillan Publishing Co., Inc., 1978.

Huck, Schuyler W., and Long, James D. "The Effects of Behavioral Objectives on Student Achievement," *The Journal of Experimental Education* (Fall 1973): 40–41.

Morse, Jean A., and Tillman, Murray H. "Achievement as Affected by Possession of Behavioral Objectives," *Engineering Education* (June 1973): 124–126.

Olsen, Robert C. "A Comparative Study of the Effects of Behavioral Objectives on Class Performance and Retention in Physical Science," *Journal of Research in Science Teaching,* no. 3 (1973): 271–277.

Taylor, Curtis et al. "Use of Inferred Objectives with Non-Objective Based Instructional Materials." Arizona State University, research sponsored by Air Force Human Resources Laboratory, Williams Air Force Base, Arizona Flying Training Division, October 1973.

8

Instructional Techniques

FUNKY WINKERBEAN by Tom Batiuk © 1981. Field Enterprises, Inc. Courtesy of Field Newspaper Syndicate.

Objectives

This chapter provides information to help the reader to

1. Recognize that individual instructional techniques are best evaluated in terms of the purposes they are to serve.
2. Note that there are a limited number of *events of instruction* that need to take place during an instructional sequence to promote learning.
3. Point out strengths and weaknesses of individual instructional techniques in terms of the events of instruction.
4. Describe procedures for implementing a number of instructional techniques.

Pretest

Directions: Using your own paper, answer each of the following true/false questions. For each correct statement, write the word "true." For each incorrect statement, write the word "false."

_____ 1. The lecture is a bad instructional technique that has no place in secondary school teaching.

_____ 2. It is desirable for teachers to explain to students clearly the objectives or purposes of a given lesson.

_____ 3. The idea that students need to apply new learning if they are truly to master it is highly overrated; in fact, there is little to be gained by providing students with this kind of hands-on experience.

_____ 4. Secondary students need help in distinguishing between important and unimportant information in new lessons.

_____ 5. The technique of brainstorming can never be used to solve real problems; it is always an exercise in simple creativity.

_____ 6. Discussion is a technique that, among other things, can be used to help students recall previously learned material.

_____ 7. Role playing can help students to learn the perspectives of others.

_____ 8. The project method has been used frequently by secondary school industrial arts teachers.

_____ 9. Discussion generally is not regarded as an instructional technique that is an especially strong choice for introducing material to students for the first time.

_____ 10. All instructional techniques work equally well for (a) presenting new information to students and (b) asking students to apply new information.

INTRODUCTION

Lecture? discussion? simulation? case study? brainstorming? independent study? or still another technique? Which is *best?* An astonishing amount of writing has addressed this question. Debates on the issue have punctuated discussions in secondary school faculty lounges for years. Not a few speakers have made a modest name for themselves by taking to the stump in support of the "excellence" of a favorite teaching technique. Although a good deal of noise has been generated by these speculations, not much wisdom has come down to us. This lack comes not so much from an absence of honest effort to arrive at a defensible answer as it results from a focus on an inappropriate question.

The question should not be "Which instructional technique(s) is (are) best?" This presupposes a uniformity among teachers, students, and situations that runs counter to reality. Further, it presumes that differences in the sorts of things that a given instructional technique might logically be able to accomplish are not substantial. In fact, there are dramatic differences among what individual instructional techniques can accomplish. In selecting instructional techniques, teachers need first to consider their own personality variables and characteristics of the youngsters in their classes. For example, some teachers are very good at organizing role-playing exercises, others are not. Some feel personally more comfortable with other techniques. As for the students, some will be poor readers, others will be excellent readers. Some will have short attention spans, other will be able to work quietly for a long period of time. And there will be still other differences.

In looking at themselves and their students, teachers individually must assess their own strengths and weaknesses and those of students in their classrooms. Once this has been accomplished, teachers can begin thinking about which instructional techniques to employ. This decision cannot be made just on the basis of a personal whim. There are dramatic differences in what individual instructional techniques can do. Therefore, the question for beginning teachers as they begin to think about instructional techniques is "Which instructional technique is good *for what purpose?*"

In responding to the "for what" aspect, we will need to think about the kinds of things a teacher needs to accomplish during a given lesson. Then individual instructional techniques can be appraised in terms of their relative effectiveness in helping the teacher to perform these necessary tasks. In the next section, these key *events of instruc-*

tion will be identified along with a selection of instructional techniques having various properties in terms of their abilities to help teachers discharge some of their important responsibilities.

THE EVENTS OF INSTRUCTION

Two well-known instructional design specialists, Robert Gagné and Leslie Briggs (1974), have pointed out that teachers must pay attention to certain events of instruction in every lesson. When all these "events" are included, students tend to learn more efficiently. When some of them are eliminated, learning will be more difficult for many students. We might think of the events of instruction as steps that must be included in any lesson. These steps are not at all complex. But they are very important. The following events of instruction or steps ought to be included in every lesson:

1. Emphasizing objectives
2. Motivating learning
3. Recalling previous learning
4. Presenting new information
5. Recognizing key points
6. Applying new information
7. Assessing new learning

Let us take a look at each of these events.

Emphasizing Objectives

Students need to know what it is that they are supposed to learn from a lesson. Many beginning teachers assume that the objective of instruction is obvious to students. Frequently it is not. In new lessons, students may be provided with a tremendous amount of information. Some of this will be important to the teacher's purposes, some of it will not. To help students recognize the difference, it is wise for teachers to provide students with a statement of objectives at the beginning of the lesson. This may be done in several ways. A printed version of the objective or objectives can be given to each student to be followed by some teacher comments. Alternatively, the teacher may state the objective orally.

To appreciate the importance of emphasizing objectives at the beginning of a lesson, consider the differences between the two following sets of teacher comments:

Teacher A: All right, today I'm going to spend about 25 minutes lecturing on "Causes of World War I." Take good notes. Let's get started.

Teacher B: Today I'm going to spend about 25 minutes lecturing on "Causes of World War I." I want you to be able to identify at least two social causes of the war, two political causes of the war, and two economic causes of the war. Also, I want you to contrast reactions to the murder of the Archduke Ferdinand in Sarajevo by the press of Great Britain and the press of Austria-Hungary. Take good notes.

Clearly students in the class taught by Teacher B have a much better idea of what they should be looking for. The teacher has given them a mechanism for identifying pertinent information. Their notes are likely to be better, their test performances are likely to be better, and their attitudes toward the class are likely to be better.

Motivating Learners

The second event of instruction focuses on motivation. The purpose of motivation is to gain students' attention and interest. The purpose is much easier to define than to accomplish. This is true because of the wide range of interests of secondary school students. All have enthusiasm. But many of these can be tied to the school curriculum only with difficulty.

Although the task for teachers is a challenging one, the effort must be made. The trick is to preserve the integrity of the content to be taught while, at the same time, engaging students' interests. For example, a junior high school class in industrial arts might be approaching a unit on working with new plastics. The teacher, in thinking about projects students can make, has a good deal of discretion. If he or she decided that students are to make replicas of old-fashioned shaving mugs, a few youngsters with interests in history might perk up, but many might not get very excited about the project. On the other hand, if the teacher decided that students are to make plastic holders for cassette stereo tapes, a much larger number might approach the effort with enthusiasm.

Every lesson must include some specific and planned attention to motivation. This is such an important topic that it has been singled out for more extensive treatment in Chapter 10, "Motivating Students and Implementing Programs." In this chapter, refer to Figure 8-1 for further discussion.

Recalling Previous Learning

Beginning secondary teachers in particular are surprised by how much students forget from one day to the next. There tends to be even more erosion of learning over longer periods of time. In conducting lessons where new material is to be introduced, it is essential that teachers spend time helping students bring to mind previous material. For example,

Teacher: We're going to begin work today on the *passé composé* tense. In most cases, we'll need a helping verb. Usually this will be the present tense of *avoir*. But there are some verbs that will require us to use *être*. Let's quickly review the present tense of these two verbs together.

This kind of a review provides a logical link from previously learned information to the new material. This step needs to be incorporated into all lessons.

Presenting New Information

One of the most important events of instruction is presenting new information to students. Once students have been apprised of the objective, motivated properly, and helped to recall essential previously learned material, it is time for the introduction of the new material. Because of the variety of approaches available to the tacher to accomplish this task, there is a tendency for inexperienced secondary school teachers to schedule too much continuous or uninterrupted class time for the "presenting new information" phase of a lesson. It must be remembered that attention spans of many secondary school youngsters are rather short. Therefore, variety is desirable. With junior high school youngsters, a good rule of thumb is not to exceed 20 minutes on any one class activity before shifting to another. Even high school students find it difficult to go much beyond 30 or 40 minutes without some change of pace. Certainly it is possible to spend more time than this on presenting new information, but some consideration should be given to using a variety of approaches to accomplish this task so that students will not have to spend an excessive amount of time doing any one thing.

Figure 8-1

POSSIBLE TOPICS OF INTEREST TO SECONDARY STUDENTS
Suppose that you were a secondary school teacher and that you wanted to motivate your students. You might start by identifying some things in which they were interested. Then you might be able to link some of your instruction to these high-interest areas.

Football
Basketball
Track
Jogging
Live theater
Automobiles
Hunting and fishing
Stereo systems
Computers

YOUR OPINION, PLEASE
Look at the list above. (If you don't like this list, develop one of your own.) Then, respond to these questions.

1. How would you rate student interest in each of the topics on the list? Can you arrange these topics in order from highest interest to lowest interest?
2. What is the basis for your set of ratings? Would all students react positively and negatively to the same things? Why, or why not?
3. Suppose that you were teaching a high school French class. How do you think students would rate their interest in each of these topics? On the other hand, suppose that you were teaching a junior high school class in drafting. How do you think students in this class would rate their interest in these topics?
4. How would you go about determining what an individual student might be interested in?
5. Suppose that you had established that many students in the class are very interested in stereo systems. How could you use this information to motivate students for a lesson in your own subject area? Specifically, what would you do to take advantage of this interest? (Remember, you want to use this interest to motivate students, but you want to do so without taking anything important away from the subject matter you wish to teach.)

Recognizing Key Points

Once new information has been presented, teachers have an obligation to help students recognize the critically important information. This will not just happen. Even given the clearest of explanations and the best of learning materials, many students will need help in focusing on the key ideas. Teachers need to build specific procedures into their lessons for helping students recognize important ideas that have been introduced. A number of techniques available for this purpose will be described in detail later in this chapter.

Applying New Information

It is a basic instructional principle that information that is to be retained is information that must be used. The very best of presentations will not result in optimal retention unless students are asked to do something with the material they have learned. There is evidence that students not only do better in classes where such application activity occurs but that their attitudes toward such classes are better as well. Some areas of the secondary curriculum have had a long tradition of encouraging application. The industrial arts are particularly strong in this regard. But application has a place throughout the curriculum, and opportunities for students to apply new information deserve a place in every lesson.

Assessing New Learning

As a capstone event, assessment procedures need to be built into every lesson. Assessment provides students with feedback or information about the quality of their learning. It helps them to recognize their own strengths and weaknesses. This information is useful as they attempt to master the new material. Assessment also helps the teacher to recognize potential weak spots in his or her instructional program. For example, if a chemistry teacher finds that all the students are confused about titration, he or she might provide more instructional time on the procedure and reconsider what has already been done. Each lesson ought to include some mechanism for providing feedback about performance to the learner and general information about instructional effectiveness to the teacher.

A number of alternatives are available for accomplishing each of the events of instruction necessary for a successful lesson. Some of these teacher options involve sets of procedures that have been organized into more or less formal instructional techniques. In the section that follows, a number of these techniques will be introduced.

TWELVE INSTRUCTIONAL TECHNIQUES AND HOW TO USE THEM

Brainstorming

Brainstorming is a technique designed to help students break loose from conventional or obvious solutions to problems. Proponents of the technique believe that many of us get into an intellectual rut when we know one or two approaches to a problem. The knowledge of these approaches sometimes makes us reluctant even to think that there might be other more imaginative and, perhaps, better solutions. Brainstorming is designed to unleash our mental power in such a way that it does not get easily sidetracked to a quick acceptance of the ordinary and the conventional.

Historically, brainstorming stems from a concern of top business executives that junior-level managers were too quick to parrot the conventional wisdom of their administrative superiors. While such an approach might be safe, it may preclude better decisions regarding company policies from getting a fair hearing. The brainstorming approach ensures that *all* responses to an issue will be heard and considered.

Rules for conducting a brainstorming exercise are simple:

1. Students are presented with a problem to consider.
2. Students are invited to call out their ideas as rapidly as they can. A student is free to speak whenever there is an opening. The idea is to generate a rapid outpouring of information. (Students are cautioned to say whatever comes into their minds, *so long as it is relevant* to the problem being considered.)
3. Students are told that they must not comment on any remarks made by others. This applies to negative as well as to positive ideas.
4. The teacher or a designated student record keeper writes down every suggestion made. The individual doing the writing will have to work very fast to keep up with the group.
5. The exercise should be stopped by the teacher when there begins to be a noticeable falling off in the rate of presentation of new ideas. (Usually a high level of participation cannot be sustained for more than 10 or 15 minutes.)

6. The teacher and the class discuss and debrief the ideas that have been introduced. (Which are the better suggestions? Why? Which could be most easily implemented? Are some more costly than others? What should be done first? etc.)

Some beginning teachers who try brainstorming find that it generates tremendous initial student enthusiasm but that it is difficult to decide just where the discussion should lead once information has been gathered. A variant of the basic brainstorming technique known as the "analytic brainstorming approach" has been designed by Dunn and Dunn (1972). The analytic brainstorming approach builds a step-by-step structure into the process that many teachers have found attractive. In general, the Dunn and Dunn procedure helps students to resolve a problem by solving it with increasing precision over a series of steps:

1. The teacher poses a problem in the form of a statement about what an "ideal" solution to a problem might be. (Students brainstorm responses. These responses are written in a place where they can be seen easily by all students.)

   "The best thing we could do to prevent pollution of Gulf Coast beaches would be to . . .". (Students brainstorm appropriate responses.)

2. With responses put forward in step 1 in full view, the teacher asks students to describe why the "best things" mentioned have not already taken place. (Students brainstorm responses. These responses are written in a place where they can be seen easily by all students.)

   "What things are getting in the way of those 'best things' we could do to prevent pollution of Gulf Coast beaches?" (Students brainstorm appropriate responses.)

3. The third phase involves a question about what might be done to overcome obstacles noted in responses to question posed in step 2. (Students brainstorm responses. These responses are written in a place where they can be seen easily by all students.)

   "How could we overcome difficulties that keep us from doing what we have to do to prevent pollution of Gulf Coast beaches?" (Students brainstorm appropriate responses.)

4. In step 4, the teacher asks students to point out difficulties of implementing ideas noted in step 3 responses. (Students brainstorm responses to the step 4 question. These responses are written in a place where they can be seen easily by all students.)

   "What might stand in the way of our overcoming difficulties that keep us from taking necessary action to prevent pollution of Gulf Coast beaches?" (Students brainstorm appropriate responses.)

5. In step 5, the teacher asks students to decide what should be done first to begin a realistic solution of the problem. (Students brainstorm answers.)

   "Considering all our thinking on this problem, what steps should be taken first to solve it?" (Students brainstorm responses.)

Brainstorming and the Events of Instruction. Brainstorming is not well suited to emphasizing objectives. The technique does have some value as a means of motivating learning. Since it depends exclusively on what students say based on what they already know, the technique is not one that can be used for reminding students about important information they may have forgotten. Although students may learn some things from what other students say, the technique is not particularly well suited to presenting large quantities of new information. Since all ideas are welcomed, brainstorming is not at all suited for accomplishing the event of recognizing key points. The real strength of brainstorming is in the area of allowing students to apply information. With its focus on a problem, brainstorming provides an excellent opportunity for youngsters to apply information they have acquired. Brainstorming, too, has some utility for assessing learning. By listening to students' responses, the teacher can gain information about the nature of students' understandings regarding the focus issue.

Case Study

The case study technique is designed to help students develop understandings from an intense scrutiny of a specific episode or situation. The focus of a case study must be selected with care. To be useful, the case should be fairly representative of a general problem or condition. Obviously, if the case is not a good example of the general problem or condition on which it focuses, students may well go away from the learning experiences with some understandings that do not transfer well to the real world.

Case studies, when prepared with care, can prompt a good deal of student interest. Many students find it much easier to identify with the characters and situations depicted in a case study than with the sometimes sterile treatment of topics in a course textbook. When well written, students identify closely with pressures and problems facing characters described in the case.

In preparing a case study for classroom use, the teacher must follow three basic steps:

1. Identify the purpose of the lesson
2. Select an appropriately illustrative case
3. Prepare suitable debriefing questions.

To illustrate how each step might be completed in preparing a case study for classroom use, let us consider an example.

Purpose

To illustrate how attitudes of other family members toward a child can influence that child's conception of his or her self-worth.

Illustrative Case*

Myrna was a pretty, blonde, blue-eyed girl, attractive to her teachers who felt baffled in their attempts to help her. At home there was her mother, a step-father, and a small sister who was a child of her mother's present marriage. The mother complained about Myrna's poor health and encouraged her to stay home when she felt ill. The mother also complained about her husband, who she said was neglecting her. The step-father was a factory worker, a fairly steady man but quite harsh in his treatment of Myrna and sometimes cruel to his wife.

Eventually Myrna reached the ninth grade at the age of 16. By this time she was grown-up physically but quite incapable of doing high-school work. She was reading at about the fourth-grade level and was discouraged about herself. She was convinced she was stupid, and she was so unsure of herself that she avoided talking to adults in the school for fear they would make too great demands on her.

---

*From Havighurst, et al. (1962, p. 41). Some cases will be a good deal longer than the example provided here.

Possible Debriefing Questions*

1. What kinds of pressures do you think Myrna was under? What were the sources of those pressures?
2. How do you account for Myrna's failure to do high school work?
3. How, specifically, might Myrna's mother's behavior have contributed to Myrna's problems? What might have been the impact on Myrna of her father's behavior?
4. Do you think that behavior of family members influenced Myrna's opinion of herself more than behavior of people outside of her family? Why do you think so?

Case Study and the Events of Instruction.   Case studies are not particularly well suited for emphasizing learning objectives. They can serve to motivate when they are well constructed. It is possible, too, for case studies to be written in such a way that previously learned material can be re-emphasized. But, in general, most case studies are not written with a view to helping students review material learned earlier.

Case studies are excellent vehicles for presenting new information to learners. When written with care, they can also help students to recognize key points. The debriefing questions, if framed skillfully by the teacher, can also involve students in applications of the new information they have acquired. The debriefing process, too, provides an opportunity for the teacher to listen and assess students' grasp of the newly learned material.

Debates

The classic format of a formal debate generally does not represent a very practical technique for most secondary school classes. (Of course *debate* frequently exists as a separate course where students prepare for interscholastic competition. In these classes, the classic format is appropriate.) The difficulty with the traditional debate is that only two youngsters are involved actively at any one time. This situation places others in the roles of observers. While a good debate may engage the interest of a large class of students, a real danger exists that the enthusiasm of the observers will diminish and classroom control problems will develop.

A more useful variant on the traditional format is the class debate (Armstrong 1980). While preserving the spirit of confrontation characterizing the classic debate, the classroom debate actively involves more students. Consider, for example, a teacher who wants at least nine students at a time to be active participants. These might be assigned the following roles:

Four students are assigned to take a "pro" position.

Four students are assigned to take a "con" position.

One student is assigned to be a "skeptical critic."

---

*To use to guide a discussion after students have read through the case. Some teachers find it useful to allow students to discuss the case among themselves for a few minutes before conducting a general class discussion. A good number of additional questions might also be asked. These are just illustrative of the kinds of questions a teacher might use during the debriefing phase of a case study lesson.

As in a traditional debate, members of the pro team attempt to make a case in support of the proposition being debated. Con team members try to make a case opposing the proposition. The skeptical critic listens carefully to arguments presented by both sides. He or she takes notes. The function of this individual is to ask probing, penetrating, and perhaps embarrassing questions of members of both the pro team and the con team after both sides have concluded their arguments.

A class debate of approximately 52 minutes could follow this general sequence.

1. Each pro team and each con team member speaks for two minutes. Speakers alternate (pro then con then pro and so forth). *Time required:* 16 minutes.
2. Each member of the pro team questions one or more members of the con team. Then, each member of the con team questions one or more members of the pro team. Each individual may have the floor for one minute. *Time required:* 8 minutes.
3. Each member of the pro team and each member of the con team make final arguments lasting no longer than one minute each. *Time required:* 8 minutes.
4. The skeptical critic asks difficult questions of members of both the pro team and the con team. The skeptical critic may ask all individuals questions or only a few individual questions. There should, however, be an effort to ask about the same number of questions of pro team members as are asked of con team members. *Time required:* 8 minutes.
5. Other class members vote to determine winning team. *Time required:* 2 minutes.
6. Debriefing by teacher. *Time required:* 10 minutes.

The teacher has a wide range of options in identifying focus topics for classroom debates. Topics such as the following might be appropriate:
Resolved that

1. The United States should establish something like the French Academy to prevent rapid changes in English language usage over the years.
2. Women should be assigned to combat roles in the U.S. military forces on the same basis as men.
3. High schools should require four years of mathematics for graduation.
4. No student should be allowed to graduate from high school who cannot pass a test on grammatical usage.
5. Auto emission standards should be lowered to allow automobile manufacturers to make higher-mileage cars.
6. The "rules" of French classic theater promoted rather than prevented creativity.
7. William Faulkner was the most influential American writer of the first half of the twentieth century.

Debate and the Events of Instruction.   Debate is not a suitable vehicle for providing students with information about the purpose of instruction. Provided that topic selection is sound, they can motivate learning. Generally, debates are not organized with a view to helping students bring to mind previously learned information that is essential for the understanding of new material.

Debates can be used for presenting new information to students. This is especially likely to occur as members of debate teams prepare for the event. The debate format is particularly good for focusing attention on key points and issues. This is likely to occur during questioning during the debate itself, questioning by the skeptical critic, and in the teacher's follow-up comments. Another strength of the debate as a technique is in the area of applying information. Students are required to think on their feet and to draw on information as they frame their positions and respond to questions. The debate also provides an opportunity to assess the depth of students' understanding by listening to comments made during the debate and during follow-up discussions.

Discussion

Discussion is a popular instructional technique though new secondary school teachers often find it difficult to implement. Many student teachers have reported to the authors that their discussions "just don't get anywhere." Discussions planned for 10 or 15 minutes often seem to run out of steam after only 2 or 3 minutes.

As with other instructional techniques, no recommendations will guarantee a successful discussion every time, but some principles can be followed to increase the likelihood of success. We will look at some of these general guidelines in this section.

First, we need to consider that a teacher typically engages in two kinds of responses during a discussion. The first is what we might call "questioning behavior." As the name suggests, teachers frequently ask questions to focus the discussion and move it along in a purposeful manner. But skillful questioning alone is not enough to ensure a productive discussion. It is also necessary for the teacher to develop sensitive "response skills." These response skills require the teacher to listen carefully to what students say and to respond in a manner that encourages additional participation and that maintains the flow of dialogue.

Let us consider the issue of questioning and how questions can be sequenced to improve the overall quality of a discussion (see Figure 8-2). In thinking about ques-

Figure 8-2

SEQUENCING QUESTIONS

Suppose that a teacher had just shown a film on modern Japan to his or her class. Following the film, the teacher planned to ask some questions of the students as part of a debriefing exercise. The teacher was considering using one of the following sequences of questions:

SEQUENCE 2		SEQUENCE 1	
Question 1:	What was the man in the factory doing?	Question 1:	What did the film mean to you?
Question 2:	How were the steel worker and the office worker alike and different?	Question 2:	Should we have a government like Japan's?
Question 3:	How would you compare the Japanese steel plant with an American steel plant?	Question 3:	What was the man in the factory doing?
Question 4:	Should we have a government like Japan's?	Question 4:	How would you compare the Japanese steel plant with an American steel plant?
Question 5:	What did the film mean to you?	Question 5:	How were the steel worker and the office worker alike and different?

YOUR OPINION, PLEASE

Look at the two sequences above. Then, respond to these questions.

1. Are there any questions that students might find more threatening than others? If so, which questions are they? Why do you think that they would be higher-threat questions than the others?
2. Do you think you would get more student participation using one of these sequences rather than the other? Why do you think so?
3. Which one of these sequences would you use? Why?

tioning, we need to recognize that many students feel exposed when a teacher asks a question. They may be inclined to say something, but they may hold back out of a fear of making a comment that the teacher might not like. Particularly, students initially may be wary of answering questions that require them to voice an opinion or to make a value judgment. However, particularly at the beginning of a discussion, they are generally not quite so reluctant to respond to a question asking them only about a fact or some other relatively simple piece of information. In this situation, provided that they know the appropriate answer (or at least think they do), they can say something that will not expose a personal value or attitude to potential teacher displeasure.

One sequence of asking questions that may teachers have found useful has been developed by the Northwest Regional Educational Laboratory (Northam 1972, p. 321). There are three basic questioning categories in this sequence. Teachers are advised to begin with category 1 questions first, then to move on to category 2 questions, and finally to conclude with category 3 questions. These categories are as follows:

Category 1. Analysis of specifics questions

Category 2. Analysis of relationships questions

Category 3. Generalizing or "capstone" questions

Analysis of Specifics Questions.   Teachers are asked to begin a questioning sequence with questions from this category. These questions are nonthreatening, low-risk questions for students. Students are asked simply to recall specific pieces of information to which they have been exposed prior to the questioning sequence. They are not asked to make opinions or judgments. This is a confidence-building phase. Some analyses of specifics questions are

What was the occupation of the main character?

How many elements were there when radium was discovered?

What French word for "trouble" did the policeman use?

What did the speaker say the first step in factoring was?

Analysis of Relationships Questions.   One purpose of analysis of specifics questions is to build a sound understanding of basic information. Once this has been established, then more sophisticated analysis of relationships questions can be asked. These questions require students to compare, contrast, and analyze materials to which they have been introduced. Responses tend to involve going beyond the facts and, hence, an element of personal judgment. Some examples are:

All right, we saw what Hamilton thought about the federal government, and we saw what Jefferson thought. How would you compare their views?

What similarities and differences do you see in the rhyme schemes, caesura placements, and beats per line between seventeenth-century French poetry and this contemporary French poem?

How would you explain the reaction that took place after the ammonium nitrate was added?

Generalizing or "Capstone" Questions.   Questions in this category are the most sophisticated of all. They require students to go well beyond given information. Further, they require students to make some rather sophisticated personal judgments. In short, they are high-risk questions. But, provided that an appropriate base has been built through use of a sequence of questions from analysis of specifics through analysis of relationships, a good many students prove willing to respond to questions of this kind. Some examples of questions in this category are:

What does the poem mean to you personally?

What basic message was the author trying to convey to the reader?

How do you feel about nuclear proliferation and why?

What consequences do you see for a continuation of the high rate of population increase in Brazil?

A productive discussion, of course, is more than simply an array of properly sequenced questions. Teachers who are good discussion leaders are careful listeners who have mastered techniques for responding to students in ways that keep the discussion moving forward in a productive manner. One of the most basic of these techniques involves nothing more than allowing students sufficient time to respond once a question has been asked. Many beginning secondary school teachers forget this point and become impatient when there is no instantaneous response to a question they have asked.

Teachers who are inexperienced in discussion leadership techniques often will ask a question and wait no longer than two seconds for a student to reply. If no reply is forthcoming, these teachers tend either to answer their own questions or to ask new questions. Experienced discussion leaders have found it prudent to ask a question and then wait at least seven or eight seconds before rephrasing the question or going on to something else. Generally, a student will respond before the seven or eight seconds has elapsed. The basic principle at work here is that thinking takes time. Particularly when questions are complex, it is illogical to presume that students can deliver a reasoned response without the benefit of a few moments of thinking time.

When a question has been asked and a student has answered it, the teacher needs to think about how he or she will respond to the student. The teacher's response should serve a specific purpose. The purpose should be tied clearly to what the student has said. The Northwest Regional Educational Laboratory has identified a number of specific teacher skills in this imporant area (Northam 1972). These skills include the following:

1. Refocusing
2. Clarifying
3. Summarizing
4. Mapping the conceptual field
5. Accepting
6. Substantiating

Refocusing. This skill seeks to help the teacher keep the discussion from wandering off the subject. Certain secondary students are adept at injecting comments that lead the group into topics having little logical connection to the lesson. To prevent this from happening, we, as teachers, need to listen carefully and to make comments that refocus group attention on the main topic of interest whenever we note the first signs of drift. Consider the following example:

Rexanna: I was just thinking about those trinity symbols in *Crime and Punishment*.

Teacher: Yes?

Rexanna: Well, on the late movie last night they had this space thing. People on the ship had these weird suits with triangle patches. I mean, you know, three-sided patches. I mean that might mean something.

Nancy: That was a b-a-a-a-d movie. I mean it was *gross.*

Tim: Yeah. Remember the part where they dumped the head dude into the giant blender? I mean, *whoosh,* and he was *gone.*

Teacher: Rexanna, let's get back to your point. How do you see symbols in the film related to the trinity symbols in *Crime and Punishment?* No, let's go back even a bit farther. Tell me what you see as trinity symbols in *Crime and Punishment.*

Clarifying. Some students have difficulty expressing themselves. Often the intent of their contributions is unclear. Students need help in expressing themselves clearly and specifically. Teacher comments can help develop this skill. Consider this example:

Sandra: I heard they're going to make Maple Street into a one-way street. That just makes me mad. They can't do that.

Teacher: Now, just who are this "they" you're talking about?

Sandra: You know, the government.

Teacher: All right, I am beginning to understand. You're saying some government officials have decided to make Maple Street one way. Now let's get a little more specific. Just what government are you talking about?

Sandra: You know, those people who decide about streets and that sort of thing?

Teacher: Well, which people do make these decisions.

Sandra: My dad said something about a planning commission. I think that's a local outfit, but I'm not sure.

Teacher: Yes, I believe that's right. So, to get back to your point, you're saying you are unhappy because the city planning commission has decided to make Maple Street a one-way street. Why don't you like that idea?

Summarizing. Discussions, unless they are very brief, can deal with a tremendous quantity of information. At points during the discussion, it is useful for the teacher to pause and take a moment to pull together points that have been made. Once this has been accomplished, the discussion can move on to still other issues. Consider the following example:

Teacher: Let's stop a minute and think about what we've said so far. Paul pointed out that Dr. Friedman said the main cause of inflation was the government printing too much money. John said that other economists say other factors are important. Renée pointed out that people don't save money like they used to and that this drives prices up. What else? Have I missed any other points that were made?

Sally: Well, Rhonda said that she read that the big tax cut last year made people spend too much and that all the stores jacked up prices.

Teacher: Thank you, Sally, I forgot about that. Anything else I missed?

Mapping the conceptual field. There is a tendency for secondary students to seek quick answers to complex questions. In general they are not comfortable with ambiguity. Consequently, during a discussion often they will rally behind the first solution to a problem that is mentioned. When this happens, further willingness to discuss may cease. One important task for the teacher in his or her role as a discussion leader is to prevent students from jumping to conclusions prematurely. Consider these examples:

Teacher: Well, most of you seem to be nodding your heads in agreement with Paul's idea that the reason this writer seems so pessimistic is that he was an orphan and must have had an unpleasant childhood. Are there some possible problems with this explanation? Are there some other possibilities?

Nora: Well, just because we know he was an orphan doesn't mean that he had a bad life. Even if he did, he might not be pessimistic now.

Teacher: That's an interesting observation, Nora. Phil?

Phil: Maybe he had a bad experience in the war.

Teacher: Peter?

Peter: He might have been on drugs and got off. I read someplace that makes you pessimistic.

Teacher: That may be a possibility for us to think about. Sarah?

Sarah: He maybe is afraid of dying. Sometimes that makes people pessimistic.

Teacher: These are all good comments. Anyone else have some ideas?

Accepting. Many secondary school students are afraid to speak up during discussions. Part of their fears stem from some unpleasant past experiences when teachers have reacted to something they have said in a way that made them feel uncomfortable. Teachers need to be as supportive as possible during discussions. In particular, obvious errors of fact students make need to be treated gently. Many students feel criticized when teachers contradict something they have said. Certainly teachers do have a responsibility to see that the correct information gets aired. But, to the extent possible, corrections should be solicited from members of the class. When the teacher finds it necessary to make the correction himself or herself, every effort needs to be made to ensure that the correction is made in a way that permits the student to maintain a sense of personal dignity.

Substantiating. While students do need to be encouraged to participate in discussions, teachers sometimes must ensure that students' statements are based upon reliable information. Substantiating helps students to look at the logic of their statements. Consider the following dialogue.

James: So what if Jefferson said it? I mean people in those days didn't know much. So why should we pay any attention?

Teacher: That's an interesting comment. Let me ask you a question or two just to help me understand your answer. Do you think an understanding of languages, mathematics, and architecture would indicate somebody who "knew something"?

James: Well, I suppose so.

Teacher: Did Jefferson know anything about languages, mathematics, or architecture?

James: I really don't know.

Teacher: I think you might find the answer to that question interesting. Let's get together at the end of the period. I can tell you where to find some things about President Jefferson you might find interesting.

Discussion and the Events of Instruction.   Discussion is not a particularly suitable technique for informing students about learning objectives. This is true because discussions typically follow the introduction of new material. For the same reason discussion is not one of the stronger techniques to use for motivating students at the beginning of a sequence of instruction.

Discussion, because of the central role the teacher plays, is a technique that serves well to help students to recall previously learned material and to recognize key points. The technique is not a particularly strong choice when the purpose is to introduce youngsters to new content for the first time. Ordinarily discussion follows presentation of content that has been introduced by some other means.

Discussion can be used to help students apply information they have learned. Use of discussion for this purpose depends on the teacher's skill in framing good discussion questions that require students to apply material they have learned. Discussion also can play a useful role as teachers seek to assess students' learning. This can be accomplished as the teacher listens carefully to student responses as the discussion goes forward (see Figure 8-3).

Independent Study

Independent study is an instructional technique that can make some students blossom. For others, it can be disastrous. It is a procedure that almost never is appropriate for use with an entire class of young people. Teachers who use the technique successfully select students who are involved very carefully.

Teachers interested in having some of their students involved in an independent study exercise must develop specific responses to five basic questions:

1. Which students are to be involved?
2. What are those students to do?

Figure 8-3

DISCUSSION ON POVERTY

LAURA: The reason those people live that way is because they're just plain lazy. Look at those filthy houses. And those yards! I don't care how poor they are; if they weren't lazy they'd never live with all that junk.

TEACHER: As a matter of fact, Laura, those people work long, long hours. And they don't get a decent wage. A lot of them hold down two jobs and still don't take home a hundred dollars a week. They work in sweat shops. They can't read and often are taken advantage of. When they get home, they're just plain beat. But I assure you, young lady, they are *not* lazy.

YOUR OPINION, PLEASE

The exchange above took place in a secondary school classroom. Think about what was said. Then, respond to the following questions.

1. What is your general reaction to the teacher's response?
2. Would your reaction to the teacher's response be different if you knew whether or not the teacher's information was accurate? Why, or why not?
3. What impact do you think this kind of response might have on this student's willingness to participate in future discussions?
4. What kind of a response would you have made to this student if you had been the teacher?

---

3. What relevant materials are available?
4. What is to be done about grading?
5. What will students who are not involved be doing?

Students selected for participation must be capable of working well without constant supervision. They will need to follow directions that may be in written form and may be read at a time when a teacher is not available for consultation.

Once the students have been identified, the teacher needs to identify the task they are to accomplish with a good deal of precision. The better the task is defined, the less the likelihood of misunderstanding once students begin work. Directions instructing students what to do must be very clear. This is particularly true when there is an intent to provide only written directions.

It is very frustrating for students to begin work on an independent study project and find that few relevant materials are available. Part of the teacher planning process involves identifying appropriate learning materials and making sure that they are in a place where independent study students can use them. Some teachers find it useful to gather pertinent information from the library and other sources in their own classrooms. Others work with librarians to organize a shelf of relevant material in the school library. Whatever procedure is adopted should enable students to get to the pertinent information easily and efficiently.

Teachers contemplating an independent study program for some students need to consider how student work from this project is to fit into the overall grading project. If students fear that the independent study work is just to be something extra that they must do for no credit, few will be enthusiastic about getting involved. Teachers with successful programs manage to integrate grades from independent study work into the overall grading scheme in a way that does not penalize a student for participating in the experience.

Finally, there is a need to think about what students who are not involved in the independent study program will be doing. In most cases, a relatively small number of students will be working on an independent study basis. This means that the teacher must plan another set of learning experiences for the rest of the class (probably a large majority). Independent study then means more teacher planning time. Not only must the independent study program be organized and monitored, but a whole separate set of learning experiences must be planned and delivered to the other students.

Independent Study and the Events of Instruction.   Independent study can be designed in such a way that directions emphasize learning objectives; the technique also has potential for motivating learners. Again depending on a good set of directions, students can be reminded of important previously learned information that they will have to work with.

One of the strongest features of an independent study program is its potential to present talented youngsters with a great deal of new information. Because no teacher is usually available to check on students' understanding, independent study is not especially useful in helping students to recognize key points and to distinguish them from less important information. Good directions, however, can be beneficial. Independent study does provide a good opportunity for students to apply new knowledge. Often this is done when students are asked to write a paper incorporating some new information they have acquired. Student projects and papers prepared during independent study exercises can be used by the teacher in assessing the quality of students' learning.

Lecture

Few instructional techniques have been as maligned as the lecture. Some cynics have been known to suggest that, when educational speakers run out of topics, they reach down into their bag and trot out their address on the evils of the lecture method. This address, among many audiences of educators anyway, is almost certain to win a good number of enthusiastic nods of agreement as alleged deficiencies are noted one by one.

While the myth that the lecture is evil persists, the lecture is a perfectly legitimate instructional technique, provided that it is used properly. Regrettably, the very legitimate concerns about misuse of the method have led some people to the false conclusion that there is something inherently wrong with the technique itself.

If misuse is the real culprit, what constitutes misuse? The question has no easy answer. To understand why, we need to understand a basic feature of the lecture that sets it apart from a good many other techniques. The lecture has the capability of introducing an incredible amount of information in a very short period of time. On the one hand, this makes it a very efficient technique. On the other hand, it can provide too much to students too quickly. Thus, one element of misuse is observed when the lecturer provides students with more information than they can be expected logically to absorb during the time period provided.

A second misuse again relates to the students. Specifically it relates to students' ability to maintain a good concentration on what a lecturer is saying over an extended period of time. As noted earlier, middle school and junior high school students (or at least large numbers of youngsters in this age group) have great difficulty listening carefully for more than about 20 minutes at a time. Even older students in the upper high school grades find their attention wanders when lectures last much more than half an hour.

A third misuse of the lecture concerns bad organization. If the lecturer is unorganized and jumps randomly from point to point, even the best note takers in the class will have difficulty in finding the message when they review their notes. Good lectures have a clear point-by-point flow.

In organizing to use a lecture technique, the teacher should attend to the following points:

1. *Identify students' present level of knowledge.* Do not presume they know something many may not know. If in doubt ask some questions. (Many students, even in high school, will not have the foggiest idea of the geographical location of Philadelphia. One student of a friend of the authors' found her shoulders sagging in despair when, after a lecture on political trends, one bright-eyed 17-year-old asked, "Ms. H., what's a 'trend'?")
2. *Keep length as short as possible consistent with the need to cover a reasonable amount of material.*
3. *Highlight key points.* During the lecture these can be emphasized. They will be cues to vary pitch and general intonation.
4. *Prepare an outline of the lecture for students to follow.* A list of major points and space for students to write notes will provide students with an organized array of information. The process of producing the outline also may help the teacher to develop a lecture with more logical point-by-point development.

A sample outline for students might look something like this:

Topic: The Roaring Twenties

1. Politics and Social Tensions of the 1920s
   1.1 Prohibition
   1.2 Immigration Problems
   1.3 The Ku Klux Klan and Other Fringe Groups

2. American Culture in the 1920s
   2.1 A Rich New Society
   2.2 Literature of the 1920s
        2.21 The Americans in Paris
        2.22 The Americans Who Stayed Home

3. Government and Big Business in the 1920s
   3.1 Republicans and the Role of Government

Lecture and the Events of Instruction.   The lecture format is very versatile. It is quite possible, for example, for a teacher to remind students of the particular objective that is to be emphasized. Although some lecturers are capable of prompting a tremendous amount of student interest in a subject, in general the technique is not regarded as one of the most suitable for motivating student interest in an area. Part of the difficulty in this regard may result not so much from any real problem with the lecture as a technique as from students' exposure through the years to so many untalented lecturers.

The lecture, when organized properly, can prompt students to recall important previously learned material. Perhaps the greatest strength of the lecture is the capability of the technique to present new information to students quickly. (As noted, this characteristic also accounts for some of the problems associated with the lecture.) A skilled lecturer also can use the technique to help students recognize key points and other essential information.

Because students during a lecture tend more typically to be taking in new knowledge than doing something with the knowledge they have already acquired, the lecture is a poor technique for involving students in applying information. Likewise, the lecture is ill suited for assessing students' grasp of new learning. A skilled teacher can watch for frowns and looks of "aha, I've got it" during his or her lecture, but beyond this kind of information, not much assessment can go on during a lecture.

Project Approach

The project approach has long been used in industrial arts and in crafts courses in the secondary school program. Its use, however, is by no means restricted to these areas of the curriculum. Nearly all teachers have experimented with student projects from time to time.

The project approach emphasizes doing. Students are expected to utilize basic information that they have gathered as they produce something tangible that can be evaluated by the teacher. With proper planning, the project approach can be highly motivating for students. They have an opportunity to see some tangible evidence of the utility of their school learning. In preparing for instruction emphasizing student preparation of projects, teachers must answer these questions:

1. What problem is to be solved by the students? (Students are expected to go beyond the facts to produce something that to some extent reflects their own personalities and thinking.)
2. What motivating features are built in? (The project, to the extent possible, should focus on something in which students have some interest.)
3. What constraints and limits are to be imposed? (For example, there may be a need to specify what materials can be used, what maximum costs can be incurred, and what length of time can be used for completion of the project.)
4. What provisions are made to take advantage of students own creativity? (It is better

for students to be asked to build something defined only in terms of basic principles that are to be incorporated than to have them re-create a clone of a finished product.)

A project assignment described by Bernard Dutton (1976, p. 30) meets these criteria well. Dutton provided students with the following instructions:

> *Design and construct a holder for either 8-track or cassette tape cartridges. The holder should be able to accommodate a minimum of eight cartridges in such a manner that the titles can be easily seen. The holder must be made from only one sheet of plastic no more than $\frac{1}{8}$ inch thick. Either clear, transparent or opaque plastics may be utilized. It must include thermoforming of the materials, but must not include any cementing processes. Your design, including complete specifications, must be approved before you start construction. You must have a full scale layout of the approved design before the materials for the project will be issued. The time allowed for this project is 15 class sessions.*

Note Dutton's selection of a project likely to whet students' interest. Tremendous numbers of secondary students have stereo systems at home. The tape carrier represents an instructional outcome for which they likely will see a good deal of utility. Also, motivation is well served by leaving the final design up to the students. The integrity of the content is preserved in that students' designs must meet certain production and materials' standards. A well-designed project exercise of this kind can be a very sound learning experience for secondary school students.

The Project Method and the Events of Instruction.   The project method accommodates quite well the need to advise learners of the intended outcomes of instruction. Directions for the project ordinarily will make this point quite clear. Additionally, projects that have been planned carefully have a high potential for motivating learning. Because most projects require application of a variety of old and new information, they may well help students to recall previous learning. Good directions can help in this regard.

Generally, the project method alone is not used to teach new information. Rather, its emphasis and real strength is on encouraging students to apply information they have learned in a way that yields some kind of a tangible product. Directions guiding students in their work can do a good job of highlighting key points that students will need to recall from recently taught information that will be useful to them in completing their projects. The project method can serve as a mechanism that the teacher can use in assessing the quality of students' learning. Finished projects will reveal a good deal about what individuals have acquired.

Role Playing

Role playing is a technique that is useful for helping students to see things from the perspectives of others. Many secondary school students approach the world with a certain lack of flexibility. They are reluctant to acknowledge that points of views and perspectives other than their own might be legitimate. Role playing can help to sensitize them to alternative ways for explaining the world around them.

Successful role playing must be preceded by careful planning. The following steps need to be accomplished:

1. The specific roles need to be identified.
2. Role descriptions that students will play need to be prepared. (These may be writ-

ten, recorded, or provided to students in some other way. Attention to detail is essential if students are to do a credible job of portraying assigned roles.)

3. A general situation must be developed. (The teacher needs to establish a situation or set of circumstances in which the various characters find themselves. For example, in a role-playing exercise featuring Lincoln and Douglas, the teacher might describe a county fair setting in the rural Midwest.)

4. Time must be scheduled for role players to familiarize themselves with the parts they will play.

5. Key questions for the debriefing session following the role-playing exercise need to be prepared. (Some examples: How realistically did each person play his or her part? Were arguments logical? Is there any way you might have reacted differently to some of the situations that developed? Do we tend to feel the same or differently about these issues today as the people being played felt in their day? And so forth.)

In thinking about preparing for a role-playing technique, we need to keep three important points in mind. First, descriptions of the individual roles that students are to play should be as brief as possible. (Of course there must be sufficient information to give students a feel for the "flavor" of the characters they are to portray.) Very-long-winded descriptions of characters tend to confuse students.

Second, the situation or setting into which the characters are placed for the role-playing exercise must be plausible. Absolute historical accuracy is not necessary, but the situation ought to have had at least the potential to have existed. Whereas some adults might appreciate a role-playing exercise involving a meeting of Julius Caesar, Mahatma Gandhi, and Cher, secondary students (or at least large numbers of them) have trouble accepting the legitimacy of this kind of fanciful grouping. (Certainly some classes would be well served by this kind of an imaginative arrangement. But, in the main, role playing that involves situations that students regard as real has more legitimacy for most students.) A group of characters including Ben Jonson and other literary figures of the time meeting in a London coffee house to discuss a play of the period is a setting that most students would regard as plausible.

Third, particular attention should be paid to planning the debriefing session. Many beginning teachers make the mistake of assuming that the follow-up discussion will simply happen even in the absence of planning. It will not. Further, the debriefing is perhaps the most important part of the entire instructional technique. It is during this phase that key points can be emphasized and students truly engaged with the essence of the ideas that have been introduced.

Role Playing and the Events of Instruction.   Although role playing character descriptions, if prepared carefully, can remind students about the objective of the instruction, ordinarily this kind of a function is secondary in such an exercise. Role playing can be very motivating for students. The technique might be capable of helping students to bring to mind previously learned information if this kind of material is included on the role descriptions prepared for each character. Many role-playing exercises, however, are not designed in this way, and this function is perhaps not as well served by role playing as by some other instructional techniques.

Some new information can be introduced via role playing. The quantity may be limited somewhat given the need to keep descriptions of individual roles relatively short. In general, role playing is more productive when students have received some of the basic information in another way. Providing students with an opportunity to apply knowledge in a free-flowing situation is a real strength of role playing. The debriefing phase of a role-playing exercise provides teachers with an opportunity to help students grasp key items of information and to assess general levels of understanding as reflected in student comments.

Simulation

Long used by the military and business, simulation enables teachers to place students in situations characterized by much of the reality of the world without subjecting them to some of the world's pitfalls. This feature was grasped early by military leaders who realized that mock battles could prepare men for war without the injuries and loss of life encountered in actual combat. Business executives, too, recognize in simulation an opportunity to train middle-management people without exposing the company to real-world losses arising from mistakes made during the learning process. This element of realism accompanied by few heavy costs for errors also played a part in educators' decisions to adapt simulations to the classroom.

Further, students' interest in games of all kinds has long been noted. The gamelike quality of simulations provides an opportunity to capitalize on this in the classroom. Many simulations are highly motivating to students, and teachers who use them report that even reluctant learners frequently become eagerly involved.

In planning for simulations, teachers typically follow a four-part sequence:

1. Assignment of students to parts or roles.
2. Time for students to learn parts and become familiar with the rules of the simulation.
3. The activity phase of the simulation
4. The debriefing phase of the simulation.

Simulations vary enormously in their complexity. A good many have rules that first-time players find confusing. Teachers need to plan sufficient time for students to grasp the parts they are to play and the rules they are to play by. It usually is not sufficient simply for students to be told to "read the rules." Most teachers find it necessary to play a leadership role in explaining rules carefully to the class.

As is the case with the role-playing technique, debriefing is a critically important part of any simulation. Well-framed questions during a debriefing session can do a great deal to help students to take important new learning away from the experience. Some have gone on to say that it is the quality of the debriefing that truly distinguishes educational simulations from parlor games that youngsters find under the Christmas tree.

Simulation and Events of Instruction. Rarely is simulation appropriate to use in emphasizing learning objectives. The technique is one of the best available for motivating learning. Only rarely do simulations build in information related specifically to items that have been previously learned and that are necessary for an understanding of some new material. Indeed, only rarely are simulations learned exclusively for the purpose of introducing brand-new material.

The real strength of the simulation technique is in providing students with an opportunity to apply information in a realistic setting. During a debriefing session, teachers are able to highlight key points and to evaluate the quality of students' learning as reflected in responses to questions.

Teacher Demonstration

Teacher demonstration has long been used in secondary school science classes. The technique has been particularly favored as a mechanism for familiarizing students with procedures that they are to follow as they perform laboratory exercises. Despite a long history of use in science classes, teacher demonstration is a technique that has a place in many other secondary school classes as well.

Successful teacher demonstrations build in steps that give students an opportunity to give evidence that they truly understand what has been demonstrated to them. It is not enough for the teacher to conduct a demonstration without providing some opportunity for students to do something that will reveal that desired information, processes, or principles have been acquired. Many teachers who have used the teacher demonstration method successfully follow a planned sequence as the demonstration goes forward. An example of such a sequence follows:

Step 1. Demonstrate to students the steps they must follow to accomplish an assigned task. (Obviously, students must also be apprised of the nature of the task and what successful completion is.)

Step 2. Respond to questions students might have about what has been demonstrated. (If no questions arise, the teacher cannot assume no questions exist. It is well for the teacher to ask a few questions on his or her own to be sure that students truly understand what has been demonstrated.)

Step 3. Review steps that students are to follow. (Clarity is a must. It is wise to write out appropriate sequence on a reference card to assure that nothing is left out as instructions are given to students.)

Step 4. At random, selected students should be asked to tell the teacher the appropriate sequence of steps that are to be accomplished. Students should be encouraged to state these steps in their own words. The teacher can listen carefully and correct any errors.

Step 5. Students should be provided an opportunity to practice what they have learned. The teacher can check on individual students' progress as they attempt to follow steps explained during the teacher demonstration.

The demonstration technique, when planned and executed properly, can give students a solid understanding of what they are to do. Beginning teachers who have difficulty with the technique frequently fail to attend to steps 4 and 5 in the sequence noted. There is evidence that students retain material better when given an opportunity to state new understandings in their own words. Further, when students recognize that they will be expected to use information presented in a demonstration, they tend to pay closer attention to the demonstration and to learn more from it.

Teacher Demonstration and the Events of Instruction.   It is possible for teachers to take a few moments at the beginning of a demonstration to remind students of objectives that are being emphasized. Some demonstrations are excellent vehicles for motivating learning. Because the teacher is the center of attention during a demonstration, it is possible for him or her to help students recall certain previously learned information relevant to the new learning task.

While demonstrations can be used to introduce entirely new material, frequently teacher demonstrations are designed to suggest to students how they should go about applying information they have already acquired. In preparing students for application tasks, teachers can organize demonstrations in such a way that key facts and principles are highlighted. Perhaps not always a formal part of a teacher demonstration lesson, but frequently flowing from the instructional technique, are opportunities for students to apply knowledge and to be assessed on the quality of their performances.

Team Learning

Large numbers of secondary teachers are interested in organizing students into groups for learning. Many group learning techniques are better suited for applications of knowledge rather than for acquisition of knowledge. An exception to this general characteristic is the team learning technique. Team learning provides an opportunity for teachers to introduce new material to students in a group setting and in a way that many students find a refreshing change from more traditional techniques.

For the teacher interested in a team learning exercise, the first step is to identify a topic area to be introduced to students. Once this has been accomplished, it is necessary to gather together in the classroom a variety of learning materials that students can use. It is essential that a large number of materials be available. It is desirable that there be a good range of difficulty represented among these materials so that students having different levels of ability will be able to find something they can use. Having identified a topic and gathered together appropriate materials, the teacher next must generate a number of focus questions. These must pertain to the topic and must be answerable given the materials students will have available to them.

Next, the class is divided into a number of teams. Groups of from four to six students each work best. Each team selects an individual to act as its recorder. The recorder is responsible for keeping notes about decisions the team will make about the several questions that will be asked. Next, the teacher distributes a set of questions to each team. The teacher points out the locations in the classroom of the relevant materials, explains to each team that the idea is to answer all the questions and reminds them to look at the available materials, and reminds team recorders to take notes.

Dunn and Dunn (1972, pp. 155–159) have suggested some rules for a sound team learning exercise.

1. Any team member may help any person on his or her own team but not any member of another team.
2. Talking is encouraged. But the noise level must be kept low enough so that work of others can go forward without disruption.
3. Each team attempts to answer all questions. The group recorder will write down all answers to questions developed by the team of which he or she is a member.

As the exercise goes forward, the teacher moves throughout the area giving assistance as needed. When all teams have answered all questions, the teacher begins to work with the class as a whole. During the debriefing, the following steps are followed:

1. A recorder for one of the groups is asked to give answers to questions found by his or her team.
2. Next, the teacher asks if any other recorders have different answers. If so, the class listens to these other answers.
3. The class discusses any discrepancies among answers to any of the questions. This discussion concludes with a determination of a "class consensus" answer. (Some teachers like to have individual recorders mark "right" or "wrong" at the side of the responses made by their groups for each question. In this variant of the exercise, a "winner" team can be identified at the end. The winner team will have the most correct responses.)
4. As a summary, the teacher can write consensus responses for each question on the board (or have students do so). Some teachers like to follow this with a distribution of these answers on paper to students the next day.

Team Learning and the Events of Instruction.   The team learning exercise is not especially well suited to helping students recognize the objectives of instruction, though in explaining the procedures teachers certainly can emphasize this information. The technique can be highly motivating for some students who do not respond favorably to more traditional procedures for acquiring new information. The technique is not particularly strong as a mechanism for helping students to recall previously learned information. The strongest feature of team learning is its capacity to introduce new information to students in an unusual way.

The technique does lend itself to highlighting key points for students in situations when the teacher does a responsible job during the debriefing phase. The debriefing phase, too, can provide the teacher with insights regarding the depth of individual students' learning as responses to questions are revealed. The technique is not a strong choice when the intention is to provide students with an opportunity to apply new learning.

Telelecture

Telelecture is an instructional technique involving classroom application of contemporary communications' technology. The technique is remarkably simple, not expensive, and highly motivating for many students. Yet its use is not widespread.

In terms of the bare essentials, telelecture involves a class of students in direct telephone contact with another individual at a site some distance from the classroom. In arranging for a telelecture, the telephone company fits an amplified voice box to a classroom. This enables the words of the party at the other end of the line to be amplified so all can hear. Typically, a microphone on a very long cord (sometimes more than one) is provided so that students can speak to the telephone guest to ask questions. To begin a telelecture, nothing more sophisticated is required than placing a telephone call (usually dialed on a mechanism that comes with the amplified voice box) to the telephone guest. Aside from the relatively modest cost of the amplified voice box installation, the only other charge is for the call. Even over long-distance lines, the call charge is not likely to be exorbitant.

The following steps are suggested in preparing for a telelecture.

1. Contact the individual to be called. Explain what the class is studying, why you would like the individual to share some thoughts with your class, whether he or she would be willing to have your class call, and whether he or she would mind responding to students' questions.
2. Assuming an affirmative response to the questions in step 1, set a time and a date. Explain that you will place the call. Get a telephone number where the guest can be reached. Be sure to consider time zone differences in agreeing about the time for the call.
3. Work with students to prepare an appropriate set of questions.
4. Decide who will place the call and determine the order of the questions.
5. Appoint one student or a committee of students to take notes on what is said for a class discussion to take place after the telelecture.

In general, half an hour is plenty for a telelecture. Certainly they can be longer if the discussion proves to be provocative and the guest is willing. However, many suitable telelecture guests are busy people, and some consideration must be given to their schedules.

Among the advantages of the telelecture technique, a most important one is the relative comfort that most secondary students have in talking to someone on a phone line. They are much less intimidated by a well-known personality who is present via the telephone system than by one who is present in person. Generally, students experience little stage fright in asking questions.

Second, it is relatively easy to get a telelecture guest. Certainly it is much simpler than arranging for an individual to come to the school in person. The guest can speak in the comfort of his or her office or home. Normal routine does not have to be disrupted.

Finally, telelecture can help students in small relatively isolated communities reach out to people hundreds and even thousands of miles away. One of the authors had no difficulty in arranging telelecture appearances for his class in the State of Washington of U.S. senators, governors, and famous literary personalities (one of whom chatted from the comfort of her Manhattan apartment, talked about the literary life, and thoroughly energized the enthusiasms of some aspiring 17-year-old writers). In short, the telelecture is a technique that probably deserves greater attention in secondary classrooms than it generally has received.

Telelecture and the Events of Instruction.   Telelecture tends to be a technique that centers attention on the invited guest, not the teacher. Consequently, telelecture is not a procedure that, by itself, is well adapted to emphasizing objectives or helping learners to recall information learned previously. The technique is a generally effective motivator. This and the capacity to introduce new information are the real strengths of the telelecture.

Good teacher follow-up can help students to get a focus on key points that are introduced during a telelecture, but the technique alone is not particularly well suited to accomplishing this task. Further, telelecture is not a sound choice when the teacher is seeking a technique that will permit students to apply new information and to provide evidence that new information has been mastered.

Posttest

Directions: Using your own paper, answer each of the following true/false questions. For each correct statement, write the word ''true.'' For each incorrect statement, write the word ''false.''

_____   1. The lecture is a bad instructional technique that has no place in secondary school teaching.

_____   2. It is desirable for teachers to explain to students clearly the objectives or purposes of a given lesson.

_____   3. The idea that students need to apply new learning if they are truly to master it is highly overrated; in fact, there is little to be gained by providing students with this kind of hands-on experience.

_____   4. Secondary students need help in distinguishing between important and unimportant information in new lessons.

_____   5. The technique of brainstorming can never be used to solve real problems; it is always an exercise in simple creativity.

_____   6. Questioning is a technique that, among other things, can be used to help students recall previously learned material.

_____   7. Role playing can help students to learn the perspectives of others.

_____   8. The project method has been used frequently by secondary school industrial arts instructors.

_____   9. Discussion generally is not regarded as an instructional technique that is an especially strong choice for introducing material to students for the first time.

_____ 10. All instructional techniques work equally well for (a) presenting new information to students and (b) asking students to apply new information.

Key Ideas In Review

1. It is inappropriate to ask whether a given instructional technique is ''good'' or ''bad.'' No instructional technique can be evaluated in these terms. Rather, it is necessary to think about the purpose to be served by a technique we are thinking of using. Clearly, certain techniques do serve some purposes better than they serve others. The ''goodness'' or ''badness'' of a given technique, then, relates to its appropriateness for a specific instructional purpose.

2. Successful lessons include specific teacher actions undertaken with a view to (a) emphasizing objectives, (b) motivating learning, (c) recalling previous learning, (d) presenting new information, (e) recognizing key points, (f) applying new information, and (g) assessing new learning. These seven considerations collectively are known as the "events of instruction."

3. Individual instructional techniques have strengths and weaknesses in terms of their appropriateness for responding adequately to each event of instruction. No technique alone can accommodate all seven events of instruction.

4. It is not enough to understand what tasks can be accomplished logically by a given instructional technique. Beyond this information, teachers need to know steps to be followed in implementing individual techniques. When such steps are adhered to, potentials of selected techniques to produce desired results are enhanced.

SUMMARY

Despite abundant talk about some instructional techniques as being good and others as being bad, these conversations go forward on a false assumption. That assumption is that a given technique can be good or bad regardless of the context within which it is used. Nothing could be farther from the truth. The appropriateness of an instructional technique can only be evaluated in terms of the purpose it is to serve. Thus, no technique is *always* good; similarly, no technique is *always* bad.

In thinking about instructional techniques and the tasks that a teacher has to accomplish, it is well to think about the components of a successful lesson. Gagné and Briggs (1974) point out that such lessons include a number of important events of instruction. The events of instruction provide a framework against which the appropriateness of individual instructional techniques can be judged. Some techniques are eminently well adapted to taking care of certain of the events of instruction but woefully inadequate choices to accomplish tasks associated with others. The successful teacher then must exercise his or her creativity to select and sequence a number of instructional techniques that collectively respond to all seven of the events of instruction. Subsequent chapters will provide illustrations of how this might be accomplished.

References

Armstrong, David G. *Social Studies in Secondary Education.* New York: Macmillan Publishing Co., Inc., 1980.

Dunn, Rita, and Dunn, Kenneth. *Practical Approaches to Individualizing Instruction.* West Nyack, N.Y.: Parker Publishing Company, Inc., 1972.

Dutton, Bernard. "Individualizing the Project," *Industrial Education* (September 1976): 30–31.

Gagné, Robert M., and Briggs, Leslie J. *Principles of Instructional Design.* New York: Holt, Rinehart and Winston, Inc., 1974.

Havighurst, Robert J.; Bowman, Paul Hoover; Liddle, Gordon P.; Matthews, Charles V.; and Pierce, James V. *Growing Up in River City.* New York: John Wiley & Sons, 1962.

Northam, Saralie B., ed. "Instructor's Manual: Development of Higher Level Thinking Abilities." Portland, Ore.: Northwest Regional Educational Laboratory, 1972.

9

Formalizing Unit and Lesson Plans

"I don't care *how* good your lesson plan is. If you don't change that crazy outfit, they're *never* going to speak up in class."

Objectives

This chapter provides information to help the reader to

1. Prepare instructional units following a systematic approach.
2. Recognize strengths of the instructional unit as a mechanism for organizing instruction.
3. Point out relationships among elements included in an instructional unit.
4. Follow a plan for developing lesson plans.
5. Prepare an instructional sequence utilizing the events of instruction.

Pretest

Directions: Using your own paper, answer each of the following true/false questions. For each correct statement, write the word "true." For each incorrect statement, write the word "false."

_____ 1. Because of the care with which today's textbooks are prepared, it is no longer necessary or desirable for teachers to develop their own instructional units.

_____ 2. Teaching situations vary so much from place to place that there are no general kinds of teacher tasks that have been found to be associated with good instruction in the vast majority of classrooms.

_____ 3. In planning an instructional unit, the last thing a teacher does is identify instructional objectives.

_____ 4. Instructional units represent a way for teachers to plan learning experiences that are suitable for the particular classes of students with whom they work.

_____ 5. Lesson plans should include references to both what teachers are to do and what students are to do.

_____ 6. An instructional unit requires more clock time to teach than a lesson plan.

_____ 7. A more complex instructional strategy is needed for an analysis-level objective than for a knowledge-level objective.

_____ 8. Instructional units should be designed so that, after they have been taught, teachers can identify strengths and weaknesses that can be modified before the material is taught again.

_____ 9. Instructional units interfere with teachers' creativity.

_____ 10. Lesson plans sometimes include plans for instructional sequences lasting more than a single class period.

INTRODUCTION

Once content has been selected, there is a need to organize it systematically. One approach that many teachers have found useful involves the development of instructional units. Typically, these units are built around course topics requiring from two to six weeks of instructional time. (This time frame represents only averages. Certainly some perfectly acceptable units may be shorter than two weeks or longer than six weeks in length.)

Instructional units enable teachers to exercise their creativity as they plan systematic instructional sequences for students in their classes. Since units are developed most frequently by the teachers who will be using them in the classroom, they can be organized to take advantage of what a teacher knows about his or her students. Further, the teacher is free to incorporate the kinds of instructional techniques in which he or she has confidence. A properly prepared unit is tailored carefully to meet the special needs of youngsters in a given course and the preferences of the teacher who will be working with these youngsters.

Units are designed to be taught over a number of instructional days. Once units have been developed, more specific plans must be prepared that focus on what is to be done during a given instructional period or, perhaps, during a limited number of instructional periods. Called "lesson plans," these very specific outlines detail what the teacher and students will be doing to implement the more general purposes described in the instructional unit. These lesson plans provide a means of giving each day's instruction purpose. They promote a sense of direction and organization both for the teacher and for students. In the sections that follow, we will look at some general features of units and lessons and then at some specific examples of each.

INSTRUCTIONAL UNITS

Instructional units represent a pulling together in a systematic fashion of all elements in a master plan for instruction focusing on a given topic for a specific period of time within a course. Careful specification of each element is important. This is so because, after the unit has been taught, we want to be able to evaluate the effectiveness of the unit. If we were less than pleased with how certain parts of the unit worked in the classroom, we need to be able to pinpoint specific components that might be modified before the material is taught again to another group of students. Often a minor alteration of one or two elements within a unit can result in a substantially improved unit.

Many frameworks for unit development are available. The one we will be working with here includes elements that frequently are encountered in instructional units. Mastery of this system will enable a teacher to adjust to another framework without too much difficulty. In the unit planning system we prefer to use, the following elements must be specified:

1. Title of the unit
2. General goal(s)
3. Focusing generalization(s)
4. Major concepts
5. Instructional objectives
6. Diagnostic tests and recommended prescriptions
7. Instructional strategies
8. Formal evaluation procedures
9. Needed learning resources

Each of these elements is included in a complete unit. In preparing the unit, clearly some of them will consume more teacher planning time than will others. Let us take a brief look at each of these nine basic unit components.

Title of the Unit

The function of this unit element is self-evident. Selection of a title involves nothing more complex than selection of a few words (or even a single word) that describe the general nature of the material to be taught in the unit. For example, a unit in a chemistry course might be titled "The Halogen Family." A unit in a U.S. history course might be called "The Progressive Era." Some districts provide new teachers with curriculum guides that include unit titles. In other areas, teachers are free to select topic titles they themselves consider to be appropriate given the focus of an individual unit they might prepare and teach.

General Goal(s)

Unit goals seek to describe in very general terms the teacher's expectations about the benefits that will come to students as a consequence of their exposure to this given body of instruction. Much less specific than instructional objectives, goals express a general area of teacher hopes regarding the kinds of learnings students will take away from the instructional experiences they confront during a given unit. For example, an English teacher who prepared a unit on the "Epic Hero Theme in American Novels" might develop the following general goal: "This unit is designed to foster students' appreciation of the form, extent of use, and purposes of the 'epic hero theme' in American novels." Clearly such a statement does not tell us exactly what students should be able to do as a consequence of their exposure to instruction on this topic. But the goal statement does suggest a general area of concern that is useful for communicating rather broad-sweeping intentions to students and to parents of students with interests in the focus of a given instructional program. Additional information about goals is provided in Chapter 7, "Selecting Content and Establishing Instructional Objectives."

Focusing Generalization(s)

The purpose of the generalizations provided in the unit is to point out specific important principles that students should come to grasp as a consequence of their exposure to this segment of instruction. Generalizations summarize in a succinct fashion the "findings" of leading scholars. Generalizations tend to represent a distillation of "truth" insofor as "truth" can be determined given our present state of knowledge. (A generalization is always subject to revision when new knowledge refutes the generalization's "truth.") In form, generalizations are statements of relationship among concepts that are not limited by reference to a specific place or time. They tend to be universally applicable explanations of the nature of the world. Consider this social studies generalization: "When urbanization occurs rapidly in a country, differences in status among people in various social classes become more pronounced." Given our present level of knowledge, the generalization is thought to be "true" and universally applicable regardless of time or of place.

Major Concepts

The focusing generalization (sometimes there may be more than one) of a unit should determine the concepts that are selected for emphasis. Recall that a generalization is a statement of relationships among concepts. Clearly students cannot be expected to grasp the generalization unless they have an understanding of the concepts embedded within the generalization. It is likely that some concepts taught will be those stated directly in the generalizations. Others may not be stated directly but, rather, be necessary for an understanding of some of the concepts that *are* stated directly.

There are many complex definitions of the word "concept." To simplify matters, let us consider concepts to be terms. What are we after in identifying the major concepts of a unit are simply those terms that we think students must understand to grasp the focusing generalization(s).

For beginning teachers, there is sometimes a tendency to identify too many concepts as major in planning an instructional unit. In looking at the selected generalization, some prudence must be exercised in identifying as major concepts primarily those terms and definitions that students are not likely to have acquired previously. Consider this generalization as an example:

> *When urbanization occurs rapidly in a country, differences in status among people in various social classes become more pronounced.*

Most secondary school students probably would have a reasonably good grasp of the concept "country" (though a few still will experience difficulty in differentiating among county, country, and continent). Most, too, we would expect to have long since mastered the concept "people." It would make little practical sense to identify either "country" or "people" as major concepts when planning an instructional unit. On the other hand, concepts such as "urbanization," "status," and "social class" may well not be understood by these students. Quite properly, then, they might be selected as major concepts. Further, a unit developer might decide that the generalization seemed to imply an understanding of the important concept "socialization." Socialization and perhaps a few other implied concepts might well be selected for inclusion in the unit as major concepts. Figure 9-1 includes an exercise designed to improve facility at identifying major concepts associated with a given generalization.

Figure 9-1

IDENTIFYING MAJOR CONCEPTS FROM GENERALIZATIONS

YOUR OPINION, PLEASE
The generalizations provided below might well be used as focusing generalizations for instructional units.* Look at each generalization. Then, for each generalization, determine the major concepts you would select were you to prepare an instructional unit centering on the generalization.

1. If the amount of money in circulation increases and the quantity of goods available for purchase remains the same, in the absence of governmental price controls, average price levels will rise.
2. If temperatures rise, then objects expand; conversely, if temperatures fall, then objects contract.
3. As the number of large cities in a country increases, there is an increasing tolerance for religious diversity.
4. In the absence of government intervention in the area of property rights, as the average annual rainfall decreases there is an increase in the average size of the land parcels held by individual owners.
5. Opinions that originate in an earlier period continue to be influential in a later period, both within a single lifetime and over generations.

*This material is adapted from Bernard Berelson and Gary A. Steiner, *Human Behavior: Shorter Edition* (New York: Harcourt Brace Jovanovich, Inc., 1967), p. 104.

Instructional Objectives

Instructional objectives make specific reference to the kinds of new behaviors that students should be able to demonstrate as a consequence of their exposure to material taught during the unit. Objectives are tied closely to the identified major concepts. It is essential that the importance of the major concepts be recognized by developing instructional objectives that will focus students' attention and teachers' instruction on these concepts. Without this important tie, the major concepts may simply become a cosmetic feature printed at the beginning of the unit but not addressed seriously as the actual teaching of the unit goes forward.

Instructional objectives can focus on outcomes related to students' abilities to manipulate academic or subject-matter-centered content (cognitive-domain objectives), to changes in students' values, attitudes, and feelings (affective-domain objectives), to students' abilities to exercise careful control of their muscular systems (psychomotor objectives). Specific characteristics of these basic objective types are outlined in Chapter 7, "Selecting Content and Establishing Instructional Objectives." The mix of cognitive, affective, and psychomotor objectives will vary with the nature of the guiding generalization(s) selected for the individual instructional unit.

A good deal of teacher artistry is required in selecting an appropriate number of objectives to frame instruction for a given unit. For a unit requiring four to six weeks' teaching time, generally six to ten objectives will be adequate. (Certainly in some units fewer objectives may suffice. Certainly, too, in some units more than ten may be required.) In general, when the number of objectives is too small, each objective sometimes is stretched artificially across too much content. On the other hand, when there are too many objectives, the content may be sliced into artificially small and insignificant pieces. Even experienced teachers have some difficulty in preparing a number of objectives appropriate for a new unit they are developing. Often, once a new unit has been taught, teachers will increase or reduce the number of objectives they had selected when they prepared the unit originally.

Diagnostic Tests and Recommended Prescriptions

Identification of specific objectives for a given unit always requires the teacher to make some assumptions about what students already know. For example, a teacher planning a unit titled "Symbolism in the Short Stories of Poe" presumes that his or her students, at a minimum, possess certain basic reading and comprehension skills. Teachers' knowledge about the general level of students' understandings, attitudes, and skills may have been drawn from informal observations of their work when previous units were taught. Possibly, too, formal diagnostic tests of a general nature may have provided some indication of students' general level of development in a variety of areas. Certainly in almost every case teachers have some reason for presuming that students will be able to do the work being proposed in a new unit.

But teachers, like everyone else, sometimes make errors in judgment. For this reason, it is desirable that some more specific diagnoses of students be undertaken after instructional objectives for a new unit of work have been identified. Examination of these objectives can suggest rather specific assumptions the teacher is making about what students know at the time instruction in the unit begins. Development of some simple diagnostic tests can reveal whether or not these assumptions are accurate. Suppose, for example, that we were preparing a unit entitled "Progressivism: An Example of an Organized Reform Movement." One instructional objective might be

Each student will correctly associate nineteenth-century reformers with the reform movement he or she led by responding correctly to eight of ten items on a matching exercise.

Note that this objective implies that the student already is familiar with the concept "reform" even before instruction begins. (The task here is for the student not to demonstrate an understanding of "reform," but, rather, to apply this understanding by identifying individuals and associations exemplifying the philosophy implied in the concept "reform.")

In this situation, a teacher might wish to develop a very short diagnostic test to determine whether the presumption of student familiarity with the concept "reform" were accurate. A very short true/false test might suffice. Note this example.

Reform

Directions: Look at the following sentences. Some of them are consistent with the idea of reform. Some of them are inconsistent with the idea of reform. In the blank provided, print the word "consistent" before the sentences consistent with the idea of reform and print the word "inconsistent" before sentences inconsistent with the idea of reform.

_____ 1. Flaws exist in every society. Man should not attempt to change them.

_____ 2. Society can be made better through deliberate political action.

_____ 3. Humans are inherently evil. Nothing can change this basic truth of our existence.

_____ 4. Better politicians will result in a better tomorrow for all of us.

_____ 5. Human beings are perfectable. Things can be changed for the better.

_____ 6. Child labor must be abolished because it is *wrong*.

Results of this diagnostic test can provide an interesting profile of the adequacy of students' understanding of the concept "reform." Teachers who have thought carefully about their students ordinarily will have developed instructional objectives that reflect fairly accurately students' existing states of development. In such cases, few students will have difficulty on a diagnostic test centering on what the students are presumed to know at the beginning of a new unit of instruction. But, in almost every case, a few students in a class will miss sufficient items to indicate some confusion. Extremely poor scores on a diagnostic test signal a need for special help.

In deciding which students need special assistance, it is desirable to identify primarily students who have received extremely low scores on the diagnostic test. Opinions vary as to what minimum standard of performance ought to trigger a decision to develop special help in the form of a learning prescription. Armstrong, Denton, and Savage (1978) suggest that students missing over half the items on diagnostic tests might well be designated to receive a special learning prescription to eliminate whatever "gap" might have been identified through the use of a diagnostic test. Using this standard, teachers who have selected their instructional objectives after a careful consideration of the characteristics of their students should not be faced with a need for preparing learning prescriptions for a very large number of youngsters.

As indicated in Chapter 6, "Diagnosing Students' Needs," a specific prescription can be provided for a student from among a number of alternatives. For example, a student with a very poor score on the diagnostic test centering on the concept "reform" might be given a short paragraph to read that explains the concept. Another student with poor reading skills might be directed to listen to a short tape-recorded explanation of the concept. Still another student might be scheduled for a teacher-student conference during which time the concept "reform" might be discussed. Whichever alternative is selected, it is important that it be something appropriate for the individual student and something that shows promise of bringing the student to an adequate level of understanding in a short period of time. See Figure 9-2.

Instructional Strategies

Instructional strategies are systematically arranged teacher activities that are undertaken to help students achieve the instructional objectives that have been developed for a given unit. Some of these teacher activities represent formal instructional techniques such as those described in Chapter 8, "Instructional Techniques." Others represent teacher activities that in all likelihood will be briefer in duration and less complex in structure than a formal instructional technique.

Properly, strategies are devised by individual teachers in light of their understanding of their students and of their own particular strengths as instructors. It is quite possible that two teachers working in the same topic area with very similar types of students may develop quite different sets of instructional strategies. Possibly, too, each may prove to be equally effective in helping students to master established instructional objectives.

While the content of individual instructional strategies may vary tremendously from teacher to teacher and from situation to situation, all instructional strategies must respond to certain important instructional tasks. These tasks have been described as events of instruction that, through some means or other, ought to be accomplished if careful and efficient instruction is the teacher's purpose. Based on the work of Gagné and Briggs (1974), the relationship between events of instruction and development of instructional strategies was described by Denton, Armstrong, and Savage (1980). A modification of the Denton, Armstrong, and Savage list of the events of instruction appears below.

Figure 9-2

WHAT INSTRUCTIONAL OBJECTIVES SUGGEST STUDENTS ALREADY KNOW: TESTING ASSUMPTIONS WITH DIAGNOSTIC TESTS

YOUR OPINION, PLEASE

In selecting instructional objectives when planning units, teachers make some assumptions about what students already know. In some cases these assumptions may not be correct. Look at the following instructional objectives. Decide what assumptions the teacher who wrote each of them seems to have had about what students already know. What kind of diagnostic tests would you recommend to test the accuracy of these assumptions? What kinds of prescriptions would you develop for students who did poorly on these diagnostic tests?

1. Each student will solve at least nine of twelve factoring problems each of which features at least three unknowns.
2. Laura's group will identify selected pollutants as being air, water, noise, or landscape pollutants by responding correctly to at least seven out of ten multiple-choice items.
3. Each student will distinguish among legislative proposals dealing primarily with (a) social issues and (b) economic issues that were made during the Theodore Roosevelt administration by responding correctly to eight of ten items on a test requiring an identification of given proposals as primarily "social" or "economic."
4. Students will identify parts of the cell by answering correctly eight of ten multiple-choice questions focusing on a provided diagram of a cell.
5. On an essay, each student will describe stylistic features of American naturalistic novelists of the late nineteenth century by citing at least six specific similarities and six specific differences in stylistic features used by American realistic novelists of the last nineteenth century.

---

1. Emphasizing objectives
2. Motivating learning
3. Recalling previous learning
4. Presenting new information
5. Recognizing key points
6. Applying new information
7. Assessing new learning

This list provides guidance to the teacher in planning a specific instructional strategy. To be complete, an instructional strategy must respond specifically to each of the seven necessary events of instruction. When this is done, the strategy rests upon a solid learning theory foundation. In simple language, the probability that students will learn what we hope they will learn is increased.

Let us see how an instructional strategy might look that responds to each of these seven events. To simplify our notation, let us develop a shorthand for each of the seven events of instruction as follows:

O = emphasizing objectives
M = motivating learning
R = recalling previous learning
P = presenting new information
KP = recognizing key points
APP = applying new information
ANL = assessing new learning

Suppose that we were teaching a geography course and that the following knowledge-level objective was among the instructional objectives we had developed to guide instruction during the unit:

> *Each student will identify capitals of Europe on a matching test with at least 80 percent accuracy.*

The instructional strategy we developed to help students grow toward mastery of this objective might look something like this (note the use of the symbols to indicate each of the seven events of instruction):

O	Remind students orally of the instructional objective related to identifying capitals of Europe. Remind them, too, that the objective is printed in their topic outline.
M	Show a short 15-minute film to prompt interest entitled "Europe's Capitals: Centers of Tradition and Power."
R	Conduct a brief discussion directed at helping students recall concepts "Europe," "country," and "capital." With a wall map available for reference, ask selected students to point to Europe, to several countries, and to several cities indicated as national capitals.
P	Divide students into groups for a team learning exercise. Using student atlases as information sources, each group will be asked to list as many European countries and capitals as possible in a ten-minute period. There will be follow-up activities including a teacher-led questioning and debriefing session.
KP	As the team learning exercise goes forward, go from group to group asking questions to assure himself or herself that students are focusing on *European* countries and *European* capitals.
APP	Provide each student with a map of Europe with individual countries labeled and stars printed at locations of each capital city. A list of capital cities will be printed on the chalkboard. Students will be asked to write in names of capitals on their maps at the places starred on their maps.
ANL	Provide students with a worksheet to take home. They will be provided with names of European countries and asked to supply the correct names of capital cities. Students should miss no more than 10 percent of these items.

This sequence of events comprises a complete instructional strategy for teaching the content contained in the indicated knowledge-level instructional objective. The specific responses to the seven events of instruction selected by the teacher designing this strategy may be quite different from those that another teacher would select. Since this objective requires students to operate only at the knowledge level, the strategy is not complex. Neither would it consume much instructional time. Conceivably all necessary steps might be accomplished in one class period. Certainly in most cases two periods would be adequate.

Note that the final step, assessing new learning (ANL), is *not* identical to the conditions of assessment mentioned in the instructional objective. The objective mentions that learning will be tested via a matching test. In the instructional strategy, the reference is to a take-home worksheet. Note that in the assessing new learning event we are interested in gathering information about how well students have acquired information to which they have just been exposed in the strategy. On the other hand, the assessment mentioned in the objective (the matching test) is designed to test retention of the new material during an examination given after instruction has been completed focusing on several of the instructional objectives in the unit. Indeed, in some cases (where only a few objectives frame instruction for an entire unit), the matching test may not be administered until the end of the unit. In this case the ten matching items focusing on locations of European capitals would be part of a much larger examination over the entire unit content.

The complexity of the identified instructional strategy will vary in accordance with the sophistication of learning required by the instructional objective. For example, we would expect a much more complex strategy to be required to prepare students for mastery of an instructional objective requiring them to function at the cognitive level of analysis than for mastery of an instructional objective requiring them to function at the cognitive level of knowledge. Some general frameworks for developing instructional strategies at each level of the cognitive taxonomy are illustrated in Figure 9-3.

Look carefully at this figure. Notice that the general strategy framework becomes more complex as we move from knowledge in the direction of evaluation. Notice that

---

Figure 9-3

FRAMEWORKS FOR DEVELOPING INSTRUCTIONAL STRATEGIES AT DIFFERENT LEVELS OF COGNITIVE SOPHISTICATION

SYMBOL	EVENT OF INSTRUCTION
O	Emphasizing objectives
M	Motivating learning
R	Recalling previous learning
P	Presenting new information
KP	Recognizing key points
APP	Applying new information
ANL	Assessing new learning

The term "Ex" will be used to identify a specific type of presenting new information which the teacher illustrates how students are to use information learned during an earlier part of the instructional sequence.

COGNITIVE LEVEL OF
THE INSTRUCTIONAL
STRATEGY   STRATEGY FRAMEWORK

Knowledge and
comprehension   O–M–R–P–KP–APP–ANL

Application   O–M–R–P–KP–APP–ANL–Ex–KP–APP–ANL

Analysis   O–M ⟨ R–P–KP–APP–ANL–Ex–APP–ANL
                       R–P–KP–APP–ANL–Ex–APP–ANL ⟩ Ex of analysis–KP–APP–ANL
                       R–P–KP–APP–ANL–Ex–APP–ANL

Synthesis   O–M ⟨ R–P–KP–APP–ANL–Ex–APP–ANL
                       R–P–KP–APP–ANL–Ex–APP–ANL
                       R–P–KP–APP–ANL–Ex–APP–ANL ⟩ Ex of synthesis–KP–APP–ANL
                       R–P–KP–APP–ANL–Ex–APP–ANL

Evaluation   O–M– ⟨ R–P–KP–APP–ANL–Ex–APP–ANL
                        R–P–KP–APP–ANL–Ex–APP–ANL
                        R–P–KP–APP–ANL–Ex–APP–ANL ⟩ Ex of developing
                        R–P–KP–APP–ANL–Ex–APP–ANL   evaluation–KP–APP–ANL
                        R–P–KP–APP–ANL–Ex–APP–ANL   criteria

                                                    Presentation
                                                        of
                              ANL–APP ———   problem

each strategy beginning at the level of analysis and continuing through the level of synthesis contains a number of repetitions of R–P–KP–APP–ANL–Ex–APP–ANL. In the example in the figure, this basic sequence is repeated three times at the level of analysis, four times at the level of synthesis, and five times at the level of evaluation. We do not mean to imply that it is necessary to follow exactly this number of repetitions in planning for instruction directed toward each of these levels; we suggest only that a strategy designed to help students to function at the level of synthesis will generally encompass more elements than a strategy designed to help students function at the level of analysis. Similarly, we would expect a strategy directed toward promotion of evaluation-level thinking skills to be more complex than a strategy directed toward synthesis-level thinking skills.

The notation used in Figure 9-3 may have something of an other-worldly look to it for a teacher unfamiliar with the symbol scheme. Remember that the symbols are just abbreviations for different steps in an instructional strategy. Once the symbols are mastered, they provide a useful notation system for teachers to use in planning their own instructional strategies. The utility of the system can be seen in some examples of instructional strategies that have been designed using this notation system. We have already introduced an example of an instructional strategy directed toward producing knowledge-level thinking. Now let us look at two additional strategies. The first will be a strategy designed to help students master an application-level objective. The second will be a strategy designed to help students master an analysis-level objective. Note the increasing complexity of the instructional strategy designed for use with the analysis-level objectives.

Application-Level Instructional Objective.   Each student will determine the shortest air distance between at least 10 of 12 pairs of cities using a globe with an inches-to-miles scale. To achieve this objective, student answers must be within 50 miles (either more or less) than the actual shortest air distance.

Strategy framework: O–M–R–P–KP–APP–ANL–Ex–KP–APP–ANL

O	Provide students with the objective orally. Remind them that the objective also is printed in the course outline.
M	Demonstrate with (1) a 12-inch globe, (2) an 18-inch globe, and (3) a 22-inch globe. A student volunteer will be asked to measure distances between New York and London on each globe with a tape measure. This will be followed by a questioning sequence. Some sample questions: Why do measured differences appear different on each globe. Why do London and New York seem farther apart on one globe than on another? And so forth.
R	Discuss (for review) basic concepts of English-system measurement with a special focus on the layout of information on a tape measure. Draw attention to tape-measure lines indicating full inches, half inches, quarter inches, eighth inches, and sixteenth inches.
P	Show film on how scale is used to build reliable models of the earth in the form of globes.
KP	Use a questioning sequence to debrief film. Draw students' attention to the relationship between the measured distance separating two points on a globe and the particular scale used in construction of that globe.
APP	Ask students to write a short paragraph in which they explain in their own words how it is possible for distances between two cities on two different globes to be unequal distances apart as measured by a cloth tape measure while, in fact, the real-world distance between the two cities never changes.
ANL	Correct student responses on the exercise noted in the previous step. Point out mistakes. Return papers with corrections to students.

Ex   Using a large globe (perhaps one where 1 inch equals 350 miles), demonstrate to students how distances between a pair of cities can be found by (1) using a tape measure, (2) determining measured distance, and (3) multiplying inches of measured distance by 350 to find actual distance in miles.

KP   Remind students to pay particular attention to the printed scale on the globe before they attempt to compute distances in miles.

APP Using globes and tape measures, ask students to find distances between selected pairs of cities. Students will write down answers and provide them to the teacher for critiquing.

ANL Using three different globes of different scales, have each student attempt to determine correct distances between two pairs of cities on each globe. Answers that fall within 50 miles plus or minus of the correct distances in each case will be considered correct.

Analysis-Level Instructional Objective.   Each student in a three- to five-page essay will comment on a letter written by James Madison to John Hancock. Each essay will point out how the letter reveals (1) basic political, economic, and social beliefs of Madison and (2) basic political, economic, and social beliefs of Hancock.*

$$
\textbf{Strategy framework:} \quad 1 \quad \text{O–M–} \left\langle \begin{array}{c} \overset{2}{\text{R–P–KP–APP–ANL–Ex–APP–ANL–}} \\ \text{R–P–KP–APP–ANL–Ex–APP–ANL–} \\ \underset{3}{} \end{array} \right\rangle \text{–Ex anal.–} \overset{4}{\text{KP–APP–ANL}}
$$

Phase 1

O   Students will be provided with an oral reminder of the instructional objective. Ask if all understand it. Point out that the objective is printed in the course guide.

M   The teacher will read a two-paragraph selection to the class from a political essay written by James Madison. Do not tell students Madison wrote the material. Tell them nothing at all about the writer. Follow with some questions to students designed to get them thinking about the author. Some examples:

> When did this author probably live?
> What might he or she have thought about the issue of a strong central government?
> Can you guess where this person was living and what he or she was doing at the time this essay was written?

Phase 2

R   The students will read handouts focusing on James Madison's activities at the time the U.S. Constitution was being written. Follow with a discussion.

P   The teacher will deliver a lecture on James Madison's political, economic, and social philosophy.

KP Using a questioning technique, the teacher will guide students toward a tight focus on elements of Madison's political, economic, and social philosophy.

---

*The numbers in the strategy framework are provided to indicate the four major divisions of the strategy. To facilitate understanding, these divisions are used to note exactly what part of the overall strategy is being accomplished by each cited event of instruction.

APP   Students will prepare short written summaries of their understandings of Madison's political, economic, and social philosophy.

ANL   These summaries will be critiqued and returned to students.

Ex   From a hat, the teacher will draw a "problem" likely to have been faced by James Madison, for example, "How should slaves be regarded?" With this problem in hand, the teacher will play the role of Madison and address the class on this issue much as Madison himself might have addressed them.

APP   Students will be divided into groups. Each group will be given a problem likely to have been faced by James Madison. Each group will outline a short speech Madison might have given. A spokesperson from each group will play the role of Madison and deliver the speech to the class as a whole.

ANL   The class members together with the teacher will orally critique the authenticity of each presentation.

Phase 3

R   Students will read handouts focusing on Alexander Hamilton. Follow with a discussion reviewing previously learned material about Hamilton's role at the time the U.S. Constitution was being prepared.

P   The teacher will show a film on Alexander Hamilton that places particular emphasis on his positions on political, economic, and social issues.

KP   In a questioning session following the film, the students will be guided toward an appreciation of the essential elements of Hamilton's political, economic, and social philosophy.

APP   In a very short written exercise, students will prepare summaries of their own understandings of Hamilton's political, economic, and social philosophy.

ANL   The teacher will critique these summaries and return them to the students.

Ex   The teacher will ask the class to suggest a problem likely to have been important at the time of Alexander Hamilton. When a problem has been named, the teacher will play the role of Hamilton and deliver a short speech to the class using the same logic that Hamilton might have brought to bear on the identified problem.

APP   Students will be divided into three groups. One group will be given an important political problem of Hamilton's day. One group will be given an important social problem of Hamilton's day. One group will be given an important economic problem of Hamilton's day. Each group will engage in a ten-minute brainstorming session on the general question, "What would Hamilton have wanted to do about this problem?" A person selected as group secretary in each group will take note of all responses. At the conclusion of this exercise a general class discussion will focus on likely responses of Hamilton to these issues.

ANL   At the conclusion, the teacher will provide an oral critique of suggestions made during the brainstorming activity and the subsequent discussion.

Phase 4

Ex
anal   The teacher will provide students with an essay that compares and contrasts the thought of Madison and Hamilton.

KP   There will be a class discussion focusing on similarities and differences of Madison and Hamilton as revealed in the essay.

APP   In a class discussion and activity session, students will fill in data retrieval charts featuring the names Hamilton and Madison along one axis and the terms political views, social views, and economic views along the other axis. Subsequent to the completion of the charts, students will refer to the information they have written during a classroom discussion centering on similarities and differences and potential explanations for similarities and differences in the thought of Madison and Hamilton.

ANL   Students will prepare papers in which, in their own words, they compare and contrast Madison's and Hamilton's positions on political, social, and economic matters.

In summary, the use of general frameworks for preparation of instructional strategies allows for a good deal of teacher creativity. Further, they allow for systematic and sequential development of instructional activities that are tied clearly to learning theory and that have solid potential for helping students master stated instructional objectives. Finally, such frameworks point out clearly that development of higher-level thinking skills is a complex and time-consuming process. Development of an instructional objective at the level of analysis, for example, must be accompanied by a rather elaborate instructional strategy if students are truly to be expected to function at the analysis level.

We believe that use of these general frameworks for instructional strategies will quickly demonstrate the folly of attempting to cover all of the content and, at the same time, developing higher-level thinking skills in all covered areas. Clearly a trade-off has to be made between the number of issues treated and the level of student sophistication developed regarding these issues. As the framework for strategies suggests, the time required for students to succeed at tasks requiring them to analyze, synthesize, and evaluate is considerable. Given the limited amount of instructional time available, the teacher must make some decisions regarding which issues deserve time required to promote the development of higher-level thinking skills and which ones will be treated less intensively. There is no right answer to the question of what is the proper mix between breadth and depth of coverage. What is clear, however, is that the issue is one that teachers must face. As can be seen from the general instructional strategies framework, we cannot develop synthesis- or evaluation-level understandings while, at the same time, we seek after the broadest possible content coverage (see Figure 9-4).

Formal Evaluation Procedures

Teachers use a tremendous variety of informal assessment techniques. But, almost universally, they rely on more formal procedures for evaluating student performance for the purposes of awarding grades. If grades are to reflect something meaningful about

---

Figure 9-4

DEVELOPING AN INSTRUCTIONAL STRATEGY FROM AN INSTRUCTIONAL OBJECTIVE

CAN YOU DO IT?

A procedure for using a framework for preparing general instructional strategies is illustrated in Figure 9-3. On separate pieces of paper try to accomplish the following:

1. Develop three instructional objectives. Focus on something you would see yourself teaching during your first year in the classroom.
2. Using the symbol system introduced in Figure 9-3, sketch the general strategy framework you will use for each objective.
3. Using these strategy frameworks, explain what would be going on in your classroom to accomplish each of the cited events of instruction.
4. Ask your instructor for comments about the strategies you have developed.

---

the content that has been taught, there must be a logical relationship between this content itself and tests used to assess student understanding of the content. For this reason, it is desirable to include tests to be used in the instructional unit plan.

Development of tests at the same time other elements in the unit are being prepared helps to ensure congruence between what is taught and what is tested. Certain kinds of tests, for example, are not suitable for assessing students' higher-level thinking skills. This means that, if we have an instructional objective written at the level of synthesis, we must have a testing procedure capable of telling us whether the student is functioning at this level. Some suggestions for matching appropriate kinds of test items to the level of thinking indicated in the instructional objective are provided in Chapter 11, "Measuring, Evaluating, and Reporting Student Progress."

Needed Learning Resources

Many an inexperienced teacher has begun a new topic area with great enthusiasm only to find that learning materials he or she assumed to be on hand were not available. To avoid this difficulty, it is a sound practice to identify the specific resources needed to support instruction while the unit is being planned. This practice assures the presence of suitable support resources to give students a reasonable chance of meeting the learning expectations stated in the instructional objectives.

Resources cited as the unit is being developed may be of two basic types. Usually most numerous will be mentions of resources intended for direct student use. These might include such things as books, periodicals, films, filmstrips, cassette tapes, and files of maps and posters. Additionally, the learning resources list often also notes items that are primarily of interest to the teacher. These materials usually are not used directly by students. Rather, they provide a source for additional teacher enrichment that can augment the depth of teacher understanding in the focus topic of the unit. Some items, of course, can be used directly both by students and by teachers.

In preparing a list of needed learning resources, we have found it wise to make an error on the side of too much rather than of too little. It is a relatively simple task to cut back on what is used. On the other hand, few teachers enjoy stretching limited numbers of resources when they have a genuine need for more. The suggestion to go for more rather than for less should be tempered with a caution to select only materials that truly are related to the topic at hand. Padding of resource lists simply to add bulk makes no sense at all.

Putting It All Together

Complete instructional units include all the pieces discussed in the previous sections. Each part of the unit contributes to the effectiveness of the whole. Therefore, each part deserves careful consideration as the unit development process goes forward. An example of a completed unit is presented in the appendix to this chapter. As you study this unit, take care to note how the unit developer has addressed each of these nine basic unit components:

1. Title of the unit
2. General goal(s)
3. Focusing generalization(s)
4. Major concepts
5. Instructional objectives
6. Diagnostic tests and recommended prescriptions
7. Instructional strategies
8. Formal evaluation procedures
9. Needed learning resources

LESSON PLANS

As noted, lesson plans focus on a much shorter span of time than do plans for entire instructional units. As the name suggests, lesson plans specify what is to be accomplished during a given lesson that is presented as part of a unit. Sometimes lesson plans are referred to as "daily plans." This usage suggests that frequently lessons are designed to be completed within a single instructional period on a given day. Although many lessons will be completed in a single class period, some may require more time. However, almost never will a lesson plan cover a time longer than two successive instructional periods.

Lesson plans contain detailed information about what will be happening in the classroom during the time period covered. They are practical, detailed, "nuts-and-bolts" descriptions of a small segment of instruction that takes place within a larger and more general planned unit. A number of frameworks for planning lesson plans are available. The one we introduce here contains elements found typically in most guidelines for lesson plan preparation. We suggest that a complete lesson plan ought to include each of the following elements:

1. Lesson topic
2. General-purpose statement
3. Lesson objective
4. Sequence of teacher activities
5. Sequence of student activities
6. Description of needed materials
7. Lesson evaluation procedure
8. Long-term evaluation procedure

Let us look briefly at each one of these lesson plan components.

Lesson Topic

This component of the lesson plan is self-explanatory. The lesson topic simply is a statement of the general area of focus of the particular lesson to be taught. The topic, of course, should bear a clear connection to the subject matter of the unit of which the lesson is to be a part.

General-Purpose Statement

The general-purpose statement indicates the aims of the lesson. Ordinarily concise in form, the general-purpose statement is capable of communicating the general intent of the lesson to a principal, another teacher, or some other interested party. It is somewhat similar in form to the general goal statements found in instructional unit plans.

Lesson Objectives

As complete instructional unit plans include instructional objectives that identify desired student learning behaviors related to an important section of the unit, lesson plans have lesson objectives that specify what students ought to be able to do as a consequence of their exposure to the lesson. Lesson objectives help teachers to keep their instruction in focus and targeted toward helping students achieve the behaviors stated in the objectives. Mastery of lesson objectives might be thought of as checks on students' incremental progress toward mastery of the instructional objective in the unit toward which the lesson is directed.

Sequence of Teacher Activities

It is desirable to lay out an intended sequence of teacher activities in developing a lesson plan. Particularly in situations characterized by a rapid-fire interchange between the teacher and students, it is easy for the teacher to become disoriented and forget exactly where he or she is in the development of the lesson. This lapse happens to experienced teachers as well as to newcomers to the profession. A lesson plan with a written sequence of intended teacher activities can be an invaluable resource for the teacher when this happens. A quick glance at the plan can get instruction back on track.

In preparing intended sequences of teacher activities, it is important to recognize that these sequences do not have to be followed rigidly. The ebb and flow of activities as a lesson unfolds may suggest alternative sequences preferable to those that have been written on the plan. The listed teacher activities are best thought of as statements about the kinds of things the teacher hopes to do as the lesson unfolds. These may provide a useful point of reference should he or she need a quick reminder about his or her planned instructional actions.

Sequence of Student Activities

Lesson plans often include statements about what students will be doing at various points in the lesson. Thinking through this sequence can be most helpful to teachers in planning in advance for students to be engaged productively as the lesson unfolds. For example, suppose a teacher planned to work with students who were organized in small groups. Some advance planning would be desirable regarding what those groups of students with whom the teacher was not working at a given moment should be doing. Careful thought to such issues can result in much smoother lessons and can diminish considerably the likelihood that serious classroom control problems will develop.

Description of Needed Materials

Perhaps nothing frustrates beginning teachers so much as to find themselves well launched into a new lesson only to be lacking some needed equipment or materials. Careful thinking in advance can eliminate many such problems. For example, if a film is to be shown, is the projector and screen available for use? If the room is an old one with only two-pronged plug receptacles, is there a three-way plug adapter available to fit the projector cord? Are there spare exciter bulbs and projection light bulbs? Careful description of needed support materials and equipment prompts teachers to ensure that all those things that are needed are on hand before the lesson begins.

Lesson Evaluation Procedure

It is sound practice to incorporate a mention of a lesson evaluation procedure into the lesson plan. Tied closely to the lesson objective, the lesson evaluation procedure specifies what will be done to ascertain whether or not students have achieved the lesson objective. Lesson evaluation procedures do not have to be rigorous and formal. But some effort ought to be made to specify how student learning in a given lesson will be assessed.

Long-Term Evaluation Procedure

The inclusion of the long-term evaluation procedure in a lesson plan represents an attempt to establish a clear tie between the lesson and the unit instructional objective toward which the lesson is directed. The long-term evaluation procedure is nothing more than a restatement of the evaluation procedure noted in the unit instructional objective. An analysis of the lesson should reveal a readily discernible connection between what is being taught and what students will be required to demonstrate when their degree of mastery of the instructional objective is assessed.

Putting It All Together

Let us see how these various components might look in a completed lesson plan. Such a plan is introduced in Figure 9-5.

Figure 9-5

SAMPLE LESSON PLAN*

LESSON TOPIC
Human Traits That Are Inherited.

GENERAL-PURPOSE STATEMENT
This lessons helps to familiarize students with some of the more common human characteristics and to acquaint them with whether selected characteristics are dominant or recessive.

LESSON OBJECTIVE
Each student will be able to cite three or four examples of inherited human traits and point out whether they are dominant or recessive.

SEQUENCE OF TEACHER ACTIVITIES
1. Short introduction to human genetics via a lecture (about 15 minutes). Conclude by asking students to think about what traits they think they have inherited from their parents.
2. Using an overhead projector and water-soluble pencil, write such human characteristics as hair color, eye color, ear lobe attachment, ability to taste PTC paper, and other easy-to-determine human traits. Discuss these items with students and respond to questions.
3. Ask students to determine whether they individually have the dominant or recessive form of each of the traits noted in item 2 above.
4. Tell students to check with members of their family and determine which have dominant and recessive forms of each of these traits.
5. Show short film entitled *Different Peoples, Different Traits.*
6. Debrief film by highlighting reasons why certain areas of the world have large populations of people with a certain expression of a given trait. For example, discuss reasons that Sweden has many blonde-haired, blue-eyed people and Italy has many dark-haired, brown-eyed people.

SEQUENCE OF STUDENT ACTIVITIES
1. In response to teacher activity 1, students will respond with their own ideas about potentially inheritable human traits.
2. During the discussion in teacher activity 2 and the question noted in teacher activity 3, students will take notes. These notes should include some mention of their own traits.
3. Students will go home and note how these traits are expressed in their family. They will write this information in their notebooks.
4. Students, as an assignment, will attempt to identify areas in the world other than those mentioned in class where there tend to be abundant expressions of a certain trait that, taking the entire population of the world as a whole, is not common.

DESCRIPTION OF NEEDED MATERIALS
Overhead projector
Roll of clear overhead projector acetate
Water-soluble overhead projector pencil
16mm film projector
Extension cord
Three-way adapter plug
Different Peoples, Different Traits, 16mm film (color), 21 minutes

LESSON EVALUATION PROCEDURE
Students will be divided into groups of approximately six students each. Each group will complete a chart listing 15 human traits. For each trait, they will note which form of the gene expression is dominant and which is recessive.

LONG-TERM EVALUATION
Each student will make genetic crosses using both Punnett square and mathematical techniques by solving correctly at least eight of ten problems that will include at least one monohybrid, one dihybrid, and one sex-linked problem.

*This unpublished lesson plan, developed in 1979 by Rose Ann Blough, has been edited, adapted, and printed here with permission.

Posttest

Directions: Using your own paper, answer each of the following true/false questions. For each correct statement, write the word "true." For each incorrect statement, write the word "false."

_____ 1. Because of the care with which today's textbooks are prepared, it is no longer necessary or desirable for teachers to develop their own instructional units.

_____ 2. Teaching situations vary so much from place to place that there are no general kinds of teacher tasks that have been found to be associated with good instruction in the vast majority of classrooms.

_____ 3. In planning an instructional unit, the last thing a teacher does is identify instructional objectives.

_____ 4. Instructional units represent a way for teachers to plan learning experiences that are suitable for the particular classes of students with whom they work.

_____ 5. Lesson plans should include references to both what teachers are to do and what students are to do.

_____ 6. An instructional unit requires more clock time to teach than a lesson plan.

_____ 7. A more complex instructional strategy is needed for an analysis-level objective than for a knowledge-level objective.

_____ 8. Instructional units should be designed so that, after they have been taught, teachers can identify strengths and weaknesses that can be modified before the material is taught again.

_____ 9. Instructional units interfere with teachers' creativity.

_____ 10. Lesson plans sometimes include plans for instructional sequences lasting more than a single class period.

Key Ideas in Review

1. Once content to be taught has been selected, it needs to be organized systematically. Instructional units, formal guidelines for instruction covering a two- to six-week period, represent a response to this need. Tailored by individual teachers to respond to the needs of their own students, instructional units provide a mechanism for careful organization and precise evaluation of instruction.

2. Instructional units include a number of interrelated elements. In reviewing the impact of a given unit on students, it is possible for each of these elements to be examined independently. Often it happens that modification of only one or two elements in a unit may enhance the effectiveness of the unit as a whole. Systematically contructed units enable teachers to become much more sophisticated in their analyses of their instructional programs by providing them with the capability of pinpointing specific problem areas.

3. Perhaps one of the most important sections of an instructional unit is the section focusing on instructional strategies. These strategies can be organized for the purpose of accomplishing certain critical events of instruction that, collectively, are thought to enhance the likelihood that students will master the material. Instructional strategies vary in complexity according to the sophistication of the anticipated learning. For example, strategies directed toward producing cognitive learning at the knowledge level tend to be less complex than strategies directed toward producing analysis-level learning.

4. Lesson plans are specific and detailed blueprints for what occurs in a classroom as a given lesson unfolds. Lesson plans ordinarily cover a rather short period of instruction. Indeed, many are written to describe what will be going on during a single class hour. In almost no cases are lesson plans written to cover a time period in excess of two successive class periods.

5. Lesson plans contain a number of elements that are analogous to those found in complete instructional units. For example, each lesson plan includes an objective that describes what students sbould be able to do as a consequence of their exposure to the instruction provided in the lesson. Further, there is a lesson evaluation component that teachers can use to determine the degree to which students have acquired the understandings introduced during the lesson.

6. Lesson plans should be tied clearly to the instructional unit. In analyzing a given lesson plan, an observer should be able to discern a clear relationship between what is proposed in the lesson and one of the instructional objectives in the guiding unit plan. In short, lesson plans guide students toward incremental mastery of unit instructional objectives.

SUMMARY

Instructional units, organized in a systematic fashion, help teachers define and describe specifically what is to be accomplished during a two- to four-week block of instruction within a given subject area. Instructional units that are teacher prepared take advantage of individual teachers' academic strengths, diagnostic skills, and creativity. Units are tailored by the developing teachers to meet the specialized needs of their own students in a way that is consistent with the prescribed curriculum and is responsive to the peculiar characteristics of the population of youngsters to be served.

When instructional units are developed systematically, teachers' abilities to assess the impact of their instructional program is enhanced. For example, should a teacher be dissatisfied with the performance of his or her students during a given unit, a precise analysis of possible causes for problems can be undertaken once the unit has been completed. Often some minor adjustment in instructional objectives, diagnostic procedures, instructional techniques, or other elements can be made that will make a subsequent teaching of the unit a much more satisfactory experience.

Unit preparation that incorporates instructional strategies formulated to accommodate the events of instruction brings home to teachers the necessity to make choices about the level of sophistication of student understandings that might be expected with regard to each concept taught. It is clear that instructional strategies designed to promote cognitive understanding at the level of knowledge, for example, require less elaborate planning and less instructional time than do those designed to promote cognitive understanding at the levels of analysis, synthesis, and evaluation. The unit planning process forces the teacher to establish some important priorities with regard to which content merits the time necessary for students to achieve higher-level understandings.

Lesson plans organize instruction for short periods of time. In many cases, a lesson plan will specify what is to occur in a classroom during a single instructional period. Only rarely will lesson plans cover a time period extending beyond two successive instructional periods. Lesson plans represent clear and concise descriptions of what is to occur in a classroom at a particular point of time while a given instructional unit is being taught.

References

Armstrong, David G., Denton, Jon J., and Savage, Tom V. *Instructional Skills Handbook.* Englewood Cliffs, N.J.: Educational Technology Publications, 1978.

Berelson, Bernard, and Steiner, Gary A. *Human Behavior: Shorter Edition.* New York: Harcourt Brace Jovanovich, Inc., 1967.

Bloom, Benjamin S., ed. *Taxonomy of Educational Objectives: Handbook I: The Cognitive Domain.* New York: David McKay Co., Inc., 1956.

Denton, Jon J., Armstrong, David G., and Savage, Tom V. "Matching Events of Instruction to Objectives," *Theory Into Practice* (Winter 1980): 10–14.

Gagné, Robert M., and Briggs, Leslie J. *Principles of Instructional Design.* New York: Holt, Rinehart and Winston, Inc., 1974.

Martorella, Peter H., with Jensen, Rosalie S., Kean, John M., and Voelker, Alan M. *Concept Learning: Designs for Instruction.* Scranton, Penna: Intext Educational Publishers, 1972.

McNeil, John. *Toward Accountable Teachers.* New York: Holt, Rinehart and Winston, Inc., 1971.

Popham, W. James, and Baker, Eva L. *Systematic Instruction.* Englewood Cliffs, N.J.: Prentice-Hall, Inc., 1970.

Pratt, David. *Curriculum: Design and Development.* New York: Harcourt Brace Jovanovich, Inc., 1980.

Appendix

Example of a Completed Unit*

TITLE OF UNIT: MECHANISMS OF INHERITANCE

GENERAL GOAL

The purpose of this unit is to help students gain an understanding of the processes through which characteristics are inherited in plants, animals, and humans.

FOCUSING GENERALIZATION

Inherited characteristics of living organisms do not occur randomly; rather, they follow predictable patterns consistent with the findings of Gregor Mendel.

MAJOR CONCEPTS

a. Genetics
b. Heredity
c. Principle of dominance
d. Principle of segregation
e. Principle of independent assortment
f. Laws of probability
g. Genetic cross
h. Chromosome hypothesis
i. Gene theory

Relationship of Instructional Objectives to Major Concepts

Identification Numbers of Instructional Objectives

	1	2	3	4	5	6	7
Letters denoting major concepts	a	c, d, e	c, d, e	f	g	h, i	c, d, e

---

*This unpublished unit, developed in 1979 by Rose Ann Blough, has been edited, adapted, and printed here with permission.

INSTRUCTIONAL OBJECTIVES—COGNITIVE DOMAIN

Ident. Number	*Cognitive Level*	
1	*Knowledge*	Each tenth-grade biology student will define the vocabulary terms associated with the topic of genetics by responding correctly to at least 22 of 25 items on a matching test.
2	*Knowledge*	Each student will identify contributions of Mendel, Sutton, Morgan, and Muller by responding correctly to at least eight of ten items on a multiple-choice test.
3	*Analysis*	Each student will compare and contrast the relative importance of the work of Mendel, Sutton, Morgan, and Muller on an essay to be completed as a formal class examination. Each essay must include specific reference to each man's (a) general body of completed research, (b) the results of this research, and (c) the theories or principles derived from this research.
4	*Comprehension*	Each student will identify the role played by the laws of probability in interpreting the results of genetic crosses by responding correctly to at least eight of ten items on a multiple-choice examination.
5	*Application*	Each student will make genetic crosses using both Punnett square and mathematical techniques by solving correctly at least eight of ten problems that will include at least one monohybrid, one dihybrid, and one sex-linked problem.
6	*Analysis*	On an essay examination, each student will compare and contrast the chromosome hypothesis and the gene theory. Each essay must include specific references to (a) essentials of each position, (b) modifications that have been made to each, and (c) strengths and weaknesses that have been associated with each view.

INSTRUCTIONAL OBJECTIVES—AFFECTIVE DOMAIN

Ident. Number	
7	Each student will demonstrate an interest in genetics by coming in before school to participate in a fruit fly breeding experiment without receiving any credit toward a course grade. The objective will be considered attained if a student is present on at least 30 percent of the days when the experiment is in progress.

DIAGNOSTIC TESTS AND RECOMMENDED PRESCRIPTIONS

Diagnostic Test A*

Directions: Circle the letter preceding the "most correct" answer for each of the following multiple-choice items.

1. Meiosis occurs in organisms that reproduce
   a. sexually.
   b. asexually.
   c. either sexually or asexually.
2. Meiosis results in cells that are _____ in chromosome number.
   a. diploid
   b. triploid
   c. haploid
   d. normal
3. Which of the following is the correct order of the phases for the first cell division of meiosis?
   a. telophase, anaphase, metaphase, prophase
   b. prophase, metaphase, anaphase, telophase
   c. metaphase, telophase, prophase, anaphase
   d. anaphase, telophase, prophase, metaphase
4. In sexual reproduction, gametes that have _____ chromosomes unite to form zygotes that are _____ in chromosome number.
   a. 2n, 4n
   b. 2n, n
   c. n, 3n
   d. n, 2n
5. Male gametes are called
   a. eggs.
   b. sperms.
   c. chromosomes.
   d. manocytes.
6. Oogenesis of the female germ cell results in
   a. one egg and three nonfunctioning polar bodies.
   b. four eggs and no polar bodies.
   c. two eggs and two functioning polar bodies.
   d. two eggs and two nonfunctioning polar bodies.
7. Chromosomes are
   a. threadlike structures in the cell nucleus.
   b. constant in number for each species.
   c. the carriers of the genes.
   d. all of the above.
   e. none of the above.
8. DNA is arranged in fixed patterns to form thin strands of _____ in the nucleus.
   a. genes
   b. ribosomes
   c. chromosomes
   d. nucleotides
9. A segment of a chromosome that carries a unit of genetic information and controls hereditary characteristics is a
   a. chromatid

---

*Students who miss more than four of these questions will be provided with supplementary reading material as a remedial prescription.

  b. spermatocide.
  c. gene.
  d. nucleocyte.
10. Any change in the chromosome pattern of an organism results in
  a. abnormalities.
  b. death.
  c. inability to reproduce.
  d. illness.

Diagnostic Test B*

Directions: Using your own paper, solve the following problems involving multiplication of fractions.

1. $1/2 \times 1/4 =$
2. $1/2 \times 1/2 =$
3. $1/4 \times 1/2 =$
4. $3/4 \times 1/2 =$
5. $1/2 \times 17 \ =$

6. $1/4 \times 3/4 =$
7. $2/3 \times 1/3 =$
8. $1/2 \times 1/2 \times 1/2 =$
9. $1/3 \times 1/4 =$
10. $3/4 \times 2/4 =$

Prescription for Low Scorers on Diagnostic Test A

Students in this group will listen to a tape and view a series of slides explaining the concept "meiosis." This program discusses chromosomes and genes in relation to meiosis and reproduction. Each phase of meiosis is covered. Additionally, students will listen to a second tape including explanations of male spermatogenesis and female oogenesis. This tape also reviews the process of zygote formation. Students will be provided with handouts to observe as they listen to the tapes. These handouts are coordinated with the tapes. Among other things, these handouts will include the following diagrams:

Male Spermatogenesis: Male Gamete Production by Meiosis

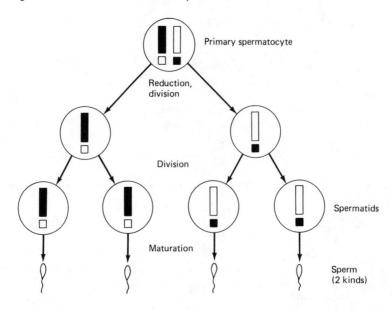

*Students who miss more than four of these items will be provided with appropriate supplementary material as a remedial prescription.

Female Oogenesis: Female Gamete Production by Meiosis

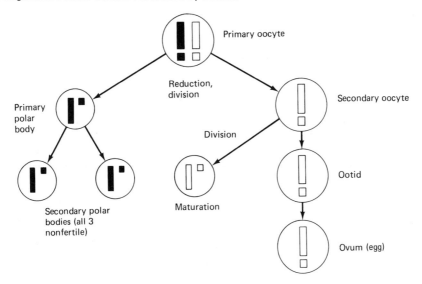

Zygote Formation

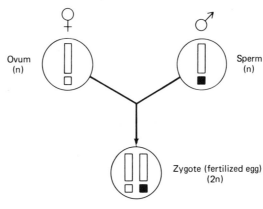

n = haploid
2n = diploid (normal chromosome number)

Prescription for Low Scorers on Diagnostic Test B

The following material will be presented to these students.

Let us review how we multiply fractions. To multiply two or more fractions, multiply the numerators together and make the product the numerator of the new fraction. Next, multiply the denominators together and make the product the denominator of the new fraction. Let us look at some examples.

$$\frac{1}{2} \times \frac{1}{2} = \frac{1 \times 1}{2 \times 2} = \frac{1}{4} \qquad \frac{2}{3} \times \frac{1}{2} = \frac{2 \times 1}{3 \times 2} = \frac{2}{6}$$

$$\frac{1}{4} \times \frac{1}{1} = \frac{1 \times 1}{4 \times 1} = \frac{1}{4} \qquad \frac{1}{2} \times \frac{1}{2} \times \frac{1}{2} = \frac{1 \times 1 \times 1}{2 \times 2 \times 2} = \frac{1}{8}$$

Remember: $\dfrac{\text{Numerator} \times \text{numerator}}{\text{Denominator} \times \text{denominator}}$

INSTRUCTIONAL STRATEGIES

Instructional Objective 1:

Each tenth-grade biology student will define the vocabulary terms associated with the topic of genetics by responding correctly to at least 22 of 25 items on a matching test.

Strategy framework: O–M–R–P–KP–APP–ANL

O   Teacher will remind students orally of this objective and remind them that the objective has been included in their printed unit outline.

M   Referencing important vocabulary items displayed via the overhead projector, teacher will tell students importance of genetics to their lives and emphasize the need for understanding of basic terminology associated with the subject.

R   Teacher will conduct a brief class discussion focusing on generations, inheritance, cell structure, and division. Students have encountered all these topics previously.

P   Students will be organized into groups for a team learning exercise. Each group will be given a set of vocabulary flash cards. Students will be asked to quiz one another regarding meanings of terms. Ask each team to come up with a team champion at the end of the 15-minute exercise. In a brief 5-minute exercise before the whole class, the teacher will try to select a class champion by quickly flashing cards and asking the team champions for definitions.

KP   Teacher will go through all vocabulary cards drawing students' special attention to those terms considered to be most critically important for understanding the material in this unit.

APP   Students will be provided with a vocabulary worksheet including a list of terms and a list of definitions. Students will be asked to match terms with their appropriate definitions. Work will be checked in class.

ANL   Students will be asked to complete a written exercise calling upon them to (1) use selected vocabulary words correctly in a sentence and to (2) provide brief, written definitions of these terms.

Instructional Objective 2:

Each student will identify contributions of Mendel, Sutton, Morgan, and Muller by responding correctly to at least eight of ten items on a multiple-choice test.

Strategy framework: O–M–R–P–KP–APP–ANL

O   Teacher will remind students of the objective orally, ask if any have questions about the objective, and point out that it is printed in the unit outline.

M   Teacher will call students' attention to a bulletin board featuring photos of Mendel, Sutton, Morgan, and Muller along with some examples of their work. Teacher will describe some of the more interesting facets of the work of each individual.

R   Teacher will conduct a short review of basic procedures followed in scientific research. Students have previously been exposed to this material. Also, quickly review essentials of plant reproduction and insect reproduction.

P   Teacher will provide for students a tape/slide presentation focusing on work of Mendel, Sutton, Morgan, and Muller.

KP   Immediately following this presentation, teacher will debrief students regarding key points made during the preceding session. Teacher will use an overhead projector to write important points about each of the four scientists as the discussion goes forward.

APP Teacher will ask students to prepare, in their own words, brief written summaries of the work of Mendel, Sutton, Morgan, and Muller. They will be free to use any reference materials available in the classroom.

ANL On a worksheet, students will match the work, results, and conclusions provided with the scientist responsible for them.

Instructional Objective 3:

Each student will compare and contrast the relative importance of the work of Mendel, Sutton, Morgan, and Muller on an essay to be completed as a formal class examination. Each essay must include specific reference to each man's (1) general body of completed research, (2) the results of this research, and (3) the theories or principles derived from this research.

Strategy framework:

$$O–M \begin{cases} R–P–KP–APP–ANL–Ex–APP–ANL \\ R–P–KP–APP–ANL–Ex–APP–ANL \\ R–P–KP–APP–ANL–Ex–APP–ANL \\ R–P–KP–APP–ANL–Ex–APP–ANL \end{cases} Ex\ anal.–KP–APP–ANL$$

O Teacher will review instructional objective orally, remind students that it is printed in the course outline, and respond to any questions related to the objective.

M Teacher will show film focusing on important advancements in genetics that have come about because of the research efforts of certain important scientists.

R Teacher will conduct a brief oral review of plant reproduction with emphases on self-pollination and cross pollination of flowering plants.

P Teacher will deliver a formal lecture on the work of Mendel focusing on the nature of his observations and the conclusions he drew from them.

KP Teacher will use a series of overhead transparencies to highlight some of the cross results Mendel obtained and to reinforce information regarding three important principles Mendel formulated.

APP Students will individually produce charts or models, according to directions provided, that will illustrate Mendel's principles.

ANL Students will respond to questions in the text regarding the essential contributions of Mendel.

Ex Students will read a short selection entitled "Analyzing Mendel: Was He Lucky or Was He a Genius?"

APP Students will participate in a classroom debate on this topic: "Resolved that Mendel had great results but was not a great scientist."

ANL Students will prepare a paper in which they utilize their understanding of the term "scientific method" to either support or attack the procedures of Mendel.

R Teacher will conduct a brief oral review of chromosomes, cell division, and reproduction.

P Students will read handout materials focusing on the work of Sutton.

KP Teacher will conduct a review with students regarding highlights from the Sutton materials. Teacher will use an overhead projector to write key points as this discussion unfolds.

APP Working in groups, students will prepare charts referencing key contributions of Sutton. These will be put up on the wall for display throughout the remainder of the unit.

ANL Students will be asked to prepare short written summaries of their understanding of Sutton's key contributions.

Ex Teacher will conduct a critique of Sutton's work in terms of his methodology.

APP Given what they know about how Sutton proceeded, in brainstorming groups, students will generate as many "positive aspects of Sutton's methodology" and "negative aspects of Sutton's methodology" as possible in a 15-minute period. Each group will share results with the class.

ANL Students will utilize their understanding of the term "scientific method" in a paper they prepare commenting on Sutton's methodology.

R Teacher will review the chromosome hypothesis.

P Teacher will show a filmstrip on Morgan's fruit fly experiments and his gene theory.

KP Teacher will review key points orally after the showing of the film strip.

APP Students will complete a worksheet featuring a number of key questions about Morgan's contributions.

ANL Students will take a short true/false quiz centering on Morgan's work with fruit flies.

Ex Students will read a copy of a speech made by an individual who had looked carefully at Morgan's approach to research.

APP Students will prepare charts showing "strengths" and "weaknesses" of Morgan's approach to research.

ANL Students will prepare short papers in which they comment on Morgan's methodology.

R Teacher will review the concept "mutation."

P Teacher will present slides accompanying a lecture centering on Muller's investigations of the causes of mutations.

KP In a postlecture discussion, teacher will ask probing questions to determine whether students have acquired key points.

APP In groups, students will prepare charts for display summarizing Muller's work in the area of mutation.

ANL Given a list of potential mutators, students will be asked to identify which are likely to, in reality, be mutators and to describe their reasons for their choices.

Ex Students will study carefully a critique made of Muller's methodology.

APP Students will interview someone who role plays Muller in a "Meet the Press" format during which "Muller" is questioned sharply about his research methodology.

ANL Students will prepare short papers in which they comment on Muller's use of the scientific method.

Ex. of anal. Teacher will lead a class discussion centering on comparisons of the work of Mendel, Sutton, Morgan, and Muller. Emphases will be on the similarities and differences of their research methods and their individual use of results to jump to novel conclusions.

KP As a conclusion to this discussion, teacher will highlight important differences and similarities of the four scientists.

APP Students will divide into two teams to play "Biology Baseball." "Getting to base" involves answering questions from the teacher (i.e., the "pitcher"). Teams will score points and stay at bat each inning until three teacher questions on Mendel, Sutton, Morgan, and Muller are missed.

ANL   Students will complete a data retrieval chart with the four geneticists (Mendel, Sutton, Morgan, and Muller) listed on one axis and the other axis labeled with (1) the research completed, (2) the results obtained, and (3) the theories and/or principles derived from the research.

Instructional Objective 4:

Each student will identify the role played by the laws of probability in interpreting the results of genetic crosses by responding correctly to at least eight of ten items on a multiple-choice examination.

Strategy framework: O–M–R–P–KP–APP–ANL

O   Teacher will remind students orally of the objective, point out to them, as well, that the objective is printed in the unit outline, and answer any questions related to the objective.

M   Teacher will ask each student in the class to flip a coin and determine whether the coins turned up heads or tails. On the board, teacher will write the number of heads and the number of tails that resulted from this single flip by each class member, and ask students whether they think the ratio of heads to tails determined after this one flip reflects what one would expect the ratio to be. Teacher will ask probing questions designed to engage students' interest in the general area of probability.

R   Teacher will explain to students that a knowledge of multiplication of fractions is necessary in working with probability ratios. Teacher will review processes using the chalkboard.

P   Students will view a film in which the two laws of probability are explained and their use in interpreting and predicting the results of genetic crosses are introduced.

KP   Teacher will provide each student with a handout explaining the operation of the two laws of probability and some examples of their application to genetic problems. Teacher will discuss this material with the students.

APP   Students will be divided into groups. Members of each group will flip a coin 50 times and count the numbers of heads and tails obtained. After recording these results, each group will determine whether these findings follow the first law of probability. Next, each student in every group will flip two coins (one after the other) 10 times and record the results. Members of the group will pool results and determine whether they follow the second law of probability.

ANL   Students will complete successfully a take-home assignment requiring them to complete some problems related to the laws of probability and their relation to genetics.

Instructional Objective 5:

Each student will make genetic crosses using both Punnett square and mathematical techniques by solving correctly at least eight of ten problems that will include at least one monohybrid, one dihybrid, and one sex-linked problem.

Strategy framework: O–M–R–P–KP–APP–ANL–Ex–KP–APP–ANL

O   Teacher will tell students objective, remind them that it is printed in the unit outline, answer any questions related to the objective.

M   Teacher will describe briefly some fascinating kinds of problems that geneticists have answered over the years. Teacher will describe the problems first of all in terms of what they wanted to know, point out the large number of variables involved, and ask students for some ideas about how they think geneticists might have established procedures to organize variables in a systematic way for prediction.

R   Teacher will review laws of probability with students, question individual students to see whether they can express laws of probability in their own words, and correct mistaken impressions.

P   Students will be provided with a handout explaining the operation of the Punnett square technique and with alternative mathematical techniques.

KP   In a debriefing discussion, teacher will highlight key features of the Punnett square technique and of alternative mathematical techniques.

APP   Students will be organized into groups for a team learning exercise. Each team will be given a set of problems to work. Problems will include monohybrid, dihybrid, and sex-linked crosses. For each provided problem, students will be instructed to use either Punnett square or mathematical techniques. They will be free to refer to notes or handouts.

ANL   Each student will be given a worksheet of problems to complete. These will be checked and returned to students with appropriate remedial comments, as needed.

Ex   Teacher, using the overhead projector, will work several genetic cross problems. At least one monohybrid, one dihybrid, and one sex-linked problem will be worked using both Punnett square and mathematical techniques.

KP   Teacher will discuss situations when it is preferable to use Punnett square and situations when it is preferable to use mathematical techniques.

APP   Each student in class will be provided with a number of genetic cross problems to solve. He or she will be asked to solve them with no reference to information related to the use of Punnett Square or mathematical techniques. He or she will be free to choose whichever technique seems appropriate. The teacher will check the results of this work and provide remedial feedback where necessary.

ANL   On a take-home exercise, students will successfully work 80 percent of the provided genetic cross problems provided.

Instructional Objective 6:

On an essay examination, each student will compare and contrast the chromosome hypothesis and the gene theory. Each essay must include specific references to (1) essentials of each position, (2) modifications that have been made to each, and (3) strengths and weaknesses that have been associated with each view.

Strategy framework:

$$O\text{–}M\text{–}\left\langle \begin{array}{c} R\text{–}P\text{–}KP\text{–}APP\text{–}ANL\text{–}Ex\text{–}APP\text{–}ANL \\ R\text{–}P\text{–}KP\text{–}APP\text{–}ANL\text{–}Ex\text{–}APP\text{–}ANL \end{array} \right\rangle \text{–Ex of anal.–}Kp\text{–}APP\text{–}ANL$$

O   Teacher will review the objective orally, remind students that it is written in the unit guide, and respond to any questions related to tbe objective.

M   Teacher will show a film on chromosomes and genes and their role in inheritance to prompt interest and engage students in a lively postfilm discussion.

R   Using the overhead projector, teacher will review with students cellular components, the location of chromosomes, and their actions during cellular reproduction.

P   Teacher will deliver a short, tightly focused lecture on the chromosome hypothesis. This will be reinforced by distribution of a handout capsulizing much of this information in a highly readable fashion.

KP   In a follow-up discussion, teacher will write key points relating to the chromosome hypothesis on the board.

APP   Alternatively, students may elect to summarize the chromosome hypothesis in a short paper or to make a short tape recording of their comments that can be turned in to the teacher.

ANL   In class, students will take a short true/false quiz focusing on characteristics of the chromosome hypothesis.

Ex   Students will view slides on corn cell meiosis. With the teacher's direction, they will focus particular attention on the actions of the number 9 chromosome. The teacher will explain how this movement is consistent with what might be expected from the chromosome hypothesis.

APP   Students will write a short paper describing the actions of chromosomes during reproduction and how these actions tend to support the chromosome hypothesis.

ANL   Teacher will provide written feedback to each student regarding the general acceptability of the response rendered to the exercise cited immediately above.

R   Teacher will review previously introduced material regarding chromosomes and the location of genes.

P   Teacher will show to class and discuss pictures of the salivary glands of drosophilia larvae and follow with a short lecture on gene theory.

KP   Teacher will provide students with a handout summarizing key points of gene theory and ask if there are any questions regarding any of the listed points.

APP   Working in groups and using notes taken from lectures and other available learning resources in the room, students at each table will attempt to formulate as complete and succinct a statement of the gene theory as possible.

ANL   Students will complete a short take-home worksheet focusing on characteristics of the gene theory.

Ex   Students will be provided a handout of the genetic map of *drosophilia*. They will be organized into groups. Students will be asked to study the genetic map and think on how changes in the arrangement of genes on the chromosomes can be expressed as physical changes in the flies. Moving from group to group, the teacher will explain the connection between these physical characteristics as consistent with what gene theory would predict.

APP   Working in groups, students will develop a large wall poster that presents in a graphic and succinct fashion an explanation of gene theory including (1) what the theory states, (2) how the theory was proved, and (3) any modifications that have been made to the theory.

ANL   Students will complete take-home worksheets focusing on gene theory.

Ex. of anal.   Students will read a short selection providing a brief summary of arguments made comparing and contrasting the chromosome hypothesis and the gene theory with some judgmental comments included regarding views.

APP   Students will be organized into groups. Each group will be asked to engage in a brainstorming activity designed to generate (1) as much support as possible for the chromosome hypothesis, (2) as much opposition as possible for the chromosome hypothesis, (3) as much support as possible for the gene theory, and (4) as much opposition as possible for the gene theory. A spokesperson for each group will share findings with the class. A general discussion will ensue.

ANL   Students will write imaginary "letters to the editor" in which they take a position either in support of the chromosome hypothesis or of the gene theory.

Instructional Objective 7:

Each student will demonstrate an interest in genetics by coming in before school to participate in a fruit fly breeding experiment without receiving any credit toward a course grade. The objective will be considered attained if a student is present on at least 30 percent of the days when the experiment is in progress.

Enabling Procedures: At the beginning of the unit, each student in the class will be invited to participate in this activity. The general nature of the activity will be explained. Special emphasis will be placed on its voluntary nature and its total divorce from the grading system. Further, a simple written summary of the activity will be provided to each student. Further invitations to participate will be made at the beginning of each week the activity is in progress.

FORMAL EVALUATION PROCEDURES

Instructional Objective 1: Part 1

Directions: Definitions listed on the left define terms listed on the right. There is only one correct term for each definition. In the blank provided, place the letter identifying the term described by the definition.

_____	1. Inherited resemblances and differences among organisms.	a. linkage
	2. The study of heredity.	b. allele
_____	3. An organism that is heterozygous for one or more characteristics.	c. phenotype
_____	4. An allele that is always expressed when it is present in an organism.	d. genotype
	5. All allele that is only expressed homologously.	e. genetics
_____	6. Having two like alleles for a trait.	f. heredity
_____	7. Having two different alleles for the same trait.	g. hybrid
		h. autosome
		i. selection
		j. recessive
		k. dominant
		l. heterozygous

_____	8. One of two or more alternative inherited traits.
_____	9. Outward physical appearance of a trait.
_____	10. The genetic composition of an organism.
_____	11. Inheritance in which neither allele is dominant, but which shows a mixing of the two alleles.
_____	12. Tendency of different traits to be inherited together because the genes controlling them are located on the same chromosomes.

m. homozygous
n. blending
o. polyploidy

Instructional Objective 1: Part 2

Directions: Definitions listed on the left define terms listed on the right. There is only one correct term for each definition. In the blank provided, place the letter identifying the term described by the definition.

_____	1. Permanent change in a gene or chromosome, which is transmitted to the offspring.
_____	2. Nonsex chromosome.
_____	3. Exchange of sections between homologous chromosomes.
_____	4. A segment of a chromosome that carries a unit of genetic information and controls heredity characteristics.
_____	5. The condition in which the cells of an organism have more than two full sets of chromosomes.
_____	6. Propagation between two close relatives.
_____	7. Chart giving the ancestry of an animal, plant, or person.
_____	8. Offspring of the parental cross.
_____	9. Traits whose genes are carried on the sex chromosome.
_____	10. Separation in its offspring of traits that are combined in a hybrid.
_____	11. Process of choosing certain desired organisms for breeding.
_____	12. Mating between two pure-breeding organisms.
_____	13. Offspring of the first filial generation.

a. pedigree
b. inbreeding
c. gene
d. blending
e. mutation
f. crossing over
g. linkage
h. autosome
i. segregation
j. F_2
k. selection
l. polyploidy
m. F_1
n. sex-linked
o. P

Instructional Objective 2

Directions: This is a multiple-choice test. For each item, only one answer is correct. Please circle the letter of the answer you believe to be correct.

1. Gregor Mendel experimented with
    a. fruit flies.
    b. garden peas.
    c. four o'clocks.
    d. corn plants.
2. Which of the following conducted the first scientific studies of heredity?
    a. Walter Sutton
    b. Theodor Boveri
    c. Gregor Mendel
    d. Thomas Morgan
3. Through his investigations, Morgan discovered and developed
    a. the gene theory.
    b. sex-linked traits.
    c. crossing over.
    d. a, b, and c.
    e. none of the above.
4. Hermann Muller uses X rays to increase the natural rate of mutation by about
    a. 10 times.
    b. 50 times.
    c. 100 times.
    d. 1,000 times.
5. Besides X rays, other agents that Muller discovered that can produce mutations are
    a. high temperature and cosmic rays.
    b. low temperature and nitrous acid.
    c. radiation and formaldehyde.
    d. a, b, and c.
    e. a and c.
6. According to Morgan, a(n) _____ was a segment of a(n) _____ that controls a particular genetic trait.
    a. chromosome, gene
    b. gene, allele
    c. autosome, allele
    d. gene, chromosome
7. From his experiments, Morgan formulated the principle of dominance, the principle of independent assortment, and the principle of
    a. segregation.
    b. separation.
    c. selection.
    d. recessiveness.
8. Walter Sutton and Theodor Boveri developed a hypothesis stating that _____ carry the genetic factors of heredity.
    a. alleles
    b. genes
    c. chromosomes
    d. nucleic acids
9. Who proved the Sutton chromosome hypothesis?
    a. Sutton
    b. Boveri
    c. both a and b
    d. neither a nor b
10. Which of the following genetic researchers was ignored during his own lifetime?
    a. Morgan
    b. Mendel

     c. Muller
     d. Sutton

Instructional Objective 3

Directions: Prepare an essay no more than three or four pages in length in which to compare and contrast the importance of the work of Mendel, Sutton, Morgan, and Muller. In your essay, make specific mention of each individual's (1) general body of completed research, (2) results coming out of this research, and (3) theories or principles derived from this research.

Instructional Objective 4

Directions: This is a multiple-choice test. For each item, only one answer is correct. Please circle the letter of the answer you believe to be correct.

1. The chance that a coin will turn up heads when tossed once is
     a. 1/2.
     b. 1.
     c. 2/3.
     d. 0.
2. The chance that two coins can be tossed and both will be heads is
     a. 1/2.
     b. 1.
     c. 1/4.
     d. none of the above.
3. The results of one trial of an event _____ the results of later trials of the same event.
     a. do affect
     b. do not affect
     c. change
     d. indicate
4. The chance that two independent events will occur together is the _____ of their chances of occurring separately.
     a. sum
     b. product
     c. quotient
     d. result
5. The _____ the number of samples taken of a chance event, the _____ it follows the laws of probability.
     a. larger, closer
     b. larger, less
     c. smaller, closer
     d. smaller, less
6. The chance that a male with genotype TtRr will produce a tR sperm cell is
     a. 1/2.
     b. 1/4.
     c. 1.
     d. 0.
7. A short, blonde female has what chance of producing an egg that carries a gene for a tall, blonde trait?
     a. 1
     b. 3/4

    c. 1/4

    d. 0

8. If you flip a quarter, a penny, a dime, and a nickel, the chance that all will be tails is

    a. 1/2.

    b. 1/4.

    c. 1/8.

    d. 1/16

9. What is the probability of a heterozygous tall, homozygous blonde, heterozygous right-handed male producing this sperm cell?

    a. 0

    b. 1/2

    c. 1/4

    d. 1/8

10. The results of a first trial event do not affect the results of a second, different trial event.

    a. This is always true.

    b. This is never true.

    c. This may or may not be true depending on the events.

Instructional Objective 5

Directions: Solve each of the following problems. Use the method given in the problem. Show all genotypes, phenotypes, and ratios as specified in the problem.

1. A homozygous black female guinea pig is mated with a homozygous brown male. Black coat color has complete dominance over brown. Let B represent the dominant gene and b the recessive gene. Solve the the Punnett square method. Show P genotypes and F_1 and F_2 phenotypic ratios.

2. Cross a homozygous tall pea plant with a heterozygous tall pea plant. Show the P phenotypes. Solve F_1 and F_2 ratios by the Punnett square method.

3. A homozygous red-flowered four o'clock is crossed with a homozygous white-flowered plant. Using the Punnett square method, solve for the F_1 and F_2 ratios.

4. Cross a homozygous tall, yellow pea plant with a short, green pea plant. Obtain the F_1 and F_2. Solve by Punnett square.

5. Cross a homozygous black, shorthaired male guinea pig with a homozygous brown, longhaired female. In guinea pigs, black coat color is dominant. Also in guinea pigs, short hair is dominant to long hair. Solve using the mathematical technique. Show the phenotypes and genotypes of the F_1 generation.

6. Cross a roan, polled (hornless) bull with a white, horned cow. In cattle, red is incompletely dominant over white, the heterozygous condition being roan. The polled condition is dominant over the horned. Give the genotype, phenotype, and number of F_1.

7. In humans, normal color vision is dominant to color blindness. Color blindness is a sex-linked characteristic. If a normal man marries a woman who is also normal but carries the gene for color blindness, what are the chances that one or more of their children will be color blind? Solve by using a Punnett square.

8. In humans, hemophilia is a sex-linked, recessive trait. If a boy and his father both have normal blood clotting, his mother and sister also have normal blood clotting, but his new little brother is a free bleeder, show the Punnett square for the family. List the genotypes of the entire family.

9. If gene A is lethal when it is homozygous, and two organisms that are hybrid for this trait produce a large number of offspring, what percentage of the offspring

can be expected to die? Solve either by Punnett square or by the mathematical method.

10. Cross a tall, yellow, round pea plant with a short, green wrinkled pea plant. Find the genotype and phenotype of the F_1 and the phenotypes of the F_2. Use the mathematical method.

Instructional Objective 6

Directions: Prepare an essay of about four pages in length. In your essay, compare and contrast the chromosome hypothesis and the gene theory. Include specific mention of (1) essentials of each position, (2) modifications that have been made to each, and (3) strengths and weaknesses that have been attributed to each view.

Instructional Objective 7

Teacher Tasks: The teacher will keep track of the number of sessions attended by each student who participates in the before-school fruit fly breeding experiment. The number of sessions attended will be divided by the total number of sessions held to determine what percentage of the total sessions was attended by each participating student.

Needed Learning Resources

Books

Baker, Myron S., and Jackson, B. Norton. *Contemporary Biology.* New York: Poston and Company, 1979.

Chester, Quenton V. *Burbank: The Master Hybridizer.* Santa Clara, Calif.: Denvy Press, 1964.

Lipscomb, Farley R. *The Great Geneticists.* Boston: P. Strand and Company, Publishers, 1976.

Lockridge, Cecile. *A Brief Review of Probability Theory.* Chicago: State Street Press, 1980.

Films and Filmstrips

Dolby Films, Inc. *The Monte Carlo Caper or Probability Made Simple,* 16mm sound film (color), 21 minutes.

B. Jackson Company. *No Blue Jeans These: The Small but Important World of Genes and Chromosomes,* 16mm sound film (b/w), 18 minutes.

Noland and Company. *The Amazing Fruit Fly,* color filmstrip (81 frames).

Wagner Brothers Films. *Achievements of the Great Geneticists,* 16mm sound film, 28 minutes.

Other Commercially Prepared Materials

Adams Scientific Supply. "Photo Set #104" (includes photos and background materials on Mendel, Sutton, Morgan, and Muller).

Knickerbocker School Products. *Genetics' Big Four* (series of 35mm slides accompanied by sound tape focusing on work of Mendel, Sutton, Morgan, and Muller).

Kraatz, Henry V. "Analyzing Mendel: Was He Lucky or Was He a Genius?" *Inquiries in Genetics* (Winter 1980): 117–124.

Lowery, L. Byron. "Morgan's Techniques: A Reappraisal," *Methodological Review* (September 1978): 432–451.

Munson Scientific. *Muller and Mutation* (set of 35mm slides accompanied by sound tape).

Nelson Supply Co. *Corn Cell Meiosis* (set of 35mm slides).
Wright Biological Instruction, Inc. "Salivary Glands of Drosophilia Larvae" (a large graphic representation).

Teacher-Prepared Materials

Genetic map of *drosophilia* (dittos needed for each student).
Handout explaining operation of Punnett square technique and the mathematical technique (one for each student).
Handout focusing on work of Sutton (one for each student).
Overhead transparency containing important vocabulary words associated with genetics.
Overhead transparencies summarizing Mendel's work.
Set of vocabulary flash cards including terms and definitions of words associated with genetics. (Prepare six sets.)
Take-home sheets explaining laws of probability and their relationship to genetics (one for each student).
Vocabulary worksheet including terms associated with genetics.
Worksheet of problems for students to solve using Punnett square and the mathematical technique.
Worksheet on gene theory.

10

Motivating Students and Implementing Programs

FUNKY WINKERBEAN by Tom Batiuk © 1979. Field Enterprises, Inc. Courtesy of Field Newspaper Syndicate.

Objectives

This chapter provides information to help the reader to

1. Recognize differences between intrinsic motivation and extrinsic motivation.
2. Describe how certain aspects of intrinsic motivation and extrinsic motivation can be used in the classroom.
3. Identify basic components of the act of communication and state how they may apply to classroom interactions.
4. Describe special teacher skills needed in working with large groups, small groups, and individuals.
5. Point out factors that influence classroom climate and suggest several things teachers can do that are designed to produce a positive classroom climate.

Pretest

Directions: Using your own paper, answer each of the following true/false questions. For each correct statement, write the word "true." For each incorrect statement, write the word "false."

_____ 1. Basically, intrinsic motivation results because of something that occurs within the learner.

_____ 2. Most theorists believe that extrinsic motivation is more powerful then intrinsic motivation.

_____ 3. Maslow has pointed out that the self-actualization need is the most basic and fundamental of all human needs.

_____ 4. A person's desire to be like someone else has been called the identification motive.

_____ 5. Provision of exploratory activities in the classroom is one way in which classroom teachers can provide an instructional program that responds to the curiosity drive.

_____ 6. Generally, individuals become more interested in things in which they are proficient than in things in which they are not.

_____ 7. Grades are effective incentives for all learners.

_____ 8. Sometimes students do not attach the same meanings to words and symbols as do their teachers.

_____ 9. A common reason for student failure in small-group instructional settings is that the student has not been instructed properly with regard to what he or she, specifically, is supposed to do.

_____ 10. Classroom climate, to a large degree, is shaped by what the teacher does.

INTRODUCTION

Jerry Smith: Boy Scout

Jerry developed his interest in scouting late. In fact, he didn't join Troop 16 until he was 12 years old. The scoutmaster welcomed him to the group, but told him he would have to do a lot of work to get himself sufficiently informed to go along on the overnight bike trip. Jerry was told that he would have to have all his basic scouting memory work in hand (the scout oath and so forth) and also be able to describe basic safety procedures to be followed when biking and when preparing an overnight camp site. Jerry received this information on Monday night. Mr. Sweeney, the scoutmaster, told him that, provided he could pass an oral test on the required material on Friday night, he could go along on the bike ride and overnight camp out on Saturday and Sunday.

Jerry studied furiously all week. His parents had never seen him approach anything with so much enthusiasm. When Friday night came, he answered Mr. Sweeney's questions with confidence. He was cleared for the trip. He had a great time and regaled his parents with all the details for days afterward.

Jerry Smith: Junior High School Student

Jerry Smith is in the seventh grade. He does well enough in most subjects. But not in math. He hates math. He has always hated math. He just can't seem to "get it."

Jerry's teacher, Ms. Holland, is worried about Jerry's progress. He has been late in turning in a lot of assignments. In fact, some of them he hasn't turned in at all. Ms. Holland has spoken to Jerry. She has spoken to the school counselor. She has spoken to Jerry's parents. Still, she just isn't seeing any real change. "He just seems to be in another world," she has told several of her teacher colleagues. "I just can't get him to care."

Teachers' frustrations in the area of motivation are legendary. (One recent point of view is expressed in Figure 10-1.) Indeed, concerns about the apparent indifference of some youngsters to classroom instruction must rank among the half a dozen most frequently discussed topics in secondary school faculty lounges. Countless instances can be cited of youngsters who seem to thrive on challenges outside the school setting but who remain apathetic, at best, to what goes on in the school classroom.

As we begin to think about the problem of motivation, we must first keep the issue in perspective. Motivation *is* a problem. No one argues that. But at least part of the problem may result from expectations of certain teachers that they ought to be able to inspire every single student who lands in their classroom. Setting out to reach everyone as a goal is a laudable intention. But developing feelings of failure and frustration when some students continue to be indifferent to our program despite our most valiant attempts to interest them is an inappropriate response. We need to remember the tremendous diversity of youngsters who enroll in middle schools, junior high schools, and senior high schools. Literally, we take them all. Given the spread of personalities and interests across this diverse group of youngsters, it is unavoidable that some youngsters (not too many, it is hoped) will simply not develop much enthusiasm for what we are teaching. The objective, therefore, should be to get through to as many as possible. And, provided that we have made an honest attempt to reach as many youngsters as we can,

Figure 10-1

ARE TODAY'S STUDENTS LESS MOTIVATED?

Today's youngsters *are* less motivated. One of the culprits is television. These kids watch these talented performers who are supported by legions of gag-line writers. Then, they come to school and expect us to turn them on too. There is just no way we can compete with television.

There's another thing too. Today's youngsters have an anti-intellectual bias that kids a few years ago didn't have. I think it's part of this antiestablishment thing. They just have no respect for learning.

Finally, I think youngsters' time perspectives have changed. They aren't interested in waiting for *anything*. Ten years in the future simply does not exist in their thinking. They want to live for the here and now. They want to have fun. They want immediate gratification. Regrettably, many of them don't see much fun or gratification in school. So, they raise hell and in general just make life miserable for the small number of good kids who are still in the schools.

Statement by a teacher

YOUR OPINION, PLEASE

Read the comments above. Then, respond to these questions.

1. Do you think that today's students have changed? If so, in what ways? How do you account for any changes?
2. Do you think the causes of change cited by the teacher who made this statement are valid? Why, or why not?
3. Have changes in society made it more difficult for teachers to motivate youngsters? Why, or why not?
4. What kinds of things motivated you when you were in secondary schools? Do the same kinds of things motivate youngsters today? Why do you think so?
5. How do you feel about your own abilities to motivate students? What are your strong points and weak points?

---

we need harbor no deep-seated feelings of guilt if several remain unconvinced that what we are doing is either interesting or important. It is to be hoped that the "chemistry" will be better with some future teacher for these youngsters and that their enthusiasms will be ignited later if not sooner.

Our task then is to capture the interests of as many of our students as possible. Without some interest, without at least a small spark of curiosity about what they are studying, it is difficult for students to perform well. We want them to perform well because there is abundant evidence that youngsters' learning in areas in which they sense themselves to be competent far outstrips that in areas in which they sense themselves to be less able.

One fundamental problem for teachers is the fact that they generally meet their students every day. There simply is not enough lead time for teachers to develop elaborate motivational strategies for each day, let alone for each different class of students. Further, teachers have no special resources to back them up as they think about how they might motivate their students. Many teachers have reflected enviously on what might be done were they able to meet their classes only once a week and introduce new material using ideas generated by a platoon of gifted script writers—sort of a "Saturday Night Live" in the classroom.

Regrettably, the possibility of such circumstances coming to pass in public school classrooms in the foreseeable future is remote. (Indeed, a superintendent approached by a teacher with such a proposal could be excused for describing the suggestion as "hallucinatory.") So we are left to work with what we have. Namely, we must do what we can do given the nature of our own personalities and the nature of the time constraints under which we work. This by no means, however, suggests the issue of motivation is hopeless. Rather, it points out the necessity of utilizing our precious time wisely.

Because teachers' personalities, students, and instructional responsibilities vary widely, it makes more sense for beginners interested in motivation to master certain basic principles than to be introduced to a set of effective motivational tricks. (A soft shoe and a banjo might work brilliantly for one teacher with one group of students. It could become an unqualified disaster for another.) In our view, the teacher who is well grounded in some fundamental principles of motivation can generate some specific responses consistent with these principles that have potential for success in the setting in which he or she is instructing.

Motivation is a part of the larger issue of implementing instruction. After plans for instruction have been completed, the time at last arrives for a "trial by fire" in the classroom. While no single set of procedures can guarantee moving lessons to a productive conclusion, there are things that we can do to increase the likelihood that learners will profit from our instruction. A number of specifics in this regard will be introduced in subsequent sections of this chapter.

Finally, as a conclusion to this introduction, we would like to point out that expertise in the area of motivation and implementation of instruction develops rather slowly. The tasks of diagnosing students, selecting content and establishing objectives, and identifying instructional techniques all occur *before* the teacher is confronted with the necessity of coming face to face with students as instruction unfolds. Decisions regarding these issues can be made in the relative calm of the faculty lounge or faculty office or at home. On the other hand, decisions related to motivation and implementing instruction often must be made as the actual instruction goes forward in the classroom. Frequently, such decisions must be made quickly and in a setting where the teacher's attention may be diverted into a dozen or more separate directions. Consequently, beginning teachers need not feel bad if they sense themselves less expert in the motivation and implementation of instruction areas. Often it takes several years of classroom experience for teachers to begin to feel that they are developing real competence in discharging these responsibilities.

THE GENERAL ISSUE OF MOTIVATION

For beginners unfamiliar with all of the implications of motivation, sometimes there is a tendency to think of it as something that must be dealt with only at the beginning of a lesson. In reality, the issue of motivation has to be considered at various points in a lesson. In general, we need to think about motivation at the beginning of a lesson ("How can I establish initial interest?"), at important transition points during the actual implementation of the body of the lesson ("How can I maintain interest?"), and at the conclusion of the lesson ("How can I wrap this up so students will want to learn more tomorrow?"). Answers to these questions will vary depending on such factors as teacher personality, student population being served, and subject matter being taught. Clearly there are no "right" kinds of motivation that will work for all teachers in all settings.

In thinking about motivation, we must recognize that it is a phenomenon that has been much studied but that, even today, is not fully understood in all its dimensions. Although all the answers are not in, enough is known about motivation to provide some principles useful for suggesting classroom practices that hold promise of working as motivators. We do know that there seem to be two basic types of motivation: *intrinsic* and *extrinsic*.

When a student does something, perhaps an assigned task, because he or she is intrinsically motivated to do so, that student finds the task itself to be personally satisfying. For example, a youngster might spend hours on perfecting a hook shot in basketball because acquiring the skill provides some kind of personal satisfaction. There is some feeling that intrinsic motivation is the most potent force there is. When a person does something because it satisfies a deeply held personal need, that individual usually needs no convincing that the task that satisfies the personal need ought to be accomplished.

When a student accomplishes a task because of a promise of being rewarded with something other than the satisfaction that the task has been brought to completion, he or she is said to be extrinsically motivated. The real motivation in this case is the "something else." Grades are good examples of extrinsic motivators. Some students (certainly not all) will study subjects they do not care for because they wish to receive good grades. Good work, then, results not because of any intrinsic love of the subject matter but rather out of an intrinsic love of high grades.

A premise behind the use of extrinsic motivation is that it will prompt students' interest in topics toward which, initially, they may be indifferent. In time, such students may develop a keen interest in this unfamiliar subject matter. When this happens, they may continue to study it because they have developed an intrinsic interest. Thus, in theory at least, extrinsic motivation can be used to promote the development of intrinsic motivation. In the next sections we shall explore more fully the nature of intrinsic and extrinsic motivation.

INTRINSIC MOTIVATION

In thinking about intrinsic motivation, we need to recognize that the motivation occurs because whatever activity is being pursued satisfies a deeply felt personal need. The nature of some of these needs has been explored by the distinguished motivational theorist, A. H. Maslow.

Maslow's Needs Theory

Maslow (1943) developed a theory of motivation based on needs gratification. Maslow pointed out that there are certain needs that all human beings strive to satisfy, some of which are more basic than others. These basic needs must be satisfied before higher-order needs can be considered. Maslow's list of needs, presented here in order from most basic to least basic, is as follows:

1. Physiological needs
2. Safety needs
3. Love needs
4. Esteem needs
5. Self-actualization needs

Speaking about these needs, Maslow (1943, pp. 394–395) has written that they

are related to each other, being arranged in a hierarchy or a prepotency. This means that the most prepotent goal will monopolize consciousness and will tend of itself to organize the recruitment of the various capacities of the organism. The less prepotent needs are minimized, even forgotten or denied. But when a need is fairly well satisfied, the next prepotent ("higher") need emerges, in turn to dominate the conscious life and to serve as the center of organization of behavior, since gratified needs are not active motivators.

According to Maslow, then, we cannot expect a youngster who is hungry to be greatly motivated on issues related to personal esteem or personal development (self-actualization). He or she must respond first to the more basic physiological need of hunger. An implication of Maslow's scheme for teachers is that care must be taken to ensure that students' more basic needs have been met. Unless they have been met, youngsters will be unable to generate much interest in the kind of knowing and understanding they need to more toward self-understanding (self-actualization). Free lunch programs in schools, regulations relating to yougsters' safety and behavior, and school counseling programs all are examples of actions taken by educators to ensure that the basic needs of students are met.

A basic need of particular importance for secondary school teachers to recognize is the need for love. Many adolescents work very hard at feeling loved. They want to be accepted or, in Maslow's terms, loved by others in the school. Youngsters who feel that they are not accepted by others in the school setting may reject school in favor of activities in other settings where, in fact, they do feel accepted. As teachers, we need to do whatever we can to make youngsters feel welcome. This is both in the interest of the youngster whose sense of personal security will be enhanced and in the interest of the teacher who will see a student who is much more likely to develop a greater appreciation of the academic program.

In summary, the work of Maslow suggests to us a need to be keen observers of youngsters in our classes. Through our observations we can make determinations of instances when individual youngsters' basic needs have not been met. With such information in hand, it is hoped that we can take specific remedial action.

Jerome Bruner's Perspectives

Jerome Bruner, like Maslow, has also written widely on topics related to motivation. Bruner suggests that all people have an innate curiosity drive or need (Sprintall and Sprintall 1977). When this curiosity drive is activated, powerful motivation results. The curiosity drive is triggered when an individual experiences an appropriate level of uncertainty. If a given task or challenge is too easy, then the curiosity drive will remain dormant. If the task is too difficult, the curiosity drive likewise may not be stimulated. The individual may be simply too confused or frustrated to care much about the problem at hand.

A number of instructional techniques have been devised that are designed to trigger the curiosity drive. A generalized procedure, often referred to as the "inquiry approach," is an example. In inquiry instruction, the teacher presents students with a problem that appears to describe a situation that conflicts with what the students believe to be true. Presented properly, inquiry techniques prompt youngsters to resolve conflicts or uncertainty by arousing their curiosities and encouraging them to offer explanations that "make sense" in the light of information available to them.

In general, the curiosity drive is well served when teachers provide opportunities for youngsters to engage in exploratory activities in the classroom. Bruner implies that individuals have a built-in "will to learn." The task of the teacher is to establish conditions that will allow this will to learn to flourish. To accomplish this end, instructional programs need to encourage active student participation. It is insufficient for teachers to provide all the answers. Some of them, at least, must be generated through the efforts of the students themselves.

The Identification Motive

The identification motive is a basic principle associated with motivation. All individuals are thought to have some desire to increase their similarity to certain other people who are viewed as commanding powerful resources of some kind. This desire is referred to as the identification motive. In the secondary school realm, youngsters activated by the identification motive may dress, talk, or act like some persons whose behaviors they would like to emulate. If these role models are characterized by interests in intellectual pursuits, the teacher will likely have little difficulty in generating interest in classroom work. But, if the role models selected demonstrate no interest in academic pursuits, the teacher likely will find school subjects a very "hard sell" indeed. ("My old man makes 40 grand a year, and he doesn't give a damn about the War of 1812.")

The identification motive tends to present secondary school teachers with more difficulties than elementary school teachers. Indeed, particularly with very young children in the primary grades, the identification motive often proves to be a real plus for elementary school teachers. Many youngsters at this age idealize their teachers and are more than willing to behave in ways that will please this role model. By the time they are in junior and senior high school, however, youngsters are likely to hold the teacher in much lower esteem. Pop music stars, certain political figures, well-known professional athletes, and even some other students in the school may be held in higher esteem than the teacher.

As a result, we as secondary teachers need to do some digging to identify the particular kinds of individuals with whom youngsters are identifying. When possible, we need to slant instruction to take advantage of students' tendencies to identify with certain kinds of individuals. Suppose, for example, we were working with a junior high school mathematics class that included a good number of youngsters with high interest in professional football players. We might take advantage of this interest to create problems around the theme of football when we prepared exams. (We want to emphasize that such adjustments cannot *always* be made. We must preserve the integrity of what we are teaching. But, when we can link a student's identification interest to something we are teaching, there is a good possibility the student will find the instruction interesting.)

The Drive for Competence

Another aspect of intrinsic motivation is the drive for competence. Quite simply, the drive for competence means that we seek to do things that we are good at and to avoid things that we are not good at. For teachers, an implication of the drive for competence is that students will become motivated to pursue further learning when they have experienced some success in prior learning. Without some feelings of confidence inspired by success in mastering material previously introduced, many youngsters may lose their confidence. A fear of failure may keep them from working as hard at an assigned task as they might otherwise do. They may well appear to be a good deal less interested in their school work.

Concern for the drive-for-competence aspect of intrinsic motivation is especially critical during the middle and at the conclusion of a given lesson. A teacher may have done a fine job of engaging students' interests at the beginning, but unless they experience some feelings of success as the lesson progresses, their enthusiasms are likely to diminish. Similarly, unless students leave a given lesson with at least some feeling of personal achievement, they probably will not approach subsequent lessons on the subject with any great enthusiasm.

Teachers can do a number of things to help youngsters achieve feelings of competence. First, instruction can be broken up into small enough segments so that students are not required to master too much at once. Satisfaction growing out of mastering one small part of a lesson can serve as a motivator for going on to master other parts of the lesson. In general, it is better to acknowledge students in terms of their mastery of specified bits of content than to place them in highly competitive situations where their scores are measured against those of others in the class.

Suppose that a youngster received a score of 89 on a test requiring students to compute lengths of missing sides of right triangles. A teacher interested in developing youngsters' feelings of confidence might make this comment: "Well, Mark, you seem to have the Pythagorean theorem down pretty well. Except for that simple multiplication error, you got all of the problems right. A fine job!"

Another teacher, someone emphasizing competition, might make quite a different remark to this student. The teacher might say, "An 89. Let's see. That places you in the bottom fifth of the class on this test."

Clearly, the student in the second teacher's class is not likely to feel very competent given the teacher's assessment of his performance relative to those of others in the class. Surely he or she is less likely to generate as much personal enthusiasm for the next topic to be introduced in the class as is the student whose teacher praises the 89 score as evidence that learning has taken place.

There is evidence that not only do positive teacher comments help students to expand their confidence in dealing with new information but that competence-based motivation is further increased when these kinds of positive teacher comments are made relatively frequently. What is needed here is not simply a continuous outpouring of positive comments but, rather, comments that tell the youngster precisely what he or she might do to make future work even better. This kind of teacher feedback requires teachers to monitor student work closely and to make frequent comments designed to help youngsters move toward mastery. Such practices can be demanding. But given the potential for improving both youngsters' performances and attitudes toward school work, many teachers find the effort worthwhile. Consider this discussion as you respond to the questions asked in Figure 10-2.

EXTRINSIC MOTIVATION

Recall that extrinsic motivation refers to motivation to accomplish a task that is prompted by something other than an inner satisfaction that the task itself is worthy of accomplishment. Suppose that a man had a filthy dumpster outside of his apartment complex that he wanted cleaned. No one was eager to accomplish the task. But, when he offered two high school students $25 each to clean it, they agreed to do so. Obviously, they had no intrinsic interest in cleaning the dumpster. But they got to work because of an extrinsic interest in the $25. In summary, then, a person who does something because of an extrinsic interest does not do so because this activity satisfies some inner need or drive.

Some theorists say that teachers really cannot do much about intrinsic motivation. It may be impossible to know precisely the inner needs and drives of each youngster. On the other hand, some extrinsic motivators seem to work well with large numbers

Figure 10-2

SOME INTRINSIC MOTIVATION ISSUES

YOUR OPINION, PLEASE

1. Do you believe that everyone has an innate curiosity drive? What evidence can you cite that supports your view?
2. Assuming the existence of a curiosity drive, how would you capitalize on it to motivate your students?
3. How would you relate Maslow's ideas of basic human needs to motivating students in your subject area? Specifically, what would you do?
4. Do you think that there is such a thing as an identification motive? Did you personally ever identify with someone you really wanted to be like? Specifically, what characteristics of this individual appealed to you?
5. Did teachers you had in school work systematically to build youngsters' confidence? What kinds of things do you think you could do to accomplish this objective?

---

of people. (Large numbers of people are motivated by material rewards of various kinds, for example.) Whether teachers should focus exclusively on extrinsic motivation is an arguable point. Few, however, quibble with the suggestion that teachers should have a professional acquaintance with extrinsic motivators of various kinds. In the sections that follow, a number of these will be described.

The Token or Work-Incentive Program

The token or work-incentive program exemplifies external motivation. In this scheme, certain incentives are provided for students to accomplish certain tasks. Often these incentives are tokens that the student can turn in for something he or she might want. For example, tokens may be given for such things as good classroom behavior, for completion of assignments, for participation in classroom discussions, for getting a certain number of problems correct on a take-home assignment, or for almost any other task the teacher might deem appropriate. When enough tokens are gathered, the student might exchange them for such things as free time, talking privileges in the cafeteria, ice cream cones, or any of a host of other things that he or she might desire.

Recently, a junior high school in a large West Coast city experienced a very serious problem of absenteeism. Low achievement scores on standardized tests were thought to be due, in part at least, to youngsters' irregular attendance patterns. To encourage attendance, the school principal instituted a policy of providing youngsters with 25 cents for each day they attended all their classes. His presumption was that the students were not willing to attend school simply because it met some internal need (intrinsic motivation) but that the youngsters would attend school if some external incentive (the money) were provided. The long-term result of this school's policy is not yet clear. We mention it here not as something "good" or "bad" but rather as an example of a school practice flowing clearly from the premises of external motivation. Another view of this issue is given in Figure 10-3.

As we examine the world around us, it is clear that extrinsic motivation plays an important role. Most of us are quite anxious to receive a paycheck for our services. Often we do some things we do not particularly enjoy doing to gain free time to pursue those things we do enjoy doing. Most of us generally feel better when we (and others) pursue objectives and complete tasks because of an intrinsic need. However, in an imperfect world, we must recognize that all of us do some things in response to incentives that are clearly external.

Figure 10-3
_____

SOME CONCERNS ABOUT REWARD SYSTEMS

I don't believe it, Minervie, I don't believe it. I hear tell over at the school now they're giving the eighth-grade kids a ticket every day that they bring their history homework in. As I understand it . . . now listen closely to this . . . every time a kid gets twelve tickets together, the teacher gives out a free pass to the movies. Such nonsense! In my day those teachers made us *want* to learn. We did our homework because it was interesting. It's just plain corrupt to pay these kids for doing what they ought to want to do. Why, it's nothing but out and out bribery!

YOUR OPINION, PLEASE

Read the comments reported above. Then, respond to these questions.

1. Do you agree with the basic position taken by this individual? Why, or why not?
2. Do you think an incentive system such as the one described can have harmful long-term effects? Why, or why not?
3. Why don't youngsters show an interest in their school work if this is something they ought to do?
4. Are salaries bribery? Should people be paid only just enough to keep from starving? Shouldn't they have a personal interest in their work that is so profound they will do it with little regard for monetary rewards? Why, or why not?
5. Thinking about how schools might be operated 40 years from now, would you expect to find more teachers using token incentive systems than now or fewer teachers? Why do you think so?
_____

Limitations of Grades as Extrinsic Motivators

Perhaps because grades played a rather important role in prompting their own efforts in high school (and later in college or university), large numbers of individuals preparing to teach presume that grades are important to nearly all students in secondary school. While certainly many secondary students are concerned about grades and are willingly work hard to get high grades, large numbers of other students in middle schools, junior high schools, and senior high schools are not particularly upset when they receive low grades. Particularly for youngsters who have experienced little success in school and who have as their objective dropping out of school as soon as it becomes legally possible for them to do so, appeals from the teacher to "work hard and earn a good grade" have little impact. For this reason, the traditional incentive of grades has not worked well in many inner-city schools.

We should not infer that, because youngsters who have experienced little success in school may not be motivated by grades, they are incapable of being motivated. Indeed they can be. But motivators must consist of something that they view as worthwhile. Teachers who communicate effectively with youngsters with a past history of failure in the school typically have done their "diagnostic homework" to determine what motivators do work with these students. We gain little by wringing our hands and suggesting that "all students *ought* to want good grades." Whether they ought to or not is not the point. The fact is that many students do not care much about grades. As a result, professional teachers search for alternative motivators.

Three General Principles for Using Extrinsic Motivation

In thinking about implementing extrinsic motivators other than grades, one approach might be to describe particular details related to a number of specific techniques. The number of such techniques, however, is large. Consideration of techniques one by one would require an entire volume. We have decided that a more productive approach here would be to suggest three general principles that run through most extrinsic motivational procedures.

One fundamental principle in this area is to *be positive*. Too often in the schools students are publicly reprimanded or in other ways punished for failing to accomplish what is desired. Generally, it is much more motivating for a youngster to hear praise when he or she does something right than to hear negative comments when a mistake has been made. Positive comments for good work encourage many youngsters to do additional good work in the future.

A second principle is that *interest is created by novelty*. Most of us are drawn to something that is new or unusual. This may be related to the curiosity drive that Bruner (Sprintall and Sprintall 1977) has described. In recalling our own secondary school years, many of us can remember specific lessons or teachers that were memorable because of the unusual approaches taken to the introduction of subject matter.

Novelty alone will not sustain interest over a great span of time. Clearly something must be done to hold whatever enthusiasm is generated by a new and unusual introduction. But the power of novelty should not be underestimated. As teachers we need to be on the look out for new ways in which to present our material to students in our classrooms.

A third general principle is to *minimize failure*. There is abundant evidence that students who experience consistent failure do not respond well to teachers' attempts to motivate them. Certainly we are not implying that difficult subjects should be eliminated from the curriculum. But we are suggesting a need to concern ourselves with how materials are sequenced and paced. Decisions in these areas can result in dramatic differences in the numbers of youngsters who experience success. In general, the more success experienced by an individual youngster, the more motivated he or she is likely to be to perform future tasks well.

"Today's lecture will consist of sparkling wit mixed with a bit of academic drivel."

Figure 1O-4

TOMORROW'S TEST

Tomorrow's exam is going to be a lulu. You better be ready! Now, it'll cover the stuff in that supplementary book. You know the one I mean. The third one we looked at last Tuesday. Now, there will be essay questions *and,* especially for you objective-items *aficianados,* some true-false questions. You'll have to do a bit of extrapolating, but mostly the inferences will be pretty low-inference, clear cause-and-effect stuff. Take a quick peek again at the ecological and technological treatments in the first section of those three chapters. Oh, before I forget, there'll also be some emphasis on the map work. You know the kind of thing your author does in all of those chapters. OK, everybody understands, right. Good. Let's hit it then first thing tomorrow.

Directions given by a teacher to a group of high school sophomores

YOUR OPINION, PLEASE

Read the material above. Then, respond to these questions.

1. How well do you think students in this class would understand what the test will deal with?
2. If you were a student in this class, how would you go about preparing for this examination?
3. What reactions do you have to this teacher's choice of words? Might some specific words cause youngsters problems? Which ones? Why?
4. Suppose that you were giving test directions to a group of youngsters. Think about what you would say. Write some brief remarks. Ask another person in your class or the instructor to critique your directions in terms of their clarity.
5. When you were a secondary school student, did you ever have a teacher who was not an effective communicator? If so, how did you feel about this person and about his or her class?
6. Specifically, what advice would you give to the teacher who gave the directions quoted here?

Closely related to the issue of motivation is the area of classroom communication. To a large degree, youngsters' success in the classroom is related to how well they comprehend what the teacher is attempting to communicate. In the section that follows, we examine some dimensions of communication as it relates to classroom instruction. For a discussion, see Figure 10-4.

TEACHING AND COMMUNICATION

The teaching act, primarily, is one of communication. Teachers who are successful implementors of their instructional plans understand how the communication process works. Some have this knowledge intuitively. Others have learned it. Let us look at some of the basics of classroom communication.

The most basic communication system involves three elements: a sender, a message, and a receiver. We might diagram this system as follows:

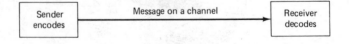

Using this simple system, a sender has a message that is to be forwarded to a receiver. The "channel" that might be selected could vary among a number of options. For example, a verbal channel might be selected and a spoken message sent. Alternatively, a written message might be transmitted. Certainly it would be possible to opt for a nonverbal channel of some kind and communicate the message via something such as a glance or gesture. Regardless of the type of channel selected, the potential for this basic system to generate misunderstanding is enormous.

One cause for this breakdown is the difference between the experiences of the person receiving the message (the receiver) and those of the person sending the message (the sender). Take the example of two people coming from different cultures. In some cultures children have been taught that it is disrespectful to look an adult directly in the face. A teacher from an American middle-class background might mistake the meaning of a child from such a culture. The looking-away behavior could be interpreted by such a teacher as evidence the youngster was misbehaving. Such an inference could be followed by a demand that the youngster "tell me the truth and look me straight in the eye when you're talking."

Another source of potential confusion when this basic model is used results from our tendency to send several messages concurrently. There is nothing basically wrong with this. But, if the messages are in conflict, misunderstanding can result. For example, a teacher might tell a student, "You've done a good job on that lathe turning" while, at the same time, creasing his or her brow in a deep frown. The student receives a positive signal via the verbal channel ("good job") and a negative signal via the nonverbal signal (the frown). When the student tries to interpret the message, he or she is likely to be confused.

To eliminate some problems associated with communication, it is desirable to add another element to our basic communication system: specifically, a feedback loop. Our new system can be diagramed as follows:

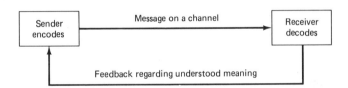

Using the expanded communication system, we see that the receiver (person receiving the message) sends his or her understanding of the message back to the sender (person sending the message). When this happens, the sender is able to discern whether or not the message has been understood properly.

In thinking about the implications of this expanded system in classroom teaching, we might begin by suggesting that an effort should be made to determine exactly how well youngsters have understood directions or other bits of information that have been presented. Asking a random selection of students to repeat the essence of a "message" can provide useful information regarding whether or not what was heard squares with what was said. In the case of misunderstanding, we can make another attempt to get the information communicated.

Some problems of communication can be prevented if we think carefully about the words we select in making an explanation or in presenting new information. There is a tendency for teachers to say too much. That is, they tend to include extraneous material in their statements to students. Particularly when directions related to assignments are being given, we must strive for clarity. One way to check on our verbal patterns in this regard is to make tape recordings of our verbal behavior when giving assignments. (A small tape recorder and microphone can easily be fitted in an open desk drawer.) Beginning teachers who followed this practice often are surprised at the enormous quantity of nonessential information that clutters up their messages on assigned work to be completed.

If a problem in direction giving is diagnosed, one remedy is to write directions down on a sheet of paper before class. This exercise tends to clarify thinking with regard to exactly what students are to do. Written guidelines can then be used as a rough script when verbal directions are given. (We don't recommend they be read word for word. Such a practice tends to make for a wooden, mechanical classroom performance. A close paraphrasing is generally much more effective.)

Finally, in communicating with youngsters, teachers need to think carefully about their choice of words. Beginning teachers almost invariably report shock at the limited vocabularies of many students, even of those in the last two years of senior high school. Important messages should be couched in simple, unadorned terms. Although we may lament the fact that students do not have a broader acquaintance with words, our first priority must be to help youngsters understand what our expectations are. Clearly they cannot be expected to become engaged productively in learning activities that, in time, have potential to expand their mastery of the language if they do not know what they are to do. (Refer again to Figure 10-4.)

GROUPING LEARNERS FOR INSTRUCTION

One of the most important decisions teachers must make as they begin putting instructional plans into operation is how to group students in their classes. Traditionally, many teachers have elected simply to work with the entire class of 30 to 35 students as a single group. For some purposes that arrangement works well. For others, however, it may be desirable to organize students into a number of small groups. On certain occasions, too, there may be merit in totally individualizing instruction (in this case, every student, in effect, becomes a "group" of one for instructional purposes).

Different grouping arrangements require different kinds of behaviors from the teacher. Specific types of groups and related teacher responsibilities are introduced in sections that follow.

Large Groups

There definitely are times when it is most efficient to work with a class of youngsters as a single large group. For example, when we have specific information that each member of the class needs to have, it makes little sense for us to break the class into small groups and deliver the same message three, four, or even five times.

In working with large groups, we face the problem of monitoring youngsters' understanding. Quite simply, it is easy for an individual to become lost in a lesson directed toward a large group of learners. Unless we, as teachers, check systematically on individual student understanding, a good many students may simply miss whatever message is being delivered. This situation particularly has a likelihood of occurring in classes taught by inexperienced teachers. Often they mistake nodding heads on the part of a few bright students as evidence that everybody understands. On the contrary, seldom does everybody understand. Almost always, some students in a large group will miss out on some important information.

To identify as many of these youngsters as possible so that we can clear up their misunderstandings, we must remain alert during a large-group lesson. For example, how many youngsters are participating? Do some students have quizzical or confused looks on their faces? Do some students refuse even to attempt to answer a question when they are called upon? Experienced teachers who work well with large groups are very sensitive to issues suggested by these questions.

When we suspect that some youngsters are not understanding, we need to take time to ask some questions and to clear up any confusion—in a sensitive manner. Students must feel free to ask questions and participate even when they do not have personal confidence in the accuracy of what they are saying. To establish an environment in which students will be willing to participate, it is essential that they in no way be made to feel inadequate. A student who senses himself or herself to have been diminished personally in any way in the classroom becomes a reluctant participator. Thus, to determine how youngsters are understanding the substance of a lesson, we must not only listen and observe carefully but also establish conditions that make it comfortable for students to take an active part in classroom discussions.

Small Groups

When there is an intention to establish conditions conducive to active participation by large numbers of students, small groups may be a good organizational choice. Small groups provide an opportunity for each individual to speak up. Further, many students feel psychologically more secure and comfortable in a small-group setting. Hence they are more likely to participate actively in a small group than in large-group instructional setting.

There are special challenges for teachers in working with small groups. In particular, attention must be directed toward providing students with sufficient directions that the small-group arrangement will be productive. It must be remembered that most students have spent almost their entire school careers in large-group settings. Generally, by the time they are in secondary school, they know what their roles are in these large-group arrangements. For many (perhaps most), small-group schemes are something of a novelty. They need specific instruction with regard to their behavior in this kind of a learning configuration.

When planning small groups, we must clarify to all members of each group the general purpose of the group. Their task should be described in terms precise enough so they will be able to know when they have completed their assignment. Some teachers find it useful to insist that some kind of instructional product be developed by each group. ("All right, when you people have finished reading these short articles on Jefferson's attitudes toward a strong federal treasury, I want you to prepare a master list of his arguments on this butcher paper. Use this magic marker to write with. When we finish this exercise, we'll hang your butcher paper on the wall. Then I will call on someone from your group to refer to the butcher paper and make specific comments about Jefferson's attitudes.")

In addition to general group assignments, specific responsibilities of each member need to be clarified. ("Paul, I want you to be recorder. Edna, you organize the distribution of materials. Phil, you and Joanne can be discussion leaders. James and Beth, I would like you two to find any flaws in the arguments presented either in the articles or by members of the group during your discussion. I will be asking for your comments when we finish.") With precise directions, youngsters in small groups embark upon their exercises with direction. Delivery of clear expectations to participants enhances the possibility of small-group learning being a productive experience.

Small groups must be provided with materials sufficient to accomplish the tasks they have been asked to complete. If there is to be work with maps, plenty of maps should be available. It is folly to organize a group of youngsters and send them to the school library with no materials and vague instructions to the effect that they should "find whatever you need in the library." Moreover, such an approach will win no goodwill from the library staff professionals. (These people are anxious to serve. But they cannot provide good help without some prior warning that will allow them time to gather pertinent materials.) On the other hand, youngsters sent off to "find something in the library" are very likely to become frustrated. Little learning is likely to result from such ill-planned instructional ventures. Consider this discussion as you respond to questions posed in Figure 10-5.

Individualized Programs

In general, an individualized program is one that is planned for a single individual. There are many kinds of individualized programs. Some require each student, in the end, to complete exactly the same work. The individualization in programs of this type

Figure 1O-5

SMALL-GROUP INSTRUCTION

I know we haven't done small groups before, but I think you really will like them. Look on the board here. See, I have divided you into five groups of six students each. Now I want the "A" group to work on Paraguay. The "B" group can do Argentina. The "C" group can work on Honduras. The "D" group can do Chile. And the "E" group can do Ecuador. Now I want you to go to the library and get to work. I will expect each group to present a ten-minute report to the class tomorrow."

YOUR OPINION, PLEASE

The directions above were given by a teacher to a class of secondary school students. Read these remarks. Then, respond to these questions.

1. Were these directions clear? Why, or why not?
2. What do you think the scene in the library was like when these students arrived?
3. Would some of these students have more difficulty than others? Would some groups face a more difficult time in getting ten minutes' worth of oral report material together?
4. How do you think you would feel about small-group learning if you had been in this class and received these instructions?
5. Were you ever in a small-group learning situation in your secondary school years that proved to be a disaster? If so, what went wrong?
6. Suppose that you had been teaching this class. What kind of directions would you have given to these students? Why do you think your directions might have been better than those given by this teacher?

---

ordinarily means only that particular youngsters will progress through the same material at different rates. (Brighter students will go through faster than will average students, for example.) A second type of individualized program is designed so that all students will pursue a similar broad learning objective but using different kinds of learning materials and experiences (tailored to their own special needs) as they progress toward mastery of this objective. A third general type of program permits students to choose and define both their own objectives and their preferred modes of learning material related to these objectives. (Programs of the third type are rarely found in public schools.)

All individualized instructional programs place heavy demands on teachers' planning time. Special provisions have to be made (or at least approved) for each student. This means that a very complex record-keeping system must be devised. Time must be found to counsel with individual youngsters on a one-to-one basis. Typically evaluation in an individualized program occurs at different times for different youngsters. Finally, teachers who manage individualized programs are faced with the general problem of keeping track of who is doing what and in which place.

Many teachers who initially are extremely enthusiastic about individualized programs find that the allure of such programs fades once they confront the management tasks inherent in such efforts. Certainly new teachers interested in developing individualized programs ought to move slowly. Perhaps individualized instruction focusing on one or two units of work in a single class would represent an appropriate beginning. Should the program succeed and the teacher enjoy operating in this mode, consideration might be given to expanding the range of the individualized program. Relatively slow, incremental growth has more promise of resulting in a strong individualized program than do ill-advised attempts to individualize instruction for all students in all classes simultaneously. Hasty efforts to do too much too quickly are likely to produce more frustration than satisfaction both for students and for the teacher.

CLASSROOM CLIMATE

Classroom climate relates to the character or nature of interactions that occur between students and the teacher in a given instructional setting. The character of these interactions can have an important impact on students' learning. Factors that combine to shape the climate of a particular classroom include the way in which the teacher exercises authority, the degree of support that individual students feel, the nature of competitive and cooperative relationships among students, and the freedom that youngsters feel to express themselves openly.

Clearly many of these dimensions relate directly to the behavior of the classroom teacher. For example, when the teacher encourages open expression of student views and provides good emotional support to students who speak up in class, the classroom is likely to be characterized by more free-flowing interactions between teacher and students than when the teacher tends not to welcome free expression of ideas and frequently makes judgmental comments to students who say something that was not "right." When teachers stress high-powered competition, classes may well be characterized by relatively high levels of student anxiety. (After all, in a highly competitive environment everbody cannot be a winner.)

Each teacher needs to make some decisions about the climate he or she would like to have in his or her classroom. (We are not suggesting that any one classroom climate is necessarily appropriate for all situations. In large measure, the teacher needs to define the kind of environment in which he or she can function in a professional manner.) Once the general characteristics of the desired classroom climate have been identified, the teacher needs to ask himself or herself some questions about his or her own behavior and how this behavior might be contributing to or inhibiting the development of the preferred kind of classroom climate. Such questions as the following might be asked.

How many of my comments are positive and how many are negative?

How do I react when students make contributions? Am I accepting? Do I build on students' contributions? Or do I reject them?

How do I use my power and authority? Do I use it to respond to student needs? If so, how? Do I use it to enforce rigidly what I believe to be right for the students? If so, why?

Do I find critical comments by students threatening? Do I accept critical comments by students as a challenge to modify my program to make it better?

Do I see students as basically good and, therefore, generally expect the best from them? Do I see students as basically bad and, therefore, expect the worse from them?

Do I favor competition over cooperation? Do I seek a balance? Do I favor cooperation over competition?

Do I respect students as individuals with real rights of their own? Or do I regard students as subordinates with few rights of their own?

These questions represent only a small sampling of those that might be asked. The precise questions are not nearly so important as the decision to develop a set of questions that focuses on the nature of teacher-student relationships in the classroom. When teachers have a clear idea of the kind of classroom climate they want, they can go about the task of modifying their own behaviors to achieve this kind of a climate. It is clear that the teacher is the important variable in establishing the tone of the individual classroom. Teachers who work hard to establish a pattern of relationships with their students that they like generally derive much more satisfaction from teaching than do those who fail to recognize the important role of the teacher in shaping the classroom environment. Too frequently teachers in this latter group have assumed that "there is something wrong with these students" when patterns of interaction have not been what they would like to see. In our view, in the vast majority of cases, problems related to classroom environment result not from the nature of a particular group of students so much as from the failure of the teacher to modify his or her own behavior to create a satisfactory pattern of teacher-student relationships.

Posttest

Directions: Using your own paper, answer each of the following true/false questions. For each correct statement, write the word "true." For each incorrect statement, write the word "false."

_____ 1. Basically, intrinsic motivation results because of something that occurs within the learner.

_____ 2. Most theorists believe that extrinsic motivation is more powerful than intrinsic motivation.

_____ 3. Maslow has pointed out that the self-actualization need is the most basic and fundamental of all human needs.

_____ 4. A person's desire to be like someone else has been called the identification motive.

_____ 5. Provision of exploratory activities in the classroom is one way in which classroom teachers can provide an instructional program that responds to the curiosity drive.

_____ 6. Generally, individuals become more interested in things in which they are proficient than in things in which they are not.

_____ 7. Grades are effective incentives for all learners.

_____ 8. Sometimes students do not attach the same meanings to words and symbols as do their teachers.

_____ 9. A common reason for student failure in small-group instructional settings is that the student has not been instructed properly with regard to what he or she, specifically, is supposed to do.

_____ 10. Classroom climate, to a large degree, is shaped by what the teacher does.

Key Ideas in Review

1. Motivating students and implementing programs are skills that do not come easily to new teachers. Success in these areas involve complex sets of interactions between teacher and students. Competency in these areas tends to develop gradually as teachers gain in experience in working with youngsters. There are, however, certain things that teachers can do to facilitate their professional growth as it pertains to motivating students and implementing programs.

2. *Intrinsic motivation* is motivation that results when some deeply felt personal need is satisfied. *Extrinsic motivation* is motivation not related to personal satisfaction with a task that is to be done but rather to personal satisfaction with something else that will occur as the task is being done or completed. In general, intrinsic motivation is thought to be more powerful than extrinsic motivation.

3. A. H. Maslow has developed a needs theory according to which lower-level, more physical needs must be met before more higher-level needs can be met. An implication of Maslow's

work is that teachers must diagnose whether students' lower-level needs have been met before they can present them with programs targeted toward satisfying higher-level student needs. Unless lower-level needs are satisfied, students (and, indeed, people in general) will not respond to programs directed toward satisfaction of higher-level needs.

4. Jerome Bruner has suggested that all people have an innate curiosity drive. When this drive is triggered, people become highly motivated. For teachers, an implication of Bruner's work is that students be presented in classrooms with puzzling and challenging situations that will bring forth the motivating curiosity drive.

5. All people are thought to have some desire to increase their similarity to other individuals whom they idealize as role models. This tendency is referred to as the identification motive. For secondary school teachers, the identification motive can provide challenges. This is especially true when students identify strongly with individuals whose interests and behaviors are inconsistent with the content of school courses. In some cases, it is possible for teachers to take advantage of the identification motive by building linkages between school content and characteristics of role models with whom students identify.

6. People have a strong drive for competence. For teachers, this means that students who achieve success in an area are likely to derive more satisfaction than are those who experience failure. Success is a strong motivator. To the extent possible, then, school programs need to be designed in ways that maximize students' potential for success.

7. Rewards of various kinds have frequently been used as extrinsic motivators. For some students grades are rewarding. For others, however, grades are not very important. Use of rewards for extrinsic motivation depends on what the teacher sees as a reward as being seen likewise as a reward by the student. Extrinsic motivators characterize much of life both in and out of the school. Although some people would like to see a heavier reliance on intrinsic motivation, it seems safe to suggest that extrinsic motivation probably will always play some role in school programs.

8. Communication in classrooms is an important variable that bears heavily on student achievement. In general, there is a necessity not only for teachers to make initial communications clearly, but also to attempt to determine how well such communications have been understood.

9. A number of different grouping patterns are found in secondary school classrooms. Perhaps the most common of these is large-group instruction in which all students in a class are treated as a single unit for instructional purposes. Many teachers also employ some small-group instructional experiences in their programs. Finally, independent study, an instructional mode characterized by instructional procedures directed at students one at a time, has been favored by some teachers for specific purposes. Large-group, small-group, and independent study procedures require different kinds of planning and implementation responsibilities of teachers. Executed properly, each format can make significant contributions to the secondary school program.

10. The nature of interactions between teacher and students contributes to the creation of an environment often referred to as classroom climate. In shaping classroom climate, teacher behavior is the most critical variable. Teachers through their actions can create classroom climates characterized by openness, authoritarianism, or competitiveness or by any one of a number of other variables that somehow pertain to the nature of teacher-student relationships.

SUMMARY

Teachers tend to require more ''percolation time'' in developing expertise in the areas of motivating students and implementing programs. Other areas of instructional planning can be accomplished largely in settings away from the classroom itself. Motivation and implementation, however, must occur in the classroom as instruction is unfolding. In this setting the teacher is confronted with making a great many decisions relatively quickly as the lesson unfolds. It simply takes time for teachers to learn to manage all that goes on during a given class period and to develop confidence in making responses to students that engender motivation and smooth program flow.

There are, however, some basic principles that beginning teachers can learn that tend to characterize behavior of teachers with real expertise in the areas of motivation and implementation. A number of these relate to basic psychological principles that have been determined to have a connection to individuals' willingness to pursue tasks. Some refer to alternative organizational patterns and their implications for teacher responsibilities in the classroom. Still others have to do with the nature of the communications process itself. With information related to these areas and some sound experience in the classroom, in time most teachers do develop a sense of competence in the areas of motivation and program implementation. But even "old hands" are not universally successful in these areas. All teachers have days that simply do not go as well as they would have wished. But, with some understanding of basic principles in hand and a willingness to learn, the numbers of these days can be reduced.

References

Armstrong, David G.; Denton, Jon J.; and Savage, Tom V. *Instructional Skills Handbook.* Englewood Cliffs, N.J.: Educational Technology Publications, 1978.

Biehler, Robert F. *Psychology Applied to Teaching.* 2nd ed. Boston: Houghton Mifflin Company, 1974.

Bigge, Morris L. *Learning Theories for Teachers.* New York: Harper and Row, Publishers, Inc,. 1964.

Clarizio, Harvey F.; Craig, Robert C.; and Mehrens, William A., eds. *Contemporary Issues in Educational Psychology.* 3rd ed. Boston: Allyn & Bacon, Inc., 1977.

Long, Lynette. *Listening/Responding: Human-Relations Training for Teachers.* Monterey, Calif.: Brooks/Cole Publishing Company, 1978.

Maslow, Abraham H. "A Theory of Human Motivation," *Psychological Review* (July 1943): 370–396.

Sprintall, Richard C., and Sprintall, Norman A. *Educational Psychology: A Developmental Approach.* Reading, Mass.: Addison-Wesley Publishing Company, 1977.

Weisgerber, Robert A., ed. *Perspectives in Individualized Learning.* Itasca, Ill.: F. E. Peacock Publishers, Inc., 1971.

Measuring, Evaluating, and Reporting Student Progress

FUNKY WINKERBEAN by Tom Batiuk © 1981. Field Enterprises, Inc. Courtesy of Field Newspaper Syndicate.

Objectives

This chapter provides information to help the reader to

1. Recognize the need for sound measurement and evaluation procedures.
2. Define the terms and explain the relationships among measurement, evaluation, and grading.
3. Identify different types of measurement tools.
4. Identify the strengths and weaknesses of different types of test instruments.
5. Note the relationship between the cognitive level of learning that is sought and the kind of procedure used to assess this learning.
6. Distinguish among several alternative schemes for awarding students grades.

Pretest

Directions: Using your own paper, answer each of the following true/false questions. For each correct statement, write the word "true." For each incorrect statement, write the word "false."

_____ 1. "Measurement" refers to the process of gathering information about the absence or presence of an attribute or behavior.

_____ 2. Informal and impressionistic evidence is satisfactory for making decisions regarding educational programs.

_____ 3. Students frequently infer the real purposes of a course (which may be quite different from the stated purposes) by looking carefully at the kinds of assessment procedures used.

_____ 4. When developing a rating scale, it is important that the various points on the scale be easily distinguished.

_____ 5. In general, essay tests should not be used to assess students' cognitive thinking at the level of knowledge.

_____ 6. One difficulty in preparing true/false tests is the need to develop statements that are either entirely true or entirely false.

_____ 7. In norm-referenced grading, a student's grade is determined by his or her performance as it compares with scores of other students in the group.

_____ 8. In criterion-referenced grading, a student's grade is determined by his or her performance as it compares with scores of other students in the group.

_____ 9. Grading students on the basis of how much progress each person in the class makes as compared with his or her standing at the beginning of the term may be to the disadvantage of very bright students.

_____ 10. Because of regression toward the mean, students who score at very low levels on a given test may score much higher on that test if it is given a few days later even though they may have learned nothing new about the material.

INTRODUCTION

"Is my program working well?" "Are my students learning anything?" These questions are of consuming interest to professional teachers. Those who can answer both questions with a resounding "yes" tend to feel good about themselves and what they are doing. Those who have some concerns about the quality of their programs and about how much students are profiting from their classes often doubt their own adequacies as classroom instructors. While an interest in the quality of our instructional program generally is a healthy impetus to do our best in the classroom, it is important that we make judgments about our progress on the basis of evidence. Sometimes subjective impressions may get us in trouble. Consider, for example, the case of a Ms. Beth Jones, a high school social studies teacher with two years of experience.

Ms. Jones

The bell had sounded ending the class two minutes ago. The last students had clattered their way out of the room. Sighing, Ms. Jones slumped into her chair. "One of those days," she thought, "one of those days when nothing clicks. How come?"

The planning had been solid. In fact, several hours had gone into preparation for the mock Congress exercise. "And," she mused, "they were able to really get

involved in our discussions on the legislative process. There was lots of involve-
ment. But then our simulation . . . a big, grade 'A' flop."

It had begun well enough. The youngsters had seemed interested. "But," won-
dered Ms. Jones, "why didn't they know how to act out the assigned roles. Even
the 'A' students who had performed brilliantly in the discussion seemed totally
unaware about how a legislature works. They couldn't have forgotten everything."

Ms. Jones eased herself up from her chair. "Time for a quick cup of coffee." she
thought to herself. "Maybe tomorrow will be better. Right now I feel like I just
can't teach anybody anything. I hope it's just one of those days. I'm sure it's one
of those days . . . I hope."

What was the problem here? Well, probably several things. But one factor that
may have contributed to Ms. Jones' self-doubts could have been her willingness to
draw conclusions about what students could or could not do based on inadequate evidence. Let us look for a moment at the general issues of measurement, evaluation, and
grading. Then we will make some comments about the adequacy of Ms. Jones' self-
judgment given her understanding (or lack of understanding) of how each task is
accomplished and how information about each should be interpreted.

Measurement

Measurement refers to the process of gathering information relating to the presence or
absence of a student behavior or attribute. For the teacher, the important understanding
in performing this task is the recognition of which measures of a given attribute or
behavior are *valid*. For example, a yardstick is not an appropriate tool of measurement
if there is an interest in determining the attribute of student weight. A test requiring a
student to translate a page of French into written English is not a valid measure of the
student's ability to listen to rapid-fire oral French and make a simultaneous oral
English translation. The technique selected for gathering the information must be
capable of providing information that is related clearly to the behavior or attribute of
interest.

Well, now, how did our Ms. Jones do with regard to measurement? Recall that
she had involved youngsters in a discussion in which they had done a good job of identifying various facts relating to the legislative process. She used this as a measure of
their ability to apply these concepts to a mock Congress. Was this a valid measure of
their ability to apply information? Probably not. Learning psychologists tell us that
the ability to recall information is quite different from the ability to apply information.

Evaluation

Evaluation refers to the process of making a value judgment or decision. The evaluator
must decide whether the student is able to demonstrate a particular behavior at an
acceptable level of proficiency. Consequently, those who evaluate must have had adequate training so that they know what level of performance is acceptable. Beyond a
professional ability to set acceptable standards, evaluators must base their decisions on
a broad base of information. For teachers, this ordinarily means that a variety of measurements should occur before evaluative judgments are made. If judgments are made
on the basis of only one or two measurements, the evaluation may not be an accurate
reflection of a given youngster's abilities.

In the case of our Ms. Jones, a judgment of personal failure was made on the
basis of very limited information. (Although Ms. Jones tried to convince herself that

maybe it had been "just one of those days," we get the distinct impression that she had been let down by the experience and that she wasn't really holding out too much hope for tomorrow.) She made a judgment on her adequacy as a teacher based almost exclusively on the youngsters' difficulty with the role-playing exercise. Certainly this data base was far too narrow to serve as a rationale for the kind of negative self-judgment she engaged in after the class.

Grading

A grade is a shorthand means of communicating teachers' evaluations to other interested parties. In this country, the most common system involves the use of letter grades. Whether letter grades or some other scheme is used, it is important that the grades communicate clearly to the parties who will see them. That is, it is essential that people have a clear understanding of what grades of "A," "B," "C," "D," and "F" *mean* (assuming that a letter-grading system is in use).

In general, there are two widely used schemes for determining how grades should be awarded. One scheme is referred to as a "norm-referenced" system. Under norm-referenced grading, a student's grade is determined by how well he or she does relative to other students in his or her class. An example of a norm-referenced system is the scheme found in many schools that students refer to as "grading by the curve." Grading by the curve requires teachers to fit all student scores into what mathematicians call a normal curve and award a certain percentage of students each letter grade. In general, there will be relatively few very high and very low grades. Most students will receive grades in the middle of the distribution (more "B's," "C's," and "D's" than "A's" and "F's" in a letter-grading system, for example).

A second scheme for awarding grades is referred to as a "criterion-referenced" system. Students are graded according to how their scores measure up against a given standard or criterion. For example, a criterion of 90 percent correct might be established for an "A," 80 percent correct for a "B," and so forth. This system permits all students or no students to achieve any grade. (If everybody in a class met our 90 percent level, then everybody would get an "A." If nobody had 90 percent, no "A's" would be awarded.) More detailed information regarding norm-referenced and criterion-referenced schemes is provided later in the chapter.

Regardless of the grading system selected, it is essential that grades be awarded on the basis of supportive data. It is totally unacceptable to award grades to students based only on subjective feelings about which youngsters deserve "A's," "B's," "C's," "D's," and "F's." Teachers who follow such a practice may find themselves in very hot water should any student or his or her parents challenge a grade in court.

Did our Ms. Jones tell us anything about the adequacy of her grading practices in her musings about the mock Congress lesson? She did indeed. Recall her concern that the "A" students in the discussion had had difficulty assuming their roles. This suggests that Ms. Jones had made some subjective judgments about which students were the "A" students based on her intuitive feelings about how they ought to have been able to perform. Although these youngsters may indeed have been stellar performers in a discussion or on a test asking for factual recall, they definitely were not "A" students in terms of their ability to perform the simulated legislature exercise. (This may not have been their fault. It seems quite possible that the teacher had asked for too large a jump in going from classroom discussion directly to an application activity.) The point here is that Ms. Jones seems not to have a clear grasp of what an "A" grade means. It would suggest a need to think through very carefully the kind of student competencies that she would expect to be demonstrated by any youngster to whom an "A" grade ought to be awarded.

PRINCIPLES OF PLANNING A MEASUREMENT AND EVALUATION PROGRAM

In planning our measurement and evaluation programs, we need to keep in mind three general principles:

1. What we are measuring ought to be related clearly to what we are trying to teach (our expected learning outcomes).
2. Measurements should be taken at frequent intervals so that random chance factors do not cause us to make judgments about students that may not reflect accurately their true abilities.
3. Because we as teachers have a clear understanding of the expected learning outcomes established for our students, we should play an active part in selecting the kinds of measurement instruments to be used in gathering information about performance levels of individuals in our classrooms.

Let us look at each of these principles individually.

The first principle suggests that measurement and evaluation should be tied clearly to our expected learning outcomes. It makes no sense whatever to develop a test that requires youngsters to demonstrate their understanding of material unrelated to what we have been focusing on in class. Few teachers intentionally set out to develop test items that are unrelated to what they have been teaching. Frequently such test items do result, however, when exams are developed in haste with little serious thought about the content to which students have been exposed. Obviously, such practices set students up for failure. Test results clearly cannot be regarded, in such cases, as adequate indicators of youngsters' grasp of the contents introduced during the preceding classroom instruction. To avoid development of testing procedures that are inconsistent with our expected learning outcomes, we need to plan our measurement program at the same time we identify the expected learning outcomes we will be seeking during the instructional phase of our program.

Some teachers have found it useful to develop a measurement and evaluation plan as they begin to think about planning their overall instructional program. Once such a plan has been completed, the expected learning outcomes and identified measurement techniques can be included in the instructional objectives developed to guide instructional planning. (For an explanation of instructional objectives and the ABCD format for preparing them, see Chapter 7, "Selecting Content and Establishing Instructional Objectives.") An example of a simple measurement and evaluation plan is provided in Figure 11-1. Once these techniques have been identified, of course tests and other identified measurement instruments will need to be developed.

The second principle speaks to the necessity to measure youngsters' progress at relatively frequent intervals. There are several advantages to this approach. First, students tend to become very nervous when their course grades are being awarded on the basis of only one or two major exams given during an entire grading period. They are likely to feel much less intimidated by the testing program when tests are given at more frequent intervals.

Further, frequent tests provide us with results that can help us identify problems that youngsters may be having. This kind of evidence can suggest a possible need to review material that has been introduced or expand upon what we have done. When we identify such difficulties relatively early, we may be able to help some youngsters who, left unattended to for a longer period of time, may become hopelessly lost.

Finally, frequency of measurement tends to provide us with a more reliable basis for making a judgment about an individual student's real understanding of our material than does infrequent measurement. Suppose that we gave only one test and that John Jones was not feeling well on the day we gave it. He might score lower than he would

Figure 11-1

SAMPLE MEASUREMENT AND EVALUATION PLAN

EXPECTED LEARNING OUTCOMES	EVALUATION TECHNIQUE ALTERNATIVES
1. Ability to distinguish among positions of members of President Lincoln's cabinet.	Multiple choice; matching; true/false.
2. Ability to locate sources of historical data.	Essay; short answer test; multiple choice.
3. Ability to write a paper that demonstrates ability to incorporate historical research in a logical and consistent way.	Rating scale.
4. Ability to identify biases contained in different accounts of historical events.	Essay; multiple choice.
5. Ability to take an active part in class discussions of historical issues.	Observation scale; checklist.

Note that the specific techniques listed under the heading "Evaluation Technique Alternatives" are not intended to be definitive. They simply reflect one teacher's judgment. Another teacher might develop a list that would look quite different from this one.

---

otherwise. We could erroneously conclude that he did not know as much of the material as, in fact, he did. On the other hand, Carla Smith might have "guessed lucky" on several questions. Her high score might lead us to conclude that she knew more of the material than, in fact, she did. Frequency of measurement can help to eliminate difficulties of these kinds.

In our concern for frequency of measurement, we do not wish to imply that teachers should give no midterm or final examinations. On the contrary, we believe that these kinds of exercises do have an important role to play. They can help youngsters to review, pull together, and, in general, make sense out of a body of content. For teachers, questions that sample content that has been presented during half a term or over a whole term can pinpoint areas in the instructional program in need of revision. For example, low student scores on questions related to certain content areas can suggest a need to revise that part of the total instructional plan before the same material is taught to a different group of students. Our point regarding frequency of measurement is not that examinations over half a term's work or a whole term's work should be avoided but, rather, that there should also be other measurements taken at more frequent time intervals.

The third general principle suggests that we as classroom teachers should be involved directly in preparing the measurement and evaluation program we use with our own students. It is imperative that we do this if we are truly serious about our desire to measure those learning outcomes we have identified as important. It is highly unlikely that examinations developed by others will be perfectly congruent with the learning expectations we have established for our own youngsters. To the extent that we have the authority to do so, we should attempt to use test items developed by others only after we have assured ourselves that they are capable of measuring those kinds of learning we want to measure.

We do not wish to suggest that standardized tests developed by well-known national testing firms are unimportant. They do have some value in helping individual school districts and schools understand in a general sort of way how their students compare with national averages. But such tests generally should not be used for the purpose of measuring and evaluating youngsters in a given class. Individual items on such tests are likely to be assessing students' learning on issues that, in too many cases, may be far removed from the learning expectations established by the individual classroom teacher.

Once we have a basic understanding of some of these fundamental principles associated with planning the measurement and evaluation program, we are ready to consider some of the options available. A number of these are described in the next section.

MEASUREMENT AND EVALUATION OPTIONS

When many people contemplating a career in teaching hear references to "measurement and evaluation," they think immediately of formal tests. Certainly pencil-and-paper tests are important. But by no means are they the only available alternatives. For example, depending on what we may be teaching, we might be interested in having youngsters demonstrate their proficiencies by doing things as diverse as baking a cake, playing a difficult selection on a French horn, or rebuilding a carburetor and installing it in an automobile.

Despite the differences among individual measurement instruments, all those that are selected wisely are characterized by their capacity for measuring the specific kinds of learnings we wish to have measured. Some of these instruments, for example, rating scales and checklists, are completed by the teacher as he or she makes observations regarding an individual student's proficiency in a given area. Others, such as multiple-choice, true/false, and matching tests, require students themselves to make marks on paper. These marks, when judged by a teacher against a correction key, provide information that is used as a basis for deciding how much a particular youngster has learned. Types of tests vary considerably in terms of how much they can tell us about what a student understands. Later in the chapter we will examine some special strengths and limitations of a number of techniques. Before looking at these procedures, we need to pause a moment to reflect on the kinds of "messages" our testing program might send to students in our class.

Although many classroom teachers make a practice of telling students what the purposes of their courses are, youngsters tend to infer the real purpose of a given course from the measurement and evaluation program that is used. Suppose, for example, that a history teacher told his or her students that "the primary purpose of this course is to help you analyze major historical issues." Suppose, further, that this same teacher's tests contained only fill-in-the-blanks items that required students to recall very specific pieces of isolated information from the text. Youngsters in this class very early in the game would conclude that the real purpose of the course (as opposed to its stated purpose) was to convey unrelated bits of factual information.

As a result of students' making this kind of a judgment about the course, the teacher almost certainly would suffer a certain loss of credibility. ("If we can't trust what he or she says about the purpose of the course, can we trust anything else he or she might say?") Additionally, many students in the class almost certainly would modify their study patterns to focus on isolated facts rather than on material useful for historical analysis. In this unhappy situation, the teacher might wonder why students "can't seem to do any real thinking," and students might wonder why the teacher doesn't want to be candid about his or her "real" expectations. This kind of situation can quickly undermine a positive classroom climate. For this reason, we believe that it is essential for us, as teachers, to work for a congruence between our stated learning expectations and the kinds of learning we really are assessing in our measurement and evaluation program.

To ensure this kind of congruence when we engage in the preparation of formal tests (matching, multiple choice, true/false, and so forth), we can play close attention to the level of cognitive thinking we want youngsters to demonstrate and take care to select testing techniques that are appropriate for testing thinking at this level. As noted in Chapter 7, "Selecting Content and Establishing Instructional Objectives," instructional objectives may vary in terms of the complexity of the thinking they demand. In planning our testing program, this means, for example, that, if the objective requires thinking at the level of analysis, our testing procedure must demand analysis-level thinking. A discussion of the relative merits of individual testing techniques for measuring student thinking at the respective levels of (1) knowledge, (2) comprehension, (3) application, (4) analysis, (5) synthesis, and (6) evaluation is provided later in the chapter as part of the general description of each procedure.

Once we have identified alternative procedures that possess the technical capacity to assess thinking at a given level, we have to consider how much time is required for test development and correction. For example, an essay question takes very little time for a teacher to prepare, but correction time can be considerable. On the other hand, good multiple-choice questions require a great deal of time to prepare, but, once they are ready, they can be corrected quickly. We need, then, to give some serious consideration to the issue of time as we make our final decisions regarding the specific testing procedure we will select to assess youngsters' learning.

We will want to keep some of these general considerations in mind as we look at a selection of measurement instruments that are available.

Rating Scales

Some instructional objectives require youngsters to engage in certain kinds of physical tasks that preclude assessing proficiency using a paper-and-pencil test. Objectives relating to such things as using laboratory equipment, delivering speeches, completing art projects, and turning finials on a lathe are examples. A rating scale is a measurement tool that can be used to gather information about student proficiency on tasks of this type.

Typically, a rating scale identifies a specific set of characteristics or qualities. Indications are made along the scale in such a way that a judgment is made about the degree to which the identified quality (or qualities) is (are) present. The developer of a rating scale must take pains to ensure that the qualities identified on the rating scale are consistent with those noted in the instructional objective. Further, clear descriptions of the kind of performance implied by each point on the scale are essential. Otherwise, the rater will have difficulty in deciding exactly where along the scale a mark should be made that references the quality of an individual student's performance.

Suppose that a music teacher was interested in determining how well a given youngster could sight-read a given piece of music. He or she could develop a rating scale that might include the following directions and sample item:

Directions: Circle the appropriate number for each item. The numbers represent the following values.

$$5 = \text{outstanding}$$
$$4 = \text{above average}$$
$$3 = \text{average}$$
$$2 = \text{below average}$$
$$1 = \text{unsatisfactory}$$

1. To what extent does the student play the appropriate note?

5   4   3   2   1

The rating scale shown does not give the rater very specific information regarding what is implied by each rating. For example, what, specifically, separates "outstanding" from "above average," "above average" from "average," and so forth? The item might be improved somewhat by changing the descriptors for each step on the scale in the following way:

> 5 = always
> 4 = frequently
> 3 = occasionally
> 2 = seldom
> 1 = never

While there still may be some confusion of exactly which rating a given performance ought to be given, in general these descriptors are more informative than the initial set. (For example, few would have difficulty with "always" or "never." There may be some problems with "frequently, occasionally," and "seldom," but they probably would occasion less difficulty than "above average," "average," and "below average.")

Sometimes it is useful to add descriptive phrases at various points along the scale to indicate behaviors that youngsters should demonstrate to earn a given point rating. Suppose, for example, that a teacher was evaluating performances of students who were giving individual speeches. He or she might wish to use a rating scale something like this:

5	4	3	2	1
Demonstrates a continuous unity of thought. Points are clear and related to the topic.		Demonstrates a generally logical flow. There are occasional "drifts" from main topic.		Rambles consistently. Presentation lacks coherence. Topic never comes into focus.

Inclusion of these descriptors contributes to the accuracy of the rating process. Also, if this scale is shared with students in advance of their speeches, it provides them with useful cues as they prepare for their presentations.

In summary, then, rating scales are useful for making judgments about physical kinds of student performances where proficiency cannot be assessed properly through the use of pencil-and-paper tests. Probably the most difficult part of constructing good rating scales involves providing clear descriptions of the specific kind of performance that would merit a rating at each point on the scale.

Evaluative Checklists

Checklists share certain characteristics with rating scales. Both are used to gather information about physical kinds of student behavior that do not lend themselves well to assessment techniques of a pencil-and-paper test variety. Both depend upon the student behaviors that are the focus of interest as being clearly observable. (The teacher has to be able to see or hear what the student is doing to make a judgment and note this information on the rating scale or checklist.)

A major difference between rating scales and checklists is that rating scales generally provide teachers with more flexibility in determining the degree of adequacy of a given youngster's performance. While nearly all rating scales allow teachers to make judgments at any one of a number of points along a scale (for example, on a five-point scale, a teacher might choose to mark any one of the following: 5, always; 4, frequently;

3, occasionally; 2, seldom; 1, never), large numbers of checklists allow only for a "yes/ no" decision. That is, a checklist usually is employed when there is an interest only in the presence or absence of a given behavior. When the behavior is indeed present, the checklist format does not lend itself well to making judgments about the relative quality of the behavior.

Suppose, for example, that a teacher was interested in monitoring the progress of individual youngsters on a term-paper project. The teacher might prepare a checklist such as the following to note how far along each youngster was on the term-paper assignment.

STUDENT'S NAME: _____

	Yes	No
Topic selected and approved		
Rough outline turned in		
Final outline turned in		
Note cards turned in		
First draft turned in		

Norman Gronlund (1976, pp. 445–447) suggests subscribing to the following principles in developing a sound checklist:

1. Identify and describe clearly each of the specific actions desired in the performance.
2. Add to the list those actions that represent common errors, provided that they are limited in number and can be easily defined.
3. Arrange the desired actions and likely errors in the approximate order in which they are expected to occur.
4. Provide a simple procedure for numbering the actions in sequence or for checking each action as it occurs.

When these procedures are followed and when our interest is in determining the presence or absence of a given student performance, a checklist represents a reasonable choice.

Essay Items

Essays are very powerful test items in that they have the technical capability of assessing students' thinking at virtually any level of the cognitive taxonomy (knowledge, comprehension, application, analysis, synthesis, and evaluation). Although essays are capable of testing students' thinking skills at a variety of levels, as a practical matter, they are used best to assess thinking at the higher levels (application, analysis, synthesis, and evaluation) than at the lower levels (knowledge and comprehension).*

In general, essays are not preferred for testing students' abilities to think at the levels of knowledge and comprehension because they require so much time to correct. Alternative testing techniques, such as multiple choice, matching, and true/false, are available. These require much less correction time, and they are perfectly capable of assessing knowledge-level and comprehension-level thinking.

A significant "plus" for the essay format is that questions can be generated rela-

---

*For a discussion of each of these levels of the cognitive taxonomy, see the major heading "Kinds of Instructional Objectives" in Chapter 7, "Selecting Content and Establishing Instructional Objectives."

tively quickly. In fact, essay questions are so easy to write that sometimes it is a temptation for us to prepare them too hastily. Carelessly written essay items are likely to produce frustration for students taking the test as well as for the teacher who, when working through a stack of student papers, may wonder "how could so many of them missed the point?"

In thinking about preparing an essay item, one problem we face is that of content coverage. Because of the time required for students to write responses to essays, typically only very few essay items can be included on a given exam. This can result in a very limited sampling of content unless the few essay questions (typically one or two, rarely four or more) are written carefully. One of the authors, for example, remembers vividly his own frustration when a final examination in a course in Western civilization (a course characterized by an incredible diversity of content) included only a single essay question focusing on an obscure event in Greek history (*very* obscure in the mind of the author of your text!). It was doubtful that responses even of those who did brilliantly on the question gave the instructor an adequate picture of students' understanding of the range of content covered in the course.

Maintaining a consistent pattern of scoring when correcting essays prepared by different students presents the teacher with a real challenge. Correction takes a long time, particularly when large numbers of students are involved, and fatigue can interfere with even our best intentions to apply the same standards to the last paper as to the first.

One interesting dimension of the consistent-grading issue is sometimes referred to as the "halo effect." A halo effect may be initiated when a teacher notes that an essay he or she is about to read has been written by one of his or her "good" students. Because of a predisposition to believe that such an individual would be unlikely to do anything but good work, there is a tendency for the teacher to be less critical of what the student has written in response to the essay question. Thus, the halo the teacher sees surrounding the student in terms of his or her general performance is transferred to his or her work on this specific task, namely, the essay. The halo effect can result in a youngster's receiving a higher grade on an essay than he or she would have received had the teacher been unaware of the name of the individual who prepared the essay response in question.

Although problems of content selection and correction consistency are very real, they can be overcome. We can begin by clearly structuring the essay task for the student. This means that we need to be as precise as possible regarding what the student should include in the essay and the approximate quantity of prose that should be provided. Note the differences between the two following sets of instructions for completing an essay item that were provided to students in a high school biology class:

A. Write an essay in which you discuss the chromosome hypothesis and the gene theory.
B. Write an essay, about five pages in length, in which you compare and contrast the chromosome hypothesis and the gene theory. In your response, include specific references to (1) essentials of each position, (2) modifications that have been made to each position since it was initially developed, and (3) strengths and weaknesses that have been attributed to each view by critics.

A student receiving instructions similar to those in A may be inclined to ramble. There is little precision of language used to describe the task. (The word "discuss," for example, is a very vague guide to what the student should write about.) Further, there are no references to how long the response should be. A student might write a paragraph, or he or she might write eight pages. In light of these vague instructions, the teacher would likely receive a set of papers that would be difficult to assess because each youngster was forced to determine more or less for himself or herself what the task was.

The set of directions in B is much better. Youngsters have a clear focus regarding the topics to be covered in their response. Further, a specific length condition is imposed ("about five pages"). Because of these guidelines, the teacher is likely to have a much better set of papers. Further, correction will be easier than in the case of the set of papers coming from students given the A directions, because, at a minimum, the teacher can look to see whether each essay (1) compares and contrasts the chromosome hypothesis and the gene theory, (2) outlines essentials of each, (3) notes changes in each position since it was first postulated, and (4) describes strengths and weaknesses of each position as viewed by critics. These common "must-be-included" features help the teacher to look at each essay in the same way. They help to maintain consistency of grading from paper to paper. Figure 11-2 is an exercise in writing essay test questions.

In preparing and grading essay items, a number of procedures can be used to professionalize our practices. Among these are the following:

1. Complete a sample response to each essay item administered to students.
2. Take steps to keep ourselves from learning the name of the writer of a given response until after we have graded it.
3. Read all answers provided by all students related to one essay item before going on to consider answers to other items on the test.
4. Read responses to each item more than once.
5. Adjust scoring criteria in light of a content analysis.

Let us look at each of these procedures in some detail.

Completing a Sample Response.   Once we have written a essay question, it makes sense to sit down and write out an answer ourselves. Although this procedure takes time, it can help us spot potential weaknesses in the language of our question. Further, the contents of our own answer can suggest some criteria that can be used for grading student responses. If we wish to do so, we can assign a certain number of points to each piece of specific evidence we provided in our own responses. When the same kinds of evidence surface in the student papers, those points can be awarded to the students. (Of course there will be evidence in the student papers we may not have thought of which we will want to credit. But, in general, this

Figure 11-2

IMPROVING THE QUALITY OF ESSAY TEST QUESTIONS

Below are a number of poorly written essay questions. Try your hand at rewriting each question to turn it into a better item. Be prepared to tell the instructor why your rewritten version is superior to the original.

1. Compare and contrast the underhanded versus the overhanded method of shooting a free throw.
2. Analyze the president's policy on Iran.
3. Suggest possible changes in the nature of plane geometry theorems that might result in a new geometry based on the assumption that parallel lines meet at some point this side of infinity.
4. Contrast alternative explanation for the growing of suburbs.
5. Contrast the two poets' use of alliteration.
6. Analyze critically the theory of plate tectonics.

YOUR OPINION, PLEASE

Write an essay item that you might give to students focusing on a subject you might be teaching. Be sure that your essay requires thinking beyond the levels of knowledge or comprehension. Ask your instructor to comment on the adequacy of your item.

---

system does begin to give us some idea of the kind of content we are expecting to see in our student responses.)

Maintaining Anonymity of the Essay Writer. Because of the halo effect and other problems that might interfere with the fairness of our judgment when we know the identity of the individual who has written an essay, it is desirable to establish some scheme to obscure the identity of the writer until after we have completed the grading process. Some teachers cover over student names with a card paper clipped to student answers and then shuffle the stack. Others assign students a code or a number at the beginning of the term. Students write their codes rather than their names on their papers. The teacher does not determine the identity of the student until after the correction process has been completed and grades are entered into a grade book where numbers or codes assigned to each student are identified. Certainly other schemes might be devised to achieve the same objective of maintaining name anonymity until after grading has been completed.

Grading All Student Answers on One Item Before Going On to the Next. When faced with a stack of examination papers, there is a natural tendency to start with one student's answers and grade his or her answers to all questions that have been asked before going on to another student's paper. Because criteria for grading one item may differ markedly from criteria for grading another, it makes better sense to grade all student responses to one item before grading responses to others. That is, we should grade all answers to question 1, then we should grade all answers to question 2, and so forth. This procedure will make for greater consistency in scoring than will the alternative of reading through responses one student has made to all questions before going on to responses of another youngster.

Repeated Readings of Responses to Essay Items. If time permits, it is a sound practice to read responses that students have made to an individual essay item several times. Although we try to keep our general mood from influencing our judgment, there are times when we are likely to be more generous than others when reviewing students' responses. If possible, if we read papers once, then wait at least 24 hours before shuffling and reading them again, we should have reduced the likelihood of making serious judgment errors because of our particular mental frame of mind at the time we were correcting the student responses.

Adjusting Scoring Criteria in the Light of Content Analysis. The first step in a content-analysis process is for the teacher correcting students' work to note on a sheet of paper each different piece of significant pertinent information that students have provided in response to the question. The "significant pertinent information" might be in the form of key words, of concepts, or of short phrases. The first time that an individual item of information is encountered in a student paper, the teacher writes it on his or her sheet. Subsequent references to similar information on papers written by other students are noted as tally marks following the original key word, concept, or short phrase.

When this process has been completed, the teacher has a profile of the information provided by the class in response to the essay item. The frequency of mention of certain information can suggest how well the youngsters understood pertinent points. It may be that this content analysis would prompt the teacher to rethink his or her weighting of the importance of certain of the points that might have been included. In this event, the teacher might wish to adjust his or her scoring of individual student responses.

Some teachers we know have found it useful to post all responses and tallies from the content analysis on the board. This information can serve as a good basis for a debriefing session. Further, with this material before them, the class might even be involved in a discussion centering on how much credit or weight ought to be given to each element of information in a completed essay. Such a discussion can help to sharpen students' understandings of the components of a high-quality essay response.

In summary, essays are especially useful for making judgments about students' abilities to engage in higher-level thinking skills. Among difficulties with essays are (1) the time required for correction, (2) the inability to sample a broad range of content by asking large numbers of essay questions on a given test, and (3) maintaining consistency of grading practices. There are, however, procedures we can follow to deal with these problems. Properly constructed and evaluated, essay tests represent a powerful tool in our assessment repertory.

Completion Items

Completion items share with essays the feature of requiring youngsters to write responses in their own handwriting. However, they are much less powerful in terms of the kinds of thinking they can assess. Generally, completion items are most useful for assessing student thinking at the lower cognitive levels of knowledge and comprehension. It is very difficult to prepare completion items capable of testing higher-level thinking abilities of students.

Completion items are easy to construct. They are capable of sampling a broad range of content. Ordinarily individual items do not require a great deal of time to correct. Consequently, a teacher can include a large number of completion items on a given test or examination.

A problem with completion items relates to their scoring. It is very difficult to construct items for which only one answer is logically correct. It is especially difficult to decide what to do about student answers that are partially correct. To get some perspective on this correction issue, look at the following completion-type item:

The individual elected president of the United States in 1980 was _____.

Now probably most students would write in Ronald Reagan. But there are other plausible answers as well. For example, how would a teacher deal with such alternatives as "a man," "an actor," "a Republican," "a conservative," "a Californian"?

To avoid correction problems, it is essential that completion items be written so that the type of response is very clear. For example, the item about the president could have narrowed the range of acceptable (or potentially acceptable) answers considerably had it been phrased like this:

The name of the president of the United States who was elected in 1980 is _____.

The inclusion of the word "name" would eliminate the possibility of many of the alternative responses that would have been logically acceptable given the original phrasing of the item.

In addition to providing for clarity of expected response, it is important that each completion item have only one blank space in which students can write. Further, this blank ought to come toward the end of the item. This arrangement gives the student time to pick up relevant cues regarding the nature of the expected response. An item with many blanks that are placed at random is almost sure to result in little other than confusion. Consider this horrible example:

_____ *affects* _____ *independently of* _____ *except on those occasions when* _____ *and* _____ *stand inversely related.*

To eliminate some scoring problems, teachers often provide students with a selection of answers, some correct and some incorrect, from which they are to draw their responses. Students must use only answers provided on the list. Thus, students can be held accountable both for correct word choice and for spelling (the word is there; the student has only to copy the word correctly to spell it right).

But this kind of revision does somewhat alter the format of the completion item into a kind of modified matching item. Further, it introduces the possibility of being able to guess and get the item right. However, some teachers are willing to make this exchange to simplify their correction chores. An example of this kind of a modification is provided here:

STUDENT'S NAME: _____

Completion Item

Directions: A number of blanks appear in the following short paragraph. Below the paragraph you will find a list of terms. Select appropriate terms from this list and print them carefully in the proper blanks. Include only terms included in the list at the bottom of the page. You will be expected to spell these terms correctly.

In recent years, there has been a trend for people to move away from the core of a city toward the surrounding suburbs. Sociologists call this movement _____. Another urban phenomenon involves movement of people from one social class to a part of the city occupied by people in another social class. This is termed _____. When a new group in a city succeeds in taking over a neighborhood, a situation termed _____ results. When minority members of a community are removed by majority members, we have a situation called _____. When this causes married couples to move to a locale where neither set of parents is resident, their new family residence is said to be _____. The group an individual interacts with over time on a more or less continuous basis is called a (an) _____ group.

recurrent	suburbanization	succession
allotropic	invasion	concession
neolocal	separation	expulsion
patrilocal	segregation	deviance

In general, completion items do not represent a particularly good technique for assessing youngsters' proficiencies. In most cases, multiple-choice, true/false, and matching items are to be preferred. Multiple-choice, true/false, and matching items have the capacity to assess knowledge- and comprehension-level thinking, as do completion items; but, unlike completion items, they are much easier to correct.

Matching Items

Matching items are used to measure students' thinking at the levels of knowledge and comprehension. (Although it may be possible to construct matching tests to assess higher-level thinking, this is not usually done.) Matching items enjoy a number of "pluses" in the eyes of classroom teachers. They are relatively easy to construct. They can be corrected quickly. And there is little danger that one student's test will be graded according to a standard different from that used for another student's test.

Difficulties that do arise with the use of matching items are usually associated with poor item construction. These problems can be overcome if we pay attention to a limited number of basic principles of sound matching item construction.

First, all terms in a given matching item should focus on a single topic or theme. Students become confused when they are confronted with a matching item containing an array of unrelated terms and definitions. To avoid this possibility, we want to restrict our focus and to cue youngsters to what that focus is by mentioning it by name at the beginning of the matching item. For example, a test including the names of a number of Confederate generals on one side and a number of exploits associated with them listed on the other ought to be labeled "Matching Quiz: Confederate Generals."

As a rule of thumb, the list on the right-hand side (the one providing alternative answers from which students are to select answers to put in the blanks before items on the left-hand side) should contain about 25 percent more items than the list on the left-hand side. For example, if there were 10 definitions with blanks on the left, then there might be 12 or 13 terms from which students might choose on the right.

The practice of placing more options on the right makes it possible for a student to miss one question without being forced, as a consequence, to miss another. When there is an identical number of items in both left- and right-hand lists, this double penalty for a missed question comes into play. (In such a situation, for example, a student who incorrectly identifies term "d" as his or her response to definition 1 rather than to definition 3, which is correct, will end up having wrong responses both for definition 1 and definition 3.)

Another principle of matching test construction is to have the entire test printed on one page. It is absolutely unacceptable for any portion of either the left-hand list or the right-hand list to be carried over to a second page. When this formatting error is committed, many students fail to realize that part of the test is on another page, which results in additional errors.

Always provide clear directions for matching tests. Students must be given instructions that direct them specifically to place the letter identifying a particular term in the right-hand column in the blank provided before the appropriate definition in the left-hand column. When explicit directions are not provided, students tend to draw lines connecting definitions to terms. This results in a confusing spider web of lines that can tax a teacher's weary eyeballs beyond endurance when there are many tests to correct. Further, directions should make clear to students that only one correct term is provided for each definition listed in the left-hand column. See Figure 11-3 for an example of a properly formatted matching test.

When these principles of construction are followed, students should have few difficulties with matching tests that can be attributed to formatting problems. The principles are learned easily, and teachers who are comfortable with them find matching tests to be very useful vehicles for gathering data about youngsters' control of definitional kinds of information.

Multiple-Choice Items

Experts in measurement hold multiple-choice items in especially high regard. Multiple-choice items can be adapted to a tremendous variety of subject matter content. They can be scored easily. And they have the capacity to test not only for knowledge and comprehension but for some higher-level thinking abilities as well.

In terms of basic format, a multiple-choice item consists of two basic parts: (1) a stem and (2) some alternative choices only a few of which (usually only one) logically relate to the stem. Among the alternative choices there is (are) a (some) correct answer(s) and some others that are called distractors. The difficulty of the item depends in large measure on the level of sophistication needed by a student if he or she is to identify the correct answer(s) from the distractor alternatives.

It is no easy task to prepare multiple-choice items where distractors appear as really plausible answers. It requires a great deal of time to prepare these items. But the effort is necessary if we really want to check on students' understanding. If we are too hasty and prepare items where distractors are not plausible, we are likely to reveal the correct answer even to students with only marginal knowledge of the material on which they are being tested. A number of basic principles need to be kept in mind as we prepare multiple-choice items.

Figure 11-3

SAMPLE MATCHING TEST

MATCHING TEST: TENNIS TERMINOLOGY   YOUR NAME: _____

Directions: Find the term in the right-hand column that is defined by the definition in the left-hand column. Place the letter identifying this term in the blank space provided before its definition. Only one term is correct for each definition. Please do *not* draw lines connecting definitions to terms.

_____ 1. The point that, if won, wins the match for a player.	a. ace
_____ 2. The area between the net and the service line.	b. backswing
_____ 3. Hitting the ball before it bounces.	c. center service line
_____ 4. Stroke made after the ball has bounced, either forehand or backhand.	d. deep shot
_____ 5. The line that is perpendicular to the net and divides the two service courts.	e. forecourt
	f. set point
_____ 6. The initial part of any swing. The act of bringing the racket back to prepare for the forward swing.	g. lob
	h. match point
	i. serve
_____ 7. A ball hit high enough in the air to pass over the head of the net player.	j. volley
	k. dink
_____ 8. A ball that is served so well that the opponent fails to touch it with his or her racket.	l. ground stroke
_____ 9. A shot that bounces near the baseline.	
_____ 10. Start of play for a given point.	

First, we need to be sure that the stem of the item is clear and grammatically correct. The alternative answers should be grammatically consistent with the stem. Consider this example:

> Nils Johannsen, in his novel of the Canadian prairies, *West From Winnipeg,* called trapping an
> a. science.
> b. art.
> c. duty.
> d. nuisance.

A student totally unfamiliar with the novel who read the question carefully would identify "b" as the correct answer simply because it is the only choice logically consistent with the article "an" at the conclusion of the stem. To correct this problem, the writer of the stem might have concluded it in this way: " . . . called trapping a (an)". This version makes any of the four alternatives grammatically plausible.

A stem that is too brief fails to cue the student regarding what kind of information he should be looking for in the list of alternatives. Consider this example:

> Roger Williams
> a. sailed on the Mayflower.
> b. established the Thanksgiving tradition.
> c. founded the Rhode Island colony.
> d. developed the first rum distillery in the New World.

Because the stem is so incomplete, the students really is faced with four true/false items to ponder than with one good multiple-choice item. The task for the student, in other words, is not well defined. A far better way of formatting this question would be this example:

> The founder of the Rhode Island colony was
>   a. Sir Walter Raleigh.
>   b. John Winthrop.
>   c. Roger Williams.
>   d. William Bradford.

As noted earlier in this discussion, multiple-choice items can be designed to test students' ability to think at a number of cognitive levels. Let us examine some examples of multiple-choice items designed to assess thinking a different levels of sophistication.

Knowledge Level.   Recall that at the level of knowledge we are interested only in determining the extent to which youngsters can recall specific information. Multiple-choice items are easy to construct for this purpose. Indeed, it is likely that most teacher-prepared multiple-choice items are designed to test thinking at this level. The following is an example of a knowledge-level multiple-choice item:

> A belief that an individual has not only the right to succeed but also has the duty or obligation to succeed is referred to by sociologists as the
>   a. multiplier theory.
>   b. mobility ethic.
>   c. transference syndrome.
>   d. neolocal tendency.

Comprehension Level.   Multiple-choice tests designed to test students' thinking at the level of comprehension require them to demonstrate an understanding of a number of elements in a given situation that are related to one another in some kind of a systematic fashion. Comprehension requires students to demonstrate an ability to perceive the proper interrelationship of these elements. The following is an example of a comprehension-level multiple-choice item:

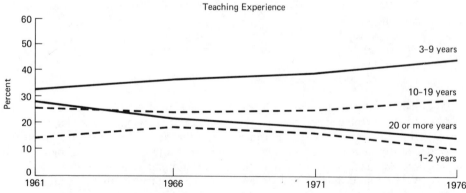

Chart is from Nancy B. Dearman and Valena White Plisko., *The Condition of Education* (Washington, D.C.: National Center for Education Statistics, 1979), p. 83.

> **Directions:** Look at the chart. This chart suggests that between 1961 and 1976 the percentage of teachers with one to two years' experience did what as compared with the percentage of teachers with three to nine years' experience? (Circle the letter before the best choice. There is only one correct response.)
>   a. The percentage increased.
>   b. The percentage stayed about the same.
>   c. The percentage decreased.
>   d. It is impossible to tell, given this information.

Application Level.   Application-level multiple-choice items require students to take information learned in one setting and use it correctly in another. Suppose, for example, that students had been exposed to the concept of "horizon of worker expectation" in a previous lesson focusing on the economy of Yugoslavia.* We might develop an application-level test item related to this concept that would look like this:

> In a social system where workers were allowed to vote on how profits of their employing firms were to be spent, we logically would expect a worker near retirement to
> a. support expenditures for plant improvement projects rather than expenditures for workers' benefits.
> b. support expenditures for workers' benefits rather than for plant improvement projects.
> c. support nearly all efforts of younger workers to improve plant efficiency.
> d. support nearly all efforts of younger workers to gain agreements to improve working conditions at a time to begin ten years after a contract settlement had been reached.

Analysis Level.   Analysis requires students to make inferences. That is, they are asked to go beyond what is given. To accomplish this, they examine information that may provide some relevant clues and that will provide a data base for their analytical thinking activities. Analysis-level multiple-choice questions are difficult to construct. They require considerable teacher time to prepare. For this reason, some teachers prefer to use essay examinations when testing for analysis-level thinking. We do not mean to suggest, however, that it is not worth committing the time to develop analysis-level multiple-choice questions. Despite the preparation time required, there is some compensation in that they take little time to correct.

Often multiple-choice items at the level of analysis present a good deal of information to students along with the stem and the alternative answer options. This information becomes the data base to which the student refers in responding to the multiple-choice item. Often a number of multiple-choice items at the level of analysis will require the student to work with a single set of presented information. An example of an analysis-level multiple-choice item is presented here:

> *Ellison had the flair of genius. But he was not a genius. Though pedestrian in his approaches, he was yet a phenomenon. His was a talent of concentration, not of innovation. No other man of his time rivaled his ability to shunt aside irrelevancies to focus on a problem's essentials. For him, non-critical considerations were trifling bits of detritus to be swept away in a moment. His resolute attack on the nuggety essence of an unresolved issue obviated even the serious probability of egregious error. Contemporaries described his reason as "glistening." Only an audacious few ventured public challenges to his positions. It is not too much to say that he lived out his days surrounded by a nervously-approving silence. Later generations have seen his conclusions as less than revolutionary. But, in his own time, Ellison's ability to "will" an impeccable solution to a complex issue made others seem small figures who were destined ever to walk lightly in the dark shadows of a giant.*

---

*Very briefly, the concept "horizon of worker expectation" involves the idea that workers tend to vary in terms of the kinds of benefits they would like from their employer in ways that are related to the amount of time they continue to see themselves working for their employer. Workers who see themselves working for an employer for only a short time want maximum benefits immediately. Those who see themselves working for a longer period of time may be willing to defer present benefits if there is a promise of more benefits at some future time.

One assumption revealed in the preceding paragraph is
   a. Ellison was not truly competent, but he had a flair for impressing people with the logical structure he built to support his solutions.
   b. Ellison really was a genius whose "glistening" logic resulted in novel solutions to problems.
   c. Today, people tend to be more impressed with Ellison than they were in his own day.
   d. Ellison's form probably was a more significant contributor to his reputation than was the substance of his thought.

Synthesis Level and Evaluation Level.   It is possible to prepare multiple-choice questions at levels higher than that of analysis. Time requirements for development of individual items at these levels prevent many teachers from considering multiple-choice items as a vehicle for testing students' thinking at these levels. For those who may be interested in some models for developing multiple-choice items to measure thinking at the levels of synthesis and evaluation, we would like to recommend a very good book. It is Benjamin S. Bloom, J. Thomas Hastings, and George F. Madaus, *Handbook on Formative and Summative Evaluation of Student Learning* (New York: McGraw-Hill Book Company, 1971).

True/False Items

True/false items, though generally used by teachers to assess knowledge-level thinking, do have some limited applications at a few higher cognitive levels. True/false items can be prepared relatively quickly. They provide a format whereby each student is likely to have his or her work graded in the same manner as every other student. They can be graded quickly.

But a number of disadvantages of true/false items should be noted. For one thing, they tend to encourage guessing. Since there are only two choices, a student has a 50:50 chance of getting an item correct even when he or she has no grasp whatsoever of the material.

Another difficulty with true/false items has to do with having to prepare statements that are absolutely "true" or absolutely "false." Much content we treat in our courses tends more toward gray than toward black or white. For this reason, some teachers feel constrained by the true/false format, which, they feel, forces them to steer away from the main focus of the instruction to find the odd example that indeed is absolutely true or absolutely false.

When a decision has been made to prepare a true/false test, we ought to follow several basic principles. Items we select must be unarguably either "true" or "false." Further, very specific instructions must be provided for students regarding how they should note their answers.

It is typical for true/false tests to be prepared in such a way that a blank space is provided before each item. Students should be directed either to write the entire word "true" or "false" (as appropriate) in each blank or to place a symbol such as "+" (for true items) or "0" (for false items) in each blank. It is *not* a good idea to direct youngsters to write the letter "t" in the blank before "true" items and the letter "f" in the blank before "false" items. Some students have mastered the technique of producing a hybrid letter that, when looked at one way, appears to be a "t" and, when looked at another way, appears to be an "f." When asked for clarification, the student is certain to define his or her intentions in terms of whichever choice, "t" or "f," was appropriate for the item in question.

As noted at the beginning of this discussion, most true/false tests are developed to test students' ability to think at the level of knowledge. With some work, other levels can be assessed using this format. Figure 11-4 provides an example of a true/false test designed to test students' comprehension-level thinking.*

FUNKY WINKERBEAN by Tom Batiuk © 1980. Field Enterprises, Inc. Courtesy of Field Newspaper Syndicate.

USING TEST RESULTS TO MAKE JUDGMENTS ABOUT THE INSTRUCTIONAL PROGRAM

One use of test results that inexperienced teachers sometimes overlook is to determine strengths and weaknesses of the instruction that preceded the test. Suppose that we had given a test during a unit we had developed according the framework introduced in Chapter 9, "Formalizing Unit and Lesson Plans." Had we done this, our test would be tied to one or more of our instructional objectives. In turn, each objective would be tied to some specific major concepts, some diagnostic procedures, some instructional strategies, and some learning resource materials. If, after giving the test, we found that a large number of youngsters had done poorly, we would want to identify some potential causes of this unhappy turn of events. In searching for these causes, we might consider a number of questions.

For example, were the diagnostic procedures adopted sufficient to identify possible gaps in students' grasp of prerequisite information? Were there weak spots in the general instructional strategies selected to help youngsters master the objective(s)? Were materials selected for use in this situation appropriate? Finally, what about the test itself? Did it adequately sample the student behavior we were trying to assess?

If we are able to engage in this kind of analysis after we have given a test, it is essential that our programs be designed systematically. It is critical that test items be tied clearly to individual instructional objectives. This does not necessarily mean that a given test will relate to only a single instructional objective. For example, we might choose to give a 40-item test consisting of 10 matching items, 20 multiple-choice items, and 10 true/false items. Questions 1 to 10 might be related to instructional objective 1, questions 11 to 20 to instructional objective 2, questions 21 to 30 to instructional objective 3, and questions 31 to 40 to instructional objective 4.

When test items are identified clearly with individual instructional objectives, it is relatively easy for us to look at test results and make some general conclusions about which parts of our unit students learned relatively well and which parts they may have

---

*Examples of tests provided in this section of the chapter because of space limitations have been drawn from only a very limited number of subjects taught in the secondary school curriculum. Other examples of excellent test items covering the areas of language arts, social studies, art, science, mathematics, literature, expository writing, and industrial education can be found in Bloom, Hastings, and Madaus (1971).

Figure 11-4

SAMPLE COMPREHENSION-LEVEL TRUE/FALSE TEST

Data to Be Used in True/False Test

	Minority Percentages in Schools Attended by Blacks		
REGION	RACIALLY INTEGRATED (0–49% MINORITY)	PREDOMINANTLY MINORITY (50–89% MINORITY)	RACIALLY ISOLATED (90–100% MINORITY)
Northeast			
1970	20.1	26.3	53.6
1976	16.9	24.0	59.1
South			
1970	37.9	27.8	34.3
1976	43.8	32.7	23.4
Midwest			
1970	15.5	18.6	66.0
1976	20.9	19.7	59.4
West			
1970	25.0	23.8	51.2
1976	25.5	30.6	43.9

Source: N. B. Dearman and V. W. Plisko, *The Condition of Education* (Washington, D.C.: National Center for Education Statistics, 1979), p. 56.

Directions: Look carefully at the table. Respond to the following true/false questions. Write the word "true" before correct items and the word "false" before incorrect items.

_____ 1. Between 1970 and 1976, there was a greater percentage drop in the numbers of blacks attending racially isolated schools in the South than in the Northeast.

_____ 2. In 1976, a higher percentage of blacks living in the Northeast attended racially integrated schools than attended "racially integrated" schools in any other region.

_____ 3. Between 1970 and 1976, the smallest percentage change in the numbers of blacks attending racially integrated schools occurred in the West.

_____ 4. Between 1970 and 1976, there was an increase in the percentage of blacks attending racially integrated schools in every region except the Northeast.

_____ 5. Between 1970 and 1976, there was a decrease in the percentage of blacks attending racially isolated schools in every region except the Northeast.

_____ 6. In 1976, a higher percentage of black students in the South attended racially integrated schools than in any other region.

_____ 7. In 1976, the two regions where the highest percentages of blacks attending racially isolated schools were the Northeast and Midwest.

_____ 8. In 1970, the region with the highest percentage of black students attending predominantly minority schools was the South, but in 1976 the highest percentage of black students attending predominantly minority schools was in the West.

learned less well. When this kind of analysis is not possible (a situation likely to occur when test items are not tied clearly to individual instructional objectives), there is a tendency, especially for inexperienced teachers, to feel that their whole program has been a failure when students miss more than a few questions. In fact, there is a possibility that youngsters have mastered most of the material presented very well and that the missed items related only to certain parts of the content that was presented. But, when individual questions are not identified clearly with specific objectives, it is not possible for a teacher to locate with confidence a potentially minor component of his or her instructional program that youngsters may not have understood well.

In addition to preventing unnecessary self-criticism by allowing for ready identification of isolated weak spots in the instructional program, tying test items to specific instructional objectives saves time. Obviously it is much more efficient to spend a little time revising an occasional weak spot in a unit than in scrapping the entire unit out of a faulty conviction that the entire instructional plan was a failure. For some practice in using test results as an aid in revising an instructional unit, see Figure 11-5.

USING TEST RESULTS TO GRADE STUDENTS

Of all the tasks they must perform, awarding grades ranks close to the bottom of the preferred activities list of many teachers (perhaps even of a majority). Grading requires

Figure 11-5

USING TEST RESULTS TO REVISE INSTRUCTIONAL UNITS

Suppose that you had developed and were teaching the instructional unit depicted in the appendix to Chapter 9, "Formalizing Unit and Lesson Plans." You have completed teaching a good portion of this unit, and you have just given your class a 45-item test. These items relate to instructional objectives for the unit as follows:

Question 1 to 25: Relate to instructional objective 1
                     (22 of 25 correct needed to master this objective)
Questions 26 to 35: Relate to instructional objective 2
                     (8 of 10 correct needed to master this objective)
Questions 36 to 45: Relate to instructional objective 4
                     (8 of 10 correct needed to master this objective)

Suppose that you were teaching this unit in three of your classes with a total of 100 students involved. After all three classes had taken the tests, you made these determinations with regard to the numbers of students passing each of the three focus objectives.

INSTRUCTIONAL OBJECTIVE	NUMBER PASSING	NUMBER NOT PASSING
1	85	15
2	81	19
4	69	31

YOUR OPINION, PLEASE
Note these figures. Then, respond to these questions.

1. How do you feel about the overall quality of the instructional design related to each of the three instructional objectives?
2. To what do you attribute the success of the instructional program as reflected in the objective or objectives you identify as having been mastered by an acceptable number of students?
3. Specifically, what would you do as a teacher to change elements within the instructional program related to instructional objective 4? (To respond to this question, you will need to look carefully at the appendix to Chapter 9 to determine what was done in the unit plan regarding this objective. Then, you will need to identify potential weak spots that might be revised before this material was taught again.)
4. If you were to do any revising of the unit plan, how would you allocate your time among revisions respecting instructional objective 1, instructional objective 2, and instructional objective 4?

us to look at test scores and other evidence for the purpose of making judgments about individual students. Typically, these judgments are converted to letter grades ranging from "A" for the most outstanding work through "F" for failing work.

In grading, we need to consider two basic concepts: fairness and specificity of communication. Fairness requires that grades not be awarded capriciously. Grades must reflect some levels of performance that are known to individual students. Should youngsters ever infer that this is not the case and that grades are being awarded on the basis of some arbitrary whim of the teacher, their performance levels are sure to fall off.

Grades should communicate something specific to parents and administrators. This means that a grade of "A" in a given class should communicate something clearly different from what is communicated by a grade of "B." Levels of competence implied by grades of "A," "B," "C," "D," and "F" should be clear to students, parents, and administrators who see these grades. Regrettably, these differences, in many schools, have been and continue to be poorly defined.

Three basic schemes have been used in secondary schools as bases for awarding letter grades. There are differences among them in terms of their individual capacities to communicate differences in the levels of competence of youngsters receiving different grades. These basic schemes are designed to award grades, respectively, on the bases of (1) individual improvement, (2) individual performance as compared with group performance, and (3) individual performance as compared with a predetermined standard. Let us look at each of these arrangements in some detail.

Individual Improvement

Grades awarded on the basis of individual improvement require the teacher to administer an initial test of a student's understanding and then a second test (or tests) after he or she has been exposed to the instructional program (typically an instructional unit). When this has been accomplished, youngsters receive grades based on the amount of improvement shown between scores on the initial test and scores on the test(s) given at the end of the instructional program. Students showing the high improvement scores receive the better grades.

There is a certain humanistic appeal to the idea that youngsters should be awarded grades based on their individual improvement scores. Clearly the scheme does place the teacher's focus on the individual student. Too, the approach suggests a grading practice consistent with many educators' enthusiasm for individualized instruction. But there are dangers associated with the procedure that may be overlooked by its proponents.

When individual improvement becomes the basis for grading, students showing the greatest individual gains will be awarded the highest letter grades. Suppose that we had a youngster who, on an initial test, received a score of 9. On the test given at the conclusion of the instruction unit, this same student received a score of 50. Subtracting the initial score of 9 from the final score of 50, we would find that this youngster had achieved a very large gain, namely, 41 points.

Now let us suppose in this same class that there was another student who had an initial test score of 80 and a final test score of 93. The difference between this individual's initial and final test was only 13 points. Following the principle that the highest grades should go to youngsters with the largest point differences between initial and final test scores, the first student would be awarded a higher letter grade than the second student. Yet, the final test score clearly implies that the second student mastered more of the course content than did the first.

Of the problems associated with this grading approach, the first relates to something that statisticians call "regression toward the mean." Regression toward the mean tells us to be very suspicious of scores on an initial test that are either extremely low or extremely high. Very low scores are thought to be due in part to some chance factors or "bad luck" that caused students to miss more items than they really ought to have missed. Very high scores are thought to be due to chance factors or "good luck" that caused students to get a few more items correct than they really should have gotten correct.

Regression toward the mean tells us that, on any subsequent test (as, for example, the test given at the end of a unit of instruction), extremely low scorers may well score higher than they did on the initial test (that is, their scores might be higher or closer to the average or "mean") and extremely high scorers may well score lower than they did on the initial test (that is, their scores may be lower or closer to the average or "mean"). What all this means for a grading scheme based on individual improvement is that those youngsters who score very poorly on an initial test enjoy a considerable advantage over students who score very well in an initial test in terms of their ability to "improve" their performances as measured by tests given at the end of an instructional unit. This scheme makes it easier for a student who does poorly on the initial test to receive a high letter grade than for a student who does well on the initial test.

Another problem for students who score high on the initial test is something called the "topping-out effect." Let us see how this might work. A student who scores 9 out of a possible 100 on an initial test enjoys a logical possibility of improving his or her score by 91 points, assuming that the second test also has 100 points possible ($100 - 9 = 91$). On the other hand, a student who scores 83 on the initial test has his or her improvement limited by the topping-out effect. Since only 100 points can be awarded on the second test, this individual has the possibility of improving his or her score only by 17 points ($100 - 83 = 17$). In a system that awards letter grades on the basis of improvement scores, the latter student is a severe competitive disadvantage relative to the youngster who does poorly on the initial test.

A final difficulty with this arrangement is that a given letter grade does not necessarily imply something specific about the level of competence of each student who receives this grade. For example, suppose that we decided to award grades of "A" to students who "improved" at least 50 points between an initial test of 100 total points and a final test of 100 total points. Note the initial test and final test scores for each of the following students who received a grade of "A":

	Initial Test Score	Final Test Score
Noel Baker	9	60
Sam Johannsen	44	95
Sydney Lofflin	4	55
Wendy Pharr	48	99

Clearly students Johannsen and Pharr, as measured by their final test scores, seem to have mastered the content more adequately than have students Baker and Lofflin. Yet all four students qualify for a grade of "A" under this "improvement" system. Although all receive "A's," it seems clear that these "A's" do not refer to a common level of competence.

In summary, the defects of the individual improvement approach are so severe that it should not receive serious consideration for use. Other alternatives are much more attractive from the standpoint of being fair to youngsters at all ability levels and from the standpoint of assuring that a given grade refers to a specific level of competence.

Individual Performance as Compared with Group Performance

More commonly used than individual improvement grading is a scheme that awards letter grades to students in a class based on how their performance compares with that of other youngsters in the class. Sometimes this kind of grading is referred to as norm-referenced grading. The idea here is that an individual student is graded in reference to the "norm" for the group of which he or she is a part. Norm-referenced grading awards higher grades to students scoring above class averages and lower grades to students scoring below class averages (see Figure 11-6).

In implementing a norm-referenced system, we ordinarily make some sort of a determination of the percentages of youngsters in our class who will receive each letter grade. Because of differences in courses, students, school settings, and other variables, there is no established set of "correct" percentages of "A's," "B's," "C's," "D's," and "F's" for every classroom situation. For example, one teacher might have a class of very bright and hard-working youngsters. Another might have a group characterized by large numbers of indifferent students of modest intellectual gifts. It would hardly be fair to allow the grading system to require that the same percentage of "A" grades, for example, be given by each of these two teachers.

A leading authority in the field of measurement, Norman E. Gronlund (1976), recommends that school personnel consider establishing an official range of percentages

Figure 11-6

BASING ALL GRADES ON THE NORMAL CURVE

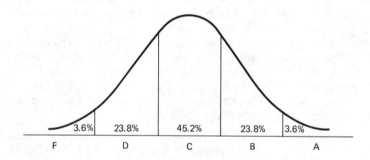

Mr. Jones, a new teacher, read that human ability tends to be distributed in a fashion that can be depicted graphically by a bell-shaped curve. That is, there are smaller numbers of higher- and lower-ability people than average-ability people.

Mr. Jones decided that this information could be used as a rational basis for awarding grades to the 32 students in his class. After some further reading, he decided that the top 3.6% would receive "A's," the next 23.8% "B's," the next 45.2% "C's," the next 23.8% "D's," and the lowest 3.6% "F's."

YOUR OPINION, PLEASE

Think about this scheme. Then, respond to these questions.

1. In general, how do you think students would respond to this scheme? Why?
2. Would students tend to work harder or to do less work given this arrangement? Why?
3. Would this be a fair grading arrangement? Why, or why not?
4. What would grades awarded under this system tell us about the individual competence of youngsters' receiving each grade?
5. Suppose that you decided to write a letter to Mr. Jones commenting critically on this system. What would you say?

to which teachers might refer in deciding upon the numbers of "A's," "B's," "C's," "D's," and "F's" to award in their individual classes. Percentages of each grade then could be varied in accordance with unique characteristics of individual courses and students. Gronlund (1976, p. 528) suggests the following possible distributions of percentages for each grade in an introductory course:

"A" = 10 to 20 percent of the learners

"B" = 20 to 30 percent of the learners

"C" = 30 to 50 percent of the learners

"D" = 10 to 20 percent of the learners

"F" = 0 to 10 percent of the learners

Note that in this scheme the teacher is not required to give any failing grades. It is important in using a norm-referenced system that youngsters recognize that the adopted system does not require some students to fail. This is important for several reasons. First, youngsters approach courses in a more positive frame of mind when they realize that everyone in the class has the potential, at least, to pass. Second, mandating a certain percentage who must fail makes little educational sense. In a single class of youngsters, perhaps one with students who are academically talented, even youngsters who score at the bottom of the class on tests may have mastered enough material to go on to more advanced work with little difficulty. In such a situation, clearly they have not failed. Rather, they simply have not mastered course work at as high a level of sophistication as have many of their classmates.

Proper use of norm-referenced grading schemes requires that careful attention be given to the issue of how much content individuals receiving various grades have mastered. It is never sufficient to disregard this issue entirely and award grades based *only* on how well a given student does as compared with others in the class. An incident that occurred several years ago will illustrate the importance of tying norm-referenced grades to some kind of a performance standard.

A high school in a large urban area had established a policy of awarding grades based only on students' performances in classes as they compared with performances of other students in those classes. When the end of the school year came, as was the traditional practice, a valedictorian was established. This individual had a "straight A" average. Clearly, in terms of the competition in this school, this person was at the top. Shortly after graduation, it was revealed that the valedictorian had not been admitted to the public university in the area because of deficient scores on the Scholastic Aptitude Test.

How could this have happened? Probably several factors were at work, but certainly one was that "A's" given in the student's high school, though correctly reflecting the student's achievement relative to others in the school, were not tied clearly to any kind of standard of performance. In a sense, this student's grades simply said that this individual was first in a group of people who knew very little. Failure to get admitted to the university was devastating to the individual concerned (who, because of the high grades received, had the illusion of being academically competent) and very embarrassing to the high school.

To prevent this kind of thing from happening, it is important that we take some pains to tie norm-referenced grading standards to some collateral kinds of assessment that might tell us soemthing about the level of content mastery of an individual youngster. Gronlund (1976) suggests, for example, that we might want to devise a special mastery test covering "the minimum essentials of the course" (p. 529) with a view to assuring that all youngsters whom our norm-referenced grading system has identified as "passing" possess certain basic knowledge. As Gronlund points out, "even when grading is done on a relative basis [norm referenced], the pass-fail decision must be based on an absolute standard of achievement . . . if it is to be educationally sound" (p. 529).

Individual Performance as Compared with a Predetermined Standard

Criterion-referenced grading is the term generally used to describe practices according to which letter grades are awarded on the basis of a comparison made between a student's performance and some pre-established standard. Typically, different levels of performance are required of youngsters who will receive different letter grades.

Criterion-referenced grading allows for clear communication of the level of competence implied by each letter grade. The standards for individual letter grades can be disseminated easily to students, parents, administrators, and others who may have an interest in this matter When this is done, little doubt remains regarding what is meant by an "A," a "B," a "C," and so forth.

In a criterion-referenced grading system, each student is potentially capable of achieving any grade. No arbitrary percentages of "A's," "B's," "C's," "D's," and "F's" are established in advance that must be awarded. In this system, there is no particular advantage given to very-low-achieving students (as in individual improvement) and no particular disadvantage is given to very-high-achieving students (again, as in individual improvement grading). It is logically possible for all students to get "A's." Similarly, it is logically possible (though unlikely) for all students to receive any other available grade. The determinant of the grades that are awarded is simply student achievement in terms of the pre-established performance standard for each letter grade.

As might be imagined, the real challenge for the teacher in using a criterion-referenced grading system is establishing the appropriate standards of achievement for each grade level. Beginning teachers and experienced hands who are new to this grading approach often find that they must teach units several times before they are satisfied with the criteria they have established for each grade. In general, we want to keep grading standards rigorous enough to prevent students from doing hasty and sloppy work but not so rigorous as to make it impossible for them to earn "A's" and "B's."

Some teachers find it useful to specify criteria in the form of grading contracts. Each contract specifies what must be done to earn a given grade. There are different contracts for students interested in seeking each grade. (Usually there are no contracts for "D's." "D's" tend to be awarded to students who fail to complete part of the work on "A," "B," or "C" contracts. "F's" are awarded to those who fall hopelessly short of their contractual obligations.)*

Another possibility for awarding grades using a criterion-referenced scheme involves the use of instructional objectives. Recall that each complete instructional objective includes a reference to a "condition" or kind of testing and a "degree" statement about how well a student must do to achieve the objective. The test mentioned in each instructional objective is not, itself, tied directly to letter grading. These tests are used only to determine whether or not the teacher should consider a given student to have achieved the objective. In a criterion-referenced grading scheme, letter grades are determined by considering the total number of instructional objectives a particular student has mastered.

Let us see how such a plan might work. Suppose that during a given grading term students had had an opportunity to achieve a maximum of 40 instructional objectives.

---

*Those interested in specifics regarding the development of grading contracts are directed to chapters in Section 2 "Developing Contracts," in Rita Dunn and Kenneth Dunn (1972).

Under these conditions, we might develop a grading system based on instructional objectives' attainment that would look like the following:

Total Number of Instructional Objectives = 40

Grade	Number of Instructional Objectives Achieved
"A"	36–40
"B"	32–35
"C"	28–31
"D"	24–27
"F"	23 or fewer

In this scheme, a determination was made to award grades of "A" to students achieving 90 percent or more of the objectives, grades of "B" to students achieving 80 to 89 percent of the objectives, grades of "C" to students achieving 70 to 79 percent of the objectives, grades of "D" to students achieving 60 to 69 percent of the objectives, and grades of "F" to students achieving fewer than 60 percent of the objectives. These percentages were selected purely for purposes of illustration. A teacher is free to choose percentage figures that he or she thinks are appropriate in view of his or her own teaching situation.

A grading system of this kind establishes a clear tie between the instructional program and grading. When students are provided with copies of the instructional objectives and information concerning the number of mastered objectives needed to earn each grade, they have an incentive to focus on the content associated with the objectives that will be used in grade determination. Instructional-objectives-based grading establishes a connection between what occurs in the classroom and the grading process. This kind of a system is likely to reduce the possibility that students will see grading as capricious and arbitrary.

Whether framed by learning contracts or around instructional objectives' attainment, criterion-referenced grading systems have much to commend them. They can communicate clearly the levels of competence implied by each letter grade. Further, no particular groups of students are placed in positions of either special advantage or special disadvantage. Finally, they serve well the need to let students know that grades are being awarded according to practices that are consistent and equitable.

Posttest

Directions: Using your own paper, answer each of the following true/false questions. For each correct statement, write the word "true." For each incorrect statement, write the word "false."

1. "Measurement" refers to the process of gathering information about the absence or presence of an attribute or behavior.

2. Informal and impressionistic evidence is satisfactory for making decisions regarding educational programs.

3. Students frequently infer the real purposes of a course (which may be quite different from the stated purposes) by looking carefully at the kinds of assessment procedures used.

——————— 4. When developing a rating scale, it is important that the various points on the scale be easily distinguished.

——————— 5. In general, essay tests should not be used to assess students' cognitive thinking at the level of knowledge.

——————— 6. One difficulty in preparing true/false tests is the need to develop statements that are either entirely true or entirely false.

——————— 7. In norm-referenced grading, a student's grade is determined by his or her performance as it compares with scores of other students in the group.

——————— 8. In criterion-referenced grading, a student's grade is determined by his or her performance as it compares with scores of other students in the group.

——————— 9. Grading students on the basis of how much progress each person in the class makes as compared with his or her standing at the beginning of the term may be to the disadvantage of very bright students.

——————— 10. Because of regression toward the mean, students who score at very low levels on a given test may score much higher on that test if it is given a few days later even though they may have learned nothing new about the material.

Key Ideas in Review

1. Students infer much about the reality of a course from the kinds of tests they are required to take. For example, if a teacher states that he or she is interested in developing analytical thinking but gives tests asking students only to recall specific information, students may determine that the teacher has no real interest in developing their analytical thinking skills. To maintain their credibility, tests must be congruent with their stated intentions.

2. The processes of measurement, evaluation, and grading are interrelated. Measurement refers to the process of gathering data. Evaluation concerns the making of judgments based on these data. Grading focuses on the communication of these judgments to other interested parties.

3. In deciding upon the specifics of a measurement and evaluation plan, it is prudent to consider the nature of the instructional objective about which student attainment information is to be gathered. Further, attention needs to be given to such issues as the ease of item construction, the relative difficulty of scoring, and the potential for sampling a reasonable range of content.

4. Of the most frequently used kinds of recognition-type tests (true/false, matching, and multiple choice), multiple-choice tests can be used to test for the broadest range of cognitive-domain competencies. Multiple-choice tests can be used to test at the levels of knowledge, comprehension, application, analysis, and, sometimes, even synthesis and evaluation.

5. Essay items are capable of assessing complex levels of cognitive thinking. They allow for a great deal of response flexibility. But they do have some limitations. Although items are relatively easy to construct, scoring can be very time consuming. Further, consistency of evaluation of papers prepared by different students is difficult. Also, because of the time required for students to answer a given question, the essay format is not well suited when the intent is to sample a very broad range of content.

6. Sound grading schemes are fair. Students must believe that they have a chance to succeed, in terms of grades, if they are going to work hard in a course. Additionally, grading systems should allow for clear and consistent communication. Differences in competence among students receiving letter grades of ''A,'' ''B,'' ''C,'' ''D,'' and ''F'' should be understood easily and observed consistently.

7. Grading students according to their individual improvement is a scheme that has initial humanistic appeal but that suffers from logical flaws. Because of regression toward the mean, this system penalizes very bright students and provides a means for very poorly performing students to receive better grades than they may deserve. Further, letter grades awarded by the

system do not refer consistently to specified levels of competence. One person earning a grade of "A" might have much less adequate grasp of content than another person earning a grade of "A."

8. Norm-referenced grading schemes award letter grades to a student based upon how well his or her performance compares with that of others in his or her class. In using a norm-referenced system, it is essential for the teacher to be somewhat flexible in determining which percentages of youngsters will receive each letter grade. It is especially important that the adopted plan does not require the teacher to give a minimum percentage of failing grades. (Should this occur, many students will have less than positive feelings about the class.) Finally, it is desirable that some attention be given to assuring that there is some relationship between letter grades awarded and the actual level of understanding of youngsters receiving a common grade.

9. Criterion-referenced grading systems award grades based on how well a student's achievement compares with predetermined standards. Typically, a separate standard is identified for each grade awarded. Criterion-referenced grading makes it relatively easy for interested parties to determine exactly what a given letter grade means in terms of a student's level of competence. In some criterion-referenced systems, contracts are used to specify exactly what students must do to earn a given grade. In other arrangements, students' grades are determined by referring to the number of instructional objectives they have mastered. (In general, the more objectives achieved, the higher the grade.)

SUMMARY

Today, teachers are under increasing pressure to defend the precise meaning of the grades they award and to identify the means used in arriving at these grades. Consequently, educators have become increasingly concerned about (1) the degree to which an individual grading system communicates clearly to parents and other interested parties and (2) the relative equity or fairness of the system used to determine grades.

The kinds of data that are gathered and the techniques used to gather these data have come under considerable review in recent years. Several considerations come into play as teachers attempt to make reasoned choices from among the many evaluation techniques available.

First, the procedure selected ought to be capable of providing a direct focus on the student behavior the teacher wishes to measure. Second, the technique selected ought to have the capacity to test students at the cognitive level of the instructional objective that has guided instruction. In other words, if there has been an expectation that students should be able to analyze material, then the testing technique selected should be capable of testing the analysis-level thinking abilities of students.

Once data are in hand, teachers have available a number of alternative schemes for awarding grades. Three that have seen use in the schools have been procedures that have focused, respectively, on (1) awarding grades according to individual improvement, (2) awarding grades according to how a given student's performance compares with that of others in the class, and (3) awarding grades according to how a student's performance measures up to a predetermined standard of excellence. In general, the practice of awarding grades based on individual improvement has certain logical flaws that make it a dubious choice. Schemes associated with norm-referenced or criterion-referenced grading are much to be preferred.

References

Armstrong, David G.; Denton, Jon J.; and Savage, Tom V. *Instructional Skills Handbook.* Englewood Cliffs, N.J.: Educational Technology Publications, 1978.

Bloom, Benjamin S., ed. *Taxonomy of Educational Objectives: Handbook I: The Cognitive Domain.* New York: David McKay Co., Inc., 1956.

Bloom, Benjamin S.; Hastings, J. Thomas; and Madaus, George F. *Handbook on Formative and Summative Evaluation of Student Learning.* New York: McGraw-Hill Book Company, 1971.

Dearman, Nancy B., and Plisko, Valena White. *The Condition of Education.* Washington, D.C.: National Center for Education Statistics, 1979.

Dunn, Rita, and Dunn, Kenneth. *Practical Approaches to Individualizing Instruction: Contracts and Other Effective Teaching Strategies.* West Nyack, N.Y.: Parker Publishing Company, Inc., 1972.

Gronlund, Norman E. *Measurement and Evaluation in Teaching.* 3rd ed. New York: Macmillan Publishing Co., Inc., 1976.

Hunkins, Francis P. *Curriculum Development: Program Improvement.* Columbus, Ohio: Charles E. Merrill Publishing Co., 1980.

Popham, W. James, ed. *Criterion-Referenced Measurement: An Introduction.* Englewood Cliffs, N.J.: Educational Technology Publications, 1971.

Sax, Gilbert. *Principles of Educational Measurement and Evaluation.* Belmont, Calif.: Wadsworth Publishing Company, Inc., 1974.

III

STUDENTS IN THE SECONDARY SCHOOL

12

Profiles of Secondary School Students

FUNKY WINKERBEAN by Tom Batiuk © 1980. Field Enterprises, Inc. Courtesy of Field Newspaper Syndicate.

Objectives

This chapter provides information to help the reader to

1. Identify changes in the nature of the secondary school population being served today as compared with that 50, 60, or 70 years ago.
2. Note trends that are occurring that have implications for numbers of students expected to be in secondary schools in the years ahead.
3. Recognize some generalized patterns of physical development of secondary school youngsters.
4. Point out some factors associated with differences in attitudes and aspirations of individual secondary school students.
5. Suggest patterns of intellectual development expected in students of secondary school age.
6. Recognize the tremendous diversity existing within the total population of secondary school students.

Pretest

Directions: Using your own paper, answer each of the following true/false questions. For each correct statement, write the word "true." For each incorrect statement, write the word "false."

_____ 1. Prospects are good that there will be a steady increase in secondary school enrollments through the 1980s.

_____ 2. By the end of the century, students who are native speakers of Spanish are likely to comprise the largest minority within the secondary school population.

_____ 3. There is little evidence that the economic background of a student's family has anything to do with his or her feelings about the importance of academic courses offered by the school.

_____ 4. In general, high schools have tended to become larger than they were in the earlier years of this century.

_____ 5. Secondary schools in the United States tend to enroll a higher percentage of adolescent youngsters in the total population than do secondary schools in Europe.

_____ 6. There are more students of Indochinese descent in the schools today than there were ten years ago.

_____ 7. Girls in the 11- to 14-year-old age range tend to be shorter than boys in the same age range.

_____ 8. Secondary school teachers perceive discipline to be less of a problem than do elementary school teachers.

_____ 9. The vast majority of Spanish-speaking secondary students attend school in rural areas.

_____ 10. There is evidence that youngsters in secondary schools who come from higher socioeconomic levels are more popular in school than are youngsters coming from lower socioeconomic levels.

INTRODUCTION

Larry Larsen and the Chair

Larry Larsen, architecture student, believed he "had it made." Professor Sackett had given each person in the class a design task. "For once," Larsen thought, "I got lucky." When Sackett had reached his name, the good professor had looked up over his half-lens spectacles, and said, "For you, Larsen, something a little different. I want you to think about some school furniture. More specifically, I would like you to design a school chair for a 13-year-old."

Convinced that this was a task he could acquit with distinction, Larsen now found himself seated in a corner at the back of Mrs. Alderson's eighth-grade social studies classroom at Parker Junior High School. "A little on-site work to look at some 13-year-olds, then a quick trip to the drafting table, a few deft strokes of the pencil, and . . . presto . . . , the thing will be done," thought Larsen.

The second hand of the large clock in the front of the room reached twelve. A bell sounded. The halls exploded into cacophony as lockers slammed, animated conversations sprang up, and minor scuffles punctuated the between-classes life of the corridors. In groups of twos and threes, students began bouncing into the room.

From his vantage point in a rear corner, Larsen took up his pen, prepared to take notes, and began looking over the arrivals. In the first "wave" two enormous six-footers came careening in. Behind them were three chattering girls. One of them could have been a finalist in a campus fraternity's queen contest. One was a very obese girl who had to struggle into her seat. The third was a tiny birdlike creature who couldn't have weighed 80 pounds.

In a matter of moments, this initial stream of students became a flood as highly excited youngsters chatted and elbowed their way into the room. Eighty-five-pound lightweights who still looked up to five-footers tromped in along with several giants who could have played line positions on high school football teams. Once seated, some students' feet fell well short of the floor. Others found themselves with knees high in the air as impossibly low seats refused to accommodate comfortably their adult-sized legs.

Surveying this scene, Larsen sensed a sinking feeling in the pit of his stomach. "Sackett has done it to me," he thought. "A chair to fit a 13-year-old! Impossible! There are big ones, little ones, skinny ones, fat ones . . . and they're all 13! A chair to fit them all? Sackett's got to be kidding. What did I do to get this turkey of a problem? Well, maybe bean-bag chairs, or some kind of an inflatable job that can be blown up to fit around the person sitting in it, or . . . or? Maybe I'll tell Sackett that they should just sit on the floor. No, better not. Underdeveloped sense of humor there . . . a chronic professorial condition. Ah well, no revelry tonight. To the drawing board!"

If one word could be summoned up to describe the nature of the secondary school population, that word might well be "diversity." Youngsters in middle schools, junior high schools, and senior high schools represent a range of characteristics that is almost a mirror image of what we might find in the population as a whole. Indeed, there is some evidence that differences existing among individuals of secondary school age are even greater than those found among other age groups in the general population (National Panel on High School and Adolescent Education 1976). These differences do not just relate to the kinds of physical differences observed by our architecture student, Larry Larsen. They include differences in aspirations, intellectual capacities, interests, and values as well. Secondary school teachers today must be prepared to work with youngsters of many kinds. Beginning secondary teachers in particular need to understand that large numbers of the youngsters with whom they will be working will have a view of the world that may be very different from the teacher's.

Evidence mounts that teachers today must deal with a greater variety of students than ever before. Today, secondary schools in the United States enroll more than 90 percent of all students of secondary school age. This is truly a remarkable figure considering that the total population includes youngsters with severe handicaps, with unsupportive home backgrounds, with native tongues other than English, and with a host of other characteristics that have potential for interfering with their success in school. The magnitude of the American accomplishment can be put into better perspective through a comparison with secondary education programs elsewhere. In the most developed nations of Western Europe, formal schooling for adolescents is provided for a low of about 4 percent of the total adolescent population to a high of less than 20 percent of the total adolescent population (National Panel 1976, p. 1). This comparative information underscores the fact that American secondary school teachers deal with a much broader cross section of the adolescent population in their classrooms than do their counterparts in many other parts of the world.

Not surprisingly, this diversity brings with it certain problems. No matter how responsive teachers and schools attempt to be in establishing programs to meet needs of specialized groups of youngsters, many students still find little satisfaction in their school programs. Perhaps, given the range of students in secondary schools, it is folly to hope for programs that will make every youngster happy. Some critics suggest that we may already be spreading resources available for secondary education too thin and that we should cut back on the range of services provided to secondary school youngsters. Others argue that more needs to be done. We shall look at some of the arguments related to this general question later in the chapter.

One conclusion that almost no one disputes is that the dissatisfactions with the school program felt by some secondary students create difficulties for secondary school teachers. Although there may be similar dissatisfactions among elementary school youngsters, this population tends to be a much less diverse group than secondary school youngsters. Further, younger learners are less inclined to dispute teachers' authority openly. A recent survey found that 20.9 percent of secondary school teachers reported that student discipline was the problem that "hindered them most" (Williams 1979, p. 74). For elementary school teachers, the figure was 12.8 percent (p. 74).

We do not intend to give too negative an impression of secondary school students by citing these figures. We do feel an obligation, however, to point out that the population of secondary school youngsters in the school is diverse and that this diversity can pose challenges for secondary school teachers. Further, it is our hope that future secondary teachers will recognize the futility of trying to conjure up an image of a "typical" secondary school student. While statistical averages could be used to develop a profile of such a person, he or she would exist only in the mind of the person making the computation. The real world of today's middle schools, junior high schools, and senior high schools is peopled by youngsters who range so widely from any such average as to make it of almost no value to the classroom teacher. The teacher must be prepared to accept and work with individuals who vary in terms of almost any trait we might wish to imagine.

In the remainder of this chapter, we look at some representative patterns that occur in the secondary school population. Certainly other patterns could have been added as well, but we feel that these are reasonably representative of the categories of difference we find today in secondary schools. Among other things, we consider changing enrollment patterns in secondary schools, major subgroups within the secondary school population, patterns of intellectual development of secondary school youngsters, physical characteristics of secondary school students, and attitudinal differences among secondary school students. Figure 12-1 describes some age-related concerns in this regard and poses some important questions.

CHANGES IN NUMBERS OF SECONDARY SCHOOL STUDENTS

Widespread availability of birth control technology has been largely responsible for important changes in the age makeup of the American population. This technology came to be almost universally accessible in this country during the middle to late 1950s. Prior to this time, especially during the 15 years following the end of World War II, the fertility rate was very high. This rate peaked in 1957 when there were 3.8 births per female. Since 1957, the fertility rate has been in decline, reaching, for example, 1.8 per female in 1978 (U.S. Department of Education 1980, p. 2).

For educators, an important implication of this change has been the steady decrease in the proportion of the population under age 18. In 1965, 36 percent of the population was under 18. The anticipated percentage of people under 18 had fallen in 1980 to an estimated 28 percent (U.S. Department of Education 1980, p. 2). Clearly the American population has been aging. The impacts of this trend on school enrollments are complex.

Through about 1990, it appears that secondary school enrollments will be in a decline. But beginning in the mid-1980s, elementary school enrollments will begin to climb, as the extremely large number of people who were born in the post–World War II baby boom will have youngsters old enough to be in elementary school. Thus, even though fertility rates have remained low, the extremely large number of females of childbearing age has produced a very large number of children. Stated in another way, the large number of youngsters results not because individual mothers are having lots

Figure 12-1

DO HIGH SCHOOLS ARTIFICIALLY PROLONG "YOUTH"?

Only in the last 25 years has a majority of teenagers, through high school attendance, been increasingly separated from significant contact with older adults, other than parents and teachers. The successful achievement of a high school experience for nearly everyone has been accompanied by a decoupling of the generations—for the young, delayed entry into the real adult world, prolongation of the institutional controls of childhood, delay in the early transmission of adult culture patterns.*

YOUR OPINION, PLEASE

Read the paragraph above. Then, respond to these questions.

1. Do you feel that high schools cut off young people unnecessarily from adults? Why do you take this position?
2. Some have argued that high schools are needed to keep young people out of the labor force until at least age 18. Without the high school, some allege, young workers would flood the market and mass unemployment problems would ensue. How do you react to this reasoning?
3. Suppose that you accept the premise that there needs to be more systematic contact between adolescents and adults. How would you go about promoting an increase in such contacts? Would the high school have to go? Or could it be modified?
4. Without the institution of the high school, would we have such a word as "teenager"? Does the word, and all it stands for, result simply because we have created youth ghettos called high schools? Support your case with evidence.

*National Panel on High School and Adolescent Education, *The Education of Adolescents,* Final Report and Recommendations (Washington, D.C.: U.S. Department of Health, Education, and Welfare, 1976), p. 4.

---

of children but, rather, because there are so very many mothers who are having one or two children. The swell in the numbers of elementary school-aged children that will be noticed in the mid-1980s will result in an eventual growth in secondary school enrollments. But this will not be felt until the 1990s. For a graphic representation of these changes, see Figure 12-2.

At first glance, the revelation that numbers of secondary students are declining would seem to suggest that employment possibilities for new middle school, junior high school, and senior high school teachers wold not be good throughout the 1980s. This conclusion is not supported by a more careful examination of relevant information. We need to remember that teacher employment demand is a function of two variables. One is the number of students. (This figure bears a direct relationship to the number of classrooms needing teachers.) The second is the number of teachers seeking employment. These two variables acting together determine the relative scarcity of teachers. Let us see what has been happening to teacher supply.

The supply of new teacher graduates has declined each year since 1972. This decline has been dramatic. Further, this trend is expected to continue. For example, by 1987, the number of new teachers completing college or university training programs is expected to be *less than one half* of the number of teachers who completed their programs in 1972 (U.S. Department of Education 1980, p. 72). What all this tells us is that the supply of new teachers is decreasing at a faster rate than the numbers of students to be taught are decreasing. This suggests, then, that during much of the 1980s teachers are going to be in greater demand than they have been for some years. Of course there are likely to be great variations in the intensity of this demand from one region of the country to another. Clearly high-growth areas such as the states of the

Figure 12-2

POPULATION OF SELECTED AGE GROUPS IN THE UNITED STATES

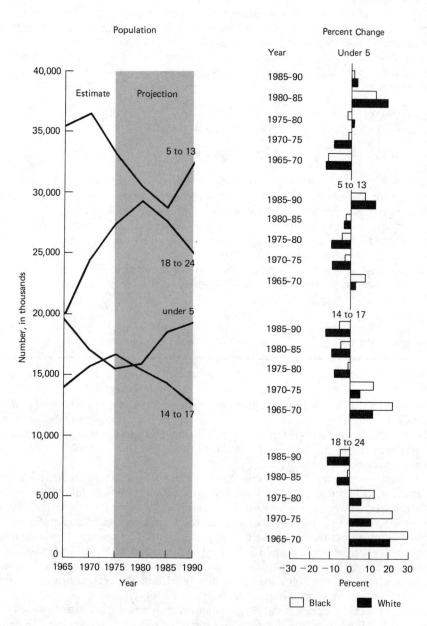

Source: U.S. Department of Education, *Condition of Education, 1980* (Washington, D.C.:
National Center for Education Statistics, 1980), p. 11.

Sunbelt will likely generate a higher need for teachers' services than will states suffering a net outflow of population. Even with these variations, it is safe to assert that the
decade of the 1980s will see an improved employment environment for teachers relative
to that of the 1970s. See Figure 12-3 for a discussion of and questions about related
concerns.

Figure 12-3

ADULT ATTITUDES TOWARD YOUNG PEOPLE

Given the negative or indifferent climate of opinion toward children and youth today, any thought that they are suddenly going to be accorded the priority attention they deserve seems naively optimistic. This is especially true of children from disadvantaged backgrounds. As the conservative mood of the nation deepens, appeals for attention to the needs of young people will no doubt increasingly go unheard, and negative perceptions of them will probably thrive—if for no other reason than that these perceptions serve as a convenient rationalization for failure of conscience and compassion. Young people will probably continue to be seen as economic burdens rather than as assets, their problems will go unrecognized or be subordinated to the claims of older groups, they will be given little chance to play a constructive role in the nation, and they will be regarded essentially as a threat to the comfort and security of adults.*

YOUR OPINION, PLEASE

Read the paragraph above. Then, respond to these questions.

1. To what extent do you think there is a ''negative or indifferent climate of opinion toward young people today''? What is the basis for your opinion?
2. As the average age of the American population continues to increase, is it likely that concerns for affairs of youth will diminish? Why, or why not?
3. How do you react to the argument that, since young people in the years ahead will be relatively small in numbers, they will be pampered and cherished as scarce assets? What is the basis for your opinion?
4. Do you see any evidence that young people increasingly are being seen as threats by older citizens? If so, how do you account for this perception?
5. Looking ahead 30 years from now, would you expect relationships between young people and older citizens to be more cordial or more hostile than they are today? Why do you think so?

*Alan Pifer, ''Perceptions of Childhood and Youth,'' 1978 Annual Report, Carnegie Corporation of New York, 437 Madison Avenue, New York 10022, p. 10.

MAJOR MINORITIES WITHIN THE SECONDARY SCHOOL POPULATION

Within the total secondary school population, clusters of individuals belonging to various minorities can be identified. Indeed, carried to its logical extreme, it would be possible to divide, subdivide, and divide again the secondary school population to so fine a point that each youngster himself or herself became identified as a minority of one. Obviously we cannot describe general characteristics of every youngster in the schools. So, realizing that some important groups must be slighted because of space limitations here, we will try to highlight certain characteristics of some of the larger minority populations likely to be encountered by secondary school teachers.

Ethnic and Language Minorities

The two largest minority groups in schools are blacks and Hispanics. Blacks today constitute about 11 percent of the total population. The fertility rate for black Americans is somewhat higher than is that for the white American population. One consequence of this difference is that the black population, on average, is somewhat younger than the white population. Therefore, blacks constitute somewhat more than 11 percent of the school population.

The black population is overwhelmingly urban. Over three quarters of the black population live in major metropolitan areas (Pifer 1978). Blacks in rural areas tend to be concentrated in states of the Old South. Although for many years educated in schools that were legally segregated in many southern states and in schools that were de facto segregated in many areas in the north because of residential settlement patterns, today only a minority of blacks attend schools in buildings where 90 to 100 percent of the students are of a minority race (Williams 1979). Progress toward achieving the goal of integrating schools has varied considerably from region to region.

Given the early federal attention to the South, perhaps it is not surprising that most progress toward achieving integrated public school systems has been made in this part of the country. Note the information in the following table.

	Percentages of Students Attending Schools with		
	0 to 49 % (minority enrollments)	50 to 89 % (minority enrollments)	90 to 100 % (minority enrollments)
U.S. total	33.0	26.3	40.5
Northeast	19.0	23.2	57.8
Border and D.C.	28.1	13.5	58.4
South	44.5	32.2	23.4
Midwest	19.4	18.4	62.2
West	26.6	28.3	45.1

Source: Jeffrey W Williams, compiler, *Students and Schools* (Washington, D.C.: National Center for Education Statistics, 1979).

Like blacks, Hispanics also are a minority that is overwhelmingly urban. Hispanics are thought to comprise about 5 percent of the total population (Pifer 1978). This figure is believed to be suspect, however, as it is based on the official Hispanic population; given the large numbers of undocumented Hispanics thought to be in the country, Hispanics may well comprise considerably more than 5 percent of our population. Pifer suggests that there may be as many as 17 million Hispanics. If this is so, then Hispanic-Americans constitute 8 percent of the population. Pifer's estimates were made before the 1980 exodus from Cuba of more than 100,000 people. When these Hispanics are added to the estimates cited here, it is possible that this minority will comprise an even more significant proportion of the population.

Fertility rates among Hispanic-Americans are among the highest for any group in the country. Pifer estimates that over half of the Hispanics in the United States are under 18 years of age. Given the young age of this population and the high birth rates characterizing this group, it seems quite possible that by the end of the century Hispanics may be the largest minority group in the country (Pifer 1978).

There is evidence that both black and Hispanic students experience more academic difficulty in schools than do white students. A variety of explanations for this situation have been forwarded. Certainly economic conditions of black and Hispanic families and language problems seem to be among factors contributing to the failure of black and Hispanic students, on average, to perform as well on measures of academic achievement. Too, there may be unintended cultural biases embedded in tests being used to measure levels of achievement. For whatever reasons, the evidence seems clear that the measured achievement levels of blacks and Hispanics tends to worsen relative to whites as they progress through the school program.

The National Assessment of Educational Progress has tested thousands of youngsters in the schools at ages 9, 13, and 17. Results of these tests demonstrate that black and Hispanic youngsters perform farther below national averages (in most academic areas) at 13 than at 9 and at 17 than at 13. Patterns of these differences can be seen in the table presented in Figure 12-4.

Figure 12-4

DIFFERENCES FROM NATIONAL MEAN SCORES IN LEARNING AREAS BY AGE AND RACIAL/ETHNIC GROUP*

Learning Areas	Age 9		Age 13		Age 17 (In School)	
	Percentage Point Difference from Mean Achievement Score	Standard Error of the Difference	Percentage Point Difference from Mean Achievement Score	Standard Error of the Difference	Percentage Point Difference from Mean Achievement Score	Standard Error of the Difference
Social Studies (1971–72)						
White	2.73	0.30	2.07	0.20	2.39	0.21
Black	−12.16	0.62	−12.42	0.79	−13.56	0.56
Hispanic	−10.59	1.03	−10.05	0.66	−13.12	1.13
Science (1972–73)						
White	3.12	0.25	3.49	0.32	2.13	0.20
Black	−13.36	0.58	−16.63	0.60	−10.32	0.61
Hispanic	−9.53	0.86	−11.55	0.85	−11.08	1.08
Mathematics (1972–73)						
White	2.76	0.24	3.74	0.35	3.63	0.32
Black	−12.38	0.54	−18.23	0.68	−19.83	0.60
Hispanic	−7.77	0.83	−11.71	1.00	−14.36	1.02
Career and Occupational Development (1973–74)						
White	3.23	0.26	3.50	0.34	2.19	0.19
Black	−14.21	1.18	−18.77	0.72	−15.96	0.89
Hispanic	−14.08	1.77	−12.44	1.59	−7.65	2.08
Reading (1974–75)						
White	2.54	0.21	2.73	0.22	2.78	0.22
Black	−10.94	0.58	−13.95	0.61	−16.44	0.74
Hispanic	−10.77	1.11	−11.25	1.38	−11.42	1.54

*All differences from the national mean scores are significant at the 0.05 level.

Source: U.S. Department of Health, Education, and Welfare, National Center for Education Statistics, *Hispanic Student Achievement in Five Learning Areas: 1971–75* 1977. Reprinted from U.S. Department of Education, *Condition of Education, 1980* (Washington, D.C.: National Center for Education Statistics, 1980), p. 26.

The data displayed in Figure 12-4 suggest that schools in the years ahead will be intensifying efforts to meet needs of black and Hispanic students. Although predictions of future program emphases are always open to debate, we feel that current trends will likely continue. For example, a good deal of work is being done at present to develop evaluation procedures that are free from "culture bias." That is, educators want to be sure that a test score a student receives on a test is truly a measure of his or her true understanding and not a score that is either too high or too low because of factors associated with the particular cultural group of which he or she is a part. A good deal of controversy surrounds the issue of culture-free assessment. It seems to be an issue that will continue to draw attention and to prompt debates in the years ahead.

Another trend we note in the effort to enhance the school performance of blacks and Hispanics has to do with the issue of language. In some parts of the country, efforts are being mounted to provide some school programs taught in black English. The idea here is to establish initial communication with black youngsters in a language they know and understand and to build a systematic language bridge to standard American English. This programmatic thrust has been enormously controversial both within and without the black community. Some argue that black English programs will be the salvation of black students in the schools. Others suggest that such instruction delays acquisition by black students of patterns of standard English that they need to move comfortably in the larger society beyond the black community. The debate over this issue seems certain to be with us for some time to come.

The language issue is also very important with respect to the Hispanic population in the schools. The federal government has taken a great interest in problems of youngsters speaking native languages other than English. This interest has resulted in the passage of legislation calling for bilingual education in the schools. What this means, basically, is that a youngster is entitled to be educated in his home language in school until such time as his or her proficiency in English is equal to his or her proficiency in the home language. This legislation has prompted considerable debate. Much of it has paralleled to large degree the arguments made in support of or in opposition to black English programs. Some feel that bilingual programs facilitate an adjustment of non-native speakers of English to the school program. Others contend that they delay youngsters' acquisition of English usage skills. Although bilingual education is law, the arguments continue.

Black and Hispanic students have been in American schools in large numbers for years. Enrollment of large numbers of native speakers of Vietnamese in the schools has been a very recent phenomenon. With the collapse of the government of South Vietnam and the subsequent integration of that region into a Vietnam state under the authority of the Hanoi government, thousands of Vietnamese from the south fled their homeland. Large numbers have come to the United States since 1978. A government estimate indicated about 600,000 Vietnamese refugees to be in the country in 1981 (U.S. Department of Education 1980, p. 3).

In 1980, more than 67,000 children of Vietnamese parents were in the schools. These young people tended to be concentrated in a relatively small number of school districts. The National Center for Education Statistics reports that 275 school districts in the country enrolled more than three quarters of all Vietnamese students. Figure 12-5 provides a graphic representation of the distribution of Vietnamese students among the states.

Teachers and administrators in school districts where substantial numbers of Vietnamese-speaking youngsters are enrolled have faced some real challenges. Large numbers of these students, for example, have spoken no English when they have arrived to enroll in school. It has been extremely difficult for school districts to find individuals to teach who are qualified for professional teacher certification and who are fluent in both Vietnamese and English. Meeting the needs of the younger generation of Vietnamese refugees who are enrolled in the schools promises to be a continuing concern of educators in the years ahead.

Figure 12-5

CHILDREN OF VIETNAMESE REFUGEE PARENTS IN ELEMENTARY AND SECONDARY
SCHOOLS

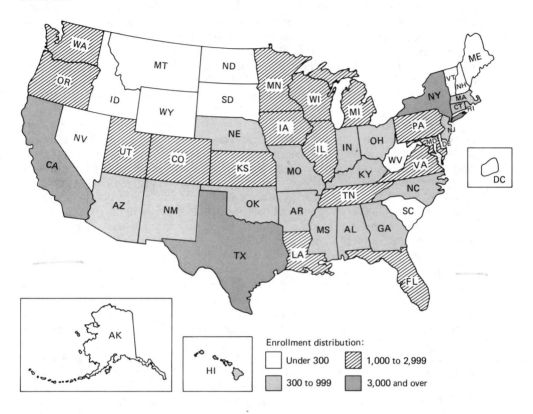

Enrollment distribution:

- Under 300
- 300 to 999
- 1,000 to 2,999
- 3,000 and over

Source: U.S. Department of Education, *Condition of Education, 1980* (Washington, D.C.: National Center for Education Statistics, 1980), p. 15.

Students from Impoverished Families

Educators have long been concerned about students who come to schools from impoverished family backgrounds. Dietary deficiencies, potential health standards deficiencies, and other problems frequently associated with poverty can have a dramatic impact on youngsters' performance in school. Further, there is some evidence that students growing up in lower economic strata tend to have a different emotional reaction to the school program than do youngsters coming from more financially secure family backgrounds.

The incidence of poverty varies somewhat from one part of the country to another. One survey noted that the percentage of families falling below the federal poverty level was lowest in the North Central region, next lowest in the Northeastern region, somewhat higher in the West, and highest in the South. Present trends seem to suggest that the poverty rate in the South is dropping at a relatively rapid pace and that it is increasing in the Northeast at a relatively rapid pace (Williams 1978, p. 12).

In general, poverty rates tend to be higher in central cities than in the suburban fringes surrounding these cities. This configuration has important meaning for the level of school services likely to be available for students from impoverished home backgrounds. To sketch the case in very general terms, it is fair to say that central cities have been losing populations and tax bases to suburban areas. What this has meant is that central-city school districts have not been able to raise as much money through imposition of taxes on city property as was true in years gone by. This situation has made it very difficult for inner-city schools to provide well-funded educational programs for youngsters coming from economically deprived home backgrounds.

The general erosion of the inner-city tax base has been compounded by pressures to spend tax monies that are available on social programs other than education. For example, from 1961 to 1976, educational expenditures as a proportion of the total budget in New York City declined by 7 percent. During the same period, the proportion of the total New York City budget spent on welfare programs climbed by 10 percent (Williams 1978, p. 9).

A number of legal challenges have been mounted in recent years that have sought to provide adequate funding for schools regardless of where they are located. The logic has been that a youngster should not be penalized in terms of the kinds of school experiences that he or she receives simply because he or she lives in an inner city or in some other place with a meager tax base. The ultimate outcome of these challenges is not yet certain. But there does appear to be some movement in the direction of decreasing differences in funding levels among schools and school districts in different parts of a given state. For the present, however, great differences continue to characterize schools and school districts located in different places.

The high schools in the United States sometimes are referred to as "comprehensive" high schools. This means that they are designed to serve the entire population of students regardless of their family backgrounds, their talents, and their individual aspirations. Deeply embedded in the American view of secondary education is the idea that there is some benefit for all students in coming together in a school setting where they rub elbows with "everybody." The comprehensive high school has been seen as some kind of a social melting pot where all kinds of youngsters come together and grow in confidence and maturity as they interact with and learn the perspectives of others. Today, some observers are beginning to question whether the comprehensive high school truly does enhance mutual understanding among the various groups in the school. In particular, there is concern about whether the comprehensive high school may be reinforcing stereotypes about students from impoverished home backgrounds and from minority ethnic and racial groups.

Critics of the present organization of the comprehensive high school point out that youngsters from economically deprived home backgrounds have lower aspirations regarding future careers than do youngsters from more well-to-do families (National Panel 1976). In part, this situation may result from a feeling that "it is hopeless" to compete against youngsters from more affluent family backgrounds. The National Panel on High School and Adolescent Education found that students from economic impoverished backgrounds tended to be much less actively involved in the whole school program. Indeed, their findings suggest that many arrangements in the typical comprehensive high school may act to diminish the self-esteem of these youngsters (p. 37):

> *Children of higher socioeconomic levels are more popular as friends and enjoy greater status. Middle-class children are more likely to get higher grades, hold student office, and take active part in extra-curricular activities.*

PATTERNS OF PHYSICAL DEVELOPMENT IN SECONDARY SCHOOL STUDENTS

Physical differences among youngsters of the same age are enormous in the total population of young people enrolled in secondary schools. Speaking to these diferences, Dorothy Eichorn (1972) has written: "Between the ages of 11 and 17, the range of individual differences in physical structure and physiological functioning at any given chronological age is greater than at any other time in the human life span" (p. 34). For secondary school teachers, this means that typically there are profound physical differences among youngsters in any given classroom. This reality has caused despair for years among producers of schoolroom furniture, particularly those interested in serving the junior high school market.

To get some perspective on the range of physical differences among youngsters of a given age, let us consider the case of 15-year-old boys. There is evidence that early- and late-maturing boys of this age may vary as much as eight inches in height (sometimes even more). There may be weight differences in excess of 30 pounds. Differences in physical maturation rates result in a tremendous disparity in the coordination, physical strength, and general appearance of youngsters of this age.

Differences in physical development, to some extent, at least tend to be accompanied by differences in interests. A group of 14-year-olds in a ninth-grade class may have patterns of interest ranging from concerns of typical middle-grades elementary school youngsters to enthusiasms of adults. Some interest differences have rather obvious connections to physical differences. For example, large early-maturing boys who do well in sports are likely to be much more interested in athletics than are later-maturing youngsters who are unable to compete successfully in the athletic arena with their earlier-maturing counterparts.

Earlier-maturing girls, who at age 13 or 14 may have the appearance of 17-, 18-, or 19-year-olds, tend to be treated differently by adults from their later-maturing age mates. They tend to have broader interests than later-maturing girls, and these interests tend to more closely parallel interests of girls who are two, three, four or even five years older than themselves (National Panel 1976).

Delayed physical maturation can have important psychological impacts on students in secondary schools. The National Panel on High School and Adolescents, for example, reported that "some late maturing boys may not be able to compete successfully until the time has passed when skills linked to size, endurance, and strength have considerable social pay-off" (1976, p. 35). This may mean that expectations of adolescents regarding who among them are "leaders" are set rather early during the secondary school years and that the "leaders" tend to be largely youngsters whose earlier physiological development allows them to succeed at tasks that cannot yet be accomplished by many of their age mates. Given this possibility, teachers in secondary schools need to be particularly sensitive in dealing with late-maturing youngsters. Their failure to achieve social status as a result of maturational factors may be presumed falsely by these students to have resulted because there is something fundamentally "wrong" with them.

Differences in rates of physiological development vary by sex. Girls, in general, tend to develop at an earlier age than do boys. For example, on average, girls in the 11- to 14-year-old age ranges tend to be taller than boys. Between the ages of about 9 or 10 through about age 14 and $14\frac{1}{2}$, the average girl tends to be heavier than the average boy. What in casual conversation is sometimes referred to as the adolescent "growth spurt" typically begins for girls somewhere in the $9\frac{1}{2}$ to $14\frac{1}{2}$ age range. For boys, this occurs somewhat later, typically falling somewhere in the $10\frac{1}{2}$ to 16 age span (National Panel 1976).

Within single classes, teachers may find physiological differences among youngsters to be even greater than what might be expected by students of a given age. For example, although the typical ninth-grader is about 14 years old, most ninth grades will include youngsters of a much broader age range. For example, there may be youngsters as young as 12 in the classroom, and it is not unusual to find ninth-grade classes with several 16- or 17-year-olds enrolled.

Because of recent trends to expand the number of course offerings in secondary schools, teachers today probably find a greater age range in their classes than historically has been true. The expansion of curricular offerings has tended to break down traditional practices of reserving specific courses as "freshman-," "sophomore-," "junior-," or "senior-level" offerings. Although many courses tied to grade level remain in the secondary school program, today many courses may be taken by students of different grade levels. This has caused many secondary school classrooms to be filled with students who are widely scattered in terms of their progress through the entire secondary school program (see Figure 12-6). Teachers in these courses find an extraordinary range of physiological development among the youngsters in their classrooms.

SCHOOL SIZE AND STUDENT ATTITUDES

Centralization has been an enduring theme in American public education during the twentieth century. With regard to school district organization, this trend has been observed in the tremendous decline in the number of school districts. Today, for example, there are only about one fourth as many school districts in the country as existed here during the 1920s. Consolidation of school districts has resulted in the creation of districts that today enroll many more students, on average, than the districts of 60 or 70 years ago.

The trend toward bigness at the school district level has been paralleled by consolidation of scattered small schools in districts into lesser numbers of large schools. Today, over one half of the adolescents enrolled in public schools attend classes in buildings that enroll in excess of 1,000 students (National Panel 1976). The National Panel on High School and Adolescent Education pointed out that, while consolidation doubtless has resulted in some advantages for certain kinds of students, the trend also has tended to promote a cluster of difficulties that generally are referred to as "big school problems" (1976, p. 23).

Some critics have charged that increasing school size has put too much pressure on administrative officials to develop management systems that will allow them to handle the enormous load of paperwork. This pressure, some allege, has resulted in the development of cold, uncaring, and inflexible attitudes toward students. It is not simply

---

Figure 12-6

WORKING WITH LATE-MATURING STUDENTS

Suppose that you were teaching a class of eighth-graders. In your class you had two boys who still had yet to reach a height of five feet. Each weighed less than 90 pounds. These two youngsters were the butt of a continuous series of pranks dreamed up by a group of very physically mature students. Among other things, these youngsters have been put in student wall lockers. They have been tossed as "human footballs" outside the school building at noon and after school. And they have generally been told by other students that they are "losers" who should be back in the fifth grade.

YOUR OPINION, PLEASE

Think about your reactions to this situation. Then, respond to these questions.

1. Do you recall any similar situations from your own school years? What impact did the behavior of others have on the physically immature youngsters?
2. What specifically would you do to help these late-developing students to develop a sense of personal confidence?
3. Is there anything you would do to prevent the early-maturing youngsters from taking advantage of their much smaller age mates? If so, what?
4. Have you personally ever been either on the giving end or the receiving end of a situation where there was a confrontation between early maturing and late maturing youngsters? What happened? How did you feel about this situation?

---

a matter of "bad-hearted" administrators not wanting to do "the right thing." Rather, the critics allege, the huge increase in the average size of secondary school buildings has forced basically good people to devote an inordinate amount of time to bureaucratic paper shuffling. This, some say, has resulted in the establishment of a false sense of priorities for those who manage secondary schools. Speaking to this issue, the National Panel on High School and Adolescent Education made the following comments (p. 4):

> *Large high schools, organized for reasons of economy and tradition around the classroom unit, have tended to be inflexible in their capacity to adopt newer instructional forms and procedures. The recent history of efforts to deploy teachers in different instructional modes (e.g., team teaching, use of paraprofessionals, modules, and minischools) demonstrates the institutional rigidity inherent to bigness: the priorities of management must override the interest of clients.*

Certainly there is potential for some students to feel lost in large secondary school buildings. This possibility places a special burden on secondary school teachers to provide a welcome and caring atmosphere in their classes. Moreover, it suggests the necessity of engaging students in conversations and otherwise seeking contacts with them outside the formal classroom setting. Clearly this kind of contact is more difficult to achieve in the large secondary schools where the majority of today's teachers are employed. No longer do teachers and students necessarily live in the same neighborhoods. No longer are teachers and parents likely to be acquaintances or in any way associated personally outside the school setting. It takes a real effort on the part of secondary school teachers today to develop close relationships with students. But, when such relationships can be established, they can do a great deal to build youngsters' sense of belonging. Youngsters who enjoy this kind of psychological security in their schools tend to do better scholastically and are less likely to develop unproductive behavior patterns in class. Given their concern for these matters, teachers in large secondary schools have a self-interest in taking the time to get to know well the youngsters in their classes.

PATTERNS OF INTELLECTUAL DEVELOPMENT IN SCHOOL LEARNERS

There is evidence that youngster's intellectual development does not follow a random pattern. Rather, the kinds of thinking in which youngsters can engage seems to follow a predictable, age-related sequence. This implies that youngsters of certain ages have thought processes that are describably different from those of youngsters who are either older or younger. For the teacher, this sequence suggests, for example, that a student's failure to learn may not necessarily result from his or her "failure to apply himself or herself" but, rather, from a confrontation with an intellectual task that demands thinking more sophisticated than he or she is capable of performing given his or her current level of intellectual development. Clearly instruction must be designed with some attention to the intellectual development of the students to be served. Speaking to this issue, Sprinthall and Sprinthall (1977) observe: "Everything in the right time and the right season might be the motto for child adolescent growth and development" (p. 117).

Perhaps the best known figure in the area of sequential development of intellectual abilities has been the late Swiss psychologist Jean Piaget. Piaget suggested that young people pass through a series of four stages as they mature toward adult thinking patterns. Let us examine briefly each of these stages.

Sensorimotor Stage: Ages 0 to 2

Intellectual activity during this first intellectual stage involves almost exclusively phenomena that can be perceived directly through the senses. As the young child matures and begins acquisition of language skills, there is some preliminary application of language labels to concrete objects. The child begins to understand the connection between the name of an object and the object that is referenced by the name.

Preoperational Thought Stage: Ages 2 to 7

Language development occurs at a dramatic rate during this stage. Increasingly verbal symbols are used to reference concrete objects. Decisions tend to be made on the basis of intuition, not rational analysis. Youngsters at this age frequently amuse adults by examining unfamiliar situations and arriving at some bizarre conclusions. In part this behavior results from their tendency to focus excessively only on selected parts of a total situation and to generalize excessively from very limited information. For example, a youngster at this age may conclude that airplanes are small objects about 12 inches in length because that is how they appear to him or her when he or she looks up and sees them flying in the sky.

Concrete Operations Stage: Ages 7 to 11

Rational logic begins to make its appearance during these years. At this stage youngsters increasingly are able to use systematic reasoning to arrive at solutions to certain kinds of problems. The kinds of problems for which they develop this facility are what we call *concrete* problems. That is, they are [problems involving phenomena that can be perceived directly through the physical senses.] They are much less adept, at this stage, in using logical reasoning to analyze abstract problems.

Youngsters at this stage have great difficulty in "going beyond the givens" to make sense of a school task that tends to demand more than a simple explanation of immediately available evidence. For example, these youngsters frequently become very frustrated when asked to search for "hidden meanings" in literary selections. They tend to be extremely literal minded. In general, school instructional programs that demand a great deal of sensory contact with tangible objects tend to be successful with youngsters at this age. They like problems that have answers. They are not at all happy when confronted with ambiguity.

Formal Operations Stage: Ages 11 to 16

As they move into the formal operations stage, the stage characterizing adult thought, they are able to apply rational logic to all categories of problems, abstract as well as concrete. They are able to deal with content asking them to go beyond the givens. They tend to be much less willing to take anything except formal logical explanations as evidence that something is either "true" or "false." Sometimes, particularly during the early phases of experience at this stage, youngsters become so enamoured of the power of logic that they become very upset by what they perceive to be contradictions between "the nature of the world" and what logic suggests to them the world really "ought to be" like. Many become very idealistic at this time of life. The differences between their idealistic view of what a logical world would be like and what the real world seems to be frequently make these young people very suspicious of the motives of adults whom they see to be defending an "unjust" or "unfair" society on illogical grounds.

To recapitulate, Piaget's stages suggest to us that human beings' intellectual development follows a predictable sequence. Each ascending stage is in all cases preceded by the stages that come before. The order of stages a person goes through en route to the formal operations stage are constant from individual to individual. The age ranges given are general guidelines. Some individuals enter and exit stages at ages somewhat younger than the suggested age points mentioned. Others enter and exit at somewhat older ages. The specific ages a given individual may enter or leave a stage will vary. But the passage of each individual through all four stages in the order noted is thought to be unvarying.

Implications of Piaget's Stages for Teachers

Some evidence suggests that teachers at the junior high school level are less happy than those at any other level of education. (This same pattern may be true of middle school teachers, as well. To date, insufficient descriptive data have been gathered about this group focusing on their general levels of satisfaction.) Social status of teaching at this level, sparse funding levels for buildings and materials, and many other factors doubtless contribute to junior high school teachers' dissatisfactions. Certainly among the issues to be considered is the issue of intellectual stages of junior high school students.

Particularly in the early junior high school years (or middle or late-middle school years), many learners may well still be functioning at the concrete operations stage (remember this stage runs roughly from age 7 through age 11). Highly dependent on concrete learning experiences, these students may well tax the teacher's ingenuity to provide for large numbers of "hands-on" experiences. In the very same classrooms, there may be youngsters who have passed into the early stages of the formal operations stage. Recall that many of these youngsters tend to become extremely idealistic and potentially suspicious of adults who they may see as defending a real world that is not logical. Given the potential for this kind of a classroom mix of youngsters at the concrete operations and formal operations stages, some junior high school teachers sense themselves to be pressed on the one hand by the needs of some youngsters for "touch, feel, and grasp" kinds of learning experiences and on the other hand by youngsters who are suspicious, if not hostile, toward the teacher's judgments.

Those who seek to work with younger secondary school students need to be aware of the kinds of student needs and attitudes that are to be expected given the age levels of these youngsters. Old hands have had time to observe the miraculous transformation that time works on the intellectual capacities and attitudes of junior high school students. Most can speak of several students who appeared beyond salvation as eighth-graders but who today are pillars of their local communities. New teachers can benefit greatly from conversations with some of these old hands. Further, by taking time to become familiar with the work of Piaget and others who have focused on patterns of intellectual development in learners, they can develop the kind of knowledge base that is essential for understanding and appreciation of early secondary school youngsters. Certainly time spent in acquiring such an understanding has the potential for helping teachers develop more realistic expectations of student behavior patterns during this interesting time of life.

FUNKY WINKERBEAN by Tom Batiuk © 1981. Field Enterprises, Inc. Courtesy of Field Newspaper Syndicate.

Posttest

Directions: Using your own paper, answer each of the following true/false questions. For each correct statement, write the word ``true.'' For each incorrect statement, write the word ``true.''

_____   1. Prospects are good that there will be a steady increase in secondary school enrollments through the 1980s.

_____   2. By the end of the century, students who are native speakers of Spanish are likely to comprise the largest minority within the secondary school population.

_____   3. There is little evidence that the economic background of a student's family has anything to do with his or her feelings about the importance of academic courses offered by the school.

_____   4. In general, high schools have tended to become larger 'than they were in earlier years of this century.

_____   5. Secondary schools in the United States tend to·enroll a higher percentage of adolescent youngsters in the total population than do secondary schools in Europe.

_____   6. There are more students of Indochinese descent in the schools today than there were ten years ago.

_____   7. Girls in the 11- to 14-year-old age range tend to be shorter than boys in the same age range.

_____   8. Secondary school teachers perceive discipline to be less of a problem than do elementary school teachers.

_____   9. The vast majority of Spanish-speaking secondary students attend schools in rural areas.

_____   10. There is evidence that youngsters in secondary schools who come from higher socioeconomic levels are more popular in school than are youngsters coming from lower socioeconomic levels.

Key Ideas in Review

1. The population of American secondary schools is incredibly diverse. Nearly the entire population of secondary-school-aged children is actually enrolled in secondary schools in this country. This contrasts sharply to conditions in Europe where a much smaller percentage of such youngsters is enrolled. This diversity presents secondary school teachers with a demanding and challenging professional work environment.

2. Numbers of students in American secondary schools are declining. This decline reflects smaller rates of population increase following the general availability of birth control technology beginning in the late 1950s. This decline does not mean, necessarily, that demand for secondary school teachers is slacking. In fact, the opposite is likely to be true through the 1980s. The potential increase in demand for secondary teachers' services can be attributed to the very large decreases in the numbers of students in colleges and universities who are preparing to enter public education.

3. Blacks are the largest minority group in secondary schools today. However, given present population trends, Hispanics may well be the largest minority by the end of the century. Both blacks and Hispanics have not fared as well in school as majority group youngsters (at least as measured by scores on standardized achievement tests). Out of this recognition, many special school programs have been targeted toward black and Hispanic youngsters. This trend seems likely to continue in the future.

4. Vietnamese students represent a relatively new element within the population of secondary school students. Today, there are more than half a million Vietnamese refugees in the United States. Nearly 70,000 children who are native speakers of Vietnamese are in the schools. They tend to be concentrated in a relatively small number of school districts.

5. Secondary teachers everywhere have to deal with some students coming from economically impoverished home backgrounds. In general, poverty rates tend to be higher in central urban areas than elsewhere. In recent years, various court cases and other legal challenges have been directed toward dispersing educational funds in a way that students living in impoverished school districts have educational programs every bit as adequate as those available to youngsters in more affluent areas. Today, great differences continue to characterize school districts in poor and affluent areas. But there seems to be a trend toward equalizing educational funding that, in the long run, seems likely to reduce the dimensions of these differences.

6. Differences in physical development among individual youngsters are dramatic. This is particularly true at the secondary school level. There are thought to be more differences among youngsters of the same age at this time of life than at any other period. A classroom of 14-year-olds is likely to have some youngsters who appear to be almost adultlike and others who look like they would be perfectly at home in a fifth-grade classroom. In general, physical maturation among girls comes earlier than for boys. Many 13-year-old girls are taller and heavier than 13-year-old boys.

7. Intellectual development of young people has been found by Jean Piaget to follow certain predictable patterns. These stages of intellectual development are passed through by all individuals en route to maturity. Thinking processes at each stage differ from thinking processes at all other stages. This is an important consideration for teachers. For example, if a youngster is still operating at the concrete operations stage, he or she is incapable of using logical thinking processes to deal with abstract concepts. It is not that the youngster is unwilling to engage in this kind of thinking; it is, rather, that he or she is incapable of doing so.

SUMMARY

An enormous diversity characterizes youngsters in secondary school classrooms. This is particularly true of secondary schools in the United States. In this country, the vast majority of youngsters of secondary school age are actually enrolled in secondary schools. This contrasts sharply to the situation in Europe where a much smaller fraction of this population is enrolled in secondary schools. The diversity of the American secondary school population makes teaching in U.S. middle schools, junior high schools, and senior high schools a very challenging proposition.

Teachers confront in their classrooms nearly every aspect of the entire U.S. population. The poor youngsters are there. The middle class youngsters are there. The affluent youngsters are there. Youngsters of every hue people the classrooms. Native speakers of Spanish, French, Punjabi, and dozens of other languages are present. In short, teaching in secondary schools requires teachers who are sensitive to differences, flexible, and willing to accept an employment environment where many youngsters may well reflect attitudes and values different from their own.

Perhaps the most challenging environment of all for teachers is the upper middle school or junior high school age group. Many of these youngsters are still operating at the concrete operations stage of intellectual functioning. They require instruction featuring lots of work with tangible objects or other experiences allowing them to perceive things directly through the senses. Further, those of this age who have begun to cross over into the formal operations stage may well be in the extremely idealistic phase of the stage when they tend to reject much of the world "as it is," including the teacher and his or her perspectives.

Finally, youngsters at this age are likely to vary tremendously in size. Some will be as developed as 18-year-olds. Others will have physical characteristics of much younger children. These differences make it difficult for the school to provide classroom furniture appropriate for each student. Further, these differences also tend to associate with dramatic differences in interests and enthusiasms among these youngsters. Teachers who work with students of this age must be prepared to abandon any notions about what a "typical" middle school or junior high school youngster is and work, instead, to deal effectively with the incredible array of individual student characteristics likely to show up in a given classroom.

References

Eichorn, Dorothy. "Biological, Psychological and Socio-Cultural Aspects of Adolescents and Youth." Unpublished paper, 1972.

Elkind, David, and Flavell, John H., eds. *Studies in Cognitive Development.* New York: Oxford University Press, 1969.

McCandless, Boyd R., and Coop, Richard H. *Adolescents: Behavior and Development.* 2nd ed. New York: Holt, Rinehart and Winston, Inc., 1979.

National Panel on High School and Adolescent Education. *The Education of Adolescents.* Final Report and Recommendations. Washington, D.C.: U.S. Department of Health, Education, and Welfare, 1976.

Sprinthall, Richard C., and Sprinthall, Norman A. *Educational Psychology: A Developmental Approach.* 2nd ed. Reading, Mass.: Addison-Wesley Publishing Co., Inc., 1977.

U.S. Department of Education. *The Condition of Education, 1980.* Washington, D.C.: National Center for Education Statistics, 1980.

Williams, Jeffrey W., compiler. *Students and Schools.* Washington, D.C.: National Center for Education Statistics, 1979.

13

Legal Rights and Responsibilities of Students

FUNKY WINKERBEAN by Tom Batiuk © 1973. Field Enterprises, Inc. Courtesy of Field Newspaper Syndicate.

Objectives

This chapter provides information to help the reader to

1. Identify the basic rights of students in school settings.
2. List the substantive principles and the procedural steps of due process procedures.
3. Identify the three basic categories of student rights and the types of cases that apply to each.
4. State the basic principles that influence court decisions in cases of student rights.
5. State the implications for teachers of changes in student rights.

Pretest

Directions: Using your own paper, answer each of the following true/false questions. For each correct statement, write the word ''true.'' For each incorrect statement, write the word ''false.''

_____ 1. The teacher in the classroom has the authority to establish any rules that he or she deems desirable.

_____ 2. Public education is a privilege, and therefore a denial of an education does not interfere with the rights of a student.

_____ 3. A high school student who is married can be excluded from high school.

_____ 4. Teacher advisors and school principals may exercise any censorship they desire over student publications.

_____ 5. A basic principle that is used in deciding whether a school regulation is reasonable is whether or not the behavior prohibited results in a substantial interference with normal school operation.

_____ 6. Generally, a student who is suspended from school for a period of ten days or more has a right to legal counsel.

_____ 7. School lockers are the same as private property and therefore may not be searched without a search warrant under any circumstances.

_____ 8. In an overwhelming number of cases, the courts have established that a student who fails to learn may collect damages from a teacher who has neglected to teach him or her what he or she was supposed to have learned.

_____ 9. Public schools are not required by law to provide educational services for handicapped students.

_____ 10. According to recent court decisions, rules designed to govern student behavior ought to be written in an ambiguous manner to accommodate unforeseen circumstances.

INTRODUCTION

Few areas in secondary education have generated so much controversy as has the issue of student rights. In recent years, the relationship between students and authorities charged with administering school programs has changed dramatically. While some changes have come about as a consequence of school-related legislation, most have occurred because of court decisions having to do with the status of youngsters in the schools. In general, these decisions have tended to endow students with more legal rights than they enjoyed in earlier times.

These decisions have not been welcomed uniformly by professional educators. Some have viewed them as serving to undermine the authority of school officials to the extent that the capacity to maintain order and productive levels of discipline has been jeopardized. Others have countered that these decisions have quite properly served to ensure that students in the schools are not subjected to arbitrary and capricious actions of those few school administrators and teachers who might be inclined to act in a less than professional manner toward students. The pros and cons of recent court decisions in the student rights area have been discussed widely.

For administrators, one public relations problem resulting from many of these court decisions has been that of apprising the local community of the implications of these rulings. Some school patrons, for example, do not understand why schools do not have rigid dress codes, strict regulations regarding what can and cannot go in student publications, and procedures to arrange for quick expulsions of disruptive students. Unless the public is aware that the courts have placed many constraints on administrators in these areas, there is tendency for some citizens to believe that school administrators simply are "unwilling to do what ought to be done."

Recent changes in how the legal relationship between students and schools are defined reflect some changes in societal perspectives toward young people. To better understand the nature of the changes, some grasp of historical underpinnings of the currently eroding view that youngsters should be considered as legal inferiors of school officials will prove helpful. Some of these historical issues are explored in the next section.

STUDENTS AND SCHOOLS: AN HISTORICAL PERSPECTIVE

A frequently encountered character in literature is the harsh and unbending schoolmaster. This historic figure often established rules arbitrarily and enforced them with a heavy hand (and frequently with a rod in that hand). The schoolmaster's authority was unquestioned. Legally, students and parents of students had little recourse were they to take issue with the appropriateness of any decision made by a school official. For example, as late as 1959, a student suspended from school had no legal way to appeal such a decision.

While, to modern eyes, such a situation seems to place students in a "no-win" situation, historically the move to give school authorities broad powers over students resulted from very humane motives. Going way back in time, the whole concept of childhood did not exist. A person was either an infant or he or she was an adult. Legal implications of this perspective were that very young children could be (and were) charged, tried, and imprisoned much as adults were charged, tried, and imprisoned. There are records of young children even being executed.

In time, general knowledge about growth and development of young people came to be known more widely. The concept of childhood as a period unique and distinct from infancy and adulthood emerged. Individuals sensitive to children's special qualities began pushing for laws and regulations that would help young people to survive to a productive maturity. A general principle supporting these efforts was that children, above all, needed protection.

As the Industrial Revolution unfolded and horror stories about exploitation of children in the workplace spread, intensive efforts were mounted to secure passage of laws regulating child labor. In the field of education, this general reform effort resulted in the evolution of a system whereby children in the schools were provided with what was seen as protective custody. In other words, children in the schools were seen as being transferred for the duration of the school day from the protective custody of their parents to the protective custody of the school. The rights of youngsters in the school were viewed as rights of safety, security, and protection. For their own good, children were thought of as being placed in the hands of responsible adults who would seek after their interests in much the same manner as their parents. It was, then, as a consequence of an effort to *protect* youngsters *from* the full rights of citizens (a doctrine that had resulted in unconscionable exploitation of young people) that children were placed in the protective arms of the school. That youngsters were placed in a position where they could not legally challenge school authority was considered of minor consequence given the perceived gain in terms of their protection from dangers that might accrue to them were they simply regarded no differently from adult citizens.

In the days before public secondary schools enrolled large percentages of the pre-adolescent and early-adolescent population, there was little public resistance to the idea that youngsters should be viewed as legal wards of the school. For years there were no mandatory attendance laws beyond elementary schools. Even after such laws became common, enforcement frequently was lax. Well into the twentieth century, percentages of youngsters staying in school and completing the entire secondary school program remained relatively small. Unlike elementary education, then, secondary education tended for much of its history to be viewed as voluntary rather than as mandatory.

Youngsters who enrolled in secondary schools were thought to be turned over to school authorities voluntarily by their parents. There was a widespread perception that secondary education was not a right that was available to all but, rather, a privilege for those willing to do the work and obey the rules. As long as parents (and the society in general) viewed themselves as having a real choice regarding whether to enroll or not to enroll youngsters in secondary schools, little resistance developed against the idea that schools should exercise almost absolute legal authority over students. It was only when conditions changed and an overwhelming majority of youngsters of secondary school age were compelled to attend school that questions began to emerge about the fairness of the relationship between school officials and students.

Certainly by 1960 (and probably well before that date), it had become clear that there was little voluntarism involved in a parent's decision to send a son or daughter to secondary school. School attendance in most states was mandated through about age 15 or 16. Put simply, there was almost nothing voluntary about a parent's decision to send a child to secondary school by this time. As a result, substantial pressures began building related to the nature of secondary education in general and, more specifically, to the appropriate legal relationship between students and schools.

One watershed court case of this period was the *Dixon* case [186 F. Supp. 945 (1960)], in which the court ruled that tax-supported education had become so fundamental that it could no longer be regarded as a privilege; rather, it ought to be viewed as a "substantial right." In essence, this decision meant that, as a right, such an education could not be denied to a student unless due-process-of-law provisions were followed. In other words, school officials could no longer act in a custodial relationship with students when questions of suspensions and expulsion were involved. Students had to be provided the legal protections afforded any other citizen when a right was potentially jeopardized (see Figure 13.1). This decision meant that students threatened with actions affecting their ability to continue attending school had a right to counsel,

Figure 13-1

SHOULD SCHOOLING BE THOUGHT OF AS A PRIVILEGE?

OK. OK. So who has a problem agreeing that *some* schooling is necessary for everybody? I won't argue that. I mean, look, everybody knows that kids in elementary schools have to be there. It's not something for just a few lucky ones.

But what about these jokers who are 16 and 17 years old? I think if they screw up, they should be sent down the road. No way should teachers have to put up with a few of these bad apples. I don't see any mention in the Constitution of a "right" to raise hell in class and keep other kids from learning. If they'll sit and do as they're told, fine. But, if they abuse the privilege, then I say they should be escorted to the door and told to not come back.

Statement by a caller on a late-night radio talk show

YOUR OPINION, PLEASE

Read the paragraphs above. Then, respond to these questions.

1. Are there some students for whom schooling is a right and others for whom it is a privilege? Why do you think so?
2. The caller says that "*some* schooling is necessary for everybody." Do you agree? Does this mean schooling ought to be regarded as a right?
3. What justification do you see for regarding schooling as a basic right? What implications does this view have for teachers (i.e., what does this mean in terms of the kinds of youngsters who will be in classrooms, and so forth)?
4. What justification do you see for regarding schooling as a privilege? What does this mean for teachers?
5. In general, how do you react to the message of the caller? If you were the host on this talk show, how would you respond?

to be confronted with the evidence, and to all the other appurtenances associated with the legal principle of due process.

Many of the early challenges to the authority of school officials occurred at the college and university level. The so-called "free speech" movement of the 1960s swept across many of the nations' campuses during these years. A consequence of this movement was that administrators' authorities increasingly came to be viewed as negotiable rather than as unassailable prerogatives of office.

During this time society in general began to question seriously the legitimacy of authority of all kinds. Perhaps the episode in our national history that acted as a catalyst to bring a large cross section of the population to question decisions of leaders of establishment enterprises (including, certainly, education) was the war in Vietnam. Concerns about the adequacy of government policies regarding the war made it much more respectable to challenge authority of all kinds. School authorities, of course, were not immune from these kinds of critical appraisals.

The controversy over Vietnam bore directly on one of the most important court decisions in the student rights area. In Des Moines, Iowa, children of several families who opposed governmental policy in Vietnam decided to demonstrate their opposition to the war by wearing black armbands to school. When school officials learned that this protest was to take place, they met and adopted a policy stating that any student who arrived at school wearing an armband would be asked to remove it. A failure to comply would result in suspension from school.

Three students—John Tinker, Mary Beth Tinker, and Christopher Eckhardt—wore armbands to school. In accordance with the school policy, they were suspended. Attorneys for the students filed suit in the U.S. district court. The end result of the ensuing legal battles was the now-famous case of *Tinker* v. *Des Moines Independent Community School District* [393 U.S. 503 (1969)]. In its decision, the Supreme Court stated that neither teachers nor students left their constitutional rights at the schoolhouse door. The court viewed the wearing of armbands as symbolic speech. Therefore, the students' rights to wear armbands were protected under the First Amendment to the U.S. Constitution (the free speech amendment).

The court's decision in the *Tinker* case prompted considerable debate in the educational community, creating an initial confusion as to just what school authorities could and could not require students to do (or refrain from doing). Some saw the *Tinker* decision as an example of unwarranted judicial interference in the school management process. Certain critics of the decision identified strongly with the minority dissent of Mr. Justice Black who argued, "One does not need to be a prophet or the son of a prophet to know that after the Court's holding today some students . . . in all schools will be ready, able, and willing to defy their teachers on practically all orders."

The *Tinker* decision was by no means regarded universally with dismay. Many educators felt that the court had moved responsibly to redress an imbalance in the legal relationship between students and school authorities. In their view, the schools had not lost their authority to make reasonable rules. Rather, the court's decision had simply helped to define the kinds of rules that could be imposed without putting students' rights as citizens in jeopardy.

Recent court decisions have attempted to define more precisely the appropriate legal relationship between school authorities and parents. For purposes of examination, it is useful to group these court cases into three major categories. The first includes those that concern the extent of school authorities' power to interfere with students' actions. The second has to do with the extent of school officials' responsibility to ensure that learners profit from instruction provided by the school. The third involves cases centering on the issue of fairness or appropriateness of processes followed by school officials in making decisions affecting rights of students. We will examine each of these categories in the sections that follow.

SCHOOL AUTHORITY AND INTERFERENCE WITH ACTIONS OF STUDENTS

A review of court cases in this area reveals one trend. In general, courts have tended to oppose restrictions on actions of students unless those actions can be shown to harm other students or to interfere with the educational process. For example, in deciding for the students in the *Tinker* case, the court found, among other things, that there was no evidence that school authorities had clear evidence that armband wearing was associated either with harm to students or with disruption of the school program. In the sections that follow, we will take a look at some of the specific issues related to school regulations and student behavior that have come before the courts.

Protest Symbols

The *Tinker* case represented an instance in which a judicial decision supported students' rights to wear protest symbols. But not all cases of this type have resulted in decisions favoring student complainants. For example, in one case a regulation adopted by school officials prohibiting the wearing of protest buttons was upheld. In this situation, school officials were able to document numerous instances of fighting between wearers of protest buttons and other students opposed to sentiments expressed by the buttons. The decision reflected a view that the school regulation represented a prudent precaution against the very real possibility of physical danger to students in the school.

A general result of decisions in this area has been a tightening of language used in school regulations related to protests and protest symbols. It is no longer acceptable for schools to have vague regulations requiring students to behave "responsibly" or "correctly." Any regulation must pinpoint the precise nature of any forbidden behavior. The language of any rule must be clear enough so that a student can easily determine whether or not his or her behavior is in violation of the rule. Finally, school officials must be able to establish that, in the absence of such a rule, possible harm might come to students or to the school program.

Student Publications

In general, the courts have held that student publications enjoy the same constitutional protections as adult publications. Not too many years ago, it was a common practice for teachers acting as sponsors of student newspapers and for school principals to censor what was printed in these publications. Today, the legal grounds for this practice have become very shaky. (This is *not* to say censorship no longer exists. In many places it does. *But* should affected students have the resources to pursue the issue in court, they stand a good chance of carrying the day.)

Consider this example. Suppose that a school newspaper article made unkind or even libelous statements about certain school officials. Could the principal or the publications' sponsor force students to remove such statements from the article in advance of publication. From a legal standpoint, probably not. Such an act might well be seen by the courts as potentially illegal interference with free expression. While the student who wrote the article might later be found guilty of violating libel laws, the article would first have to be published for libel to be established (Blackman, Broussard, and Mundt 1968). See Figure 13-2 for another example.

Another issue that comes up frequently in cases involving student publications has to do with obscenity. There is much disagreement about what is and what is not obscene. In obscenity cases, the issue has not been so much a question of students' possession or nonpossession of a right to print obscene material as it has been a question of determining whether what has been printed is, in fact, obscene. If it can be demonstrated that school authorities have suppressed the publication of something that cannot be established definitely as being obscene, then it may be that these authorities have interfered illegally with free speech and freedom of expression. In one case, at least,

Figure 13-2

LIMITS OF EXPRESSION IN STUDENT PUBLICATIONS

Several years ago, some students in a secondary school in the state of Illinois decided to produce a so-called "literary journal" called *Grass High*. They proceeded with these plans and produced a publication that contained comments that were believed by school officials to be a direct and unconscionable challenge to administrative authority. School attendance was described as "idiotic and asinine." The senior dean of the school was described as having a "sick mind." Further, students were urged to refuse to take home to parents any "propaganda" issued by the school. Should such material be passed out to them, the editorial suggested they destroy it.

The journal was sold to a number of students and faculty members in the school. The episode led to a great deal of controversy. In the end, the editor of *Grass High* was expelled. Subsequently, the student took the matter to the U.S. district court.*

YOUR OPINION, PLEASE

Read the paragraphs above. Then, respond to these questions.

1. Do you believe that students had a right to produce and disseminate this publication in the school? Why, or why not?
2. Would you feel any differently had these comments been made in the regular school newspaper rather than in a publication a number of students simply launched on their own? Why, or why not?
3. What do you think the proper administrative response would have been in this situation?
4. How do you think the court ruled in this case? On what legal basis do you suppose the decision was made?

*The situation described was a real case, *Scoville* v. *Board of Education of Joliet Township High School District 204 (Ill.),* 425 F. 2nd 10 (1970). You might be interested in reading the actual court decision in this case. A summary of the court's findings is provided in David V. Martin, "The Rights and Liberties of Students," *The High School Journal* (October 1973): 24–38.

---

the Supreme Court has ruled that school officials' beliefs that something may be obscene is not grounds for suppressing publication [*Papish* v. *University of Missouri Board of Curators*, 410 U.S. 667 (1973)].

Student Dress and Appearance

School dress and appearance regulations have been challenged frequently in the courts in recent years. Although there have been a number of court decisions regarding these regulations, no clearly consistent pattern has emerged. In some cases, judicial decisions have upheld dress and hair-length codes. In others, the decisions have supported the challenges brought forward by students' legal representatives. At this time, a trend does seem to be developing for courts to uphold regulations where school officials have been able to demonstrate a clear need in terms of preserving student safety and the orderly functioning of the instructional program. For example, given this emerging trend, a school legitimately might require hair nets to be worn both by male and female students with long hair when they work as food servers in school cafeterias. Similarly, students working with power grinders in shop classes might be required to wear protective goggles.

Search and Seizure

Do school authorities have a right to search students' lockers for drugs or other illegal substances or materials without first securing students' permission? Can students' persons be searched for the same purposes? Actions of school authorities in the general area of search and seizure have led to a number of lawsuits. In general, complainants have raised the issue of whether actions of school authorities violate Fourth Amendment guarantees against unreasonable search and seizure. Compare this with the example outlined in Figure 13-3.

In numerous decisions, the courts have pointed out that the Fourth Amendment does *not* prohibit all searches and seizures. Only *unreasonable* search and seizure is prohibited. Decisions in individual cases have tended to turn on whether school officials have been able to demonstrate that actions they have taken are not unreasonable.

Before reviewing some interesting cases involving search and seizure, we need to get a fix on some important legal principles that are relevant to court decisions in this area. The first of these principles is *probable cause*. Probable cause implies a set of circumstances that, given available evidence and circumstances, cause a reasonable person to believe that an individual is guilty of an offense. Issuance of search warrants ordinarily are based on the principle of probable cause.

Reasonable suspicion as a ground for action in search and seizure cases is less stringent than probable cause. Reasonable suspicion is established when a reasonable person concludes that an individual might be guilty of wrongdoing of some kind. Probable cause can be established only when there is corroborating evidence. Reasonable suspicion does not require corroboration.

Figure 13-3

THE SEARCH AND SEIZURE ISSUE

The Coordinator of Discipline in a high school, while escorting a student to his office, observed a bulge in his pants pocket. As they neared his office, the student bolted for an outside door. Noticing a policeman who was standing outside his office, the Coordinator shouted to him, "He's got junk and he's escaping." The Coordinator then chased him three blocks away from the school. He grabbed the wrists of the student's left hand, which was in his pants pocket. The hand emerged from the pocket, revealing the nipple of an eyedropper with other material clenched in his fist. On demand, the student opened his fist and displayed a set of "works." This material was then given to the policeman, who arrived on the scene at this point. In trial court prosecution tried to use it as evidence of illegal possession of drugs. . . . *

YOUR OPINION, PLEASE

1. How would you have reacted had you been the coordinator of discipline in this school?
2. Do you think the action of the coordinator of discipline was correct or incorrect? Why? Was the action of the coordinator of discipline legal? Why, or why not?
3. Suppose that the student involved argued in court that the evidence gathered by the coordinator of discipline and the policeman could not be used against him because the evidence had been obtained through illegal search and seizure? Would the court, in your view, have been receptive to this argument?
4. A court case did result from this situation. Do you think the decision favored the actions of the school official? Or, do you think the decision favored the student who claimed evidence used against him had been gathered illegally?

*The episode described is from a real court case. If you would be interested in learning how the court ruled, you might like to read the decision in *People* v. *Jackson*, 65 Misc. 2d 909, 319 N.Y.S. 2d 731 (1971). A summary of the decision is contained in David V. Martin, "The Rights and Liberties of Students," *The High School Journal* (October 1973): 24–38.

In applying probable cause and reasonable suspicion principles to school search and seizure cases, action based on probable cause rather than on reasonable suspicion seems more likely to be sustained by the courts when a search of an individual is involved. The case of *Doe* v. *Renfrow* illustrates this point [*Doe* v. *Renfrow*, No. H 70-233 (N.D. Ind., 30 August 1979)].

This case involved the use of dogs to search for drugs in a high school. When one of the dogs acted in a manner suggesting that Diane Doe had drugs on her person, school authorities required her to empty her pockets and purse. Further, a strip search was conducted. No illegal substances were found. Infuriated at what had happened, Diane Doe filed suit in district court on the grounds that the sniffing of the dogs, the search of her pockets and purse, and the strip search violated her rights.

In the decision, the court held that the sniffing of the dogs was not a search and was therefore permissible and reasonable. Too, the emptying of pockets was also ruled justifiable because the action of the dog provide reasonable suspicion that an illegal substance might be present. But the court held for Ms. Doe on the issue of the strip search. The strip search was declared an invasion of privacy that could not be tolerated only on the basis of reasonable suspicion. The court suggested a need for a search warrant that would have been issued only under circumstances where probable cause could be established.

In general, court decisions have supported school officials' rights to search school lockers and desks when there is reasonable suspicion of an existence of illegal items. Part of the logic here is that students do not own these lockers or desks. They, therefore, are not items of a clearly personal nature.

The legality or illegality of searches conducted by school officials in part seems to be related to the intended purpose of the search. In two cases involving the search of college dormitory rooms, *Moore* v. *Student Affairs Committee of Troy State University* [284 F. Supp. 725 (M.D. Ala. 1968)] and *Piazzola* v. *Watkins* [316 F. Supp. 624 (M.D. Ala 1970)], the courts ruled that school officials did have a right to conduct the search so long as the objective was restricted to the maintenance of discipline and an educational atmosphere. However, if there were an intent to use whatever evidence might be found for purposes of criminal prosecution, then school officials would be obligated to obtain a search warrant. Such a warrant would be issued only if probable cause could be established.

As can be inferred from the cases cited, what teachers and other school officials can do in the area of search and seizure is governed by technical legal principles. Obviously this is an area in which educators must proceed with caution. Today, school officials tend to rely heavily on advice from legal counsel before undertaking action.

FUNKY WINKERBEAN by Tom Batiuk © 1981. Field Enterprises, Inc. Courtesy of Field Newspaper Syndicate.

RESPONSIBILITY OF EDUCATORS FOR STUDENTS' LEARNING

Court decisions have tended to define education as a right of students rather than as a privilege. This view of education, which obliges teachers and administrators to provide educational services to all school-aged youngsters, represents a break with many historic practices in American education. For example, not too many years ago, it was common for schools to refuse entry to married students. Youngsters with severe behavioral problems were summarily expelled. Many handicapped youngsters received no educational services. Today, schools legally cannot do any of these things.

Suspension and Expulsion

Until fairly recent times, suspension and expulsion from school programs was a standard method for dealing with discipline problems. Today, suspension and expulsion procedures will be sustained only when school officials can demonstrate that a given student's presence constitutes a real danger to other individuals in the school or clearly disrupts the school program. Even when such circumstances can be established, very careful procedures must be followed. (Many of these are detailed in a subsequent section of this chapter: "Students and Due Process.")

For years married students and especially married females who were pregnant were regularly excluded from school programs, often on the grounds that the presence of married students would encourage teenage marriages. The presence of pregnant students was widely believed to have a possibly "corrupting" influence on morals of other students in school. School authorities used to argue that presence of such students would create an uproar among other students and, therefore, would cause a severe disruption of the instructional mission of the school. This logic failed to stand up when challenged in the courts. A general thrust of judicial decisions in this area has been to declare school regulations barring married or pregnant students to be unreasonable. Such policies are a rarity today.

Some schools, in response to some early court decisions, did admit married and pregnant students. But often these youngsters were forbidden to participate in any extracurricular activities. Court cases in more recent years have acted to undercut the authority of school officials to impose these kinds of restrictions. In general, these decisions have declared the extracurricular program to be an essential part of schooling. Therefore, it should be available to all students. Today, most secondary schools attempt to treat married and pregnant students just as other youngsters in the schools are treated.

Bilingual Education

Historically, public schools were viewed as an agency that could "acculturate" youngsters from a variety of ethnic groups. To speed this process, it was considered essential that youngsters rapidly learn English. To prompt learning, it was believed wise to prevent youngsters from using their native languages at school. In some parts of the country, punishment was meted out to youngsters who used a language other than English even on the playground. This placed a burden on youngsters who came to school speaking something other than English as a first language. They were expected to learn a new language at the same time they were expected to compete effectively with native speakers of the language.

The issue of language discrimination in the schools came before the Supreme Court in *Lau* v. *Nichols* [414 U.S. 563 (1974)]. The court ruled that regulations requiring learners who did not understand English to use the same materials as native speakers of English constituted unequal treatment. As a result of this and subsequent decisions, bilingual programs in schools have come to be mandated by the courts.

Today, a student who has difficulty with English has a right to be taught in his or her native tongue until English proficiency is attained.

Teacher Malpractice

Should teachers be held liable if students in their classes do not learn? Several legal actions have been brought by students who have attempted to hold teachers responsible for their inability to master subjects taught in school. These cases have prompted a great deal of public interest. A number of them have been covered widely in the press. To this point, courts generally have taken the position that a student's failure to learn cannot be attributed to the actions or inactions of the teacher alone. Certainly individual student motivation plays a role, but many factors other than teacher actions contribute to whether a student does or does not learn. Although courts generally have taken the view that many variables beyond the control of teachers and schools influence learning, the issue of teacher malpractice is by no means dead (see Figure 13-4). We may expect to see additional suits relating to this issue in the future.

STUDENTS AND DUE PROCESS

Court decisions have declared that, when school officials act in a manner that might interfere with rights of students, they must act in an appropriate manner. In most instances this means that school officials must follow due process provisions. The Fourteenth Amendment of the U.S. Constitution states that no citizen can be deprived of

Figure 13-4

SHOULD TEACHERS BE ACCOUNTABLE FOR STUDENTS' LEARNING?

I hired this young guy in my shop. Sharp as a whip. Been with me six months now. I almost canned him the first week. I had him write up some past due notes for a couple of customers. He was just about to send them out when I thought, "uh-oh, better do a quick check on these first." When I saw them, I hit the ceiling. He had at least six misspellings on each one of them. I mean they were simple words like "receive," "parcel," and "collect." Every one of them had "a lot" spelled as one word.

Well, I got him straightened out in a hurry. We fixed them up before sending them off. Good grief. My customers would have thought my business was being run by some nitwits if they'd seen all those spellings. Anyway, I got him a word division book and he began looking seriously at what he writes. He hasn't made a serious mistake in months. I mean he's an intelligent guy.

Now, what I want to know is how did he get out of high school in this condition? I think it's a case of almost criminal neglect. As far as I'm concerned some of those teachers sat on their duffs and didn't get the job done. If I'd canned him, I think he would have had a good case if he'd gone to court and charged some of those turkeys he had in high school with negligence.

Statement from an employer

YOUR OPINION, PLEASE

Read the paragraphs above. Then, respond to these questions.

1. What is your general reaction to the position taken by the employer?
2. Should teachers be held liable for what students learn in their classes? Why, or why not.
3. Some have said that what a student learns in school is almost totally up to the student himself or herself. Do you agree or disagree with this view? Why?
4. Why do you suppose the employee mentioned in the paragraphs above suddenly became a proficient speller?

"life, liberty or property, without due process of law." Since the courts have defined public education as a substantial right for all citizens, logically they have also held that such an education cannot be denied unless due process provisions are met.

Due process involves two basic components: the *substantive component* and the *procedural component*. Protections associated with the substantive component of due process reference the basic principles of due process. The following principles associate with the substantive component of due process:

1. Individuals are not to be disciplined on the basis of unwritten rules.
2. Rules must not be unduly vague.
3. Individuals are entitled to a hearing before an impartial tribunal.
4. Identities of witnesses are to be revealed.
5. Decisions are to be supported by substantial evidence.
6. A public or private hearing can be requested by the accused.

The procedural component of due process relates to the guidelines that must be followed to meet due process requirements. With respect to school practices, the following steps are consistent with the procedural component:

1. Rules governing student behavior are to be given to students and parents at the opening of school.
2. Whenever a student is accused of breaking rules that could result in due process procedure, the charges must be given in writing to the student and his or her parents.
3. A written notice of a hearing needs to be given so that the student has time to prepare a defense. Usually the hearing must take place within two weeks.
4. A fair hearing must be held that includes the
   a. right of the accused to be presented by legal counsel.
   b. right of the accused to present a defense including the presentation of evidence.
   c. right of the accused to face his or her accusers.
   d. the right of the accused to crossexamine witnesses.
   e. the right of the accused to receive a complete transcript of the hearing.
5. Decision of the hearing board must be based on evidence presented. Further, the decision must be rendered within a reasonable period of time.
6. The accused must be informed of the right to appeal the decision of the hearing board.

Let us consider how due process might apply in situations pertaining to suspension and expulsion. Suspension is defined as a temporary separation from school. Expulsion, on the other hand, is a permanent separation from school.

A suspension lasting for a period of time shorter than ten days is considered to be a short-term suspension. When a student is faced with a short-term suspension, only minimal due process procedures need be observed. In this situation, the student in question must receive (1) at least an oral (preferably a written) notice of the specific charges that have been made, (2) an explanation of the evidence to support these charges, and (3) an opportunity to present his or her version of the issue at question. In this case, it is not necessary for legal counsel to be present. The procedures ordinarily can be accomplished in a very short time. Usually this abbreviated hearing procedure will precede a student's removal from school. But, if the presence of the accused students threatens disruption of the normal school program or endangers the safety of others, then the student can be removed immediately. In such a case, the official notice of the problem and the scheduled hearing will follow as soon as possible.

A suspension exceeding ten days in length is considered to be a long-term suspension. Long-term suspensions require full due process procedures. All steps noted under the procedural component of due process must be adhered to strictly. A failure of school officials to follow these procedures may make them legally vulnerable should litigation result from their actions.

Expulsion is the most serious action the school can take against a student regarding his ability to attend school. Expulsion places a permanent bar against school attendance. Consequently, in cases where expulsion is likely to be the end result, the strictest due process procedures must be observed. In most cases, a teacher or an administrator of a school cannot make an expulsion decision. It tends to be the prerogative of the highest governing officials of a district. It is they who will oversee the due process hearings in most expulsion cases.

DUE PROCESS AND TEACHERS

The days when the classroom teacher was the ultimate and unquestioned authority are over. The courts have spoken clearly on this issue. Students have constitutional rights. And those rights, like those of all citizens, must be respected.

Teachers tend not to be of one mind in terms of their attitudes toward these changes. Some feel that extensions of student rights have represented an unwarranted invasion by the courts into the affairs of public schools. A few argue that the capacity of teachers to set rules and discipline youngsters has been undermined. Others, however, point out that, while court decisions have required educators to pay close attention to decision-making processes, courts generally have affirmed rights of educators to adopt rules and regulations necessary to ensure a safe and orderly educational environment. Disciplinary actions can be taken against students who violate these rules and regulations. But enforcement must take student rights into consideration.

One important implication for teachers that flows out of recent judicial decisions regarding student rights is that they must be very careful in framing rules governing behaviors of students under their charge. Such rules must be justifiable in terms of either assuring students' safety or assuring a maintenance of a productive educational atmosphere. In thinking about rules and regulations, we might wish to consider such questions as these:

1. Is the purpose behind the rule clear?
2. Is the rule consistent with local, state, and federal law?
3. Is the rule described in clear and precise language?
4. Does the rule have a clear relationship to maintaining discipline or to preventing a disruption of the educational process?
5. Do all students know that the rule has been established?

In the past, many educators were reluctant to spell out rules for fear that their flexibility in responding to individual problems would be limited. The courts have been unsympathetic to this argument. One of the most successful defenses that students have made when charged with violations is that they "didn't know what the rule was." To prevent this kind of situation from arising, many secondary teachers now make a practice of publishing and distributing to students copies of classroom rules and regulations at the beginning of each term. Some go as far as to obtain a signed form from students indicating that rules and regulations have been read and understood.

In conclusion, it is fair to say that the legal relationship between educators and their students has changed dramatically over the past 20 years. This is an area that is still very much in an evolutionary state. As a consequence, beginning teachers would do well to read widely, seek out counsel from administrators and fellow teachers who track developments in this area, and make other actions appropriate to keeping on top of changes. There are certain to be lots of them.

Posttest

Directions: Using your own paper, answer each of the following true/false questions. For each correct statement, write the word "true." For each incorrect statement, write the word "false."

_____ 1. The teacher in the classroom has the authority to establish any rules that he or she deems desirable.

_____ 2. Public education is a privilege, and therefore a denial of an education does not interfere with the rights of a student.

_____ 3. A high school student who is married can be excluded from high school.

_____ 4. Teacher advisors and school principals may exercise any censorship they desire over student publications.

_____ 5. A basic principle that is used in deciding whether a school regulation is reasonable is whether or not the behavior prohibited results in a substantial interference with normal school operation.

_____ 6. Generally, a student who is suspended from school for a period of ten days or more has a right to legal counsel.

_____ 7. School lockers are the same as private property and therefore may not be searched without a search warrant under any circumstances.

_____ 8. In an overwhelming number of cases, the courts have established that a student who fails to learn may collect damages from a teacher who has neglected to teach him or her what he or she was supposed to have learned.

_____ 9. Public schools are not required by law to provide educational services for handicapped students.

_____ 10. According to recent court decisions, rules designed to govern student behavior ought to be written in an ambiguous manner to accommodate unforeseen circumstances.

Key Ideas in Review

1. Historically, schools were seen to have a custodial relationship with students. The student enjoyed a right to custody, not a right to full protection of the law enjoyed by adult citizens. Thus students were not entitled to challenge rules and regulations adopted by school authorities. Schooling tended to be regarded as a privilege. There was no concept of a "right to schooling" to support a legal challenge of a student who had been suspended or expelled by a school administrator.

2. With the extension of compulsory school laws and, more important, actual enforcement of such laws, it became clear that schooling really was not a matter of free choice either for parents or students. This situation began to change attitudes toward education. Rather than being seen as a privilege, education increasingly came to be seen as a right.

3. In about 1960, a series of court challenges began to chip away at the traditional conception of the student as a ward of the school. Taken together, court decisions in the student rights area have redefined the relationship between school officials and students. In general, students today enjoy the full rights of citizens and all the constitutional protections these rights imply. This means that any actions of school officials that may impinge on student rights must be taken only after procedures designed to protect student rights have been observed.

4. In cases involving suspension, expulsion, and other actions relating to potential restrictions on students' Fourteenth Amendment rights, due process must be observed. Today, the formal hearing, calling of witnesses, representation by legal counsel, and other practices associated with procedural due process are a regular feature of administrative practice in the schools.

5. In cases where students have challenged the legitimacy of school rules regulating student behavior, the courts have tended to uphold regulations characterized by (a) a clear relationship

to preserving the well-being of students and (b) a clear relationship to maintaining the integrity of the ongoing school program. Where such connections have not been made in a convincing manner by school officials, courts have tended to support positions taken by student complainants.

6. Teachers and other educators today must be very careful in the selection of language used in rules and regulations. Students must know whether a given action is consistent or inconsistent with any adopted rule or regulation. They must understand the language of the rule or regulation. All this has meant that today's rules and regulations tend to be stated in much more specific language than the more ambiguous rules and regulations of former times.

SUMMARY

Court decisions in recent years have had a dramatic impact on the legal relationship of school officials and students. Traditionally students were regarded as wards of the school. They enjoyed not the full rights of citizenship but, rather, something that might be described as a "right to custody." In these circumstances they were unable to mount legal challenges to decisions made by school authorities. Originally this custodial relationship was thought to be a protection for students against the actions of a larger society that was insensitive to the special needs of childhood. In more recent times, this legal relationship came to be challenged as critics pointed out that it afforded youngsters no legal remedy against arbitrary and capricious actions of school officials.

Numerous court cases dating from the late 1950s and early 1960s have by this time accorded students in the schools the full legal status of citizens. Today, these youngsters enjoy the same constitutional protections as do adults. Decisions of school authorities can be challenged in courts of law, and the new legal environment has resulted in many changes regarding the kinds of rules and regulations that school authorities may logically impose.

In general, courts have tended to support rules and regulations that can be demonstrated to be necessary to protect students' safety or to avoid disruption of the school program. The burden of proof that such a necessity exists has been placed on school officials. As a result, the tendency has been to frame school rules and regulations in much more specific language than was formerly the case. Rules referring to such things as "appropriate" or "suitable" behavior are no longer sufficient. They will not survive a court challenge.

The issue of student rights is still very much with us. Numerous cases are presently being litigated. For teachers, an important need is to keep apprised of changing developments in this area. Failure to do so could result in decisions to act toward students in a manner that would not be supportable should actions face a legal challenge by a student or his or her legal representatives.

References

Bible, Jon. *Student Rights and Responsibilities: A New Generation of Law.* Austin: The Texas Association of School Boards, 1977.

Blackman, C. Robert; Broussard, Joseph; and Mundt, Whitney R. "Before You Judge Your Next Student Press First Amendment Case," *Phi Delta Kappan* (October 1968): 105–107.

Flygare, Thomas J. "Detecting Drugs in School: The Legality of Scent Dogs and Strip Searches," *Phi Delta Kappan* (December 1979): 280–281.

Haubrich, Vernon F., and Apple, Michael W., eds. *Schooling and The Rights of Children.* Berkeley, Calif.: McCutchan Publishing Corporation, 1975.

Hazard, William R. *Education and the Law.* 2nd ed. New York: The Free Press, 1978.

Hookel, Clifford P., ed. *The Courts and Education.* The Seventy-Seventh Yearbook of the National Society for the Study of Education. Chicago: University of Chicago Press, 1978.

Manley-Casimir, Michael E. "Procedural Due Process in Secondary School Discipline," *Theory into Practice* (October 1978): 314–320.

Martin, David V. "The Rights and Liberties of Students," *The High School Journal* (October 1973): 24–38.

14

Gifted and Talented Students

FUNKY WINKERBEAN by Tom Batiuk © 1980. Field Enterprises, Inc. Courtesy of Field Newspaper Syndicate.

Objectives

This chapter provides information to help the reader to

1. Recognize the general historical support for education for the gifted and talented.
2. Describe procedures used to identify gifted and talented students.
3. Describe some common school practices that have been developed to serve the needs of gifted and talented students.
4. Point out some of the arguments used by proponents and opponents of expanded programs for gifted and talented students.
5. Note the provisions being made to train teachers to work with gifted and talented students.
6. Describe some myths about gifted and talented students that have tended to slow expansion of programs to meet special needs of these young people.

Pretest

Directions: Using your own paper, answer each of the following true/false questions. For each correct statement, write the word "true." For each incorrect statement, write the word "false."

_____ 1. Gifted and talented students tend to suffer from more emotional problems than do "normal" students.

    _____ 2. There is considerable dispute today regarding kinds of procedures that should be used to identify gifted and talented students.

    _____ 3. The vast majority of states require teachers who work with gifted and talented students to hold special teaching certificates certifying their competence to work with students of this type.

    _____ 4. About 3 percent of the school-aged population in the United States is gifted and/or talented.

    _____ 5. Today, there is nearly universal agreement that standardized tests alone should be used to identify students who are gifted and talented.

    _____ 6. Some critics argue that special programs for gifted and talented students promote undemocratic elitism in the schools.

    _____ 7. There tends to be more support for gifted and talented programs that involve enrichment activities for these students in regular classrooms than for programs that provide special accelerated classes for these students.

    _____ 8. Students who are gifted and talented tend to "burn out" early. Most do not make significant contributions in later life.

    _____ 9. Some critics of gifted and talented programs are concerned about value received for monies expended.

    _____ 10. Since the early 1970s, the federal government has taken an active role in support of education for the gifted and talented.

INTRODUCTION

"Item 4 on the agenda," intoned the school board clerk, "is the proposal to spend $75,000 on the pilot gifted and talented program at the high school next year."

Hearing this information, the superintendent suppressed a wince, discretely popped another Tums tablet into his mouth, and set his face into his best "I-don't-want-to-take-sides-on-this-one" stare.

Members of the audience rustled in their seats. Some slid purposefully forward, eager to jump to their feet at an appropriate time. A few nodded knowingly to political allies scattered at strategic points throughout the room. One or two gritted their teeth and looked angrily toward the front. A reporter in the back of the room whispered to a friend, "This is going to be a war."

Mrs. Llewelyn, chairperson of the school board, covered her own anxieties with her best political smile as she looked out over the group. She began to speak. "I understand that there is a good deal of interest in agenda item 4. On behalf of the board, I want to welcome all of you to tonight's meeting. We are delighted to have such an expression of interest in the affairs of our schools. Now, since we are so many, we are going to follow certain ground rules. No more than five minutes per speaker. And no speaker gets the floor more than one time. If some of you feel that you would like to share additional remarks with the board, please feel free to write them up. You can give them to the clerk either tonight or send them to him in the mail. All right, who would like to be first?"

Ten people were on their feet immediately. Nodding to a gentleman in the back, Mrs. Llewelyn said, "Please state your name and address before you begin. Remember, now, five minutes. When you have one minute left, the clerk will raise his right hand."

"Thank you, Mrs. Llewelyn," the man began. "I am Howard Rodman. I live at 4651 Northwest Ely Street. I represent the 500 members of the Northwest Parents Association, and tonight I come to you to speak in opposition to the gifted and talented project. Our members feel that this program represents an unconscionable expenditure of our tax monies for a narrow intellectual elite. We all know the bright youngsters are going to succeed in life. We all know that they are doing well in school now. By what conceivable logic then are we proposing to take money and divert it to the benefit of youngsters who already enjoy life chances much superior to those of our more typical students? These students are already an intellectual elite. This program is going to go beyond that to make them a social elite as well. They are likely to become arrogant prima donnas who will look down on students not involved in the special program. In summary, our group feels that the program will spend money for an unnecessary end and that it will result in the creation of a special group of elite students who derive more benefit from the school program than other youngsters. The proposal clearly is undemocratic. The proposal clearly is inconsistent with our desire to serve all of the students."

"Mr. Rodman, the board appreciates your comments. They will receive careful consideration." Looking away from Mr. Rodman, Mrs. Llewelyn asked, "Who would like to be next?" Nearly a quarter of the people in the room jumped to their feet. A few looked angrily at Rodman. Making a quick selection, Mrs. Llewelyn said, "the second person in the fifth row, please."

"Thank you, Mrs. Llewelyn. I am Sondra Jacobsen of 331 Tamarack Lane. I am speaking on behalf of the hundreds of members of Citizens for Quality Education. We are absolutely delighted that the school district has *at last* decided to do something positive for bright students. Our own studies reveal that nearly every new program in this district that has been mounted in the past ten years has been designed to help slow learners, handicapped students, or some other students with learning problems. We certainly applaud these efforts. But isn't it time to do something for our leaders of tomorrow? Isn't it time we put a special effort into helping exceptionally bright youngsters to reach their learning potentials? We think both questions should be answered with an unequivocal 'Yes!' Nothing is sadder, no loss is more profound than a good mind wasted. Intellectual talent needs special care. These youngsters need challenges that are not being provided by regular classroom instruction. For the good of our school district, for the good of our community, please, members of the board, do not be swayed from making the decision you know in your hearts is right. Give us the gifted and talented program."

"Our thanks to you, Ms. Jacobsen. The board appreciates your willingness to share your views. We will think long and hard on them." This public relations gesture completed, Mrs. Llewelyn looked again at the audience. "Anyone else?" she asked. Once more, large numbers of people were on their feet, waving their hands to seek recognition. Mrs. Llewelyn nodded at a woman seated near the front of the room.

"My name is Victoria Lopez. I live at 1914 South Thomas Street. I am speaking tonight in support of the unanimous position adopted by the United Minorities Coalition at its special session Monday evening. While we are not opposed, in principle, to special programs for gifted and talented students, we are concerned that the board has failed to speak out on specific procedures to be used to identify students who will qualify for the program. Our review of programs elsewhere has led us to conclude that most rely almost entirely on standardized test scores. This approach is totally unacceptable to us. Because of cultural biases in these tests, children of minority parents do not score as well as children of majority parents. These tests simply are not valid indicators of true talent. If the board uses standardized tests and nothing else to identify gifted and talented students, then the board will select a group of all-white youngsters for inclusion in the program. This is simply a mechanism to perpetuate racism under the more acceptable label of 'gifted and talented' education. We reject racism. We don't believe that the board wishes to promote racism either. Please, then, no gifted or talented program without protections that will guarantee a reasonable level of participation by minority group children."

"Ms. Lopez, the board certainly wishes to do *nothing* of a racist nature. We thank you very much for sharing your concerns with us. We appreciate your help." Once more, Mrs. Llewelyn looked over the audience. "Next?" she asked. Looking through the crowd of waving hands, she nodded at a man in the back.

"T. J. Smalley. 41511 Winding Hill Drive. I'm representing the Taxpayers for Responsible Schools group. We have studied the proposal for the gifted and talented project for the past month and have concluded that it provides very poor value for the money to be expended. We have no objection to quality education. We're all for that. But, in looking at what the pilot project will provide, we simply can't see that much that is new, different, and better is to result from the expenditure of 75,000 dollars. The program proposes to provide these students with special classes where they will read more books, go on a few field trips, and in general have opportunities to apply what they learn. Presumably this means that they will write some papers, build some projects, and so forth. All of this sounds wonderful. But isn't this what is supposed to be going on in the classrooms now? Does the board mean to suggest that *all* students are not being asked to apply what they learn? Is the kind of education that we, in our apparent innocence, presumed was being offered to all the students now to be offered only to a few? And to those few only after the expenditure of an additional $75,000? We feel that no case has been made that this money will result in something truly different being offered to youngsters selected for the program. In summary, we believe that the taxpayers are being asked to pay an additional $75,000 for which they will receive something that may be no better than what they are getting now. The proposal should be rejected."

"Thank you, Mr. Smalley. As taxpayers ourselves, members of the board are always pleased to hear comments from a group who gives such careful study to expenditures of public money. Certainly we want to do nothing that will not result in a good value for the dollars expended."

Looking out at the audience again, Mrs. Llewelyn recognized the next speaker. The process repeated itself until the large round oak clock at the back of the room indicated 1:30 A.M. Incredibly, over 75 people remained in the room. Incredibly, too, large numbers still wanted to speak. Finally, at 1:45, having thanked the representative from the Ad Hoc Parents Committee Against Elitism group for his remarks, Mrs. Llewelyn once again looked over the audience.

"There seems to be even more interest in this issue than the board had anticipated," she began. "We are very concerned that we make no decision until we have benefited from the counsel of all who wish to speak. So, at this point, I am going to table further consideration of this issue and a final vote until Tuesday. We will hold a special board meeting at that time restricted to completing work on this issue. We thank you all for coming."

With a few grumbles, parents and other interested school patrons began filing out of the room. A few came forward to lobby school board members personally. The newspaper reporter gathered up his notebooks, headed for the door, and began thinking of the task of reducing his notes to three to five column inches of final copy for the morning edition. The superintendent, still showing no emotion on his face, fought down a potential stomach cramp. Sighing, he popped another Tums. Turning to Mrs. Llewelyn, he commented, "A nice meeting, Mrs. L. I can't wait until next month when we have something controversial—forced busing. Have a nice evening."

With some variations, some of the themes played out during this board meeting have been sounded over and over again at school board meetings throughout the country when special programs for gifted and talented students have been discussed. Some people are opposed to gifted and talented programs of any kind. Others, probably a much larger group, agree that such programs have a place. But there is bitter disagreement over "proper" characteristics of a gifted and talented program and over procedures to be followed in identifying students who will be enrolled in the program.

Emphasis on programs targeted specifically toward gifted and talented students for many years was not heavy. Only within the last 10 to 15 years has political muscle been placed behind the idea that these students ought to be provided with school programs tailored to their special needs. Much debate rages regarding what characterizes "good" programs for the gifted and talented (and even over whether such programs ought to be provided at all). In this chapter, we will outline some of the major concerns of people interested in education for the gifted and talented. These concerns, we feel, will continue to be much debated by educators in the years ahead. To provide a context for the consideration of major issues in dispute, let us begin with a short historical overview of the concern for educating gifted and talented students in the schools.

GIFTED AND TALENTED EDUCATION: AN HISTORICAL PERSPECTIVE

Early secondary education in the United States was directed primarily at preparing sons of an aristocratic leadership to assume a responsible stewardship for business and governmental affairs. With few exceptions, education was unapologetically elitist. In general, the "talent" was assumed to reside almost exclusively in the minds of the sons of the upper classes. A few, Jefferson, for example, suggested that there might be such a thing as a "natural aristocracy." These natural aristocrats might be sons of quite ordinary people. Jefferson recommended the establishment of procedures to identify these youngsters for special training (Schnur 1980). In a sense, this might be thought of as an effort to identify gifted and talented youngsters who were to be educated to assume positions of leadership. This conclusion, however, must be tempered with the observation that Jefferson envisioned only a very small number of natural aristocrats. The basic assumption continued to be that academic talent and aristocratic birth were, if not inseparable, then very very closely associated.

During the Age of Jackson, the view that an aristocratic elite ought to be the major target of education began to break down. Horace Mann's crusade for the common school spun out a scenario in which youngsters from all social classes would learn together in school. The success of Mann's effort to create a public school system that was viewed as a crucible for democracy for years provided an obstacle to serious consideration of special school programs for gifted and talented students. Schnur has commented on this situation as follows (1980, p. 5):

> The egalitarianism of Jackson and the public school of Mann significantly altered education in the United States and made it unique in the world. The result was the notion of education for all. Once this was accomplished, to educate the gifted began to suggest some sort of caste system within education that some find repugnant.

From the middle of the nineteenth century into the first two decades of the twentieth century, it was not only the philosophical commitment to egalitarian education that prevented secondary schools from establishing special programs for gifted and talented students. Probably an even more compelling reason was that secondary schools at this time tended to enroll only an intellectual elite. That is, a significant percentage of students enrolled in secondary schools at this time would be what, today, we might call gifted and talented. How could this be? Were people smarter in those days than they are now? Not at all. It was simply a question of who went to school. Let us look at some figures.

In school year 1899–1900, only 519,000 students were enrolled in grades 9 through 12 in the entire United States. There were only 62,000 high school graduates in the entire country in that year (National Center for Education Statistics 1979). Seventy-five years later, there were over 14 million students in grades 9 through 12 and between $2\frac{1}{2}$ and 3 million high school graduates (National Center for Education Statistics 1979). What these figures tell us is that only a very small percentage of young people of secondary school age attended secondary schools in 1899–1900. (This same general pattern obtained, with some improvement, through 1920.) Those youngsters in schools tended to be an intellectual elite who attended high school to prepare for college work. Although there were exceptions, a high percentage of these youngsters were intellectually talented. Therefore, school programs placed heavy challenges on all youngsters enrolled. No need was seen for providing special programs for gifted and talented students. Almost by definition a student in a high school was presumed to be gifted and talented, and he or she was taught accordingly.

During the 1920s with an expansion in the percentage of the secondary school-aged population actually enrolled in secondary schools, there began to be a recognition that differences among students were becoming so great that a common pattern of instruction for all was no longer practicable. There were proposals during this period for special programs for gifted and talented youngsters that were designed to challenge their special abilities. A number of forward-looking school systems had special tracks for academically talented youngsters by the end of the decade. Much of the progress that was made in this direction was undone with the onset of the Great Depression of the 1930s.

The contracting American economy of the 1930s resulted in diminished employment opportunity for all. Even some of the most highly qualified college and university graduates were unable to find employment. As a result, the public schools found it difficult to justify expenditures for special programs designed to send eminently prepared young people on to colleges to pursue degrees leading only to the unemployment line. Many school officials had no difficulty voting to cut programs for the gifted and talented in this kind of an environment.

After World War II, schools had to work so hard to expand facilities to accommodate the huge expansion of the population of school-aged children that little attention was devoted to establishing special programs for distinct populations of students, such as the gifted and talented. School officials in many cities felt themselves lucky simply to find places for youngsters to sit. Certainly they were disinclined to do anything that would result in added responsibilities for school planners, administrators, and teachers. This situation began to ease by the mid-1950s. During the latter part of this decade, the Soviet launch of an earth satellite, Sputnik I, prompted a public debate that for a time brought the issue of the education of gifted and talented youngsters very much to the fore.

Some observers saw the Soviet success with Sputnik as direct evidence that American public schools were doing precious little to educate talented young people to their maximum potentials. How else, they reasoned, could the Soviets have launched an earth satellite before the United States? As a result of these concerns, large numbers of scholars with distinguished national and international reputations in their respective subject areas began to interest themselves in public school curricula. Many of them took part in curriculum development efforts during the early 1960s that resulted in the development of secondary school curricula that were thought to have much more intellectual rigor than those they replaced. The National Defense Education Act of 1958 provided monies for many teachers to return to school to receive intensive training to enable them to use these materials effectively.

Many new curricula of the early 1960s were aimed specifically at gifted and talented students. Some developers of these programs went so far as to say that they were designed to provide a solid intellectual base for students who not only would complete college but who would go on to do doctoral-level work. These curriculum development efforts might have proved more successful had the schools of the 1960s been enrolling the same kind of intellectual elite as high schools of 1900 enrolled. But by the 1960s only a minority of all high school graduates went on to complete baccalaureate programs at colleges and universities. Certainly only a tiny percentage of this minority completed doctoral-level work. As a consequence, increasing numbers of students came to see these high school programs as irrelevant to their own interests.

The perception that the new school curricula had little to do with their own aspirations coincided with two cataclysmic events of the mid-1960s. The first was the explosion of the inner cities as blacks and other minorities directly challenged established governmental authority to improve their conditions of life. The second was the war in Vietnam, an episode that increasingly divided the priorities of government policy makers and the population at large. The rise of tensions in the inner cities and the national heartbreak of Vietnam resulted in an increasing suspicion on the part of all citizens of governmental authority. This suspicion came down on the heads of school officials as well. Students and their parents began pressing for more relevant programs. Traditional expectations of school principals and teachers that students would do what they were told to do began to break down. Rigorous academic curricula devised in response to Sputnik could not stand up in this new environment. Schools hurried to develop new programs that appeared more genuinely responsive to the interests of students and their parents.

One result of the social upheavals of the 1960s was a new perception on the part of many groups of students and parents that, when organized, they could influence school practices in a desired direction. Once recognized, this new power prompted the formation of many groups of parents and other patrons who had special interests they wanted served. Many such groups mounted highly sophisticated lobbying campaigns at the local, state, and federal levels on behalf of school programs they favored. Special programs were established for handicapped youngsters, for bilingual students, and for other special populations in the school. Not surprisingly, parents and others interested in gifted and talented youngsters began pressing for more school programs for these youngsters.

Responding to this concern, the U.S. Commissioner of Education in 1971 prepared a status report for Congress on education for the gifted and talented in the United States. This report pointed out that specific programs for the gifted and talented were extremely few in number. This report prompted a great deal of additional interest in programs for gifted and talented students. In 1972, Congress established the Office of Gifted and Talented within the U.S. Office of Education. Gifted and talented children were defined as follows in Public Law 91-230 (*United States Statutes at Large* 1971, p. 153).

(1) The term "gifted and talented children" means, in accordance with objective criteria prescribed by the Commissioner, children who have outstanding intellectual ability or creative talent, the development of which requires special activities or services not ordinarily provided by local educational agencies.

In 1974, responding to additional public interest, Congress, in Public Law 93-380, provided federal funds for local and state educational agencies for the specific purpose of improving programs for the gifted and talented.

Since the middle 1970s, there has been a steady expansion of programs to serve gifted and talented students in the schools. At least some schools in all areas of the country have such programs. Increasing numbers of colleges and universities are offering courses on education for the gifted and talented (Mitchell and Erickson 1978). At this time, only a few states require teachers who work with gifted and talented students to hold a special teaching certificate (Mitchell 1980). However, requirements in this area are tightening, and we may expect more states to have such requirements in the future.

In summary, political factions supporting expansion of programs for gifted and talented youngsters have enjoyed a large measure of success over the past 10 to 15 years. There is reason to expect a continued expansion of special programs for gifted and talented students in the years ahead. This by no means suggests that controversies regarding these programs do not continue to rage (see Figure 14-1). We will be exploring some of these in subsequent sections.

Figure 14-1

ARE PROGRAMS FOR GIFTED AND TALENTED STUDENTS RACIST?
Recently, a caller on a radio talk show made these comments about a proposed new program for gifted and talented students in the school district.

> Look, let's think about this thing as it really is. Whose kids are really going to benefit from this program? In my mind these classes are going to be filled with the kids who live in the fancy houses on the hill. This whole program is simply a political ploy to get the enthusiastic support of these upper-income people. Lots of these folks have all but had it with public education. I mean they are hacked off about busing, about special programs for minorities, and a bunch of other programs that primarily have benefited blacks and Hispanics. They can't oppose these programs directly. To do so would be to leave themselves wide open to the charge of racism. Instead, they have adopted the code words "gifted and talented" programs to hide behind. These programs will result in setting up a situation in the school where their youngsters, disproportionate numbers of whom will be identified as gifted and talented, will not have to rub shoulders in their classes with blacks and Hispanics. The gifted and talented program is a godsend for racists who have long sought a legal mechanism for resegregating the schools.

YOUR OPINION, PLEASE
Read the comments carefully. Then, respond to these questions.

1. Are gifted and talented programs promoters of racism? Why, or why not?
2. How do you assess the general logic of this caller's arguments?
3. Suppose that you were interested in establishing a gifted and talented program that would not be open to charges that it was promoting racism. How would such a program be organized?
4. Suppose that you were the superintendent of the school district that had established the gifted and talented program to which this caller was referring. Suppose that the radio station gave you time to respond to the caller's concerns. What would you say?

WHO ARE THE GIFTED AND TALENTED?

Much of the controversy surrounding programs for the gifted and talented centers on difficulties in deciding exactly which students are gifted and talented. Some have argued that gifted and talented students should be identified by standard intelligence tests. Various cutoff points have been suggested. A number of programs have used minimum measured IQs between 120 and 135 as evidence of "giftedness" (Daurio 1979).

Others have challenged the reliance on standardized IQ scores to identify gifted and talented children. Some have argued that measured IQ, by itself, is too narrow a criterion to use for identifying students of exceptional ability. Others, particularly those concerned with education of students from minority groups, point out that standardized IQ tests are culturally biased. That is, they fail to account for the special values, abilities, and specific cultural-based knowledge of young people from racial and ethnic minorities (Bruch and Curry 1978). Consequently, large numbers of minority group students who are truly gifted and talented will not score well on standardized IQ tests. Note that the arguments of minority critics are not against the importance of intelligence as one characteristic of gifted and talented students. Rather, they charge that standardized test scores are an inappropriate measure of this intelligence.

In addition to intelligence, it has been suggested that gifted and talented students are characterized by an ability to pursue a given objective tenaciously over a long period of time until it is achieved. The high level of personal involvement in their work of gifted and talented individuals has been well documented through the years (Roe 1953;

Terman 1959; MacKinnon 1965). Task commitment then is thought to complement intelligence as one of the characteristics of gifted and talented students.

The elements of intelligence and task commitment suggest that gifted and talented students not only have above-average intellectual abilities but that they characteristically bring these abilities to bear on some task in a purposeful way (see Figure 14-2). It is not just the intelligence itself but what is done with the intelligence that is important. Some specialists in gifted and talented education contend that the simple willingness of a student with high intelligence to keep at a task is not sufficient evidence of the existence of giftedness. There must also be some measure of the nature of what is achieved as a result of the commitment to the task. People such as E. Paul Torrance (1970) have advocated expanding the definition of gifted and talented students to include the dimension of creativity. That is, students who are gifted and talented not only have above-average intellectual abilities and a commitment to task completion but they also tend to complete tasks in unusual, nontraditional ways.

A leading authority in gifted and talented education, Joseph S. Renzulli, has pointed out that a long history of research supports the conclusion that giftedness involves an interaction among the factors of intelligence, task commitment, and creativity (Renzulli 1978). Logically, then, selection procedures used to identify students for inclusion in gifted and talented programs ought to include evidence related to all three areas. As Renzulli (1978) points out, too frequently measures of general intellectual ability alone have been used to identify gifted and talented students. Selection procedures of this type tend to include some students who properly ought not to be included. And they tend to exclude some students who properly ought to be included.

Perhaps the overreliance on measures of intelligence noted by Renzulli results from the abundance of tests to measure general intellectual ability and the relative scarcity of reliable measures of "task commitment" and "creativity." It may well be that the availability of the tools of measurement has prompted undue attention on the factor of intelligence.

Figure 14-2
THE INGREDIENTS OF GIFTEDNESS

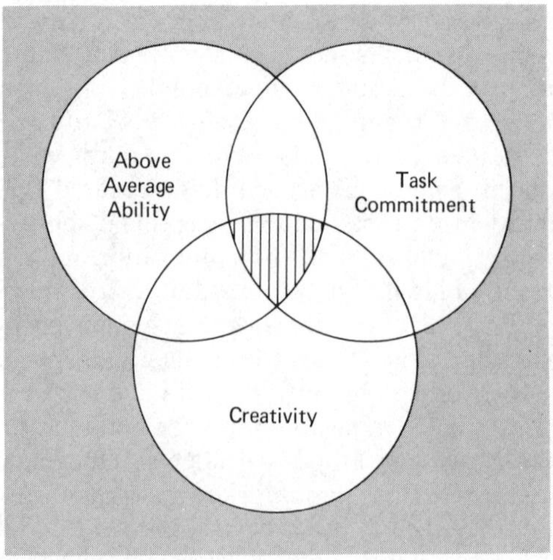

Source: Reprinted with permission from Joseph S. Renzulli, "What Makes Giftedness?" *Phi Delta Kappan,* November 1978, pp. 180–184, 261.

An increasing appreciation of the point that giftedness is a composite of several variables has led administrators of many programs for the gifted and talented to use a variety of sources of information as bases for making decisions about which youngsters will participate. The program for Mentally Gifted Minors in California, for example, selects youngsters based on (1) tests of intellectual ability, (2) records of school achievement, and (3) judgments of teachers, psychologists, and administrators. Further, because of concerns about culturally biased intelligence tests, "scores from IQ tests are inadmissable as the main criterion for excluding or including the child in the program" (Olstad 1978, p. 187). Although there are differences in specific procedures, the California pattern of looking at several kinds of information is one supported today by large numbers of administrators of programs for the gifted and talented.

Through a variety of procedures, today's programs for the gifted and talented seek to identify a very select group of young people. In very rough terms, it has been estimated that about 3 percent of the population of students can be classified as gifted or talented (Mitchell and Erickson 1978). These figures would suggest that between 1 and $1\frac{1}{2}$ million school-aged children can be classified as gifted and talented. About half this number are enrolled in secondary schools. Evidence suggests, however, that fewer than one half of these youngsters presently are provided some sort of school programming that is directly aimed at gifted and talented learners (Mitchell and Erickson 1978). This evidence suggests potential for considerable additional expansion of programs for the gifted and talented.

How do the youngsters involved in these programs feel about them? As one would expect, some like them, some are indifferent, and some are hostile. In general, however, studies reveal that many students who are involved are quite enthusiastic about their experiences. One survey found gifted students to appreciate their inclusion in the special program so long as their involvement did not lead to conflicts with regular class teachers or to antagonistic attitudes on the part of students not in the program. Apparently, most students had no difficulties in these regards because, in the same survey students noted indifferent attitudes toward their participation in the program on the part of other teachers and on the part of friends (Ford 1978).

In a discussion of research reporting on impacts of special gifted and talented programs on students who were enrolled, Tremaine (1979) noted one study where researchers found that students in the program had higher educational goals than did students not in the program. Further, they were found to have higher regard for school in general and their teachers in general than did other students. Finally, they tended to be more involved in school activities and community projects than were students not in the program. Tremaine also reported an absence of data supporting the contention of some critics that students involved would develop condescending attitudes toward other students.

In summary, gifted and talented students are individuals who are characterized by a blend of (1) high intelligence, (2) high task commitment, and (3) high creativity. Most programs for the gifted and talented today consider information from several sources as bases for making decisions regarding which students should enroll in programs (See Figure 14-3). Students who do enroll, in general, have been found to react favorably to their experiences.

KINDS OF PROGRAMS FOR GIFTED AND TALENTED STUDENTS

In general, programs for gifted and talented students sort into two broad categories: enrichment and acceleration. Enrichment programs try to meet needs of these youngsters by providing them with additional or different kinds of learning experiences from those provided for other learners. In programs of this kind, gifted and talented students progress through the school program at the same rate as other students.

Figure 14-3

CRITERIA FOR SELECTING STUDENTS FOR A GIFTED AND TALENTED PROGRAM

YOUR OPINION, PLEASE
Suppose that you had been asked by your principal to provide a set of guidelines for identifying students for a pilot gifted and talented program to be started in your school. How would your guidelines address these questions?

1. How much emphasis would you attach to information you might have about a student regarding (a) his or her IQ, (b) his or her task commitment, and (c) his or her creativity?
2. How would you propose to measure the quality of task commitment?
3. How would you propose to measure the quality of creativity?
4. What provisions, if any, would you suggest to (a) enable students selected initially to drop out of the program and to (b) enable students not selected initially to qualify for the program at a later date?
5. To what extent would your selection guidelines make provisions for selecting minority group students who might not score well on ordinary IQ tests because of culture bias?

Acceleration programs, on the other hand, are designed to increase the pace at which gifted and talented students complete their schooling. For example, a given gifted or talented student might complete the high school program in only two years. As in enrichment programs, students in acceleration programs generally are provided with more challenging content than that provided to other students.

Profound philosophical differences tend to divide proponents of enrichment programs and acceleration programs. In the sections that follow, we shall look at some practices recommended by partisans of each view. We shall also examine some arguments that have been made to support and to criticize each of these positions. A status report on the enrichment versus acceleration debate will conclude this discussion.

Enrichment

Enrichment consists of learning experiences and activities that are above and beyond those of the regular curriculum (Renzulli 1977). Enrichment programs attempt to stretch gifted and talented youngsters by exposing them to experiences that challenge them to make maximum use of their considerable capabilities. Enrichment is thought to be democratic in that it provides opportunities for gifted and talented youngsters to be exposed to learning experiences appropriate to their needs without removing them from contact in regular classes with more typical students.

A number of authorities have developed guidelines for enrichment programs. One of the best known of these is the "enrichment triad model" developed by Joseph S. Renzulli (1977). Renzulli suggests that an enrichment program ought to provide three categories of experiences for learners: (1) general exploratory experiences, (2) group training activities, and (3) individual and small group investigations of real problems.

General exploratory experiences. Learning experiences in this category are designed to introduce students to contents not ordinarily treated in the regular school curriculum.

Group training activities. Learning experiences in this category seek to familiarize students with rational thinking processes and with feeling and valuing processes.

Individual and small-group investigations of real problems. Learning experiences in this category involve students in activities where they apply what they have learned to solve real problems. There is an emphasis on students' developing learning products for which there is a demonstrated need in the real world.

Programs for the gifted and talented that are built around the enrichment triad model attempt to accommodate two key concerns. On the one hand, there is an effort to provide learning experiences that are different from what youngsters otherwise would encounter in the school program. Provision of different experiences assures that these students are not simply being introduced earlier to material that they might encounter at a later date in the regular school program. Where this principle has not been observed, gifted and talented students in the ninth grade, for example, have simply been exposed to eleventh- or twelfth-grade content early. This then creates a problem for teachers when these youngsters reach the eleventh or twelfth grade in that they have already been exposed to the learning experiences typically provided during those years. Because of these difficulties, it has become fairly common for enrichment programs to avoid duplication of content offered in the regular curriculum.

A second concern addressed by the enrichment triad model has to do with a conviction that giftedness implies not simply a set of descriptive characteristics about a given youngster but, rather, a capability to utilize innate talents in a productive way (Delisle 1980). According to this understanding, many enrichment programs require gifted and talented students to engage in activities that result in some kind of "observable end product" (p. 11). In the enrichment triad model, the category of experiences labeled "individual and small group investigations of real problems" attempts to accommodate this need.

The enrichment triad model is one of several frameworks for organizing meaningful programs for gifted and talented students. All these guidelines are efforts to assist teachers in systematic development of enrichment programs. Even programs developed in accordance with these comprehensive planning frameworks have not escaped controversy. Enrichment programs of all kinds continue to generate debate. Let us look at some of the issues that have been raised in these disputes.

Arguments Supporting Enrichment.   Enrichment is democratic. It avoids segregating gifted and talented students from other youngsters in the school. Special needs of gifted and talented students are met within the regular classroom by providing them with learning experiences appropriate for their needs. This arrangement mirrors a real world in which people of all kinds must live and work together. It prevents gifted and talented students from coming to think of themselves as a pretentious elite who need not interact with others.

Enrichment is convenient administratively. Traditionally, American schools have been organized according to an age-based grading scheme in which youngsters progress through school one grade at a time. All age mates remain at a common grade level throughout their school experience. Scheduling patterns, staffing arrangements, and other administrative practices have evolved out of an assumption that age grading is and will remain the norm. Enrichment programs accommodate well with these traditional practices. Gifted and talented students progress through school one year at a time much as do all other students in the school. Consequently, such programs pose few management concerns.

Gifted and talented students benefit from associating with other students of their own age as they progress through the school program. In terms of their social development, these youngsters are no different from others in their age groups. Thus, it makes good sense for them to grow to social maturity with youngsters in their classes who are, socially, at about the same level of development.

There is a psychological advantage to keeping gifted and talented students in regular classes and serving their special needs by providing them with enriched learning experiences. In such classes, they are unlikely to feel such heavy psychological pressures as might result were they to be assigned to special classes including nothing but gifted and talented youngsters. There has been some evidence that, when placed in special classes, gifted and talented students feel that parents, teachers, and administrators expect too much of them. Some, too, are concerned that grading practices in such situations may be unfair. For example, a student who receives a "B" in a special gifted and talented class may well ask himself or herself whether he or she might well have received an "A" in a regular class with a lot less effort. In summary, then, use of enrichment classes has potential to diminish psychological problems for gifted and talented youngsters.

Arguments Opposing Enrichment.   There is no evidence to suggest that gifted and talented students who are in enrichment programs tend to be any more democratic in their outlooks than those in other kinds of programs. Indeed, there is evidence to suggest that most gifted and talented youngsters do not develop into pretentious and condescending snobs. This is true *regardless* of the nature of the school program in which they are enrolled. A number of studies reveal that gifted and talented youngsters enjoy a wide range of positive social relationships with people at every intellectual and social level.

Enrichment may well be administratively convenient, but does that make it "good"? Perhaps yes, perhaps no. The question here is whether administrative convenience ought to be allowed to determine whether a given program is good or bad. Administration, after all, should not be the end but, rather, the means to the end. If an arrangement other than enrichment shows promise, then administrative tradition should not be allowed to stand in the way. It is much more appropriate to change the administrative structure to serve a good end than to abandon a good end because it is not convenient administratively.

It is nonsense to suppose that a great social benefit results because gifted and talented youngsters happen to be enrolled in classes where they sit side by side with regular students. Although a computer may print out a roster of youngsters who are assigned to a given class period, there is no assurance that every youngster in the class will enjoy close social relationships with all others. Such an expectation denies the existence of profound individual differences. What happens in most classes is that youngsters of like interests (and, to some extent, like abilities) tend to develop patterns of association. What we get, then, is a classroom full of many small subgroups. While, certainly, some gifted and talented youngsters may develop warm personal relationships with students in the class who are not gifted and talented, it is folly to predict that this will be a natural result of enrichment programs.

The fear of psychological problems of gifted and talented students is unfounded. Abundant research evidence suggests that gifted and talented youngsters tend to have more positive self-concepts and fewer psychological problems than the general population of young people. Teachers and administrators tend to remember the isolated case or two where a gifted and talented youngster has suffered severe psychological crises. From this unrepresentative sample, they have inferred, incorrectly, that gifted and talented youngsters are prone to psychological problems. In fact, these youngsters probably can stand up to pressures of all kinds as well, if not better, than other youngsters in the school.

Enrichment: Status Report.   Today, enrichment tends by an overwhelming margin to be the preferred mode of dealing with gifted and talented youngsters in the schools (Cohn 1979). The approach enjoys considerable support from parents, counselors, and administrators. It is consistent with the view of the school as a melting pot for students of all kinds. The approach is consistent with the view that we need to produce leaders, but these leaders must be familiar with and able to communicate with people of all kinds. There is a strong cultural bias supporting programs that allow gifted and talented and other students to rub elbows in the schools. Although the approach certainly will continue to draw challenges from some critics, evidence suggests that enrichment will remain the predominant mode for dealing with gifted and talented students in the schools for some time to come. Think about this discussion as you respond to issues raised in Figure 14-4.

Acceleration

Acceleration involves gifted and talented students in "progress through an educational program at rates faster or ages younger than conventional" (Pressey 1949, p. 2). Advocates of acceleration reject the premise that students in schools must proceed through the program one grade and one year at a time. Rather, they take the position that, when capable, students should be provided opportunities to complete the program more quickly. Partisans of acceleration suggest that any potential benefits of keeping bright students in classes with their age mates are outweighed by the potential for boredom and failure to make maximal use of their capabilities (see Figure 14-5). Gifted and talented students, so say advocates of acceleration, should be provided with opportunities to progress through school at rates consistent with their abilities.

There are two basic types of acceleration: subject matter acceleration and grade acceleration. Subject matter acceleration permits a student to take a given course earlier than would normally be the case. For example, a student in grade 8 might be allowed to take an introductory calculus course, usually a grade 12 elective. Grade acceleration

Figure 14-4

CAN ENRICHMENT BE DEFENDED?
Recently, the following letter appeared in a local newspaper in the "Letters to the Editor" column.

Initially, I applauded the efforts of our school board to do something for our gifted and talented students. Like other thinking parents, I said, "About time!" But, now that I have had a chance to look at some of the program specifics, I have some concerns.

It seems that youngsters in the program are going to be exposed to experiences in the arts, in music, in drama, in creative writing, and in the dance. My first blush to this information was "great!" After all, our youngsters need to know about these things. I still feel this way. My concern now is simply this. The gifted and talented program will enroll only about 50 students. That's less than 3 percent of the high school enrollment of 1,800.

Surely these experiences would benefit a much larger group of students than a mere 50. What is there about them that makes them "uniquely suited" to the needs of these select 50? In my judgment, the answer to this question is "nothing." I must protest the restriction of these valuable learning experiences to such a minuscule proportion of the student body.

YOUR OPINION, PLEASE
Read the letter carefully. Then, respond to these questions.

1. In general, do you agree or disagree with the position taken by the writer?
2. If you agree with the writer, what kind of an enrichment program would you develop that would be "uniquely suited" to the needs of the gifted and talented?
3. If you disagree, what response would you make to the writer's logic?
4. If you had a free hand to develop an enrichment program of your own, what would you include? How would you defend your program against charges that it was not "uniquely suited" to the special needs of the gifted?

Figure 14-5

SOME CONCERNS ABOUT ACCELERATION
At a recent school board meeting, a district patron, Mr. Clark Robertson, spoke these words.

My son is very talented in math. I know this sounds a bit pretentious, but he really is. And I have the evidence to support my statement. If some of you would like some independent verification, I would be happy to provide it. But, for now, let's assume I have my facts right.

I am concerned that Robert (that's my son) is not being challenged at school. He has mastered the content they are going to be teaching at the *end* of the course already, and it's only October. He is simply bored silly with having to mechanically solve problems using techniques he's mastered ages ago. I've spoken to his teachers about putting him in a more advanced course and have been told simply that "it can't be done." Now, this seems more than a little unreasonable. I realize the need for administrative policies and all of that, but I think in this case the priorites have been misplaced. It seems to me that my son is suffering because of administrative stone-walling.

It seems to me that we need an accelerated program for students such as my son. I would like to see these kids challenged with as much content as they can handle. If this means they have to take advanced courses, well that's fine. If it means they may have to skip over some required courses, that's all right too. I would even like for them to take some work at the college if they can handle it.

YOUR OPINION, PLEASE
Read the remarks of Mr. Robertson carefully. Then, respond to these questions.

1. Do you generally agree or disagree with his comments?
2. What specific problems might result were the school board to adopt his suggestions? What benefits might come to the district?
3. Suppose you were a member of this school board. How would you comment on Mr. Robertson's remarks?
4. How do you think teachers and other students would react to Mr. Robertson's proposal?

---

occurs when a student is allowed to skip an entire grade to take a complete program of courses that is more advanced than that ordinarily taken by a student of his or her age.

One of the best known acceleration programs that has evolved over a number of years has been part of Julian C. Stanley's Study of Mathematically Precocious Youth (SMPY) (Stanley 1978). In the SMPY program, mathematically talented youths are permitted to take advanced mathematics classes. They are assigned to work with a mentor who is another mathematically talented young person who has mastered the content of at least the first year of university-level calculus. Further, provision has been made for students in the program to earn college credit for advanced work in mathematics when they are able to complete advanced college-level courses successfully. Stanley's program has been in operation for over ten years. It has proved to be highly successful. A number of youngsters in the program have entered college with a substantial number of hours completed at entrance. Many have gone on to complete advanced degrees at an unusually early age. Despite the success of SMPY and other acceleration programs, the principle of acceleration continues to inspire a good deal of debate. Let us look at some arguments that have been put forward both by proponents and opponents.

Arguments Supporting Acceleration.   Acceleration focuses on the needs of the student, not on the needs of the school administration. If a student is capable of doing advanced work, then the administrative structure bends to permit the student to do such work. Acceleration places the focus where it should be—on the individual youngster.

A great deal of evidence suggests that students who are working up to their academic potentials are happier than are students who do not find themselves challenged by the school program. Accelerated programs enable such students to develop a sense of personal satisfaction as they master advanced content in a systematic way. Contrary to the speculations of some opponents of acceleration, gifted and talented students in such programs experience few emotional or behavioral problems.

Acceleration rejects the unstated premise of many of its critics that "there is something wrong" with gifted and talented programs. Only a view of unusual brilliance as something aberrant could underlie a decision to keep gifted and talented students in age-graded classrooms and force them to consume a school program designed more to help them conform than to help them progress. Acceleration takes the position that giftedness is a blessing. Acceleration represents a response that is truly consistent with this view.

Students in accelerated programs do not think of themselves as so different from the rest of the population that they cannot communicate with typical students or adults. Indeed, evidence suggests that they have very broad social interests. The notion that they see themselves as some kind of a pampered elite may be a popular view. But it simply is not supported by evidence.

Youngsters who are involved in accelerated programs are overwhelmingly supportive of their experiences. These students are eager to move ahead faster than they could were they to be locked into the traditional grade-by-grade and course-by-course structure. Acceleration permits them to achieve goals that require a satisfying stretching of their capacities. These youngsters are not bored. They tend to become increasingly alert, confident, and proud of their achievements.

Arguments Opposing Acceleration.   Acceleration puts too much pressure on gifted and talented youngsters to succeed. Parents, teachers, counselors, and other students expect such youngsters academic performance to be an unbroken string of excellence. These expectations can lead to frustration, self-doubt, and finally a decision to give up. The potential for academic "burn-out" of youngsters in accelerated programs is high.

Social adjustment of youngsters in accelerated programs can be difficult. This is particularly true when they find themselves in classrooms with students who are much older. A bright eighth-grader, for example, who finds himself in classrooms with twelfth-grade students may have a difficult time accommodating to the male-female role relationships common among high school seniors. These social difficulties may lead to profound self-image problems.

Acceleration programs frequently do not resolve the problem of what to do with the youngster who has completed the program. Suppose, for example, a student completes high school at age 11 and college or university at age 15. Is he or she really capable of functioning in the world at such a tender age? Given widespread legal restrictions that prevent hiring of people under 18 years of age, there may well be no place for youngsters who complete educations while very young.

Tests of academic talent that are employed frequently as part of the criteria used to select youngsters for acceleration programs are anything but foolproof. Consequently, underqualified youngsters who have been enrolled have not stood up well under pressures associated with acceleration programs. When they have returned to regular classrooms, some have felt themselves to be failures. Involvement in acceleration programs may well result in a perfectly capable boy or girl inappropriately deciding that he or she will not make much of a mark in life.

Acceleration Programs: Status Report.   Despite the substantial research that points to the success of acceleration as a response to dealing with gifted and talented students, the percentage of gifted and talented students in accelerated programs is very small as compared with the percentage in enrichment programs. There continues to be a strong bias against acceleration on the part of administrators, teachers, and parents. If evidence of the success of acceleration programs continues to mount, in time we might expect to see a larger number of them in the schools. For the foreseeable future, however, acceleration probably will continue to take a back seat to enrichment.

TEACHERS OF GIFTED AND TALENTED STUDENTS

In recent years, there have been a number of attempts to specify the teacher characteristics associated with success in teaching gifted and talented students. James O. Schnur (1980) has reviewed certain of these efforts and has identified some common themes running through most descriptions of capable teachers of the gifted and talented. Let us look at some of these themes.

Maturity and Security

Successful teachers of gifted and talented youngsters are themselves very bright people who do not feel threatened by very bright students. These teachers tend to have unusual depth and expertise in their respective teaching specialties. They have a desire to work with gifted and talented students. They are able to deal calmly and rationally with the unexpected.

Creativity and Flexibility

These teachers tend to have a versatility of interests. Many of these interests tend to be of an intellectual nature. In general, successful teachers of the gifted and talented tend to be individuals who are regarded as among the more stimulating and imaginative teachers on the staff. They tend to embrace and enjoy original and creative ideas.

Ability to Individualize

Many educators talk about the need to individualize. Successful teachers of the gifted and talented are able to go beyond a verbalized concern for individualization to an actual implementation of individualization in the classroom. They are able to tailor programs to the special needs of youngsters with whom they work. To accomplish this objective, they know how to utilize a wide variety of instructional techniques.

Teaching for Depth of Understanding

Successful teachers of the gifted and talented recognize a need to teach students to apply, analyze, synthesize, and evaluate what they have learned. They know that true understanding demands mental processes going beyond simple recall of facts. Generally, teachers who work well with gifted and talented students have demonstrated their instructional effectiveness with ordinary students in regular classrooms.

General Operating Characteristics

These teachers are characterized by a strong drive for achievement. They tend to have very warm working relationships with their students, whom they tend to like very much as individuals. Successful teachers of gifted and talented tend to be very student oriented. They also generally recognize that all productive learning need not take place in the classroom. Typically they support the practice of releasing students from formal classroom settings to study topics on their own initiatives.

Preparation of Teachers

Few states require special teaching certificates for those who aspire to work with gifted and talented youngsters. A very small number require such teachers to take some special courses. The vast majority of states have no special degree, certificate, or course requirements for teachers seeking to work with gifted and talented youngsters (Mitchell 1980). This situation may be changing in the years ahead as the expansion of gifted and talented programs generates a greater demand for teachers to work with these youngsters. Indeed, there is evidence that teacher preparation institutions are beginning to respond to this situation. In recent years there has been a great expansion in the number of courses on the gifted and talented offered. Such courses are now available in at least one institution in all but a handful of states.

Because of an absence of widespread special degree and certification requirements, most teachers of the gifted have moved into this role from regular classroom teaching positions. These moves have come about for a number of reasons. In some districts, teachers have been asked to volunteer for such programs. In others, they have been "volunteered" by the superintendent or by other school officials.

Teachers new to the role of teaching gifted and talented youngsters have developed expertise in working with these students through on-the-job training and through special in-service programs. There has been a great expansion in the past ten years of the number of in-service programs provided to help refine the skills of teachers of gifted and talented youngsters. Surveys reveal a trend for these programs to be increasing in number (Mitchell and Erickson 1978).

In summary, the demand for teachers of gifted and talented youngsters is on the upswing. It is likely that the many courses now available in teacher preparation institutions for students interested in teaching gifted and talented youngsters will begin to be clustered into more formal areas of emphasis. There is a good probability that specialized degree patterns and certificates for teachers of the gifted and talented will become more common in the years ahead than they are today.

Posttest

Directions: Using your own paper, answer each of the following true/false questions. For each correct statement, write the word "true." For each incorrect statement, write the word "false."

_____ 1. Gifted and talented students tend to suffer from more emotional problems than do "normal" students.

_____ 2. There is considerable dispute today regarding kinds of procedures that should be used to identify gifted and talented students.

_____ 3. The vast majority of states require teachers who work with gifted and talented students to hold special teaching certificates certifying their competence to work with students of this type.

_____ 4. About 3 percent of the school-aged population in the United States is gifted and/or talented.

_____ 5. Today, there is nearly universal agreement that standardized tests alone should be used to identify students who are gifted and talented.

_____ 6. Some critics argue that special programs for gifted and talented students promote undemocratic elitism in the schools.

_____ 7. There tends to be more support for gifted and talented programs that involve enrichment activities for these students in regular classrooms than for programs that provide special accelerated classes for these students.

_____ 8. Students who are gifted and talented tend to "burn out" early. Most do not make significant contributions in later life.

_____ 9. Some critics of gifted and talented programs are concerned about value received for monies expended.

_____ 10. Since the early 1970s, the federal government has taken an active role in support of education for the gifted and talented.

Key Ideas in Review

1. Programs for the gifted and talented have prompted considerable controversy. Some say that such programs are undemocratic and promote unhealthy elitism. Others contend that selection procedures are faulty and that students of ethnic and racial minorities are underrepresented. Still others point out that the real impact of these programs, which may be expensive to maintain, has not been demonstrated. On the other side, supporters argue that brilliant students are not challenged by the regular school program. They contend that programs for the gifted and talented are needed to prevent underutilization of the mental capacities of bright students.

2. One impetus for the creation of gifted and talented students in secondary schools has been the change in the makeup of the student population over the past 80 or so years. At one time, only an intellectual elite attended secondary schools. Consequently, nearly all students, by today's standards, might have been regarded as gifted and talented. Today, nearly the entire population of young people of secondary school age actually attends secondary schools. This means that there has been a great broadening in the range of intellectual abilities in middle schools, junior high schools, and senior high schools. Consequently, there is a need, some say, for special programs for gifted and talented students.

3. There has been a great increase in the interest of the federal government in programs for gifted and talented youngsters since about 1970. Today there is a federal Office of Gifted and Talented. Further, the federal government provides some support money for gifted and talented programs that is paid to states and to local school districts.

4. Proper selection of youngsters for inclusion in gifted and talented programs has been a problem. There has been a disinclination, in most cases, to rely only on standardized tests of intelligence. These have been felt to measure only one dimension of giftedness. Further, there have been concerns about possible cultural biases of such tests. Today, information from a variety of sources (tests, teacher recommendations, counselor recommendations, and so forth) is used to identify program participants.

5. One leading authority (Renzulli 1978) suggests that giftedness includes a combination of three basic trait categories: above-average ability, task commitment, and creativity. In considering how an individual ranks in terms of each of these categories there are some problems. For example, creativity is difficult to measure.

6. The kinds of programs provided to gifted and talented students tend to be of two basic types. One type attempts to provide enrichment experiences for gifted and talented students who continue to be enrolled in regular classrooms. The other type attempts to accelerate the progress of gifted and talented youngsters through school by allowing them either to skip grades or to enroll in more advanced course work. There tend to be vastly more enrichment programs in existence than acceleration programs.

7. Today, although courses providing information about working with gifted and talented students are widely available, few states require teachers of these youngsters to hold special degrees or certificates. This situation may be changing with the increased demand for teach-

ers of the gifted and talented. Most teachers of these youngsters have gotten their training through a combination of in-service work and on-the-job experiences.

SUMMARY

Because of the diverse population of youngsters now enrolled in secondary schools, there is increasing concern that members of certain subgroups have not been well served. These concerns have prompted an interest in establishing special programs for such youngsters. One such group for whom special services have been proposed and implemented consists of gifted and talented students. Since 1970, there has been a tremendous expansion of the number of programs for the gifted and talented in secondary schools.

Perhaps one of the biggest controversies that has surrounded education for the gifted and talented has to do with criteria to be applied in identifying students. In particular, members of cultural and ethnic minorities have been concerned about potential abuse of culturally biased tests as a basis for a selection. To protect themselves from charges of racism and because evidence suggests that measured intellectual ability is not alone a sufficient ground for assuming giftedness, most administrators of programs for gifted and talented students select participants using a variety of criteria.

In general, there are two types of programs for gifted and talented students. Most programs are of the enrichment variety. In enrichment programs, gifted and talented students progress through school at the same rate as their age mates, but they are provided with learning experiences tailored to their own special needs. In acceleration programs, students are encouraged to progress through the school program at a faster rate than normally would be expected. Students in such programs may skip grades or they may take courses that are well beyond what a student of their age would ordinarily take.

In general, programs for gifted and talented students are increasing in number. This increase may spawn an expansion of special degree and certification requirements for teachers who work with gifted and talented youngsters in the schools. Today, however, most teachers of the gifted and talented have learned to work with these students through a combination of in-service work and on-the-job training.

References

Bruch, Catherine B., and Curry, James A. "Personal Learnings: A Current Synthesis on the Culturally Different Gifted," *The Gifted Child Quarterly* (Fall 1978): 313–321.

Cohn, Sanford J. "Acceleration and Enrichment: Drawing the Base Lines for Further Study," in William C. George, Sanford J. Cohn, and Julian C. Stanley, Eds., *Educating the Gifted: Acceleration and Enrichment,* pp. 3–12. Baltimore: Johns Hopkins University Press, 1979.

Daurio, Stephen P. "Educational Enrichment Versus Acceleration: A Review of the Literature," in William C. George, Sanford J. Cohn, and Julian C. Stanley, eds., *Educating the Gifted: Acceleration and Enrichment.* Baltimore: Johns Hopkins University Press, 1979.

Delisle, James. "Education of the Gifted: Coming and Going," *Roeper Review* (May–June 1980): 11–14.

Ford, Barbara. "Student Attitudes Toward Special Programming and Identification," *The Gifted Child Quarterly* (Winter 1978): 489–497.

MacKinnon, Donald W. "Personality and the Realization of Creative Potential," *American Psychologist* (April 1965): 273–281.

Mitchell, Bruce M. "What's Happening to Gifted Education in the U.S. Today?" *Roeper Review* (May–June 1980): 7–10.

Mitchell, Patricia Bruce, and Erickson, Donald K. "The Education of Gifted and Talented Children: A Status Report," *Exceptional Children* (September 1978): 12–16.

National Center for Education Statistics. *The Condition of Education, 1979.* Washington, D.C.: U.S. Government Printing Office, 1979.

Olstad, Deborah. "The Pursuit of Excellence Is Not Elitism," *Phi Delta Kappan* (November 1978): 187–188, 229.

Pressey, S. L. "Educational Acceleration: Appraisal and Basic Problems." Bureau of Educational Research Monographs, No. 31. Columbus: Ohio State University Press, 1949.

Renzulli, Joseph S. *The Enrichment Triad Model: A Guide for Developing Defensible Programs for the Gifted and Talented.* Wethersfield, Conn.: Creative Learning Press, 1977.

———. "What Makes Giftedness: Re-examining a Definition," *Phi Delta Kappan* (November 1978): 180–184, 261.

Roe, Anne. *The Making of a Scientist.* New York: Dodd, Mead & Company, 1953.

Schnur, James O. "Teachers for the Gifted—Past, Present, and Future," *Roeper Review* (May–June 1980): 5–7.

Stanley, Julian C. "SMPY's DT-PI Mentor Model: Diagnostic Testing Followed by Prescriptive Instruction," *Intellectually Talented Youth Bulletin,* Vol. 4, No. 10 (1978): 7.

Terman, Lewis M., and others. *Genetic Studies of Genius: The Gifted Group at Mid-Life.* Stanford, Calif.: Stanford University Press, 1959.

Torrance, E. Paul. "Broadening Concepts of Giftedness in the 70s," *Gifted Child Quarterly* (Winter 1970): 199–208.

Tremaine, Claire D. "Do Gifted Programs Make a Difference?" *Gifted Child Quarterly* (Fall 1979): 500–517.

United States Statutes at Large. 91st Congress, 1970–1971, Vol. 84, Part 1. Washington, D.C.: U.S. Government Printing Office, 1971.

15

Teaching Handicapped Students

"I welcome you to our conference on the handicapped. I can see that some of us are not too familiar with the mainstreaming concept."

Objectives

This chapter provides information to help the reader to

1. Describe requirements of Public Law 94-142.
2. Define "appropriate education" as it applies to handicapped students.
3. Point out what must be included in individualized educational plans designed for handicapped students.

4. Define the term "least restrictive environment."

5. Distinguish among different handicapping conditions.

6. Suggest general responses that teachers can make in responding to the needs of students with different handicapping conditions.

Pretest

Directions: Using your own paper, answer each of the following true/false questions. For each correct statement, write the word "true." For each incorrect statement, write the word "false."

_____ 1. It has been a practice in American schools for generations to provide some educational experiences for *all* handicapped youngsters.

_____ 2. To fulfill the "appropriate education" component of legislation relating to handicapped youngsters, a school must do nothing other than place handicapped youngsters in classes designed exclusively for handicapped learners.

_____ 3. By law, parents are to be included when individualized educational plans for handicapped students are developed.

_____ 4. The language "least restrictive environment" means that every handicapped youngster must spend the entire school day in a regular classroom alongside nonhandicapped learners.

_____ 5. Most classroom teachers in the schools today, as undergraduates, received extensive training on procedures for working with handicapped students who were enrolled in regular classrooms alongside nonhandicapped students.

_____ 6. Emotionally disturbed students are included among those classified as "handicapped."

_____ 7. Students categorized as "educable" tend to have relatively short attention spans and to become frustrated easily.

_____ 8. In working with hearing-impaired students, teachers are advised to face the class at all times when they are giving information orally.

_____ 9. "Learning disabled" students have problems in understanding or using spoken or written language.

_____ 10. There is no existing federal legislation relating to treatment of handicapped learners in the schools.

INTRODUCTION

As sensitive people, educators have had a long history of concern for working with students having special needs. For years, large numbers of handicapped students have received some training in public schools in so-called "special classrooms." Teachers interested in working with these youngsters took specialized courses during their undergraduate years in preparation for this work. In general, there was an assumption that these youngsters would not be served by regular teachers in regular classrooms. The expectation was that they would be taught in special classrooms that enrolled small numbers of youngsters with handicaps (and no nonhandicapped students).

This long-standing method of dealing with handicapped learners first began to be questioned seriously about 15 years ago. Two specific arguments began to draw public attention to the issue of educating the handicapped. On the one hand, it was pointed out that, although many handicapped children were receiving some services from public schools in so-called "special education classrooms," many others were not enrolled. Investigations revealed that, if youngsters were characterized by conditions with which existing special education classrooms were not equipped to deal, these students frequently received no education at all. Many of them simply stayed at home.

Further, concern developed for the adequacy of the education being provided for those handicapped youngsters for whom schools were providing some services. Some argued that programs that put youngsters with a variety of handicaps into single classrooms assured that many of their needs could not be met adequately. Differences among individuals were simply felt to be too great. Further, critics pointed out that these youngsters were being unfairly isolated from contact with nonhandicapped youngsters and with the kinds of instruction available to these nonhandicapped learners.

A bottom-line result of these concerns was that parents and others interested in handicapped learners in the late 1960s and early 1970s increasingly protested what they felt to be inadequacies in school services provided for handicapped youngsters. Numerous lawsuits were brought that, in general, attempted to establish the point that school practices, in effect, were depriving handicapped children of "life, liberty, and property" and that this was happening without due process of law as required by the Fourteenth Amendment to the U.S. Constitution.

A watershed case was brought to court in 1972, when the Pennsylvania Association for Retarded Children sued the State of Pennsylvania on behalf of mentally retarded learners in the state. The suit charged that these individuals were receiving instruction that was inadequate or that they were receiving no instruction at all. The court decided for the plaintiffs. The case established an important precedent giving mentally retarded learners a right to access to educational services provided by public schools.

Soon, numerous other cases were filed. A number of basic principles flowed from the decisions. Generally, it was held that handicapped individuals were capable of benefiting from educational services. Second, it was determined that handicapped learners had a right to education in a public school setting. Finally, it was determined that schools must provide due process safeguards when classifying individuals as handicapped or making arrangements regarding the placement of handicapped students in school programs.

These court cases and continued pressures by interested groups of parents and citizens began to attract the attention of federal legislative leaders in the early 1970s. Ultimately, interest in the issue of educational services for the handicapped resulted in the passage of federal laws laying down specific standards for treatment of handicapped learners in the schools. This legislation has had an important impact on school programs in every school district in the country. In the sections that follow, particular features of key federal legislation and some implications for those who have handicapped youngsters in their classrooms will be introduced. See Figure 15-1, which considers this problem further.

PUBLIC LAW 94-142

As a result of citizen interest, the Senate in the early 1970s held a number of hearings on the status of education for handicapped individuals in the public schools of the United States. Among other things the senators learned that over 1 million handicapped youngsters in the country were receiving no educational services whatever from the schools. These findings and continued pressures from constituencies representing the interests of handicapped individuals led to the enactment in 1975 of the Education for All Handicapped Act, Public Law 94-142. This piece of legislation has been called the "Bill of Rights for Handicapped Children."

Public Law 94-142 was a very different kind of federal legislation for educators. Traditionally, most federal laws had established certain goals or objectives. Means of achieving these goals or objectives had been left largely to state and local school authorities. Public Law 94-142, on the other hand, not only specified goals and objectives but went on to speak in very specific terms about how schools should achieve these goals and objectives. Some of these required processes have resulted in dramatic changes in

Figure 15-1

SHOULD THE GOVERNMENT TELL SCHOOLS *HOW* TO SERVE THE HANDICAPPED?

I think it's great for the federal government to tell public schools that they ought to provide services to the handicapped. I mean, if the government didn't do this, some irresponsible school districts (and even in the 1980s, there are still some of them around) would just do nothing for these kids.

But where I part company from the federal government is when they tell districts exactly *how* they should serve the handicapped. Take this Education for All Handicapped Law, for instance. The law *tells* school districts that the only appropriate way they can teach handicapped youngsters is through the use of individualized programs. Well, that may or, more importantly, *may not* be true. I mean, certainly there are likely to be *some* handicapped students for whom individualized programs are not the best answer. I think the professionals in the local schools should be able to judge how to provide educational services to handicapped kids. They are closer to the youngsters. They know the parents. They know the general environment each youngster comes from. I think we would be a lot better off if the federal government would keep its nose out of specific program planning. Let Washington tell us the general problem that has to be solved. But let the people at the local level decide the specific steps that are to be taken to solve it.

Statement made by a concerned citizen at a school board meeting

YOUR OPINION, PLEASE

Read the comments above. Then, respond to these questions.

1. Do you believe that the federal government should pass no laws regarding the conduct of education in local school districts? If you do, why do you take this position? If you do not, why do you oppose this position?

2. If we accept the reality that there will be federal legislation related to education, should this legislation be limited to identifying broad goals to be met? Or should it make reference to specific steps that must be taken at the local level?

3. The Education for All Handicapped Act represented something of a break with tradition in that, unlike many previous laws, it prescribed very specific steps to be taken by local school officials rather than simply requiring that something be done, but leaving the means of accomplishment up to local officials. Why do you suppose that Congress chose to include such specific language in this law? Do you expect future education legislation to continue to impose very specific requirements on local school districts? Or would you anticipate a return to the more traditional practice of leaving specific responses up to the discretion of state and local authorities?

---

schools' responses to the needs of handicapped learners. To understand some of these changes, let us look at the specific provisions of the law.

Appropriate Education

Public Law 94-142 requires that all handicapped learners be provided an "appropriate education." Congress chose to define an appropriate education as one that is designed to meet the particular needs of the individual handicapped youngster. To accomplish this end, the law requires that an individualized educational plan (I.E.P.) be designed for every handicapped student. The I.E.P. must include the following elements:

1. An assessment of the student's entering level of achievement. This must include academic achievement, vocational skills, psychomotor skills, self-help skills, and social skills.
2. An identification of long-term goals to be achieved.
3. Measurable short-term objectives that begin with a student's entry-level attainment and proceed forward to the long-term goals.

4. A description of the educational services that will be provided to meet the unique learning needs of the handicapped individual.
5. The dates when these services will be started and when they will be terminated.
6. Objective criteria that will be used to make an assessment (to be accomplished at least once a year) of whether or not short-term objectives are being achieved.
7. An indication of the extent to which the individual may participate in regular educational programs.

A completed I.E.P. is a document that functions as management tool. It allows school professionals and parents to learn what school resources have been committed to support the education of their handicapped youngster. Further, it enables them to monitor the effectiveness of these services as the instructional plan goes forward. A sample I.E.P. form is presented in Figure 15-2.

Figure 15-2

SAMPLE INDIVIDUALIZED EDUCATIONAL PLAN FORM

STUDENT: _____   SUBJECT AREA: _____

TEACHER: _____   ENTRY DATE: _____

SUMMARY OF ENTRY-LEVEL PERFORMANCE: _____

_____

_____

PRIORITIZED LONG-TERM GOALS: _____

_____

Behavioral Objectives	Materials or Resources Needed	Person Responsible to	Date Started	Date Ended	Date of Evaluation

Continuum of Services	Hrs. Per Week	Committee Members:
Regular Classroom	_____	_____
Resource Teacher in Regular Class	_____	_____
Resource Room	_____	_____
Specialists (specify)	_____	_____
Counselor	_____	_____
Special Class	_____	Date I.E.P. Approved _____
Others	_____	Meeting Dates _____

The I.E.P. requirement of Public Law 94-142 imposes several responsibilities on classroom teachers. First, teachers are expected to be capable of diagnosing entry-level achievement of youngsters for whom I.E.P.s are being planned. Further, they must be capable of identifying long-term learning goals and of developing a sequential set of program objectives that, when completed, will result in achievement of the established long-term goals. Finally, the teacher has to be competent in the area of evaluation. I.E.P.s include specific reference to objective criteria that are to be used in evaluating student progress.

This kind of expertise represents nothing new. For years certain educators have been advocating the kind of diagnostic-prescriptive model of teaching that is described in the I.E.P.s for handicapped learners. In the past, however, there was no external requirement that this kind of an approach be used. Some teachers elected to organize their programs in this way. Others chose not to do so. What Public Law 94-142 has done is to require all teachers to become familiar with the components of diagnostic-prescriptive planning. Clearly, this has meant more of a transition for those who have not used the approach previously than for those who have.

The requirement to develop I.E.P.s for each handicapped student has placed additional time burdens on secondary school teachers. Typically parents and other professionals are involved as I.E.P. planning goes forward. This usually necessitates meetings before or after school. Further, because several individuals are involved, it can take time to come to a consensus on how a given youngster might be served best. Although they are generally interested in serving the needs of the handicapped as well as those of other youngsters in their classes, some teachers have found themselves frustrated by the time demands imposed by Public Law 94-142. Certainly this legislation continues to be a topic of lively debate in the nation's faculty lounges (see Figure 15-3).

Figure 15-3

IS THERE A HIDDEN AGENDA BEHIND THE I.E.P. REQUIREMENT?

Now, I don't mind working with these handicapped kids. I don't even object to these endless meetings we have with parents, counselors, administrators, and who knows who else. But I am *very* suspicious about these I.E.P.s. I mean, I don't like the fact that we commit everything to writing and turn them into almost a contract.

The difficulty is just this. We have a group of people deciding what the goals, objectives, and so forth are to be for a given student. But the only person who has the responsibility for *accomplishing* these goals is me. I feel like I am left holding the bag for decisions made by a bunch of other people. If the youngster doesn't achieve what the group has said he or she is supposed to achieve, then I'm the guilty party. I just don't like to be put in the spot of having to guarantee success for every handicapped student I work with.

Statement by a senior high school teacher

YOUR OPINION, PLEASE

Read the statement above. Then, respond to these questions.

1. Do you agree with this individual's statement? Why, or why not?
2. Do you believe that the objective of the I.E.P. requirement of Public Law 94-142 is to make the teacher totally responsible for learning of a handicapped student, or do you believe that it is simply a management device designed to identify specifically what is to be done?
3. Should teachers be responsible for what their students learn? Why, or why not?
4. Would you favor legislation requiring development of I.E.P.s for *all* students in schools, not just for the handicapped? Why, or why not?

Least Restrictive Environment

Public Law 94-142 requires that handicapped students be taught in the "least restrictive environment." This means that the handicapped youngster will be placed in the least restrictive environment where he or she can be expected to profit from the provided educational experiences. This does not mean that all handicapped learners must be placed in regular classrooms. This does not mean that there will be no remaining special classes for certain kinds of youngsters. What it *does* mean is that, if the individual can function for the entire day or for part of the day in a regular classroom, then he or she must be placed in a regular classroom for the entire day or for part of the day.

The least restrictive environment provision means that there are great differences in how different handicapped youngsters spend the school day. Some spend all day in a regular classroom. Some spend part of the day in a regular classroom and part of a day in a special classroom. Some spend all day in a special classroom. The policy of placing handicapped youngsters, to the extent possible, in regular classrooms is called *mainstreaming*. Public Law 94-142 encourages mainstreaming for handicapped youngsters who can profit from it. They are thought to benefit not only from the instruction in regular classroom settings but also from their associations with non-handicapped youngsters.

The mainstreaming concept represents a break with the tradition of placing handicapped youngsters in special classrooms where they spent the school day in isolation from other learners in the school. Critics of this formerly common practice suggested that it tended to attach an unfair stigma to handicapped youngsters that would stay with them throughout their lives. Further, surveys revealed that in some places disproportionately high numbers of racial minority youngsters were enrolled in special classrooms for handicapped youngsters. This raised suspicions that special education placements, in some instances at least, had resulted more out of an interest in keeping minority youngsters out of regular classrooms than in determining whether they were handicapped and in actual need of special services.

Individuals who have argued in favor of mainstreaming point out that benefits accrue not only to the handicapped youngsters but to the nonhandicapped students as well. The "regular" students learn to overcome fears and prejudices they may have harbored against handicapped learners as they work with them in their classrooms and increasingly come to recognize that, in most respects, "they are just like us."

Mainstreaming has caused teachers to make certain adjustments. We need to recall that all teachers who were trained prior to the mid- and late 1970s likely received no instruction on working with handicapped youngsters in regular classrooms. When they were undergraduates, it was assumed that such youngsters would be assigned to special classrooms. Therefore, little mention (if indeed any) was made of the handicapped learner in most undergraduate teacher preparation programs (except, of course, those directed toward future special education teachers). The presence of handicapped youngsters in regular classrooms has increased the range of differences among individuals with whom teachers must work. Many districts have provided teachers with training to prepare them to work with those handicapped students who now spend a part, or all, of their day in regular classrooms. Although certainly adjustments have had to be made, large numbers of teachers have come to recognize that handicapped youngsters are simply not all that different from the other students in their classes (see Figure 15-4). As one of the authors' colleagues put it, "these are just some of the kids who come to school."

Procedural Safeguards

To guarantee that provisions of Public Law 94-142 were met, a number of procedural safeguards were mandated. Generally, these procedures relate to the issues of safe-

Figure 15-4

HOW DO YOU FEEL ABOUT HAVING HANDICAPPED YOUNGSTERS IN YOUR CLASSROOM?
  You are teaching in your subject area at the junior high school level. Your principal informs you that you will have some handicapped youngsters in your classes this year. You haven't been to the I.E.P. meetings yet, but you suppose that some of these students might be in class every day, while others may be attending only part of the time.

YOUR OPINION, PLEASE
Think about the situation described above. Then, respond to these questions.

1. What are your initial feelings about having handicapped students in your classes?
2. What assumptions about the entry-level learning capabilities of your students might you have to reconsider?
3. What specific things you had planned to do might prove difficult for students with certain kinds of handicaps?
4. What will you do first to prepare yourself?
5. How will you prepare other youngsters in your class for the inclusion of these handicapped learners?

---

guarding students' due process rights and including parents or guardians of handicapped youngsters in the educational decision-making process.

Once a student is identified as an individual having a handicapping condition, both educators and parents must be involved in determining how the school will serve this youngster. Often a committee known as an admissions, review, and dismissal (ARD) committee is formed. Such a committee is likely to include a representative from the school district who is qualified to supervise or provide services to handicapped learners, the teacher or teachers of the student in question, the parents or guardians of the students, and, sometimes, the student himself or herself. The committee takes responsibility for gathering all information needed before decisions can be made resulting in preparation of an individual educational plan for the student.

Procedural safeguards related to due process, among other things, permit parents to demand a hearing if they disagree with what is written in the I.E.P. The content of these hearings varies from state to state. Typically parents have the right to have decisions reviewed by a disinterested and impartial hearing officer. Usually, too, they can demand an independent evaluation of their youngster should they be dissatisfied with what the school district has done in the areas of diagnosing and making recommendations for their child.

Some teachers and administrators have been a little uneasy about the due process protections afforded to parents under Public Law 94-142. There has been some concern that parents with unrealistic expectations about what their handicapped youngster can do might tie up school officials in long and tedious hearings. While certainly such incidents have occurred, generally the inclusion of parents as planning for the I.E.P.s goes forward has served to open lines of communications between parents and school officials. Concerns of parents, generally, have been reflected in I.E.P. documents. Consequently, the incidence of challenges by parents to I.E.P.s has been relatively low.

Personnel Development

Public Law 94-142 recognized the need to train teachers to work in regular classrooms with handicapped youngsters. The law requires each local school district to specify procedures to be used to prepare personnel to work with handicapped students. This feature of the law is designed to ensure that teachers will have the knowledge base thought necessary for provisions of Public Law 94-142 to be implemented successfully. In keeping with this concern, workshops on mainstreaming have become a common feature of teacher in-service programs across the country.

Public Law 94-142: Status Report

Implications of Public Law 94-142 continue to be much debated in the educational community. As might be expected, some educators feel that the law has resulted in the first positive actions in years to improve the level of school services being provided to handicapped youngsters. These individuals point with pride to the large increases in enrollments of handicapped youngsters in school programs since passage of this watershed federal legislation. They take satisfaction, too, from what they see as a dramatic increase in the quality of programs being provided to handicapped youngsters.

On the other side, some educators express concerns that the law requires them to spend so much time preparing I.E.P.s and in meeting other requirements of the law that the services provided to so-called "normal" students have suffered. Many of these critics have been especially unhappy about the extensive paperwork involved in managing programs for handicapped youngsters. Further, substantial numbers of teachers have experienced feelings of anxiety about how they should work with handicapped youngsters in their classrooms. Many have had no formal course work on this issue, and some say that district in-service support has been inadequate.

What we need to keep in mind as we consider points made both by proponents and critics of Public Law 94-142 is that the debate tends to be over "means," not over "ends." This is not a debate between one faction that supports educational services for the handicapped and another that opposes such services. Educators on both sides of the controversy, in general, are sincerely interested in helping handicapped students to extract the most possible benefit from their school experiences. The debate centers on *how* this ought to be accomplished. Some say that Public Law 94-142 provides an appropriate answer. Others say that it does not. This general debate appears certain to be one that will be with us for some time to come.

KINDS OF HANDICAPPING CONDITIONS

As we begin to think about the issue of working with handicapped youngsters in the classroom, we need some basic understandings of the different types of handicapping conditions we might encounter. Any attempt to categorize handicapping conditions is risky. First, broad categories often mask considerable differences among individuals within each category. Further, a good many youngsters are likely to have multiple handicaps. For example, we might have a youngster who is both visually impaired and emotionally disturbed. The categories to be described in later sections should not be regarded as exclusive. A good many handicapped students in our classes may have several concurrent handicaps.

In general, a handicapped student can be defined as "an individual who has a mental or physical condition that prevents him or her from succeeding in a program designed for individuals who are not characterized by this condition or these conditions." Various authorities use different schemes to organize handicapping conditions into categories for purposes of description and analysis. For our purposes, we will consider the major kinds of handicapping conditions to be (1) mental retardation, (2) hearing impairment, (3) speech impairment, (4) visual impairment, (5) learning disability, (6) physical and health impairment, and (7) emotional disturbance. In the following sections, we will outline major characteristics of each condition and provide suggestions for adapting classroom instruction to meet special needs of youngsters having conditions cited.

Mental Retardation

Mental retardation is a term that is difficult to define with any degree of precision. In general, a person is thought to be mentally retarded when his or her intellectual development is (1) significantly below that of age mates and where (2) potential for academic achievement has been determined to be markedly less than for so-called "normal" individuals who are otherwise similar to the individual in question.

Historically, IQ scores were much used to determine whether a person properly could be categorized as mentally retarded. A problem with using IQ scores for this purpose is that people who may appear to be mentally retarded on the basis of an IQ test may be perfectly capable of functioning in a normal fashion under other conditions. For example, people with very low IQ scores may do very well in certain kinds of job roles after leaving school. Because of this, the American Association of Mental Deficiency (AAMD) advocates a broader measure of mental retardation than the IQ test. The AAMD suggests that a person who is mentally retarded is characterized by "deficits in adaptive behavior." This means that an individual who is mentally retarded cannot function as a normal person might function within the typical range of life situations. The individual who can function within this typical range is not classified as mentally retarded regardless of how he or she might fare on an IQ test (Payne et al. 1979).

We need also to remember that mental retardation is not in every case a permanent condition. There are people who, because of early home and family environments, may appear to be mentally retarded at some fairly early point in their lives. Such individuals may appear to be perfectly normal at later periods of their lives if they have been placed in enriched environments where special help is provided (Payne et al. 1979).

Traditionally, it has been a practice to describe several categories or levels of mental retardation. Generally the terms "educable," "trainable," and "severely" or "profoundly retarded" are used. The type of mentally retarded individual most likely to be assigned to spend part of the school day (perhaps a full day) in the regular classroom is the individual classified as "educable." Educables represent by far the largest percentage of individuals who are mentally retarded. The U.S. Office of Education estimates that about 2.3 percent of the entire population is mentally retarded. Of these, nearly 2 percent fall into the educable category (Payne et al. 1979).

We cannot speak with great authority regarding what kinds of achievement might be expected from educable youngsters. Some experts suggest that they cannot be expected to succeed at work much more demanding than that offered in a typical sixth-grade classroom. But there are so many differences among individuals in the educable category, that generalizations of this kind are hazardous. It is fair to say that these youngsters can profit to some extent from the school program. To the individual teacher falls the task of diagnosing each educable youngster with whom he or she works and of devising learning experiences (in concert with parents and other school officials) that are reasonable.

Working with Educable Students.   Educable students tend to have rather short attention spans. Further, they tend to become frustrated rather easily. Many educable students, by the time they reach secondary school, have experienced a long history of failure in school. Consequently, these youngsters tend to see themselves as failures even before they start on a new task. Some may not even be willing to try. In general, these youngsters have difficulty in grasping abstract ideas or complex sequences of ideas (see Figure 15-5).

In teaching educable learners, lessons should be short, direct, and to the point. Material should be presented in short sequential steps. There ought to be large numbers of very concrete examples to illustrate new ideas. Material that is introduced in prose form should be reinforced with additional visual and oral presentations. Some

Figure 15-5

SENSITIVE TREATMENT OF EDUCABLE LEARNERS IN THE REGULAR CLASSROOM

When you were in school, there may not have been any students in your classes who would be formerly categorized as "mentally retarded-educable" (though perhaps there were). But you very likely had some classes that included individuals who simply appeared to be much less bright than most others in the class.

YOUR OPINION, PLEASE

Spend a few moments trying to recall any students similar to those mentioned in the paragraph above. Then, respond to these questions.

1. In general, how did your teachers treat these youngsters? Can you recall some specific examples?
2. How did these youngsters react to school? Were they active in the extracurricular program? Were they generally popular? How would you assess their general social standing in the school?
3. Have you kept track of what has happened to any of these people in the years since you graduated from high school? What are they doing? Are some of them doing things that you never would have predicted?
4. How would you prepare other students in your class if you learned that you would have some "educables" on your roster? Would you say anything at all? Would you choose to remain silent? Or would you follow some other course of action?
5. Knowing what you know about "educables," how might you make assignments in such a fashion that they would enjoy some potential for success? Would everybody in the class be doing the same thing at the same time? If not, how would you manage several different kinds of activities at the same time?

---

teachers have found it useful to assign one of the nonhandicapped youngsters in the class to work with an educable student as a tutor. Frequently a peer tutor will be able to explain material in simpler, more direct language than the teacher. Certainly, peer tutoring programs can offer a good supplement to what the teacher does.

Teachers must monitor their vocabularies very carefully when directing comments to educable students. This is particularly true when providing directions. Often, educable students' failures can be attributed as much to their lack of understanding regarding what they are to do as to their difficulty with accomplishing an assigned task.

Educable youngsters frequently require more time to accomplish a given task than do nonhandicapped youngsters. Teachers need to be cautious about establishing tight, overly restrictive deadlines for these students. Often it is better to have them accomplish fewer tasks, even though each task takes some time to complete, than to push them to work on more tasks than they can get done. Self-esteem is enhanced when a youngster has an opportunity to get the job done. Consequently, allowing educable students sufficient time to complete their work can enhance their self-images.

Finally, teachers need to be very careful about exposing educable youngsters to situations that are highly competitive. It is particularly important to avoid placing them in situations where they have to compete against nonhandicapped students. An educable youngster can be absolutely devastated when he or she is forced to compete in a situation where he or she has almost no prospect of doing anything but losing. Such an experience can be a great humiliation, and it can lead to a greatly diminished interest in the school program.

Hearing Impairment

Students who are hearing impaired tend to fall into two broad categories. On the one hand, there are students whose hearing loss is so profound as to preclude their ability to acquire normal use of the oral language. These individuals are classified as "deaf."

On the other hand, there are students with a hearing loss that is serious but not so serious as to have prevented them from acquiring normal speech patterns. These individuals are classified as "hard of hearing."

There are great differences among hearing-impaired youngsters. For example, some are unable to hear certain pitches. Others require different levels of amplified sound. Some will have had a hearing loss since birth. Others may have suffered a hearing loss after some oral language proficiency has developed (Turnbull and Schulz 1979). A characteristic shared by large numbers of hearing-impaired youngsters is a difficulty in developing proficient oral language skills. A great deal of emphasis in school programs for these youngsters is placed on improving their performance capabilities with the spoken language.

About 5 percent of the school-aged population is estimated to suffer from some degree of hearing loss. Of this 5 percent, only about 1.5 percent are thought to require special educational services (Payne et al. 1979). Even youngsters with quite severe hearing losses are capable of functioning satisfactorily in regular classrooms. Teachers of these youngsters do need to exercise care to assure that these youngsters understand what is going on. School hearing specialists can provide practical guidelines.

Working with Hearing-Impaired Students.   Large numbers of youngsters who suffer severe hearing losses have been taught to attend very carefully to visual cues. Many know how to read lips. Because of their dependence on visual signals, students with hearing losses must be introduced to learning material in such a fashion that they can take advantage of their visual learning skills. For teachers, this suggests a need to face hearing-impaired students when introducing new information and providing directions. Teachers with hearing-impaired youngsters might also consider using overhead projectors rather than blackboards. (Overheads permit teachers to face the class while writing information on the acetate sheets. On the other hand, when writing on the blackboard, a teacher may be talking with his or her back turned to the class.) It is a good idea, as well, for teachers of hearing-impaired youngsters to remain relatively stationary while they are speaking. Trained lip readers find it difficult to follow comments being made by a person who is in motion.

Assignments and other directions ought to be provided in written form. (They can be oral as well, but the written material can go a long way toward eliminating potential confusion.) When a lecture format is used, it is helpful to provide class members with a general printed outline (including at least major headings) of the material to be presented. This will help students to keep up as the lecture is presented. In advance of the lecture, it is a good idea to provide students with lists of important and potentially confusing words. This is particularly critical when words to be used may have multiple meanings. (Consider, for example, the differences in meaning attached to the term "market" as it is used in everyday conversation and the term "market" as it is used in the discipline of economics.) Specialized usages need to be explained on the lists themselves. A follow-up discussion in advance of the lecture will also prove helpful.

In general, hearing-impaired students do best when instruction is well organized and systematic. The easier it is for such students to recognize the organizational scheme of the lesson, the better they are likely to do. All students tend to become confused when they do not understand what a teacher is attempting to accomplish at a given point during a lesson. For hearing impaired students who lack all the communication channels open to nonhandicapped youngsters, the task of keeping on track with the teacher presents a real challenge. For these students, well-organized instruction (which, indeed, can benefit *all* students) is essential.

Some hearing-impaired youngsters may wear hearing aids or other mechanical devices designed to enhance their ability to compensate for their hearing loss. Teachers need to understand how these devices work. For example, they should know how batteries are replaced in a hearing aid. It may be a good idea for them to have a supply of batteries (and perhaps certain other critical components) on hand so that minor repairs can be made in the classroom. Certainly some advice from school hearing specialists ought to be solicited regarding what properly can and cannot be done in this connection. Figure 15-6 specifies some techniques for working with this group of youngsters.

Speech Impairment

Identification of students with clearly defined speech impairments is difficult. Even the most clear-cut definitions of speech impairment still require the individual making a decision about a given student to use a good deal of personal judgment. In general, an individual is thought to suffer from impaired speech when his or her speech differs significantly from the speech of others of the same age (McLean 1978). Speech problems encompass a wide range of difficulties. These relate to such things as voice quality, problems of articulating certain sounds, and stuttering.

Because speech impairments do not present so clear-cut and obvious obstacles to learning as do such handicaps as hearing impairment and visual impairment, there is a tendency for some teachers not to take them as seriously as probably they should. A very important side effect of speech impairment, and one that occurs in a distressingly

Figure 15-6

SUGGESTIONS FOR WORKING WITH HEARING-IMPAIRED STUDENTS IN THE CLASSROOM*

1. Help the hearing impaired learn differences among sounds by pointing out these differences.
2. Help the learner hear sounds by speaking clearly and in your normal tone of voice. Speak as you do normally.
3. Use the overhead projector for pointing out visually the sounds in words. Write the word. Then say it clearly.
4. When working on connected sentences, point out the rhythm of the sentences to the class. Have the learners repeat them.
5. Discuss the hearing-impaired learner's speech with the speech clinician to find out what skills the clinician and the student are working on. Seek to reinforce these skills in class.
6. If a hearing aid sputters, check
   For battery fluid leak in battery chamber. Remedy by wiping out corrosion with a cloth or pencil eraser and replacing damaged battery with a new one.
   Contact between hearing aid and cord. If aid sputters when plug is wiggled, rub accessible contacts with a pencil eraser. If pins are clean, replacement of the cord may be needed. This is the parents' responsibility.
7. If hearing aid causes a high-frequency whistling known as feedback, check
   Fit of ear mold. If loose, contact parents.
   For volume turned too high.
8. Keep the classroom reasonably quiet for best hearing-aid usage.
9. Do not pretend to understand what the hearing-impaired student says if you do not truly understand what he or she is saying. Provide honest and authentic feedback. This will help the student to learn appropriate patterns.

*This material has been adapted from Texas Learning Resource Center, Division of Special Education, Texas Education Agency, "Tips for Teachers in Programming for Learners with Problems" (Austin: Texas Education Agency, 1978), pp. 13–14.

---

high number of youngsters suffering from this problem, is a low self-image. Out of their frustration at their inability to speak normally, there is a tendency for large numbers of youngsters with speech impairments to conclude that they are inferior or even incompetent. The dropout rate among students with speech impairments is quite high.

Working with Students with Speech Impairments. Many students with speech impairments can profit from work with a trained speech therapist. A good many districts have such individuals on their professional staffs. But classroom teachers, too, can do a great deal to help these youngsters. In general, these students need a good deal of emotional support. As noted, they tend to suffer from negative self-image problems. Thus teachers must take care to avoid placing youngsters with speech impairments in situations that call unnecessary attention to their handicap.

For example, in classroom discussions, it may be wise to call on students with speech handicaps only when they raise a hand and indicate a willingness to volunteer a response. When such a student begins to speak, he or she should be allowed to complete what he or she has to say without interruption or correction. Praise and other kinds of positive reinforcements should be provided when these youngsters volunteer a remark in class.

Some teachers have found it prudent to talk to other members of the class, at a time when speech-impaired students are absent, about the desirability of not criticizing or making fun of their speech handicap. Support from other students in the class can make it much more comfortable for a youngster with a speech impairment to speak up.

Finally, it is a good idea for the teacher to provide opportunities for speech-impaired students to speak with the teacher on a one-to-one basis. This kind of a setting provides an opportunity for the teacher to boost the morales of such students by making sensitive supportive comments to them individually. Further, it affords the student an opportunity to talk to the teacher about course work (or other matters) without fear that he or she will experience a communication difficulty that might prompt ridicule from other class members.

Visual Impairment

The term "visual impairment" implies a variety of deficiencies related to the sense of sight. Some visually impaired individuals have no sight whatever. However, most in this category have some sight. Some see a world that is blurred, dim, or out of focus; others may see only parts of objects. Federal education officials have estimated that about one tenth of 1 percent of the school-aged population is blind or partially sighted. This translates to about 50,000 students who are visually impaired and who require special educational services in the schools (Payne et al. 1979).

Working with Visually Impaired Students. In the past, rarely were students with severe visual impairments placed in regular classrooms. Today, large numbers of such youngsters sit alongside nonhandicapped students in public school classes. While certain adaptations of the instructional program are necesary if instruction is to be delivered successfully to these individuals, in general these youngsters are able to derive a great deal of benefit from participation in the activities of a regular classroom.

To assist teachers in working with visually impaired students, some states provide braille editions of textbooks used in required courses. Other districts provide typewriters for blind youngsters to use in classrooms. Large numbers of blind students have been taught to type using the touch system. Those who have acquired this skill can type written work associated with assignments and examinations. Where typewriters are available, it has usually been the practice to make some classroom modifications to provide typing carrels or other areas where typewriters can be used.

Whenever assignments are written on the chalkboard or written information is passed out to the class, the teacher must make special arrangements to communicate with visually handicapped youngsters in the class. In some cases it may be sufficient to explain this information orally. In other situations, it is useful to provide a recorded version of the material that visually handicapped youngsters can take with them to play on personally owned cassette recorders.

A problem shared by all individuals with severe visual handicaps has to do with personal mobility. In time, people with visual handicaps develop good mental pictures of areas they visit frequently. But they require some experience in a new environment before a mental picture develops. Thus it is useful for teachers to arrange for students with severe visual handicaps to visit classrooms at times when class is not in session, which will allow them to learn configurations of furniture and other features of the room. When changes in these arrangements are made, teachers must make a special effort to familiarize visually handicapped youngsters with the new classroom configuration.

Learning Disability

The term "learning disability" is a very broad one. Some students who are not learning disabled at all have been so labeled simply because certain teachers have experienced difficulty in communicating with them. Properly, a student classified as learning disabled is one who exhibits a disorder in one or more of the basic psychological processes involved in understanding or using spoken or written language. These disorders may be revealed in such areas as listening, writing, reading, spelling, or computing. Sometimes learning disabilities are referred to by such terms as "perceptual handicaps," minimal brain disfunctions," and "dyslexia." Fundamentally, then, the student who is characterized as having a learning disability experiences difficulty processing sensory stimuli.

Youngsters with learning disabilities often experience difficulty in following directions. They may appear disorganized. Teachers often find that they are unable to get started on assigned tasks. Many learning disabled youngsters have a low tolerance for frustration. Some learning disabled students will become tense and appear to be incapable of doing anything when they sense that they are being pressured by the teacher. Handwriting of these youngsters often appears disorganized. Letters within words may be inconsistent in size. There may be letter reversals. In terms of their oral communication, some learning disabled youngsters have unusual speech patterns in which, for example, words may be out of sequence.

Working with Learning Disabled Students.   Most students who suffer from learning disabilities need special help in the area of organization. The teacher needs to assist them in organizing their learning materials and their thinking processes. Such youngsters, for example, frequently experience great difficulty in differentiating between critical material in an assignment and other information that is much less important. In working with learning disabled students, it is desirable for teachers to take time to highlight key ideas and to provide students with ways of organizing these ideas into a meaningful pattern.

Because of a typically low toleration for frustration, learning disabled youngsters often have a hard time dealing with alternatives. Teachers can reduce unnecessary anxieties of such youngsters by limiting the number of alternatives confronting them.

In general, by the time they reach the secondary school level, learning disabled students have experienced a good deal of frustration and failure. Consequently, many of them suffer from low self-concepts. Anything the teacher can do to help these youngsters grow in terms of their own self-confidence should be encouraged. In a supportive classroom environment, many of these students *can* learn.

Physical and Health Impairment

Physical and health impairment is a broad category encompassing many different kinds of specific conditions. In general, students in this category include those who have limitations that may interfere with school performance or attendance that are related to physical abilities or medical conditions (Payne et al. 1979).

The National Advisory Committee on the Handicapped has estimated that there are approximately 328,000 physically and health-impaired youngsters of school age in the United States. About half of these are individuals who have suffered from cerebral palsy or some other crippling disease. The other half is composed primarily of students suffering from some kind of chronic health problem (Payne et al. 1979).

Working with Students with Physical and Health Impairments.

The range of conditions in this general category makes it impossible to provide recommendations that would be appropriate for every handicapped youngster who is either physically or health impaired. For the teacher, the appropriate initial step is to gather complete information regarding the specific physical and health handicaps of youngsters in his or her classes. Meetings or conversations with parents, counselors, and others with relevant information are certainly appropriate. Once specific information is in hand, the teacher can consider what modifications might have to be made in the instructional program to make it appropriate for each physically or health handicapped student.

Information about specific handicaps may result in any one of a number of actions being taken by the teachers. For example, a physical or health limitation may make it impossible for a given student to complete certain tasks at as fast a rate as nonhandicapped youngsters. In such a case, special time allowances may need to be made. For another youngster, perhaps one who must use a cumbersome walker, it might be necessary to rearrange furniture in the room to make it possible for this individual to move into the area and slip into a seat. Space for special equipment needed by some physically or health handicapped students will need to be found.

In general, physically and health handicapped students are fully capable of meeting the intellectual challenges of instruction in regular school classrooms. The challenge comes not so much in devising unique methods of presentation as it does in accommodating limitations pertaining to youngsters' physical and health characteristics. When arrangements can be made, many youngsters in this category do very well as students in regular classrooms.

Emotional Disturbance

Emotionally disturbed students have been defined as those who display "a marked deviation from age-appropriate behavior expectations which interferes with positive personal and interpersonal development" (Turnbull and Schulz 1979, p. 41). Many classroom teachers find emotionally disturbed students difficult to work with. In part this results from a tendency of some emotionally disturbed youngsters to engage in behaviors that are disruptive to classroom instruction.

A number of schemes have been developed to categorize types of behavior of emotionally disturbed youngsters. One scheme identifies five separate kinds of behaviors thought to be characteristic of these students. According to Payne et al. (1979, p. 35), these individuals are thought to

1. Have problems in achieving in school that cannot be explained by sensory or health factors.
2. Have problems establishing and maintaining satisfactory interpersonal relationships with others.

3. Have a tendency to demonstrate inappropriate feelings and actions under normal circumstances.
4. Be characterized, in many instances, by a pervasive mood of unhappiness or depression.
5. Have a tendency to develop physical symptoms such as pain or emotional symptoms such as fear as a consequence of their problems.

Some emotionally disturbed students may be defiant, rude, destructive, and attention seeking. Others may be fearful and withdrawn. One of the authors once taught a group of emotionally disturbed youngsters, one of whom, at a moment's notice, would explode and begin to throw books, desks, and any other available objects. In the same class, there was a boy who would begin to cry and start running to a corner of the room when he was greeted with a friendly "good morning" from the teacher.

Officially, the U.S. Office of Education estimates that about 2 percent of the school-aged population is emotionally disturbed. Some experts think this figure is too low. They cite as evidence that behaviors associated with emotional disturbance tend to occur with such a frequency that it is likely more than 2 percent of the students are involved (Payne et al. 1979).

Most emotionally disturbed students have difficulty coping with their environments. Their difficulty in making needed adjustments frequently distracts them from tasks associated with completing school-related work. Consequently, a lack of academic success often ensues. Problems in the academic area often lead to self-concept problems. Self-concept problems lead to anxieties, and these anxieties often result in behaviors that are unacceptable in the context of the school. In essence, many of these become caught up in a cycle of failure. Teacher efforts in working with youngsters of this type are directed at breaking this destructive pattern of behavior.

Working with Emotionally Disturbed Students.   Teachers need to attend to four basic concerns in planning instructional programs for emotionally disturbed students. First, activities need to be success oriented. That is, there must be a reasonable chance for the youngster to accomplish what he or she is asked to do. Second, teachers must be specific in terms of communicating their behavioral expectations to these students and consistent in enforcing these expectations. (We cannot be "hard nosed" one day and a "soft touch" another day.)

Third, teachers must minimize distractions. These youngsters tend to be diverted very easily from assigned tasks. Efforts must be undertaken to reduce the potential for shifting their attentions away from required work.

Fourth, the teacher needs to help emotionally disturbed youngsters realize that there is a clear and definite relationship between their behaviors and consequences flowing from these behaviors. Many such students do not make an immediate connection between something that happens to them (receiving a low grade, for example) and what it was that they did that resulted in the occurrence of that "something." Large numbers of these youngsters believe the world to be a totally capricious place where anything that happens to them occurs because of random chance or bad luck. Teachers need to make the effort to help them appreciate that there is a connection between what a student does and what happens to him or her.

A general concern related to some extent to all four of these major areas is the issue of motivation. By the time many emotionally disturbed youngsters reach even the junior high school level, they have experienced so much failure that they begin to doubt that anything taught in school can be mastered. Further, many suspect that school learning simply isn't useful. Many emotionally disturbed youngsters go to great lengths to avoid becoming involved in academic tasks. In considering the issue of motivating emotionally disturbed youngsters, the teacher needs to devise ways to convince these students that the subject, if mastered, will really do something for these learners. Identified benefits need have immediacy. It does little good, for example, to tell an emotionally disturbed student, "You should do this because ten years from now it will help you get a better job."

Beyond motivation, there is a need to develop instruction in such a way that potentials for success are maximized. One approach to this problem is to cut large tasks into small pieces. Emotionally disturbed youngsters are much less likely to be intimidated when a small piece of a larger task is assigned than when they are asked to complete the entire larger task before being credited with satisfactory performance. When material is introduced in small steps and positive feedback is provided at the successful conclusion of each step, the emotionally disturbed student is encouraged to keep on task.

Behavior patterns of emotionally disturbed children are variable. We must recognize that not all emotionally disturbed youngsters are likely to engage in disruptive behavior in class and, hence, immediately catch the teacher's attention. Some emotionally disturbed youngsters may be withdrawn and passive. Sometimes these students are experiencing more severe problems than those whose outward symptoms may appear

Figure 15-7

FEELINGS ABOUT WORKING WITH HANDICAPPED STUDENTS

YOUR OPINION, PLEASE
Please respond to each of the following questions.

1. As you review the different handicapping conditions, which ones do you think would be most difficult for you to teach? Why?

2. What could be done to alter your instruction to accommodate students with that particular handicap?

3. The attitude of the teacher is very important in working with handicapped learners. What is your attitude regarding teaching these learners? Is it positive or negative? What can be done to improve your attitude?

4. As your review this chapter, what particular skills and knowledge do you still need to acquire to be successful in teaching handicapped learners? How will you acquire these skills and knowledges?

---

to be more obvious. With such youngsters, the teacher needs to work to build trust and to eliminate a potentially debilitating fear of failure.

Finally, teachers with emotionally disturbed youngsters in their classes must understand that such problems are not likely to go away overnight. In many cases, emotional disturbance has developed over a period of years. Consequently, even teachers who approach such youngsters with compassion and understanding do not achieve quick results. In working with emotionally disturbed youngsters, we have to take satisfaction from small, incremental changes. If we can be tolerant and if we can take a long-term perspective, eventual changes in behavior patterns of these young people can provide a great sense of professional satisfaction.

Handicapped Students: A Final Observation

It has been found that a critical element in teaching handicapped students successfully is the attitude of the teacher (see Figure 15-7). Successful teachers of handicapped youngsters tend to be characterized by accepting attitudes. They do not experience great anxieties regarding the abilities of these youngsters to perform. When teachers approach handicapped learners in a positive manner and expect the best, generally these youngsters will do well. But if the teacher really does not expect much from these students, he or she is likely to get very little from them.

Posttest

Directions: Using your own paper, answer each of the following true/false questions. For each correct statement, write the word "true." For each incorrect statement, write the word "false."

_____ 1. It has been a practice in American schools for generations to provide some educational experiences for *all* handicapped youngsters.

_____ 2. To fulfill the "appropriate education" component of legislation relating to handicapped youngsters, a school must do nothing other than place handicapped youngsters in classes designed exclusively for handicapped youngsters.

_____ 3. By law, parents are to be included when individualized educational plans are developed.

_____ 4. The language "least restrictive environment" means that every handicapped youngster must spend the entire school day in a regular classroom alongside nonhandicapped learners.

_____ 5. Most classroom teachers in the schools today, as undergraduates, received extensive training on procedures for working with handicapped learners who were enrolled in regular classrooms alongside nonhandicapped students.

_____ 6. Emotionally disturbed students are included among those classified as "handicapped."

_____ 7. Students categorized as "educable" tend to have relatively short attention spans and to become frustrated easily.

_____ 8. In working with hearing-impaired students, teachers are advised to face the class at all times when they are giving information orally.

_____ 9. "Learning disabled" students have problems in understanding or using spoken or written language.

_____ 10. There is no existing federal legislation relating to treatment of handicapped learners in the schools.

Key Ideas in Review

1. Although educators have always had an interest in serving handicapped students, historically, large numbers of such youngsters were not served. Those who did attend school tended to be placed in special classrooms where they had almost no contact with the so-called "regular" school program. Today, federal legislation has changed this traditional practice. To the extent possible, handicapped students are "mainstreamed" (placed in regular classes alongside nonhandicapped students). As a consequence, teachers today tend to have a mixture of handicapped and nonhandicapped students in their classes.

2. The key federal legislation relating to handicapped students is Public Law 94-142. This law guarantees handicapped students a right to a free and appropriate education. Special provisions mandate the establishment of individualized programs for these youngsters and lay down procedures for assessing progress. Education is to be provided in what the law describes as the "least restrictive environment." The law further requires joint participation by school officials and parents.

3. Students classified as "mentally retarded" are characterized by levels of intellectual development that (1) are significantly below those of age mates and (2) suggest a potential for academic achievement that is markedly less than that of so-called "normal" individuals. Historically, individuals were categorized as mentally retarded on the basis of IQ test scores. Today, authorities favor a broader range of measures.

4. About 5 percent of the school-aged population suffers some degree of hearing loss. About half of these individuals require some special educational services from the schools. Many youngsters with hearing losses are capable of functioning very well in regular classrooms where they work alongside nonhandicapped learners. Teachers who take care to ensure clear communications with these youngsters find that they adjust very well to the regular classroom.

5. Youngsters with speech impairments are characterized by speech patterns that differ markedly from those of other individuals of the same age. A big problem faced by many speech-impaired students has to do with negative self-images. One challenge for teachers of these students is to help them develop a sense of personal competence.

6. Students suffering from visual impairments may have one or more of a variety of deficiencies having to do with sight. About 50,000 visually impaired students require special services from the schools. In general, these youngsters have the intellectual capabilities to do work in regular classrooms. Teachers need to take care that these individuals are provided information via a sensory mode that does not depend on vision. Given attention to this need, these youngsters adjust well to regular classroom work.

7. Learning disabled youngsters suffer from disorders in one or more of the psychological processes involved in understanding or using spoken or written language. In general, they have difficulty in processing sensory stimuli. Often such students appear disorganized and unable to stay on assigned tasks. Many have low tolerances for frustration. Teachers need to work hard to help such individuals overcome anxieties. If they are to profit from instruction, a warm and supportive classroom environment is necessary.

8. A number of students in school suffer from physical or health impairments. These are very diverse. In general, teachers having youngsters who suffer from serious physical or health conditions need very specific information about what they can and cannot do. Parents, counselors, and others can be appropriate sources for this information. When specific knowledge about individual conditions is in hand, instructional programs appropriate to these students' needs can be devised.

9. Emotionally disturbed students deviate greatly from appropriate patterns of behavior. These deviations tend to interfere with personal development and with abilities to interact positively with others. About 2 percent of the school-aged population is emotionally disturbed. In general, teachers need to help these youngsters to learn to cope with their environments. As is true of students with certain other handicapping conditions, many emotionally disturbed youngsters suffer from low self-images. They need a supportive, understanding teacher.

SUMMARY

Historically, students with handicaps who attended schools were placed in classrooms relatively isolated from those of so-called "normal" students. Many handicapped youngsters did not go to school at all. Today this situation is much changed. Spurred on by federal legislation, handicapped students today are educated in "the least restrictive environment." This means that, to the extent possible, they are taught alongside nonhandicapped youngsters in regular classrooms.

The introduction of handicapped youngsters into regular classrooms has required some adjustments on the part of those classroom teachers who did their undergraduate work at a time when it was assumed that handicapped youngsters would not be in regular classrooms. School districts across the country have mounted numerous in-service programs to provide teachers with information related to working with such youngsters. In general, teachers have found that there are more similarities between handicapped youngsters and others in their classes than there are differences. While certainly some program elements must be tailored to meet unique requirements of certain handicapped youngsters, most now concur that these individuals (or at least a great many of them) can profit from experiences afforded them in regular school classrooms. As newly trained teachers begin flowing into America's classrooms and as older teachers become more familiar working with youngsters with special needs, it seems likely that most secondary teachers will increasingly come to regard handicapped youngsters as "just some of the students in class."

References

Glick, Harriet M., and Schubert, Marsha. "Mainstreaming: An Unmandated Challenge," *Educational Leadership* (January 1981): 326–329.

McLean, J. E. "Language Structure and Communication Disorders," in N. G. Haring, ed., *Behavior of Exceptional Children*. 2nd ed. Columbus, Ohio: Charles E. Merrill Publishing Co., 1978.

Payne, James S.; Kaufmann, James M.; Patton, James R.; Brown, Gweneth; and DeMott, Richard M. *Exceptional Children in Focus: Incidents, Concepts, and Issues in Special Education*. Columbus, Ohio: Charles E. Merrill Publishing Co., 1979.

Smith, Sally L. *No Easy Answer: Teaching the Learning Disabled Child*. Cambridge, Mass.: Winthrop Publishers, Inc., 1979.

Stearns, Marian S., and Cooperstein, Rhonda Ann. "Equity in Educating the Handicapped," *Educational Leadership* (January 1981): 324–325.

Texas Learning Resource Center, Division of Special Education, Texas Education Agency. "Tips for Teachers in Programming for Learners with Problems." Austin: Texas Education Agency, 1978.

Turnbull, Ann P., and Schulz, Jane B. *Mainstreaming Handicapped Students: A Guide for the Classroom Teacher*. Boston: Allyn & Bacon, Inc., 1979.

16

Reading Problems of Secondary School Students

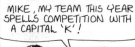

MIKE, MY TEAM THIS YEAR SPELLS COMPETITION WITH A CAPITAL 'K'!

EXCUSE ME, COACH, BUT COMPETITION IS SPELLED WITH A 'C'!

THAT TELLS YOU SOMETHING, DOESN'T IT?

FUNKY WINKERBEAN by Tom Batiuk © 1980. Field Enterprises, Inc. Courtesy of Field Newspaper Syndicate.

Objectives

This chapter provides information to help the reader to

1. Suggest the nature of the relationship between the teacher's behavior with respect to reading and the student's behavior with respect to reading.
2. Describe procedures for identifying the grade-level readability of prose material.
3. Point out the nature of vocabulary problems of secondary school students.
4. Follow a systematic set of procedures in preparing students to learn from textbooks.
5. Recognize steps in a strategy designed to maximize students' learning from prose material.
6. Note the importance of establishing a purpose for reading when assigning secondary school students to work with prose materials.

Pretest

Directions: Using your own paper, answer each of the following true/false questions. For each correct statement, write the word "true." For each incorrect statement, write the word "false."

_____ 1. The Fry readability graph produces a score that will tell a teacher how well an individual student might fare with a given prose selection.

_____ 2. The level of reading sophistication of the typical senior high school student today is no different from the level of reading sophistication of the typical senior high school student in 1910.

_____ 3. When a textbook is described as being written on the tenth-grade level of readability, this does not necessarily mean that every student in the tenth grade will be able to read the book without difficulty.

_____ 4. It is possible for a book to have low grade-level readability and yet still contain many vocabulary words students find very difficult.

_____ 5. To encourage students to develop and use reading skills, it is important that at least some parts of tests that are administered require students to use information that they have learned from their reading.

_____ 6. When students are asked to read an assignment, it is a sound instructional practice to explain to them what the purpose of their reading is to be.

_____ 7. By the time students are in secondary school, all are proficient users of book indexes and library indexes.

_____ 8. The SQ3R technique is a procedure that has been developed for the purpose of helping students to develop a systematic and purposeful approach to the skill of reading material in course textbooks.

_____ 9. Obsolete word usages frequently present problems to readers of secondary school age.

_____ 10. In general, reading difficulty of a passage can be reduced by rewriting it in such a way that average sentence length is decreased and the number of words with large numbers of syllables is decreased.

INTRODUCTION

It is 1:30 in the afternoon of a sparkling mid-November day. At Quentin B. Meyer High School, the fifth period has ended. A number of teachers with a sixth-period planning period have wearily pushed the door to the faculty lounge, noted a vacant place on one of the ancient couches, and sagged mercifully down to regather their energies. A few are sipping coffee. Others are making some half-hearted efforts to grade papers. One or two just sit silently looking out into space. In one corner, a first-year teacher, Katherine Holleman, still has not wound down from her fifth-period class. She is bending the ear of an old hand from the English Department, Dolby Ormisher.

Katherine Holleman

"Dolby, I am stunned, just stunned. I thought I had made a breakthrough with Larry Cornwall, and now . . . this! As I said, I thought I'd spark it up a bit today with something a little different. I mean it's Friday, we've just finished a unit test, and there's this game with Prep tonight. Well, anyway, I decided I'd whip something together about last week's presidential election. You know the data service I subscribe to sent me some terrific background information.

"Well, to make a long story short, I whirled into action every night this week to get my act together for today's class. I ginned up some posters, a couple of transparencies, and some charts. I even found some campaign buttons that I could bring

in. Anyway, I planned for a big show. For openers, I wrote "ELECTION TRENDS" on the board in letters 18 inches high. Then, I was off! I really cranked up the wind machines, the visuals, and all manner of props. I slipped in one deft anecdote after another. I mean it was a super experience for me! The kids were with me. They really were.

"Well, when this all wound down, I was feeling really great. The kids had enjoyed it, and I felt I had done a good job. Just as an afterthought, I asked whether there were any questions. Imagine my surprise when Larry Cornwall raised his hand. Larry Cornwall! He's slept through at least half of my classes. I was stunned when I saw that hand waving for recognition. I thought I had reached the unreachable for sure. Not wanting to delay this unexpected "dessert," I said, "Yes, Larry, what would you like to know?"

"Ms. Holleman," Larry began in that slow twang of his, "I liked what we did real well today. But there's something I just don't get. It's one of the words you used. One of them you used right at the beginning."

"Yes, Larry, which one was that?" I replied.

"Well, just what is a trend*?"*

"I couldn't believe it. Trend! *He doesn't know what a* trend *is. And these kids are juniors. His comment just ruined my day. I mean what's the use of planning when these people haven't learned anything in ten years of school?"*

Ms. Holleman's reaction to vocabulary problems of her student typifies the shock that many beginning teachers experience when they begin working with secondary school students. Many prospective teachers anticipate that students in junior and senior high schools will not be familiar with specialized vocabulary peculiar to the subjects they will be studying. For example, "titration" is a term that might be unfamiliar to a group of twelfth-graders at the beginning of their chemistry course. It is not students' lack of familiarity with these specialized terms that surprises newcomers so much as it is the students' lack of understanding of words that many teachers presume everybody should know.

Because they tend to focus on helping students with unfamiliar *technical* vocabulary, often new teachers do not recognize that it is difficulty with much more ordinary terminology that is causing a reading problem for students. Because they assume students to have much broader vocabularies than they often, in truth, have, a good many teachers fail to recognize reading difficulty as an important cause of academic difficulties experienced by some members of their classes.

In this chapter, we will examine some explanations for student difficulty with certain kinds of words. But, before getting into this material, let us reflect for a moment on the makeup of the student population itself and how this makeup may have changed over time. It may well be that changes in the nature of the student body explain why, in the minds of some educators at least, students in secondary schools today experience greater difficulty with printed materials than did secondary school students of 60 and 70 years ago.

At the beginning of the twentieth century, only about 10 percent of the students who completed the eighth grade went on to high school. The vast majority of this select group was preparing to enter colleges and universities. In brief, high school students at this time represented an academic elite of very talented young people. Contrast this population of high school students to enrollment patterns of the 1980s. Today's high schools enroll well over 90 percent of those students who have completed the eighth grade. It is evident that this student population is significantly different from the academic elite enrolled in high schools at the turn of the century.

It is thus logical to presume that these students represent a much broader range of talents and aspirations than did students in high schools in 1900. Today, large numbers of high school students do not plan to attend colleges or universities. In this connection, the National Center for Education Statistics reported that 22.4 percent of the 1977 high school graduates enrolled in a college or university (1979, p. 144). What all this means is that teachers today have students in their classes who have intellectual capacities that run across a spectrum nearly as broad as that found among the entire population. It is not surprising, then, that some students in secondary schools have active reading vocabularies that teachers find to be shockingly small. (After all, many adults in our society are very poor readers. Thus, it is logical that many students in secondary schools also experience problems with prose materials.)

Although the characteristics of the student population in secondary schools have changed dramatically during this century, some teachers continue to have the same expectations about what students ought to know that teachers had years ago when a much more select group of youngsters pursued study at the secondary school level (Shuman 1978). Compulsory attendance laws have so broadened the intellectual base of students in secondary schools that expectations of these teachers regarding what students ought to know have come to be hopelessly at odds with what, in fact, students *do* know. Commenting on reactions of some teachers to changes in the high school student body, Shuman (p. 206) writes that

> *Teachers who had been used to teaching students who were preparing for college were completely baffled by the deficiencies in the background of the new students appearing on the scene. Many, under the guise of "maintaining standards," refused to change and reached an impasse with their students, many of whom became overtly hostile toward school or hopelessly apathetic.*

In responding to the change in the makeup of the secondary school student body, teachers have tended to take one of two basic positions. Some have refused to acknowledge the changes in the student population. They have continued to make their assignments and to demand levels of performance appropriate for an academic elite. The relatively small number of intellectually talented students in the secondary schools has been served adequately by such teachers. Other students have experienced little but frustration. Not a few of these students have emerged from their school experiences with a diminished sense of self-worth and contempt for education in general and their teachers in particular.

Other teachers have adapted to changes. They have adopted the practice of beginning with students at their present levels of proficiency (regardless of where that might be). These teachers have faced a difficult task. They have set out to challenge the academically talented, serve the average student, and provide meaningful instruction for the slow learner. This has meant a willingness to identify individual differences and to prepare learning experiences appropriate for youngsters having an incredible variety of talents and interests.

In the area of reading, teachers in this group have been willing to work with students having reading skills deficiencies rather than to simply lament their shortcomings. It is in this spirit of helping students to cope with prose material that initially, at least, may prove discouraging to them that we believe the issue of reading should be approached (see Figure 16-1).

TEACHERS' BEHAVIOR AND STUDENTS' BELIEF IN THE IMPORTANCE OF READING

Secondary students have been around. They tend to infer what is true at least as much from what a teacher *does* as from what he or she *says*. In the short run, a group of secondary students may believe something simply because a teacher says it, but, in the long run their willingness to believe depends on the teachers' actions being congruent with what he or she espouses. For example, as was noted in Chapter 11, "Measuring,

Figure 16-1

MAINTAINING STANDARDS

Mr. Van Oaken, an English teacher at Briarwood Senior High School for the past 30 years, made these comments to his building principal:

> I feel as if I am taking the heat for irresponsible actions of others in my department. I know students are making requests to transfer out of my classes. Let's be honest now; the real reason this is happening is that I'm the only one left with the gumption to hold these kids to some kind of reasonable standard of performance. By golly, in my class when they get an "A" they deserve an "A."
>
> Just between the two of us, the standards in the rest of the department have gone to seed. These students are not being pushed to meet a responsible level of expectation. Rather, we, or rather some of my colleagues, have lowered their standards to the level of the student. How can a youngster learn anything this way? My grading standards are no different now from those when I started teaching. But these students certainly resist them a lot more than they used to. I wish you'd talk to the whole faculty to see if we can't get these students shaped up to perform the way they used to perform. I do know one thing. We'll never get the job done if we pass out "A's" and "B's" for substandard work.

YOUR OPINION, PLEASE

Read the statement above. Then, respond to these questions.

1. What assumptions about the students is Mr. Van Oaken making? Are these assumptions valid? Why, or why not?
2. Why do you suppose that students are requesting transfer from Mr. Van Oaken's classes? Is this reasonable behavior on their part? Should such transfers be permitted? Why, or why not?
3. Why do you suppose other faculty members seem to be using different grading standards than Mr. Van Oaken is using? Are these other faculty members behaving in a professional way? Why, or why not?
4. Suppose that you were the principal. How would you respond to Mr. Van Oaken?

Evaluating, and Reporting Student Progress," students will not continue to believe that a teacher has a sincere interest in developing higher-level thinking skills if tests recall only recall of memorized information. Similarly, the teacher who says that reading is important must signal to students that he or she really holds reading competence as a high personal value.

A basic test for the existence of a deeply held value is a person's willingness to take a public action consistent with this value. That is, we must do something to show students that we truly believe reading to be important. For example, we can tell students about books, magazine articles, and newspaper accounts that have excited us. We can bring in copies of reading materials we have read and offer to share them with students who might be interested. Before school, at noon, or after school, we can make a practice of reading books, magazines, and newspapers in a place where students can see us involved in reading. In summary, we can take a number of actions designed to flash to students the message that we think reading is important and that we derive personal enjoyment from the activity.

Additionally, the classroom can be arranged to emphasize the importance of reading. Many teachers provide a reading corner (perhaps a table, a carrel, or some other area) where high-interest materials can be kept. When students have completed assignments or otherwise have some available time (perhaps before or after school), they can be invited to use the materials in the reading corner. These items need to be updated periodically. Further, the reading corner needs to be "sold" to the students. It is not sufficient to establish a reading corner, tell students how and when to use it, and expect them to become wildly enthusiastic about it. They need to be reminded periodically about what is there, about new additions, and about items the teacher has personally found intriguing that have been included. Students, too, should be invited to suggest items for inclusion.

In addition to a reading corner, bulletin boards featuring print materials further underscore what a teacher might say about the importance of reading. These need to be changed with some frequency and to include high-interest items. Again, the teacher needs to call specific attention to items on the bulletin board. ("Have you seen the new collection of *Doonesbury* cartoons on the bulletin board. We're going to be studying Watergate. These cartoons were drawn during this period. I think you'll enjoy looking them over.") It is not enough to put up a bulletin board and assume that students will take the time to look at it. They need to be motivated.

In many communities, newspaper publishers will make newspapers available to students in a class at very low rates. (In a few favored places, they will be provided at no charge.) Occasional lessons built around the use of the newspaper that involve the teacher and the students in some joint activities centered on articles and advertisements can reinforce in students' minds the importance of reading. Many local newspapers underwrite special teacher training programs designed to prepare teachers to make productive use of newspapers with their students. Many teachers have found these "Newspaper in the Classroom" workshops beneficial. The authors have been involved in a number of these, and we recommend them highly to beginning teachers.

Finally, if we tell students that it is important for them to read the assigned material, we need to require them to do something with what they have read. In particular, when it is time to test students on a segment of instruction, some test items should relate to information presented in the required reading. In a survey reported in 1977, one researcher found that large numbers of teachers had devised tests that students could pass with a very high score without doing *any* of the assigned reading (Rieck 1977). Certainly we do not mean to suggest that there are not many ways for students to obtain information other than by reading. But we do feel that, if we are telling students that reading is important, an effort should be made to underscore this importance by requiring them to be accountable at test time for at least some information introduced in prose form.

READABILITY OF SCHOOL MATERIALS

Readability refers to the relative difficulty of a given prose selection. The readability of a selection varies with the complexity and length of sentences, the number of abstract and multisyllabled words, and the number of words that, for some reason or other, students simply do not know. In the sections that follow, we will look at some of the kinds of vocabulary items that stump many secondary students and at some procedures for identifying approximate difficulty levels of prose selections and matching individual students with materials they can read successfully.

Kinds of Words Students Find Difficult

A well-known secondary reading specialist, Robert C. Aukerman, has identified a number of categories of words that frustrate many secondary school readers (1972). Let us look at categories, adapted from Aukerman, and some examples of terms associated with each.

Obsolete Terms or Phrases.   Our language is dynamic. New terms and phrases enter our language continually. Some pass out of familiar usage over time; others remain by undergoing changes in nuance or meaning. Since many prose materials students must read were written by individuals who employed usages that no longer are common, students frequently find themselves puzzled over terms and phrases that seem foreign to their own experience.

Aukerman cites as examples such terms as the following (1972, p. 23). For those who do not recognize these terms, an explanation has been provided.

arctic   a rubber overshoe reaching to the ankle or above.

hooch   liquor (particularly illicitly distilled liquor).

lizzie   a Model T Ford.

nosegay   a small bouquet of flowers.

Colloquial Vocabulary.   Colloquial vocabulary occurs frequently in prose selections that attempt to provide the reader with the flavor of regional speech. To accomplish this objective, words are misspelled deliberately by the author in an attempt to capture the sound of regional speech (or of speech of a certain element within the larger population). Many students find such writing almost incomprehensible. For example, Mark Twain's attempts to present to the reader the speech of the Mississippi borderlands in Missouri charm many sophisticated readers but baffle many high school students. ("How come he didn't spell right?" they may ask.) The "Irish" English of Mr. Dooley presents even more serious challenges to the typical secondary school youngster. The Cornwall dialect in Winston Graham's *Poldark* novels makes no sense whatever to large numbers of high school students. In general, the more distant the depicted dialect is from the common speech of the students, the more difficult they will find it.

When students are asked to read materials containing heavy doses of colloquial speech, they need some specific preparation. First, students need to be informed that not all people speak the English language in the same way. Some specific usages in the dialect presented in the material they will be reading need to be pointed out to students. It is also helpful if the teacher reads some of the dialect material aloud so that students can begin to grasp what the author was striving for in spelling words in a way that, to the students, may appear beyond reason.

Unfamiliar Vocabulary.   Unfamiliar vocabulary includes two kinds of words. Words of the first kind include those that a student knows and may use as part of his spoken vocabulary but that he or she may never have seen in print. For example, some secondary school students may have heard such phrases of foreign origin as *comme ci, comme ça,* and be reasonably certain of their meanings. Yet these same students may never have encountered such terms in print and may fail to recognize them when they first see them in a prose selection.

A second type of unfamiliar vocabulary includes those nontechnical words that are simply not known to students. As Aukerman (1972) points out, words of this kind are especially prevalent in the writing of college and university professors who fail to appreciate the somewhat limited range of the vocabularies of many secondary school students. Students who run into large numbers of such words in their reading material may well become very discouraged.

To help teachers who are interested in looking over their texts and other intended prose materials they may wish to use to determine the extent to which unfamiliar vocabulary words are used, Aukerman (1972) has developed several lists of what he calls "impedilexae." Impedilexae is a contrived term that means words that create reading problems. He has identified lists of impedilexae for the social studies, English; science; mathematics; business, industrial arts, and vocational education; and home economics. Teachers can use the appropriate subject area impedilexae to determine which of two alternative reading materials are likely to cause students more difficulty because of their failure to understand some of the included nontechnical words. The following words are a sample of those included on the *Impedilexae in English List* (Aukerman, 1972, pp. 35–36). (Readers interested in the complete set of impedilexae lists are referred to Robert C. Aukerman 1972, Chap. 3.)

A Selection of Terms from the Impedilexae in English List

abashed	gable	raiment	vagrant
abated	galvanized	rancor	valet
abeyance	gangling	ravenous	variegated
abject	gangrenous	realization	venerable
absurdly	garrulous	recalcitrant	verbose
acclimate	gendarmes	reconnoiter	verdant
accouterment	genteel	regime	vernal
acquiescent	gingerly	reiteration	vestiges
acumen	girth	reminiscence	vicious
admonition	gloaming	remonstrance	vilify
adventitious	gnarled	remuneration	visage
adversely	gradation	renegade	voluptuous
aesthetic	grapple	replete	vortex
affliction	gravity	repugnant	vulnerable

Source: From *Reading in the Secondary School Classroom* by Robert C. Aukerman. Copyright © 1972. Used with the permission of McGraw-Hill Book Company.

Technical Vocabulary.   Each subject has specialized vocabulary that is used to describe the phenomena with which it is concerned. Of all vocabulary problems, teachers probably are most prepared to deal with difficulties associated with technical vocabulary. In part this results because they do not usually expect students to be familiar with technical terms before a course begins. Indeed, it may even be argued that much of what a course teaches is a facility in the use of the technical vocabulary experts use to communicate with one another.

The kind of technical vocabulary that presents the least problems is that consisting of words that are used rarely except in dealing with a specialized subject area. For example, the specialized term "external validity" used by historians in describing procedures followed to establish the authenticity of source material is used in almost no other context. We do not find people chatting about "external validity" in casual social conversations (except, perhaps, those engaged in by overzealous professional historians unable to lay down their professional vocabulary at the end of the day).

Another kind of technical vocabulary causes teachers many more problems. Technical words of this type have two "lives." On the one hand, they are used in a very precise and specialized way by experts in various academic subjects. On the other hand, the very same terms are used by the general public to connote things that may be far different from what the terms connote to the academic specialist. For example, the statistician in his or her specialized use of the term "significant" means to imply only that something occurred with a frequency that is demonstrably greater than one would expect from chance or luck. On the other hand, the general public uses the term "significant" almost synonomously with the term "important." Thus, when a student (or, indeed, an adult layperson) reads that some scientist has found that a method of brushing the teeth is "significantly better" than an alternative method, the student may well think that an important discovery has been made. The scientist may not see a "significant" difference as a difference that is important at all.

Terms that are used one way by specialists and another by members of the general public present students with problems. They read a term such as "market" in their economics text and presume that they know what it means (a place to buy groceries).

Untroubled by the term, they tend to skim over the material without realizing that they are missing some important basic information because they do not understand the specialized way a very familiar term is being used. The potential for difficulties of this kind makes it imperative for teachers to read prose materials carefully to identify and explain vocabulary that students may think they know but that is being used in a very specialized and technical way.

Determining Levels of Reading Difficulty

Reading specialists over the years have devised numerous techniques for assessing the approximate grade-level reading difficulty of individual prose selection. Generally these techniques are referred to as readability formulas. Although they vary greatly in terms of specific procedures to be followed, most presume that reading difficulty increases with (1) increases in the percentage of long sentences and (2) increases in the number of words with large numbers of syllables.

Readability formulas are used to identify approximate grade-level readabilities. That is, a given selection might be described as grade 8, grade 9, grade 10, or some other grade depending on what resulted from the application of the reading formula. In using readability formulas, it is important to recognize that grade levels are described in terms of averages. That is, simply because we find a given book to have a grade 11 readability does *not* mean that every student in grade 11 can read the material without difficulty. It means that the average eleventh-grader should be able to read the material. The very term "average" suggests that half the students will be able to read more challenging material and that half will not be able to read materials at this level of difficulty. In truth, there likely will be large numbers of eleventh-graders who are unable to succeed with prose materials that we find to have a grade 11 level of readability.

One of the most commonly used readability formulas is the Fry readability graph developed by Edward Fry. The graph and directions for use are presented in Figure 16-2. Figure 16-3 tests your ability to rewrite materials for lower grade-level readability.

To match reading materials to students' present levels of reading ability, we need to know more than the average grade-level readability of a given prose selection. We need to know how well an individual student will fare with this material. To get this kind of information, we might wish to use a *Cloze procedure*. This procedure, you may recall, was introduced in Chapter 6, "Diagnosing Students' Needs." The Cloze procedure will result in a measure of each student in the class that will tell us whether he or she is at the "independent" reading level, the "instructional" reading level, or the "frustration" reading level with regard to the specific prose selection we used in building the Cloze test. In practice, there is merit in following a two-step procedure to determine the appropriateness of a given selection for an individual student:

1. Use a Fry readability graph to identify material that is approximately correct given the grade level you will teach. (It is better to find material written at a reading level below your grade rather than material written at a more sophisticated reading level.)
2. Prepare a Cloze test based on this material to identify students who will be operating at the frustration level if asked to read the selection(s) you have identified.

This two-part sequence identifies a number of youngsters who are operating at the frustration level. An effort should be made to identify alternative reading materials. Of course, if no other materials can be found (and, indeed, even when they can), it is wise to think about a variety of ways to introduce content that will supplement assigned reading.

Figure 16-2

GRAPH FOR ESTIMATING READABILITY—EXTENDED*

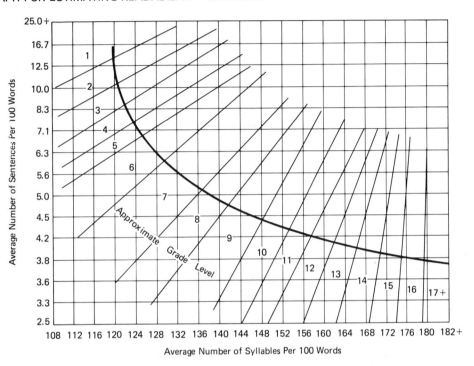

Average Number of Syllables Per 100 Words

Expanded Directions for Working Readability Graph

1. Randomly select three sample passages and count out exactly 100 words each, beginning with the beginning of a sentence. Count proper nouns, initializations, and numerals.
2. Count the number of sentences in 100 words, estimating length of the fraction of the last sentence to the nearest one tenth.
3. Count the total number of syllables in the 100-word passage. If you do not have a hand counter available, simply put a mark above every syllable over one in each word; then when you get to the end of the passage, count the number of marks and add 100. Small calculators can also be used as counters by pushing numeral 1, then push the + sign for each word or syllable when counting.
4. Enter graph with *average* sentence length and *average* number of syllables; plot dot where the two lines intersect. Area where dot is plotted will give you the approximate grade level.
5. If a great deal of variability is found in syllable count or sentence count, putting more samples into the average is desirable.
6. A word is defined as a group of symbols with a space on either side; thus, *Joe, IRA, 1945,* and & are each one word.
7. A syllable is defined as a phonetic syllable. Generally, there are as many syllables as vowel sounds. For example, *stopped* is one syllable and *wanted* is two syllables. When counting syllables for numerals and initializations, count one syllable for each symbol. For example, *1945* is four syllables, *IRA* is three syllables, and & is one syllable.

*This extended graph does not outmode or render the earlier (1968) version inoperative or inaccurate; it is an extension.
Source: Edward Fry, "Fry's Readability Graph: Clarifications, Validity, and Extension to Level 17," *Journal of Reading* (December 1977): 249.

Figure 16-3

REWRITING MATERIALS TO LOWER THEIR MEASURED GRADE-LEVEL READABILITY

CAN YOU DO IT?

1. Find a secondary school textbook for a subject you would like to teach. Using the Fry readability graph, determine the approximate grade-level readability of this book.

2. Suppose that you were using this book and found that most of your students were able to read material successfully only if it had a measured grade-level readability at least two years below what you had found to be the grade-level readability of this text. State what you might do to help these students.

3. Take 1 of the 100 word samples from the text that you used to determine the grade-level readability of the book. Rewrite this sample so that it will have a grade-level readability at least two grade levels below what you determined it to be in its original state.

4. Find a professional journal in your academic major. Choose one that is directed primarily to an audience of college professors. (Usually such articles use many complex terms and feature a good number of very long sentences. They usually have a very high measured readability level.) Prepare a 500-word summary of the contents of this article that is written at about a grade 7 level of readability. Use the Fry readability graph to check on your success in writing material at this level of reading difficulty.

An additional response, and one whose practicality may be limited because of heavy demands on teachers' time, is for the teacher to rewrite certain key passages in such a way that the reading level is lowered. Basically this amounts to shortening sentences and to substituting shorter words for longer words (when this can be accomplished without doing violence to the meaning). Teachers rarely have difficulty in mastering the technique of reducing readability levels. But the process does take time. Certainly no teacher has time to rewrite his or her entire textbook. But there is merit in rewriting selected critical passages when time can be found to accomplish the task (perhaps during the summer).

PREPARING STUDENTS TO WORK WITH TEXTBOOKS

Nearly all secondary school courses feature the use of textbooks. Certainly sound instructional planning provides opportunities for students to be introduced to content in many ways that do not require reading. Certainly, too, where reading is required, this reading by no means is always tied to a course textbook. Nevertheless, with very few exceptions, secondary school students will be required to spend at least some of their time working with textbooks. Consequently, it makes sense for us to prepare them to work productively with these learning materials (see Figure 16-4). This preparation can focus students' attention on the structure of the textbook.

The Text Overview

Campbell (1978) recommends that teachers take time at the beginning of the course to engage in a series of text overview lessons with students. The text overview focuses primarily on the table of contents. Several levels of organization are included in the table of contents that can be brought to students' attention. Nearly all texts are broken down into individual chapters. Typically, clusters of chapters are organized together around major unit titles. Subordinate unit titles may be used to organize even smaller numbers of chapters within major units. Campbell suggests that the general organization scheme be discussed with students and that they be asked to respond to some

Figure 16-4

PREPARING STUDENTS TO USE TEXTBOOKS

CAN YOU DO IT?
Select a textbook for a course you might teach. Be sure that it is a textbook designed for use in a middle school, junior high school, or senior high school. (A college or university textbook will not do.) Describe a set of procedures you would follow to prepare students to work with this textbook. Do all of the following:

1. Prepare a set of exercises based on the table of contents of the textbook.
2. If your table of contents includes references to subtopics in individual chapters, then prepare a set of questions you would ask students about subtopics in one chapter. If your table of contents does not include references to subtopics in individual chapters, devise an exercise that will require students to work with individual chapters to identify subtopics and pages where they are found.
3. Prepare a set of exercises designed to reinforce students' alphabetizing skills.
4. Select a portion of the index in your textbook and prepare a set of questions you would ask students requiring them to demonstrate an ability to use the index.

---

questions requiring them to look closely at the information provided in the table of contents.

To refresh our memories regarding how a typical table of contents looks in a secondary school text, let us look at the table of contents for Preston E. James and Nelda Davis' high school geography text, *The Wide World* (1972), on p. 372. Notice that this table of contents includes both major unit titles and subordinate unit titles.

In terms of its design, *The Wide World* is typical of the massive secondary school texts that attempt to deal with a tremendous quantity of content in a single volume. To help students focus on the nature of the content, the organization of the content, the sequence of the content, and the relative importance of the content (at least as it can be inferred from the extent of its treatment), students might be asked to respond to some questions such as the following:

1. Look at the subheadings. (They are the ones under the major part titles. For example, the first subheading in Part 1 is "Before the Age of Discovery.") Would you say that these authors are more interested in teaching you about maps, globes, and locations of countries and cities or are they more interested in teaching you about how different peoples live? How do you know?
2. Usually authors try and explain basic information students need to know in the first part of their book. Look at the information provided in the chapters in Part 1. Make a list of the kinds of information the authors explain in these chapters. (Just include the major ideas that they try to get across in this section.)
3. Compare the numbers of chapters under each of the major parts of the book (Part 1, Part 2, and Part 3). Do differences in the numbers of chapters under each part tell you anything about what the authors believe to be important? If so, what?
4. Look at the first subheading under Part 2 ("Man on the Land"). Why do you think chapters under this subheading have been introduced before rather than after the other chapters in Part 2? (Hint: Do you need to understand information presented in the "Man on the Land" chapters to understand the other chapters in the unit?)
5. Why do you suppose the authors have organized chapters focusing on the European culture region, the Soviet culture region, and the Anglo-American culture region before those focusing on other culture regions described in Part 2?

Table of Contents

Source: From *The Wide World,* 3rd rev. ed., by Preston E. James and Nelda Davis. Copyright © 1972. Used with the permission of Macmillan Publishing Co., Inc., New York

6. Compare the number of pages devoted to each of the subheadings under Part 2. Are there great differences in the number of pages devoted to the various culture regions? If so, does this tell you something about how important the authors feel it is for students to learn about one culture region as opposed to another? Explain your answer.

7. If you were not interested in learning about specific countries but were concerned only with understanding something about general differences among each of the culture regions in Part 2, which chapters would you read? Which would you not read?

8. Identify chapters that deal with more than four countries each. Identify other chapters that deal with only one or two countries. Why do you suppose the authors decided to deal with only one or two countries in some chapters and a great many countries in other chapters?

9. A "glossary" is a part of a book in which specialized words are explained. Where would you find the glossary in this book?

10. An "index" is a part of the book in which you can find out the numbers of the pages where the authors discuss specific ideas or topics. Where does the index begin in this book?

11. Some world countries may have names you do not recognize. In what chapters would you find information about these countries: Malawi, Lesotho, Togo, Malta, and Albania?

12. If you were concerned about the problem of running out of natural resources, your best source of information in this text would be which chapter?

These questions are simply samples of those that might be asked. Clearly the level of question difficulty must be geared to the abilities of class members. Constructed properly, an exercise such as the one illustrated here provides a very worthwhile supplement to a lesson focusing on the table of contents and what it says about the nature of the textbook. Students who receive a formal introduction to their texts via some systematic instruction based on the table of contents have the potential for beginning their courses with a much better "feel" for the kind of help their books can provide them.

Once a general overview of the book has been provided via a careful exploration and explanation of the table of contents, we might narrow our focus and deal with the structure of a single chapter. Some texts provide a good deal of detail in the table of contents with regard to what individual chapters contain. Major subtopics in *The Wide World*, for example, are identified by page number for each chapter. Note the layout of information in the table of contents for Chapter 19.*

Source: From *The Wide World*, 3rd rev. ed., by Preston E. James and Nelda Davis. Copyright © 1972. Used with the permission of Macmillan Publishing Co., Inc., New York.

When this kind of detail is provided in the table of contents, we can ask students a number of questions to which they can respond by referring to the subtopics noted under the major chapter listing. For example, we might ask such questions as these about Chapter 19:

1. How many communist countries are described?
2. What specific information about each country is revealed by the subtopic title?
3. Why do you think the authors have organized the chapter to discuss Poland first, Czechoslovakia second, and so forth?
4. Do you think that the authors provide much detailed information about each of these countries in the chapter? Why, or why not? (Hint: Look at the number of pages devoted to a discussion of each country.)

Regrettably, many texts do not have such detailed information about chapter subtopics provided in the table of contents. When a textbook to be used is deficient in this regard, it is productive to organize students into groups to develop expanded table of contents listings for selected chapters. Students might be organized into five groups of about six students each. Students might be advised to proceed as follows:

Teacher: All right, now we have everybody in a group. I want you to select someone to be the group recorder. I want this group to work with Chapter 4, this group with Chapter 9, this group with Chapter 11, this group with Chapter 15, and this group with Chapter 19.

At the top of the butcher paper sheet I have placed at each table, write the title of your chapter and the page number in the book where it starts. For example, the Chapter 4 group will write "Brave Men Negotiate a Continent" and page 49 at the top of their sheet.

Now, I want people in each group to go through the assigned chapter to look for major topics in the chapter. You will find these identified with the heavy type. See, I am holding up the book, and it is opened to the middle of Chapter 1. See this very dark printing at the beginning of this paragraph. It reads, "New Lands, New Challenges." This is one of the subtopics in Chapter 1. Locate these subtopics and write them on your butcher paper. Also write down the page on which they occur. When you have finished, we will put the butcher paper sheets on the wall with masking tape and take a look at what we found. Are there any questions?

Once the information has been logged on the butcher paper sheets, students can be asked to respond to similar kinds of questions regarding chapter contents that were illustrated in the discussion of Chapter 19 from *The Wide World.* This exercise helps students to recognize the major emphases within chapters. A subsequent discussion can be directed toward helping them grasp the idea that headings indicating subtopics provide useful cues about what things the author (or authors) believes (believe) to be important.

Another section of the textbook students need to know how to use is the index. Students who are familiar with the index can save themselves a great deal of time as they attempt to locate specific information in the textbook. Successful use of the index requires good alphabetizing skills. Although they have been exposed to the alphabet and alphabetizing skills during their elementary school years, many secondary school students need some refresher work on these topics before they can use a book index successfully. Shuman (1978) recommends a series of short exercises in which students are asked to alphabetize lists of words. Each successive exercise is somewhat more difficult. Let us assume that we wished to develop three sets. We could set them up in this way:

> **Directions**: Look at the list of words. Place a "1" before the word that comes first alphabetically, a "2" before the word that comes second alphabetically, and a "3" before the word that comes third alphabetically. Continue in the same fashion, concluding with a "6" before the word that comes sixth alphabetically.

Easiest List

_____ tether
_____ husking
_____ lignite
_____ volt
_____ mystery
_____ contour

Slightly More Difficult List

_____ yoke
_____ yang
_____ yield
_____ yucca
_____ yew
_____ year

Most Difficult List

_____ wiring
_____ wired
_____ wirra
_____ wirehaired terrier
_____ wireless
_____ wiretap

Note that, on the second list, students must look beyond the first letter (and in two instances beyond the second letter) to make the appropriate decision. In the third list, the student in every case must look beyond the third letter (and in four instances beyond the fourth letter) to make the appropriate decision. A brief, sequential exercise of this kind, supported by a brief discussion ("Remember, when two words start with the same letters, we have to look at the point in each word where letters begin to differ before we can decide which should be alphabetized first"), can be of great value in preparing students to work with a book index.

After a review of basic alphabetizing procedures, we may wish to have students begin applying these skills by working directly with a book index. This exercise can also help them to understand the specific use of the index as a source of information regarding where particular topics are treated in the text. One method of preparing an index use exercise involves reproducing part of a page from the textbook index along with questions related to the items indexed. Sufficient copies of this material are made so each student may have one. An example of such an exercise follows:

Using the Index

> **Directions:** Below, you will find part of a page taken from the index in your text. Below this part of the index you will find some questions. You can find answers to these questions by referring to the portion of the index reproduced for you here.

Answer each question. Use your own paper.

Source: Index items from *The Wide World,* 3rd rev. ed., by Preston E. James and Nelda Davis. Copyright © 1972. Used with the permission of Macmillan Publishing Co., Inc., New York.

1. On what page(s) would you find mention of Mongolia?
2. On what page(s) would you find information about surface features of Mexico?
3. Are there more pages in this textbook devoted to Mexico or to Micronesia? How do you know?
4. If you wanted to find out some very general information about industries of Middle America, on what page(s) would you look? Where would you look if you wanted more detailed information?
5. Suppose you knew quite a bit about agriculture in the United States. You might be interested in comparing agriculture in the United States with agriculture in Mexico and in Middle America. If you had such an interest, on what page(s) would you look to find information?

An exercise of this kind can give students some practical experience in using the index in their course textbook. Potential problems students might have can be inferred from mistakes they make on the index-based questions. Once the exercise has been completed, it is a good idea to review index use with the class and clarify any misconceptions.

In considering these suggestions about preparing students to work with textbooks, inexperienced secondary school teachers may find themselves a bit skeptical regarding their importance. They do, after all, seem to be dealing with some skills that are very basic and that, in many cases, have been introduced in elementary schools. A novice secondary school teacher may be forgiven for wondering whether time spent teaching secondary school students how to use a textbook might be "a waste of valuable time."

"Shouldn't secondary students know all these things?" they may well ask. Well, whether they should or should not is a debatable point. But what is beyond dispute is that large numbers of middle school, junior high school, and senior high school students do not come to their courses well grounded in procedures associated with efficient use of their textual materials. As a result, some time spent at the beginning of the course in reviewing textbook use skills may pay dividends in terms of improved student learning.

Teacher-Prepared Glossaries

In addition to working with students to improve their general abilities to locate specific information quickly, we can also take some specific action to help youngsters with vocabulary problems they may encounter as they read the course textbook (or other assigned prose materials). This can be accomplished by our skimming the text and attempting to identify words that might cause problems for some students. Some teachers who have adopted this procedure prepare lists of these words and ask students to look up meanings in the dictionary. In general, this is not a productive procedure.

First, dictionary definitions may themselves use words that students do not know. Suppose a student looked up "chicken pox" in the dictionary and found something like this:

> **chicken pox** an extremely contagious virus-related disease characterized by a low-grade fever that is accompanied by the formation of vesicles.

If the student does not know the terms "contagious," "virus," "low-grade fever," or "vesicles," he or she is not likely to be much enlightened by this dictionary definition. It is true that some school dictionaries try to use simplified vocabularies in their definitions. But even these may confront poor readers with words they do not understand. The bottom line is that students with reading problems (and they are often the ones who would find it necessary to look up large numbers of unfamiliar words) tend to be frustrated when they are asked to expand their vocabularies by looking up dictionary meanings.

An approach that some teachers have found to be more beneficial involves development of teacher-prepared glossaries. Teacher-prepared glossaries can be developed through a two-stage process. First, the teacher scans the textbook and circles or otherwise identifies words that might prove difficult for students. (It is important that nontechnical as well as technical words are identified.) Second, the teacher develops definitions of these words that are written at a level that students understand.

The task of developing a teacher-prepared glossary is not so overwhelming as might be imagined. Textbook authors tend to fall into patterns of word usage. Words used in the first chapters tend to occur many times throughout subsequent chapters. Consequently, the teacher's task gets progressively easier as he or she works through the text identifying words to include on the glossary. In chapters toward the end of the book, relatively few terms may need to be added to those already on the list.

When reading assignments are made, terms from the master textbook glossary can be reproduced and distributed to students. Numbers of terms on the sheets provided to students should be limited only to words that they will encounter in the assigned reading. The lists should be provided to *all* students, not just to the poor readers. This procedure assures that no student will feel that he or she has been singled out as a slow learner in need of special help. Further, even some of the better readers may find it useful to refer to definitions on the list as they work through their reading assignments. Distribution of these lists from teacher-prepared glossaries, at least in some instances, has been shown to promote dramatic improvements in students' abilities to learn from prose materials (Blossom 1973).

To see how a teacher-prepared glossary project might begin, let us suppose that we will be teaching a course using as our text *The Wide World* (James and Davis 1972). As we read through the text, we might identify words on each page that we propose to include on our mastery glossary list. One page in the text might look like this once we had identified these words:

The Hot and Humid Season

The second season is from March to early June. This is the hot season, when winds are gentle, and the sun-baked dry earth is parched and the vegetation is brown. Notice that the hottest time of the year is in May. Look also at the map on page 117. You can see that in the Ganges Valley, north of Bombay, there is a belt of land within which the temperatures climb to 110° at least once a year. The air is so hot and humid that people who wear heavy clothing and neckties suffer great discomfort. One writer suggested that even the brass doorknobs get mushy.

The Monsoons

The third season is from June to September. The beginning of this rainy season is dramatic. For several days there are great rolls of dark storm clouds on the southern horizon and at night there are vivid flashes of lightning. When the first big drops of rain come to the parched earth, people rush outdoors to feel the wetness. A fragrant smell fills the air as the dry earth is moistened. Then the rains begin in earnest. With the brilliant flashes of lightning and roars of thunder, it seems as if the clouds break open. Sheets of rain come pouring down while the people stand in the open, letting the life-giving water run over them.

These are no ordinary rains. Once they start they go on for months without stopping. The weather data for Bombay show that the rainfall is *very heavy* from June until the end of September. The winds have now shifted from the northeast to the southwest. The heavy clouds shield

Source: From *The Wide World*, 3rd rev. ed., by Preston E. James and Nelda Davis. Copyright © 1972. Used with the permission of Macmillan Publishing Co., Inc., New York.

The identified words then can be defined in terms that students understand:

Bombay   a very large city located on the west coast of India.

data   facts; specific pieces of information.

fragrant   having a sweet odor something like we might notice when we smell fresh flowers or good perfume.

horizon   when we look across the land, this is the place where the earth and sky seem to touch.

in earnest   seriously.

parched   very dry.

These terms and accompanying definitions then would be grouped together with others from the textbook to form the master glossary.

Because of the many demands on teachers' time during the school year, many teachers find it more convenient to prepare glossaries during times of the year when they are not teaching. One very successful project of this kind involved teams of teachers from individual subject areas who worked together to develop a master glossary for the textbook they were using (Blossom 1973). When arrangements can be made, this kind of cooperative effort has much to commend it.

PREPARING STUDENTS FOR READING ASSIGNMENTS

"For tomorrow, read pages 45 through 54." Some beginning teachers think a short statement such as this one is all the preparation students need for a reading assignment. They are mistaken. This painfully bare-boned explanation of the assigned task does nothing to motivate students. It does nothing to point out the purpose of the reading exercise. It is so sparsely detailed that a student may be forgiven for saying to himself or herself "Why should I do this?"

Many teachers have found that more students will do the reading and profit from it when a more detailed and systematic approach to making reading assignments is followed. Typical of these systematic approaches is the following three-part sequence:

1. Survey the content and introduce potentially difficult words to students to prepare them for the reading assignment.
2. Point out potentially difficult areas in the reading and mention specific pages students should read with particular care.
3. Establish a specific purpose for reading.

Using such a sequence, there is a good chance that larger numbers of students will be able to profit from reading the assigned material. Some specific explanations of each step in this sequence are provided in the following sections.

Content Survey and Introduction

The content of the intended reading assignment should be reviewed to identify potential vocabulary problems. The same general procedure can be followed as was suggested in the section describing teacher-prepared glossaries. These terms can be written on the chalkboard, printed on butcher paper, or projected on a screen from an overhead projector transparency.

Once these words are available for student viewing, the teacher can take time to explain meanings of each. Special care should be taken to point out instances where the meaning of a term as used in the assigned reading may be different from a more common meaning with which students are familiar. For example, many students readily recognize the meaning of the word *precious* as "valuable, or high priced." But many are not familiar with the alternative meaning of *precious* as "affected or overly refined." If the assigned reading uses the word in this less familiar sense, the teacher should take time to explain this usage of the word and provide students with sample sentences illustrating this usage.

To provide students with a feel for the context within which terms appear, it is a good idea to read sentences from the reading assignment aloud in which these terms appear. Assuming that some introduction to the meaning of the terms has taken place, students can be questioned about the meaning of these sentences as a check on their level of understanding of the focus terms. For example, suppose that we were teaching an economics course. We might have identified "market" as one of the terms we felt might pose a problem. We might select a sentence from the assigned reading and ask students some questions such as the following:

Sentence: The activities of numerous buyers and sellers are coordinated by the marvelous market mechanism.

1. Is the author talking about a grocery store when he uses the word "market" in this sentence?
2. How would you define the term "market" as it is being used in this sentence?
3. In your own words, tell me what this sentence means?

Any problems that surface as these sentences are discussed cue the teacher to provide additional explanations. To reinforce work with potentially difficult words, students can be provided individually with lists of words and definitions that have been written at a level they can understand.

Pointing out Difficult Parts

In many printed materials there are great differences in the idea content and in the general degree of difficulty from one section to another. The more difficult parts of the reading assignment should be identified by the teacher and pointed out to students as the reading assignment is being made. Often, a clarifying comment or two by the teacher will help students to cope with some of the more challenging parts of the reading assignment. For example, suppose that we were working with a group of middle school youngsters on a unit focusing on geographic skills. We might say something to them such as the following to call their attention to a part of the reading assignment that might prove confusing:

> *All right, remember now we have talked about these two terms "rotation" and "revolution." In your book, there is a discussion of these two terms on pages 14 and 15. Read this material very carefully. Remember, these two terms do not mean the same thing. Take your time reading the material on these two pages. I think it will help you see the differences between "rotation" and "revolution" more clearly.*

A brief reference will frequently result in students' paying particular attention to targeted sections of the reading assignment.

Establishing a Purpose

The statement of purpose should be tied to the content in the material students are asked to read. (The purpose is not to read pages 12 to 17 but, rather, to get something important out of this experience.) The best statements of purpose cue students to what they can expect to derive from their reading. They also serve to motivate students to complete the reading.

Visual aids can also be used to advantage to help students to understand a purpose for their reading and stimulate interest. Suppose, for example, that we were teaching a world history course. We had arrived at the post–World War I period and were about to begin a study of the German economy during this time. We might establish a purpose for reading by using a visual aid and making comments such as the following to our students:

> *"In my right hand I have a German banknote from the early 1920s. Remember that instead of dollars the Germans used marks. This is a bill for 500,000 marks.*
>
> *"Sounds like a lot doesn't it. I mean, wouldn't all of us love to have 500,000 dollars? I know I would.*
>
> *"Now there were some strange things going on in Germany in the early 1920s. Would you believe me if I told you that lots of people had 50,000-mark, 100,000-mark, and even larger bills in Germany at this time? Does this mean everybody was rich? Maybe yes, maybe no. Now as you read your assignment for tomorrow, on pages 56 through 65, I want you to think about these two questions. First, why were there so many big bills in circulation in Germany at this time? Second, were people really well off at this time? You might wish to take some notes about these questions as you read the assignment. Tomorrow we'll talk about what you found out."*

Some teachers have found it productive to take advantage of the enthusiasm of many secondary school students for competitive situations. One approach to giving assignments that build on this interest involves dividing members of the class into several teams. For example, we might be teaching a biology unit focusing on genetics. In preparation for reading an assignment in which explanations of the chromosome hypothesis and the gene theory are included, we might divide the class into two teams. Directions might be something like the following:

"Now do all of you know what team you're on? Good. All right, I want all of you to pay very close attention to the information on pages 119 through 127 in your text. You will find a description of something called the chromosome hypothesis and of something called the gene theory here. Read the arguments for and against both the chromosome hypothesis and the gene theory.

"Tomorrow, at the beginning of the period, we'll let the team 1 people meet briefly in the back of the room and the team 2 people in the front of the room. I'll give each team some butcher paper and a marker. I will want each team to list all the arguments supporting and as many arguments opposing both the chromosome hypothesis and the gene theory. I don't want you to use any notes. So read your assignments carefully and try to remember as many arguments supporting and opposing the chromosome hypothesis and the gene theory as you can. Let's see which one of our two teams can come up with the largest number of arguments supporting and opposing each point of view."

When students have a purpose for reading, they are encouraged to read much more selectively. The purpose provides them with a device for identifying important information and skipping over less essential material. Without these guidelines, students may feel themselves to be lost in a confusing forest of details. Teacher time spent helping students to identify a purpose for reading can help them to develop the capacity to develop their own purposes for reading, independent of teacher direction. A technique for helping students develop informational objectives of their own as they read is introduced in the next section.

TEACHING STUDENTS TO LEARN FROM TEXTBOOKS

Reading a textbook is not the same as reading a novel or a magazine article. Even students who are proficient readers often do not derive as much as they should from reading textbooks. In part, this is because they are unaware that there are different purposes for textbook reading than for recreational reading. Much recreational reading is undertaken for relaxation or even for "escape" from the cares of the day. Consequently, details tend to be skimmed. Enjoyment can be had even when much of the specific content is forgotten almost as soon as it has been read.

On the other hand, textbook reading is directed toward providing students with understandings that may be rather specific. Students will acquire these understandings only if they adopt an approach to textbook reading that is different from their approach to recreational reading. Large numbers of students can profit from specific instruction designed to help them make this necessary transition.

SQ3R

One of the best known schemes for approaching textbook reading systematically is the SQ3R technique (Robinson 1972). SQ3R describes a series of steps to be followed in reading textbook materials that can result in improved understanding of the content.

There are five elements or steps in the system: one "S," one "Q," and three "R's." These are as follows:

Step 1. S = Survey of content

Step 2. Q = Question development

Step 3. R = Read to answer question

Step 4. R = Recite to check on grasp of answers

Step 5. R = Review to check on understanding

Survey of Content.   In step 1, the reader is encouraged to skim over the entire reading assignment. He or she is advised to look only at major headings and to attempt to get a "feel" for no more than about half a dozen key ideas. The survey of content phase of SQ3R should take no more than about one minute. Students who are new to the technique should be warned to avoid the temptation to pause to read carefully for details during this step.

Question Development.   During this step, students look only at each major heading in the pages covered by the assignment. (The assignment might be part of a chapter, an entire chapter, or parts of more than one chapter.) Students are asked to look at each major heading and are directed to rewrite each as a question. Some teachers have found it useful for the questions developed from each major heading to be written by students at the top of separate pieces of paper. (These can be used in later steps when students are taking notes as they read relevant material in their attempts to respond to their questions.) To see how questions might be framed from major headings, suppose that we had assigned students to read some material about Italy contained on pages 249 through 254 in our course textbook, *The Wide World* (James and Davis 1972). Note the major headings and the example of a question a student might develop from each:

Population: Urban Versus Rural
    Possible question: "What is the pattern of rural and urban population in Italy?"

Agriculture in the North
    Possible question: "What are the characteristics of agriculture in Northern Italy?"

Agricultural Poverty in the South
    Possible question: "What are the characteristics of agriculture in Southern Italy?"

Booming Manufacturing in the North
    Possible question: "What things are manufactured in Northern Italy?"

Bringing the Industrial Revolution to the South
    Possible question: "What is being done to industrialize Southern Italy?"

Italy and the EEC
    Possible question: "What is Italy's role in the European Economic Community?

Read to Answer Question.   The questions formulated in step 2 provide students with a purpose for reading. This purpose is to find information to answer their questions. In step 3, students read material under the major heading related to each question they have developed. This means that they read only one major section of the assignment at a time. For example, they would read and stop at the end of the major section "Population: Urban Versus Rural" before going on to the material under "Agriculture and the North." As they read, students are encouraged to take brief notes. These notes should refer to specific information that may help them to respond to the question they have developed from the major heading title. In no case should notes be written in complete sentences. In no case should material be copied directly from the book. Notes should be quick, shorthand reminders that relate to the question. For example, a student might have jotted down the following brief notes related to this question:

"What is the pattern of rural and urban population in Italy?"
45 percent overall in cities
More in cities in North Italy than in South Italy
North Italy more industrialized
South Italy little industry, few cities
South Italy: more population growth than North Italy
Problem: too many people for land
Many left country; still too many there

These notes are very sketchy. But they are sufficient to remind the student of the key points he or she has read.

Recite to Check on Grasp of Answers.   Once a part of the assignment has been read (the part related to a single question developed from a major heading), students are encouraged to engage in a kind of self-test to see how well they recall what they have read. They are encouraged to look away from the text and to think about the question they have devised. They are encouraged to try to respond to this question as best they can without looking at notes. Some teachers suggest that students try writing certain key points from memory. When this has been done, answers can be checked against notes. This same process is repeated for each major section in the reading assignment.

Review.   During the final step, students are encouraged to look at each of the questions they have developed from the major headings. As they do so, they are asked to cover up notes they have taken as they have read material related to each of these major sections. They are encouraged to recall from memory as much information about each section as possible. When necessary, they may look at notes to fill in gaps.

The SQ3R technique, as introduced here, can help students approach textbook reading in a manner that differs from their approach to recreational reading. Formulation of questions helps them to establish a need for certain information included in the assigned reading. In summary, SQ3R enables students to work efficiently as they attempt to learn from textbook reading.

Posttest

Directions: Using your own paper, answer each of the following true/false questions. For each correct statement, write the word "true." For each incorrect statement, write the word "false."

_____   1. The Fry readability graph produces a score that will tell a teacher how well an individual student might fare with a given prose selection.

_____   2. The level of reading sophistication of the typical senior high school student today is no different from the level of reading sophistication of the typical senior high school student in 1910.

_____   3. When a textbook is described as being written on the tenth-grade level of readability, this does not necessarily mean that every student in the tenth grade will be able to read the book without difficulty.

_____ 4. It is possible for a book to have a low grade-level readability and yet still contain many vocabulary words students find very difficult.

_____ 5. To encourage students to develop and use reading skills, it is important that at least some parts of tests that are administered require students to use information that they have learned from their reading.

_____ 6. When students are asked to read an assignment, it is a sound instructional practice to explain to them what the purpose of their reading is to be.

_____ 7. By the time students are in secondary school, all are proficient users of book indexes and library indexes.

_____ 8. The SQ3R technique is a procedure that has been developed for the purpose of helping students develop a systematic and purposeful approach to the skill of reading material in course textbooks.

_____ 9. Obsolete word usages frequently present problems to readers of secondary school age.

_____ 10. In general, reading difficulty of a passage can be reduced by rewriting it in such a way that average sentence length is decreased and the number of words with large numbers of syllables is decreased.

Key Ideas in Review

1. A much higher percentage of the total population of secondary-school-aged youngsters is in school today than was true at the turn of the century. In 1900, nearly all students in secondary schools were headed toward additional academic work in colleges and universities. Today, this situation is much changed. Many students are enrolled in secondary schools today who would never have gone beyond the elementary grades in earlier times. Consequently, the number of students with severe reading skills problems is much higher today than it was in secondary school classrooms at the turn of the century.

2. If teachers wish students to accept the idea that reading is important, teachers must act in ways that communicate to students that they believe reading is important. For example, teachers can see to it that students have opportunities to see teachers reading for enjoyment. Books and articles that the teacher has read can be discussed with and recommended to students. Tests can be developed in such a way that at least some of the questions build on knowledge students have gained through reading.

3. Readability refers to the relative level of sophistication of some given reading material. A number of procedures are available that can be used to determine the approximate grade-level reading difficulty of prose materials. In general, material becomes more difficult as lengths of sentences increase and as numbers of words with many syllables increase. When a book is found to have a given grade-level readability, this does not mean that every student at this grade level should be able to read the book without difficulty. Grade-level readability is based on a class average. Clearly some students will be above this average, and others will be below this average.

4. Although large numbers of teachers expect students to be unfamiliar with technical vocabulary introduced in textbooks, many are surprised by the large numbers of nontechnical terms that many students do not know. In particular students have difficulty with obsolete terms, with colloquial vocabulary, and with unfamiliar vocabulary. Robert C. Aukerman (1972) has developed lists of nontechnical terms for a number of subjects that stump many students. These lists can be used to compare potential reading problems students might encounter with alternative reading selections.

5. Students' success in working with textbooks can be proved when teachers take time to explain the structure of the text and how the text can be used productively. In particular, time spent introducing students to the table of contents and the index can help students to use the textbook more efficiently. Further, provision of some kind of systematic approach to textbook reading, such as SQ3R, may help students to learn efficiently from textbook sources.

6. Teacher-prepared glossaries can help students as they read assigned prose materials. Such glossaries, including definitions written in simple prose that students can understand, can be distributed to students when reading assignments are made. When this practice has been followed, there is evidence of enhanced student learning (Blossom 1973).

7. It is a mistake for teachers to make a reading assignment simply by saying, for example, "For tomorrow, read pages 93 through 100." It is much more productive to give students a purpose for reading. When students have a purpose, they have a mechanism for sorting relevant from irrelevant information. An additional consideration in making assignments involves discussing problem vocabulary in advance of the assignment and pinpointing sections of the material to be read to which students should pay particular attention.

SUMMARY

Many beginning secondary school teachers are astonished at the number of students in their classes who have difficulty in reading. This problem is more pronounced today than it was in earlier years when only an intellectually talented elite attended school beyond the elementary years. Today, nearly the entire population of secondary-school-aged youngsters is enrolled in secondary schools. Because some lower-ability students, who in earlier times might have dropped out of school after their elementary school years, are today enrolled in high schools, the number of students with reading problems in secondary school classrooms is larger now than it was, for example, in 1900.

Many secondary students do not have large vocabularies. Consequently, they have a hard time with textbooks and other print materials that use words unfamiliar to them. Secondary school teachers must be prepared for students who have no idea at all about the meanings of words that teachers, it seems, think "everybody ought to know." Students have particular difficulty with obsolete terms, colloquial words, and words that they have never encountered directly in their own experience. Some teachers have found it useful to develop glossaries of their own to pass out to students when reading assignments are made. These glossaries include potentially difficult words with definitions written in a language students can understand.

Students' likelihood of success with textbooks can be increased when teachers take time to teach students how to use them. Exercises based on the table of contents and the index may prove helpful. Further, large numbers of students may profit from an introduction to a systematic procedure for studying material introduced in textbooks such as the SQ3R technique.

In making reading assignments, students must sense some purpose for reading. It is not enough for them to be told simply to read from page 111 to page 119. They must have a reason for accomplishing this task. They can be provided with questions to answer, hypotheses to be tested, or with other tasks that can convince them of some personally felt need to acquire the information presented in the prose material.

Teachers themselves need to practice what they preach when it comes to reading. Because secondary school students are inclined to "do what teachers do rather than what teachers say," teachers who want students to enjoy reading must, themselves, be observed in situations when they are enjoying reading. They need to talk enthusiastically with students about what they have read. In short, they need to show to students that their interest in reading is real, and not just something they talk about to students.'

References

Aukerman, Robert C. *Reading in the Secondary School Classroom.* New York: McGraw-Hill Book Company, 1972.

Blossom, Grace A. "The Tolleson Story: The Tolleson Six School Reading Project: A Pilot Project to Help All Students Read Grade Level Textbooks with Adequate Comprehension," ERIC No. ED 086 967. Phoenix: Arizona State Department of Education, 1973.

Campbell, John J. "Staff Development for Content Teachers: An Ice-Breaker," *Reading World* (March 1978): 205–209.

Fry, Edward. "Fry's Readability Graph: Clarifications, Validity, and Extension to Level 17," *Journal of Reading* (December 1977): 242–252.

James, Preston E., and Davis, Nelda. *The Wide World,* 3rd rev. ed. New York: Macmillan Publishing Co., Inc., 1972.

Manning, Maryann Murphy, and Manning, Gary L. *Reading Instruction in the Middle School.* Washington, D.C.: National Education Association, 1979.

National Center for Education Statistics. *The Condition of Education, 1979.* Washington, D.C.: U.S. Government Printing Office, 1979.

Rieck, Billie Jo. "How Content Teachers Telegraph Messages Against Reading," *Journal of Reading* (May 1977): 646–648.

Robinson, Francis P. *Effective Study.* 4th ed. New York: Harper & Row, Publishers, Inc., 1972.

Robinson, H. Alan. *Teaching Reading and Study Strategies: The Content Areas.* 2nd ed. Boston: Allyn & Bacon, Inc., 1978.

Shuman, R. Baird. "Teaching Teachers to Teach Reading in Secondary School Content Classes," *Journal of Reading* (December 1978): 205–211.

Taylor, Wilson L. "Cloze Procedure: A New Tool for Measuring Readability," *Journalism Quarterly* (Fall 1953): 415–433.

IV

TEACHERS IN THE SECONDARY SCHOOL

17

Profiles of Secondary School Teachers

"Just got his master's degree. He's trying out his sweeping generalizations."

Objectives

This chapter provides information to help the reader to

1. Recognize kinds of backgrounds from which large numbers of secondary school teachers come.

2. Identify patterns of commitment to the teaching profession of secondary school teachers.

3. Note attitudes toward change characterizing many secondary school teachers.

4. Suggest several characteristics of effective secondary school teachers.

5. Describe a number of factors that may contribute to secondary school teachers' levels of job satisfaction.

Pretest

Directions: Using your own paper, answer each of the following true/false questions. For each correct statement, write the word ''true.'' For each incorrect statement, write the word ''false.''

_____ 1. Secondary school teachers who held white-collar positions prior to entering teaching are more likely to leave the profession than are those who held blue-collar positions prior to entering teaching.

_____ 2. A good many secondary school teachers find boredom with their work to be a problem.

_____ 3. The vast majority of secondary school teachers report that they would choose to go into teaching again were they given an opportunity to go back and choose whatever career they wanted.

_____ 4. There is some evidence that older teachers (those over 50) tend to be more satisfied with teaching as a profession than are younger teachers.

_____ 5. A majority of individuals who go into teaching come from small towns and rural areas.

_____ 6. In recent years, there has been an increase in the average age of females accepting their first teaching position.

_____ 7. More secondary school teachers who are members of minority groups were trained in private colleges and universities than were secondary school teachers who are not members of minority groups.

_____ 8. Because of recent interest in bilingual education, there has been a dramatic upsurge in the percentage of teachers who have linguistic competencies in a second language. More than 10 percent of recent teacher graduates are prepared to work in bilingual programs.

_____ 9. More teachers tend to be drawn from managerial and professional families than from families where parents are laborers or craftspersons.

_____ 10. Secondary school teachers must deal today with students representing a much broader cross section of the population than did those who taught in the schools 50, 60, or 70 years ago.

INTRODUCTION

For every 225 people in the United States, 1 is a secondary school teacher. About 1 million secondary school teachers work in schools scattered across the breadth of the continent. They teach in schools that range from the finest money can buy to schools that are dilapidated monuments to public neglect. They represent every racial group found in the population. Their politics range from the far right to the far left. In short, secondary school teachers are a very diverse group (see Figure 17-1).

Yet, despite the range of personal interests and concerns that make individual teachers fascinating as people, secondary school teachers tend to fall into some basic patterns in terms of their hopes, attitudes, and aspirations. It would be a mistake to presume that every secondary school teacher fits a general description of the group. Many clearly do not. But general discriptions are useful for identifying characteristics

Figure 17-1

TEACHERS' *REAL* INTERESTS

Not long ago, Norman Phillips, a teacher in a senior high school, was holding forth to a couple of colleagues in the faculty lounge. Among other things, he said the following:

> And P. J., you know he's the math head over at South Central, and I had been eyeballing cheap apartment houses in that area for over a year. Well, we got word that this owner was in a bind. So we sharpened our pencils and made the guy a ridiculously low offer. Bid the whole building at a price of seventeen dollars a square foot. We spent a couple of "white knuckler" days wondering if he'd bite. Finally, two weeks ago, the owner called P. J. and told him he'd sell the place to us at our offering price. We transferred the mortgage, and the owner's carrying a small second. We've got enough cash flow coming in to cover the payments plus lay aside a hundred or two a month.
>
> Well, the deal is, with an apartment like this, you don't get very classy tenants. Had a call last night from a guy on the first floor who was screaming his head off about his ceiling falling in on him. I calmed him down and told him I'd be out. Well, when I got there there was this goshawful mess of plaster on the floor. What remained of the ceiling was dripping wet. Something was leaking from the apartment above.
>
> To make a long story short, I whipped up the stairs and pounded on the door of the second-floor apartment. A real weirdo opened it up . . . one of our "esteemed" tenants. I explained the situation and he let me in. Well, would you believe that this guy was trying to raise ducks in his apartment. Swear to God, he was trying to raise ducks. Anyway, he had this bathtub full of water and he'd put in a couple of female mallards and this really excited drake. Well, the darned drake was flapping around so enthusiastically that water from the tub was slopping out all over the place. I'm surprised the tub hadn't fallen through to the apartment below.
>
> Well, we got the lawyer on the phone, got the "duck breeder" out of the unit. We're going to have to come up with 750 dollars to fix the ceiling. Good thing this teaching money is coming in every month. Without it, a guy just wouldn't stand a chance of making some big bucks on the outside ventures. We figure when we get this one paid off that we'll take a look at a franchise for some exercise equipment. The say the return is . . .

YOUR OPINION, PLEASE

1. Have you encountered teachers who were in the business only to finance other ventures?
2. Should teachers be prevented from engaging in other money-making (or potential money-making) ventures while they are teaching? Why, or why not?
3. How exciting do you think Norman Phillips finds teaching? Why do you think so? What might have shaped his attitudes?

---

that describe large numbers of secondary school teachers. An understanding of these characteristics can provide some perspective on the group.

As we attempt to gain insight into some of these broad descriptions of secondary school teachers, we might begin by focusing on some general interests of these people. Most of us reveal our enthusiasms in casual conversation. In these settings, we have free choice of topics. We elect to talk about things that interest us. An observer can learn a good deal about us simply by listening to what we talk about.

Let us suppose that we were able to spend a day as an invisible presence in a secondary school faculty lounge listening to teachers talk to one another during their planning periods. We might hear such conversations as the following:

Mrs. Smalley
"and I told Roger that we just had *to get the chandelier for the living room now that Stoverud's has them on sale. I mean, that's what I work for. What's the use*

of putting up with these kids if you don't get some benefit? Well would you believe that he came around to the idea of buying the chandelier, but we got into this violent argument about the kind of cut-glass droplets we wanted to order for it. I mean he held out for the pear-shaped *droplets. Now isn't that just* gauche! *They've been out for years. Sometimes that man just has no taste at all. Well, anyway, they're . . ."*

Mr. Jackson

"so, I was hard charging out my classroom last night to jump in the car and pick up Elaine and the kids. We were going to go out to the valley to have dinner at the new place there on the west side. Well, I got myself organized in a hurry for a change, slammed and locked the door, whipped out of the building, hustled over to the parking lot, and got in the car. I turned the key on and got some of the sickest sounds I've ever heard. I mean that car was groaning. *You know I'm as klutzy as they come when it comes to cars. I had this horrible vision of two to three hundred dollars floating into the hands of some smiling mechanic. Well, just to go through the motions, I decided to throw open the hood and pretend I knew what I was looking for. So, up goes the hood, in goes my head, and, presto, all is revealed. Some jerk of a kid had jammed an apple core onto my carburetor. I made a few choice remarks, extracted the shriveled remains, slammed down the hood, and climbed back in the car. Saying a silent prayer, I tried the starter. It caught immediately. I tell you I felt like I'd just earned a couple of hundred dollars. I could almost see the look of disappointment on that mechanic's face. I was really burned that some kid would do this. But then, what the heck, I've been here 20 years and never had a problem like that before. Not too bad a record considering the number I work with. Besides, as I was telling Elaine, we don't put up with much at all compared with the stuff I used to pull. Did I ever tell you about the time we lit the sulfur in the central ventilating conduit? Well, you know how rotten eggs . . ."*

Ms. Jameson

"Have you read And Now, Eleuthra, And Now? *I read it over the summer and liked it so much that I've put a group of my better students to work on it. I just came back from the* best *class with these people. They are doing a splendid job of picking up on the symbolism. Some of them are developing analytical skills I never suspected were there. You know they've made a film of the book. It's playing down at that theater in South Bay City where they feature foreign films. Four of the kids have talked me into taking them over to see it Saturday afternoon. When I see youngsters 'catch fire' like this after I've taught them something, it's a real emotional high for me. The way I feel now, I could teach for ten hours straight and love every minute of it. Say, would you like to borrow my copy of the book? It's about this repressed . . ."*

Mr. Nobel

"and I was telling the wife this morning, just two more years. Whewee. Hope I last that long. These kids are just too much. Too much. When I started, teachers used to get respect. Not these days. It's all that television. They expect to be entertained. And I mean not just once in a while, they want it to be fun and games every day. I can't do that. Never could. Didn't used to even be expected to. I mean, Johnny Carson, he's got platoons of these thousand-a-week guys writing his stuff. Now how can I compete with that? I mean how could I even if I wanted to, which I don't. I stopped trying to play that game years ago.

Say, did you see the new retirement pay formula. They're going to use an average of your last two years' salary. The way you figure what you'll get is to multiply 2 percent times the number of years you've been teaching. Then you use that per-

cent figure and multiply it by the average of your last two years. In my case, I'll have 42 years in. So, I'll get 84 percent of the average of my last two years. Not too bad. Alice and I'll be able to get out of here for a bit of the winter. Of course this darned inflation may . . ."

Mr. Andrews

"and did you see that baloney the administrators fed the school board last night. Look, it's right here in this newspaper article. 'The Deputy Superintendent reported that the ratio of certified personnel to students had dropped to 23 to 1. He commented that this was a marked improvement over last year's 27 to 1 ratio.' Can you believe such malarkey! I mean, John Q. Public's going to read that and think that there are fewer kids in the classroom. You and I both know that isn't true at all. In fact, they've hired about 30 new administrators to sit on their duffs and shuffle paper downtown. And each of these birds has a certificate of some kind. So of course there are more 'certified' personnel than ever. But it sure as heck doesn't mean there are more teachers in the classrooms. If these guys had even an ounce of integrity they would cut out this nonsense and tell the people that we're working with 35 and even 40 kids in a class. How some of these folks sleep at night is beyond me."

Mrs. Newton

"Just got back from the Curriculum Council meeting. I am very sorry to report that our 'enlightened legislators' have done it to us again. Remember how thrilled we all were to be told that we had to devote time in all classes to teaching the crime prevention units? And before that when we had to 'infuse' economic education content into every course. Isn't 'infuse' a lovely bureaucratic word? Seems to suggest that we have an infinite amount of time and that we can put something in without taking it out. Well, from the great citadel of wisdom at our capital comes word now that we have been falling down on the job in yet another area. 'Too much drug abuse,' the politicians are saying. We've got the usual remedy. To wit: 'units in drug abuse are to be included in all required courses in the K to 12 curriculum.' That's sure to solve the problem, right? Do I detect a cynical look? Come now.

"Kidding aside, isn't this just too much? Drug education! Isn't there a danger we're opening up an interest in drugs for some kids who wouldn't have considered using them at all under normal circumstances? Isn't the former record of these state mandates sufficiently dismal to discourage any more of these 'do gooder' ideas? I don't know about you, but I've about had it with being told by these outsiders how and what to teach my kids."

These comments and the issues to which they refer certainly do not include all teacher attitudes and concerns. They do, however, represent the feelings of a number of secondary school teachers. In the sections that follow, we will look at backgrounds of secondary school teachers and at other factors that tend to color their perceptions of their professional roles.

SOME GENERAL STATISTICS ABOUT SECONDARY SCHOOL TEACHERS

Because secondary school teachers are so numerous and play such diverse roles, we probably could visit dozens of schools before encountering a teacher who represented a statistical average of characteristics. Were we to locate such an individual, we would find our average teacher to be a male in his middle to late thirties. He probably would have some work completed on a master's degree program. He would devote about 48 hours a week to teaching and preparing for teaching. He would spend between seven and seven and one half hours a day of required time at school (this includes his lunch period). He would teach in a middle school or junior high school. And, probably, he would teach courses in English, mathematics, science, or social studies. He would have taught about eight years (National Center for Educational Statistics 1979, p. 56).

In terms of where they grew up, secondary teachers continue to reflect a historic pattern characterizing all public school teachers. Large numbers continue to be drawn from small-town and rural backgrounds (National Center for Educational Statistics 1977b). It may be that schools as institutions charged at least in part with transmitting mainstream values tend to attract as teachers individuals from parts of the country where these mainstream values are accepted most widely.

Of teacher education graduates in recent years, there has been a marked change in the average age of females completing teacher preparation programs. Over a third of female teacher education graduates are now in their twenty-fourth year or older (National Center for Education Statistics 1977b). This trend reflects a growing tendency for mature women to seek a professional outlet for their talents. It appears likely at this time that such women will be coming into education in increasing numbers in the years ahead.

In terms of family background, more teachers tend to come from families where the principal occupation of the income earners derived from either business management or the professions. Relatively few come from families where wage earners work as equipment operators, craftspeople, or laborers (National Center for Education Statistics 1977b).

About 12.1 percent of graduates of teacher education programs are members of major ethnic groups. Of these, by far the largest percentage consists of blacks. Blacks constitute 7.5 percent of the total population of graduates from teacher preparation programs. Figures for other minority groups are as follows: Hispanics (1.8 percent), Asians (0.9 percent), and American Indians (0.5 percent). In terms of where they did their college or university work, about two thirds of minority students going into education studied at public four-year colleges. Much smaller numbers enrolled in large public universities or in private schools. In terms of what they teach, a disproportionately large number of minority group teachers teach in occupational and vocational areas. A disproportionately small number teach in the area of special education (National Center for Education Statistics 1977b).

Recent graduates in teacher education are not well grounded in foreign languages. The National Center for Education Statistics (1977b) reports that fewer than three tenths of 1 percent of recent graduates are sufficiently fluent in a second language that they could use this language as the language of instruction in their subject specialty. Given the recent federal push for expansion of bilingual education, this information suggests that problems of implementation of bilingual instruction may be severe. Clearly, to this date at least, there has been no mass movement of large numbers of individuals into education who are fluent in two or more languages.

In summary, the statistical picture that emerges of the "typical" teacher is consistent with traditional patterns (see Figure 17-2). Teachers continue to come from middle-class nonurban backgrounds. They continue to be overwhelmingly white. For a vast majority, English is the only language that has been mastered sufficiently well to serve as a vehicle for classroom instruction. In most respects, the characteristics of new teachers today vary hardly at all from characteristics that for many years have typified public school instructors.

TEACHERS' COMMITMENT TO THE PROFESSION

Once they have begun to teach, remained in the profession long enough to develop an understanding of the dimensions of teaching, and had time to reflect on whether they made a "good" or a "bad" choice, different teachers not surprisingly arrive at different

Figure 17-2

HOW DO YOU THINK TEACHERS "SEE THE WORLD"?
There is evidence that most teachers today continue to be drawn from middle-class backgrounds. Large numbers come from nonurban backgrounds. Although members of minority groups have made gains within the profession, the overwhelming majority of teachers are white. Very small numbers of teachers have a proficiency in a language other than English that is sufficiently well developed to allow them to instruct in this language.

YOUR OPINION, PLEASE
Read the paragraph above. Then, respond to these questions.

1. Would you describe teachers, in general, as rather conventional sorts of people? Why, or why not?
2. What kinds of political attitudes would you expect teachers to have? Why?
3. How do you think the average teacher, given the characteristics cited, would react to a proposal to give students much more power in determining what is taught in secondary schools and in determining how grades are awarded?
4. If teachers have general characteristics such as those noted above, what forces in our society tend to draw people of this type to teaching?
5. If you were to look into a crystal ball 30 years into the future, would you expect teachers of this future time to have many of the characteristics noted above? Why, or why not?

---

conclusions. Some become more committed to teaching than ever. Others grow luke-warm in their enthusiasms. Still others grow increasingly convinced that they made a terrible mistake in selecting teaching as a career choice. In this section, we will look at some issues that play a role in shaping teachers' attitudes.

Reactions Toward Administrative Directives

Because of the different roles that they are expected to play, perhaps it is inevitable that teachers and administrators do not always see eye to eye. Many teachers, probably a majority, may not always agree with administrative decisions, but they generally do not feel ill used by administrators. Nevertheless, there is evidence that large numbers of teachers do not feel comfortable around school administrators. In one recent survey, only 23 percent of the teachers responding reported that they had "high-quality" relationships with administrators in their buildings (Sparks 1979).

Teachers who are extremely unhappy with school administrators have been found to act according to several fairly well-defined patterns. Some engage in "brinkman-ship," for example, challenging the authority of the administrator by opposing administrative decisions in every way possible short of getting in trouble for obstructionist behavior. Other dissatisfied teachers engage in "tight roping." In tight roping, teachers neither obey administrative rules nor disobey them. They tend to act in as vague a manner as possible so as to make it extremely difficult for an administrator to establish clearly whether a directive is being observed or not being observed. Still other dissatisfied teachers engage in behavior that has been labeled "boundary testing." In boundary testing, the teacher deliberately breaks the rule or disobeys a directive, but only slightly. The idea here is to test the commitment of the administrator to the directive. If the rule is broken and nothing much happens, then the teacher may conclude that the administrator may be willing to modify his or her stand (Stapleton, Croft, and Frankiewicz 1979).

One recent study revealed that the key figure in promoting harmonious relationships between teachers and administrators was the building principal (Stapleton, Croft, and Frankiewicz 1979). Where relationships between the principal and building teachers are warm, cordial, and open, there tends to be much less suspicion between teachers and all building administrators. Those administrators who maintain cordial relationships with teachers tend to be flexible.

The issue of flexibility is an important one. As Sparks (1979) has noted, a good deal of teacher frustration results from feelings that they are trapped in an inflexible teaching environment. In one recent survey, 91 percent of the teachers who responded reported that they had almost no influence on policy decisions in their schools (Sparks 1979). This situation has the potential to create a good deal of teacher anxiety and concern. The anxiety and concern relate to a feeling that teachers are caught in a situation where the public is expecting them to perform in a given way but the administrative staff is not allowing them a voice in making decisions that will help them teach in such a way that public expectations will be met. This situation, in some cases at least, contributes to feelings of powerlessness that have been reported by a large number of teachers.

The feeling of powerlessness may contribute to negative feelings toward teaching on the part of at least some career teachers. The inability to participate directly in decisions affecting the nature of their work is a contributory factor to the emotional exhaustion reported by some teachers. Feeling trapped by forces they believe they cannot control, some teachers today report great feelings of stress (Sparks 1979). Certainly not all teachers have these feelings. But numbers reporting these attitudes are sufficiently high to suggest that educators for some time will be interested in looking closely at possible negative consequences of unpleasant administrator-teacher relationships.

Boredom

Once basic procedures have been mastered, there is a tendency for secondary school teachers to fall into rather predictable routines of doing things. Some teachers appreciate the security and stability associated with routine. For others, however, too much of the same thing can produce feelings of boredom (see Figure 17-3).

In a study of teachers' attitudes over a four-year period, Gehrke (1979) found that boredom was cited as a major problem by a large number of teachers after their second year of teaching. A number of factors seemed to contribute to the development of this condition. One of these factors was inflexible scheduling of classes. In most secondary schools, classes occur day after day in a predictable pattern. Each class lasts a fixed number of minutes. Time between classes is unchanging. For teachers this means that they must distribute their instructional time in almost exactly the same way every day.

Another factor contributing to boredom was found to be associated with the subject matter of teaching. Gehrke noted that teachers who had been through their courses a few times tended to become so familiar with the material that it was no longer novel or particularly interesting to them. Further, because of the lack of sophistication of most secondary school students, teachers cannot go very deeply into their subjects. While many teachers may have sincere interests in more complex aspects of their subjects, some of them find little satisfaction in simply scratching the surface of their subjects to communicate with secondary school youngsters.

Gehrke also reported that many teachers find little stimulation in attending to highly routinized housekeeping duties. Roletaking, distributing hall passes, signing admit-to-class forms, and other administrative details present a brief challenge for teachers during their first few months on the job. In time, these duties tend to become tedious chores that must be accomplished to keep administrative personnel happy.

Some teachers report that they find little stimulation in their interpersonal relationships with other faculty members. It does not take long in most buildings for teachers to become well acquainted with other teachers in the school. In time, what other teachers are likely to do or say becomes wearisomely predictable. The lack of new adult

Figure 17-3

TEACHER BOREDOM

So why did we do it? I mean, I spent four years grinding through some really tough math courses to get certified. I did all the advanced calculus courses. Spent some time slogging through vector analysis and even a little jewel called "Matrix Theory with Hermitian and Quadratic Forms." And what am I doing now? I'm teaching remedial seventh-graders that two plus two is four. What a waste!

This is my third year. Let's see, we're three weeks into the term, and we're beginning that electrifying chapter on long division. Now I *really* needed all that high-powered math training in college to teach that! What bugs me, too, is that I'll probably be into the same boring chapter during the third week of the next term. That job at the computer factory is getting to look better all the time.

                                     Statement of teacher

YOUR OPINION, PLEASE
Read the paragraph above. Then, respond to these questions.

1. What are the prospects that this individual will stay in teaching? Why do you think so?
2. Do you think complaints of this individual are justified? Why, or why not?
3. Should someone be expected to have so much advanced mathematics to teach remedial arithmetic to seventh-graders? Why, or why not?
4. Is there anything that this individual could do to make his or her job more interesting? If so, what?

---

personnel in secondary schools causes teachers to confine conversational relationships to the same group of people over a long period of time. Some teachers miss the stimulation of meeting new people on a continuing basis and report that seeing the same old faces contributes to their feelings of boredom (Gehrke 1979).

Many teachers recognize the potential for boredom in their positions and take deliberate action to overcome it. Some seek to broaden their professional perspectives by attending in-service meetings, taking graduate courses at night during the school year, and planning interesting activities during school holiday periods. Gehrke reports that a number of teachers make deliberate efforts to avoid routine by changing the procedures they follow in their classrooms to reduce the repetition. For example, some teachers make changes in the kinds of work they assign, in the instructional techniques they use to introduce learning experiences, in the configuration of chairs in the room, and in the material decorating room walls and bulletin boards.

Others seek relief from potential boredom by changing their roles within education. Teachers may go back to school and prepare to teach another subject or to teach at another grade level. Some become school counselors. Others begin work on administrative certificates and leave teaching to work up the administrative ladder in the school system. Others gain depth in their subject areas and in the curriculum development process and become district-level coordinators and consultants. The array of occupational roles within professional education today is sufficiently broad to afford many opportunities for the classroom teacher who feels that he or she must make some changes to remain challenged and satisfied.

Some teachers, of course, find themselves so bored by what they are doing that they decide to leave education entirely. For those who have honestly explored other career options within education and determined that none of them appears particularly attractive, such a decision may well make sense. In the late twentieth century, people in all occupational roles tend to change the kinds of things they do more frequently and more dramatically than in former times. It is not surprising, then, that teachers who are bored with what they are doing do not hesitate to move on to other things (see Figure 17-4). Indeed, for the individual who is truly unhappy in education, such a move makes sense both for the individual and for the profession. This trend could leave education with a cadre of teachers who are reasonably satisfied with what they are doing.

Personal Background and Commitment to the Profession

Secondary teachers who decide to leave teaching make this decision for a variety of reasons. In looking at those who decide to leave, however, some interesting patterns have come to light. Recent evidence suggests that the decision to leave teaching may be related to whether a teacher was on scholarship as opposed to being self-supported or parent-supported while enrolled in a teacher preparation program. The decision also may be related to the nature of work experience prior to teaching. Finally, there is evidence that the decision to stay in teaching may be connected to a teacher's level of aspiration for a position in a higher-status occupation than teaching (Gosnell 1977).

Gosnell found that teachers who had been supported on scholarships during their undergraduate years tended to be much more likely to leave teaching than students who either supported themselves or were supported by their parents. Reasons for this difference are not clear. One explanation may center on the social and economic class from which most scholarships students are drawn. More scholarships tend to be given

Figure 17-4

TEACHERS WHO LEAVE TEACHING

Recently, the National Education Association polled its membership to determine teachers' attitudes on a variety of topics. When asked to comment on whether they would choose teaching again (if they had a chance to start over) and on whether they intended to stay in teaching, these responses were obtained.*

Percentage of Teachers Who

Would go into teaching again, 59%
Would *not* go into teaching again, 41%
Plan to stay in teaching until retirement, 43%
Do *not* plan to stay in teaching until retirement, 57%

YOUR OPINION, PLEASE

Look at the information presented above. Then, respond to these questions.

1. Are you surprised by any of the figures listed? If so, which ones and why?
2. In a poll taken a year before the one discussed, it was found that only 32% of the teachers responding would not go into teaching again (*Phi Delta Kappan* 1980, p. 49). How do you account for the change between this figure and the 41% figure reported in this more recent poll?
3. What sorts of things do you think might be contributing to the high percentage of teachers who do not plan to stay in teaching until retirement?
4. Suppose that you were asked to suggest a set of conditions for teachers that, five years hence, would result in a significantly higher percentage of teachers (a) saying they would choose teaching again if they had to start all over and (b) saying they planned to stay in teaching until retirement. What conditions would you propose? Could they be implemented? Why, or why not?

*Data have been adapted from "NEA Survey Investigates Teacher Attitudes, Practices," *Phi Delta Kappan* (September 1980): 49.

to students from lower social- and economic-class backgrounds than to students from middle social- and economic-class backgrounds. There has been a cultural tradition for teaching to be regarded as an honorable calling for students from middle-class backgrounds. It may be this tradition that is the real reason for these students tending to stay in teaching. The fact that they tended to work themselves through college or university or be supported by their parents may simply be incidental.

Students whose work experience prior to becoming teachers tended to be blue-collar rather than white-collar were found by Gosnell to be more likely to remain in teaching. The explanation may be that teaching, for individuals coming from a blue-collar employment background, may be viewed as an improvement in their position. On the other hand, for individuals who had worked in white-collar occupations, teaching may be perceived as a lower-status position.

In his study, Gosnell also asked a number of teachers to identify what occupation they would choose to follow if, ten years hence, they were to do something other than teaching. The teachers involved in this study were followed over a period of years and records were kept of those who chose to leave the profession. Gosnell found that there was a tendency for those teachers who had identified an occupation generally regarded as higher in status than teaching to leave the profession in significantly higher numbers than did teachers who had identified a potential future occupation equal to or lower in status than teaching. This finding seems to suggest that teachers who consider teaching as an occupation whose status is sufficiently high to satisfy their own needs for status are more likely to remain in the profession than are those who perceive teaching as an occupation that is too low in status for them.

There has been a suggestion that, in the future, some teacher preparation institutions might take into account such factors as students' prior work experience and perception of the status of teaching in determining whether or not to admit prospective students to teacher education programs. At this time, however, a good deal more groundwork needs to be done to identify student characteristics that are associated with individuals who are effective teachers and with individuals who plan to make a long-term career of teaching.

Teaching Experience and Attitudes Toward the Profession

"Do we have to do *all* of this? Mr. Smith never made us work this hard. You must be a new teacher." The informal communication network in many secondary schools has it on "good authority" that beginning teachers tend to be a bit hard nosed. They have a reputation of demanding more work and of being less flexible than more experienced teachers. Many middle school, junior high school, and senior high school students believe that teachers, like good wine, mellow with age.

In fact, there is evidence to support the idea that teachers with more experience in the classroom tend to be less disturbed by the status quo. They feel generally more favorable toward themselves and their conditions of work. Harmer (1979), for example, found that teachers over 50 years of age tend to enjoy teaching. They do not perceive themselves as having lost any "edge" in terms of their understanding of their respective areas. They do not especially resent extra assignments of a nonteaching nature. Their attitudes toward education as a profession tend to be positive. They see themselves and the schools as doing a good job.

There is some evidence that those people who stay in teaching tend to begin identifying quite positively with the profession after only a few years on the job (Lipka and Goulet 1979). Some kind of sorting process appears to be at work among beginning teachers. This results in a decision on the part of some beginning teachers to leave the profession after only a few years. Those who remain tend to come to terms with dissatisfactions and, in a few years, become attached quite positively to their chosen profession.

TEACHERS' REACTIONS TO INNOVATIONS

The culture of the schools is strongly supportive of innovations. Pressures for change come from a variety of sources. Perhaps one of the major influences for change comes from teachers themselves. Many teachers recognize that they do not make an impact on every student. Hence, they are very receptive to the idea that changes in their procedures may help them to work more effectively with their youngsters. Few teachers oppose the idea of change or innovation. Where resistance develops, it tends to center on change that appears to be being imposed by individuals who have not consulted the teachers who will be affected by the change (see Figure 17-5).

When innovations seem to be imposed in an arbitrary fashion, it is not uncommon for teachers to resist. Dwyer (1977) has identified a number of tactics that some teachers have adopted to show their unhappiness when they are faced with implementing an innovative practice with which they have experienced little or no direct personal involvement. Some teachers under these circumstances use the tactic of "denial." That is, they deny that anything is wrong with present practices. They challenge those in authority to prove that present practices are not at least as good as those that have ever been used in the district's schools.

Another response that is often observed is what Dwyer calls "first go out and slay the dragon." Teachers who use this tactic suggest to those who are responsible for the innovation that any problems that exist are societal problems far larger than anything inherent within the school. Individuals using this line of logic are likely to tell school

---

Figure 17-5

TEACHERS AND INNOVATION

In the main, the impetus for the installation of new ideas has come from outside the four walls of the classroom. University professors, researchers, military experts, or literary crusaders have often convinced the general public, and through the electoral power the local boards of education, of the value of a particular panacea. Very seldom has the front line soldier, the teacher, been admitted into the war councils. Too often teachers have been given what amounts to an ultimatum. The teacher is required to attend a brief workshop or institute in which the new ideology or methodology is expounded. Little attention is paid the teacher's own feelings or attitudes toward the new arrangements or techniques.*

YOUR OPINION, PLEASE

Read the comments above. Then, respond to these questions.

1. Do you accept or reject the basic position that teachers have had little direct involvement in the process of making decisions resulting in changes in school practices? What is the basis for your decision?

2. Presuming that the description of teachers' roles in the decision-making processes in the comments above is accurate, how do you account for this situation? Why have teachers been left out?

3. Given what is said in these comments, do you get a picture of schools as institutions that lead public opinion or as institutions that follow public opinion?

4. Suppose that you were given a free hand to develop a set of procedures for involving teachers and members of any other group you would like to include in a committee charged with making recommendations that would result in some innovative changes in school practices. What sorts of people would you involve? How much authority in the final decision-making process would you grant to representatives of each group? On what basis would you make this determination?

*Carolyn Stern and Evan R. Keislar, "Teacher Attitudes and Attitude Change: A Research Review," *Journal of Research and Development in Education* (November 1970): 71.

district officials that first we must "eliminate poverty" or "abolish the last vestiges of racism" or accomplish some other socially revolutionary task before any changes are installed in the school program.

Still another tactic involves falling back on the argument that the root of present difficulties is "inadequate funding." According to this line of thinking, nothing is wrong with present practices. Any deficiencies that might be found are attributable to underfunding of what presently is being done. What is needed, so say supporters of this view, is not a change but rather more of the same. To get more of the same, additional funds must be provided for present programs.

In addition to concerns about the whole idea of implementing changes in which they have not been involved, teachers tend to be interested in the specific nature of whichever change is being proposed. Some changes tend to be greeted with more enthusiasm than others. This is particularly true when a proposed change involves subject matter content to be taught in the school program.

Teachers often resist teaching content in their courses that might be described as "nontraditional" (Stern and Keislar 1977). For example, in some places requirements for teachers to deal with such topics as sex education, alcohol abuse, and drug use have engendered considerable teacher unhappiness. Some even feel that devoting class time to discussion of social problems such as drug abuse may prompt an undesirable interest in drugs on the part of students who, otherwise, would have little interest at all in the drug scene (Stern and Keislar 1977).

When innovations related to subject matter have not involved teaching of nontraditional content but have focused on methods of teaching the subject matter, many teachers have been similarly unenthusiastic receptors of change. For example in the area of reading, many teachers who manage secondary school reading clinics have emerged from preparation programs giving them certain philosophical biases with regard to how reading instruction ought to proceed. When an innovative program prescribes practices that are inconsistent with these biases, teachers are likely to resist the installation of the suggested changes.

There is evidence that teachers tend to be most resistant to changes that seem to run counter to deep-seated biases they may have about the students they serve. Stern and Keislar (1977, p. 73) note that

> *With reference to the general issue of effecting teacher attitude change, it should be pointed out that even in the most strongly held beliefs about organization, methods, and content of instruction, there is far less resistance to modification than when deep-seated emotional feelings are tapped. Attitudes toward children from different religious and racial groups, from different cultures and environments, are based on the teachers' own lifetime history of conditioning and are far more impervious to short-term, superficial training models.*

With regard to teacher attitudes toward students from minority groups, there is evidence that teachers, in an intellectual sense, may believe themselves to be unbiased. But observations of teacher behavior suggest that many teachers do have biases that are reflected in their actions and attitudes toward students from minority groups. Stern and Keislar (1977) report, for example, that "both white and black teachers have biased attitudes toward black students. Black children are described as being more introverted, more distractable, and more hostile than white children. Teacher attitudes toward Mexican-American students are also extremely negative, becoming increasingly more so with [each] grade level" (p. 67).

Compounding difficulties associated with negative teacher attitudes toward innovations in which they have had no part in formulating and in innovations that run counter to deep-seated biases is the traditional approach used by many districts in preparing teachers for these changes. Typically, teachers expected to implement a change will be provided with a brief in-service program. The in-service program will attempt to explain the mechanics of implementing whatever has been proposed. Many in-service efforts, perhaps even a majority, last no longer than a single day. The short duration of these preparation programs frequently proves insufficient either to change teachers' basic attitudes toward the change or to make them truly proficient in implementing the change. Indeed, some teachers leave such in-service sessions more convinced than ever that "the old way was better."

Today, school districts are becoming increasingly sensitive to the need to involve teachers directly in the development of policies that might result in innovations and changes in the schools. There is evidence that teachers who are involved personally in decisions resulting in the installation of innovative practices are more supportive of these innovations than are teachers who have had no such involvement (Stern and Keislar 1977). In light of this condition, sensitive school administrators who want whatever innovations that are adopted to be supported enthusiastically by teachers (or at least not actively opposed by them) more and more are looking for teacher assistance when policies resulting in changes are contemplated.

THE CHANGED STUDENT POPULATION: A CHALLENGE FOR SECONDARY SCHOOL TEACHERS

Clearly the schools' most obvious expectations of secondary school teachers is that they will teach learners. Without the instructional component of their responsibilities, we could almost say that our whole concept of the teacher would have to be revised. Today's secondary school teachers face great challenges in terms of the students with whom they work. Not only is a broader cross section of the population enrolled in schools today than in earlier years, but a much higher percentage of these youngsters is in daily attendance. To gain some perspective on this situation, it is worth noting that in 1920 only 74.8 percent of students, on average, attended classes each day (National Center for Education Statistics 1977b, p. 178). In school year 1978–1979 that figure had risen to 92.1 percent (National Center for Education Statistics 1980, p. 82). Today's secondary school teachers have to deal with youngsters representing a much larger proportion of the total population of students in the secondary-school-age group than did their counterparts of 50, 60, and 70 years ago.

A number of factors have contributed to the increased percentages of students attending school. Certainly, passages of laws restricting employment opportunities for youngsters under 18 years of age have had an influence. Many youngsters who remain in today's schools and graduate at the end of grade 12 in earlier times would have dropped out of school to go to work.

Another social force acting to keep a higher percentage of youngsters in secondary schools has been the development over the last 50 years of an expectation that a person who has attained the age of 18 or 19 will have completed high school. With few exceptions, employers insist on a high school education as a minimum qualification for employment. People in general tend to look with some real dismay at high school dropouts. A generation ago, it was much easier for individuals who failed to complete their public school program to get work. Further, such a condition was much more socially acceptable than it is today.

Still another pressure working to keep secondary school students enrolled comes from the prevailing patterns of school funding. Generally, schools are allocated money from the state based on the number of students who are in attendance. This means that it is to the financial advantage of school districts to keep as many students as possible enrolled for the entire 12-year school program. This financial incentive complements nicely intellectual arguments that are made in support of dropout prevention efforts.

The forces that have been mentioned here (and others that have not) have meant that many secondary schools have some students in their classes who, in earlier times, probably would have left school before their junior high school or senior high school years. While we certainly do not wish to suggest that all these students are unenthusiastic about their studies, some of them probably would rather not be in school. There is real potential among this group of students for discipline problems.

Secondary school teachers today report that discipline is an important problem for them. Recently, the National Education Association surveyed its membership on a variety of questions. One of the questions centered on discipline. Fully 54 percent of those responding identified student behavior as a problem. Middle school and junior high school teachers indicated that, on average, they had about six students with chronic behavior problems in each class. High school teachers felt that, on average, they had about five such students in each class (*Phi Delta Kappan,* 1980).

We do not wish to leave this section on a negative note. Certainly today's secondary school teachers must deal with discipline problems. Certainly teaching in middle schools, junior high schools, and senior high schools is no easy task. But there *are* compensations. For one thing, the increase in the range of interests and abilities among the student body has injected a variety into secondary school teaching that was lacking 50, 60, or 70 years ago. Further, the array of aptitudes and enthusiasms of today's youngsters permit teachers to exercise their imaginations to design innovative instructional approaches to meet these youngsters' needs. Quite frankly, a secondary teacher today is likely to find himself or herself intellectually and emotionally stretched in a way his or her early day colleagues never were. These conditions make for the sort of personal growth that many teachers in the schools today find to be exceptionally satisfying.

Posttest

Directions: Using your own paper, answer each of the following true/false questions. For each correct statement, write the word "true." For each incorrect statement, write the word "false."

_____ 1. Secondary school teachers who held white-collar positions prior to entering teaching are more likely to leave the profession than are those who held blue-collar positions prior to entering teaching.

_____ 2. A good many secondary school teachers find boredom with their work to be a problem.

_____ 3. The vast majority of secondary school teachers report that they would choose to go into teaching again were they given an opportunity to go back and choose whatever career they wanted.

_____ 4. There is some evidence that older teachers (those over 50) tend to be more satisfied with teaching as a profession than are younger teachers.

_____ 5. A majority of individuals who go into teaching come from small towns and rural areas.

_____ 6. In recent years, there has been an increase in the average age of females accepting their first teaching position.

_____ 7. More secondary school teachers who are members of minority groups were trained in private colleges and universities than were secondary school teachers who are not members of minority groups.

_____ 8. Because of recent interest in bilingual education, there has been a dramatic upsurge in the percentage of teachers who have linguistic competencies in a second language. More than 10 percent of recent teacher graduates are prepared to work in bilingual programs.

_____ 9. More teachers tend to be drawn from managerial and professional families than from families where parents are laborers or craftspersons.

_____ 10. Secondary school teachers must deal today with students representing a much broader cross section of the population than did those who taught in the schools 50, 60, or 70 years ago.

Key Ideas in Review

1. Family backgrounds from which secondary school teachers are drawn have changed little over the years. Most continue to come from rural or small-town backgrounds and from families adhering strongly to traditional middle-class values.

2. The typical teacher in today's secondary school is male, in his late thirties, who teaches English, social studies, science, or mathematics in a junior high school. He works about 7.5 hours a day at school, but his total workweek amounts to about 48 hours.

3. Members of minority groups constitute about 12.1 percent of teacher education graduates. The majority of these individuals are blacks. A disproportionalely large percentage of minority group teachers instruct in the occupational and vocational areas of the curriculum. Surprisingly small numbers are involved in special education.

4. Teachers face many psychological pressures. Many feel that they are helpless in the face of adminitrative decisions that they may see as arbitrary. Particularly frustrating for many are administrative decisions that result in change. Unless teachers have been involved directly in the formulation of such decisions, resistance to suggested changes is a likely consequence.

5. Some teachers find that teaching is characterized by an excess of routine. There is some evidence that, after the second year of teaching, many teachers find boredom to be an important problem. Many seek release through in-service courses, outside interests, and other mechanisms that add variety to their lives.

6. In a recent survey, a majority of teachers stated that they would not go into teaching again if they had the decision to make over. Other research on teacher dissatisfaction with their professional roles has found that teachers with previous blue-collar work experience for whom teaching was seen as a profession of sufficient status and importance were less likely to want to leave teaching for another occupation.

7. Teachers' attitudes toward the profession seem to improve with years of experience in the classroom. Teachers over age 50, for example, have been found to feel much more positive about their profession than younger teachers.

8. Traditionally, teachers have not been much involved in making many decisions about how their work is to be performed. Because of mounting evidence that teacher involvement can translate to teacher commitment, more sophisticated school administrators today are increasing efforts to involve teachers directly in the decision-making process.

9. Secondary teachers today work with students representing a much broader cross section of the population than did their counterparts 50, 60, and 70 years ago. This situation has resulted in more students having only marginal interest in the school program being taught in secondary school classrooms. While this created discipline problems, many teachers have responded well to the demands of these new professional conditions.

FUNKY WINKERBEAN by Tom Batiuk © 1981. Field Enterprises, Inc. Courtesy of Field Newspaper Syndicate.

SUMMARY

Secondary school teachers represent a diverse group of individuals. Indeed, descriptions of statistical averages, while interesting, do not communicate much information about the characteristics of the population of secondary school teachers. They are simply too diverse to be described adequately by any arithmetic mean.

Today's secondary teachers work under very challenging conditions. They have nearly the entire population of young people of secondary school age in their classrooms. Some of these youngsters, in former times, would have joined the work force long before beginning secondary school programs. As a result, some students in the classrooms have only a minimal interest in school, which has led to classroom control problems.

Despite changes in the student population, today's secondary school teachers tend to be drawn from much the same sort of personal backgrounds that teachers have come from for many years. Briefly, they tend to be products of rural or small-town environments and to be sons and daughters of parents who embrace middle-class American values enthusiastically.

Many secondary school teachers have concerns about whether they made the right decision when they elected to go into teaching. Some feel that they are trapped in a situation where they must carry out decisions that have been imposed by administrators and other nonteachers. Some feel that teaching is so routinized that it becomes a boring ritual after only a few years. To combat these perceptions, sensitive school administrators increasingly are seeking to involve teachers in decisions that will have an impact on classroom practice. Evidence grows that this kind of involvement is associated with better teacher self-images and with teacher commitment to any adopted changes.

References

Dwyer, Margaret S. "Mastering Change in Education: Understanding the Anxieties Created by Change," *Educational Technology* (January 1977): 54–56.

Gehrke, Natalie J. "Renewing Teachers' Enthusiasm: A Professional Dilemma," *Theory Into Practice* (June 1979): 188–193.

Gosnell, John W. "The Relationship Between Work Experience and Occupational Aspiration and Attrition from Teaching," *The Clearing House* (December 1977): 176–179.

Harmer, Earl W. "Veteran Teachers: Old Myths and New Realities," *Phi Delta Kappan* (March 1979): 536–538.

Lipka, Richard P., and Goulet, L. R. "Aging—and Experience—Related Changes in Teacher Attitudes Toward the Profession," *Educational Research Quarterly* (Summer 1979): 19–28.

National Center for Education Statistics. *The Condition of Education, 1977.* Washington, D.C.: U.S. Government Printing Office, 1977a.

———. *The State of Teacher Education, 1977.* Washington, D.C.: U.S. Government Printing Office, 1977b.

Phi Delta Kappan. "NEA Survey Investigates Teacher Attitudes, Practices." *Phi Delta Kappan.* (September 1980): 49–50.

———. *Digest of Education Statistics, 1979.* Washington, D.C.: U.S. Government Printing Office, 1979.

———. *The Condition of Education, 1980.* Washington, D.C.: U.S. Government Printing Office, 1980.

Sparks, Dennis C. "A Biased Look at Teacher Job Satisfaction," *The Clearing House* (May 1979): 447–449.

Stapleton, James C., Croft, John C., and Frankiewicz, Ronald G. "The Relationship Between Teacher Brinkmanship and Teacher Job Satisfaction," *Planning and Changing* (Fall 1979): 157–168.

Stern, Carolyn, and Keislar, Evan R. "Teacher Attitudes and Attitude Change: A Research Review," *Journal of Research and Development in Education* (Winter 1977): 63–76.

Williamson, John A. "Biographical Factors and Teacher Effectiveness," *The Journal of Experimental Education* (Spring 1969): 85–88.

Wright, Robert, and Alley, Robert. "A Profile of the Ideal Teacher," *National Association of Secondary School Principals Bulletin* (February 1977): 60–64.

18

Teachers' Roles and Responsibilities

"Slackmeyer, I appreciate your effort to relate to your students, however . . ."

Objectives

This chapter provides information to help the reader to

1. Name a number of different roles that teachers play.
2. Point out tasks associated with several of the roles teachers play.
3. Identify potential conflicts between and among some of the roles teachers play.

4. Describe actions teachers can take to minimize role conflicts and maximize job satisfaction.

5. Describe the phenomenon of teacher "burn-out."

Pretest

Directions: Using your own paper, answer each of the following true/false questions. For each correct statement, write the word "true." For each incorrect statement, write the word "false."

_____ 1. A teacher usually has absolute freedom to perform the instructional role as he or she deems appropriate.

_____ 2. There is consensus regarding what constitutes appropriate instructional behavior of teachers.

_____ 3. Role conflicts contribute to the problem of emotional stress known as teacher "burn-out."

_____ 4. Because most secondary schools have counselors, secondary school teachers almost never are concerned with counseling students.

_____ 5. Teachers who do a good job in handling the managerial aspects of teaching tend to develop routines that help them to accomplish often-repeated tasks efficiently.

_____ 6. If a teacher is to be effective in counseling students, it is essential that he or she endeavor to be as much like the students as possible.

_____ 7. An important counseling skill for teachers is the ability to listen carefully to students when they talk about personal concerns.

_____ 8. In evaluating their own programs, there is a natural tendency for many teachers to resist change and to seek to maintain the status quo.

_____ 9. Some teachers sense conflict in their relationships with administrators with whom they are expected to function as cooperative colleagues in the day-to-day life of the school and against whom they may be pitted when professional working conditions and salaries are being negotiated across a bargaining table.

_____ 10. Typically, professional association meetings are held during the school day.

INTRODUCTION

When most people think about what teachers do, they envision people working with students in an effort to help them to master some new information or skill. Although teachers' instructional role might be described fairly as their major responsibility, clearly teachers have to meet many other obligations. To get some feel for the range of expectations that are placed on today's teachers, let us follow a secondary school teacher through an imaginary school day.

Suzanne Nielsen: High School Biology Teacher

7.12 A.M. Suzanne Nielsen eased her economy car into the faculty lot at Meriwether Lewis Senior High School. Finding her space and braking to a stop, Suzanne mentally checked off things she had to do before her first-period class. "I'll need to go by the duplicating room to get my dittos," she thought. "Then, I'll need to see about getting an overhead projector delivered to the room from the A/V center. Finally, I've got to get grades entered into my book from these papers I graded last night," she concluded.

As she entered the building, the pre-first-period flurry of activity was already well underway. Striding down the hall, Suzanne turned and entered the main office and walked over to her mailbox. Nothing much today except a note from the vice principal. Stopping briefly to read the note, Suzanne learned that the teacher in the room across the hall from her own would be out. The vice principal asked Suzanne to keep an eye open to be sure the substitute was not running into any difficulties. The only other item in the box was a federal form. "Not another one of these!" Suzanne thought. "It seems like I spend more time filling these out than in preparing lesson plans," Suzanne fumed silently.

Moving out of the central office area, Suzanne headed for the duplicating room. She picked up her dittos and headed for her classroom. She had no sooner entered the room than the department chairperson arrived on the scene to announce a special department meeting to be held right after school. As it developed, the central science curriculum coordinator from the district administration office had called. The coordinator suggested that it would be a good idea for the science faculties in all the buildings to meet and prepare departmental evaluations of some textbooks being considered for purchase. The department meeting would be devoted to a consideration of these books.

Shortly after the department chairperson moved on to tell the other teachers of the special meeting, Suzanne remembered another after-school commitment. She was scheduled to meet with a group at the district administration building to review proposals for spring semester in-service programs. "Well," Suzanne reasoned, "I suppose I can stop by the department meeting and make a few comments before going on to the administration building."

Suzanne sat down and began to enter grades in her grade book. Just as she was completing this task, one of the school counselors began talking to her through the intercom system. He wanted to know how June Smith was getting along. He had had reports from a number of teachers that she was showing signs of great anxiety in several of her classes and that she had fallen into a pattern of not turning in her work. Suzanne expressed some concern upon hearing these comments but stated that she had noted nothing out of the ordinary in June's behavior in her class.

7.40 A.M. Suzanne entered the last grade. She looked up at the clock and decided she had time for a quick cup of coffee in the faculty lounge. As she got up, she glanced at her desk calendar and noted that her "planning" period today would be taken up with a conference designed to provide an individualized instructional plan for a handicapped student. "Another night to plan everything at home," Suzanne mused.

Halfway to the faculty lounge Suzanne remembered her need for an overhead projector. She changed directions and headed for the media center. A boy assigned to the room carried the unit to her room and plugged it in to make sure everything worked.

7.55 A.M. Just enough time to walk across the hall and meet the substitute. Suzanne entered the hall from her classroom and was about to cross over to the room on the other side when Joe Wilson, president of the Future Teachers of America Club, came running up. Breathless and enthusiastic as usual, Joe pointed out a need for a special meeting this week to plan for the Harvest Dance. Suzanne suggested a meeting for Thursday afternoon and told Joe to get the work out to the members. Finally, a quick introduction and welcome extended to the substitute, and then Suzanne found herself back in her room ready to begin with her first-period class.

The morning classes went well. The third period, as usual, was a bit "difficult," but in general things flowed quite smoothly. At noon, Suzanne stopped by the office to check her faculty mailbox. There was a phone message from a parent who had called to discuss some of the topics being covered in the biology class. Suzanne took time to call the parent. After a ten-minute discussion, the parent was somewhat more accepting of what Suzanne was trying to do but still expressed some feeling that certain topics should be reserved for parents and probably should not be treated by teachers in the classroom.

A second item in the box was a reminder for a professional association meeting. The association noted that negotiations between the teachers' group and the school district administration for next year's contract were about to begin. To gather input from all teacher members of the association, a mass meeting of the membership was being scheduled for Thursday evening.

A third memo in the box was from the principal. He noted that the school board had received many complaints from parents about students' deficiencies in the areas of writing. The board was interested in finding out exactly what teachers were doing in this area. The principal, therefore, was asking each teacher to submit a written statement outlining exactly what he or she was doing in his or her classes to help students become more fluent writers.

Having read the memos, Suzanne moved on to the teachers' lunchroom. The lunch conversation centered on the memo regarding students' writing competencies. A good many teachers expressed resentment that they should be asked to teach something clearly out of their own area of training.

After a quick lunch, Suzanne stopped at the media center. She placed orders for several films she intended to use over the next several weeks. Then she returned to her classroom.

The fourth-period bunch had a little difficulty settling down after lunch. But, once they got busy on the lab assignment, they stayed on task quite well. The fifth-period meeting to plan the individualized instructional program for the handicapped youngster also went well. For once, parents, counselors, and others involved came to relatively quick agreement regarding what should be done. The sixth-period class suffered less today from that "end-of-the-day apathy" that often characterized youngsters in this group. Most worked well at the laboratory exercise.

When the final bell rang at 3 P.M., Suzanne gathered up her materials. After the last student had left, she closed her door and went immediately to the conference room for the department meeting. She stayed until 3:30. Then, explaining her other meeting obligation to the department head, she left for the central district administration building.

"With luck," she thought, "the advisory meeting will wind up by 5:15 or 5:30. I may even get home before 6:30 tonight." As she drove out of the Meriwether Lewis faculty parking lot, she reflected on a comment of a person whom she'd met recently at a party: "Oh, so you're a teacher. It must be great to have a job that's over at 3 o'clock every day!"

"Yes," sighed Suzanne. "It must be great. Sometimes I think I'd like a job like that." She drove toward the administration building. Pulling into the parking lot, she thought, "Three days till Friday. Just three days."

Let us think about some of the roles Suzanne Nielsen played during her day. In addition to the expected role of instructor, she also acted as a manager, a counselor, a public relations specialist, and a secretary. (Probably there were other roles as well.) Part of the strain teachers face results from the number of roles they are expected to play well. Compounding the difficulty is the reality that some of these roles sometimes seem to be in conflict (see Figure 18-1).

Let us consider some potential conflicts as they relate to Suzanne Nielsen's day. On the one hand, Suzanne Nielsen is a professional instructor with responsibilities to transmit subject matter content in a manner consistent with her best professional judgment. On the other hand, she is a public relations person who must keep open and positive lines of communication with parents. In terms of the call from the complaining

Figure 18-1

THE TEACHER'S DAY

YOUR OPINION, PLEASE
Reread the material related to Suzanne Nielsen's day. Then, respond to these questions.

1. Were there any things about Suzanne's day that you found unusual or surprising? If so, what?
2. Think back on some tasks you observed your own middle school, junior high school, or senior high school teachers performing. Were some of them the same as those performed by Suzanne? Were some of them different?
3. Given some of the activities Suzanne engaged in during this day, what kind of expertise do you think secondary school teachers need? Can special training be provided in all these areas? Or must teachers learn some of these things on the job?
4. What aspects of Suzanne's day do you personally find most appealing? Most unappealing? Why?
5. If there are certain things Suzanne had to do during the day that you do not presently feel qualified to do, how could you develop the necessary expertise?

---

parent, Suzanne found herself caught between her professional responsibility as an instructor and her professional responsibility as a public relations person for the school.

Although we do not know exactly how Suzanne felt about the memo from the principal calling upon each teacher to provide a statement about what was being done to improve students' writing skills, certainly there is potential for role conflict. Some teachers might well regard such a directive as an improper abridgment of their professional ability to determine the nature of instruction provided to students in their classrooms. In such instances, there would be a clear conflict between the role of instructional specialist and the role of implementor of public policy (as reflected in school board and administrative directives).

Role conflicts of various kinds place a severe strain on many teachers. They are an important cause of teacher "burn-out," as characterized by teachers who have been so subjected to psychological strain that they simply cease to function as effective classroom practitioners. We do not wish to paint too gloomy a picture in this regard. Certainly in large numbers of school districts parents are supportive of what teachers do and administrators and teachers work hard to preserve harmonious working relationships. We do feel a responsibility, however, to suggest that teaching is a demanding profession. The many roles that teachers are expected to fulfill explain, in part, why many beginning teachers find teaching a more emotionally demanding profession than they had anticipated. In the sections that follow, we will take a look at a number of these roles.

THE TEACHER AS INSTRUCTOR

Specific instructional responsibilities of teachers are detailed in the chapters in Part II of this text. Consequently, we will not speak at length here about the specifics of what teachers do in the instructional area. Rather, we will focus more on some conditions that impinge on teachers as they attempt to fulfill the instructional role and on some conflicts between the instructional role and other important professional responsibilities.

Clearly classroom instruction is central to what teachers do. The opportunity to instruct students and observe them learning motivates many individuals to seek out a career as a teacher in the first place. Many undergraduates in education presume that, once in the classroom, they will be free to perform the instructional role in the manner they individually see to be most productive. When they assume their first teaching positions, many are surprised that they must operate under very real restraints.

For example, a new teacher sometimes experiences some feelings of self-doubt when he or she reads articles by educators and lay people describing what "good teaching is *really* like." Some of these so-called (and often self-styled) "experts" fail to agree on what kinds of practices constitute good instruction. Some see a successful instructor as someone who has tight control of students, stands in front of the room dispensing information, and gives a difficult test every Friday. Others see a successful instructor as someone who involves students in the lesson planning process, encourages free verbal exchanges among students, and rarely gives formal tests. (Of course there are dozens of other conceptions of good teaching.) When newcomers to teaching read articles or listen to talks by individuals whose conceptions of quality teaching differ from their own, there may be an erosion in self-confidence. Teachers who do not have a good understanding of the theoretical underpinnings of their own classroom practices especially are likely to suffer feelings of anxiety when classroom procedures differing radically from those they believe in are espoused as effective. A prescription for beginning teachers who wish to avoid such feelings is to work hard at developing a sound logical base for the instructional practices they use in the classroom. (See the view expressed in Figure 18-2; consider your response.)

Many new teachers are surprised to learn that they do not enjoy as much autonomy in the classroom as they had imagined they would. Discussions centering on conflicts with administrators are a regular feature in secondary school teacher lounges. For example, some administrators oppose (or are believed to oppose) instructional methods that allegedly create too much noise, result in a disorderly appearance of the classroom, or consume too large a quantity of disposable materials (perhaps an excessive number of copies from the school copy center). Teachers favoring instructional practices that administrators oppose often find themselves frustrated. They argue that their role is one of providing conditions that lead to students' academic progress. If administrative decisions seem to impede youngsters' learning, there is a tendency for affected teachers to be unhappy.

Figure 18-2

LIMITATIONS ON TEACHERS' ACTIONS

When I finish my student teaching program and get my first job, things are going to be great! I have a million ideas that I want to try. I especially want to use a lot of group work. There will be kids sitting in small groups who will discuss things, make models, and generally get pepped up about school. We'll go on lots of hikes and do a lot of observing out in the community. And I plan on having lots of speakers in. To make it more efficient, I figure I'll have the same speaker stay with me every period from the first one in the morning until the last one in the afternoon.

Statement made by an undergraduate education student

YOUR OPINION, PLEASE

Read the statement above. Then, respond to these questions.

1. How great do you think things are going to be for this student during the first year of teaching? On what do you base your opinion?
2. Of the things this student mentions, which might cause him or her the gravest problems? Why?
3. Suppose that you were going to give this person some advice. What would you say?
4. Do teachers have as much autonomy as they ought to have? Why?
5. If you were to make a prediction about what teaching might be like in the year 2000, would you anticipate teachers would have more autonomy or less autonomy than they have today?

Certainly we do not wish to imply that administrators and teachers are always at loggerheads. They are not. In many buildings, there is a cooperative spirit among administrators and teachers. But, in buildings where administrators' values and values of certain teachers are in conflict, a clear strain develops as teachers struggle to weigh their professional responsibilities to their students against their other responsibilities as employees of the school district whose individual preferences, to some degree at least, must be subordinated to administrative authority.

To reiterate a point made earlier, the best thing a teacher can do to minimize the impact of potential conflicts associated with the instructional role is to develop a sound conceptual base for making instructional decisions. It is not enough for us, as teachers, simply to develop a "bag of tricks" to use in the classroom premised on nothing stronger than a personal preference for doing this or doing that. Whatever approaches we use must be educationally sound. We need to ask such questions as "Why am I doing it this way?" "Is there a more efficient way to help students master this content?" "Can I defend what I am doing by references to sound principles of learning and development?"

Teachers with a good intellectual grasp of these principles are capable of defending their actions. When administrators, parents, or other interested parties question why something is being taught in a particular way, such teachers can defend what they are doing in a responsible way. Certainly compromises may have to be struck. Even well-grounded teachers will win a few and lose a few. But, by being able to explain the "whys" supporting their instructional practices, they need not feel guilty about what they are doing should some critic suggest that good teaching varies markedly from what they are doing.

THE TEACHER AS MANAGER

All teachers have certain management responsibilities. For example, teachers select and produce at least some of their instructional materials. They organize their instructional time. They may rearrange the furniture in their instructional spaces. They keep records and coordinate a variety of functions. And they fill out an incredible number of forms.

Many teachers do not find their managerial roles satisfying. Were we to take a poll, it would not be surprising to find that an overwhelming percentage of teachers professed to enjoy their roles as instructors much more than their roles as managers. Frequently teachers complain that management tasks, especially those associated with processing paperwork of various kinds, take too much time away from classroom instruction time.

Part of the frustration many teachers experience in acquitting themselves of their managerial responsibilities results from a difficulty in seeing any immediate payoff for these efforts. For example, taking attendance can be downright boring. But attendance figures are very important for teachers. Typically, attendance figures are fed to the state education agency where they become the basis of determining how much money from the state will flow from the state to the individual school district and, ultimately, the individual school. In a sense, the teacher's salary is tied up with the attendance figures. But this connection is often lost on the harried teacher eager to get the attendance forms completed so "the real work" of the day can begin.

Similarly, considerable time is consumed in organizing records for the purpose of awarding grades to students. While entering figures into the grade book can be time consuming, careful attention to this task does have benefits for teachers. These benefits may not be immediately evident. However, when parents visit the school during a parents' night or when a parent calls, the teacher who has specific documentation to support his or her comments about a particular youngster will be much better received than one who who must fall back on such tired, vague statements as "He's doing fine" or "She could be doing better."

Court decisions of recent years also point to the necessity to keep careful records relating to student progress. When grades a teacher has awarded have been challenged in court cases, in general the courts have been reluctant to overturn grades awarded by teachers who have had a solid record of evidence to support his or her grading decision. Careful attention to maintaining information in a grade book can provide an important part of such documentation.

Some schools require teachers to perform such managerial duties as maintaining equipment inventories, overseeing the ordering of supplies, and other kinds of management tasks. Many teachers feel that some of these responsibilities, at least, could be just as well performed by clerks or teacher aides. But many schools simply do not have the funds to pay for these kinds of support services. Although the teachers in schools lacking good clerical help are not particularly happy about the time they must spend attending to managerial matters, most strive to keep their frustration in perspective. Those who enjoy their instructional role (and in general simply like working with youngsters) recognize that the parts of the job they like would not be there if they were unwilling to attend also to some of the less satisfying aspects of teaching.

Many teachers who do not particularly enjoy the managerial dimensions of teaching have found it helpful to develop efficient routines for frequently occurring management tasks such as attendance taking. Some teachers, for example, have students take attendance, keep records relating to the whereabouts of media equipment, and distribute and collect materials. When well organized, these kinds of procedures work well and "buy time" for the teacher with greater interests in the nonmanagerial aspects of teaching.

Time devoted to developing a good system for organizing materials can pay dividends for the teacher interested in minimizing time spent on managerial tasks. For example, a well-arranged file of learning materials, student records, memos, reports, and other items allows for quick retrieval of needed items.

Finally, the principle of managerial efficiency is well served when attention is directed to the issue of long-range planning. We need to think ahead about such things as films that need to be ordered, materials that must be duplicated, records that have to be updated, and a host of other managerial chores. Careful advance planning can mitigate the anxiety caused by having to do too many things at once because plans were not made and appropriate action was not taken well before important deadlines.

There is nothing unique about the managerial skills of the teacher. The same sorts of organizational and planning skills that make for proficiency in enterprises other than education are also needed by teachers who are good managers. For many teachers (perhaps most), managerial skills do not come naturally or even easily. But those who take the time to develop proficiency in this area have vastly expanded opportunities to attend to other dimensions of teaching (many of which they may find much more satisfying than management).

THE TEACHER AS COUNSELOR

Nearly all secondary schools have professional counselors on their staffs. They play a very important role in the school. However, the presence of these counselors by no means relieves teachers of certain counseling responsibilities. Counselors simply cannot do it all. The number of students per counselor in most schools is so high that counselors find that they must spent most of their time dealing only with the most pressing cases.

Further, since students (at least a high percentage of them) are unlikely to know counselors as well as they know their teachers, they tend to seek out a sympathetic teacher when they have a problem. Often the problems are not serious, but the youngster feels a need to talk to an adult who is a good listener. Part of the teacher's professionalism in counseling relates to his or her ability to recognize when a youngster has sufficiently severe problems to require help from a trained specialist. Teachers must recognize their own professional limits and be willing to refer youngsters to trained counselors or other professionals when the need arises.

Teachers' classroom performance bears a direct relationship to the counseling function. For example, a teacher who interacts with youngsters in the classroom warmly and openly will find students much more willing to be candid when they are bothered by personal problems. Teachers who are sought out by some of their students during free periods, at lunch, or before and after school often gain valuable perspectives regarding personalities and backgrounds of these students. In turn, this information increases their effectiveness in the classroom because they have superior knowledge about the students being instructed.

Not all teachers believe that they ought to play a counseling role. ("My job is to teach history. The counselor's job is to counsel. I think I should be allowed to do my job. And I think the counselor should do the counseling.") Teachers who feel this way may become uncomfortable and impatient when students seek to turn a conversation away from academic concerns to personal concerns. Frequently such reactions are interpreted by students as evidence the teacher "doesn't really care." When this perception spreads through a group of youngsters in a classroom, the teacher's instructional role may become much more difficult.

On the other hand, some teachers get so involved with youngsters' personal problems that they fail to attend to their instructional responsibilities. Class hours may be spent on little more than weary rehashing of personal concerns of certain students.

Figure 18-3

SHOULD THE STUDENT AND THE TEACHER BE FRIENDS?

SPEAKER A: When I was in high school, none of the teachers cared about me. When *I* get my own classroom things will be different. I want my students to think of me as a friend. On the first day of class I am going to invite all of them to share any personal problems they have with me. I'll tell them it will be kept strictly confidential. I hope to have lots of students over to my home. You know, just to talk and get comfortable with one another.

SPEAKER B: When I was in high school the math instruction was simply awful. I am going to turn that situation around when I start teaching. The problem then, I think, was too many interruptions. I mean there were constant assemblies, stupid forms to fill out, and all these one-on-one conferences the teachers were supposed to have with each student. I think my job is to teach math to students . . . *period.* I know that these kids have other problems and other interests. But let's have professionals in those areas deal with those problems and interests. As for me, I intend to teach math because that's what *I* am good at.

YOUR OPINION, PLEASE

Read the comments of Speakers A and B. Then, respond to these questions.

1. Speaker A suggests that none of the teachers "cared" during speaker A's high school years. Do you think this is a common view of high school graduates? Why, or why not?
2. How successful do you think Speaker A's plan for working with students will be? Why do you think so?
3. If you were to give some personal advice to Speaker A, what would it be?
4. Speaker B implies that teachers should be concerned almost exclusively with teaching their subjects. Do you agree or disagree? Why?
5. If you were to give some personal advice to Speaker B, what would it be?
6. How would you respond to the question, Should the student and the teacher be friends?

Many new teachers who abandon subject matter content for class discussions of student concerns may be devastated when their course evaluations at the end of the term reveal that large numbers of youngsters viewed the experience as "a waste of time." By no means do all youngsters appreciate a teacher who abandons his or her traditional instructional role and turns a class into an unstructured series of rap sessions on issues the teacher perceives to be "more relevant" (see Figure 18-3).

A difficulty for many beginning teachers in the area of counseling has to do with the issue of "how close" to get to students. While it is important for the teacher to be warm and approachable, it is a mistake for the teacher to become "one of the kids." There are several reasons why such an approach has little to recommend it.

Perhaps most important, a teacher's attempt to become "just one of the gang" will not work. Students perceive their teacher as a teacher, not as a peer. By the very fact that he or she plays the role of a teacher, students will never accept a teacher as "one of us."

Second, a student who seeks out a teacher for help is not looking for a friend. Rather, he or she is looking for help. It is likely that this help is being sought out of a conviction that the teacher is not just another student but, rather, that he or she is a mature adult capable of providing some help to resolve a problem. A teacher who attempts to deal with a student with a problem as a peer rather than as a mature adult takes a chance of losing credibility with the student. When credibility is lost in a counseling situation, problems may begin to emerge in the instructional area as well. Students may simply stop taking such a teacher seriously in class. "Real teachers," after all, are not supposed to be students; they are supposed to be adults (see Figure 18-4).

Figure 18-4

TO WHOM DOES THE TEACHER OWE LOYALTY?

Sam Jones was an eighth-grade teacher. Late one afternoon, his principal called him in for a meeting in his office with parents of one of his students, a girl named Sally, and some juvenile authorities from the police department. Sam learned that Sally had run away from home and had been gone for three days.

That very evening, quite by chance, Sam ran into Sally while he was shopping at the supermarket. Sally wanted to talk. They walked out of the store and sat on a bench in the shopping mall. Sally went on for an hour about how unhappy she was at home. Sally told Sam she was telling him all this because she felt he was someone she could trust to listen and to say nothing to anyone else.

Sam tried to convince Sally to call a school counselor or to get in touch with a counselor working with the juvenile authorities. Sally listened politely, but, in the end, she said she would not contact anybody. She begged Sam not to tell anyone they had met or where she was staying.

YOUR OPINION, PLEASE
Read the paragraphs above. Then, respond to these questions.

1. Suppose that Sam decided to do nothing after this meeting. What possible consequences might result from his inaction? Would you recommend this to Sam? Why, or why not?
2. Suppose that Sam immediately called the youngster's parents after this meeting. What consequences might result? Would you recommend this to Sam? Why, or why not?
3. Suppose that Sam immediately called the school principal after this meeting. What might happen then? Would you recommend this to Sam? Why, or why not?
4. Suppose through some action of Sam's that Sally was returned to her home and began returning to school. What might be altered in the nature of the relationship between this teacher and student? Why do you think so?
5. Is there any action that Sam could take that would satisfy all parties and maintain his positive working relationship with Sally? If so, what?

Perhaps one of the most productive things that teachers can do in the area of counseling is to help youngsters to develop positive self-concepts. Adolescence is a time of profound physiological and psychological change. This time of change is accompanied by periods of uncertainty and self-doubt. Youngsters are anxious to prove to themselves and to the world that they are responsible and successful individuals; yet they are not at all sure they are. Teachers can be of tremendous help to youngsters in this age group by working to build youngsters' personal confidence.

In working with students to help them develop positive self-concepts, we need to develop some selective vision that sees and praises as much positive student behavior as possible and that overlooks at least some opportunities to comment negatively on youngsters' performance. Some teachers feel that they must be ever willing to point out student faults and weaknesses so that they will truly be prepared to face the "real" world. We do not support this approach. In our view, the best preparation for the real world is working to give students faith in their own abilities to succeed both academically and socially.

In dealing with the counseling function of teaching, we need to recognize that no teacher will reach every student. Teachers are diverse. Students are diverse. There is simply no way for a given teacher, despite the most valiant of efforts, to reach every youngster in his or her charge. This does not mean that we should give up trying. But it does suggest that we should not take an inability to help a given student resolve a problem as evidence that we have failed. Teachers who work hard to listen sensitively, to praise where praise is due, and to direct students to the attention of other professionals when necessary are acquitting themselves well in the counseling area. Those who do these things well find that their attention to the counseling role often results in youngsters who are more receptive to them when they are playing their instructional role. Certainly teachers who have managed to strike an appropriate balance among counseling, instruction, and other professional roles are likely to rank among those who youngsters will remember as having shaped their lives in positive directions during the important preadolescent and adolescent years.

THE TEACHER AS PROGRAM EVALUATOR

Most secondary school teachers will have occasion to be involved in evaluations of their own courses, courses in their department, and perhaps the entire school program. A number of teacher responsibilities exist in this area. At one level, teachers are involved in assessing the impact of their own instructional programs. This involves systematic efforts to determine whether youngsters are meeting established course objectives. Some review, too, occurs in terms of whether selected objectives are appropriate. It is likely that the amount of time teachers spend evaluating the contents of their instructional program will be increasing in the years ahead.

This prediction seems supportable given the growing interest in administering standardized competency tests to youngsters in various subject areas. As a consequence, teachers are going to be very anxious that the contents of their courses bear some real relationship to the kinds of questions being asked on these examinations. Whether these tests are a good idea or not is a separate issue. The reality is that they are either here or soon to be here and that large numbers of teachers certainly will attempt to evaluate their courses to assure that they are teaching what is being tested.

Not all teachers are enthusiastic about program evaluation tasks. Teachers who have developed a program that seems to work well with students may resist tinkering with "something that works right already." Change always means more work. And when few immediate problems with existing practices are evident, there is a tendency, for some teachers, at least, to question the need for a serious program review that might result in change. The difficulty with this view is that it can lead to a continuation of practices that may be easy for the teacher to implement but that, given the passage of time, no longer respond well to students' needs. To prevent this from happening, regular program evaluation is a must.

A frequent complaint of teachers involved in program evaluation concerns the amount of time needed to accomplish the work that has to be done. Particularly when an effort is being mounted to study a large program or several programs within a given content area, curriculum revision in schools is almost always accomplished by committees. As anyone knows who has been on a committee charged with accomplishing a given task, progress comes slowly. Teachers often go to committee meetings after they have put in a grueling day in the classroom. While most recognize that there are long-term benefits to sound curriculum review and revision, the immediate benefits seem few indeed when teachers sitting in a long committee meeting reflect on all the work they need to do to get prepared for the next day's classes.

In thinking about the program evaluation role, we need to keep several key points in mind. Perhaps the most important is that change is a way of life for teachers. There simply is no settling into a routine that will remain a constant pattern over a number of years. Indeed, frequently there are great changes even within a given school year. People who go into teaching must be prepared for a career that won't stand still for them. The nature of their students may change. Certainly knowledge that they have acquired in college and university undergraduate programs in many instances will be outdated after they have been in the classroom for only a few years. Teachers must keep up. Among the happiest educators are those who find stimulation in this kind of ongoing change. There are many opportunities for teachers to keep abreast of developments in their field (and in other areas as well) through reading, in-service workshops, self-development reading, and formal college and university course work.

We do not wish to minimize the heavy investment of time necessary to engage in program evaluation and revision activities. These things *do* take time. But time consuming or not, they have to be done. Thus we believe that it makes sense for teachers to develop sound time management skills. There is no such thing as expanding the time available to complete tasks. But we can increase our use of time that is available. For example, we can establish priorities and identify those tasks that must be completed immediately and those whose completion can be deferred. Many professional teachers who are concerned about using time wisely begin each day by preparing a short list of "things to accomplish" today. Such a list can be a great help in keeping the day productive, organized, and smooth flowing.

Time perspective is important, too, in helping us to recognize that all elements of program development do not have to be tackled concurrently. If we are focusing on our own courses, it probably makes more sense to focus on improving a portion of a single course than on completely revising every course we teach. A narrower focus helps to keep the task manageable. If the tasks established are too big, there is a tendency to become overwhelmed and simply give up. Establishing an appropriate objective is the responsibility of the individual teacher. Obviously some teachers feel that they can take on larger program review projects without experiencing pangs of anxiety than can others (see Figure 18-5).

THE TEACHER AS MEMBER OF THE ORGANIZED PROFESSION

Large numbers of teachers are members of organized professional groups. The largest of these is the National Education Association, frequently referred to as the NEA. Another powerful group is the American Federation of Teachers or AFT. The AFT is much smaller than the NEA, but because of its affiliation with the AFL–CIO and its heavy concentration of membership in large cities in the Midwest and East, it, like the NEA, is a politically potent group. In addition to these two large national organizations, there are many state and local groups to which teachers belong.

Although specifics vary enormously from organization to organization and from

Figure 18-5

CURRICULUM DEVELOPMENT AND TEACHERS

I'm just beat. I've spent the last three afternoons from 3:30 to 5:30 at the central administration building working on this social studies curriculum revision team. Then, I've had to go home and get my papers corrected and my classes planned for the next day.

I think we ought to have full-time professional people to do the curriculum development work. I mean, I think they should be people with lots of teaching experience . . . we don't want any this starry-eyed, "pie-in-the-sky" stuff . . . , but I don't think they should be people who are teaching now. It's just too much. Sometimes I think we're all so tired that we are going to come up with a final product that just isn't going to amount to anything.

Statement of a secondary school teacher

YOUR OPINION, PLEASE

Read the material quoted above. Then, respond to these questions.

1. What is your general reaction to this teacher's statement?
2. What kind of curricula do you think might result were schools to employ only full-time curriculum writers? Would these programs tend to be better or not as good as those developed with heavy involvement of teachers with concurrent classroom teaching responsibilities?
3. Is it fair for school districts to ask teachers to participate in curriculum revision and development work? Why, or why not?
4. How do you assess your own expertise in terms of designing and revising courses of study? What are your strengths and weaknesses? What kind of self-development program might you follow to increase your expertise in any areas of weakness?
5. Must teachers be involved personally in the development of programs they will teach if such programs are to be successful? Why, or why not?

---

place to place, these groups tend to pursue similar kinds of objectives. They work to seek better funding for public education in general. They provide a collective voice for teachers concerned about their working conditions. They provide a mechanism for lobbying at the national, state, and local levels for improved salary benefits for teachers. (In some cases formal negotiations take place between organization representatives and school board representatives. In others, organizations simply try to persuade school authorities of the merits of their case for improved teacher benefits.)

Teachers' association meetings ordinarily occur in the late afternoon or the evening. Almost never are they held during the regular school day. The associations are not part of the school district. Rather, they tend to be independent organizations whose members happen to be teachers. In larger towns and in cities, organizations will have some full-time employees who are charged with overseeing the groups' affairs.

Participation of teachers in professional organizations has the potential, at least, of leading to some role conflicts in terms of teachers' interactions with principals and other school administrators. Typically, administrators are seen as extensions of the authority of the school board. Their role is one of implementing school board decisions. Teachers' associations, on the other hand, tend to see themselves as autonomous groups who seek to represent the best interests of their members. When discussions between school board representatives and professional association representatives are held, the principals, in effect, are seated with representatives of the school board. This arrangement, in some schools at least, has led teachers and administrators to perceive one another as antagonists.

Perhaps this kind of suspicion cannot be avoided altogether considering that principals and teachers may have their interests represented by potentially conflicting groups when discussions regarding working conditions go forward. But much of the problem may be attributable to educators' (administrators and teachers) lack of experience in this kind of a give-and-take situation. The reality is that the administrator, as a member of management, must represent the views of the school district administration. That is how the administrator's role is defined. It does not mean that he or she is "antiteacher." Similarly, teachers representing the interests of the teachers' association are not "antiadministrator." Rather, they are charged with getting the best deal possible for the organization's teacher constituents.

Increasingly, teachers and administrators are becoming more sophisticated in terms of their perceptions of their respective roles when discussions between teachers' associations and school boards occur. Once discussions have been concluded and differences worked out, both teachers and administrators are coming to realize that disagreements need to be left behind, compromises need to be accepted, and a refocusing on the needs of youngsters in the schools needs to begin anew.

We do not wish to leave an impression that active involvement in professional organization has nothing to offer but potential conflict with administrators. This is not true. Professional organizations offer opportunities for teachers to interact with others who face many similar problems. Many teachers find it therapeutic to talk and work with others who are also "there on the firing line." Professional organization work, too, has the potential to broaden teachers' perspectives to encompass a world of education far richer and far broader than that of their own classroom or their own school. In summary, many teachers find that their work with teachers' organizations helps them to be more professional.

THE TEACHER AS PUBLIC RELATIONS SPECIALIST

Teachers operate in something akin to a fishbowl. As public employees, they are subjected to scrutiny by taxpayers' organizations and others interested in how governmental authorities expend money. As individuals who work with young people, their actions are monitored very closely by parents. To preserve their credibility with taxpayers, parents, and other elements of the general public, teachers have an important public relations function to which they must attend.

If changes in students' standardized test scores (particularly if they are lower than formerly) are reported in local media, teachers must be prepared to suggest reasons. (For example, there may have been dramatic changes in the makeup of the student body since earlier tests were given, state legislation may be requiring emphases on new topics not covered in the tests, and so forth.) When teachers are unable to speak intelligently about such matters and seek refuge in silence, laypersons may presume there to be something wrong with the schools.

Of all people in the larger community, it probably is most important for teachers to maintain positive lines of communication with parents. This task presents special difficulties for secondary school teachers. Secondary schools draw from much larger attendance areas then do elementary schools. Recent federal legislation and court decisions related to such issues as racial integration have tended to expand attendance boundaries of secondary schools even farther. Consequently, today there is not much of a sense that a given school "belongs" to the residents of a fairly close-knit neighborhood. In large cities, for example, students may live many miles from the secondary school they attend, which, in turn, makes it inconvenient for parents to visit the school or for the teacher to visit the parents. In this case it is unlikely that a high percentage of parents and teachers will know one another socially.

Many secondary schools do try to involve parents in school organizations such as PTAs (parent-teacher associations), PTOs (parent-teacher organizations), or PTSAs (parent-teacher-student associations). Although there are exceptions, it is fair to say that the level of parental involvement in such groups is very low at the secondary school level. One factor has to do with the previously noted lack of physical proximity between the school and parental residences. Another relates to the fact that parents, by the time their youngsters are in junior or senior high school, tend to be saturated with school activities. Many feel that they have participated sufficiently during the years in which their youngsters were in elementary school. Further, secondary school students rarely pressure their parents to attend parent organization meetings. (This is a big factor at the elementary school level where many youngsters will badger parents to go to a meeting so that their room will win the attendance award.) The bottom line is that teachers cannot rely upon the parent organization as a vehicle to maintain good communication with all parents in the school.

Secondary school teachers who are truly interested in keeping parents informed about what is going on in school find that they must invest personal time. They generally rely on phone calls, short notes home (sent via U.S. mail, *not* sent with students), or a combination of the two approaches. In considering the kinds of contacts a teacher might make, we should note the communications from school that most parents get (other than systematic reports of grades and meeting notices). It probably is fair to say that most calls parents get from school officials occur only when one of their youngsters is in some kind of difficulty. Many parents report feeling something of a chill when they pick up a phone and learn someone from the school wants to talk to them about "Joan" or "Sam." (They expect the worst.)

To combat the perception the school people are bearers only of bad tidings, in recent years many teachers have developed a practice of calling parents (or writing to them) when a student does something especially well. A message of this kind does wonders for a parent's ego. The call from the school is almost certain to be reported to friends of the family. A simple call or note can start a chain of events that can generate a tremendous quantity of postitive sentiment toward the school.

When youngsters feel good about school and their parents believe that they are doing well, there is a tendency for schools in a community to be seen as doing a good job. But when parents are dissatisfied, their attitudes can affect the general perspective of a community toward education in a negative way. Consequently, there is a clear personal and professional interest for teachers in maintaining sound relationships with parents. Time directed toward promoting parental goodwill can produce the kind of supportive environment for teachers that makes going to work a pleasure. Clearly these kinds of public relations efforts are a most worthwhile undertaking for classroom teachers in secondary schools.

SOME CONCLUDING THOUGHTS

Secondary school teachers must wear many "hats." For new teachers, the range of responsibilities can be overwhelming. Most undergraduate teacher preparation focuses so heavily on the teacher's instructional role that many beginners scarcely have considered the many other tasks that must be performed. The broad range of these roles suggests a necessity to establish priorities. Further, the need for an organized response to the demands of teaching is evident. Teachers who give careful attention to how they will respond to each of the many roles they must play and plan accordingly find that the job can be done in the time allotted. This kind of thoughtful anticipation can help teachers to avoid the phenomenon of "burn-out." We hope that some of the descriptions of teachers' roles we have provided here will enhance prospective teachers' grasp of the dimensions of the responsibilities they will be facing in the classroom.

Posttest

Directions: Using your own paper, answer each of the following true/false questions. For each correct statement, write the word "true." For each incorrect statement, write the word "false."

_____ 1. A teacher usually has absolute freedom to perform the instructional role as he or she deems appropriate.

_____ 2. There is consensus regarding what constitutes appropriate instructional behavior of teachers.

_____ 3. Role conflicts contribute to the problem of emotional stress known as teacher "burn-out."

_____ 4. Because most secondary schools have counselors, secondary school teachers almost never are concerned with counseling students.

_____ 5. Teachers who do a good job in handling the managerial aspects of teaching tend to develop routines that help them to accomplish often-repeated tasks efficiently.

_____ 6. If a teacher is to be effective in counseling students, it is essential that he or she endeavor to be as much like the students as possible.

_____ 7. An important counseling skill for teachers is the ability to listen carefully to students when they talk about personal problems.

_____ 8. In evaluating their own programs, there is a tendency for many teachers to resist change and to seek to maintain the status quo.

_____ 9. Some teachers sense conflict in their relationships with administrators with whom they are expected to function as cooperative colleagues in the day-to-day life of the school and against whom they may be pitted when professional working conditions and salaries are being negotiated across a bargaining table.

_____ 10. Typically, professional association meetings are held during the school day.

Key Ideas in Review

1. Teachers play a large number of roles. Among these are instructor, manager, counselor, organized professional, and public relations specialist. Teachers must strike a reasoned balance among all these roles. Teachers who are unable to do so may suffer emotional problems because of role conflicts. Severe cases of role conflict may result in the phenomenon known as teacher "burn-out."

2. In the area of instruction, teachers need to have a clear understanding of why they are doing what they are doing. Lacking a conceptual base, they may suffer feelings of insecurity when certain critics suggest they are not performing as effective teachers do.

3. Teachers must attend to a variety of management tasks. Many do not find the managerial aspects of teaching particularly attractive. In part this results because it is difficult to recognize any immediate "payoff" for many of these activities. In thinking about the area of management, it is desirable for teachers to develop some understanding of the long-term benefits that accrue from sound management principles. Further, to gain time for activities they deem more satisfying, teachers can develop time-efficient routines to handle recurring managerial tasks.

4. Although most secondary schools have counselors, secondary school teachers also play a counseling role with students. Often students will approach a teacher in search of help in resolving a problem. Teachers who appear interested and willing to listen often find that youngsters in their classes are more attentive when teachers are wearing their instructional "hats." In the counseling area, teachers need to know their own professional limitations. They

must recognize when a given youngster needs to be referred to a school counselor or other specially trained individual.

5. Teachers in secondary schools act as evaluators at many different levels. To keep course content congruent with changes in knowledge and changes in students, teachers must review and revise courses periodically. Further, teachers frequently are involved in departmentwide, schoolwide, and even districtwide curriculum development and revision tasks. Often the program evaluation role consumes a good deal of time. In large measure this results because ambitious efforts of this kind typically are undertaken by committees whose members need time to come to consensus. Teachers involved in program review and revision derive satisfaction from their participation in a process that has potential to improve classroom instruction.

6. Many teachers are involved in professional teacher organization work. In the past, such involvement, in some places at least, has had the potential to produce friction between teachers and administrators. More recently, however, both teachers and administrators have come to a better understanding of their respective positions in terms of what they are expected to do during and after discussions between school board representatives and teacher organization representatives. Many teachers find that involvement with professional teacher organizations expands their educational perspectives.

7. Teachers must play many public relations roles. Especially important is their work with parents. Positive and negative views of schools in a given community tend to relate directly to how parents see the schools. Consequently, teachers have a vested interest in maintaining open and positive relationships with parents of the youngsters they serve.

SUMMARY

Teachers play many roles in the school. Often beginning teachers are surprised at the responsibilities they must meet when they assume their initial teaching positions. Most are reasonably well prepared to instruct students. But duties in such areas as management and public relations often come as a surprise.

A continuing problem for teachers is balancing the sometimes conflicting demands of the many roles they must play. The effort to meet a multitude of responsibilities in a limited amount of time can take a psychological toll on teachers. Indeed, some experience so much difficulty in handling these pressures that, in time, they come to suffer teacher "burn-out." These teachers tend to become apathetic about their work and find themselves progressively less concerned about the world of public education.

Teachers who do cope with the multifaceted demands of teaching tend to be well organized. They utilize efficient planning and organizational skills. Such skills, when well honed, enable them to maximize their accomplishments given the limited time they have available to work on the many tasks associated with classroom teaching. This careful planning, too, permits them more time to attend to those dimensions of teaching they find personally satisfying.

References

Egan, Gerard. *The Skilled Helper: A Model for Systematic Helping and Interpersonal Relating*. Monterey, Calif.: Brooks/Cole Publishing Company, 1975.

Gross, Beatrice. *Teaching Under Pressure*. Santa Monica, Calif.: Goodyear Publishing Company, 1979.

Grovers, Cy. "What Teachers Are Not," *The Education Digest* (September 1980): 20–23.

Hawley, Richard A. "Teaching as Failing," *Phi Delta Kappan* (April 1979): 597–600.

Jarvis, F. Washington. "The Teacher as Servant," *Phi Delta Kappan* (March 1979): 504–505.

Mace, Jane. "Teaching May Be Hazardous to Your Health," *Phi Delta Kappan* (March 1979): 512–513.

Miller, Dean F., and Wiltse, Jan. "Mental Health and the Teacher," *The Journal of School Health* (September 1979): 374–377.

Solnit, Albert J. "The Adolescent's Search for Competence," *Children Today* (November–December 1979): 13–15.

Stern, Adele. "Forty Years Tomorrow: A Teacher Looks Back," *Media and Methods* (May–June 1980): 31–33.

19
Teachers and Discipline

"Then I said to the kid 'you're bluffing!' . . ."

Objectives

This chapter provides information to help the reader to

1. Recognize that all teachers must deal with issues related to classroom control and management.

2. Understand that there are sets of specific teacher actions that can reduce the probability of disruptive student behavior.

3. Identify sequences of teacher responses to unsatisfactory student behavior.

4. Recognize procedures flowing from several philosophical or theoretical bases that teachers can use to deal with persistent or difficult behavioral problems of students.

Pretest

Directions: Using your own paper, answer each of the following true/false questions. For each correct statement, write the word "true." For each incorrect statement, write the word "false."

_____ 1. In general, most secondary school students do not like to know the exact limits on their behavior.

_____ 2. Little is to be gained by providing ground rules specifying appropriate standards for behavior when beginning work with a new group of students.

_____ 3. When clear guidelines for behavior are not provided by a teacher, students tend to behave as they behave in the class taught by their least restrictive teacher.

_____ 4. Teachers who express themselves clearly and firmly may well produce a positive "ripple effect" in a classroom that serves to diminish classroom control problems.

_____ 5. A principle basic to the reality therapy approach is that the individual student must be encouraged to face up to the consequences of his or her behavior.

_____ 6. Inappropriate behavior, as Dreikurs sees it, results in student concerns for (a) attention seeking, (b) power, (c) revenge, and (d) withdrawal.

_____ 7. Teachers who use a behavior modification approach should begin by identifying precisely appropriate and inappropriate behaviors.

_____ 8. The same reinforcers work equally well with all students.

_____ 9. It is wise for a teacher to have thought through in advance some responses to potentially disruptive student behavior.

_____ 10. Teachers who do not handle their administrative responsibilities efficiently may experience more classroom control problems than do teachers who handle these responsibilities efficiently.

INTRODUCTION

Scenario 1: John Jones, Undergraduate

John Jones is preparing to become a teacher. He is highly excited about this prospect. He visualizes himself as being the kind of a teacher who can get students charged up about what he is teaching. He knows his students will be eager to come to his classroom. He pictures gaggles of students gathered around his desk after the bell has rung asking penetrating questions and making intelligent comments about what has gone on in class. Above all, John Jones remembers his own halcyon days in high school and in junior high school when he hopped eagerly from his bed in anticipation of another good day. (Of course, there were a few teachers he didn't enjoy, but he surely wouldn't be like one of them.) For John, the future holds a happy prospect of leading students to understandings in an atmosphere of warmth, caring, and excitement. Certainly, as a "good" teacher he won't have discipline problems.

Scenario 2: John Jones, Student Teacher

John Jones is nearing the end of his student teaching experience. Things have gone reasonably well. But the students are not quite as he had thought they would be. In fact, he and the other student teachers spoke about this situation the other night to their university supervisor. "The kids have sure changed since we were in school," they said. John has been surprised that some students "just don't want to learn." Classroom control has become a challenging part of his day.

But John expects things to get much better once he has his own classroom. For one thing, his supervising teacher established an unfortunate climate with these

*students before he even got here. Surely, too, these students can't be typical. He
anticipates "much better" students when he assumes his first teaching position. He
knows that he has what it takes to be a "good" teacher. And he knows that "good"
teachers don't have classroom control problems.*

Scenario 3: John Jones, First-Year Teacher

*John Jones has been teaching for two months. He wants to quit. He has never
been so frustrated in his life. The students he works with certainly aren't like students when he went to school. They are even more of a problem (at least on some
days) than those he met as a student teacher. They are rude. They are disrespectful. They take every opportunity to challenge him. Even when he laces lectures
with interesting anecdotes, not many seem to get involved. He feels that he spends
so much time handling discipline problems that he doesn't have time to "really
teach." Far from being the popular and "good" teacher he has always wanted to
be, he feels that he is viewed with little enthusiasm by students. The job his uncle
offered him at the rock quarry is beginning to look better and better all the time.*

While this scenario is a little overblown, classroom control and discipline *are* problems for most teachers. They may not appear to be problems for teachers who have
been in the profession for some time. But the appearance of calm, clear-headed control
does not mean that the problems do not exist. Rather, such classrooms signal a teacher
who has taken specific actions to do something about them. Sometimes what has been
done is subtle and all but invisible to a casual observer. But beginning teachers should
rest assured that teachers who seem to have classes of interested, eager, and controlled
learners are not exercising some kind of magic. They have taken specific actions to
create the kind of classroom demeanor students display in their courses.

Happily, certain principles can be passed on to people who hope to become teachers that can help them meet the challenge of coping with preadolescents and adolescents
in the classroom. We need to preface remarks about these procedures with a note of
caution. No single set of procedures can be learned and applied by an individual teacher
to guarantee success with any single student or group of students. Students tend to
reflect the diversity of the American population. Part of the teacher's artistry involves
adapting basic principles associated with classroom control to needs of the individual
student and classroom. But this does not mean that students and classes are unique to
the point that no general guidelines for the teacher are available. On the contrary, many
students respond well to similar kinds of teacher actions taken with a view to maintaining effective classroom control. Some procedures that successful teachers have found
useful through the years will be introduced in the sections that follow.

PREVENTING PROBLEMS

Every teacher at some time in his or her career experiences discipline problems. Probably it is unrealistic to hold out the expectation that all problems associated with classroom control can be eliminated. (Even teachers with years of experience have "bad"
days.) But teachers can take actions that promise to reduce the likelihood or the frequency of disruptive student behavior.

Beginning teachers sometimes worry about the term "discipline." Many of them
see the word only in a negative sense. Some suggest that the word conjures up images
of teachers who are heavy-handed authoritarians who delight in punishing students
(see Figure 19-1). Discipline should not be viewed in this way.

Discipline, we think, provides a positive control that helps students to grow in
terms of their acceptance of responsibility and in acquiring new knowledge. Discipline,
applied properly, reflects a teacher's attitude of concern and caring for students' development. Discipline represents a teacher's effort to create an atmosphere conducive to

Figure 19-1

"I'LL BE DIFFERENT FROM THE TEACHERS I HAD IN SCHOOL"

I just hated my freshman English teacher in high school. We had to walk in quietly, sit down, and never move an unnecessary muscle for the whole period. When somebody would talk out of turn, the teacher would really get on their case. I had to stay after school a couple of times. And once, she even called my father at work. Did I ever hear about *that* when I got home. It got to the point that I could hardly stand going to her class.

It's going to be different when I go into that classroom. If students don't have a warm friendly relationship with their teacher, what's the point? And how can you get students' friendship if you do nothing but nag, nag, nag every day? It seems to me that discipline gets in the way of real teaching.

YOUR OPINION, PLEASE

The remarks above were made by an undergraduate who was preparing to do student teaching in a secondary school. Read the comments. Then, respond to these questions.

1. What motive do you think the teacher might have had for her behavior?
2. Assuming that the student's description of her English teacher's behavior is accurate, how do you react to this teacher? Why?
3. The student says that the teacher cannot be effective if there is not an atmosphere of friendship existing between teacher and learner. Do you agree? Why, or why not?
4. How do you feel about the statement that "discipline gets in the way of real teaching"? Why do you feel this way?

---

productive individual progress of students. To be effective, discipline then demands teacher actions taken to *prevent* disruptive behavior as well as actions to deal with disruptive behavior when it occurs.

In the area of preventing problems, teachers need to pay specific heed to the following:

1. Establishing specific guidelines for behavior
2. Providing for students' success
3. Pacing and monitoring instruction
4. Completing administrative tasks efficiently

Establishing Specific Guidelines for Behavior

How should students behave? "Properly." Although "properly" does respond to the question, it does not provide a set of behavioral guidelines. What is proper behavior for one teacher in one classroom might be considered totally improper by another teacher in another classroom. Students recognize these differences. They know that they can talk in Ms. Peterson's class after completing assignments but not in Mr. Smith's.

Because there are differences in expectations of individual teachers, it is a mistake for teachers to assume that students will know what is "proper" when they come into their classrooms. If no special instructions are given, students have a tendency to behave as they are permitted to behave in the class taught by the least restrictive teacher on their schedule. Such behavior may be perfectly appropriate in this teacher's course, but it may be totally inappropriate in a class taught by another instructor. To avoid this kind of situation, the teacher should clarify his or her behavioral expectations to students when he or she first begins to work with them. There is much to be said for making these behavioral guidelines as specific as possible.

One highly successful junior high school teacher always takes a full day at the beginning of each semester to explain his "ground rules." He introduces the ground rules to the class, leads a discussion centered on them, and asks for questions. He lists and distributes them to each student and announces to the class that there will be a quiz on ground rules at the beginning of the next class period. He gives the quiz, notes errors, and returns corrected papers to students. This may appear to be a somewhat elaborate procedure. But it does result in communicating clearly to the student that (1) there is a set of behavioral expectations for this class and (2) the instructor is dead serious about his intention to hold students accountable to these standards.

In formulating ground rules, several points should be observed. First, they should be broad enough to take into account most behaviors that might be anticipated during a typical instructional period. Second, they should be made public. As suggested, they might be duplicated and distributed to each student, or they might be posted on a bulletin board. Whatever procedure is adopted, teachers must do something to assure themselves that students *understand* what the ground rules mean. (Simply distributing a list does not guarantee understanding.) Often a short discussion will clarify potential misunderstandings.

Ground rules often provide guidelines for students regarding such areas as the following:

1. What students are to do when they enter the classroom.
2. What students should look for as a signal that the teacher is ready to begin the day's instruction.
3. What students should do if they need to leave the room.
4. What students should do about making up missed work.
5. What students should do in a class discussion.
6. What students should do as they are dismissed.

Some teachers involve students in the identification of specific classroom operating guidelines. There are some psychological advantages to giving students an impression that they have had a role in their development. Whether developed jointly by teacher and students or by the teacher alone, provision of specific ground rules can result in fewer classroom control problems for students. Clear ground rules remove uncertainties regarding acceptable behavior patterns. These guidelines enable students to participate more confidently in classroom activities as they recognize the limits of acceptable classroom behavior. Moreover, the existence of formal guidelines permits the teacher to take action to enforce adopted standards of behavior without feeling that he or she is operating in an arbitrary manner.

Providing for Students' Success

Classroom control problems are especially likely to arise when students sense that the teacher has placed them in a "no-win" situation. Consider, for example, a secondary student with an undistinguished academic record who for years has listened to teachers praise students with better grades (see Figure 19-2). Such an individual may well have decided that his or her personal dignity will never be appreciated by teachers. If the teacher is not seen as a person who can support his or her psychological needs, a student will have little incentive to pay close attention to what the teacher might expect in terms of classroom behavior. For example, a student who has had a long history of "D's" and "F's" is unlikely to be motivated by a fear of getting a low grade in a course.

To prevent behavior problems brought on because of students' convictions that they cannot meet a teacher's expectations, there is a need to plan learning experiences where a real possibility exists for all students to experience success. Given the widely divergent ability levels of students in middle school, junior high school, and senior high

Figure 19-2

HOW TEACHERS' COMMENTS MAY AFFECT STUDENTS

The following teacher comment was directed at Paul Benton, a student with a D— average in Mrs. Smith's algebra class. Paul had just been caught talking to another student while Mrs. Smith was giving tomorrow's assignment to the class.

MRS. SMITH: Paul, you *can't* be talking again. I'm *trying* to give you tomorrow's assignment. You of all people should want to know what that is. The last time I looked in my grade book you needed all the points you can get.

The following teacher comment was directed at Beth Marywell, a student with a B+ average in Mrs. Smith's algebra class. Beth had just been caught talking to another student while Mrs. Smith was giving tomorrow's assignment to the class.

MRS. SMITH: Beth, I can't *believe* that you are talking. We all know what a fine student you are. It just isn't like you. Now please let's not interrupt as I give the assignment.

YOUR OPINION, PLEASE

Look over the teacher's comments to the two students above. Then, respond to these questions.

1. Do you note any differences in how the teacher answers each student?
2. How do you think each student would react to what the teacher has said?
3. Do you think the teacher may be saying something that might make one of these students generally less supportive of the teacher and of the class than the other student? Which one, and why?
4. If you found yourself in a situation similar to that of Mrs. Smith, what would you say? Why?

---

school classrooms, then, every student cannot be expected to do the same assigned work. Individual students' abilities must be diagnosed and tasks assigned in such a manner that there is real reason to expect each youngster to experience success. Instructional planning of this type requires considerable teacher preparation. But the rewards for this kind of professional behavior can result in a real decrease in classroom control problems. Students who do well in classes generally feel good about themselves and their teachers.

Pacing and Monitoring Instruction

The "flow" of instruction during a class period can do a great deal to diminish the possibility of classroom control problems. Transitions from one part of a lesson to another that are ragged break the continuity of a lesson, divert students' attention from the instructional task, and present a fertile ground in which latent behavioral problems can flower. Smooth lesson development requires careful planning.

A serious error made by many beginning secondary school teachers is abandoning the use of lesson plans that were required during student teaching. While some experienced teachers do not need to formalize step-by-step procedures, few novices are able to do a responsible job of teaching off the cuff. Planning can ensure systematic development of points. More important, a written lesson plan can provide a reminder of intended sequence that can get the teacher back on track should he or she get distracted and "go blank" during a lesson. (Going blank is a phenomenon that afflicts even the best teachers. Most students never know that it happens if the teacher has a note or plan to which he or she can refer to reorient himself or herself.)

In planning for instruction, a variety of experiences should be built into each class period. As noted earlier, middle school and junior high school students find it difficult to maintain concentrated attention on a single activity for more than about 20 minutes;

even juniors and seniors in high school find their attention beginning to wander if there is no change in 30 or 40 minutes. Some teachers have found it useful to think of a class period as being composed of about five segments of 10 minutes each. In planning, they think in terms of what will be going on during each 10-minute period. This tends to introduce more variety into the instructional plan than when the unit of planning is the entire class period. Activities requiring students to become active participants that are interspersed carefully between activities requiring more passive student seat work help students to release a little energy and tend to decrease the likelihood of classroom control problems.

In monitoring students' activities, it is wise for the teacher to circulate throughout the classroom area. Students are much more likely to stay engaged when they realize that the teacher may be stopping by to see how they are getting along than when the teacher sits at his or her desk. Moving through the area also permits the teacher to ask questions of individual students to find out whether they really understand what they are to be doing. (In talking to the class as a whole, it is not unusual for an entire class to nod a strong "yes" to a teacher question such as "Does everyone understand?" No one wants to appear "dumb" in front of the entire group. It is necessary for the teacher to do some individual checking to ensure that students really do understand what they are to do.)

Adequate preparation for instructional planning and for monitoring students' activities has an important psychological payoff for the teacher. When lessons and procedures for interacting with students have been thought through with care, teachers tend to be much more secure as they direct the activities of their students. This security translates into a feeling of self-confidence. Students tend to be much less likely to misbehave in the presence of a teacher who appears confident, well-prepared, and certain of where he or she and the class are going.

Efficient Completion of Administrative Tasks

One of the first things a person who goes to work for a radio station is taught is that he or she at all costs should avoid "dead air," as when, through a mistake, no music, no voice, nothing goes out from the station to the radios of those who are tuned in. Ordinarily dead air does not last long before someone at the station either puts on some music or says something. But even a few seconds of dead air time can be costly to a station as listeners change their dials to pick up a signal from a competitor.

There are dead air times in teaching as well. And they can cause problems as students' attention loses its focus on the teacher. For beginning teachers, it is likely to develop when administrative procedures are being attended to. Roll taking, entering grades into a record book, and numerous other administrative tasks, if not completed efficiently, can provide students with opportunities to exercise inappropriate behavior.

Administrative matters require planning if they are to be accomplished expeditiously and well. For example, it is not unusual for a disorganized first-year teacher to consume 10 or even 15 minutes of class time taking roll and posting the attendance in the hall to be collected by a student clerk from the main office. Use of seating charts, roll sheets for students to sign, or even a quick call of the roll should help to complete this task efficiently. But the teacher must (1) know exactly how he or she will proceed, (2) undertake chosen procedures without delay, and (3) have available *in advance* of students' arrival all necessary forms.

Distribution of learning materials to students can also take too much time unless it is well organized. Time spent devising schemes to get materials into the hands of students quickly is well spent. (Many teachers use students to get material quickly to students.) Again, organization of materials *before* students arrive can expedite the distribution process.

In general, the quicker administrative tasks can be accomplished, the quicker the teacher can begin the instructional phase of the class period. The shorter the slack time between the beginning of the period and the beginning of the instructional phase, the less likely classroom control problems are to develop.

Some secondary teachers have succeeded in removing all slack time from the beginning of their class periods. They assign tasks for students to perform while they take role, distribute materials, and pass back papers. Students expect that something related to course instruction is to occur from the very moment they enter the classroom. Thus, they have no time to socialize and are encouraged to get to work immediately on class-related activities.

Administrative responsibilities of teachers are not limited to processing paperwork. Teachers also have decisions to make regarding physical arrangements of students in their classrooms (see Figure 19-3). In very old-fashioned classrooms, students' seats are anchored to the floor. Clearly teachers in such settings can exercise few options. In most classrooms, however, furniture can be shifted to meet varying instructional needs.

Figure 19-3

CLASSROOM MANAGEMENT CHECKLIST

The following checklist is an example of a self-check system a teacher might develop to keep track of the number of important planning responsibilities that have been accomplished.

	Yes	No	
BEHAVIORAL GUIDELINES	____	____	Ground rules have been described, explained, and distributed to students.
	____	____	Specific steps have been taken to assure that all students understand ground rules.
PROVIDING FOR STUDENTS' SUCCESS	____	____	Students' individual capabilities have been diagnosed.
	____	____	Assignments have been differentiated so that each student has a real chance to complete assignments successfully.
PACING AND MONITORING INSTRUCTION	____	____	Specific plans have been made so that transitions from one part of a lesson to another will be smooth.
	____	____	Clear and detailed lesson plans have been developed.
	____	____	A variety of instructional experiences have been developed for each class period.
ADMINISTRATIVE TASKS	____	____	An efficient plan for taking attendance has been devised.
	____	____	A smooth procedure for distributing new material to students has been planned.
	____	____	Procedures for returning papers and projects to students quickly and efficiently have been developed.
	____	____	Plans have been prepared showing how classroom furniture will be arranged at different times during the instructional sequence.

In thinking about physical arrangements, commonsense principles apply. For example, if students are to work independently, seating that minimizes opportunities for social interaction should be developed. If a discussion is planned, a circular or semicircular arrangement makes sense. Clusters of student seats are appropriate when small-group work is required. In every configuration, space for relatively free movement through the classroom area should be provided when students need to move about at some time during the period. This provision also assures the teacher easy access to students in all areas of the classroom.

RESPONDING TO MINOR BEHAVIOR PROBLEMS

Even the teacher who works conscientiously to eliminate student misbehavior will have occasional classroom control and discipline problems. In thinking about logical responses when problems arise, we need to recall that the purpose of a teacher's disciplinary action is to help students grow in terms of self-control and acceptance of responsibility. Appropriate teacher responses are directed with these ends in mind (see Figure 19-4).

Two basic principles should be borne in mind when we think about dealing with minor behavioral problems in the classroom. First, the teacher should never threaten the student with something that he or she is powerless to deliver. For example, it is unwise to threaten a student with expulsion from school if he or she does not stop talking. Usually a teacher does not have this authority. Students soon recognize such threats as idle, and their utility as prompts to appropriate action quickly dissipates. Second, the teacher should have some idea about how he or she is going to respond before a problem calling for a response develops.

In this latter connection, many teachers have found it useful to think through a number of alternative appropriate responses that might be used. Redl and Wineman (1957) suggest a number of alternatives, categorized under the general headings of "nonverbal responses" and "verbal responses" that might be useful to a teacher when a student misbehaves. They have arranged these responses in a continuum from "least severe" to "most severe." Let us look at an adaptation of their work.

Figure 19-4

GETTING CONTROL OF THE CLASS

The scene is a drafting class in a junior high school. Students have been asked to draw a hammer. Instructions have been given, and most students have begun work. One group, in the back of the room, has yet to settle down. In fact, these youngsters are having a loud animated conversation. Very annoyed, the teacher stands up and shouts, "All right, you guys, all right now! Just knock it off! I mean business!"

YOUR OPINION, PLEASE

Read through the scenario above. Think about the teacher's response. Then, respond to these questions.

1. How effective do you think the teacher's response was? Why?
2. Do you think the teacher's response was better from (a) the standpoint of stopping the behavior the teacher did not like or (b) the standpoint of pointing out more appropriate behaviors to the students?
3. How would you have reacted if you were a student who was talking and the teacher spoke to you in this way?
4. If you were the teacher of this class, how would you have dealt with this situation? How do you justify your actions?

Nonverbal Responses

In the Redl and Wineman framework,* the first level of responses that a teacher might try involve nonverbal actions. These minimize the attention directed to a student with a problem behavior by other members of the class. Under optimal conditions, nonverbal responses can lead a student to change his or her problem behavior without being embarrassed by becoming a center of attention for other students. Some categories of nonverbal responses are described below.

1. *Planned ignoring.* Often a disruptive behavior represents an attempt by a student to gain attention. A teacher's response might prove to be the very thing that the student is seeking. Such a response might reinforce the disruptive behavior the teacher is trying to change. If the desire for attention is the motive, often planned ignoring will lead to a decrease in the frequency of the problem behavior.

    Obviously not all behaviors can be ignored. The teacher must decide whether a problem behavior can be ignored without creating difficulties for other students in the class.

    Planned ignoring frequently works well as a tactic when a difficult student attempts to win attention through a strong verbal assault on a teacher. Planned ignoring communicates to the student that the teacher is secure enough to handle the assault without responding in kind.

2. *Teacher glance.* Sometimes known in faculty lounges as the "cold, hard stare," the teacher glance is used to catch the eye of a misbehaving student and to make a strong, continuous eye contact that communicates that the teacher is aware of the offending behavior. In a good many cases, the teacher glance will result in a change of behavior. When the ploy works, it has the advantage of producing a change without either embarrassing the student with the problem behavior or disrupting the class.

3. *Proximity control.* In this response, the teacher moves physically closer to the student who is misbehaving. Often just the bare beginnings of a teacher movement in the direction of a youngster who is not behaving properly will result in a speedy change. Large numbers of students find it difficult to misbehave when the teacher is close at hand.

Verbal Responses

Nonverbal responses do not always accomplish the objective of altering a problem behavior. Sometimes verbal responses are necessary. When executed properly, verbal responses can have a dramatic impact not only on the offending student but on others in the classroom as well. Kounin (1961) reports that strong teacher statements tend to have a "ripple effect" on students in the classroom other than the youngster who is addressed. Thus, when a strong and clear statement is made to a given student describing exactly what he or she should be doing, it can have a cueing effect on others in the classroom that tends to focus their attentions more directly on the kinds of behaviors the teacher prefers.

A positive ripple effect of this kind requires clarity and firmness. Clarity requires the teacher to describe as specifically as possible (1) the behavior that is unacceptable and (2) a substitute behavior that is acceptable. Firmness implies the use of a strong, no-nonsense tone of voice. A teacher who communicates his or her point of view timidly or who simply hopes that a problem will go away by itself is almost certain to be

---

*This discussion is adapted from Fritz Redl and David Wineman, *The Aggressive Child* (New York: The Free Press, 1957).

disappointed. The tone of voice should proclaim a strong commitment to the stand that is being taken.

Some categories of verbal behavior adapted from Redl and Wineman (1957) are described below.

1. *Using humor.* Humor provides a natural release for tension. If a teacher senses a confrontation developing with a student, interjection of humor frequently can turn the situation around. Few people can stay angry and laugh at the same time.
2. *A quiet word.* A quiet and private word with a student whose behavior is becoming a problem frequently is effective. Care should be taken to avoid drawing the attention of the entire class to the student in question. For example, the teacher might move to the desk of the student, quietly and firmly request that the student stop his or her disruptive behavior, and move on. This procedure often results in an immediate change in the student's behavior.
3. *Task help.* Some behavior problems result when students are frustrated by an inability to understand an assigned task. If the teacher suspects this might be the case, a private verbal review of how the task is to be approached may turn a student's behavior into a more productive channel.
4. *Individual conference.* When the preceding three approaches have not proved effective, the teacher should have a personal conference with the student, at the end of the period, at noon, or after school. It is important that the conference involve the teacher and the student together in a setting where other students are not present.

    During the conference, the student should be encouraged to do the talking. This can be prompted by asking questions such as "What is the problem?" "How can the problem be solved?" and so forth. The situation should be one where both teacher and student can speak candidly.

Next Steps

Although teachers' attempts to use nonverbal and verbal responses can change the behavior of many disruptive students, such efforts are by no means effective in all cases. Sometimes more serious action must be taken involving participation of other individuals. Some considerations that should be taken into account in planning for more drastic actions to solve a very bad behavior problem are described below.

1. *Build a case.* Teachers' complaints to administrators and parents may go nowhere in the absence of solid evidence to support allegations of misbehavior. In preparation for involving other people, a case record must be built. This can be done in several ways. For example, $3'' \times 5''$ cards can be used to build an "anecdotal record file." To build the file, the teacher should write down on individual cards specific instances of inappropriate behaviors demonstrated by the student in question. Information should be very specific. It might include (a) the nature of the behavior, (b) the date and time of day, (c) special circumstances surrounding the behavior, and (d) other pertinent information.
2. *Involve the counselor or the principal.* The person charged with working with teachers and students when questions of classroom behavior are involved will vary from district to district and building to building. The individual charged with this responsibility ordinarily will be glad to work with a teacher who comes prepared to describe a complaint and supports his or her description with a well-developed case file. Sometimes a conference between counselor or principal and the student will be all that is required to solve the problem.
3. *Involve the parents.* This might involve a call home or a student-teacher-parent conference. If arrangements can be made, the personal conference is preferable. Parents need to be apprised of the problem and to be informed about the evidence the

teacher has gathered in his or her case file. In working together with parents and students, teachers must try hard to not place the parents (or the involved student) on the defensive. Rather, the problem should be discussed in an atmosphere that might be appropriately framed by a question such as "What can we do working together to solve this problem?" If some agreements are reached, the teacher should make specific arrangements to keep parents alerted to the nature of the student's progress.

4. *Last resort.* If problem behavior continues at an intolerable level, again the school officials charged with handling school disciplinary problems need to be consulted. If removal from class, suspension, or other serious measures are to be imposed, those decisions are the responsibility of the school administration, not the teacher. Such decisions have certain legal ramifications, and it is imperative that the teacher leave them in the hands of individuals well versed in legal implications of such moves.

In general, all responses to relatively minor behavioral problems of students are intended to solve the problem without undermining the dignity of the student. It is the spirit of helping the student grow toward a sense of responsible self-worth that disciplinary actions are properly directed.

These remarks on problem behaviors should be put into a proper context. While problems *do* exist, we do not want to suggest that classrooms are populated by huge segments of hostile and angry young people. In fact, most students work very well with their teachers. Few become serious discipline problems. But those who do can disrupt the teacher's capacity to work comfortably and effectively with the majority of students in his or her class. In the interest of this majority and in the long-term interest of the student with a problem behavior, the teacher must act.

DEALING WITH MORE SEVERE BEHAVIOR PROBLEMS

Procedures described in the preceding section include techniques designed to change relatively minor behavioral problems. In most cases, these procedures will achieve the desired result. But, occasionally, teachers will encounter students whose unacceptable behaviors continue despite efforts to use some (or even all) of the techniques described. Such long-term behavior problems may require application of more systematic and formal procedures. Some of these techniques are introduced in this section.

Reality Therapy

Developed by Dr. William Glasser (1965), reality therapy seeks to help individuals change unacceptable patterns of behavior by having them focus on likely consequences of a continuation of these patterns. Several basic principles undergird the approach. First, it is assumed that individuals can change only present and future behaviors. Therefore, an extensive focus on past causes of behavior is seen as unproductive. Second, individuals are believed to be faced with a choice of dealing with circumstances as they *are,* not as they *ought to be.* Finally, individuals are perceived as personally responsible for their behaviors. As a result, they must be prepared to live with the consequences of whichever behavioral patterns they choose.

In applying the principles of reality therapy, teachers follow these steps:

1. *The student is encouraged to identify the problem behavior.*

   Teacher: What are you doing?

   Student: There was a long line at lunch and I couldn't finish in time to get here before the bell rang.

Teacher: No, I didn't ask you *why* you did what you did. I asked you to tell me what you are doing. Now, once again, what are you doing?

Student: Well, I'm coming in late to class again.

2. *The student is asked to identify consequences of the behavior.*

Teacher: What might happen to you if you keep coming in late?

Student: Well, I might miss part of the class.

Teacher: Yes. Anything else?

Student: Well, I could get some really bad grades.

3. *The student is asked to make a personal value judgment about consequences of continuing his or her behavior pattern.*

Teacher: What do you think about the possibility of getting a bad grade in this class? Is that what you want?

Student: No. A bad grade would make me *very* unhappy.

4. *The student is asked to formulate a plan for an alternative behavior.* (To the extent possible, the plan should be the student's, not the teacher's.)

Teacher: Well, what specifically do you think you might do to avoid getting a bad grade?

Student: Well, I guess I could make a real effort to get here on time.

Teacher: What kind of plan can you develop to be sure that happens.

Student: I think I'll hurry right to the cafeteria after my third-period class instead of stopping to talk with my friends. That way the line will be shorter, and I should be able to finish sooner.

Teacher: That sounds good. Try it for a week. Then let's chat again.

Obviously this is a highly abbreviated example of the kind of teacher-student interaction that might take place were a teacher to decide to use a reality therapy approach.

In the minds of many teachers who have used the reality therapy approach, an important strength of the technique is having the student assume responsibility for the consequences of his or her behavior. The sequence of teacher questions is designed to focus attention on the behavior. ("What are you doing?") There is an effort to avoid providing students with an opportunity to rationalize what they are doing. (In a reality therapy approach, a teacher never asks, "Why are you doing this?" This question does not focus on the inappropriate behavior. Further, it implies to the student that there may not be anything basically wrong with the behavior but that what is wrong is the explanation or excuse he or she has offered in defense of the behavior.) The reality therapy approach is described in detail in William Glasser's book, *Reality Therapy: A New Approach to Psychiatry.* Available in paperback, this eminently readable volume deserves a place in a teacher's professional library.

Dreikurs and the Four Goals of Misbehavior

An approach stemming from the work of Rudolf Dreikurs (1968) provides a useful framework for dealing with serious classroom behavior problems. Dreikurs points out that all human beings seek a natural state of personal acceptance and satisfaction. When they do not have these sorts of positive feelings about themselves, they become dissatisfied and discouraged. People who are dissatisfied and discouraged tend to improve their psychological condition by seeking one of the following four goals:

1. Attention
2. Power
3. Revenge
4. Withdrawal

Problem students in classrooms often seek one of these goals because of feelings of personal dissatisfaction. Teachers' actions, unless planned with care, can promote a continuation of the unacceptable pattern of behavior by convincing students that the misbehavior is helping them to move toward one of these goals. To avoid this and to begin directing students' behaviors in more productive directions, the following steps are recommended.

1. Identify the goal being pursued.
2. Avoid expected responses.
3. Use psychological disclosure.
4. Implement specific actions.

Identifying the Goal Being Pursued.   Basically, this is achieved by the teacher's examining his or her reaction to the student's misbehavior. If the teacher is annoyed and wants to tell the student to stop, it is likely that the goal being sought is *attention*. If the teacher senses that his or her authority is being challenged, it is likely the goal being sought is *power*. If the teacher senses himself or herself to be *hurt* by what the student does, it is likely the goal being sought is *revenge*. If the teacher feels like giving up and leaving the student alone, it is likely the goal being sought is *withdrawal*.

Avoiding Expected Responses.   Once the goal being pursued by the student has been identified, the teacher should attempt to avoid responding to the student's behavior in a way he or she might be expecting. For example, a student who pursues the goal of attention might welcome a strong verbal blast from the teacher as a way of getting this attention. Similarly, a student who pursues a goal of admission of inadequacy might find a teacher's tendency to leave him or her alone to accommodate the effort to seek this goal.

By doing the unexpected, the teacher avoids the possibility of reinforcing a student's misbehavior as it relates to one of Dreikurs' four goals. In time, failure of the teacher to reinforce the misbehavior may result in a reduction in the frequency of the undesirable pattern. Thus, a teacher who checks his or her natural impulse to engage in verbal combat with an attention-seeking student may lead that student to recognize that misbehavior in class will not help him or her reach the intended goal.

Using Psychological Disclosure.   In addition to systematically avoiding natural responses that might reinforce undesirable behavior patterns, teachers also can approach students directly about behavior problems once misbehavior goals have been identified. These goals, though perhaps clear to the teacher, may well be unrecognized by misbehaving students. Psychological disclosure is a technique that can be used to help such students to recognize the specific goals they are pursuing.

In very simple terms, psychological disclosure involves nothing more than a teacher's telling a student whose behavior is inappropriate the particular goal he or she seems to be seeking. These disclosures should not take the form of accusations but, rather, should be presented to the student in an open, kind, and friendly fashion. Psychological disclosure must involve only the teacher and the student. It is never appropriate for other students to hear a discussion of this sort.

As an opener, the teacher might ask, "I wonder whether you might like to know why you're behaving this way?" If the student indicates an interest, the teacher might follow up with observations designed to apprise the student of the particular misbehavior goal he or she seems to be seeking. The teacher observations might be prefaced with remarks such as the following:

"Could it be that you . . . ?"

"I get the impression that . . ."

"I wonder if you are aware that . . . ?"

The beginnings of a change of behavior come with an understanding of what motivates present behavioral patterns. For some students, a discussion leading to psychological disclosure will provide students with sufficient insights about the real motivations for their misbehaviors that these behaviors will cease. Chances for this occurring will increase if the teacher is careful to say and do things that help the student to recognize his or her sense of self-worth.

Implementing Specific Action.   When psychological disclosure alone proves to be insufficient to change an undesirable behavior pattern, the teacher needs to take other actions. These actions will vary in terms of the specific misbehavior goal that seems to be supporting the unacceptable behavior pattern. Some representative teacher actions associated with each of Dreikurs' four goals are described below:

Actions in response to seeking after attention

To the extent possible, ignore misbehavior in class. Remember, this student is looking for an audience.

Provide attention to this student when he or she is working productively and in an appropriate manner.

Counsel the student about the nature of his or her misbehavior in a setting where no audience is present. Do not let him or her have an opportunity to be "on stage."

Actions taken in response to seeking after power

Do not give in to the impulse to engage in a power conflict with a student. Recall that it takes two to fight. If the teacher withdraws, then the student has no opportunity to demonstrate his or her power.

When appropriate occasions arise, inform the student of his or her influence over others.

Give the student some meaningful classroom responsibilities. Make every attempt to focus his or her power-seeking tendencies in productive directions.

Actions taken in response to seeking after revenge

Do not give the student the impression that you are hurt or upset by something he or she has done.

Try to establish contacts with the student in a nonclass situation. If friendship links are built, the motive for revenge will be undercut.

Avoid a temptation to exercise revenge against the student.

Actions taken in response to seeking after withdrawal

Do not give up on the student. Keep working closely with him or her regardless of his or her attempts to assure you that school work is "just impossible."

Make every attempt to make specific reference to even the smallest improvements in performance.

Do not sink the student in a sea of sympathy. When overdone, sympathy can reinforce the student's sense of inadequacy.

In summary, teacher actions based on Dreikurs' four goals of misbehavior can help students to change their behavior patterns as they come to recognize the kinds of goals that may be encouraging those behaviors. Success of teacher actions depends on students' truly coming to see themselves as individuals of worth and consequence. In the hands of a sensitive teacher, this approach has proved its worth for many students with behavior problems of long standing.

Behavior Modification

Behavior modification stems from the work of the famed American psychologist B. F. Skinner (1959). Behavior modification presumes that all behavior, good and bad, results because it is encouraged or reinforced by something external to the individual. Efforts to change behavior patterns, then, depend on identification of the sorts of things a given individual finds encouraging or rewarding and a manipulation of these things to encourage appropriate as opposed to inappropriate behavior.

The term "reinforcer" is much used by individuals favoring a behavior modification approach. A reinforcer is something external to an individual that, when it occurs, tends to increase the likelihood that the behavior it follows will increase in frequency. That sounds a bit technical. Let us see what it means. Suppose that a high school student likes to attend professional basketball games. If his or her father provided a ticket to a game each time the family car was washed, waxed, and vacuumed, the student would be likely to wash, wax, and vacuum the car more frequently than if no ticket were in the offing. The basketball ticket acts as a reinforcer that increases the likelihood of occurrence of car-cleaning behavior.

In considering how a behavior modification approach might be used to deal with serious misbehavior problems in the classroom, we need to consider four different approaches: *positive reinforcement, negative reinforcement, punishment,* and *extinction.* Let us look at each.

Positive Reinforcement.   Positive reinforcers are things that an individual views as desirable. When a behavior is followed by a positive reinforcer, there is an increase in the likelihood that the behavior will occur again. For example (assuming that a student has a good relationship with a teacher and values verbal praise from the teacher), verbal praise given after a good homework assignment has been turned in will tend to increase the probability that future homework assignments will also be done with care. In general, teacher approaches based on the use of positive reinforcement are preferred over those based on negative reinforcement, punishment, or extinction.

Use of positive reinforcement is not so simple as might be supposed. Recall that a reinforcer is something to which a given individual responds in a positive manner. This means that something pleasing to one person may not be pleasing to another. So a teacher interested in using positive reinforcement must find out what an individual with a problem behavior likes. Then, when the problem student displays acceptable behaviors, they can be reinforced. The importance of identifying individual preferences might be illustrated by considering the unhappy results likely if a teacher decided to use recordings of Viennese chamber music as positive reinforcers for a student with an ear only for Country and Western. Chamber music played for an individual with "country" tastes would not reinforce behaviors that immediately preceded the provision of the music.

While we need to make the effort to find out what appeals to the individual student, some categories of things do exist that large numbers of students respond to favorably. For example, praise works well with large numbers of students. When a teacher determines that a given student does respond positively to verbal praise, supportive comments can be made to potentially difficult students when they are behaving in an acceptable manner. This should increase the likelihood of the student's adopting these positive behavior patterns more frequently.

In addition to teacher praise, many students are reinforced when they are allowed to pursue an activity they enjoy. High-preference activities can be used to reinforce student performance of low-preference activities. Suppose that a student wastes time in class and does not get assigned work completed before the end of the period. Suppose further that this same student really likes to solve mechanical puzzles. The low-preference activity (getting classwork completed efficiently) can be reinforced by the high-preference activity (solving mechanical puzzles). This is accomplished when the teacher offers the student an opportunity to work with a set of such puzzles during the last ten minutes of the period *provided that* all class work has been completed. Obviously, to be effective, the use of a high-preference activity to reinforce a low-preference activity requires the teacher to know what really constitutes a high-preference activity for the individual involved.

Negative Reinforcement.   In positive reinforcement, a given behavior is followed by a consequence the individual sees as desirable or pleasant. In negative reinforcement, a given behavior results in the avoidance of an undesirable or punishing consequence. Suppose that a student hated to speak in front of a group. Certain behaviors might reduce the chances of his or her being called upon to speak in front of the group. The avoidance of the undesirable task would reinforce the behavior that diminished the chances of being called upon to speak. Behaviors shaped by negative reinforcers then tend to be undertaken for the purpose of avoiding something that the person views as unpleasant. Clearly what one person views as unpleasant is not the same as what another person views as unpleasant. Thus, what serves as a negative reinforcer for one person will not necessarily serve as a negative reinforcer for another.

A frequently observed problem with negative reinforcers is their tendency to increase the incidence of behaviors generally considered to be inappropriate. For example, task avoidance behaviors frequently are reinforced by negative reinforcers. Consider, for instance, students who miss a lot of school. Such students, for whatever reasons, may find school distasteful. To avoid going to school, numerous dubious "illnesses" may develop. These "illnesses" may succeed in students' convincing their parents that they should not go to school. Thus, the threat of going to school is removed. This removal constitutes a negative reinforcement of the behavior of feigned illness. Few would argue this is a desirable behavioral pattern.

Cheating is a school behavior frequently maintained through negative reinforcement. Suppose that a student has a fear of being seen as a failure by others. If cheating removes this threat, then cheating behavior is likely to reoccur because it has been negatively reinforced.

It should not be supposed that negative reinforcement must always result in encouraging an undesirable behavior pattern. A teacher can use negative reinforcers to maintain preferred behavior patterns. For example, if a teacher were to work with the student who is fearful of speaking before an audience, the teacher might say, "All right, John, if you will quietly complete the essay, you will not have to give a speech tomorrow." In this case, the desirable behavior—quietly completing the essay—is reinforced negatively by the teacher's agreement to remove the undesirable consequence of giving a speech.

Such a plan, of course, does nothing to help this student get over his fear of speaking in front of a group. Were that the teacher's objective, it would be better for the teacher to identify some consequences that this student viewed as desirable. Then, when the student did give a speech, these consequences could be used to provide positive reinforcement for the speech-giving behavior. In summary, negative reinforcers tend to support undesirable avoidance and escape behaviors. For this reason, positive reinforcers generally are preferred.

Punishment.   Whereas positive and negative reinforcers tend to strengthen the behaviors they follow, punishment tends to reduce the likelihood of a recurrence of a behavior it follows. Let us consider our reluctant speaker again. Suppose that this student was behaving in a disruptive manner while members of the class were supposed to be writing individual essays. The teacher might try to get the student to stop being disruptive by threatening him with the requirement to give an additional speech if his unacceptable behavior did not cease.

Several problems are associated with punishment. First, while punishment may succeed in suppressing an inappropriate behavior, it does not provide for or support any appropriate substitute behavior. It may well be that a new behavior that develops after an inappropriate behavior has been eliminated through punishment may be even more unacceptable than the one that drew the punishment response.

Second, what the teacher sees as punishment may not be viewed as punishment by the student. For example, in some secondary schools teachers try to punish students by sending them out of the classroom to sit in the hall. While this may be punishment for some, for others it provides a wonderful opportunity to engage in fascinating conversations with passers-by. Instead of punishing the inappropriate behavior and lessening the probability of its recurrence, it is possible that the inappropriate behavior is being reinforced by the pleasant experience of chatting with others in the hall.

A third potential problem is that the cessation of punishment may be seen as a reward. In such cases, the behavior occurring when the punishment stopped may be reinforced. Consider, for example, a parent who seeks to discipline his or her child with a spanking. The child begins crying very loudly. When this happens the parent stops. The cessation of punishment may result in an increased tendency to cry loudly as a mechanism for avoiding punishment.

While some might see differences between punishment and negative reinforcement as insignificant, it is important that a clear distinction be borne in mind for purposes of problem solving in the classroom. Let us suppose that a secondary school teacher had caught a student cheating on many different occasions. The teacher faces a task of determining what is reinforcing this behavior. Suppose that the teacher determines that the behavior is being reinforced negatively by the student's fear of being seen as a "failure" by other students. In such a case, the teacher can take action to get at the root of the problem and begin to reinforce behaviors of the student that give him or her recognition and status with other students.

If the teacher does not take the time to diagnose the particular reinforcers that are maintaining the cheating behavior and moves immediately to punish the student, there is less likelihood of achieving a desirable change of behavior. True, cheating may diminish in frequency, but other undesirable behaviors may develop since nothing systematic is being done to support maintenance of a more desirable pattern.

Extinction.   If we assume that behavior is encouraged and maintained by something external to the individual, then it is logical that a given behavior is less likely to be maintained when whatever is encouraging or reinforcing the behavior is removed. For example, suppose that the father of a student who was interested in professional basketball stopped providing tickets to games after his son washed the family car. For a while the boy probably would continue to wash the car. But, in time, the frequency of this car-washing behavior would diminish. The reduction in the frequency of a behavior through the removal of something that is maintaining it is referred to as "extinction."

Extinction has some relevance for us as we think about working with problem students. It also presents some problems. The most serious difficulty is that, like punishment, extinction may result in a diminished frequency of an undesirable behavior, but it does nothing to help establish a more desirable pattern.

Implementing a Behavior Modification Program. The following general steps are followed in a behavior modification approach.

1. Identifying precisely the inappropriate behavior that is to be removed and the appropriate behavior that is to be substituted.
2. Gathering baseline information about the frequency of occurrence of the inappropriate behavior.
3. Developing and implementing a specific plan of action.
4. Gathering data to reveal changes in rates of occurrence of inappropriate and appropriate behaviors.

Let us look briefly at each of these steps.

1. Identifying behaviors. In the behavior modification approach, appropriate and inappropriate behaviors must be specified clearly. Further, they must be so specified that some measure of frequency of occurrence can be taken. For example, a teacher's statement that "Sondra just drives me crazy in class" will not do. The description needs to be made much more specific. "Sondra jumps out of her seat and won't keep at her work." This description gives us something specific to look at. Namely, the focus will be on the frequency of getting-out-of-seat behavior. The desired behavior will be in-seat behavior or, looked at in another way, a dramatic decrease in out-of-seat behavior.

2. Gathering baseline information. Once the problem has been identified, it is necessary to get baseline information regarding the status of the student's behavior at the time the program begins. Some mechanism needs to be devised to generate frequency-of-occurrence information. For example, we might simply decide to count the number of times Sondra gets out of her seat, unbidden by the teacher, during two or three consecutive class periods. An average could be computed. This would yield a mean-number-of-times-out-of-seat-per-period figure. In implementing such a procedure, we might wish to use a data chart such as that shown in Figure 19-5.

Figure 19-5

SAMPLE CHART USED IN GATHERING BASELINE DATA ON A STUDENT WITH PROBLEM BEHAVIOR

STUDENT: SONDRA SMITH
FOCUS BEHAVIOR: OUT OF SEAT (UNBIDDEN BY TEACHER)

NUMBER OF TIMES OUT OF SEAT PER PERIOD ON DAYS INDICATED:

2/1/82	2/2/82	2/3/82
14	9	11

Averages:
2/1/82 = 14
2/2/82 = 9
2/3/82 = 11
Total   34

34 ÷ 3 = 11.3 episodes per period

Figure 19-6

COMPARING FREQUENCY OF TARGETED INAPPROPRIATE BEHAVIOR AFTER INTERVENTION WITH BASELINE FREQUENCY

STUDENT: SONDRA SMITH

FOCUS BEHAVIOR: OUT-OF-SEAT (UNBIDDEN BY TEACHER)

1. RATE BEFORE INTERVENTION

Number of times out of seat per period on days indicated:

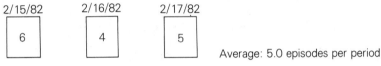

2/1/82	2/2/82	2/3/82
14	9	11

Average: 11.3 episodes per period

2. RATE AFTER INTERVENTION

Number of times out of seat per period on days indicated:

2/15/82	2/16/82	2/17/82
6	4	5

Average: 5.0 episodes per period

3. NET DIFFERENCE AFTER INTERVENTION

Rate of unacceptable behavior *before* intervention = 11.3 times per period
Rate of unacceptable behavior *after* intervention = 5.0 times per period
Net reduction = 6.3 times per period

Figure 19-7

HOW WOULD YOU DEAL WITH THIS STUDENT?

Rodney Olson is a seventh-grader. His record at school has been checkered almost from the beginning. Never an academically talented student, Rodney's grades this year have deteriorated to the point that he is passing only two of his courses. A good part of his present grade difficulties is explained by his refusal to do assigned work. Nearly all his teachers complain that they simply cannot get him to turn in assignments.

Most teachers find Rodney to be a pleasant young man. Few have ever noted any signs of hostility. He seems alert enough in class. And, in general, he gets along fairly well with his other students. He just doesn't seem to care about school-related work. His teachers and parents are afraid that, unless there is a big change, he may have to spend another year in the seventh grade.

YOUR OPINION, PLEASE

Assume that you are one of Rodney's teachers. Read the description of his behavior above. Then, respond to these questions.

1. If you decided to use a reality therapy approach with Rodney, exactly how would you proceed?
2. If you decided to use an approach stemming from Dreikurs' four goals of misbehavior with Rodney, exactly how would you proceed?
3. If you decided to use a behavior modification approach with Rodney, exactly how would you proceed?
4. If you had to make a judgment about which of the above three approaches would be most suitable in this case, which would you choose? Why?

To gather baseline data, teachers may have to enlist the services of an observer. It is difficult for a teacher to conduct a class and, at the same time, keep an accurate frequency count on the behavior of a single student in the class. Often school counselors will cooperate in a project of this kind.

3. Developing a plan. Once baseline data has been gathered, a plan of action, sometimes called an "intervention plan," needs to be developed. Specifically, kinds of reinforcers that will be used to encourage appropriate behavior need to be identified. In the case of our student Sondra, the teacher would need to devise a plan involving reinforcement of in-seat behavior. Perhaps a verbal praise of Sondra when she was engaged in productive in-seat work might be tried. Another possibility might be holding out an opportunity to do something she especially likes if she improves her behavior. Other alternatives might be devised depending upon the teacher's understanding of what Sondra might respond to in a positive manner.

Once the plan is developed, it can be implemented. In putting a behavior modification plan into operation, we need to remember that our goal is to reduce the rate of incidence of the inappropriate behavior and to increase the rate of incidence of an acceptable behavior. We should not be disappointed if the inappropriate behavior does not disappear entirely. While that might be optimal, it is unlikely to happen very often in the real world. But even a significant decrease in the frequency of occurrence of a problem behavior can make it much easier for us to work in the classroom.

4. Gathering data to observe changes. Once the plan has been implemented, data need to be gathered again to note any changes from rates of behavior noted when baseline information was collected. In general, the same format can be used to gather this information as was used in preparing the baseline data. If comparisons reveal a significant decrease in the incidence of undesirable behavior, the intervention program has accomplished its objective. If not, an alternative plan may have to be tried. Note the differences between the baseline data and the postintervention data on our student Sondra Smith as indicated in Figure 19-6.

In summary, behavior modification cannot be used to solve every difficult behavior problem in the classroom. But where the behavior is something that is clearly observable and where frequency-of-occurrence information can be gathered, the approach is worth considering (see Figure 19-7). Successful behavioral modification treatments require extremely careful preparation. They certainly should not be tried off the cuff. But when they are applied properly, they represent an excellent addition to the teacher's repertoire of responses to persistent problem behaviors.

Posttest

Directions: Using your own paper, answer each of the following true/false questions. For each correct statement, write the word "true." For each incorrect statement, write the word "false."

_____   1. In general most secondary students do not like to know the exact limits on their behavior.

_____   2. Little is to be gained by providing ground rules specifying appropriate standards for behavior when beginning work with a new group of students.

_____   3. When clear guidelines for behavior are not provided by a teacher, students tend to behave as they behave in the class taught by their least restrictive teacher.

_____   4. Teachers who express themselves clearly and firmly may well produce a positive "ripple effect" in a classroom that serves to diminish classroom control problems.

_____   5. A principle basic to the reality therapy approach is that the individual student must be encouraged to face up to the consequences of his or her behavior.

_____ 6. Inappropriate behavior, as Dreikurs sees it, results in student concerns for (a) attention seeking, (b) power, (c) revenge, and (d) withdrawal.

_____ 7. Teachers who use a behavior modification approach should begin by identifying precisely appropriate and inappropriate behaviors.

_____ 8. The same reinforcers work equally well with all students.

_____ 9. It is wise for a teacher to have thought through in advance some responses to potentially disruptive students.

_____ 10. Teachers who do not handle their administrative responsibilities efficiently may experience more classroom control problems than do teachers who handle these responsibilities efficiently.

Key Ideas in Review

1. All teachers must deal with the issue of classroom control. Although some experienced teachers may appear to have classes peopled exclusively by students who have no tendencies to misbehave, this is an illusion. There are steps that teachers can take to decrease the likelihood of difficulties with students in classrooms.

2. Students are less likely to be disruptive when specific guidelines for their behavior are known. Many behavior problems result when students do not know their limits and experiment to find out what those unspecified limits really are.

3. When teachers make assignments and require students to perform tasks at which they have a real possibility of performing adequately, students are less likely to misbehave. Unacceptable behavior problems often result when students feel that they are placed in a "no-win" situation.

4. Behavioral problems have a less fertile environment in which to develop when the flow of instruction is smooth. This demands careful teacher planning with a specific focus on provision of alternative activities for students and careful transitions from one activity to another.

5. Some teachers experience difficulty when they let necessary administrative tasks consume too much of their time and attention. Roll taking, collection and distribution of student work, and distribution of learning materials should be done systematically.

6. In many instances, minor behavioral problems can be rectified through the use of nonverbal or verbal communication. Among nonverbal options are such techniques as planned ignoring, the "cold hard stare," and proximity control. Among verbal options are humor, speaking quietly with a misbehaving student, and providing personal help on assigned tasks to students with tendencies to engage in unacceptable behavior.

7. In thinking about dealing with a severe behavior problem, the teacher needs to take a systematic approach. It is essential that specific evidence be gathered and organized in the form of a case file. When appropriate, parents and administrators need to be involved.

8. In dealing with persistent behavioral problems, reality therapy has been an approach many teachers have found useful. Reality therapy attempts to change students' inappropriate patterns by focusing their attention on long-term negative consequences of such behavior.

9. Dreikurs suggests that misbehavior results when students lack confidence in their own self-worth. When this happens, they behave in ways consistent with their efforts to seek one of four goals of misbehavior (attention, power, revenge, admission of inadequacy). Teachers are advised to diagnose which of these goals is being sought when a student misbehaves and to take appropriate action.

10. Behavior modification approaches assume that all behavior is maintained by events external to the individual. Changing undesirable student behavior, therefore, involves an attempt to reinforce appropriate patterns. The technique requires the teacher to specify problem behavior, gather initial frequency-of-occurrence information, plan and implement an intervention

strategy, and gather data to determine whether a decrease in the frequency of the undesirable behavior has resulted.

SUMMARY

All teachers experience occasional classroom control problems. There are actions teachers can take to reduce the probability of severe difficulties with students in their classrooms. In general these steps require teachers to establish sets of behavioral guidelines for students, plan instruction carefully to minimize unstructured time, and think through in advance appropriate responses to misbehavior problems.

In many cases, relatively informal verbal and nonverbal techniques of teachers will suffice to deal with a student behavior problem. For more enduring problems, systematic procedures may be needed such as reality therapy, approaches stemming from Dreikurs' four goals of misbehavior, and reality therapy.

Although student behavior problems receive a wide press, it must be recognized that most students do not misbehave most of the time. Suggestions provided in this chapter are introduced to help teachers respond on those occasions when they must act. They are not intended to imply that teaching properly is characterized as a combat zone where good, positive, and warm relationships between teachers and students are the exception.

References

Dreikurs, Rudolf. *Psychology in the Classroom.* 2nd ed. New York: Harper & Row, Publishers, Inc., 1968.

Duke, Daniel, ed. *Classroom Management.* The Seventy-Eighth Yearbook of the National Society for the Study of Education. Chicago: University of Chicago Press, 1979.

Glasser, William. *Reality Therapy: A New Approach to Psychiatry.* New York: Harper & Row, Publishers, Inc., 1969.

Kounin, Jacob S. *Discipline and Group Management in Classrooms.* New York: Holt, Rinehart and Winston, Inc., 1970.

Kounin, Jacob S., Gump, P. V., and Ryan, J. "Explorations in Group Management," *Journal of Teacher Education* (June 1961): 235–246.

Madsen, Charles H., Jr., and Madsen, Clifford K. *Teaching/Discipline: A Positive Approach for Education Development.* 2nd ed. Boston: Allyn & Bacon, Inc., 1974.

Redl, Fritz, and Wineman, David. *The Aggressive Child.* New York: The Free Press, 1957.

Skinner, B. F. *Cumulative Record.* New York: Appleton-Century-Crofts, 1959.

20

Finding a
Teaching Position

"Other than getting strung out, making the scene, and raising a little hell, what immediate goals do you have in becoming a teacher?"

Objectives

This chapter provides information to help the reader to

1. Identify personal criteria to be used in identifying desirable teaching positions.
2. Describe kinds of planning that ought to precede a job search.
3. Recognize the kinds of services provided by college and university placement offices.
4. Identify a series of steps that ought to be followed in finding a teaching vacancy and making an application.

5. Perform a self-analysis to identify individual strengths that can be communicated to school district personnel officers.

6. Suggest examples of the kinds of questions likely to be asked by a personnel official during an interview for a teaching position.

Pretest

Directions: Using your own paper, answer each of the following true/false questions. For each correct statement, write the word "true." For each incorrect statement, write the word "false."

_____   1. Under no circumstances should an undergraduate worry about securing a teaching position until he or she has completed student teaching.

_____   2. All schools tend to be pretty much the same; therefore, it makes little sense to waste time gathering information about individual schools where one might wish to teach.

_____   3. It is a good idea for undergraduate students in teacher preparation programs to gather information regarding the kind of position they might like even before they do their student teaching.

_____   4. Many individuals who seek their first teaching job falsely suppose that most schools are just like those they attended.

_____   5. A placement file (as the term is usually used in education) refers to a list of teaching vacancies kept by the individual thinking about applying for a teaching position.

_____   6. One major source of information about teaching vacancies is the college or university placement office.

_____   7. School districts should *not* be contacted directly about teaching vacancies.

_____   8. A candidate for a teaching position should not ask any questions during an interview; rather, he or she should do nothing other than respond to questions put by the interviewer.

_____   9. Typically, teaching contracts are offered at the conclusion of an interview conducted by a school district personnel officer.

_____   10. It is an acceptable practice to sign two or more contracts with different school districts.

INTRODUCTION

Securing a teaching position and going to work—that is the goal of most undergraduates in teacher education programs. Because employment is the logical conclusion of the teacher preparation program, undergraduate students should give serious thought to the issue of securing a position well before the conclusion of their programs. Nevertheless, surprising numbers of undergraduates engage in little (if any) preparation for the task of finding that first teaching position. We believe that those who fail to think and plan for the first teaching job are much more likely to be disappointed with their roles as teachers than are students who do some systematic preparation for the day they will enter the profession.

Securing a desired teaching position does not just happen. It requires preparation. Much of what needs to be done must be accomplished throughout the undergraduate teacher preparation program. Indeed, some of the information that ought to be gathered can be researched by teacher candidates even during their first year in the teacher education program.

From our work over the years with undergraduates seeking careers as secondary school teachers, we have observed that a good many well-qualified individuals fail to secure desired teaching positions because they fail to understand the process of identifying and applying for vacancies. We believe that both the individual involved as well as the profession lose when this happens. In the sections that follow, information is provided that can assist teacher candidates in identifying and securing teaching positions compatible with their own needs and interests.

WHAT KIND OF TEACHING POSITION IS DESIRED?

A surprisingly large number of undergraduates in teacher preparation programs (at least those with whom we have worked) seem to have an impression that one teaching job is pretty much like another. As a result, they give relatively little thought to the issue of identifying teaching positions that complement their own personalities and skills. As those who do even a modest review of the teaching environments in different public schools soon conclude, the diversity in the demands placed on individuals who share the common label "teacher" should encourage prospective teachers to ask themselves some questions that might bring into focus the kind of teaching position that would be appropriate for them. For example,

Am I more interested in working in a middle school, a junior high school, or a senior high school?

What subject(s) would I like to teach best?

Would I be more comfortable teaching introductory courses or more advanced courses?

Would I prefer to work in an inner-city school, a suburban school, a small-town school, or a rural school?

Would I be more interested in a school placing heavy emphasis on academic achievement or in a school placing heavy emphasis on personal development of students and counseling?

Would I prefer to work on a teaching team or alone in my own classroom?

Would I prefer to work with students with severe basic skills problems or with youngsters with few such difficulties?

We will look at some of the variables that affect the character of a given teaching position in the sections that follow.

The Teaching Level

The subject of teaching level is something that undergraduates can keep in mind throughout their entire teacher education program. Clearly there are different challenges to be met by middle school, junior high school, and senior high school teachers. For example, students in these several settings tend to be at different physiological and psychological stages of development. Problems of classroom control are not the same for teachers of twelfth-graders as for teachers of seventh-graders (see Figure 20-1). Obviously there are great differences in the kinds of subjects that are taught and in the depth of treatment of subjects at various grade levels.

In contemplating which teaching level to choose, undergraduates should seek to answer the question "What is teaching really like?" for each level. Many teacher preparation programs today arrange for undergraduates to visit different levels of secondary schools early in their programs. If visits are not built into the program, students should ask their professors to arrange some individual visits to different schools. There is noth-

Figure 20-1

TEACHING DIFFERENT AGE GROUPS IN SECONDARY SCHOOLS

Suppose that you were asked to describe different challenges teachers face who work with (1) seventh-grade students and (2) eleventh-grade students. What differences would you see regarding each of the following issues?

1. Classroom control and discipline.
2. Depth of subject matter knowledge needed by the teacher.
3. Difference in physical sizes of students in a class.
4. Receptivity to leadership by the teacher.
5. Attention span.
6. General enthusiasm for the entire school program.
7. Demands placed on teachers in the extracurricular activities area.
8. General ability to influence students' futures.

YOUR OPINION, PLEASE

Given your responses to these issues, which grade level would you prefer? Why? What kind of special preparation do you think a teacher should have to work at your preferred grade level? What do you intend to do to prepare yourself for the demands of teaching at your preferred grade level (whether it be grades 7 or 12 or some other grade)?

---

ing like an on-site visit to provide a feel for the dimensions of teaching in a building. Such visits have changed the minds of many students regarding the teaching level they would prefer. Certainly formal interviews or casual conversations with teachers who work at different secondary school levels can provide valuable additional insights regarding the pressures and pleasures of working with youngsters in different age groups.

Another consideration related to teaching level has to do with the size of the school building and the number of students enrolled. In general, high schools tend to be larger and to enroll more students than do middle schools or junior high schools. Some individuals find high schools, because of their size, to be somewhat impersonal places. Many who feel this way say that they like working in the smaller middle schools or junior high schools. On the other hand, some teachers in high schools point out that, while the number of people working in the building may be large, relationships with people in individual departments and with students are cordial. Probably, teachers' reactions to the size of a particular building has less to do with the size itself as with individual teachers' reactions to the size. Since people tend to react differently to the issue of school size, prospective teachers ought to spend time thinking about how they would react to working in buildings of different size.*

Finally, in thinking about a teaching level, differences in curricula need to be considered. Some subjects are not taught at all levels. (For example, few middle schools would have a drivers' education course.) Further, even where there is a commonality among subjects at different grade levels, the depth of treatment varies greatly from grade to grade. Generally, material introduced to youngsters in middle schools and

---

*In this discussion, we have suggested that high schools are larger, on average, than middle schools and junior high schools. While this is true, we do not wish to imply that all high schools are enormous affairs enrolling hundreds (if not thousands) of students. Clearly many small high schools remain. Indeed many high schools in small towns are smaller than junior high schools and middle schools in larger centers.

junior high schools has to be presented in a much more concrete manner than that introduced to senior high school students. In making this statement, however, we need to insert a caution. Many high school youngsters are not nearly so sophisticated in terms of what they can assimilate as many undergraduate teacher education students think they are. Many have very limited abstract thinking skills and require very concrete kinds of learning experiences. Often this reality comes as a great shock to student teachers who find that an assigned class of eleventh- or twelfth-graders (or at least many student in such a class) cannot deal analytically with much of the material to which they are introduced. To get a more realistic view of what the curriculum in the schools is and what youngsters at different levels can do with the curriculum, undergraduates in teacher preparation programs should visit schools and to talk to teachers.

The School Setting

Secondary schools exist in all settings. The setting has a great deal to do with the nature of the demands placed on the teacher. This important point is overlooked frequently by undergraduates in teacher preparation programs. There is a great tendency for these students to generalize from their own experiences as youngsters in middle schools, junior high schools, and senior high schools. In their minds, many are convinced that "most schools are basically pretty much like the ones back home." Frequently, when they go out into the schools for student teaching, these undergraduates report shock at "how schools and students have changed since we were there." Well, schools and students haven't changed all that much. What the undergraduate student teachers are seeing for the first time is the incredible diversity of secondary education. In many instances what they see is not at all like the "schools back home." Most soon adjust. But the accommodation to the change can be a good deal easier if teacher education students relatively early in their programs seriously consider the diversity of school settings and potential advantages and disadvantages in working in several kinds of places.

For example, students might consider that schools in many rural areas offer small, stable student populations. Further, teachers in many rural settings are still able to maintain systematic and regular contact with parents. (Because of busing and other considerations, this kind of contact is difficult in many urban districts.) On the other hand, rural communities can be rather close knit. Some teachers might feel themselves too visible in such a setting. Clearly certain amenities of larger centers are absent. Similar pluses and minuses could be charted for schools in other settings.

There is no "ideal" setting. Whether or not a given school is a "good" place to work depends very heavily on the perceptions of the individual teacher, which, in turn, depends heavily on personal priorities and values. Having identified these priorities, some effort should be expended in considering the school setting where, in the judgment of the prospective teacher, most of these important things might be available. Suppose a person decided that a suburban setting seemed most consistent with his or her personal priorities. Having made such a judgment, an effort should be made to visit some schools or at least to talk to some teachers working in this kind of a school setting. Such visits or conversations can go a long way to confirm (or suggest the need for modifying) the undergraduate's conception of the "right" school setting.

The School Program

There are enormous differences among schools in terms of specialized course offerings and program management. These differences are so profound that an individual who might be an abject failure in one setting might be considered a great success in another. School districts today, particularly larger ones, may have specialized magnet schools offering highly sophisticated course work in a clearly defined area of interest, specialized schools for youngsters with behavioral adjustment problems, and a number of other entities that typically one does not think of when a general reference is made to secondary education. In addition to these program differences, philosophies with regard to how classes should be managed and students handled vary greatly from school to school.

Clearly, a teacher who appreciates a great deal of formal structure may well be dissatisfied in a school with a *laissez-faire* management style. Similarly, teachers committed to the idea that instructional programs should be designed to accommodate the needs of individual youngsters may well be very unhappy in schools where administrators expect a prescribed set of materials and techniques to be used with all learners.

When an interviewer asks a candidate for a teaching position if he or she has any special questions about the school or school district, many candidates find themselves hard pressed to ask questions ranging much beyond salary and discipline issues. (What do teachers earn? and Do principals back teachers when they have problems with students?) Considering the relationship between the operating philosophy of the school and the happiness of the teacher, it is important for candidates to ask questions that will elicit information about how the job of teaching is perceived in the school where they may be employed. If the candidate finds the operating philosophy of the school to be at some considerable distance from his or her own, he or she should do some serious thinking before accepting an offer of employment.

Of course, a teacher candidate's capacity to react positively or negatively to a particular school's (or school district's) conception of the teacher's role presupposes that the candidate has a sound grasp of his or her own personal educational philosophy. To bring various attitudes regarding education and teaching into focus, candidates might ask themselves some questions that can help them delineate more clearly their own educational philosophies. Some questions such as the following might be appropriate.

How much structure do I like?

What kinds of learning do I think to be most important for students?
Do I think a prescribed curriculum should be followed by all teachers and students?

How "close" or how "distant" do I think teachers should be in their relationships with students?

What do I believe to be the most important mission of the schools?

Certainly many other questions could be added to this list. The specific questions are not so important as is the commitment to develop and respond to some that, when answered, will provide the individual with some insights regarding how he or she sees the world of education. Undergraduate teacher education students who have this kind of information in hand are much more likely to identify teaching positions that would place them in roles compatible with their own perspectives than are teacher candidates who give little thought to the issue of how they, personally, view the role of the teacher (see Figure 20-2).

LOCATING VACANCIES AND OBTAINING TEACHING POSITIONS

Once a teacher candidate has worked out a general image of the kind of teaching position with which he or she would be comfortable, it is time to begin formal preparation for the job search. A number of specific steps need to be taken at this time. Brief descriptions of these steps and the tasks associated with them are provided in the sections that follow.

Figure 20-2

___

CAN A NEW TEACHER CHANGE A SCHOOL'S PHILOSOPHY?

I interviewed with this guy. A real laid-back type. He had long hair. Wore an open neck shirt, and I could see a peace medal hanging on his chest at the end of a chain. He was into that cool, California-smooth, "mellow speak." Said he was a principal at this alternative high school. He told me he and the students "dialogued daily" about all manner of topics. He indicated that his big objective in life was to promote "self awareness and personal acceptance" among his students.

Well, then and there I decided *this* is the place I want to work. I can't imagine a place more incompatible with my own view of education! What a challenge! I mean this bird is mouthing the bankrupt sophistries of the late 60s and early 70s. Those kids are getting shortchanged. I want to get on board and reinstitute some rigor into the program. Give me a couple of years and I'll even have some of the students wearing ties to school. If they offer me a contract, I'm going to sign on the dotted line. Let the revolution begin!

                  Comments by a teacher candidate just returning from an interview

YOUR OPINION, PLEASE
Read the comments of the student above. Then, respond to these questions.

1. Suppose that you were asked to comment on this student's decision. What would you say?
2. What is the likelihood of success for this "revolution"? Why do you think so?
3. What would it really take to change the philosophy of the school described above (assuming that someone really wished to change it)?
4. What kind of intrastaff relationships problems might you foresee were this student hired to work in this school?
5. Have you met individuals who wanted to change the world and who announced that the chance would come about from their efforts alone? How did they fare?

___

Establishing a Placement File

Nearly all colleges and universities with teacher preparation programs maintain placement offices. One of the services provided by the placement office is the maintenance of a "placement file." A placement file is a comprehensive record on an individual teacher candidate that includes such information as grades, transcripts, letters of recommendation, addresses and phone numbers, and kinds of teaching positions being sought. When a prospective teacher applies for a job, the placement center will provide the interviewer with a copy of the file or will mail a copy to the district personnel office. Once a file has been established, the original remains in the placement office. When copies are provided, the placement office makes copies from its original. Most placement offices charge a small fee for this service.

Often, a placement file will be seen by a school district personnel person before he or she sees the teacher candidate to whom the file pertains. Because the placement file is a source of considerable first-impression information, it is advisable to exercise care in filling out paperwork that will be included in the file. Sloppy typing and misspellings convey an impression of someone who is, at best, careless.

Most placement offices provide candidates who are establishing files for the first time with forms that are to be given to people who will be writing recommendations (college professors, student teaching supervisors, and so forth). Because many individuals who are asked to prepare written recommendations have many other pressing obligations, sometimes they delay preparing the forms and returning them to the placement office. Occasionally they will even lose the necessary forms. Teacher candidates who have distributed the recommendation forms should check with the placement office periodically to ensure that the forms have been returned. If, after a reasonable time a recommendation form has not been returned, the candidate should follow up with the individual recommendor. Employers pay a great deal of attention to what has been said on the recommendation forms. Candidates who lack them in their professional files may be at a disadvantage.

Performing a Self-analysis

After the placement file has been established, it is a good idea for the teacher candidate to perform a self-analysis, the purpose being to highlight skills and experiences that might be of interest to a school district personnel officer. The analysis should certainly take into consideration academic preparation and subjects that could be taught with confidence. But the analysis should not stop there. School personnel people are always interested in experiences that candidates may have had working with young people in nonschool settings. For example, any work as a playground supervisor, a summer camp counselor, a music tutor, or a church school worker should be included. Involvement in activities of these kinds can signal to a school hiring official that the candidate understands adolescents and has a sincere interest in working with them.

Because teaching in schools involves responsibilities other than instruction in the academic areas, a systematic self-analysis should also seek to highlight avocational interests. Involvement in certain hobbies and recreational pursuits can suggest to a personnel director that the individual in question might fit in well to the school extracurricular program.

The self-analysis should be committed to writing. The completed effort need not be taken to an interview. (The process of writing everything down usually helps most people to remember nearly everything on the list.) The importance of writing is that it gives the self-analysis activity more importance. By formalizing "findings" in writing, more information is likely to be included than when one restricts self-analysis to "just thinking about" what he or she has done. The writing process, too, frequently helps candidates to organize information into logical categories. This organized information can then be used to respond to questions posed by interviewers.

Sharpening Interviewing Skills

Good interviewing skills are not innate. They are not something that people either have or they don't have. They can be learned. And, when learned, they can be made better through practice. In preparing for a job interview, probably the general objective for the teacher candidate is to work to anticipate what might be asked in an interview. Anxiety in interviews results more from confrontation by the unexpected than from any heavy-handed behavior on the part of the interviewer.

The admonition to "be prepared" may sound like an unattainable objective. Probably it would be were there tremendous differences in what school personnel officials ask from one interview to the next. Happily, this is not the case. Indeed, most interviews follow fairly predictable patterns. Thus information regarding what has gone on in past interviews tends to be a reasonably reliable indicator of what a teacher candidate might expect in an interview in the future. There are several sources of information regarding what goes on in an interview.

Many placement offices offer counseling services. Some placement services even put teacher candidates through "mock interviews." In addition, some professors regularly do this in their courses. (Interviewing techniques tend to be a favorite topic for seminars held during student teaching quarters or semesters.) Finally, just about every faculty member working today in a secondary school was hired after an interview. Most are more than willing to share information about their experiences with prospective teachers.

After gaining some general impressions about the kinds of issues that might be raised in an interview, the teacher candidate should prepare a set of questions that he or she thinks might be asked during an interview. Then, the candidate can follow up this effort by thinking through good responses. Some of the questions on this list (or at least some questions very similar to them) are likely to be asked when the real interview occurs. The candidate who goes in prepared to respond thoughtfully to some of the questions he or she will be asked gains in confidence. This confidence generally makes it easier to respond to other questions for which no systematic preparation may have been made.

Finally, the teacher candidate might well think about some questions he or she would like to ask the person conducting the interview. Many school personnel people appreciate a candidate who asks thoughtful questions about the school and the prospective teaching assignment. The candidate who asks good questions comes through as an individual who has enough professionalism to care about the environment in which he or she may be working.

Finding out About Teaching Vacancies

Undergraduates in teacher preparation programs generally begin to learn about teaching vacancies during the last quarter or semester they are in the program. Some vacancies become known by word of mouth. A teacher resigns, and this information passes from individual to individual until a teacher candidate hears it. Sometimes school districts advertise vacancies in local newspapers. But this practice has been infrequent in recent years. The most common source of information regarding teaching vacancies is the college or university placement office.

Typically, when school districts have openings, they notify placement offices of colleges and universities. The placement offices on individual campuses compile lists of vacancies. These lists are posted in and around the placement offices. Sometimes they are mailed to those who have expressed an interest in finding out about open positions. Typically, a placement office listing will include the specific nature of the vacancy, the name and address of the individual to contact, the salary range, and the closing date for accepting applications.

Usually, the largest number of listed vacancies for a particular college or university placement office come from the state in which the college or university is located, though a few listings come in from other states. Consequently, for teacher candidates seeking positions in other states, another approach is needed to identify additional out-of-state listings.

A candidate interested in out-of-state teaching positions should advise the placement office of this interest. Many placement offices have agreements to share placement lists with other institutions. If this is the case, the placement center may be able to arrange for the candidate to get a list of vacancies developed by a college or university placement office in the state in which he or she would like to teach.

If this kind of an arrangement cannot be worked out, the teacher candidate may need to contact out-of-state districts directly to inquire about possible vacancies. To accomplish this objective, it will be necessary to locate a source of addresses of out-of-state school districts. Many states issue an education directory that lists these addresses. Some placement centers have directories from several states. A few may be found in university or college libraries. If none can be found locally, state education directories can be purchased directly from the states in which they were issued. If a teacher candidate is interested in purchasing such a directory, he or she should write to the State Department of Education in the state capital of the state in which he or she is interested in securing a teaching position.

Once a list of school district addresses is in hand, the teacher candidate can identify some places where he or she might like to teach. The next step is to contact these districts. The best contact is a letter. A letter requesting information about vacancies will establish a formal record of contact with the school district. A telephone call, on the other hand, may catch a personnel official at a busy time. Further, it is likely no permanent record will be maintained of the candidate's contact with the district. The contact principle is important. This is true because a district that has no openings at a time an initial query letter from a candidate is received may get some later. When this happens, districts frequently will review their files and pass along this information to individuals who appear to be qualified.

Keeping Track of Contacts

Teacher candidates who mount serious job searches sometimes find that they have contacted so many districts about so many possible positions that they lose track of "what they have done where." A simple record-keeping scheme reduces confusion and helps the teacher candidate to avoid such embarrassing miscues as writing to the same school official twice about a particular position. A simple checklist that is effective appears in Figure 20-3.

The Letter of Inquiry

Frequently the first contact a candidate will have with a school district comes in the form of a letter of inquiry seeking information about possible teaching vacancies. Most school districts receive large numbers of letters of inquiry. Consequently, it is important for a teaching candidate to prepare the letter properly. This will simply ease the work of school district personnel officials and make a positive initial impression. All good letters of inquiry contain a number of common elements.

Position Preference. A letter of inquiry should always make clear the specific grade levels and subjects the writer would like to (and will be certified to) teach. Vague questions such as "Do you have any vacancies in your district?" should be avoided. Remember that personnel offices frequently are charged with filling positions for cooks, bus drivers, and custodians as well as for teachers in all subject areas and at all grade levels. The writer of a letter of inquiry makes a much more favorable impression on a personnel office with a question that indicates the specific kind of vacancy in which he or she is interested. ("I am wondering whether you anticipate any teaching vacancies for the next academic year in senior high school English. I am especially interested in teaching composition courses. By September 1 I will hold a general secondary certificate endorsed for English."

Your Availability. A letter of inquiry should specify when the writer is able to assume a position, should there be a vacancy. It is particularly important to assure the school district that you will have a teaching certificate in hand by the date you indicate you will be prepared to begin work. School districts cannot hire just anyone. They are legally obligated to employ only those who are qualified for the positions they need to fill. In the case of teachers, this means that the individual must hold a valid teaching certificate.

Because of concerns about certification, it is helpful in a letter of inquiry for a candidate to specify both the particular certificate held (or that will be held) and when it was received (or will be received). For candidates who have completed their undergraduate programs but have yet to receive their certificates, their college or university certification offices frequently will supply a letter to school districts stating that such candidates have met all legal qualifications and are awaiting action on certificate applications from the appropriate state agency.

Figure 20-3

CHECKLIST FOR A JOB SEARCH

NAME AND ADDRESS OF SCHOOL DISTRICT	CONTACT PERSON	NATURE OF OPENING	LETTER OF INQUIRY SENT	APPLICATION RECEIVED	APPLICATION RETURNED	PLACEMENT PAPERS SENT	INTERVIEW SCHEDULED	COMMENTS
Bluebell S.D. Bluebell, ID	Mr. Stone	11/12 U.S. History	3/12/83	3/19/83	3/23/83	3/23/83	5/1/83	Seems to want a coach.
Panhandle S.D. Parma, ID	Mr. Larch	Sociology, economics	3/12/83	3/21/83	3/23/83	3/23/83		Notice job filled (4/10/83).
Schoondale S.D. Holland, ID	Dr. Snow	8/9 Social studies	3/17/83	3/25/83	3/25/83	3/25/83	4/28/83	Not promising.
Corkerdale S.D. Irons, ID	Mr. Lamb	11/12 U.S. history	3/17/83	3/26/83	3/28/83	3/28/83	4/10/83	
Bar-Sky S.D. Bar, ID	Ms. Tong	World geography	4/1/83	4/11/83	4/15/83	4/15/83	4/27/83	A possible!
Granite S.D. Mica, ID	Ms. Fern	8 U.S. history	4/1/83	4/12/83	4/17/83	4/18/83	5/3/83	Also supervise bus loading.
Sila S.D. Sila, MT	Dr. Froid	World history	4/2/83	4/10/83	4/15/83	4/16/83	5/2/83	Hired! Contract approved (5/31/83)

Student Teaching Information. School district personnel are always interested in the student teaching component of the undergraduate training of a prospective teacher, especially in the case of a candidate seeking his or her first teaching position. Consequently, it makes sense to include information related to student teaching in a letter of inquiry. References may be made to (1) the school district in which the student teaching occurred, (2) the subjects taught, (3) the nature of students in the school, and (4) the names and addresses of supervising teachers with whom the candidate worked during his or her student teaching experience.

Candidate's Address and Phone Number. It is critical for a writer of a letter of inquiry to include his or her address and phone number. Personnel offices of school districts are busy places. If a vacancy develops and personnel officers find a letter of inquiry from a likely looking candidate, they will give him or her a call or write a letter. But, if address information is lacking, they frequently will keep looking through their files until they find an apparently qualified candidate who has supplied address and telephone information.

If the candidate anticipates some changes in addresses and phone numbers in the weeks and months after the letter of inquiry is sent, this information should be conveyed. ("Until May 31, I shall be living at 411 Glencourt Place, Dishman, Washington 99231. Phone: 509-672-2093. After that time, I will be living at 715 Alameda, Belmont, California 94002. Phone: 415-775-4309.")

Other Considerations. The quality of writing in letters of inquiry should be high. Personnel officials do not wish to place individuals in classrooms who may embarrass the district by sending students home with material that contains grammatical errors and misspellings. Careful proofreading of a letter of inquiry is a must.

Letters of inquiry should *never* be sent in the form of Xeroxed or dittoed copies. Neither should postcards be used. Both practices suggest that the individual is sending out hundreds (if not thousands) of letters of inquiry at random. Many personnel officials abhor receiving copies of letters or postcards on the grounds that the candidate should be willing to commit the time necessary to prepare an original letter.

Letters should be sent on standard-sized paper $8\frac{1}{2}'' \times 11''$) to accommodate districts office files that use standard $8\frac{1}{2}'' \times 11''$ folders. It also makes sense to select a heavy-weight bond paper, preferably a 20-weight grade, as heavy-weight papers have a rigidity that will help them "stand up" in a file; under no circumstances should onion skin paper be used. Onion skin papers tend to "fold up and die" when they are placed in file folders. A letter written on onion skin may become lost at the bottom of a folder.

Finally, the letter should be sent by the person who is seeking the teaching position. Letters stating that "My husband is looking for an English teaching job. Please send any information you might have about vacancies," for example, do not make a good impression. Such second-party letters create the impression that the individual looking for the position cannot have much personal interest in it. Otherwise, he or she surely would have wanted to make the inquiry himself or herself.

The Resumé

Resumés are known by many different labels in education, among them "vita," "dossier," and "personal data sheet." The resumé contains a compact summary of information related to a teacher candidate. The purpose of the resumé is to provide a personnel official with a quick impression of the candidate's characteristics and qualifications.

There is disagreement among personnel office officials regarding the usefulness of the resumé. Some see them as useful attachments to letters of inquiry. They point out that the resumé provides a quick source of ready information about a candidate that goes beyond what is ordinarily included in the letter of inquiry. Others suggest that the volume of inquiry letters is so high that they almost never look at resumés. They acknowledge a need for the kind of information contained in a resumé, but they suggest that they are not interested in it at the letter-of-inquiry stage. They believe a resumé to be more useful when they are seriously interested in a candidate and are engaged in a thorough study of his or her professional file. Given this latter observation, candidates should prepare a resumé for inclusion in their professional file at the college or university placement center.

Good resumés communicate clearly and efficiently. This kind of communication is facilitated by systematic formatting of information. Although formats vary, typically most resumés provide information related to the following areas:

1. Personal background information
2. Educational background
3. Teaching certificates held
4. Experience
5. Honors
6. Professional memberships

Personal Background Information.   This section ought to include address and telephone information. Additionally, many candidates choose to include information relating to such things as birth date, marital status, children, and military experience. (Some prefer to include military experience under the "employment experience" heading.)

Educational Background.   In this section, the candidate should include names of schools attended, graduation dates from high school and college or university, and other special kinds of training experiences.

Teaching Certificates Held.   In this section, the candidate should include names of teaching certificates held (or about to be held) and the expiration date for any of these certificates. Finally, specific subjects the certificates authorize the individual to teach must be mentioned.

Experience.   List all employment experience in this section, including names of employers and supervisors and their addresses and any experience involving either paid or unpaid work with youngsters.

Honors.   List scholarships, awards, prizes, and other special recognitions in this section. If the candidate has received a tremendous number of honors, it is wise to make a selection for inclusion on the resumé. Those having the closest ties to the world of education should be included. If a candidate has received no honors, the entire category should be eliminated. It looks bad to have a major heading "honors" with nothing but blank paper following it.

Professional Memberships.   Provide references to memberships in groups having some relationship to professional education. Positions of leadership within any such organizations should be noted. If the candidate has had no memberships in professional groups, delete the category.

In general, some artistry is needed in preparing a good resumé. As has been noted, for some individuals all the categories suggested here may not be appropriate. Other people might have certain kinds of background characteristics that do not seem to fit comfortably under any of these headings. It certainly is legitimate to develop other headings that would appropriately bring these characteristics to the attention of a school personnel official. The basic idea of the resumé is to communicate a candidate's strengths to a personnel official in a concise and efficient manner. If the resumé accomplishes this end, then the format is a good one. See Figure 20-4 for an example.

Figure 20-4

SAMPLE RESUMÉ

PAULA FISCHER COE

PERSONAL:	Address: 803 Hilda Avenue	Phone: 406-247-2980
	Missoula, Montana 59801	

Birth Date: March 10, 1961   Marital Status: Single

EDUCATION: Elementary (grades 1 to 8): Roosevelt School, Missoula, Montana, 1967–1975
High School: Hellgate High School, Missoula, Montana, 1975–1979
Montana State University: Bozeman, Montana, 1979–1983 (Bachelor of Science awarded June 1983)

TEACHING
CERTIFICATES: Montana Standard Provisional Secondary Certificate: Endorsements—High School Biology, Chemistry, Physics (date of issue: June 15, 1983; expires: June 15, 1987)

EXPERIENCE: 1. Summers only, 1978, 1979, 1980: Dairy Snacks of Montana, Mr. Paul White, supervisor, 311 West Broadway, Missoula, Montana 59801
2. Summers only, 1981, 1982: Lutheran Church Camps Northwest, Pastor Steve Lempke, supervisor, Sula Road, Darby, Montana 59829
3. 1982–1983 (part-time during school year): Montana State University Book Store, Ms. Ruby White, supervisor, Montana State University, Bozeman, Montana 59715

HONORS: 1978: Inducted into National Honor Society (Hellgate High School Chapter, Missoula, Montana)
1979–1983: Recipient of Big Sky Lumber Academic Excellence Scholarship (renewed annually for each of four years of college)
1982–1983: Dean's list, Montana State University (grade-point average in excess of 3.5 on a 4.0-point system)
1983: Most Promising Teacher Education Graduate Award (voted by faculty of the School of Education)

PROFESSIONAL
MEMBERSHIPS: 1977–1979: Future Teachers of America Club, Hellgate High School, Missoula, Montana, President, 1978–1979 school year
1979–1983: Montana State University Chapter of Student Education Association, Treasurer 1980–1981, Vice President 1981–1982
1982 to present: Kappa Delta Pi
1982 to present: Montana Science Teachers Association

Filing an Application

When school districts have vacancies or anticipate having vacancies in a teacher candidate's area, typically they will send an application in response to a letter of inquiry. Although each district includes unique categories in its forms, most applications tend to seek very similar kinds of information. Most application forms will want information related to the following:

1. Name, address, and phone number of the candidate.
2. Specific teaching position desired.
3. Specific date the candidate can begin work.
4. Teaching certificates held by the candidate and subjects the candidate is authorized to teach.
5. Coaching capabilities (if any).
6. Extracurricular interests.
7. Details regarding student teaching.
8. Reasons for applying to this district.
9. Candidate's philosophy of education. (Many applications ask for this section to be written in the candidate's own handwriting.)
10. Permission for the district to request credentials from the candidate's placement center (or a request to the candidate to order them sent to the district as soon as possible).

For the candidate who has never encountered an application, the forms can be intimidating. Because it is easy to make errors in completing the form at the outset, the candidate should make a copy of the form for a practice guide. Then, when the candidate is satisfied with the presentation, the information can be transferred to the original.

Most applications feature directions for completion. These should be read carefully. For example, some school districts (not many) will want the form filled out in the handwriting of the candidate. An individual who submits a typed form to such a district will stand little chance of being seriously considered for a position.

A good many candidates are intimidated by the "philosophy of education" section that continues to appear on many applications for teaching positions. Many candidates try to guess at what kind of a philosophical stance the district would find acceptable and to frame their remarks accordingly. In fact, few districts are tremendously interested in candidates' specific views on educational philosophy. The real intent (at least in most instances) of this section is to provide the candidate an opportunity to express himself or herself in writing. District personnel officials are likely to be much more impressed by the technical level of the writing and the general fluency of the response than by any particular philosophical stance the candidate might take. Because of this interest, it is particularly important for candidates to proofread their "educational philosophy" statement with care.

Once an application has been completed, it is sound practice for a candidate to make a copy for his or her files. A copy has several potential uses. First, districts occasionally lose applications. Second, if a district schedules an interview, the copy can be used to review responses that were made to questions on the form. Finally, applications from one district to another tend to be very similar. Thus a file copy of an already-completed application can be used as a reference when applications from other districts are being filled out.

Finally, all contacts with school district personnel offices should be kept on a high professional level. One of the authors had an experience a few years ago involving a very competent female student teacher. In fact, she was one of the best he had ever worked with. This individual did a splendidly professional job of preparing her application. But her mode of delivery proved to be a disaster. Instead of mailing the application, she picked it up and dropped it off on the way to a poststudent-teaching celebration party. Clad in a bikini, she burst into the personnel office and explained to the bug-eyed clerk, "I was on my way to the lake. Since I was going by the office I thought I'd just drop off my application." This person was not offered a teaching position. In the judgment of personnel officials, her behavior did not suggest someone capable of using common sense and good judgment. (Whether such behavior on the part of personnel offices is justified is another question. The facts are that personnel offices expect certain standards of behavior from teacher candidates. When those standards are not met, it is unlikely that offending candidates will receive job offers.)

The Interview

With almost no exceptions, interviews are required before teachers are hired. Some districts require applicants to be interviewed several times by different people. For example, a school personnel official might conduct an initial screening interview and then send a candidate on to chat with a building principal. Sometimes teachers participate in the interviewing process. This is particularly likely when a person is being hired to work as a member of a teaching team (a situation in which several teachers work together and share responsibility for a common group of learners).

Interviews serve two general purposes. First, they provide school officials with an opportunity to gather additional information about a candidate to supplement what they might have learned from reviewing his or her professional file, position application, and letter of inquiry. Second, interviews provide candidates with a chance to learn about the school district and, more importantly, about the environment in the particular building where they might be working (see Figure 20-5). Given these two purposes, interviews tend to follow rather predictable patterns.

It is common for an interviewer to begin by asking some very general questions of the candidate. Often questions about places of residence, family members, and hobbies will be asked at this time. The purpose of these "opener" questions is to relax the candidate and to get him or her in a mode of comfortable response.

After a positive climate of communication has been established, the interviewer begins to focus on more substantive issues. The interviewer looks for several kinds of things during this phase. On the one hand, the interviewer is interested in observing how well the candidate expresses himself or herself. Can the candidate think on his or her feet? How poised does this individual seem to be under pressure? Does he or she seem to have a fairly sound knowledge base concerning the real world of students and teaching? Answers to questions such as these are among those sought by interviewers as they begin moving into the substantive areas. Part of the interviewer's interest then is in the manner of the response. Part of it is in the substance of the response.

Another issue that crops up frequently during the substantative part of the interview is classroom management or discipline. Nearly all school districts have concerns in this area. Further, there is some feeling that this dimension of teaching frequently poses problems for new teachers. Given the interest in this area, teacher candidates should think through their views on classroom control and discipline and be prepared to respond to questions on these areas.

Frequently interviewers ask questions on techniques or methods of instruction. Future secondary school teachers are particularly likely to get questions of this type. This results, in part, because of a suspicion widely shared among secondary school administrators that many beginning secondary school teachers think that they can deliver content to junior high school and senior high school students simply by lecturing from the notes they took as students in college and university classrooms. Candidates would do well to think through responses indicating to interviewers that they are famil-

Figure 2O-5

WHAT QUESTIONS SHOULD A CANDIDATE ASK AN INTERVIEWER?

How much will I make my first year?

Does the district provide new teachers with help from subject matter specialists?

How are discipline problems handled in the building where I might teach?

Would I be forced to work on a teaching team?

Is the enrollment in the school district growing or declining?

If you hire me, does that mean you'll hire my husband as well?

Do teachers have discretionary money to buy supplementary materials?

Who do I see if I have a problem?

How much freedom will I have to approach a subject in my own way?

Who selects the textbooks?

Can I get a day off if I need to take care of personal business?

How long do I have to work before I get a sabbatical?

Is there a possibility I can teach summers?

Are the kids all hoods?

Do you provide teachers with weapons?

YOUR OPINION, PLEASE

In general, interviewers like to have questions from teacher candidates. Some questions are better than others. Look at the questions above. In the space provided below, list the three best questions and the three worst questions. Give reasons for your choices. Finally, write three questions of your own you would ask in an interview.

1. Three best questions.
2. Three worst questions.
3. Your three questions.

---

iar with a variety of instructional techniques and that they are cognizant of the special needs of secondary school students.

Some interviews attempt to probe the extent of a candidate's familiarity with the instructional materials available for use in his or her subject area. They may ask questions about textbooks, films, and other materials used during student teaching. A candidate who can speak knowledgeably about secondary school materials in his or her area often can make a very positive impression on an interviewer.

Recent legislation has had a dramatic impact on the nature of the student population in secondary school classrooms. Today, because of mainstreaming legislation, regular classrooms enroll youngsters having a wide variety of handicaps as well as so-called "normal" students. Interviewers increasingly are asking teacher candidates how they would adapt their instructional programs to meet specific needs of these youngsters. Candidates who have some knowledge of the nature of various handicapping conditions and some general instructional responses to these conditions stand to do well with interviewers.

Frequently there will be questions related to coaching interests and extracurricular activity interests. Schools need teachers who not only are capable classroom instructors but who can play leadership roles in the many other activities that go on in today's secondary schools. Candidates who demonstrate an interest in working with youngsters in nonclassroom settings tend to receive high marks from interviewers. (Of course, they must be also interested in doing a good job in the classroom.)

Most interviews do not last long. Although times vary, about 20 minutes represents a reasonable average. When the interviewer gives signals that the interview is over, the candidate should take the cue, thank the interviewer for his or her time, and leave. Interviewers frequently have extremely tight time schedules. A candidate who utilizes too much of an interviewer's time is unlikely to leave a good impression.

It should be recognized that teaching contracts almost never are offered at the conclusion of an interview. Typically, interviewers take notes on what has gone on that form a basis for later discussions with others in the school district. Only after these discussions are contract offers made. Given this pattern of doing business, candidates need not feel disappointed when they leave an interview having received neither positive or negative signals in terms of their employment prospects. The employment decision simply is not in the hands of the interviewer alone. It is, however, reasonable to ask the interviewer when some decision might be expected. Should this time come and go without hearing anything from the school district, it is reasonable to call the personnel office of the district and inquire about the status of an application.

Signing the Contract

When a decision is made to offer employment to a candidate, a contract will arrive in the mail. The contract will state all conditions of employment. A contract is a legally binding document. As such, it should be read carefully. If a candidate has questions about any items, he or she should seek clarification from the school district personnel office. If the contract is satisfactory, it should be signed and returned to the school district. Typically, a district allows a candidate one or two weeks to do this.

A contract does not become official until it has been received by the school district and has been acted upon by the school board. In most cases, favorable action by the school board may be assumed. Until the board acts, however, the contract has no legal force.

It is particularly important for beginning teachers to understand the importance of honoring any contract they have signed. Penalties for failing to do so can be severe. In some states, for example, a failure to honor a contract is viewed as sufficient cause for revocation of a teaching certificate. Revocation of a certificate, in effect, removes a teacher's legal authority to teach. Contractual obligations, then, should not be taken lightly. Teachers who do so expose themselves to great professional risk.

Posttest

Directions: Using your own paper, answer each of the following true/false questions. For each correct statement, write the word "true." For each incorrect statement, write the word "false."

_____ 1. Under no circumstances should an undergraduate worry about securing a teaching position until he or she has completed student teaching.

_____ 2. All schools tend to be pretty much the same; therefore, it makes little sense to waste time gathering information about individual schools where one might wish to teach.

_____ 3. It is a good idea for undergraduate students in teacher preparation programs to gather information regarding the kind of teaching position they might like even before they do their student teaching.

_____ 4. Many individuals who seek their first teaching job falsely suppose that most schools are just like those they attended.

_____ 5. A placement file (as the term is usually used in education) refers to a list of teaching vacancies kept by the individual thinking about applying for a teaching position.

_____ 6. One major source of information about teaching vacancies is the college or university placement office.

_____ 7. School districts should not be contacted directly about teaching vacancies.

_____ 8. A candidate for a teaching position should not ask any question during an interview; rather, he or she should do nothing other than respond to questions put by the interviewer.

_____ 9. Typically, teaching contracts are offered at the conclusion of an interview by a school district personnel officer.

_____ 10. It is an acceptable practice to sign two or more contracts with different school districts.

Key Ideas in Review

1. Securing a good teaching position requires work. A good deal of planning can be accomplished during the undergraduate preparation program. Careful planning can result in a good match between the individual teacher candidate and the particular demands of teaching in a given setting.

2. Teacher candidates should give careful attention to considering both the teaching level they would prefer and the teaching setting they would prefer. Characteristics of youngsters vary markedly from the beginning to the end of the secondary school years. Similarly, there are great differences in the nature of teaching as it goes on in different kinds of settings. Prospective candidates need to engage in some systematic self-analyses to determine where their own preferences lie. Once candidates have completed such analyses, they are better positioned to judge the relative attractiveness of different kinds of teaching opportunities.

3. Nearly all campuses afford teacher candidates with opportunities to establish professional placement files. These files represent collections of information related to a given candidate. Copies of the files can be released, on a candidate's request, to representatives of school district personnel offices. Personnel officials will use information in the files as part of the decision-making process that precedes issuance of a teaching contract.

4. College and university placement offices represent good sources of information relating to teaching vacancies. It is also permissible to query districts directly about possible openings. When this is done, it is far better to rely on a letter than on a telephone call. District personnel offices are busy places. Telephone messages sometimes get lost. A letter, on the other hand, is likely to be placed in a file and to prompt a written response from the district involved.

5. In preparing letters of inquiry to school districts, candidates need above all to be specific. Clear references ought to be made to the kind of position desired. References to subjects of interest and grade levels desired are a must. Further, such letters should include background relating to teaching certificates held. Finally, the school district officials should be advised of the date the candidate would be available to assume a position should one be offered.

6. Resumés are brief (typically only one page in length) summaries of information related to an individual teacher candidate. They are designed to provide a personnel official with a quick overview of a candidate. Candidates are advised to include resumés among their documents at their college or university placement office.

7. Care in preparing applications for teaching positions is a must. Most applications provide explicit instructions that candidates are expected to follow. Because some applications are long and because it is easy for candidates to make mistakes, it is recommended that candidates make copies of application forms and use them to prepare rough drafts. When the drafts are in a satisfactory condition, the information can be transmitted to the original.

8. Nearly all school districts require interviews of teacher candidates. Interviews focus on a variety of topics. In general, there is an interest in hearing responses of candidates to substantive issues and in observing how well they communicate in an unstructured setting. Frequently questions will be asked relating to such issues as classroom management, the school

curriculum, instructional materials, and extracurricular interests. Candidates should feel free to ask questions of the interviewer. The more they know about the school district, the more likely they are to determine whether or not they would enjoy working in the district.

9. Teaching positions are formally offered in the form of official contracts. These contracts typically are mailed from the district some time after an interview has taken place. Contracts should be reviewed by the candidates and, if all is in order, signed and returned to the school district. Contracts become official when they have been acted upon by the school district. Contracts are legal instruments placing obligations on individuals who sign them. It is unethical to sign more than one contract at a time. Fulfilling the terms of a contract is a professional obligation of a teacher.

SUMMARY

Getting a good teaching position requires careful planning. There is a tremendous variety represented in secondary education in this country. Beginning teachers who would be miserable in one kind of setting frequently find that they are very happy working in another. The idea, then, for the prospective teacher is to identify school districts and schools in which programs and philosophies are congruent with his own or her own.

This implies a two-pronged procedure. On the one hand, the candidate needs to think through his or her own preferences and dispositions. Once the candidate has determined the components of an appropriate teaching job, he or she is in a position to begin looking at positives and negatives that might be associated with working in different kinds of settings. Careful attention to the business of seeking a match between candidate personality and school can go a long way to assuring that the candidate will be satisfied with his or her decision to go into teaching.

Applying for a teaching job requires careful attention to details associated with letter writing, filling out applications, and interviewing. None of these tasks should be approached casually. Personnel officials look for teachers who are professionals. Consequently, candidates who appear to have been lackadaisical in their approaches to the search for employment are unlikely to make positive impressions. For individuals serious about obtaining that ''good teaching job,'' attention to the planning necessary to show their talents in a positive light will bear fruit. Although there are exceptions, it is safe to say that a higher percentage of candidates who take the job search seriously find positions that are personally satisfying than do those who approach the search in a much more casual manner.

References

Addams, H. L. "Preparing Resumes and Letters of Application," *Business Education Forum* (March 1978): 29–30.
Downs, Cal W. *Professional Interviewing.* New York: Harper & Row, Publishers, Inc., 1980.
Foster, A. G., and Schrank, H. L. "Job Acquisition Skills: How Effective Are They?" *Journal of College Placement* (Summer 1980): 68–72.
Garrison, L. "Reorganizing and Combatting Sexist Job Interviews," *Journal of Employment Counseling* (June 1980): 270–276.
Jump, C. O., and Trotter, E. E. "Preparing Student to Find Jobs by Choice, Not by Chance," *School Shop* (October 1978): 52–53.
Raygor, B. R., and Ludeman, V. L. "School Officials Prefer Closed Files in Hiring Process," *Phi Delta Kappan* (May 1978): 636–638.
Rosson, J. "Credentials: A Game Teacher Applicants Play," *Journal of College Placement* (Winter 1978): 28–30.
Simpkins, E., "Arbitration and Policy Issues in School Contracts," *Education and Urban Society* (February 1979): 241–254.
Smith, R., and Nash, S. "Videotapes Help Students Correct Interview Faults," *Journalism Education* (April 1980): 46–47.

Author Index

Subject Index